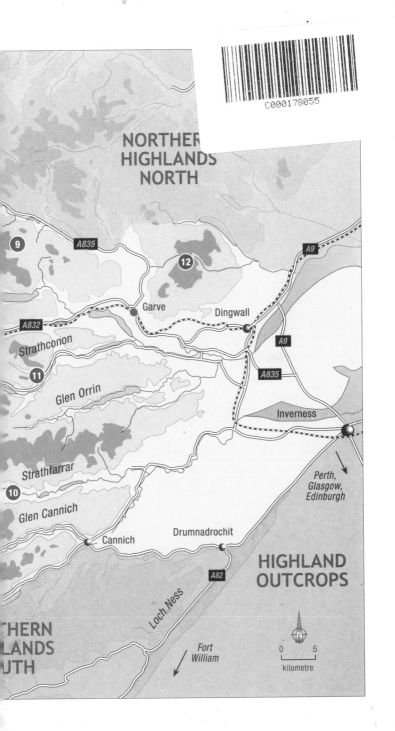

NORTHER
HIGHLANDS
NORTH

9

12

A835

A9

Garve

Dingwall

A9

A832

A835

Strathconon

11

Glen Orrin

Inverness

Strathfarrar

Perth,
Glasgow,
Edinburgh

10

Glen Cannich

Drumnadrochit

Cannich

HIGHLAND
OUTCROPS

A82

THERN
LANDS
UTH

Loch Ness

Fort
William

N

0   5

kilometre

NORTHERN HIGHLANDS CENTRAL

Rock and Ice Climbs

including

Kinlochewe, Gairloch and Gruinard Crags, Carnmore, An Teallach, The Fannaichs, Strathfarrar and Strathconon

Andy Nisbet
John Mackenzie
Andy Cunningham

Edited by Andy Nisbet
Series Editor: Brian Davison

SCOTTISH MOUNTAINEERING CLUB
CLIMBERS' GUIDE

Published in Great Britain by The Scottish Mountaineering Trust, 2006

ISBN 978-0-907521-90-7

A catalogue record for this book is available from the British Library

*Front Cover: Ian Taylor on the first ascent of Cat Burglar, E4, Stone Valley Crag
(photo Graeme Ettle)*

This guidebook is compiled from the most recent information and
experience provided by members of the Scottish Mountaineering
Club and other contributors. The book is published by the Scottish
Mountaineering Trust, which is a charitable trust.
Revenue from the sale of books published by the Trust is used for the
continuation of its publishing programme and for charitable
purposes associated with Scottish mountains and mountaineering.

Design concept: Curious Oranj, Glasgow
Production: Scottish Mountaineering Trust (Publications) Ltd
Typesetting: Ken Crocket
Diagram and map graphics: Ken Crocket, Tom Prentice
Colour separations: Core Image Ltd, East Kilbride
Printed & bound by Elkar, Bilbao

Distributed by Cordee, 3a DeMonfort Street, Leicester. LE1 7HD
(t) 0116 254 3579, (f) 0116 247 1176, (e) sales@cordee.co.uk

For details of other SMC guidebooks see inside rear endpaper

Contents

Diagrams & Maps

Introduction & Acknowledgements

This is the second and central of three volumes to the Northern Highlands. It covers the area south of the Inverness to Ullapool road (although Ben Wyvis is included) and north of Torridon, whose charms must wait for the South volume. This is quite a small area geographically, but it packs in a lot! And some of the best climbing from each style, from top quality winter climbing in The Fannaichs, An Teallach, Ben Wyvis and Slioch, to the famous mountain rock routes at Carnmore and the Bonaid Dhonn.

But the major reason for the climbing in this area more than doubling in size, is the huge number of crags which have been developed in the last ten years. From less than 100 crag routes around Gairloch and Gruinard in the 1993 edition of the guide, there are now over 1,000 and many more around An Teallach and in Strathconon. Most of these crags are smooth domes of gneiss, with rough slabby rock, providing middle grade routes. But the established Raven's Crag and Gruinard Jetty Buttress have more holds and lower grade routes, while there are plenty of steep walls around to test those with strong fingers. The accessibility and wide range of grades has seen this crag system become popular in recent years.

The quality of the roads in the area continues to improve slowly and make a significant impact on access, with none of the cliffs now involving a drive of more than 1hr 30mins from Inverness. Most of the area is served by a circular main road from Garve, via Achnasheen, Kinlochewe, Gairloch, Poolewe and Dundonnell. The last section of single track road is currently being widened, and judging by the new road around Achnasheen, should become straight and fast!

The west coast scenery is slightly balanced by the west coast climate, although the area has much less rainfall than the Fort William and Glen Coe area further south. The midges can be very bad on still cloudy days but many of the crags are open and sunny, so a breeze and fine weather solves the problem.

Enjoy the new photo-diagrams! They give much greater accuracy than drawn diagrams, but the reader should be warned that many routes have had few ascents and despite the best efforts of the author, there may be the occasional deviation which is not shown accurately.

Andy Nisbet
Summer 2006

Thanks go to the previous authors of Northern Highlands Vol I and II, in particular Geoff Cohen and Dougie Dinwoodie.

Also to those who made major contributions; Paul Tattersall, Jim Buchanan, Steve Chadwick, Blyth Wright, Simon Richardson, Dave Porter and Tom Prentice.

And to those who made comments on descriptions, grades and stars; Ian Taylor, Mike Reed, Julian Lines, Rab Anderson, Ross Jones, Dave McGimpsey, Roger Everett, Allen Fyffe, Dave Neville, Erik Brunskill, Jon Robinson, "Heavy" Whalley, Chris Cartwright, Roger Webb, Paddy Buckley, Jo George and Bob Brown. Thanks also to everyone who submitted photographs for consideration and anyone accidentally forgotten.

The authors and production team would like to express considerable gratitude to John Mackenzie who spent many hours drawing excellent diagrams for many crags in this guide, only to see them surpassed by photo-diagrams. And no guide is functional without the editing team of Brian Davison for text and Grahame Nicoll for photographs. And no guide even exists without the design and production management of Tom Prentice.

Geology

Much of the special character of the climbing in the North-West Highlands is associated with the unique variety of rocks that occur there. Only four main types of rock are present in this area, but they are all very different from the granites and lavas of the classic climbing areas of Glen Coe, Glen Etive, Ben Nevis and the Cairngorms.

Lewisian Gneiss: The rock at the bottom of the pile is Lewisian Gneiss, a coarse crystalline metamorphic rock. It is one of the oldest rocks in Europe, and can be regarded as the foundation on which the later rocks have been built. At least two major episodes of metamorphism can be recognised in the group, dated at 2,800 and 1,700 million years ago. It occurs extensively in the north-west, and tends to be confined to the lower ground. However it is generally very rough sound rock, and where it does form crags, the climbing is superb, such as at Carnmore, Gruinard and Tollie.

Torridonian Sandstone: Resting on the Lewisian Gneiss is a very old, well stratified sedimentary rock called Torridonian Sandstone. Commonly dark red in colour, it is one of the most distinctive rocks in the north-west and forms much of the high ground. Its total thickness has been estimated at more than seven kilometres. The original Torridonian sediments were deposited around 1,000 to 800 million years ago by rivers draining from a mountainous region which lay further north-west. The conspicuous pebbles present in some beds have been linked with rocks now found in south-east Greenland. There are not as many long mountain routes on Torridonian Sandstone as might be imagined from the amount of exposed rock. This is because frequent terraces break the bigger mountain faces. These terraces are less noticeable in winter when the direct lines of gullies and icefalls cut through them. The cliffs of Slioch and An Teallach provide the sandstone climbing in this guide.

Cambrian Quartzite: On top of the Torridonian Sandstone lies the Cambrian Quartzite, a pure quartz sandstone which forms a distinctive capping on many Torridonian peaks, including Beinn Eighe. The rock is white or grey and tends to break into sharp angular fragments. It is badly shattered in places, but where it is sound it provides first rate climbing, for example on The Bonaid Dhonn and the ramparts and buttresses of Beinn Eighe.

One part is known as Pipe Rock because of the conspicuous vertical markings it contains – the burrows of organisms that once lived in the sea-floor sediments about 550 million years ago. These make fine rough handholds compared to the smooth faces.

Moine Schists: The collision of two tectonic plates to the south-east caused a major mountain building episode that formed the massive Caledonian Mountain chain. The sediments in the ocean between the plates were squeezed and heated to produce the Moine Schists. An extraordinary structure called the Moine Thrust Zone developed as the metamorphic rocks were pushed up and over the block of Lewisian Gneiss, Torridonian Sandstone and Cambrian Quartzite that remained undeformed to the north-west. A great pile of schists was eventually transported several tens of kilometres north-westwards, coming to rest on top of the younger Cambrian Quartzite. The Moine Thrust runs from Whiten Head in the north to Loch Alsh on the west coast, then continues into Sleat on Skye. The Moine Schists make up most of the Highlands to the east and south of the Moine Thrust. They are sometimes rather vegetated but can then provide winter climbing opportunities, on Ben Wyvis and Sgurr na Muice for example. The sound rock gives good rock climbing, although pre-cleaning is usually involved, as on Creag Ghlas and Glenmarksie Crag.

The final moulding of all these various rocks was brought about largely by the action of the huge ice sheets and glaciers which built up and melted down many times during the ice ages of the last two million years. At times the whole of Scotland was covered by ice, with the possible exception of the highest summits. The last main ice maximum occurred 17,000 years ago. In the North-west Highlands glaciers flowed both east and west, carving out the characteristic U-shaped valleys, corries and aretes, depositing moraines and sculpting the 'scarred and silent' landscapes in which we climb today.

HISTORY

Protected by poor roads and the vagaries of the Scottish climate, the development of climbing in the Northern Highlands has been notably sporadic. Only in the last decade or so have improved roads and a greatly increased population of climbers promoted an avalanche of new routes – particularly on smaller outcrops which former generations classed only as "less than 150 feet" and certainly were unwilling to do any cleaning. While a few of the greatest enthusiasts have ranged far and wide over the whole gamut of climbing in the Northern Highlands – one thinks of Ling and Glover, Patey and, more recently, Nisbet – it is perhaps only natural that the development of certain areas was very much the preserve of dedicated groups. Thus the Fisherfield forest will ever be associated with the Cambridge University climbers of the 1950s led by Wrangham, O'Hara and others, while the exploration of the southern Fannaichs and the outcrops of Strathconon and Easter Ross was fired by the restless and insatiable John Mackenzie. In recent times the outcrop revolution has been fired by the competitive teams of Rab Anderson, Blyth Wright, Mackenzie and Paul Tattersall.

Bonaid Dhonn and Slioch

At the SMC Easter meet in 1899 Lawson, Ling and Glover climbed a route up the east end of Liathach on April 1st, and a gully on Sail Mhor of Beinn Eighe on the 2nd. For the third day Glover, Inglis Clark and Gall Inglis chose to investigate the Waterfall Buttress of Beinn a' Mhuinidh. A six hour struggle with vegetation and steep rock ensued, including much gardening and a difficult stomach traverse, but the trio were victorious, and much satisfied with their achievement.

The 1910 Easter Meet saw Inglis Clark return to this hill and record a climb on Craig Roy (now called Bonaid Dhonn), slightly left of the corner of Gleann Bianasdail. On this occasion they had excellent spring weather and 'the spirit of Pan seemed everywhere'. The next visitors were J.H.B.Bell and his wife in 1946, who climbed two splendid easier routes on Bonaid Dhonn, as well as a variation to the Waterfall climb. A steady trickle of new routes followed over the next decades. The best routes were Cunningham and March's climbs, Vertigo and The Creep, which take improbable lines up the steepest section of Bonaid Dhonn. Mention should also be made of Ginger Cain's explorations both on Waterfall Buttress and on the smaller outcrops further up Loch Maree, near Furnace. The early 1980s saw local climber Steve Chadwick take a proprietary interest in the north face of Slioch, producing several routes to add to the classic Stepped Ridge and Main Buttress. Chadwick was also the main developer of Raven's Crag around the same time. In 1984 a blizzard not only blocked the roads for the rivals but the wind blown water froze away from the watercourse and allowed Andy Nisbet and Phil Thornhill to seize a winter ascent of the Waterfall on Beinn a' Mhuinidh – a magnificent pure ice climb.

Rush hour on the outcrops has reduced visits to Bonaid Dhonn but Tom Prentice and Charles French discovered the ease of approach by abseil and on their second visit in 1996 climbed three fine routes, including the direct line up the best wall, Dream Ticket. Over two days the following year, Paul Thorburn, Rick Campbell and Alastair Robertson battled their way up North by North-West (E7 6b), the hardest mountain route in this guide. Vertigo remains the classic but word of the quality has yet to spread. Winter development of Slioch has also remained with a few connoisseurs. Roger Webb, lover of the long approach and epic day out, often partnered by Neil Wilson but sometimes by Simon Richardson, has managed to keep a low profile on a cliff which doesn't encourage the casual approach. His exploration of this large and complex cliff peaked in 1996 with the ascent of The Sea, The Sea (VII,7), a line up the awesome front face of Main Buttress. Some good easier routes may yet tempt a few more visitors. Recent visits by Roger Webb have produced four routes on the descriptively named Big Pinnacle.

Stone Valley

The crag is clearly visible from the main road, yet only a couple of quiet visits were made by locals before Bob Brown spotted the arete of Open Secret shining in the sun after a visit to Baosbheinn. Brown soon roped in John Mackenzie and the Secret was out, climbed in a snow storm and graded HVS, soon reduced to a classic Hard Severe. This was followed by several fine lines on Stone Valley Crag, including Bald Eagle (HVS 5a). A rush of development produced several fine routes such as Bold as Brass (E3 5c) and The Thug (E2 5b). They also jointly led the uphill line of Demon Razor, the crag's third E3, which indicated the rock was rarely as blank as it looked. After the publication in the SMC Journal, others began to realise that there were still gaps and Mackenzie and Blyth Wright's Blood Feud (E1 5b) on Stone Valley Crag plugged a major blank. As good and harder was Graeme Ettle and Ian Taylor's superb Golden Eagle to the left of Melting Pot, an area in which they and Wright produced several quality E3's. The blank wall to the left of The Thug was an obvious problem and this (Cat Burgler E4 6a) and the neighbouring left-slanting crack (The Flashing Blade E3 6a) were climbed by Taylor and Ettle before Mackenzie and Brown had got their act together. Wright meanwhile had scanned the existing unclimbed area and discovered Flowerdale Wall and Atlantic Wall, joining forces with Ettle, Brown and Mackenzie to effectively polish off these attractive sections of rock. In June 1998, Wright, along with Icelander Asta Parker and Ettle opened the overlooked Viking Crag. In 1998 Wright produced a mini-guide to the Gairloch and Gruinard Crags, extending from Stone Valley to Gruinard Bay. This guide soon increased to some 500 routes by 2001 before production ceased.

Loch Tollaidh Crags

Another set of crags casually admired from the road and occasionally visited by locals before being "discovered" by Rab and Chris Anderson in 1995. It became their project for 1996 when they climbed more routes that summer than the 30 climbed in the previous five years at Highland pace. Publication in the SMC Journal persuaded the locals to reclaim many of the good easier lines, although this extended to E2 with Kermit and Sprocket by Jim Buchanan in 1992 and Buena Vista, Water Lily and Malpasso by Alan Winton in 1994. Most of these routes were on the main Lower Tier, though the Andersons' thorough exploration covered many new crags on the Middle and Upper Tiers as well as the Inlet Area. The highlight of the summer was El Passe and Old El Pastits (E6 6b), by Rab Anderson and Cubby Cuthbertson in May, with Cuthbertson returning in September for Conquistador (E7 7a). Some of the best hard routes climbed by the Andersons between these visits were Lorelei and Strip-teaser (E4 5c) on Siren Slab, Dangerous Lesions (E5 6a) on Buttock Buttress and Hollow Heart (E3 5c) on Recessed Wall. After 1996, many others started to visit the crags, most notable being Paul Tattersall who first visited in 1991 with Someone Else's Dream (E2 5b) on The Cloiche Wall but later climbed many of the hard gaps as well as discovering the new buttresses of The Real Hidden Crag and Fetish Crag. In 2001, early pioneer Jim Buchanan produced a topo guide to the Loch Tollaidh Crags. This proved so popular that many other climbers came to these crags rather than the bigger Creag Mhor Tollaidh nearby. Encouraged by this, topos have been produced to many of the nearby crags (see www.wildwesttopos.com).

Creag Mhor Tollaidh

Not surprisingly, Tom Patey was first, climbing with the Edinburgh Squirrels in 1966, The Hand Rail (Hard Severe) being one of the first routes. Patey and the Squirrels climbed a few more routes before Sheffield climber Chris Jackson visited in 1967, perhaps en route to Carnmore, and upped the grade with The Trip (E1 5a) and Teddy Bears' Picnic (E1 5b). The crag became quite popular for a few years with various teams visiting, like the Alpha Club from Manchester climbing Siren (Richard McHardy, Paul Nunn and Clive Rowland), a Glenmore Lodge team climbing Stoney Broke (HVS 5b) in 1970 (John Cunningham and Bill March; Fred Harper had climbed here in 1969) and Jackson returning several times and climbing Gudgeon (E2 5c) with Tom Proctor in 1971. The crag was often used as a stopover to Carnmore throughout the '70s but fewer new routes were done, an exception being The Bug (E2 5b) by Lake District climbers Botterill and Lamb in 1974. A new phase started in 1983 when Rab Anderson and Murray Hamilton from Edinburgh climbed Decadent Days (E2 5c) and other hard routes with Dougie Dinwoodie from Aberdeen. This liaison didn't last, so when Anderson and Dinwoodie returned in 1987, they were in competition. Anderson was updating the guide for the 1993 edition and climbed or freed many routes, often with Grahame Nicoll whereas Dinwoodie's flying visit produced Rain-in-the-Face (E4 6a). 1987 was a busy year because Kev Howett climbed four long sustained routes on Loch Maree Crag, including Spirit Air. Howett was climbing well and the grades were on the stiff side; all repeats of Spirit Air were a major struggle, resulting in an upgrading to E5 6a, which may end up being generous but hopefully lead to some enjoyable ascents of a superb route. Howett returned for two more routes in 1992 as well as Shimmer (E4 6a) on the nearer White Wall Crag. In recent times, attention has switched to newer crags and vegetation has even regrown on some of the lowly starred routes, while the three star E2's of The Bug, Decadent Days and Gudgeon have remained popular.

Carnmore and Fisherfield

The end of May 1909 saw that indomitable pair Ling and Glover take an interest in Beinn Lair and Beinn Airigh Charr. Their first foray on Beinn Lair met with 'loose shaly rock, wet earth and a lamentable lack of hitches'. The next day, on Martha's Peak, they found a more satisfying climb, so much so that they were determined to return the following year. With the aid of 'some very superior rowing' a large party crossed from the Loch Maree Hotel and made their way to the foot of the face of Martha's Peak. While Charles Inglis Clark, C.Walker and R.W.Worsdell 'elected to explore the west end – as three such fashionable bachelors might be expected to do', Ling and Glover's party took a central route on the face. Glover described the upper part of their climb: 'holds were small but always dipped the right way and one could climb at a high angle with comfort and safety, which (much as I love the extreme north-west Highlands) is an unusual luxury on most of the rounded sandstone peaks which chiefly congregate there. My advice to the youth of the SMC is to explore to the west of the first half of our climb, and after that to try to the east above our cairn.' This advice was taken up by Burt, Bell and Matheson who, in 1928, tackled the prominent curved buttress left of Ling and Glover's route and reported a rib of excellent clean rock with a sensational finish.

Apart from two routes recorded by Pat Baird and party in 1933 on Torr na h' Iolaire and A' Mhaighdean, no other climbs done before the Second World War are of sufficient merit to be still remembered. The real development of the extraordinary rock climbing potential of this area began with the explorations of a variety of university student teams in the early 1950s. This followed a stimulating survey of rock climbing throughout the Northern Highlands by Frank Cunningham in the 1951 SMCJ. In 1951 parties from Glasgow, Edinburgh, Aberdeen, Leeds and Cambridge universities all recorded routes on Beinn Lair, the best climbs falling to the Glasgow team who discovered Wisdom Buttress among others. There was overlap amongst these explorations, but a clear review by Dr Bell in the 1952 SMCJ reduced the confusion to an acceptable level. Following this annus mirabilis only three summer climbs have been recorded on Beinn Lair in the ensuing fifty years, though a number of interesting winter ascents have been made. The year 1951 also saw tentative explorations on Beinn Airigh Charr, Torr na h' Iolaire and A' Mhaighdean by the team of Slesser, Dutton and Wight; followed a year later by the first climb on Carnmor – Diagonal Route by the Cambridge University climbers Wrangham and Clegg. The seed of knowledge had been sown in Cambridge, but the avalanche of new climbs awaited the arrival some years later of Mike O'Hara, George Fraser, Bob Kendell and their friends. A few days in the summer of 1955 accounted for the exploration of Maiden Buttress on Carnan Ban and the discovery of Na Bearta Buttress; 1956 saw investigation of the less awesome left wing of Carnmore and the fine Ipswich Rib on Torr na h' Iolaire; then 1957 saw their finest hour with the discovery of Fionn Buttress, Dragon and a host more routes on Torr na h' Iolaire and other outlying crags. These university vacation trips must have had a care free atmosphere. The Cambridge climbers would happily spend days of their holidays ferrying food into the Carnmore barn from Poolewe and leisurely exploring the secrets of their new playground. Competition, if it existed, was restricted to their small circle – out of the tiny number of British climbers (as compared with today) only a small proportion knew of the treasures hidden in the wilds of Colonel Whitbread's estate. After the Cambridge era new climbs tended to come from isolated visits rather than sustained campaigns, but word must have got around that intimidating lines could be climbed. Gob in 1960 by Haston and Smith; Balaton in 1966 by Higgins and Gorman; and Abomination, also in 1966, by McLean, Cunningham and Currey were all routes of the highest quality. The following year saw St George fall to Geoff Cram while a fruitful few days by a Manchester team comprising Dick Isherwood, Gordon Macnair, Bob Jones and Eddie Birch produced five more first class routes, including The Sword. As this was unaccountably omitted from Ian Rowe's 1969 Climbers' Guide, it remained something of a mystery for many years, its true worth being appreciated in the 1980s. Soon after, Rab Carrington and John Jackson explored the Ghost Slabs and the Carcase Wall on Torr na h' Iolaire, and they returned a year later to pluck the much sought after plum of Carnmore Corner.

The 1980s finally saw modern rock climbing standards reach Carnmore, the principal culprit being Dougie Dinwoodie. Wilderness, the imposing crack on the left of Carnmore Corner, was climbed on sight by Dougie Mullin in 1980 to give the first E4; Dinwoodie then produced the magnificent Orange Bow on the right arete of the corner in 1985, the first E5. He returned in 1986 with Graeme Livingston to climb three fine difficult routes on the Dragon Wall and the first E6, Death-Wolf, up the enormous roof left of Abomination. Further significant routes on several of the outlying crags were added by Dinwoodie and Nisbet in 1988. Thus the area now has a reasonable number of challenges for visitors aspiring to test their capacities in the harder grades, but its particular distinction will always be the variety of middle grade climbs it provides in a mountain ambience unrivalled in Britain.

In the last ten years, this area of Britain's most remote crags has not increased in popularity, although many parties still come for Dragon, Gob and Fionn Buttress. The easier access of using bikes on the estate roads, followed by a new path, has yet to have an effect but hopefully word will get round. Most of the hard routes have seen repeats and two new routes were climbed in 2000 by Tim Rankin and Guy Robertson. But the largest number of new routes has been on Beinn Lair, although only in winter. The long sought Bat's Gash saw an ascent in winter conditions (V,6) in 1997 by Finlay Bennet and Jamie Fisher. Previous winter visitors always had this route in mind as potentially one of the best gullies in Scotland but never found snow in it, so future visitors should not expect to find it plastered. Roger Webb is keen on the remote winter route and two of his visits have produced a winter ascent of Original Route on Beinn Airigh Charr (IV,5) with John Lyall, a superb long route when frozen, and A Ridge Too Far on A' Mhaigdean (IV,4) with Martin Hind, notable as an ascent of an unknown ridge in poor weather followed by a very long walk out in the dark. The reputedly even more remote Na Bearta Buttress has been found accessible by bicycle and been visited by both Andy Nisbet and Rab Anderson, leaving only Stac a' Chaorruinn, unvisited since 1909, as the last great remote problem.

Gruinard Crags

While it is hard to imagine the roadside Jetty Buttress untouched, the first two recorded routes were by J.H.B.Bell and Mrs Bell in 1946. During this trip, they also climbed an easy route on Goat Crag and explored the back of Carn Dearg an Droma. Since outcrops were considered less important than mountains in those days, little was made of these routes and there is no record of climbing until Kinloss Mountain Rescue Team members John Hinde, Derek Bottomer and Reid Sadler climbed Missile on Goat Crag in 1963. Jetty Buttress was probably well established by then although Tom Patey may not have arrived till later; he soloed the impressive Breach Route on Goat Crag in 1966. In the late '60s and '70s Joint Services Mountain Training Centre parties were based at Dundonnell and climbed frequently at Jetty Buttress but surprisingly there is no record of them on any of the other many crags in the area. There were occasional visits to Goat Crag, with Andy Anderson and Mike Hall climbing the overhanging Liquidator in 1971, reputedly with some aid. It seems not to have been repeated until 1998 when Andy Nisbet struggled up it with a rest point, later freed by Paul Tattersall.

A Joint Services guide to Jetty Buttress was updated by Dave Neville of the Dundonnell MRT and rescue team members started climbing a few new lines here, like Right Charlie (E1 5b) by Fraser Fotheringham and Jon Robinson in the late '80s. Robinson and Neville in particular climbed up to about E1 on many of the other crags, such as Lochan Dubh Crag (Nick the Niche E1 5b), Dog Crag (K9 and Inverianvie Corner) and Inverianvie Crag (named only as Routes 1, 2 and 3). Inverianvie Corner was graded a modest HVS by Robinson, with the reason being that before a fire in 1989, you could step over the crux on rose bushes. But the now so highly rated Gruinard Crag was left untouched for Bob Brown and John Mackenzie to climb many routes in May 1994, although the highly rated Overlord (Brown) and Red John of the Battles (Mackenzie) required a lot of cleaning. The same team also climbed on Lochan Dubh Crag that year, although some of the routes had been done before. It didn't take long for word to get round, as Martin Moran was there in spring 1995 with Call of the Wild (E3 5c) and Rab Anderson in the summer accidentally repeating many routes as well as redpointing the hard and sustained Major Domo (E6 6b) and Dead Calm (E6 6b). These outstanding routes have seen several repeats but were only flashed in 2004 by Dave MacLeod and Niall McNair. In 1997, Rab Anderson climbed several of the harder lines on Gruinard Crag and after this, the biggest crags were becoming full.

Patey knew about Carn Goraig and told Andy Anderson and Pete Boardman, who failed on a route in 1974, the day after Barefoot in the Park (E2 5b) on Goat Crag. But the first successful ascent was of the best route, Wailing Wall (E1 5b) in 1987 by Fraser Fotheringham and Alan Taylor. Fotheringham climbed two more routes before Blyth Wright found out about the crag in 1998 and went there with Mackenzie. It's hard to believe it was chance but a week later Mackenzie and Wright met Fotheringham and Andy Cunningham on the way to the crag, won the race to get there and started up The Highland Cragsman (E3 5c). When they arrived on the top tier, Fotheringham and Cunningham had "stolen" their intended finish, now called Call of the Muwazzin (E2 5b). The following year Mackenzie, either with Richard Biggar or Wright, started to develop the nearby Carn nam Buailtean, but this has yet to gain popularity.

A rare crag to be missed by both Mackenzie and Anderson was Mungasdale Crag. This powerful fingery venue was adopted by Paul Tattersall in 1999, climbing 13 routes with Angela Katzenmeier and Colin Meek, also three more in 2000. In the last few years Andy Cunningham has become interested in the Gruinard area and has developed several smaller crags, often with Allen Fyffe. These include Beach Crag, Road Crag and Fox's Buttress. The main crags have remained popular, partly because of the topos, but these smaller crags less so.

An Teallach Area & Beinn Dearg Mor

Thomas Pennant in 1772 described An Teallach as "a chain of rocky mountains ... with sides deep, dark and precipitous ... here Aelous may be said to make his residence, and be ever employed in fabricating blasts, squalls and hurricanes, which he scatters with no sparing hand over the subjacent vales and lochs." The mountains of Dundonnell were popular with the early SMC and one of the first notes of exploration of Beinn Dearg Mor appeared in 1895 when Edward Greenly of the Geological Survey spent a month at Larachantivore (then a welcome little lodge often mentioned by travellers) and made observations of the corries and cliffs. A few years later Sang and Morrison made the first ascent of the South peak of Beinn Dearg Mor, and then in 1907 came a visit from the ubiquitous Ling and Glover. They climbed the precipitous buttress of Corrag Bhuidhe rising above Toll an Lochain, up steep grass and rock, then two days later attempted the gully cleaving the Central Buttress of Beinn Dearg Mor. After 450 feet they came to a chimney blocked by a big chockstone – though the 'slighter member of the party' (Ling) might have been able to crawl through, 'it was not large enough for the more massive member' (Glover). So they descended and climbed Central Gully 'by ledges, scree and snow'.

Sang returned with Morrison in 1910 to climb Hayfork Gully on Bidean a' Ghlas Thuill and his account is astonishingly dramatic. They "kicked pigeon holes for 50 feet, thereafter it was strenuous hewing all the way". After two hours they were confronted by an 'evil looking icefall' – while Sang smoked, Morrison got to grips with it. When Sang climbed, 'the raven's harsher cry betokened the expectation of human eyes for supper' .... 'the rope ... owing to the violence of my struggles had gracefully looped itself round a hundredweight block of stone which, even as I looked, started on its downward career'. Above the icefall the gully forked and they were lured onto 'as entertaining a piece of rock climbing as heart of man could desire. All that seemed obvious was perilously untrustworthy and all that was obscure was firm and difficult. All pulling in holds pulled out promptly, nor was it possible to tell if the vegetation was rooted or merely laid on the rocks for appearance' sake.' So it continued: Morrison swarmed up a crack 'large enough to admit an unencumbered man of modest proportions', and finally intending future climbers were warned that the gully 'shows signs of being a through route for falling climbers'.

Though no doubt always a popular venue, little new was accomplished on An Teallach in the inter-war years, save for Bell's ascent of Lord's Gully in 1923. However, the decade following the Second World War saw relatively more interest in the Dundonnell area. The 1946 SMCJ had an article by E.C.Pyatt describing numerous outcrops, including Junction Buttress and Gruinard Jetty Buttress, as well as the ascents of Main Rib and the remarkable Sulphur Gully, 'Standard 3b', climbed by Barford with the aid of a jammed ice axe belay. Then in 1953 Parker climbed the Central Buttress of Beinn Dearg Mor by a route which appears from its description to have been of considerable difficulty. This route remained a winter target for many years until it saw two ascents a week apart, Chris Cartwright and Ian Stevens being the lucky first in 1995, Sandy Allan and John Lyall being the unlucky second.

But An Teallach, surprisingly neglected in winter for many years, has seen an explosion of new routes, 38 since the last guide, with many by Dave McGimpsey and Andy Nisbet in the last few years. Most impressive of these was the awesome sidewall of Hayfork Gully (VI,7). But other routes are of high quality, including (Sgurr) Fiona Verticale (III) by Martin Moran and David Litherland and two routes on Sail Liath by John Lyall and Jonathan Preston, following previous exploration by McGimpsey and Nisbet. An Teallach is in nick more often than previously thought, so may become more popular in the future. 1978 Face Route has had several highly enthusiastic repeats, with the rib to its right also climbed in 1999 and named Cnocturne (VI,6) after an all night ascent by McGimpsey and Neil Johnson.

Although the gneiss crags around Gruinard have seen all the publicity, sandstone crags close to the road to Badrallach have also seen some development in recent years. John Mackenzie and Bob Brown started off, soon followed by Nick Smith and friends. But as with many of the crags round here, local climbers like Dave Neville and Jon Robinson had previously climbed there, so the most obvious lines were reclaimed, their original grades proving how soft we've become.

Just to prove there's plenty more to go at, Colin Meek explored Corrie Hallie Crag in 2002 and climbed eight routes, but kept quiet. Dave Porter also discovered the crag in 2004 but being new to the first ascent scene and therefore extra keen, climbed another 38 routes (as well as the eight originals of course) during the year. How many more crags are waiting?

The Fannaichs

No climbs appear to have been recorded in this area before 1960. An unrecorded visit in that year by Ronnie Sellers and Jerry Smith, and their untimely death a few months later, inspired Tom Patey and his colleagues to record the first two 'summer' climbs on Sgurr nan Clach Geala. This was followed by winter exploration by the Corriemulzie Club, whose fulsome descriptions in the 1966 Interim Guide spoke of 'a noble cluster of six magnificent buttresses up to 800 feet high'. The 1970s and early 80s saw a slow but steady flow of further excellent Aberdonian contributions to the winter climbing on the Geala crags. Skyscraper Buttress (VI,7) was probably the finest climb, and the source of a little rivalry, before falling to a powerful foursome on a perfect winter's day. A thorough mopping up operations by Dougie Dinwoodie added two new difficult starts to this route and the well named Destitution Road (V,5). After a ten year lull in activity, the crag has recently become more popular, largely because of the growing reputation of Skyscraper Buttress. Several attempts have failed either due to avalanche conditions on the approach slopes or due to unfrozen turf on a start which is exposed to the sun. Attention has been distracted from the other buttresses, on which Dave McGimpsey, Andy Nisbet and friends have proved there are still new lines, Sellers' Buttress providing two fine routes.

Meanwhile, after early climbs in Garbh Coire Mor in the south-east Fannaichs by Clive Rowland and his friends, the late 70s and early 80s saw intensive development of this area by a Dingwall based group led by John Mackenzie. Although easy of access in the days before usage of the Fannaich Lodge road became restricted, this corrie remained relatively unvisited by other climbers for many years. Many of these early lines were ice routes which have rarely formed since the cold winters of the late seventies. The use of bikes to approach up the tarmac road has favoured cold lean conditions and the emphasis has switched to mixed climbs. Neither The Ramp Tramp (IV,4) by Colin Maclean and Andy Nisbet in 1985 or The Turf Accountant by Simon Jenkins and Martin Moran (IV,6) in 1987 inspired the ascentionists, but the more obvious lines have long sections of easy turf. Once attention switched to the huge left wall of the corrie, left by the pioneers who were waiting for the magical central icefall to form (it may never!), then the quality of the mixed climbing was realised. Several visits by Nisbet proved that while the appearance is blank slabs, the corner-lines sometimes have good cracks. Some recent unlikely lines with McGimpsey inspired Erik Brunskill and Dafydd Morris to get "On yer Bike" (VI,6), but the number of visitors is still small.

Mackenzie also produced several climbs on the north face of Sgurr Mor, including Resurrection (III), formidably described in Cold Climbs. But the dramatic description was counter productive and the route largely shunned until John Lyall soloed down it and opened the floodgates; it has recently been snowboarded by Paul Raistrick. Once it was realised that the crux initial icefall was optional and the rest of the route stayed in condition even after the biggest thaw, members of Martin Moran's winter climbing courses have made around 30 ascents and in a mild winter, the route is probably climbed more often than the rest of the routes in Fannaichs combined. Finally the steep cliffs of Carn na Criche, whose potential was first demonstrated by Des Rubens in 1984, gained more good routes in the early 1990s. The routes have mostly been climbed on ice but recent milder winters have rarely brought it into similar condition. Unlike Garbh Choire Mor, here the mixed climbing era has yet to happen. The fierce starts and long easier upper section are less encouraging.

Strathfarrar by John Mackenzie

If it were not for the locked gate at the entrance to Strathfarrar, climbing development on the mountain crags deep within the glen would have been completed years ago. As it is the aura of inaccessibility has deterred rather than attracted the general climbing public, something that the old SMC pioneers would never have baulked at. Fortunately for John Mackenzie and his friends, these aspects appealed with the result that cliffs such as those on Sgurr na Muice and Sgurr na Fearstaig now have over 50 routes between them. Likewise the higher crags on An Riabhachan and Sgurr na Lapaich have been recently explored both via the Strathfarrar road and from Loch Mullardoch.

Of the crags, the most important are those encircling Coire Toll a' Mhuic. Sgurr na Muice had some early rock climbing in the 1930s, briefly reported, but then nothing until 1978 when Jerry Smith, Tom Anderson, Duncan McCallum and John Mackenzie started winter exploration. The late 1970s were particularly icy and the south-east face revealed several icefalls, all of which were climbed producing some fine medium grade climbs, notable then for their lack of belays. Likewise the potential of the neighbouring Sgurr na Fearstaig was noted, with nibbles being made by the same team at the sides and a bold solo by Mackenzie of Enchanter's Nightshade (III), the best line at the time.

The cliffs then rested until the early 1990s saw a wave of winter exploration on Sgurr na Muice, commencing with the fine Pearls Before Swine (IV,4) by Graham Cullen and John Mackenzie. Many good routes followed, of which the pick were undoubtedly the very fine Wolf (V,6) by Mackenzie, Bob Brown and Cullen in 1995, Pigsticker (IV,4) and Pygmalion (IV,4) by Dave Broadhead and John Mackenzie in 1996 and culminating in The Boar, the crags first Grade VI, in 1998 by Mackenzie and Broadhead. On Sgurr na Fearstaig the obvious corners were climbed starting with Snowdrop (IV,3) in 1999, courtesy of Cathy Grindrod and Mackenzie, followed by Flower of Scotland, similar but slightly harder (IV,5) by Mackenzie and Rod Richard and, after three attempts, the glaringly challenging central corner-line of The Sorcerer (IV,5) by Mackenzie and Richard Biggar in 2001 under exceptionally favourable conditions. This line had almost been climbed (one is tempted to say under 'normal conditions' by today's standards of mild winters) by Rik Weld and Mackenzie in 1996, retreating due to desperate conditions and darkness one pitch from the top, though topping out by an easier line (Sorcerer's Apprentice) to the left. In between these highlights the numerous grooves of Sgurr na Muice were practically all climbed giving medium grade climbs often of considerable quality including the harder Tusker (IV,5) by Cullen and Mackenzie in 1996. Given car access up the glen the cliffs are accessible, and come rapidly into condition, having plenty of turf and being in the 'centre' of Ross-shire are usually snowier, colder and have more settled weather than the west.

The exploration of the various crags on Sgurr na Lapaich and An Riabhachan were much less concentrated, the initial climb being Spindrift Gully, a steep Grade II on the latter mountain by D.Smith and J.G.Stewart in 1969 followed by other routes on Coire Riabhachan in the 1980s and late '90s. Sgurr na Lapaich's crags, high up and often icy, were approached from Loch Mullardoch by John Lyall and Andy Nisbet in 1989 to produce the fine Lapland Buttress (IV,5), which pointed to the potential of several crags dotted about the east facing flank of the mountain. 1997 saw the only rock climb of note, the Lap of the Gods, an E1 by Graham Little and Justin Finlay situated not far from the summit, whilst the same cliff saw the hardest route in the area climbed in 2001 by Brian Davison and Dave McGimpsey, the appropriately named Lap Dance at Grade VI,7. One suspects that the pace of future development of these remote but beautiful mountains will remain sporadic, a place for solitude and genuine exploration in the true spirit of Scottish mountaineering.

Strathconon by John Mackenzie

Much more accessible than Strathfarrar it boasts low lying crags of excellent gneissose schist which sometimes faces south, are quick drying and more importantly, perhaps, are close to the road. It also has mountain crags, of which Creag Ghlas is the most important, a fine winter crag in Creag a' Ghlastail and possibly the best 'roadside' ice in Scotland on Creag Dubh.

Of the outcrops the most pleasant and best is undoubtedly Glenmarksie, a south facing plaque of steep slabs and walls overlooking Loch Luichart. A sun trap, it has proved popular despite bracken in summer and midges in autumn. Development started pre-1977 when Ian Ruscoe climbed Greased Lightning (HVS 5a) followed by a spate of climbs in 1979 and 1980 by Mike Birch, Bob Brown, Dave Butterfield, Duncan McCallum and John Mackenzie. The best of that era is Proteus (HVS 5a), which remains popular though not as much as the somewhat less taxing Sea of Tranquillity (HVS 5a), climbed by Mackenzie and Graham Cullen in 1990, ushering in the next phase of activity. Unbeknownst to the 1990 pioneers of Mackenzie, Brown and Cullen, Brian McDermott and Butterfield had climbed Sickle Moon, Selene and Callisto in 1982, by slightly different lines but had not recorded them. These three lines are possibly the most climbed on routes today, together with Sea of Tranquillity. Altogether harder were Mackenzie and Brown's lines of Phobos (E2 5c) and Deimos (E3 6a) (Fear and Terror!), climbed in 1990 and 1989 respectively, the latter still seeing plenty of epics. The hardest line on the main crag still remains Strategic Arms Limitation (E4 6a), climbed by Mackenzie and Brown in 1989, an overhanging one in four groove that is fortunately well protected. Other fill in routes have been climbed, including the inevitable girdle, but the best of these which deserves to become popular is The Conjuror (HVS 5b) by Richard Biggar and Mackenzie in 2000. A good clean and re-appraisal of the "blank" section of the crag in 2003 and 2004 has seen more lines, with the best being Mackenzie's The Joker (E2 5c) that follows the gunbarrel left of Sea of Tranquillity's top pitch. Strong armed desperadoes from the Lakes and the Central Belt have so far failed to make much of an impression on the wall to the right of Strategic Arms; surely there must be someone out there capable of doing it?

Meig and Aspen Crags remain the best of the outcrops in Strathconon proper. Others on the sunny side of the strath, such as Hidden Crag, remain less so despite the sun. Meig's best include good VS climbs such as Gabbro Slab and Blueberry Hill, climbed in 1992 by Martin Hind, Brown and Mackenzie, the more serious and aptly named Yellow Streak (E3 5b) by Hind and the classic crack of The Birch (E2 5c) by Mackenzie and Hind, in 1992 and '91. Aspen was almost entirely developed by Hind, Mackenzie and Brown in 1991, of which the first climb, Meridian (VS 5a), remains possibly the best, though the girdle, Uncertain Voyage (E2 5b), must be a close second. Both these crags, so utterly different in character and climbing, yet so close, offer a good day out providing they are dry.

The Scatwell River slabs epitomise some of the esoteric climbing here. Developed by members of the Inverness MC in the late '70s and '80s, this smooth sheet of schist falls into one of the finest pools of the river Conon (scene of a Joe Brown TV fishing extravaganza). The best pre-1990 route is undoubtedly Grand Central (VS 4b), a McDermott discovery, despite the rock and the ants, whilst more modern fare such as the excellent Tilting Yard (E1 5b) by Mackenzie and Justin Finlay in 1993 and its neighbour, The Joust (E2 5c), by Finlay and Mackenzie, offer more conventional experiences. The Upper Slabs are of better rock, shorter and can be climbed on in the wet in places. The VS, Stranger Than Friction, maintains its popularity as do the short but rather fierce wee routes on the Bonsai Wall, courtesy of Hind, Mackenzie and Brown.

The winter climbing further up the glen on Creag Dubh depends entirely on frost. Offering 150m routes five minutes from the road (given a frozen river!) gives excellent icefalls, the best being the classic Centrefall (IV,4). Climbed by members of the Inverness MC back in the 1970s and '80s, they come into their own on short days of hard frost when powder snow blankets the hills. The Strathconon Experience (III) to the right of Creag Dubh, climbed by Cullen and Mackenzie in 1995 was notable for a maximum daytime temperature of minus 17 °C. Creag a' Ghlastail at the back of Strathorrin is another cold spot, unfortunately facing south and at relatively low altitude. It contains two excellent climbs, namely Ghlastail GTX (V,5) by Cullen and Mackenzie in 1990, an established classic and the more recent Waterfall Gully (IV,4) which deserves to become popular, being an extraordinary deep-cut gully with hidden ice pitches. However the creme de la creme remains Creag Ghlas, a twin buttressed crag rising above Glen Meinich and the scene of a bold foray by Dave Bathgate and Robin Campbell in 1967 on the West Buttress, The Lizard (HVS 5a), and a more regular outing for Renny and Strong and later Patey on Oh Dear on the East Buttress. The West Buttress really emerges from its obscurity in the period after 1992 when Mackenzie, Brown, Cullen and Hind clean and climb a series of fine climbs culminating in routes such as Salamander (HVS 5a), perhaps the route of the crag, Hall of Mirrors (E2 5b), possibly one of the finest pitches in Scotland at its grade emerging after 14 hours of cleaning by Brown and Victory Crack (E3 6a), this latter climb showing just what the real potential is on the steep slabs here. This was soon realised when Robin McAllister, Dave McGimpsey and "Moose" Harrison climbed the slabs to the left of Victory Crack to create the first E5 here. Julian Lines, Mr Slab himself, soon paid the crag a visit repeating this and many other routes and culminating in one of Scotland's few on-sight E7s with Richard Biggar in 2002. Other good lines include Toad Hall (E2 5b) by McGimpsey, Andy and Gill Nisbet and a sorting out of the thin cracks either side of Tales of the Old Days with such routes as Garibaldi (E3 6a), a clever name, by McGimpsey and Nisbet. Interest then spread to the lower slab where a whole series of 20 to 25 metre short lines, most of good quality, were climbed by a variety of climbers. Most of the obvious routes have now been climbed, leaving a fine legacy on the West Buttress for others to appreciate and enjoy. The East Buttress, however, produced a reasonable VS in 2002 to Mackenzie and his two children adjacent to Oh Dear, showing that moderately graded discoveries are still possible.

Ben Wyvis by John Mackenzie

The remote and serious winter climbing potential of the two great corries of Wyvis, namely Coire na Feola and Coire Mor are only just coming into focus. Coire na Feola has provided the best of the bunch with the initial route, Discovery Buttress (IV,4) by Dave Broadhead and Mackenzie in 1992, taking a good strong line without being too taxing. Other routes such as Gael Force Grooves (IV,4) to Mackenzie and Hind in 1993, (climbed in a gale by Gaels) and the crag's classic, Walking On Air (V,5) by Cullen and Mackenzie also in 1993 showed the variety of pure ice and mixed possible here. A visit by Simon Richardson and Chris Cartwright involved a four hour walk-in and produced an interesting and topically named mixed line, Laird of the Rings (V,5). Also in 2001, a fine pure ice line, True Blue (IV,5), was climbed by Mackenzie and Rik Weld. Naturally epics have occurred, with a massive avalanche passing harmlessly over the heads of Pete Moffat and Mackenzie in 1994, a considerate act of nature which then allowed them to climb The Snick (III) under ideal conditions. However it is not a place to take chances with but to await those good conditions ideally allied to a good forecast! Coire Mor is higher and considerably bigger in breadth with several cliffs offering climbing. So far the best has been the mixed winter lines on the main buttress to the right of Fox Gully, with several lines climbed by Mackenzie with Dave Allan and Alan Dennis, the two best being The Last Resort (IV,4) with Allan in 2003 and the splendid Temptress (V,6) with Dennis in 2004. Mackenzie has continued to visit with three more mixed routes in 2006. It is perhaps fortunate that this big hill has two very different types of corrie, catering for tastes in both ice and mixed on epicurian turf and largely in the middle grades. Apart from the longish walk in, they both have much to offer the adventure climber.

Environment
Access
Part 1 of the Land Reform (Scotland) Act 2003 gives everyone the right to be on most land and inland water for recreation, education and for going from place to place providing they act responsibly. This includes climbing, hillwalking, cycling and wild camping. These access rights and responsibilities are explained in the Scottish Outdoor Access Code. The key elements are:

- Take personal responsibility for your own actions and act safely.
- Respect people's privacy and peace of mind.
- Help land managers and others to work safely and effectively.
- Care for the environment and take your litter home.
- Keep your dog under proper control.
- Take extra care if you're organising an event or running a business.

If you're managing the outdoors:
- Respect access rights;
- Act reasonably when asking people to avoid land management operations;
- Work with your local authority and other bodies to help integrate access and land management;
- Respect rights of way and customary access.

Find out more by visiting <www.outdooraccess-scotland.com> or phoning your local Scottish Natural Heritage office.

Stalking, Shooting & Lambing
The stag stalking season is from 1st July to 20th October, although few estates start at the beginning of the season. Hinds continue to be culled until 15th February.
There is no stalking anywhere on Sundays, although requests to avoid disturbing deer on the hills may still be made, and there is no stalking on land owned by the National Trust for Scotland.

The Hillphones scheme <www.hillphones.info>, run by Scotland's Natural Heritage (SNH) and the Mountaineering Council for Scotland (MCofS, see below), provides daily stalking information on recorded telephone messages. In this guide, only Strathfarrar is covered by Hillphones (01463 761360).

The grouse shooting season is from 12th August until 10th December, although the end of the season is less used. It is also important to avoid disturbance to sheep, especially from dogs and particularly during the lambing season between March and May.

Bird Life
When climbing, don't cause direct disturbance to nesting birds, particularly the rarer species, which are often found on crags (eg, Golden Eagle, White Tailed (Sea) Eagle, Peregrine Falcon, Razorbill, Guillemot, Puffin, Fulmar, Kittiwake, Cormorant, Shag, Buzzard, Kestrel, Raven). Often this is between 1st February and the end of July. Intentional disturbance of nesting birds is a criminal offence and if convicted, you face a fine of up to £5000 and confiscation of climbing equipment.

It is the individual's responsibility to find out from the MCofS (see below) about voluntary restrictions at any particular location and to obtain advice as to whether their presence might disturb any nesting birds.

Footpath Erosion & Bicycles
Part of the revenue from the sale of this and other Scottish Mountaineering Club books is granted by the Scottish Mountaineering Trust as financial assistance towards the repair and maintenance of hill paths in Scotland. However, it is our responsibility to minimise our erosive effect, for the enjoyment of future climbers.

Bicycles can cause severe erosion when used 'off road' on footpaths and open hillsides and should only be used on vehicular or forest tracks.

Vegetation

When cleaning routes in summer take care what you remove, some of the flora may be rare. Many crags are designated Sites of Special Scientific Interest (SSSI). This doesn't mean climbing is not allowed, but it may mean there are restrictions on activity. When winter climbing, minimise damage to underlying vegetation by only climbing when it is fully frozen. Crag and Winter Climbing Codes are available from the MCofS (see below).

Camping, Litter & Pollution

Responsible wild camping is permitted under the new access legislation, although No Camping signs can still be found in the hills. If camping, do not cause pollution, and bury human waste carefully out of sight and far away from any habitation or water supply. Avoid burying rubbish as this may also pollute the environment.

Cairns

The proliferation of navigation cairns detracts from the feeling of wildness, and may be confusing rather than helpful as regards route-finding. The indiscriminate building of cairns on the hills should be discouraged.

Car Use

Do not drive along private roads without permission – the use of bicycles is covered by access legislation (see opposite) – and when parking, avoid blocking access to private roads and land or causing any hazard to other road users.

General Privacy

Respect for personal privacy near people's homes is nothing less than good manners.

Bothies

The Mountain Bothies Association has about 100 buildings on various estates throughout Scotland which it maintains as bothies. The MBA owns none of these buildings, they belong to estates which generously allow their use as open bothies. Bothies are there for use by small groups (less than six) for a few days. If you wish to stay longer permission should be sought from the owners. The increased number of hill users have put a greater strain on the bothies and their surrounding environment. It is therefore more important than ever that the simple voluntary bothy code be adhered to. This and more information can be found on the MBA website <www.mountainbothies.org.uk>:

• If you carry it in, then carry it out and have respect for the bothy, its owners and its users;

• Leave the bothy clean and dry, guard against fire and don't cause vandalism or graffiti;

• Bury human waste carefully out of sight far away from the bothy and the water supply and avoid burying rubbish.

Mountaineering Council of Scotland

The MCofS is the representative body for climbers and walkers in Scotland. One of its primary concerns is the continued free access to the hills and crags. Information about bird restrictions, stalking and general access issues can be obtained from the MCofS. Should you encounter problems regarding access you should contact the MCofS, whose current address is: The Old Granary, West Mill Street, Perth PH1 5QP, tel (01738 638 227), fax (01738 442 095), email <info@mountaineering-scotland.org.uk>, website <www.mountaineering-scotland.org.uk>.

Safety

Participation

"Climbing and mountaineering are activities with a danger of personal injury or death. Participants in these activities should be aware of and accept these risks and be responsible for their own actions and involvement."
UIAA participation statement.

24 | TECHNICAL NOTES

Liabilities

You are responsible for your own actions and should not hold landowners liable for an accident (even if a 'no win, no fee' solicitor tempts you), even if it happens while climbing over a fence or dyke. The same is true of bolted sport climbs, or routes with any protection in place. It is up to you to assess the reliability of bolts, pegs, slings or old nuts, which over time, may have become corroded and therefore fail.

Sea-cliff and Mountain Rescue

Contact the police, either by phone (999) or in person. Give concise information about the location and injuries of the victim and any assistance available at the accident site. It is often better to stay with the victim, but in a party of two, one may have to leave to summon help. Leave the casualty warm and comfortable in a sheltered, well marked place.

Equipment and Planning

Good navigation skills, equipment, clothing and planning can all reduce the risk of accident. Mobile phones and GPS can help in communications and locating your position, but mobiles do not work in many places in the North of Scotland and both rely on batteries and electronics which can fail or be damaged. Consequently, they can never be a substitute for good navigation, first aid or general mountain skills.

Rock Climbing

Two-thirds of accidents are the result of a lengthy fall, either due to holds breaking or rockfall. About one-third are the result of planning errors – being too ambitious (trying a route that's too hard) or simply failing to judge how long a route will take and becoming benighted. When climbing on sea-cliffs remember that incoming tides may cut off your retreat even if the cliff base itself is not tidal.

Snow and Ice Climbing

These accidents are twice as likely as for rock climbing, but the fatality rate is almost half! – Perhaps the landing is softer? A substantial number are related to navigation errors, getting down from routes. Benightment and numerous other incidents are often the result of poor planning. The greatest number of accidents is caused by falls while climbing, which reflects the lack of protection and the more serious nature of snow and ice climbing!

Avalanches

Climbers venturing on to the hills in winter should be familiar with the principles of snow structure and avalanche prediction. Deposition of wind blown snow causes the largest risk, especially as snow is frequently blown around Scottish hills. Slopes between 30 and 60 degrees with fresh snow, whether freshly fallen or simply blown, should be considered suspect. The greater the amount of fresh snow, the higher the risk. Avoiding these slopes may be simple, such as choosing a buttress rather than a gully, or finding a section of cliff blown clear, but remember that some buttress routes involve steep snow at their base or more seriously, just below the cliff top. In this guide the winter cliffs of The Fannaichs and Ben Wyvis have extensive plateaus as collecting zones and east facing slopes prone to deposition. They have few ridges and may not offer a safe option in doubtful snow conditions.

On meeting snow of dubious stability, climbers should dig a snow pit and examine the snow profile, looking especially for different layers of snow with different degrees of bonding. Slab avalanches are caused when a surface layer of snow is insufficiently attached to layers below and often when a climber triggers the slide. If a witness to an avalanche it is vital to start a search immediately, given it is safe to do so. Victims will often be alive at first, but their chances of survival lessen rapidly if buried. Unless severely injured, some 80% may live if found immediately, but only 10% after a three hour delay. Mark the burial sight if known, listen for any sound, look for any visual clue, search until help arrives if possible. Again, a working knowledge of first aid may save a life, as many victims may have stopped breathing.

A Chance in a Million? by Bob Barton and Blyth Wright, published by the SMC, is the classic work on Scottish avalanches (see Books, below). While the ability to make your own assessment of risk is vital to anyone venturing into the area, avalanche predictions for the major winter climbing areas, produced by the Scottish Avalanche Information Service (01463 713191), or <www.sais.gov uk> are readily available during the winter. These can be found at police stations, sports shops, tourist information centres and on display boards in climbing areas.

Maps

Symbols are used on SMC maps to indicate different categories of summit. Tops are not marked on the maps in this guide: Munro – black triangle; Corbett – black circle; Graham – black diamond; Other – crossed circle.

Place names and map references have in general been taken from the Ordnance Survey 1:50,000 Landranger maps. The following OS 1:50,000 Landranger (L) and 1:25,000 Explorer (E) maps cover this area.

L19, E433	Kinlochewe and Loch Maree, Gairloch Crags
L19, E434	Tollaidh Crags, Rubha Mor, Gruinard Crags
L19, E434-5	Carnmore and Fisherfield
L20, E435	An Teallach Area
L20, E436	The Fannaichs
L25, E430	Glen Affric to Strathfarrar and Upper Strathconon
L26, E431	Lower Strathconon
L20, E437	Ben Wyvis Area

Books

The following SMC and SMT publications, *The Munros, The Corbetts, North-West Highlands, Scottish Hill and Mountain Names, Scottish Hill Tracks, Highland Scrambles North, Hostile Habitats – Scotland's Mountain Environment,* and *A Chance in a Million? – Scottish Avalanches* are useful for hill walking routes and general mountain interest in this area. For more information and to order SMC and SMT publications, visit the SMC website <www.smc.org.uk>. See also the publications list at the end of this guide.

Technical

Summer Grades

The grading system ranges from Easy, Moderate, Difficult, Very Difficult, Severe, Hard Severe, Very Severe (VS), Hard Very Severe (HVS) to Extremely Severe. The Extremely Severe grade has been subdivided into E1, E2, E3, E4, E5, E6 and E7 and so on.

Technical grades are given for routes of VS and above where known, also sometimes for Severe and Hard Severe. The normal range for technical grades expected on routes of the given overall grade are as follows; Severe - 4a, 4b; Hard Severe - 4a, 4b, 4c; VS – 4b, 4c, 5a; HVS – 4c, 5a, 5b; E1 – 5a, 5b, 5c; E2 – 5b, 5c, 6a; E3 – 5c, 6a; E4 – 5c, 6a, 6b; E5 – 6a, 6b. Routes with a technical grade at the lower end of the range will be sustained or poorly protected, while those with grades at the upper end, are likely to have a shorter and generally well protected crux.

Grading information is in some cases scanty or even lacking, particularly in some of the older or more obscure routes. A † symbol indicates that the overall grade is perhaps correct but there is no recent information for pitch grades. Where there is even less information, harder routes have been graded Scottish VS, which can encompass a range of difficulty from VS to E2.

French grades have been given for a very few bolted climbs.

Winter Grades

Climbs have been graded using the two-tier system. The technical grades, which are shown by the Arabic numbers, apply to the hardest move or crux sequence of a route, while the Roman numeral gives an indication of the overall difficulty of the climb. The combination of the two grades makes the system work in a similar way to how the E grades and the numerical grades are used in summer.

In this way a V,4 is normally a serious ice route and V,5 would be a classic ice route with adequate protection, V,6 would be a classic mixed route and V,7 would indicate a technically difficult but well protected mixed route. Each route has the same overall difficulty (Grade V) but with differing degrees of seriousness and technical difficulty. Both parts of the grading system are open-ended.

Grade I – Uncomplicated, average-angled snow climbs normally having no pitches. They may, however, have cornice difficulties or long run-outs.

Grade II – Gullies which contain either individual or minor pitches, or high-angled snow with difficult cornice exits. The easiest buttresses under winter conditions.

Grade III – Gullies which contain ice in quantity. There will normally be at least one substantial pitch and possibly several lesser ones. Sustained buttress climbs, but only technical in short sections.

Grade IV – Steeper and more technical with vertical sections found on ice climbs. Mixed routes will require a good repertoire of techniques.

Grade V – Climbs which are difficult, sustained and serious. If on ice, long sustained ice pitches are to be expected; mixed routes will require a degree of rock climbing ability and the use of axe torquing and hooking and similar winter techniques.

Grade VI – Thin and tenuous ice routes or those with long vertical sections. Mixed routes will include all that has gone before but more of it.

Grade VII – Usually mixed routes which are very sustained or technically extreme. Also sustained routes on thin or vertical ice.

Grade VIII – Very hard and sustained mixed routes.

A few routes have been graded Scottish IV or Scottish V, from the older I to V system, where Scottish IV can be harder than new IV but short and Scottish V could be anything new V or above.

Equipment and Style

Scotland has a tradition of climbs with leader placed protection. Pegs are nowadays considered unacceptable in summer rock first ascents due to improved equipment and the option of move rehearsal as an alternative to hammered protection. Some established climbs depend on peg runners to keep their grade; these are acceptable. Bolts are also considered unacceptable on mountain cliffs. However, bolt protected sport climbs are accepted on low lying cliffs which are not adventurous in nature, do not have a history of established traditional routes and have been agreed to be better suited to sport climbing by the local climbing community. Retrobolting of traditional routes is considered unacceptable without agreement from the first ascentionist and the local climbing community.

Left and Right

The terms generally refer to a climber facing the cliff. This always applies for route descriptions and usually for descents, which are often planned before the downhill movement starts. But for a few complex descents from mountain cliffs, the direction is facing downhill (but then the direction is specified). Routes are described from left to right and this should be assumed, unless the cliff is always approached from the right, when right to left is used and indicated in the text.

Pitch Lengths

Pitch lengths are often rounded to the nearest 5m, although pitches below 20m are sometimes rounded to the nearest 2m. The descriptions assume the use of 50m ropes.

Diagrams

If a route has been numbered, this indicates that there is a diagram depicting the cliff, which will be found close to the relevant text. The numbers of the climbs in the text correspond to the numbers on the diagrams.

Recommended Routes

A star quality system has been used. No star routes may be good although nothing special, or eliminate in line, or information may be lacking. Only a few are worthless or unpleasant.

* Good climbing, but the route may lack line, situation or balance.
** A good route but lacking one or more of the features that make it a climb of quality.
*** An outstanding route of the highest quality, combining superb climbing with line, character and situation.
**** The best climbs of their class in Scotland.

In winter, quality will vary with conditions so stars, like grades, are applied for the conditions when the route is commonly climbed.

First Ascensionists

The year of the first ascent is given in the text. The full date and first ascensionists are listed by area in chronological order at the back of the guide. If climbed originally using aid or rest points, this is listed, usually with the first free ascent. Details of variations are usually given under the parent route. An ascent in winter conditions is indicated by a W at the start of an entry and a summer route by S. Winter ascents are listed separately from their corresponding summer route.

Amenities

There is an all year Tourist Office at Gairloch (01445 712 130). Access by public transport is possible but not recommended for the area covered by this guidebook. For the determined, contact Traveline at (0870 608 2608) or <www.traveline.org.uk> for possibilities. Gairloch is a fair sized place with shop, chip shop and petrol. Old Inn is the best pub. Poolewe is more favoured by climbers, with an outdoor shop (no hardware) at the Slioch clothing factory. Also the Bridge Cottage Coffee Shop and a swimming pool. Kinlochewe has a shop, cafe, petrol, hotel (bar meals) and small climbing shop (Moru, at the village hall just on the Torridon road). The area can easily be visited from Ullapool or Torridon.
Climbing Wall: In the Gairloch Leisure Centre, open from 5pm, but quite old (DR, 8m high, 1994), (01445 712 345).
Camping: Sites at Gairloch (NG 797 773), Poolewe (NG 862 812) and Laide (NG 903 918).
SYHA Youth Hostel: Carn Dearg is 4km west of Gairloch (NG 763 776), (0870 004 1110).
Independent Hostels: Sail Mhor Croft (Camusnagaul, NH 064 893), (01854 633 224, open all year). A bunkhouse is attached to the Kinlochewe Hotel (01445 760 253).

Weather Forecasts

Weather forecasts are important as west coast weather is very changeable, but it is hard to get one with sufficient local accuracy. This is the north-west, so south-east is the best wind direction, even if caused by low pressure over England and plenty of rain in the rest of the country. The coasts often have better weather than the hills just inland. The forecasts below must be interpreted carefully. There is something to be said for "go anyway".
Radio Scotland: As well as the regular forecasts, there is an Outdoor Activities forecast. The time in summer 2005 was at 6.58pm, but 7.58pm on Sunday and an additional one at 6.58am on Saturday.
TV: Reporting Scotland forecast at 6.50 to 6.55pm is the best daily one (often starring "Heather the Weather").
Internet: The Internet has led to the withdrawal of good telephone forecasts. There is a wide variety of forecasts on the Internet (in 2006), including: <www.mwis.org.uk>. It is the best mountain forecast.
<www.metcheck.com> gives a huge range of information including mountain forecasts and long range forecasts.
<www.bbc.co.uk/weather> and <www.metro.co.uk> give fairly reliable forecasts.

KINLOCHEWE & LOCH MAREE NORTH

GLEN DOCHERTY

This is the glen above Kinlochewe taken by the road to Achnasheen. One ice climb has been recorded here in particularly cold conditions. **Helter-Skelter** (240m IV,4 1979) is "the first gully below the car park" near the top of the glen.

BEINN A' MHUINIDH

(NH 032 661)   Alt 692m

This is the hill south-east of Slioch, divided from it by the picturesque Gleann Bianasdail. The south-west and north-west flanks have a lot of rock, providing plenty of scope for exploratory scrambling, and two crags with some worthwhile longer routes on good quartzite. The views up Loch Maree and across to Beinn Eighe are superb.

Approach: Park at Incheril, 1km east of Kinlochewe (NH 038 624). Follow a path leading north-west along the north side of the Kinlochewe River towards Loch Maree and Slioch. This path is left at various points to reach crags on the hillside above.

There are two diagonal bands of cliff, the Upper and the Lower, but since they are set beside each other, the altitudes of the climbing areas are no different. The Upper is on the slopes below Meall an Ghobhar. The south or bottom end of the Upper is seen and reached first, with the north beyond it. Above is a large and unexpored buttress which looks steep, loose and heathery. Waterfall Buttress, south end of the Lower Band, is next. The Lower Band then rises northwards to the Bonaid Dhonn, situated just round the bend into Gleann Bianasdail.

CREAG RUADH

(NH 037 631)   Alt 230m   South-West facing

This small crag lies on the skyline above the car park at Kinlochewe. At the first gate across the path ascend the hillside beside a fence, then up and left to the crag, 20mins. **Watch Ma Sheep** (10m E1 5b 1996) takes a central line on the right-hand buttress. Start at a shallow corner and swing up on to the wall to a diagonal crack. Follow this to finish left.

UPPER BAND - SOUTH BUTTRESS

(NH 026 642)   Alt 160m   South-West facing

The central part of this buttress is steep, but loose, although the following route has been recorded. Towards the left there is a Severe climbed by Tom Patey (SMCJ, 1958). It takes an obvious crack set in a corner and overhangs slightly. The middle part of the crack was avoided on the left via a small tree, and regained below the top overhang, which was climbed direct. At the right of the buttress there is a pleasant slab (Difficult).

The Blitz   50m   HVS   *(2001)*
Start about 10m left of a deep tree filled recess at the foot of a left-facing corner-crack.
1. 25m 4c Climb the corner-crack to a ledge system. Move along this for 4m and climb a short steep wall (crux) to gain a short right-facing corner. Climb this and traverse left to the base of a fine right-trending gangway, followed to an eyrie stance.
2. 25m 4b Climb up 2m to gain a ledge system running rightwards into a corner. Follow this to the top.

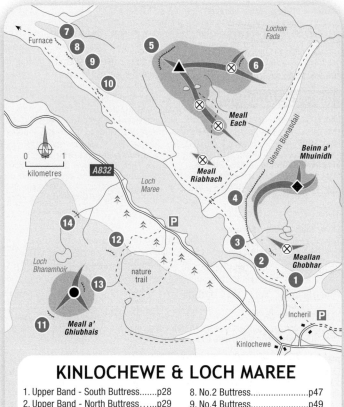

KINLOCHEWE & LOCH MAREE

UPPER BAND - NORTH BUTTRESS

(NH 025 646)   Alt 300m   South-West facing

A short steep buttress, but the rock is worrying.

Descent: Walk down about 100m north of the cliff.

The routes are described from the top left back towards the car park.

Zigzag Gully   45m   Difficult   *(1949)*

On the left of the buttress start directly up a block with a prominent yellow blaze, from which an entrenched zigzag gully leads to the top. Its position is unsure, but several easy although scrappy lines could be climbed here.

Staircase Ridge 50m Severe   (1958)
A steep stepped ridge seen in profile from the foot of Double Flake Route; the ridge section is short but well defined when seen from its base. Go up white quartzite to a ledge. Traverse left up an overhung wall and onto the ridge. Climb the ridge and continue direct to the top.

Double Flake Route 75m Severe   (1946)
Start at a tunnelled eye between two flakes. The lower flake, 20m up, is reached from right or left, and the wall behind the flake is climbed by a 25m pitch to a good belay. A cave ahead is avoided by slabs on the right to an exposed 3m crack which breaks through the canopy. This exit leads sensationally to a steep slab on the left, climbed by friction and vegetation. A further 30m of moderate climbing leads to the top.

Stepped Chimney 50m Severe   (1958)
Start right of Double Flake Route. The deep chimney on the second pitch can be seen clearly from the bottom. Go up loose blocks to a short crack on the right and up to a chockstone belay. Climb the strenuous chimney and the overhanging crack above.

Silver Slab 50m Severe   (1958)
This takes the right edge of fine steep slabs left of a deep gully. Ascend a broken wall below the slabs on the right (15m). Climb silver slabs and go diagonally right to a heather filled crack at the edge, which is climbed to a stance (25m). Climb the rib on the right to the top.

Pinnacle Gully 40m Very Difficult   (1958)
This is the deep gully right of Silver Slab. Climb grass and loose blocks to the foot of the Pinnacle. Go up between the Pinnacle and the wall at the back and belay on top. Leap onto a broad grass ledge. Move left to the face overlooking the Pinnacle. Climb the exposed ridge above to an easier finish.

Pinnacle Face 40m Severe   (1958)
Climb the face on the right of Pinnacle Gully, starting from a recess on the left. Ascend the Pinnacle on the right on friable holds and continue as for Pinnacle Gully.

For three other routes on this buttress, which are likely to be similar to the above, see SMCJ 1959.

LOWER BAND - WATERFALL BUTTRESS
(NH 024 648) Alt 220m West facing Map p29 Diagram p33
A typical quartzite crag, but distinctive because of the waterfall, which is marked on the OS 1:50000 map. The routes are steep and exposed, but with excellent holds on very clean rock. There are a few loose blocks and heather on the ledges. The original route, The West Climb, has a fine traditional flavour and the original route description is quoted here. The descriptions in general are brief and some route finding may be required; but there are plenty of holds. The waterfall itself, on the rare occasions when it is frozen, gives a superb pure ice climb.

Approach: Follow the Loch Maree path to a fork just before the burn coming down from Waterfall Buttress. The left fork is much more obvious but is a dead end unless the loch is low. Take the right fork along the base of the hillside, then strike uphill before reaching the burn.

Descent: Either walk down at the south end of the cliff or scramble down at the north end.

Routes are described right to left. The first route has not been found; there must be errors in the description.

1 Prelude   45m   Severe   (1951)
Start some distance right of the waterfall. From the bottom of the climb a steep corner and arete are seen on the immediate left of a gully and right of a reddish coloured wall with a rowan tree high on the cliff to the left. Climb the wall for 12m avoiding an overhang on the left. Go up a wall to a second overhang (20m). Turn the overhang at its left edge, move back right, then straight up on small holds to a ledge with large shattered blocks (10m). Step left and climb the wall for 6m to where it ends abruptly on a ledge. Go left again to the next wall and climb 6m to the top of a small pinnacle. Continue to the top.

2. Twoo   35m   Hard Severe 4b   (2005)
High on the right of the cliff is this big crack with a rowan at 6m. Climb the wall just right of the crack until above the rowan. Step left and climb the steep crack to a ledge. Climb the continuation crack above.

3 Blanco   100m   Severe **   (2005)
Fine clean rock with very positive holds. Start 25m right of the waterfall at the right end of the low section of the wall, 10m right of the end of waterwashed rock.
1. 15m 4a Climb up left to finish on an exposed arete.
2. 30m Climb clean walls with bits of heather until right of the second pine on Tuit.
3. 40m 4a Climb a large clean wall till it peters out, then move left to climb another clean wall right of a chimney which bounds the rib of Tuit on the right.
4. 15m 4a Finish up a final wall.

4 Tuit   100m   Severe *   (1952)
Start as for Blanco, 25m right of the waterfall and 10m right of the end of waterwashed rock.
1. 45m Take a similar but easier line slightly leftwards to a tall thin pine tree and then a slightly smaller pine.
2. 20m A chimney on the right gives access to a wall above and a ledge with a rambling pine in a corner.
3. 35m 4a The narrow rib to the right of the corner leads to a final wall.
Winter: **V,5**   (2001)
Close to the summer route except the final wall was missed by traversing right along a ledge to gain easy ground above.

5 Chiaroscuro   90m   Severe **   (1982)
Despite a possibly wet start, the best route here is steep and exposed, with good holds on clean rock. Start right of the waterfall, where the black waterwashed rock is bounded by a prominent corner (10m left of Tuit). The route may be very similar to Waterfall Corner, described in SMCJ, 1973.
1. 40m 4a Climb black rock on the left of the corner for 10m then traverse right into the grey rock in the corner. Follow the crack on superb holds to its top then go left up a wall above to the first pine ledge.
2. 50m 4a Go straight up behind the pine for a few metres, then left towards the foot of a rib with a detached block at its base. Step round the block into the corner beyond and follow the corner-crack and clean wall above, finishing by a step left round a rib. There is a possible belay on the rambling pine on the right after 35m.

6 The Waterfall   120m   V,5 ***   (1984)
On the first ascent the waterfall was not completely frozen but there was thick ice just right of the water flow. Three 20m pitches were climbed until below a curtain of icicles. The top of the icicles was gained via a hidden rock niche on the right, then easier ice led to the top. The route was considered technically easy for its grade, but thawing conditions forced the use of rock belays which were poor and hard to set up. On an attempt in 1986 the fall was well frozen and formed a magnificent free standing pillar about 60m from the bottom.

7 Linea Nigra   90m   Severe * (1972)

This follows the black rock immediately left of the waterfall. Start at a rowan sapling.

1. 25m   Traverse right 5m and follow a groove near the edge to the foot of a prominent slab. Move left over a pinnacle and along a ledge to an ash tree belay.
2. 40m   Go back to the pinnacle, step off the top and go straight up the wall. Move right and back left over a block, then up short walls until an exhilarating traverse right across a final steep wall leads to ledges, which are followed up left to a corner.
3. 25m   Go diagonally right and round the arete to the upper waterfall basin; then easily up left to a ledge below a shattered crack. Climb the crack and exit left onto a sloping ramp. Move left into an easy corner and follow this to the top.

8 Rainbow's End   90m   Very Difficult (1982)

Start left of the waterfall at a holly tree in a corner. The route takes the corner towards yellow overhangs and then curves right towards the top of the waterfall.

1. 40m   Follow the chimney-crack line behind the holly, passing various trees, to a stance in the corner below a slab.
2. 35m   Climb the slab and follow it as it curves into a gangway and ledges to the right; step across a bottomless chimney onto a hanging rib and ledges beyond. Now go up to a stance overlooking the upper waterfall basin.
3. 15m   Take the short crack above (as for Linea Nigra), or go up below this and exit on the right.

9 The Alley   90m   Severe * (1967)

Start 45m left of the waterfall at the foot of a square pillar.

1. 30m   Climb the front of the pillar and two short walls above to a large ledge and chockstone belay. (This is the large triangular ledge mentioned in The West Climb.)
2. 30m   Traverse right then go back left by a short chimney and continue slightly left to belay.
3. 30m   Finish by a steep groove some 8m left of the large overhangs obvious from below.

10 The West Climb   90m   Severe (1899)

This is the original route on the cliff and is remarkable for its standard and conception at that time. The grading may be open to debate, but if approached in the right spirit the climb will be found rewarding, with fine situations. The following description attempts to capture the atmosphere of the first ascent. Start at a 6m perpendicular crack to the left of the square pillar of The Alley, 45m left of the waterfall. The crack is flanked on the right by a square pinnacle and on the left by a large buttress.

From here, "an unsuccessful attempt was made on the crack, but the way proved to be for two men to get on to the top of the pinnacle, where there was just room for the second man giving the leader a shoulder low down, and steadying him until he reached some high hand-holds". Go up 3m, then left into a crack and up to the first tree (15m). Leave the tree platform at its left-hand corner and climb a chimney-crack on the left to a platform, a triangle with 6m sides.

"It was agreed by all that the beautiful, both in rock scenery and hand and foot holds, had been sought and found". Gain a ledge 5m above, first stepping left before ascending. Go leftwards (stomach traverse mentioned), to an overhanging cave located in the grassy fault on the left which leads to the top of the cliff. Climb the face on the left of the cave to a "comfortable platform". Climb "a few feet of rather rotten work" to a ledge whence climb a small open gully at its right-hand corner ('easy back and knee work'). Broken rocks to the top.

11 West Climb, Bell's Variation   90m   Very Difficult (1946)

Start up the buttress left of The West Climb. Moderate climbing for 9m, then 12m of steeper rock lead to a fir tree, followed by 5m of walking. Climb a hard pitch up a wall, then round a delicate corner to the right until one can climb straight up the

WATERFALL BUTTRESS

Andy Nisbet

2. Twoo	Hard Severe 4b	9. The Alley	Severe *
3. Blanco	Severe **	10. The West Climb	Severe
4. Tuit	Severe *	11. West Climb,	
5. Chiaroscuro	Severe **	Bell's Variation	Very Difficult
7. Linea Nigra	Severe *	12. Spider	Difficult
8. Rainbow's End	Very Difficult		

wall to a good stance. Go up the steep face on small rounded holds for 20m, then moderate climbing for 30m leads to the top.

12 Spider 75m Difficult *(1975)*
Start about 15m left of Bell's Variation, just left of a block pinnacle low on the face. Climb straight up in three steep sections, cross a grass ramp and finish easily.

13 Coloured Corner 60m Severe *(1970)*
Start about 30m left of Bell's Variation at an obvious corner with a crack at the back, a tree at 10m and a tree on a ledge at 20m. Climb the corner direct to a large platform and belay. Climb the left wall then pleasant slabs to the top.

LOWER BAND – LITTLE BUTTRESS

(NH 022 653) Alt 350m South-West facing

A broken band of rock continues slanting up across the hillside from Waterfall Buttress. Little Buttress is the first compact mass of rock reached to the north. It is defined on the left by a wide broken gully, and is some 300m from the corner of the glen.

Approach: Follow the Loch Maree path and its right fork to the burn coming down from Waterfall Buttress. Cross the burn and follow a small ridge diagonally leftwards up the hill to reach the Lower Band. A good narrow goat track below the Lower Band starts near Little Buttress.

Descent: A ramp about 50m to the north, sloping down and away from the buttress.

Miscellany 50m Severe *(1959)*
This route is immediately right of the gully, up a ridge, indistinct below but sharp above. Climb the ridge to a heather ledge and traverse right; go diagonally right up a yellow slab to the edge of a wide crack; climb the crack and the steep wall above. A mantelshelf leads to a ledge in 6m; turn the overhang on the right and finish by a knife edge on the right.

Refuse Cruise 50m VS 4c *(1984)*
This is the rib right of Miscellany. Climb easily up to a stance below and just right of the rib (10m). Follow the rib directly to an overhang and break through this on the left to the top.

Climax Slab 50m Severe *(1959)*
Start 15m right of Miscellany up the least heathery of three slabs. Climb 18m to a heather ledge and continue to the next but one heather ledge, below the overhang. Climb left of the overhang to a wide chimney; take the left fork, emerging with difficulty.

BONAID DHONN

(NH 022 657) Alt 450m West-North-West facing Map p29 Diagram p36

The Lower Band continues to rise round the hillside above lower Gleann Bianasdail, where it forms an impressive plaque of steep clean rock. The cliff gets the afternoon sun and the situation high above Loch Maree is inspiring, as is the view of Slioch. There are positive holds and good cracks typical of quartzite, but the compact nature of the rock here means that there are also bold fingery sections. There are still a few loose blocks on the less popular routes. For a mountain cliff, the rock dries quickly away from the vegetated ledges on some of the easier routes.

Approach: As for Little Buttress to find the goat track. It continues below the Bonaid Dhonn and beyond. This is the approach for Routes I and II, also A Walk on the Wild Side and beyond at the north end of the crag. While it is an option for the main central section, some unpleasant scrambling to its base means that an abseil approach is recommended.

The abseil point is fairly easy to find, even for first time visitors. Approach as for Waterfall Buttress, heading up the south side of its burn and crag to reach the top of the Lower Band. It is possible but unpleasant to scramble up north of Little Buttress. Follow the cliff-top northwards until almost at its high point. Here is a slight bay under the last rise (NH 022 657, alt 550m, marked by a cairn in 2005). At the bottom right of the bay, tucked under a small outcrop, is a platform from where a big south-facing sidewall of a corner can be seen on the right (climbed by North by North-West).

This platform is the abseil point, requiring medium to large wires and 8m of slings to reach the cliff edge. The abseil is close to 53m, so 60m ropes are ideal but 50m ropes and a short scramble down can be used with care. The abseil is down Dream Ticket and leads to a large boulder at the start of several routes, including Vertigo. Most other routes can be reached by an exposed traverse right or left.

Descent: There is no easy descent on foot to the cliff base; for those who have approached from below, it is better to climb with rucksacks. The options are either to head north for about 300m to a step down in the cliff-top, then make a descending traverse south before scrambling down steep broken ground and heather. Or walk about 1km north to the end of the cliff and take a U-turn back under it, making sure not to drop under a lower tier on the return.

The path contouring round to the Bonaid Dhonn passes under a small beak of rock at Little Buttress, then a much more prominent beak 5m above the path at the 'corner' of the glen, which marks the start of Route I. The most compact and steepest part of the crag is the Main Wall, about 100m further on.

1 Route I   120m   Difficult *   *(1946)*
Start from the goat track just left of the beak of rock. Climb rightwards up a clean slab and continue up short ribs (or more easily on the left) for some 80m before moving right to climb a 10m wall above a huge square block. Continue up a series of ribs to the hardest section, an exposed 25m wall. Climb it by a groove just left of the arete, stepping right on to the skyline near the top. Above this a small overhang and an easy rib lead to the plateau.

2 Route II   120m   Very Difficult *   *(1946)*
Start about 100m left of Route I, beyond smooth walls and just before the ground becomes vegetated (the scrambling approach to the Main Wall). Rounded ribs leading rightwards to a big overhang are seen above. Climb a slabby wall for 10m, then move left to climb the slabby ribs and pass left of the big overhang. Go up towards the steep upper wall, then traverse about 20m right to a chimney. Climb the wall on its right, then the chimney for a short distance and finish up the wall on the right.

Main Wall

This compact wall lies beyond Routes I and II and about 50m above the goat track.

The steep red wall of Dream Ticket is flanked well to the left by the big corner of North by North-West, and on the right by the smaller corner-line of Safari. Routes are described from right to left. All the routes look good, although some are given †, indicating no recent ascents are known and grades should be treated with caution.

BEINN A' MHUINIDH – Bonaid Dhonn

1. Route I — Difficult *
2. Route II — Very Difficult *
4. The Tallon — VS †
5. Grades of Shey — E1 *
6. Safari — VS †
7. The Creep — HVS **

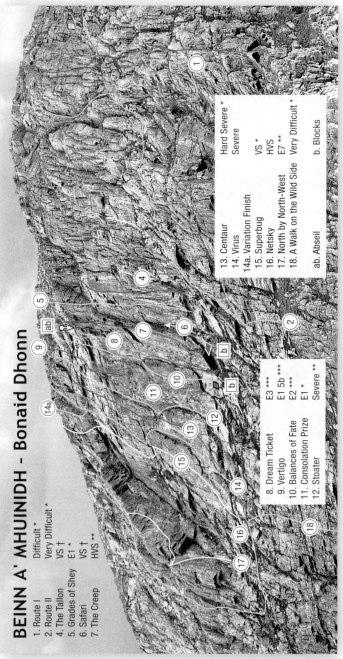

8. Dream Ticket — E3 ***
9. Vertigo — E1 5b ***
10. Balances of Fate — E2 ***
11. Consolation Prize — E1 *
12. Stoater — Severe **

13. Centaur — Hard Severe *
14. Virus — Severe
14a. Variation Finish
15. Superbug — VS *
16. Netsky — HVS
17. North by North-West — E7 **
18. A Walk on the Wild Side — Very Difficult *

ab. Abseil
b. Blocks

Tom Prentice

3 The Rebound   60m   Hard Severe *(1968)*
Start about 40m up and right of Safari at a 5m flake.
1. 30m 4b Climb to the top of the flake and then up right to a block. Climb a shallow right-facing groove to a ledge, then move 6m left. Climb the wall above, moving right at half-height, and continue to grass ledges.
2. 30m 4a Climb a wide crack in a shallow right-facing corner and continue up walls to the top.

The line of **The Bow** (Scottish VS 1969) is not certain, but it starts up the wall right of the start of Route II and above, it probably takes the obvious wide flake-crack right of a clean smooth wall.

4 The Tallon   60m   VS † *(1969)*
This takes the line of a very shallow groove, undercut at its base, about 12m right of the corner-line of Safari.
1. 10m Climb slabs and a thin crack to a stance under overhangs.
2. 25m Go left and pull over the overhangs at the highest point. Climb up and round right to enter a steep shallow groove, which is followed for 25m, until it is possible to traverse left and go up to a small stance on the rib.
3. 15m Climb directly over two overhangs, then go up slabs to belay behind a large flake about 5m right of the main corner.
4. 10m Climb a steep wall to finish.

5 Grades of Shey   50m   E1 * *(1996)*
Two pleasant pitches on the wall immediately right of Safari, lead to a fine finishing corner in the left arete of the prominent recess. Start under the overhang at the end of pitch 1 of The Tallon (reached on the first ascent by a 50m abseil down the line of the route).
1. 25m 5b Pull over the overhang 2m left of The Tallon and climb the crack and rib above to a stance.
2. 10m 5b Move left along a large projecting block and step off onto the wall, which leads to a stance in the large recess below the upper corner.
3. 15m 5b The prominent hanging corner in the arete on the left is steeper and harder than expected.

6 Safari   70m   VS † *(1969)*
The corner-line flanking the red wall on the right. Start from a huge perched block.
1. 20m Climb the crack until forced by vegetation on to the slab on the right; climb this and the flake above, then move back left into the chimney.
2. 20m Climb the chimney to a ledge on the left.
3. 20m Climb the difficult corner above to a niche, then mantelshelf strenuously leftwards. Step back right into the crack and belay in the open corner.
4. 10m Climb the open corner, passing a large flake.

7 The Creep   70m   HVS ** *(1971)*
A good climb up the right edge of the red wall climbed by Dream Ticket; not well protected on the first pitch. Start at the large block at the base of the wall, below the Vertigo flake-crack.
1. 40m 5a Move up and right on grass ledges, then traverse right across the wall until near the left edge of the corner-line of Safari. Go up to a ledge (peg runner) then straight up the wall to a roof and belay on the right.
2. 30m 4c Climb the overhanging corner directly above the belay and finish up a splendid steep crack.

8 Dream Ticket   65m   E3 *** *(1996)*
Fine sustained wall climbing in a superb position. Although slow to dry, this can be checked on the abseil descent. It is often better to climb another route first and wait for the afternoon s. Protection is good, but spaced and a double set of Friends 0.5 to 2 are useful. Start at the large block at the base of the wall, below the Vertigo flake-crack.

1. 45m 5c Climb ledges to a prominent pair of thin cracks, then move up and right to the left end of a long overlap. Return back left into the centre of the wall and continue to a small overlap level with the top of the Vertigo flake. Pull over this, climb the crack above and follow the scoop right to belay on the right edge of the wall.

2. 20m 5b Move back left and follow the right edge of the wall and easier ground to the top.

9 Vertigo 70m E1 5b ******* *(1971)*

The flake-crack and upper wall give an excellent and quite bold route. Start at the large block at the base of the wall, below the flake-crack.

1. 30m 4c Climb the flake-crack to a small ledge at its top.

2. 20m 5b Traverse left and step onto a steep grey wall. Climb up and slightly left until it is possible to pull on to the steeper wall above. Climb this until an awkward move left is made into the obvious short corner 5m above; climb the corner to a belay.

3. 20m 4b Climb over an overlap above, then move up and right towards an obvious easy corner. Avoid this by climbing a slab on the left to the top.

10 Balances of Fate 65m E2 *** *(1996)*

This counter-line to Vertigo offers excellent climbing. Start at the large block at the base of the wall, below the Vertigo flake-crack.

1. 35m 5b Ascend towards the flake-crack, but cross the small overlap on the left at its narrowest point to gain the wall. Climb straight up the wall then a small slab to belay on the flake as for Vertigo.

2. 30m 5c Traverse right onto the red wall and climb a steep undercut crack to slabbier ground above. Follow the prominent diagonal crack through a steep bulge to an awkward exit, then a groove and easier ground to belay right of a large block.

Variation: **Scales of Justice 30m E4 5c** *(2003)*

From the very left end of the flake belay, climb straight up a thin overhanging crack with difficulty to better holds and a rest below right-curving overlaps. Climb straight up to the overlaps on dwindling holds and with dwindling protection, then follow the overlaps more easily rightwards to join the normal route.

11 Consolation Prize 70m E1 * *(2003)*

Climbs the wall left of Balances of Fate and right of the wide flake-crack of Stoater. Start at a large block at the base of the wall, below the Vertigo flake-crack.

1. 15m Go up and left to belay just right of the flake-crack of Stoater.

2. 20m 5a Climb up a wall then a short groove; trend left, then up to a ledge.

3. 35m 5b Go up a scoop and flake, swing right, then go up to join Vertigo at its obvious short corner. Finish up slabs and overlaps as for Vertigo.

12 Stoater 80m Severe ** *(1971)*

This starts at a fairly wide flake-crack, the first prominent feature left of the Vertigo flake-crack.

1. 40m Climb the flake-crack, then the wall above to a small rock ledge beneath an overhang.

2. 40m Climb up and over the overhang then finish up the wall above on excellent holds, moving right through an overlap.

13 Centaur 80m Hard Severe * *(1967)*

This takes a wide shallow groove of yellow rock slanting slightly right between the flake-cracks of Stoater and Virus, about 30m right of the big corner of North by North-West. There is a flat ledge about 10m above.

1. 30m 4a Climb slabs rightwards, then climb the yellow groove to a small ledge on Stoater. Poorly protected.

2. 30m 4b Continue up the slabby right wall of the groove and the steeper wall above to a small grass ledge. An alternative (more independent of Stoater) is to climb the flake-crack left of the stance and continue up the wall above.

Tom Prentice

Charles French on the first ascent of Balances of Fate, E2, Bonaid Dhonn, Beinn a' Mhuinidh. Vertigo climbs the obvious flake-line

3. 20m 4b Climb slabs and surmount an overhang at its narrowest point. Finish up a prominent overhanging niche.

14 Virus 85m Severe *(1967)*

This route gains the stepped flake and corner-crack left of Stoater. Start as for Centaur, below the pedestal.

1. 40m 4a Climb slabs, then up onto the flat ledge. Move up and cross below an overhang into a groove on the right. Climb the groove and exit left on to grey slabs which lead to a ledge with a large flake.

2. 15m Ascend a shallow chimney and the wall ahead to a small ledge.

5. 30m Move left onto slabs. Climb these to a ledge and use flakes to reach an easy corner. Follow the corner to the top, or, for a much better finish, climb straight up the arete on the left on perfect holds.

15 Superbug 85m VS * *(2005)*

A direct line up clean slabs left of the corner of Virus. Start below and left of Virus.

1. 40m 4a Climb the slab direct to the large flake of Virus.

2. 45m 4b Move left (Virus climbs the chimney above) and climb direct up slabs

to break through a steep upper wall by flakes leading left. Step back right and finish at the top of the arete of Virus.

16 Netsky   85m   HVS   (2005)
The slabs right of the big corner are not as clean as Superbug. Quite bold but low in the grade. Start about 10m right of the big corner.
1. 35m 4c Climb slabs to an overlap. Break through this left of twin cracks (bold), then move right to break through a second overlap at the continuation fault above the twin cracks. Go up to below a big slab.
2. 50m 4c Climb the slab by a fairly direct line which leads to the top of the big corner. Step left and either climb a short arete direct (5b), or pass it on the left, to finish rightwards up easy slabs.

**17 North by North-West   45m   E7 ** **   (1997)
Climbs the left wall of the big corner, right of the crest taken by A Walk on the Wild Side. Start on a ledge below a striking vertical crack.
1. 20m 5c Climb the crack past a hollow flake until near a huge roof. Follow a thin break out left to belay on a small ledge on the arete.
2. 25m 6b From just above the belay, follow a break dipping rightwards to a low traverse line in the roof. Follow this to a spike, then climb the sustained right-slanting crack and continue in the same line to gain a good hold at the top of a faint left-facing groove. Move up left to a break and follow this, pulling over a bulge on to the arete to belay.

The following routes start from the goat track. Further left, below the big corner of North by North-West, the lower section of the Bonaid Dhonn becomes steeper and there is an overhung bay. Another 50m left, after crossing a gully, the path runs below a second, more vegetated overhung bay.

18 A Walk on the Wild Side   100m   Very Difficult *   (1967)
A good steep route on sound rock following the crest of the bulging buttress left of the big corner. Start on the path to the right of the first overhung bay, where the angle relents slightly and climb broken walls to heather. Walk left on heather to reach the foot of the buttress. Climb near the crest by cracks and grooves (easier to the left) and finish by a delightfully exposed wall on the crest. A direct start is up the steep wall on the left of the first overhung bay (40m VS †). This may be the line of **The Tappit Hen** (SMCJ 1973).

19 Aquila   150m   Very Difficult   (1980)
About 50m left of A Walk on the Wild Side at the second overhung bay. This route starts below the overhang and ascends the open convex wall above.
1. 25m Exit left from the bay and ascend a large, obvious pinnacle flake.
2. 25m Climb straight up slabs.
3. and 4. 90m Ascend diagonally right to a rib bounding the left wall of a large bay. Climb the rib then the open face above on rough solid rock.

Crypton Crack (55m Severe 1959) is about 250m left of the wide gully which splits the crag left of A Walk on the Wild Side, where the rock becomes more consistent again. It climbs a short wall to gain the crack, which is followed to a slab, a groove and insecure walls to finish.

SLIOCH

(NH 004 690)   981m

(NH 004 691)   Alt 620m   North-West facing   Map p29

Driving south-east down Slattadale and along Loch Maree the north-west face of

Slioch presents a magnificent aspect, particularly in winter. The length of both the approach and descent has deterred most climbers, although high quality climbing is available to those who find suitably cold conditions.

Approach: From Incheril near Kinlochewe along the north-east shore of Loch Maree. Follow the path to Letterewe until past Meall Riabhach, about 2km beyond Gleann Bianasdail. Follow the burn up past its source in Coire Smiorasair to a crest with a large boulder, 4hrs. Looking north-east, the Main Buttress now forms the skyline on the left.

The face is composed of Torridonian sandstone and the buttresses are therefore crossed by occasional terraces. The best rock is on the steep lower section of Main Buttress, known as Atlantic Wall. The routes on the 200m high Atlantic Wall finish on the flat top of Main Buttress. From here, another 150m of easy scrambling leads to the summit of the mountain. The routes are described right to left.

1949 Route   350m   II   *(2001)*
On the right of Main Buttress, immediately above the boulder, is a gently angled buttress. The route follows its rocky front. The lowest rocky tier was climbed by the easiest line just right of centre (moves of technical 4 initially) but can be avoided. Continue up the front face through a steepening at half-height by turfy grooves just to the left of centre to reach a level rocky ridge leading to the top of Easy Gully. In summer it gives some 30m of Difficult climbing, followed by scrambling to the top.

Easy Gully   350m   II
The gully dividing The Way Forward from Main Buttress is difficult unless there is a good build-up.

Main Buttress   245m   V,6 *   *(2000)*
Start at the right edge of Main Buttress. Move up Easy Gully for about 25m past an overhanging wall on the left, to reach an obvious turf ramp. The summer line (Severe 1952) was the result of a very impressive solo ascent, perhaps under-graded, and may coincide with Skyline Highway in places (the winter route does not).
1. 25m Climb the steepening ramp to reach the right-hand end of a large ledge.
2. 30m Move to the centre of the ledge and climb grooves to reach a steep terrace, then move left to the skyline.
3. etc. 150m Climb progressively easier grooves in the buttress edge to reach the col behind the flat top of Main Buttress.

Skyline Highway   200m   HVS *   *(1986)*
This tackles Atlantic Wall directly. Start a few metres left of the right edge of the buttress (cairn). The initial tier is steep, but gives way to more relaxed climbing above.
1. 30m 5a Follow a shallow groove right to the base of two obvious parallel cracks. Climb these on the left, then up past a ledge and awkward finger crack to a stance.
2. 25m 4c Move left then up past a small roof and continue to the first terrace.
3. 30m Scramble up the terrace to the second-tier.
4. 35m 4b Climb this tier directly, taking a blank wall at mid-height from left to right and finishing up an open corner.
5. 25m Go up the second terrace to the third-tier.
6. 35m 4c Climb a flake-choked groove leading to a smooth impending corner and an off-width crack, then more easily to a stance.
7. 70m A final easy groove leads to the flat top of Main Buttress and the long summit ridge.
Winter: **205m   VI,7 ****   *(1993)*
The first tier was climbed as for summer (crux). The second tier was climbed up a two-stepped groove left of the summer line. The third tier was climbed by a crack system 10m to the right. Continue for 70m to the flat top of Main Buttress.

Xenephon   240m   VI,6 *   (2005)
Start as for The Sea, The Sea.
1. and 2. 45m As for The Sea The Sea.
3. 40m Move right to the first line of weakness beyond The Sea, The Sea pitch 3. This comprises two narrow grooves. Climb the right-hand one to a broad ledge.
4. 40m Above is an obvious left-facing right-angled groove. Climb this to gain the left end of a narrow ledge.
5. 45m Move right towards the edge of the buttress and climb grooves immediately left of Skyline Highway (this is on the left of the buttress edge; Skyline Highway goes up the crest).
6. and 7. 70m Continue more easily in the same line to the top of the buttress.

The Sea, The Sea   240m   VII,7 ***   (1996)
The large triangular face of Main Buttress is taken on the right by Skyline Highway. This outstanding route takes the easiest line up the hardest facet of this cliff, outflanking its steep upper section. From the right edge of the buttress, walk left from beneath the start of Skyline Highway until below a very obvious corner system about three-quarters of the way to the left-hand arete. Slightly right of this point, the overhanging lower wall is threaded by a turfy line that runs about 15m up the cliff to end at a vertical wall. Start here.
1. 25m Climb the turf line until stopped beneath an undercut blank corner. Traverse right on turf for 10m to another corner.
2. 20m Climb the corner, partly on the left wall, until it is possible to step left (protection). Climb the wall above to gain a steep terrace.
3. 20m The rock is overhanging above. Traverse easily right to a bay, identified by a small chimney on the left and a high fist sized crack on the right.
4. 10m Overcome the initial bulge to a ledge below the crack.
5. 20m Climb the left wall before moving right to the crack; climb this to a ledge system.
6. 10m Move right below overhangs to a prominent groove trending slightly left.
7. 15m Gain the bottom of the groove from the left.
8. 40m Climb the groove with increasing difficulty to gain the traverse line of The Slioch Slim Plan.
9. and 10. 80m Ascend grooves with increasing ease to the flat top of Main Buttress.

The Slioch Slim Plan   300m   III *   (1994)
A left to right diagonal line up the imposing Main Buttress. Spectacular positions for the grade. Start 50m up Starters Gully where a prominent parallel sided gully cuts up right through the second-tier.
1. 40m Climb the gully, passing several steepenings, to a terrace.
2. and 3. 100m Follow the obvious line of weakness up a ramp and wide gully to a broad terrace.
4. 30m Continue up to a well defined ledge cutting across the buttress.
5. 50m Follow the ledge rightwards to near the right edge of the buttress where the angle of the upper section eases.
6. and 7. 80m Climb mixed ground, common with Skyline Highway, to the flat top of Main Buttress where Bump Start Gully emerges from the left.

Avalanche Goose   265m   VI,7 **   (2004)
To the left of The Slioch Slim Plan are a line of narrow chimneys. Start as for The Slioch Slim Plan.
1. 55m Climb the gully of its pitch 1 and 15m of easy ground to below the line of chimneys.
2. 25m Climb icy turfy grooves to the base of the lower chimney.
3. 20m Climb the first chimney to a terrace.
4. 25m Climb the second chimney, which is more of a flake at the bottom (crux), and move out left on to the terrace above.
4. and 5. 80m Traverse right, then go up short walls to gain probably Bump Start

Gully on the left.
6. and 7. 60m Climb the gully, with one steepening, to gain the col behind the flat top of Main Buttress.

Bump Start Gully   200m   III *   (1992)
The gully defining the left edge of Main Buttress. Ascend Starters Gully taking its right branch until an obvious broad gully with an icefall at its base opens out on the right. Climb the gully to gain the col behind the flat top of Main Buttress.

To the left of Main Buttress are a series of buttresses and gullies.

Starters Gully   400m   III *   (1982)
The wide gully between Main Buttress and Stepped Ridge. Climb by any one of several runnels. The best line takes the right side and a steep chimney at half-height. Where the gully joins the crest of Stepped Ridge, traverse left for 60m and climb a gully for 100m to finish just short of the west summit.

Stepped Ridge Direct   180m   VS *   (1933/1993)
A good mountain route on clean rock. This attractive feature consists of seven distinct steps. The original line avoided the major difficulties by following the gully to the left, but if climbed direct it provides a fine sustained route. Start at the foot of Starters Gully, and scramble up a grassy gully to the right of the unpleasant first step to a grass terrace.
1. 45m 4c Climb the second step, easily at first, up cracks, then make a difficult slabby exit on to a ledge. Move easily up to the base of the third step.
2. 40m 4b Take awkward parallel cracks to the top of the step, then move to the base of the imposing fourth step which is characterised by a prominent right-facing corner.
3. 25m 4c Climb the slabby corner to where it steepens and emerge on the top of an exposed tower. Climb the left edge of the knife-edge arete above (crux) to a ledge. Continue easily to the base of a prominent tower.
4. 20m 4c Climb the front face of the tower, and make an awkward exit just left of centre. Move easily along the ridge to the foot of the sixth step.
5. 20m 4c Bridge the twin off-width cracks on the right side of the tower to the top, then move along the ridge to the seventh and final step.
6. 30m 4b Climb the left of two wide cracks and continue up the prominent crack and corner system which splits the tower to reach the top of the ridge (junction with Starters Gully). Drop down left and scramble another 100m to reach the summit ridge.
Winter: **250m   V,5**   (2000)
Avoid the first step as for the summer line, then climb by grooves and cracks just left of the crest. Difficulties increase with height, the crux being the last pitch which is common with the direct summer line. From here, a further 100m of grade I ground leads to the summit ridge.

Surprise Gully   450m   II   (1984)
Left of Stepped Ridge the face opens out until another gully is reached. Start up this but soon make a long deviation right to avoid a large boulder choke (this may bank out). Continue upwards to a col high on Stepped Ridge. Traverse right from the col for 40m, crossing Starters Gully, and climb the open face above for 160m to the top.

Pinnacled Gully   450m   III,4 **   (2004)
This line follows the complete gully avoided by Surprise Gully and is defined by three spectacular pinnacles on its left side. A superb expedition. The line initially follows the right-hand base of the first pinnacle, overlooking the start of Surprise Gully before re-entering the gully.
1, 2 and 3. 150m From the start of Surprise Gully climb out leftwards towards the first pinnacle. Follow relatively easy ground skirting the base of the pinnacle to

reach a crest with a small tower overlooking the intersection of the main gully and a gully running up behind the first pinnacle.

3, 4 and 5. 150m Follow the crest a short way, then drop down to the intersection. Continue up the main gully, bounded on the right by the main cliff and on the left by the second and third pinnacles, until it ends at a final narrow col. This col separates the top of the third pinnacle from the mountain.

6. 20m Facing away from the pinnacle, traverse leftwards a short way to enter a left-facing shallow corner. Climb this to a bulge, tackled on the left, to reach easier ground and follow it for three pitches to the top.

A series of pinnacles form the left side of Pinnacled Gully (Surprise Gully). From below, there appear to be three, although their structure is more complex than appearance suggests. The highest and largest pinnacle is named Big Pinnacle.

Pinnacle Surprise   150m   Very Difficult   (1984)
The first and lowest of the three pinnacles. Start at the lowest rocks left of Surprise Gully. Follow short walls and grooves to the foot of a steep buttress. Move up and left to the buttress edge, where exposed moves lead to a groove above. Follow the crest of the ridge for two further pitches to reach the surprisingly abrupt and airy top of the pinnacle. Descent is via the south side to a col, followed by an abseil down into Surprise Gully.

Big Pinnacle

Approach: If approaching from below, traverse northwards below Main Buttress, past Stepped Ridge and Pinnacled Gully, until open hillside is reached with numerous small pinnacles denoting the left flank of Pinnacled Gully up and right. Above and to the right is a considerably bigger and more impressive pinnacle, separate from the others by a deep cut gully. But Big Pinnacle is best approached from above. Cross the ridge between Slioch summit and Sgurr an Tuill Bhain about 250m east of the summit; from here the top of Big Pinnacle can be seen. Descend due north with the pinnacle on the left and find the top of a ramp that leads to a bay (see below) with the start of the routes. 3.5hrs.

Descent: From the top of the Pinnacle, walk 100m left to gain the main hillside. A further 100m of ascent gains the summit ridge as on the upper approach.

The left edge of the Pinnacle forms a spur which descends 100m lower than the rest of its base. Beyond the spur to its left is an inset bay about 40m wide with a steep wall at its back. To the left of this bay there is a distinct steep ramp about 10m wide that leads up to the left and easy ground.

**Big Pinnacle Route 1   200m   III,4 ** **   (2005)
Start from the bay to the left of the projecting spur.

1. 40m Climb easily to the back right corner of the bay. Ascend a steepening open groove system topped by a very distinctive mushroom shaped block to reach the crest of the spur.
2. 20m Ascend the spur for a few metres until forced right by a steepening. Cut back left up a diagonal line of weakness to reach a ledge.
3. 20m Traverse rightwards passing through the line of Big Pinnacle Route 3 to the right edge of the pinnacle.
4. 30m Cut back left up a diagonal line to reach another ledge.
5. 20m Traverse back to the right edge to the foot of an attractive narrow chimney which cuts back diagonally right to left.
6. and 7. 70m Climb the steepening chimney to reach the top of the pinnacle. The last 25m is the crux, perhaps harder than 4, but it is possible to move about 5m left and join the top of Big Pinnacle Route 3 (III,3 overall).

Big Pinnacle Route 2   200m   III,4   (2005)
Climbs the chimney at the back left of the bay, opposite Route 1. Climb the

entertaining chimney to a ledge system (35m). Continue straight up to reach disappointingly easy ground after 40m. Amble easily up rightwards to below the final tier to the point where Route 3 emerges to belay under the obvious steep chimney. Instead climb the chimney-crack on the left (15m).

Big Pinnacle Route 3   200m   III,4   *(2005)*
Start on the right side of the projecting spur.
1. 40m Climb easily up a shallow gully to reach a point overlooking the separating gully.
2. 40m Continue in the line above, keeping just right of the crest, to reach a comfortable bay.
3. 25m Pull out rightwards to a groove. Climb this to where it forms an awkward chimney.
4. 10m Climb the chimney to a good ledge.
5. 50m Continue up in the same line crossing a narrow traverse line (Big Pinnacle Route 1) and continue up the groove above to a broad ledge.
6. 35m A traverse left would escape to easy ground. It is more sporting to continue straight up to a very steep chimney below the final steep tier.
7. 15m Move right to climb a far more pleasant right-facing corner to the top of the pinnacle.

Top Tower Gully   200m   I   *(2006)*
The deep gully that lies right of Big Pinnacle and curls left behind it. Straightforward snow leads to a steep exit on the right to gain the main hillside behind Big Pinnacle.
Variation: **Right-Hand Finish   150m   III**   *(2006)*
About 50m below the top of the gully is an icefall on the right wall. Climb this (or avoid it by mixed ground on the left) and climb the shallow gully line over a couple of short steps and passing under a chockstone near the top.

On a Flat Day you can see America   70m   VI,7 *   *(2006)*
About 60m below the finish of Top Tower Gully, the steep south-east face of Big Pinnacle is cut by a striking fault-line.
1. 30m Step left and climb a steep vegetated ramp that curls up and right to a steep slot. Avoid this by making steep moves up the wall on the right to reach a good ledge.
2. 25m Continue up the steep corner above moving around several large blocks. Exit steeply onto a ledge and follow this to the left for 5m to reach a good stance.
3. 15m Climb the corner at the back of the ledge and continue up easier ground to the summit of Big Pinnacle.

COIRE AN TUILL BHAIN

(NH 021 689)   Alt 750m   South-East facing   Map p29

A remote corrie with a steep headwall and one prominent buttress on the right.

Approach: Follow the Slioch path into its main south-east corrie, cross the east spur of Sgurr an Tuill Bhain at a break shown in the cliffs at 700m, then traverse the corrie to the cliffs on its north side.

Reconciliation Gully   130m   I   *(1994)*
The obvious gully at the top left end of the cliff. Well defined for 70m, then opens out to a snow fan.

Magellan's Gully   120m   II   *(1993)*
The gully immediately left of the prominent buttress.

Far Away Buttress   170m   III **   *(1993)*
The prominent buttress. Start at the lowest point.
1. 40m Climb a gully trending rightwards before breaking left at 25m to regain the

crest. Belay below a fault-line.

2. 40m Climb directly up the fault-line to belay in an open bay with no obvious escape.

3. 40m Move hard right for 5m to gain a chockstone choked chimney behind a giant flake. Continue to belay below the final wall.

4. 50m Climb the wall to a spectacular narrow ridge which leads to the summit.

FURNACE CRAGS

Above the path from Kinlochewe to Letterewe, along the north-east side of Loch Maree, are several outcrops of Horneblende schist. They are well seen from the other side of the loch at Grudie Bridge. The outcrops are bigger than they appear, have excellent rock and give pleasant climbing with a splendid outlook.

Approach: The easiest approach is directly over the loch by canoe, inflatable or other waterborne means. Failing this the path from Incheril near Kinlochewe gives a long but very scenic approach.

The crags are described from left to right, as seen from Grudie Bridge; but this is of course the inverse order if approached from Kinlochewe.

BROWN SLAB CRAG

(NG 963 706)   Alt 130m   South-West facing

This is at the west end of the ridge of crag which contains Creag Mhor at the eastern end. The crag contains a fine brown slab.

Brown Slabs Direct   30m   Severe *   (2001)
Start left of the corner by a thin crack and below a shallow rib at the top. Climb the slab to and up the rib on good crinkly rock.

Brown Slabs Left   25m   Very Difficult *   (2001)
Climb straight up 4m left of the Direct over an overlap and up brown rock above.

Brown Slabs Right   30m   Severe   (2001)
Start near the corner and straight up to near a recess. Move left up the shallow rib finishing as for the Direct.

CREAG MHOR

(NG 967 703)   Alt 150m   South-West facing

This is the clean looking buttress at the right end of the ridge and about 1km east of Furnace, identified by the grass strip leading up to its left side. The rock is friendly and often climbable in the wet, though not always protectable.

Left Wall   60m   HVS   (2001)
The wall at the base of the crag has a left-facing corner; start left of this.

1. 45m 5a Climb a vertical wall past an overlap to slabs and continue much more easily up these to a thread above a heather rake.

2. 15m Climb the easy ramp right of the heather rake to the top.

Disjointed climbing with a good start. A more balanced Very Difficult can be made by starting at the left end of the crag and moving up right to join the slabs.

Creag Mhor Cracks   60m   VS **   (2001)
A very good route. Start at a pair of short parallel cracks which lie just left of the slanting ramp of The Mad Fencer.

1. 40m 4c Climb up these cracks and over the little overhang above. Step left and climb the thin slabs direct over a brown slab to belays near the heather rake.

2. 40m 4a Move right to a shallow groove right of the rake and climb this up, then

right to the top.

The Mad Fencer   75m   Hard Severe   (1984)
Start a couple of metres right of the parallel cracks.
1. 15m Climb the good diagonal ramp right to a vertical wall. Move left under it and up to a ledge, no adequate belay.
2. 35m Move diagonally right across the slabs to below the only obvious crack on the cliff, well to the right.
3. 25m Climb the crack, then a little tower to the top.

The Mad Fencer Direct   60m   Hard Severe   (2001)
A more logical line.
1. 40m 4b Climb the first pitch of the original route but continue straight up past a heather ledge to belays 3m right of the heather rake.
2. 20m 4a Climb the shallow groove as for Creag Mhor Cracks to finish.

Creag Mhor Wall   60m   E2 *   (2001)
A good route with a bold crux. Start below the overhanging curl of rock which lies above a ramp right of the Mad Fencer.
1. 35m 5b Climb easily to the ramp, then move to the left end of the wall and up this via a short bulge to traverse right past a small tree below a steep brown slab of excellent rock. Climb the steepening slab, moving up left to gain a narrow ledge, crux. Continue to a break above and thread.
2. 25m 4a Climb up right past broken ribs to the vertical back wall left of The Mad Fencer's crack. Climb the wall leftwards via a groove to the top.

CAISTEAL MOR

No.1 Buttress

(NG 984 693)   Alt 300m   South-West to South-East facing   Map p29

This is the largest left-hand of the buttresses on the Loch Maree flank of Caisteal Mor. The buttress has its main slabby face towards the east. The southern frontage of this crag is a vertical wall starting above a grass crevasse, sheltered but midgy! Various deer trods lead above the track to the crag avoiding the worst of the heather.

Crevasse Wall   145m   HVS   (2001)
Start at a slim pillar come flake roughly mid-way along the wall.
1. 15m 4c Climb this to a ledge below a flake overhang on the left, an excellent pitch.
2. 45m 5a Climb over the overhang and trend up a diagonal leftwards line on blocky rock, under another overhang and up right past it to below a slab.
3. 40m Go up the easy slab to a heather terrace.
4. 45m 4c Climb a short steep slab via a crack, then up easy slabs to finish.

There is a route starting on the steeper front of the buttress and following the long slab above on the right (150m Very Difficult).

No.2 Buttress

(NG 987 690)   Alt 300m   South-West facing   Map p29

The next crag right of No.1 Buttress.

Riabhach Slab   120m   Severe   (1985)
1. 20m From just a few metres left of the lowest point climb steeply at first to heather ledges below slabs.

Sidewinder, VS, Furnace Crags, Loch Maree. Climber John Mackenzie

John Mackenzie collection

2. 40m Climb straight up the slab to a stance on the right.
3. 20m Continue up the slab to heather ledges below the final slab.
4. 40m Climb the crack on the right to an overhang, surmount this and continue to the top.

The right-hand boundary wall of the slab is of more continuously steep rock, avoiding some of the heather of the front face.

Sidewinder   120m   VS 4c *

(2001)

A pleasantly relaxed line with some good but mossy rock lower down. To the right of the original line is a sidewall with a flake boundary between the south and east faces. Start right of the flake at the first thin crack.
1. 35m 4c Climb this direct to a slanting crack and follow this to belays beyond the right end of a heather ledge.
2. 40m 4b Climb the pleasant slab above, then an easier slab to below a final steeper slab.
3. 40m 4b Climb the steeper slab direct to the top.

No.4 Buttress

(NG 991 686)   Alt 350m   South-West facing   Map p29

Next right is a small clean crag, No.3 Buttress, with no routes. Right again is this buttress, distinguished by an impending lower central area and a corner on the upper right. It has three routes all starting at the same point, a diagonal heather weakness at the right side of the crag.

Skeleton Lum   105m   VS   *(1984)*
1. 30m   Follow the break left to a ledge with oak and aspen at the foot of a chimney-corner.
2. 30m   Climb the chimney, strenuous at first, to the top of the crevasse.
3. 45m   The wall above leads to the top.

Norse Requiem   110m   HVS   *(1985)*
This takes the obvious large corner.
1. 5b   Follow Skeleton Lum for about 20m, then go up right to the foot of the corner. Climb to a stance under the chockstone. Surmount this to gain the steep right wall of the corner, follow thin cracks up to the arete and go up to an exposed stance.
2. 4c   Climb a pleasant slab to the base of a steep crack which is climbed to the top.

Soft Shoulder   120m   Severe   *(1984)*
1. 40m   Go up to the foot of the big corner, around the lower block of the corner via the chimney on the left, and traverse right to belay in a crevasse behind a giant flake.
2. 20m   Follow the flake round to the right and over a short crack to a stance on perched flakes.
3. 40m   Climb a shallow corner and slabs above to a stance on the right.
4. 20m   Take the steep slab above and scramble to the top.

Low Crag

Map p29

The lowest in the Caisteal Mor group, just above the path about 5km from the east end of the loch. It has two routes.

Indian Summer   70m   Severe   *(1985)*
Start in a depression near the centre of the crag, below a gnarled alder.
1. 35m   Climb the wall rightwards, then directly to a pine tree.
2. 35m   Follow a slanting wall rightwards to the top.

Phew   65m   Severe   *(1985)*
1. 25m   Right of Indian Summer is a steep wall, overhanging at the base where goats have sheltered. Climb a ramp up left into the central depression, then back right to an oak tree.
2. 40m   Move right and climb steeply to the top.

ARDLAIR CRAGS

Alt 100m   South-West facing

The crags stretch from Ardlair to Witches Point. Beyond, the more broken crags of Creag Tharbh (The Bull Rock) extend for another 2km. The geology of the crags is complex, the rock composition being basic to intermediate. As such, the lower section of the crags tends to be a variety of rather mixed amphibolite rocks whilst the upper is a rougher variety of the same. The rock improves both with height and moving from west to east, but a considerable amount is slatey, almost basaltic, unhelpful and deficient in either holds or cracks. Fortunately belays are often mature Scots pines which dot the crags at random. A further complication to this area is the prolific insect population, especially ticks, which appear from early spring onwards. Shorts are therefore not advised. The crags should also be avoided during the nesting season.

Approach: From Poolewe, take the road towards Kernsary. Leave it at NG 883 788 and follow a new path which bypasses Kersary to meet the track to Ardlair. Cycling via Kernsary shortens the approach considerably. A boat would be quickest in calm weather.

Descent: By abseil down one of the adjacent gullies, which often contain mature holly trees.

RECCE BUTTRESS
(NG 900 760)

This is the first of the buttresses, situated immediately above the ruined building by the track leading down to Ardlair. It is composed of a remarkably unfriendly rock. Protection is often noticeable by it absence.

The Wreckie   55m   VS   *(1999)*
A poor messy route with an apt name. Start at a large flake at 6m in the centre of the crag.
1. 20m 4b Climb the wall to the right of the flake and enter the chimney behind it. Gain the top of the flake and step on to the wall which is climbed for a few metres to where a left traverse leads to a tree.
2. 35m 4b Climb the pleasant slab to the right of the tree to a ledge. Move up right to reach the base of a left-slanting groove, which is followed to a point where the wall on the right can be climbed to finish, which avoids the scrappy top section of groove.

The main area is composed of three big crags separated by vertiginous gullies. Going from west to east, the first is vertical and of dubious rock. The second is the showpiece of the area with a prominent overhang cutting the right-hand edge and the third is dark and slabby with a slabby pillar overlooking a deep gully at the right end. There are also upper crags, with two routes on the crag containing a prominent corner above No.1 Buttress. To reach the crags walk along the track past a new house and on for about a kilometre to either a scree slope below No.2 Buttress or where a wall runs up the hillside. The crags are above broken rocks and scree.

Upper Tier

This can be reached by scree gullies and scrambling either side of No.1 Buttress.

The Corner   10m   HVS 5a   *(2001)*
This is the Cenotaph Corner look alike, alas a much reduced version in reality. Climb it over some loose rock but excellent gear.

Left Wall   10m   E2 5b   *(2001)*
The left wall is climbed via a crack.

NO.2 BUTTRESS
(NG 909 751)

This is the best looking buttress with a slabby apron leading to vertical rock above, bordered on the left by a flying buttress and on the right by a brown nose cut by a massive roof.

Flying Buttress   115m   HVS 4c   (1990s)
On the left side of the buttress is a flying buttress with a Scots pine on its crest. Start at an imbedded flake in the flying buttress. Climb up then right, unprotected, to the right edge; follow the flake more or less up the middle to the tree belay, (4c). Continue up the steep wall above then up slabs on much better rock to the top.

Where Eagles Nest   90m   E1 5b **   (2001)
The best route on the crag taking the right edge via the rib and huge overhang. Start at a brown rib left of a steep alcove at a grass ledge a few metres up.
1. 20m 5b Climb the rib direct to a huge block, step left, then go up the crack to a fine stance (Friend 4 belay).
2. 20m 4c Climb the groove a little, then make an awkward traverse right to a corner. Climb this over a pinnacle and traverse right easily to a tree below the roof.
3. 20m 5a Climb the rib above to an overlap, move right under this and up past the roof to step left by a small tree on the nose.
4. 30m 4c Climb a fine rib direct over a small sharp overhang to a glacis. Move left and climb a steeper nose to the top.
Abseil either down the gully immediately right of the crag or down a loose wall further right from a big tree which gives one 50m abseil to the base.

NO.3 BUTTRESS

(NG 910 750)
This is the somewhat friendlier slabby crag just right of No.2. The rock is mixed in quality on the grey section but excellent on the initial and top sections.

Serious Adventure   90m   E1 5a *   (2001)
Start at the base of the crag below a brown slab which has a small overlap a couple of metres up.
1. 20m 5a Climb the excellent slab direct, minimal protection, to the pine tree above.
2. 30m 4c Above is a steep grey massive wall of few cracks. Climb above the tree, then move up right under bulging rock to the right-hand edge (serious), then back left to a small tree. Continue up a pair of parallel cracks moving up left to a large tree.
3. 40m 4b Now the rock dramatically improves. Climb out left from the tree and straight up enjoyable slabs to a final little bulge at the top.
Abseil down from a little tree at the crest of the crag then down the line of the route in two abseils.

Slattadale Pillar   110m   VS 4c *   (1999)
This is the fine slabby rib bounding the right-hand side of the buttress. Start at the base to the right of a tree. Descend by two abseils down Holly Tree Gully on the right; prickly but unavoidable.
1. 35m 4c Climb a crack and the short wall above. Move up to a steep crack with a small tree. Climb the crack to reach an easy groove which leads to a splendid belvedere overlooking the loch.
2. 25m 4a Move up a corner to below a big roof and traverse the slab leftwards to exit up a steep corner with good holds to a pine tree above.
3. 50m 4a Above is a fine brown rib. Climb this, moving slightly left to follow the edge exactly all the way to the top, a very good pitch on rough rock.

KINLOCHEWE & LOCH MAREE SOUTH

The hills and crags in this chapter are all approached from the road from Kinlochewe along the south side of Loch Maree in the direction of Gairloch. The hills are the north end of the Torridon group whereas the crags (like the major group of the Stone Valley Crags) fit more naturally into Northern Highlands Central.

RUADH STAC BEAG

(NG 973 614)   896m

This is the outlying, seldom visited hill guarding the north-east side of Coire Ruadh-staca. Flanking its east end is a 100m triangular quartzite slab, climbed direct by **The Long Stroll** (Very Difficult 1983).

Ruadh Ridge Beag   100m   III   *(1999)*
Near the left end of the cliffs south-east of the summit of Ruadh Stac Beag is a well defined ridge right of a gully (clearly seen from the Black Carls section of the Beinn Eighe ridge). Climb the crest with two steep but very helpful sections.

MEALL A' GHIUBHAIS

(NG 977 635)   886m

CREAG BHAN

(NG 971 632)   Alt 570m   South-West facing   Map p29

On its south-west flank there is a cliff consisting of two tiers of clean quartzite, apparently with a number of routes. **Traveller** (150m Very Difficult 1980s) takes a prominent corner in the upper tier to a bay, finishing up an arete on the left.

NATURE TRAIL AREA

There are several areas of crag to the south-west of Loch Maree which are approached from the Nature Trail paths.

Quartzite Crags

Situated at about 400m, these crags are approached by the eastern trail and are at NG 998 638. Though promising from a distance, they are fairly loose and unlikely to be more than 60m high. Some are sound, particularly moving uphill and though it is possible that climbs have been done, none are recorded. The soundest and perhaps most obvious is the farthest uphill, a slabby sound buttress just right of the path.

Path Buttress   40m   Difficult   *(1999)*
Start at the lowest point, climb the rib, move right and climb the steeper top section centrally.

Great Red Slab

(NG 987 648)   Alt 400m   North facing   Map p29

The slab is composed of clean rough sandstone and despite strips of vegetation, gives good climbing in the lower grades. The slab is climbable almost anywhere so the best choice is to find the general line and keep to the best rock. There is limited protection. The routes are quite pleasant and no harder in the wet but the approach and descent are grim.

Approach: Most easily approached from the western path of the Nature Trail. Park at the car park with a large sign for Beinn Eighe, Glas Leitir Trails. The western path goes under the road, then immediately crosses the burn. The slab soon becomes visible high on the right. Follow the path to the 300m level and a set of wooden steps on a crest. Traverse across heather with a slight descent keeping well below the crags to the base of a small corrie. Go straight up through jungle for another stretch whereupon the slab becomes increasingly visible up on the left. "Jungle" is accurate because it is a nature reserve and herbivores are discouraged.

Descent: Descents are to the right (west) beside a slippery gully.

The most likely point of arrival is the base of the main slab. The slab has a vertical right sidewall overlooking the descent gully, with a 20m diagonal section between it and the base of the slab. The right end of the base has a level grass platform below a big open corner. The left wall of the corner is steep, the right forms a knobbly slab. About 100m left and below this platform is the start of the next route, which climbs a steep but scrappy lower tier before continuing above. From its top, the platform can be regained by climbing down right (about Moderate).

Money Lenders Slab   100m   Severe *(1999)*
Start at a little cave below a wide corner just right of the lowest rock (which is a big overhang). Climb the steep left wall of the corner, step right and pull over via a small tree. Move a metre right, climb a pair of wedged flakes and step right on to a slabby nose. Climb this pleasantly to a small ledge and then climb the slabby wall to the right of a short corner to easy ground. A walk right from here would gain the platform. Move up to the next tier which is of sound clean rock. Climb a shallow groove which is left of centre direct to the top; this gives the best climbing on the route.

Pawn Broker   120m   Very Difficult *(2000)*
Start from the platform, at the left (bottom) end of the left wall of the open corner. Climb out left on good holds, cross a vegetated groove and climb out left again onto open slabs. Go easily up a vague crest trending right. A scrappy route.

Lonesome Pine   120m   Very Difficult * *(2000)*
Start from the platform up the steep little knobbly slab at the right end of the base. Above this, go directly up (trying to keep to rock) to reach a large area of clean red smooth slab. Climb this trending slightly right, then back left to finish by easy padding.

Great Expectations   120m   Very Difficult * *(1999)*
This climbs the right edge of the slab, overlooking the retaining west wall. A good climb, gaining interest with height, all on superb clean rock. Start up the knobbly slab; climb this to easy slabs which lead naturally to the very edge. Climb the steeper slabs above through grooves and corners, all on the right edge, to a much steeper section. This is climbed overlooking the edge on good holds, finally moving left above a loose block. Climb more slabs and corners overlooking the right edge to a final steep wall on the left which is split by a slanting crack. Climb the left wall of the crack to a rather stretchy exit.
Variation 1:
A harder start up the sidewall. Start well up and right from the base, 2m right of a short left-slanting chimney (cairn and arrow). Climb a short steep wall to the edge.
Variation 2:
Start as for the original but before reaching the edge via the easy slabs, climb straight up a long corner-ramp (left of a recess) to regain the edge after about 25m.

CAVE CRAG

(NG 987 651)
Three hundred metres west of the Great Red Slab, and level with its base, is a small crag with a prominent cave. Climb into the cave which becomes a chasm. On the

right wall is an obvious crack. This gives an entertaining climb **Chasm Pinnacle** (2000) up slightly friable rock to a ledge from where the top of a huge detached pinnacle can be gained (Severe). Either abseil off the in-situ sling or traverse via a through route and down climb awkwardly to another large chasm.

NORTH-EAST FACE

(NG 981 638)   Map p29

The north-east side of the hill is split by a single gully which gives a winter climb, **Outrider** (180m III 1986).

Persecution Rib   200m   Severe   (1999)
The face is characterised by a long broken rib of steep tiers separated by scree and grass. The rib is left of the existing winter route but is a poor climb; a central start might improve it a little. Start at the steep wall at the base. On the left is a jutting block; climb over this from the left, move up right and climb a short chimney. Traverse left to below steep slabs which are followed to the crest. Go up easy ground to the next tier, which is taken left of centre, as is the tier above that. The final tier is of better rock and is taken by the centre of three grooves.

Lower North-East Flank - Allt Bhanamhoir Fall

Map p29

This waterfall lies in an overhung alcove of crags at 370m just above the pine woods of the Nature Reserve at NG 978 655. It is approached direct up the side of the burn from the A832, and froze into an impressive icicle topped by a cluster of canopies after a week of continuous frost. There were other icefalls hereabouts. During the hind culling season (Nov 1 to Feb 15) climbers are advised to first call the SNH ranger at Kinlochewe to check access, as shooting is carried out on these slopes (01445 760254 day, 01445 760244 evening).

Bhanamhoir Fall   35m   VI,6   (1996)
Climb 75 degree ice into a recess to the right of a free standing section (peg and screw runners). Climb the pillar (thin and watery) up leftward into a niche, then battle through organ pipes and umbrellas to the top. To finish, either climb left out of the burn on a slab of ice spray or climb ice pitches a little higher in the burn.
Variation: **Resignation Variation   45m   IV,4**   (2001)
Climbs the right-hand wall of the very steep main pitch. On this occasion the main fall did not form a complete column. Climb a steep initial section, then move right onto a heathery wall which formed a thick icefall. Return back into the main small gorge above.

On the Skyline   90m   IV,5   (2001)
Climbs the icefall draining from the obvious cleft on the skyline above and left of the falls of Bhanamhoir (NG 980 653). Consists of two pitches of good ice, the second having a 20m vertical step.

COBLE CRAGS - SRON A' CHOIT

These are a line of crags overlooking Loch Maree above Victoria Falls at Slattadale. The routes are short and steep on gneiss with good incut holds.

Approach: From the Victoria Falls car park, walk up the forestry track on the west side of the stream towards the hydro dam on Loch Garbhaig. On exiting from the top end of the wood, a line of knolls with small crags can be seen on the left skyline (to the east). These are the smaller Coble Crags Three to Seven, numbered left to right. Bear off left across the stream to the line of crags (30mins total). Coble Crag Two eventually comes into sight to the left but Coble Crag One is about 300m further left.

COBLE CRAG ONE

(NG 905 706) Alt 250m North-West facing

On the Pavement 20m E1 5b ** *(1999)*
The most obvious feature towards the left end of the crag is a holly bush below a corner. The route climbs the attractive wall left of the corner. Start at the bottom left of the wall. Climb up and right to a line of flakes which lead diagonally left, then out right near the top to a narrow ledge. Move left to the arete and up easier mossy walls.

Alter Ego 20m VS 4c ** *(1997)*
Start under the holly bush. Climb up the wall left of the holly (crux, or climb through the holly, much easier) into the obvious corner and up to a roof. Continue up left on a ramp to the easier edge and finish as for On the Pavement.

Solid Gold 25m E2 5c * *(1999)*
Start just right of the holly bush. Go up ledgy ground to the left end of the big roof. Climb the pillar left of the roof, then a right-trending crack-line to finish.

Right of Solid Gold is a section of scrappy ground with steep walls and ledges leading across to a heathery gully. About 10m right of the gully is a corner which is at the left end of a short steep red wall of good rock.

Anxiety 20m VS 4c *(1999)*
Climbs the rib left of the heathery gully. Climb steps leftwards into a steep right-facing corner. Follow it to a ledge, then climb a crack-line up short walls above. Spoiled by abundant heather in the top half.

Little Jack Horner 15m HVS 5b *(1999)*
Right of the heathery gully is an unclimbed groove, then the corner at the left end of the short wall. Climb the corner awkwardly to a ledge at its top. An interesting finish is to step out left on to the wall to reach a steep crack-line.

The Flakiest 8m E1 5b * *(1999)*
The leftmost of three routes on the wall. Start 3m right of the corner at the left end of the wall. Climb up and right into a triangular niche. Finish up a steep flake-crack above.

Ripsnorting 8m E2 5c ** *(1999)*
Climb a steep right-slanting flared crack-line near the right end of the wall, starting about 5m down from the right end. A ledge out right gives a possible rest. High in the grade, with fiddley protection.

Wasted 6m E1 5c *(1999)*
An artificial route squeezed into the right end of the wall. Climb steeply via faint twin cracks to good finishing holds.

COBLE CRAG TWO

Mutant Gene 16m HVS 5a * *(1997)*
Start under the left-hand side of a long overhang, climbing straight up and into a short corner. Continue straight up on small ledges.

Prodigal Sun 16m HVS 5a * *(1997)*
Start under the right-hand edge of the overhang. Follow a distinct linear crack to a horizontal sloping shelf, then step left and finish up a short crack.

Coble Crags Three to Seven offer several short walls with routes up to 10m. The only recorded route climbs the left arete on Crag Three at a poorly protected 4c **Blunt Edge** (8m 1997, perhaps just HVS).

STONE VALLEY CRAGS

Map p74, Diagram p57

The crags lie on the west flank of Meall Lochan a' Chleirich, which lies to the south of the A832 west of Loch Maree. The name Stone Valley was due to the numerous crags of all shapes and sizes which form a rocky wall on the hillside. The rock is clean rough gneiss although slightly gritty on first ascent. It has a splendid outlook both to Baosbheinn and the sea, although the planting of a million trees in the area as part of the Millenium Forest project will eventually alter the openness of the site. The crags are a suntrap and due to their hummocky formation, many routes dry rapidly after rain. The proximity to the mountains means, however, that the crag often catches showers when crags nearer the coast are dry. This is a very pleasant place to climb, although the quality climbing on many routes is quite short.

Approach: Park at a car park around a green barn (current colour, but known locally as the Red Barn) at NG 856 721. Follow the Loch na h-Oidhche track, which has a signpost indicating the Bad na Sgalag Native Pinewood, for about 1km and the crags will be seen facing south-west on the craggy hillside of Meall Lochan a' Chleirich. There is a hint of a path leading across the upper of two bridges and towards Stone Valley Crag. About 40mins.

The pale clean arete of Stone Valley Crag is the most obvious feature. It is barely seen from the parking place but becomes increasingly obvious the further up the track one goes, as does the clean wall on its right with the best climbs. Clearly seen from the Red Barn car park are the Domes high up at the back and Rum Doodle Crag, which lies left of Stone Valley Crag and is identified by its prominent arete.

CREAG NAN CADHAG

(NG 864 722)   Alt 160m   North-West facing

A steep crag next to the road.

Central Corner   25m   VS 4b   *(1989)*
The big central corner of this overhanging lichenous crag. The corner chimney-crack was climbed until it became too narrow and the route finished up the left wall.

The Trail of the Lonesome Pine Marten   25m   HVS 5a   *(1989)*
Start a few metres left of Central Corner, below a boulder on a ledge. Go straight up with increasing difficulty to finish by the obvious overhanging jamming crack.

SCRAGGY SLAB

(NG 868 720)   Alt 260m   West facing   Diagram p57

As seen from the parking place, the first group of skyline rocks above and right of Creag nan Cadhag contains Scraggy Slab. On the approach, this is seen as a series of smaller outcrops below and left of the more obvious Flowerdale Wall.

Scraggy Slab   30m   HVS 4c   *(1998)*
This disappointing route takes the biggest slab, about 200m left of Flowerdale Wall, on dubious rock with poor protection.

THE VALLEY WALLS

(NG 868 719)   Alt 270m   South-West facing   Diagram p57

Above and right of Scraggy Slab is a shallow valley that forms a col on the skyline.

Andy Nisbet

STONE VALLEY CRAGS

as seen from the car park as well as on the approach. The valley has the Valley Walls on its left side (hidden) and the obvious Flowerdale Wall on its right side. The walls start at a short vertical bow shaped wall at the entrance to the valley and lead to a pleasant but broken line of slabs running along its left side. Flowerdale Wall, the bigger wall facing the approach, lies on the right at the entrance to the valley. The first routes lie on the steeper bow shaped wall at the entrance to the valley.

Round the Block   15m   VS 4b   *(2001)*
At the left end of the steeper wall is a flake-line. Climb this and a short blocky crack to the top. A bit hollow.

Flash in the Pan   15m   E3 6a   *(2001)*
The thin crack immediately to the right of Round the Block is climbed with difficulty, protected by good but small wires. Continue up the more obvious crack in the final wall.

Off the Block   15m   HVS 5a *   *(2001)*
The central line. Climb up and step on to the obvious block then climb the crack to easier ground. The top of the flake was not pulled on.

The following route lies on the stepped slab a short way to the right, above the flat floor of the valley (alt 280m, south facing).

Three Stepped Slab   20m   Hard Severe 4b   *(2001)*
Just right of an obvious fault is a crack with an obvious jug at its base. Climb this thin crack up the first step. Climb directly up the wall above to easy ground and traverse left to climb the third step past a block.

One Step Beyond   15m   Severe 4b   *(2001)*
Beyond a slight bay and about 20m to the right is this rib. Leaving the ground is hard, the rest is much easier.

FLOWERDALE WALL

(NG 868 719)   Alt 270m   West facing   Diagram p57
A wall of white speckled rock on the right side of the valley but facing the main road. It also lies 200m behind Rum Doodle Crag (and Stone Valley Crag) and can easily be reached from there. It provides a pleasantly steep middle grade crag composed of juggy but blocky rock on the left and smoother red rock on the right.

Rock Around the Block   25m   VS 4c   *(1997)*
To the right of a small buttress at its left end is a narrow crack leading to a wider one. Climb the crack on sharp holds. Step across the wide crack and move right to climb the rib direct taking care of some unsound flakes.

Blyth Spirit   25m   VS 4c **   *(1997)*
Good rock. Stand on top of a rock finger right of the last route and climb direct to a small overhang. Climb over this and up a thin but helpful crack to the top.

Sun Due   25m   VS 4c *
A pair of wider cracks lies to the immediate right of Blyth Spirit. Climb the left one.

Tormentil Grooves   25m   VS 4b   *(1997)*
Climb the right crack and move up right to a wide corner-crack, climbed to the top.

Lilly of the West   25m   E1 5b **   *(1997)*
To the right is a narrow buttress with a snaking crack providing well protected steep climbing in an excellent position. Follow the crack over the crux bulge and finish directly up the edge.

Veinous Fly Trap   25m   HVS 5a *   *(1997)*
A red slab lies to the right of the buttress of Lilly of the West. A shallow corner bounds its left-hand side. Climb this corner somewhat tenuously to the top.

Blood Red Roses   25m   HVS 5a *   *(1997)*
Just right of the shallow corner, the slab has a lichenous patch. Climb the slab direct to and up the lichenous patch and exit near some heather.

Mountain Everlasting   25m   HVS 5a   *(1997)*
Climb the increasingly thin and bold red slab to the right of Blood Red Roses directly up its crest.

White Lining   25m   HVS 5a *   *(2001)*
The arete has a prominent narrow streak of white quartz running down it which stops short of the base of the crag at the start of a bottomless groove and flake-line. Climb up the fault to the right of the arete to a spike. Swing left into the bottomless groove at the base of the white line, then gain the flake-line and follow this up the right side of the arete to finish easily up slabby ground. The original line started 2m to the left and finished at the same place.

Avoid the Paint   12m   VS 4c *   *(2001)*
The centre of a slim buttress at the right end of the crag, starting up a shallow grassy corner.

ATLANTIC WALL

(NG 866 718)   Alt 210m   West facing   Diagram p57
The main line of crags features the obvious aretes of Rum Doodle Crag and Stone Valley Crag. About 150m left of Rum Doodle Crag is a shallow amphitheatre with a vertical back wall as seen from the car park. The right-hand wall of this back wall is Atlantic Wall. Though relatively short, it is vertical and varied, with reasonable protection, but the rock is brittle. The first three routes are on the concave slab immediately to its left.

Cannonade   10m   Severe 4a   *(1997)*
The concave slab climbed centrally is quite thin.

The Compleat Angler   13m   Difficult   *(1997)*
Start up the lichenous slab to the right and take a rightwards line to the top near the next route.

Casting a Line   12m   Difficult   *(1997)*
Climb the crest of a rib left of the main wall to and over a niche at the top.

Mutineers   12m   HVS 5a   *(1997)*
Start to the right of the left edge of the main wall and climb a steepening wall direct to a short crack at the top. This is best turned by a move to the left but can be climbed direct at 5b.

The Cruel Sea   12m   E2 5c **   *(1997)*
The best route on the wall; sustained, high in the grade, but with good protection although strenuous to place. Start in a shallow scoop near the centre of the crag and climb up to a slot in a horizontal crack. Go straight up to the right end of a small roof and finish up the thin crack above.

Ancient Mariner   12m   HVS 5a *   *(1997)*
Climb directly up the wall to the left of a flake to a square perch. Continue up the wall above - a strenuous top section.

The Cat   12m   Severe 4b   *(1997)*
Climbs the right edge of the wall. Move right below the flake onto the wall and climb it to the top.

Tall Tail   8m   E4 6a   *(2001)*
Beyond a bay is another small wall. Climb the centre of this unprotected bulging wall just left of a thin crack-line.

Fisherboys   8m   E1 5b   *(1997)*
The awkward thin crack-line to its right.

CATERPILLAR CRAG

(NG 866 717)   Alt 270m   South facing   Diagram p57

This is a small crag behind Atlantic Wall and Rum Doodle Crag, at the left end of a band with Playtime Wall at its right end. Go up the small gully between Atlantic Wall and Rum Doodle Crag; the crag is in front and slightly to the right.

Benny Blanco from the Bronx   12m   VS 4b *   *(2006)*
At the left side of the crag is broken scarred black rock. Start 2m right of this under a right-curving shallow groove at two-thirds height. Climb direct up a steep wall to the easier groove.

Gailes   12m   Hard Severe 4b   *(2006)*
Start 2m right of Benny Blanco under a small right-facing corner. Climb on good holds to the corner and finish direct.

Giggling Cairn   12m   Hard Severe 4b   *(2006)*
A right-leaning crack-line a metre right again.

RUM DOODLE CRAG

(NG 867 717)   Alt 220m   South facing   Diagram p57

This lies several hundred metres left of Stone Valley Crag and appears as two parallel aretes. Most of the climbing is based on the left arete (Rum Doodle Arete), which is well seen from the Red Barn car park. The main crag has two smaller buttresses to its left.

Crowded Out   12m   Difficult   *(2001)*
The slabby crack-line on the leftmost buttress.

Doodles   10m   E2 5c   *(2001)*
Climbs a steep prow on the next buttress. Start up a capped groove and pull over the roof on to a ramp. Go up the ramp to a high runner, then go left on to the front of the prow and finish leftwards.

Go Lightly   10m   VS 4c   *(1999)*
This small buttress has a chimney on its right-hand side. Climb the wall left of the chimney and just right of an arete past a tiny roof.

Heavyweights   10m   VS 5a   *(2001)*
Start up the chimney, move right and finish up the left side of the wall above a heathery ledge.

Better Things to Do   10m   Hard Severe 4a   *(2001)*
The next smooth slab to the right, some 20m left of Rum Doodle Arete.

Totter's Slab   40m   Very Difficult   *(1995)*
Follow the right edge of this smooth slab to move right and up a bigger pale slab.

Gotta Feeling   20m   Severe 4a   *(2001)*
Climbs more broken ground between Totter's Slab and the arete to finish up a cleaner slab right of Totter's pale slab.

Busy Day   20m   Severe 4a   *(2001)*
Start as for Gotta Feeling but on the top slab, climb a shallow groove to its right.

Juniper Slab   25m   Severe 4a   *(1996)*
Immediately left of Rum Doodle Arete is a narrow red slab. Start left of the central crack and climb directly up the slab keeping left of Rum Doodle Arete.

Rum Doodle Arete   35m   Hard Severe 4a *   *(1995)*
Start below the arete at a little groove to the left, gain the arete and follow the narrow edge directly, which is both bold and airy but with splendid friction. The last few metres are mossy and can be turned by a crack just to the left. Walk off at a ledge above or climb a straightforward groove on the left.

Roman Wall   35m   Severe 4a **   *(1996)*
Climbs the slabby right wall of Rum Doodle Arete. Start left of a gully which leads to small trees. Climb a central rib leading to a small tree. Step left on to the wall and climb upwards to a right-slanting ramp. Follow this to below a vertical wall with thin cracks and step left to take the final few metres of the arete direct (crux) to the ledge. Finish by the optional central crack (4c) or scramble off right.

Dear Trees   35m   Hard Severe 4a   *(2001)*
Start as for Roman Wall but move right to climb past the left side of a roof to reach and climb a left-facing corner.

The following route climbs the right arete of the chimney system but taking a harder start on the left. The arete can be climbed from the base at Very Difficult but is disappointing.

Chleirichal Error   25m   VS 4c   *(1996)*
To the right of Roman Wall lies a gully with a steep right wall. To the left of a pair of short cracks (both Very Difficult) is a groove. A steep entry gains the base of a thin grass filled groove. Step right onto the wall and climb this to step back left above the grass. Excellent rough rock to the top.

RED BARN CRAG

Diagram p57

Directly below Rum Doodle Crag lies this lower crag. It sports a narrow rib of rough rock with a smooth sidewall on the right.

Flying Circus   25m   VS 5a   *(1997)*
Start left of the line of the rib and climb a rough slab to the base of the rib immediately to the left of Curse you! Awkward moves reach a small overhang which is climbed on hidden holds, then follow the rib direct to the top.

Curse you Red Barn!   20m   VS 4b   *(1997)*
Start right of the line of the rib and climb a short wall to gain a central crack-line immediately to the right of the rib and Flying Circus. Low in the grade.

A Load of Old Bosche   15m   VS 4c   *(1997)*
To the right of the narrow rib is a smooth wall with an awkward two-step V-groove.

Hun in the Sun   15m   HVS 5a   *(1997)*
The smooth wall to the right has a wide crack which is climbed on marginally hollow holds but good gear. Quite pleasant and open.

So What   8m   Severe 4a   *(2001)*
A groove line in a wall 15m right of Hun in the Sun.

Then What   8m   5a   *(1999)*
The rib on the right of So What. Start up the rib to reach jugs on the right near the top.

VIKING CRAG

(NG 867 717)   Alt 220m   South facing   Diagram p57

Between Rum Doodle Arete and Red Wall Crag lies this small crag marked by large fallen blocks and short walls. Descend on the left (looking up).

Helga's First Time   30m   Severe 4a   *(1998)*
There is an obvious broken groove with twin cracks above. Climb the pleasant rough slab on the left of the groove to a boulder. Step left on to a wall, then by interesting moves right to finish directly up the crest of a rib.

Uphellya   30m   VS 4c   *(1998)*
Take the obvious broken groove, step left, then up right to climb the twin cracks (harder if the dubious block at the top of the cracks is not used). Follow a crack on excellent rock to finish just right of the crest.

Little Valhalla   12m   VS 4c *   *(1998)*
About 10m right of Uphellya, is a very obvious short overhanging V-groove with a pinnacle right of its base. This gives delightful, well protected climbing. Much better than it looks.

Norse Face Route   12m   E2 5c *   *(1998)*
Starting up Little Valhalla, gain the pinnacle on the right. A shimmy up the arete and mantelshelf gains a pocket with a vital Friend 3.5 runner. An extended wire into a slot on the right protects hard moves right to a crack. Further hard moves up lead to a right-trending fault-line and easier finish. The overall grade increases if the extended runner cannot be placed.

RED WALL CRAG

(NG 868 717)   Alt 230m   South facing   Diagram p57, 64

This is the steep wall left of Stone Valley Crag. The rock is more fissile but essentially sound. The red pillar of Bold as Brass at the left end is the most obvious feature. Right of it is a groove with trees at different heights. Right again is a smaller bulging pillar, then the smaller but well defined groove of Lucky Strike. From here a heather ramp slopes up right.

1 **Bold as Brass   20m   E2 5c ****   *(1996)*
Climbs the red coloured left-bounding pillar of the wall. Gain a ledge just left of Flaming June, step up right to below a flange, then climb it stepping left to below a thin curved crack. Make thin moves up the crack and easier to the top.
Variation: **Direct Start   E3 5c**
This gives a better but bolder route with RP protection. Climb direct from the ledge, near the right arete of the wall, to the upper section, thus independent of Flaming June.

2 **Burnt Offering   25m   E2 5b ***   *(1998)*
Bold as Brass is followed to below the flange, when a wall on the right is climbed to a groove with tiny tree below an overlap. This is passed on the right, with a deviation right which avoids the hardest direct moves.

**3 Flaming June   25m   VS 5a ** ** *(1995)*

A steep line with devious but good climbing, close on the left of the groove with trees. Start on a short rib just right of Bold as Brass. Climb up to a small ledge at its right end. Continue to an obvious flange above, then traverse right to a ledge with small trees. Climb up the flake-crack and step left into a niche below a small roof, then step back right towards heather. Climb up and left into a well positioned open corner to a ledge. A short arete provides a pleasant finish.

4 Flaming Crack   30m   VS 5a *(1998)*

The crack of Flaming June is followed throughout. Will improve with time.

5 The Wallace   20m   E4 5c *(1997)*

Climbs the bulging pillar. Start 2m left of the obvious groove of Lucky Strike and climb a crack in a small groove to a ledge at 4m; layback boldly left round a giant flake, leading to a vital Rock 1 runner, which may eliminate deckout potential. Continue to the nest of hollow spikes on Lucky Strike, then step left to finish more easily up good cracks. Only Bravehearts need apply.

**6 Lucky Strike   20m   VS 5a ** ** *(1996)*

Start just at the bottom of the heather ramp. Follow the obvious groove, bearing left to a nest of hollow spikes at its top. Climb the seemingly blank wall up and right on hidden holds to the ledge.

7 The Bruce   20m   HVS 5a *(1997)*

Follow the initial groove of Lucky Strike for about 5m. Take the groove on the right to a good finish right of Lucky Strike. Beware of spiders.

8 Schiltrom   25m   E1 5b * *(1998)*

Starting at a small embedded spike in the heather ramp right of Lucky Strike, make a hard move left to gain the bottom of a rightward-trending flake-line. This leads to a semidetached spike just left of Strike Two, from where a move leftwards gains an overlap which is overcome with difficulty. Climb the clean slab above, with a delicate move left to finish.

9 Strike Two   30m   HVS 5a *(1997)*

Start at the same spike as Schiltrom, below a groove. A tricky bulge gains access to the groove. Care is needed with some hollow flakes. Continue up the upper wall on good rock.

10 Short Sharp Shock   8m   E1 5b *(1996)*

A steep shallow corner in a small wall immediately above the finish of Lucky Strike.

11 Gas Bubble Wall   30m   Very Difficult *(1996)*

At the top of the heather ramp is a black vesicular wall. Climb it and up a corner on the left, then step back right and climb tiered slabs to the top. Pleasant but a bit artificial.

PLAYTIME WALL

(NG 868 718)   Alt 280m   South facing   Diagram p57, 64

About 30m further back and behind Red Wall Crag is a long line of 10m high wall of perfect rock. This is more of a bouldering wall although the routes can be led. The obvious and most tempting line is the centrally placed groove above a small triangular ledge. This is Playtime Wall. The lower left section of wall has several boulder problems around 4c to 5b.

12 Playtime Left Wall   10m   6a

Start just right of a 2m capped corner. Climb a shallow flake-line over a bulge and trend right to finish up a crack just left of Playtime Wall.

64

STONE VALLEY

Red Wall

Stone Valley Crag

1. Bold as Brass	E2 5c **
3. Flaming June	VS 5a **
5. The Wallace	E4 5c
6. Lucky Strike	VS 5a **
7. The Bruce	HVS 5a
8. Schiltrom	E1 5b *

9. Strike Two	HVS 5a
10. Short Sharp Shock	E1 5b
11. Gas Bubble Wall	Very Difficult
16. Cheesegrater Slab	VS 5a *
18. Hidden Agenda	VS 4c
19. No Beef	E3 5c *

20. Touch and Go	HVS 5a **
21. Open Secret	Hard Severe ***
22. Bald Eagle	HVS 5a **
23. Blood Feud	E1 *
24. Stone Diary	HVS *

25. Inside Information	HVS *
26. Golden Eagle	E3 6a **
27. Melting Pot	E3
28. The Beer Bottle Dilemma	E3 5c *
31. Updraught	VS 4b

Alan Leary

13 Playtime Wall   10m   6a *   *(1997)*
The narrow ledge is not reached easily (graded as a boulder problem) and the
climbing is not quite over when it is.

14 School's Out   10m   6b   *(2000)*
Right of Playtime Wall is a smooth area of rock with an obvious brown streak
running down it. Move up a thin crack and reach holds out on the left in the brown
streak, then climb the cracks to the top. Reduced to 6a by stepping left higher up.

15 Primary Care   10m   4b   *(2000)*
The cracks just right of School's Out.

STONE VALLEY CRAG

(NG 868 717)   Alt 250m   South facing   Diagram p57, 64

This is the biggest and best crag, barely seen from the car park but easily identified
from the approach track by the silvery arete of Open Secret which lies down and
left of the apparent summit crags. The base of the crag is a short steep wall with a
short crack on the left, a central chockstoned gully and some cracks on the right
near a little tree. Above this wall the angle falls back into undulating steep slabs
with a prominent water washed groove right of centre.

Descent: Easiest by the open grassy gully on the left (facing up). The central
chockstoned gully provides a Moderate ascent or descent to the upper crag and is
useful if routes on the right wish to be reached rapidly.

Left of the descent gully is a wall with two cracks. The left one starts up a lower
crack capped by a loose block, then uses a large flake for the upper crack (Hard
Severe 4b). The right crack has one hard move near the top (VS 5a). Right of the
gully and to the left of the crest of the main slabs is a sidewall of steep rock and
an inset pink slab.

16 Cheesegrater Slab   10m   VS 5a *   *(1996)*
Below the following lines and forming an excellent approach to them is a small
slab, climbed centrally.

17 No Mutton   15m   Hard Severe 4a   *(2001)*
Start in a corner on the left of the inset slab and trend up left to an open right-
facing corner and crack to easy ground.

18 Hidden Agenda   20m   VS 4c   *(1995)*
Start as for No Mutton but move right of it to aim for a slanting crack. Once at the
crack, the climb finishes thinly by stepping left (crux). Rather bold.

19 No Beef   18m   E3 5c *   *(1996)*
Climbs the steep wall; sustained and quite bold for its grade. Start on top of the
boulder left of Touch and Go and climb the wall to a ledge. Climb a shallow groove
to a flat ledge; step right and up to an overhang with an undercut hold. Surmount
the overhang to a groove and then make the crux moves diagonally left to finish
by mantelshelves.
Variation: **No Robins   18m   E2 5c**   *(2000)*
Start as for No Beef, but where that route steps right, continue up a thin crack-line
to finish at the same point. Protection is available but difficult to place.

20 Touch and Go   20m   HVS 5a **   *(1995)*
The obvious inset slab formed left of the crest. Start in the slab's centre and climb
straight up (keeping away from the right edge), then slightly left to finish up its left-
bounding corner. Reach the crest and the main slab at a niche. Step right and finish
up the crux of Open Secret.

21 Open Secret   40m   Hard Severe ★★★   (1984)
Climb cracks in the crest which forms the left edge of the main slab.
1. 15m 4a Climb a short crack on the left of the lower wall and trend left to below the crest.
2. 25m 4b Climb the crack to where it bends right. Now follow a thin snaking crack which trends left up the steep slabby headwall.
Variation: **Direct Start   35m   HVS 5a**   (2001)
Very good but poorly protected climbing squeezed between the initial pitches of Open Secret and Bald Eagle. Start at the base of the shallow corner of Bald Eagle and climb the steep crack on its left to reach the slab via a suspect flake. Climb the slab and overlap direct to join Open Secret.

22 Bald Eagle   40m   HVS 5a ★★   (1995)
The seemingly bald slab right of Open Secret, unfortunately feeling close to it, gives a very good route. Climb the initial pitch of Open Secret to the base of a corner on the right (or start from here, either reached by scrambling up left from the foot of Open Secret or traversing easily to it from the descent). Climb the corner and at its top step left and climb a thin crack to its end. Climb straight up over two small bulges above to a thin crack. Climb the thin crack to its termination, then straight up the red slab.

23 Blood Feud   40m   E1 ★   (1997)
Another fine route but rather squeezed in. Start at the foot of the lowest wall, to the right of Open Secret's initial crack, below a ledge with a cleaned lip and a small tree. Quite hard for those who have trouble finding the key hold.
1. 20m 5b Climb the bald wall behind the tree via a crack but make a blind reach straight up where the crack veers right. Step left and continue up the fine slab to the left end of a heather ledge.
2. 20m 5a Climb the left side of a scoop and the thin crack above. Continue up to finish up a crack in the headwall slab (the corner-crack on the right being Inside Information).

24 Stone Diary   40m   HVS ★   (1995)
Start just left of the central chockstoned gully in the lower wall.
1. 20m 5a Gain a plinth and climb the steep rib between the gully and a smooth pod. Step left above and friction up a fine slab to a heather ledge (belay as for Blood Feud).
2. 20m 5b From the middle of the ledge move up rightwards on friction. Reach left to a good hold over the bulge above. (Pitch 2 of Blood Feud is close on the left and the more obvious line.) Continue up and finish up the crack as for Blood Feud.

25 Inside Information   45m   HVS ★   (1995)
1. 20m 5a Climb the steep jamming crack on the right of the lower wall to exit by some blocks. Step left and climb an easy rib to avoid the heather, stepping right at the top to belay below the water worn groove.
2. 25m 5a Climb the excellent groove. Step left and climb a flake-crack to an awkward exit by a little corner.

26 Golden Eagle   30m   E3 6a ★★   (1997)
To the right of Inside Information is a steep buttress with a shield of rock on its left wall and a pair of thin cracks. The rock is uncharacteristically smooth. Scramble up the gully or climb Melting Pot to the base of the cracks. Climb the excellent left-hand crack on improving holds. The best of the cracks on this wall.

27 Melting Pot   45m   E3   (1995)
Start to the right of Inside Information at a rib to the right of a tree.
1. 20m 4c Climb the wall and continue to step right to a ledge. Climb the short wall above and scramble up heather to the base of the cracks.
2. 25m 5c Step onto a ramp and climb the left crack to a sloping hold, move right

Ian Taylor

Demon Razor, E3, Stone Valley Crag. Climbers Graeme Ettle and Bob Brown

and climb the right crack to the shield. Holds now begin and pleasant climbing leads to the top. Sustained to the shield with good protection but few holds.

28 The Beer Bottle Dilemma   30m   E3 5c *   *(1996)*
Scramble up the chockstoned gully and move right to the next crack right beyond Melting Pot. Climb cracks trending slightly rightwards to gain a ledge. Easier pleasant climbing to the top.

29 The Time Warp   30m   E3 6a *   *(1997)*
To the right of The Beer Bottle is a crack. Predictably strenuous, it gives good sustained climbing to easier rock above.

30 Divided Loyalty   30m   Hard Severe 4b *   *(1996)*
This route is most easily reached by scrambling up the central chockstoned gully and traversing right below the top pitch of Melting Pot to a narrow chimney. Climb into the chimney and up this to step left on to the front face. Continue up a slab

Ian Taylor

Graeme Ettle on the first ascent of The Flashing Blade, E4, Stone Valley Crag

and then a ramp on the right to the top on excellent rock, a fine pitch, much easier than it looks.

31 Updraught   25m   VS 4b   *(1996)*
To the right of Divided Loyalty is a prominent corner. Climb the corner to where it eases, then step right onto the fine edge and follow this on rough rock to the top. Low in the grade.

LEFT DOME

(NG 869 717)   Alt 300m   South to West facing   Diagram p57

Higher up above Stone Valley Crag is the summit buttress which is two dome like crags separated by a gully. Near the base of the left dome and 20m left of a big corner is a rightward slanting thin red slab, a pronounced feature and left of this is a lower wall, increasing in height leftwards before tailing off into the hillside The first routes start near the left end of this lower wall.

Controlled Steering   20m   VS 4c   (1996)
Left of the highest point is a pronounced V-groove above a slanting heather rake. Climb the groove to the capping roof, move left to another groove and finish up this.

Demon Razor   20m   E3 5c **   (1996)
To the right of Controlled Steering is an overhanging wall split by a thin flake-crack. Start in the "cave" and climb the crack-line to a ledge. Continue up the pleasant arete above.

Mellow Ambler   25m   VS 4c   (1996)
To the right of Demon Razor there are some boulders with a grooved arete above. Climb the groove on the left of the arete to exit right by a small tree. Continue up the edge to rough rock and climb the right side of the topmost arete via cracks to the crest.

The Thin Red Line   45m   HVS 4c   (1995)
The thin red slab was climbed on gritty rock to finish up more broken ground.

To the right of The Thin Red Line is an overhanging wall with left and right-slanting cracks forming a V above a lower wall. Three fine routes, arguably worth an extra star each.

The Flashing Blade   20m   E3 6a *   (1997)
The thin crack forming the left-slanting section of the V. Start up a right-slanting mucky groove and turn left to the base of the crack. The crack involves a very hard move but is well protected by small Friends.

Cat Burglar   20m   E4 6a ***   (1997)
The formidable looking wall between the two more definite cracks of the V. Superb sustained climbing, but better protected than it looks; high in the grade. Start up The Flashing Blade and then step onto the wall, following a thin overhanging crack all the way.

The Thug   20m   E2 5b **   (1996)
Climbs the striking right-slanting crack of the V. Start left of the crack at a right-slanting groove (as for the previous two routes). Climb the groove to a small ledge below the crack. The crack yields to a no frills approach with the crux at the top. Finish up a straightforward arete or scramble off left.

The Lum   70m   Very Difficult *   (1996)
To the right of The Thug the crag turns a right-angle which contains a vertical chimney. Climb the fine (when dry) chimney to move out right to below a shallow red corner (25m). Left of the corner is an overhung crack. Surmount the bulge and follow the crack around to the front face and follow to a terrace (20m). Either walk off leftwards or continue up easy but pleasant rocks to the summit of the dome (25m).

Lumside Phew   40m   E2   (1996)
To the right of The Lum is a red wall. Start directly below a shallow groove near the left-hand end.
1. 10m 5c Climb up the wall and groove to make the thin crux moves left into a scoop. Continue to a ledge.
2. 30m 4c Climb straight up, then left across The Lum to surmount some poised blocks, then straight up the slab to the terrace.

Questionable Crack   65m   Hard Severe   (1996)
To the right of The Lum is a red wall split by a crack at its right-hand end.
1. 25m 4b Climb the crack to an awkward landing and then more easily to the

Mark Gear collection

The Thug, E2, Stone Valley Crag. Climber Ruth Pybus

shallow red corner (stance shared with The Lum).
2. 15m 4b Climb the steep corner to the terrace.
3. 25m Either walk off left or continue up easy but pleasant rock to the summit of the dome.

The Domino Effect   25m   E3 6a   *(1997)*
Climbs the left arete of Dome Corner. Climb over a steep bulge to cracks in the wall below the arete (crux), swinging right to gain cracks in the right side of the arete. Finish up easier ground to the top.

Dome Corner   40m   Severe 4a   *(1984)*
On the left wall of the gully and starting immediately at the top of the gully's steepest section, is a corner. Climb the corner until it becomes vegetated, then move on to the right arete.

RIGHT DOME - PINK WALL

(NG 870 716)   Diagram p57
Pink Wall   25m   Difficult   *(1996)*
The upper right wall of the right-hand dome offers numerous routes up to Difficult in standard, the best line being approximately central.

Long Walk, Short Climb   50m   Severe   *(2001)*
The right-hand wall has a steep rib to the right of a pink slab. Climb the rib and step left onto the front face to reach easy ground after 10m. Pleasant scrambling to the top.

PERCUSSION WALL

(NG 870 715)   Alt 280m   South facing   Diagram p57
There are two clean walls on the next buttress to the right and towards the glen from the Domes. The upper is pink and quite short, offering various climbs of about Difficult while the lower is grey and of excellent rough rock. This is Percussion Wall. The wall has a pronounced crack system towards its right end.

Percussion Crack   25m   Very Difficult   *(1997)*
Climb the crack direct past a ledge at one-third height.

Syncopation Wall   25m   VS 5a   *(1997)*
To the left of the crack is a slabby wall; climb this to a ledge, then climb the excellent crack which leads up right to a ramp which is followed by a short wall and the top. Fine climbing.

THE SLABS

(NG 869 715)   Alt 270m   South facing   Diagram p57
Lower down the hillside are a spread of slabby walls, The Slabs, which appear from below as a lower continuation of the right-hand dome.

Wander at Will   30m   Difficult   *(1997)*
The centre of the slabs provides pleasant sport picking a line of choice.

Stratospheric Pachyderms   25m   VS 5a   *(1997)*
The right of the slabs steepens into a pair of cleft bulges. Climb the lower overhang to a cosy niche below the next bulge. Climb the top bulge more energetically.

BAOSBHEINN

(NG 871 653)   875m
A fine remote hill with many steep faces providing some winter climbing.

CREAG AN FHITHICH - NORTH-WEST FACE

(NG 857 676)   Alt 550m   North-West facing
The triangular face which is seen when driving south from Gairloch, has a very open aspect and is the result of a huge landslip in post glacial times, as per the great Beinn Alligin gash. Below and left of this landslip is a steep cliff which provides

some good icefall climbing in cold weather.

Approach: Park as for Stone Valley Crags at NG 856 721. Follow the Loch na h-Oidhche track for about 3km until a right fork leads to a bridge across the Abhainn a' Garbh Choire. Head across country to the face.

Descent: The icefalls end on a terrace. From here, either traverse left along the terrace to a belay on the crest. Continue up and right on turfy steps until an easy ridge is reached leading to the top (100m), or traverse right along the terrace to the left side of the landslip (60m) and a quick descent (both options are Grade II).

Scalagwag   90m   V,6 *   *(2001)*
The leftmost icefall, which features a prominent column forming over an overhang. Climb ice to the base of the column (rock runners high on right). Step left onto the column and climb it to a terrace (30m). Cross the terrace (20m) and climb the continuation icefall via a steep ramp. Go slightly left and finish up a vertical corner to the upper terrace (40m).

Beachcomber   85m   V,5 **   *(2001)*
A central line. Start up and right where the ice is more extensive.
1. 30m Go up easy iced slabs to an icy corner-chimney. Climb this to a small snowy bay.
2. 55m Continue up the line of steep icy corners above to a terrace (this pitch could be split).

Right Icefall   60m   IV,5   *(2001)*
The rightmost ice line. An iced groove at the start was incomplete but can form, so the route was started by traversing in from the right. Climb the rightmost icy groove, then move left to climb steep ice to the terrace.

Leading up right from the icefalls is an open chute line, the left side of the landslip, which provides an easy Grade II (1987) while a broader right-hand line which runs right to left and converges with the other is Grade I. It can be used as descent.

North-West Ridge   150m to scrambling   II   *(2001)*
The attractive looking ridge on the right of the landslip starting at NG 855 675 has a disappointing upper half.

RONA FACE

(NG 867 657)   Alt 680m   West-South-West facing

Approach: Park as above at NG 856 721 and follow the track to cross the outflow from Loch na h-Oidhche about 400m downstream from the loch (wide but shallow). Head up into An Reidh Choire and follow it to the col at NG 869 664. Descend a gully to the bottom left-hand corner of the face.

Merlinswanda   210m   IV,5   *(2002)*
This interesting route climbs the left edge of the highest section of cliff. Start at the lowest left toe of the buttress below an obvious steep groove.
1. 15m Climb the groove to belay up and left at a good thread.
2. 40m Follow the groove directly above to a terrace.
3. 20m Climb the shallow groove trending first right then back left to below an obvious deep chimney.
4. 20m Climb the fine chimney and continue up to a spike.
5. 45m Climb up and right aiming for an obvious ramp which slants left to the top of the tower. Belay halfway up the ramp.
6. 30m Continue to the top of the ramp, then climb straight up by a series of grooves to a terrace.
7. 40m Follow the easiest line to the top.

Andy Nisbet

Scalagwag, V,6, Baosbheinn. Climber Dave McGimpsey

NORTH-EAST FACE

(NG 873 653)   Alt 620m   North-East facing

Directly below the summit is this large triangular face. Approach by following the track almost to Loch na h-Oidhche and crossing by a bridge reported just below its outflow.

Direct Route   300m   III,4   *(1999)*

Take a line directly to the apex of the face, more clearly defined in the upper third.

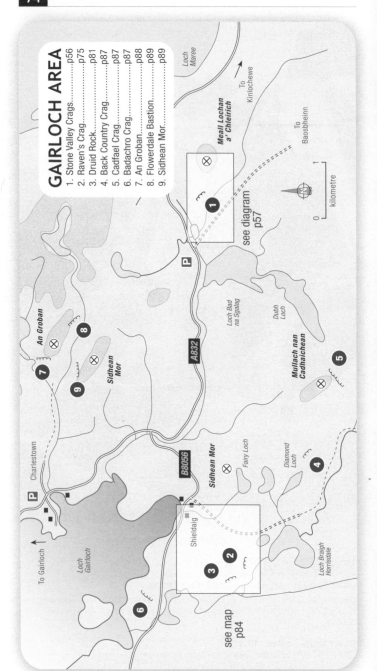

To Kinlochewe

To Baosbheinn

Loch Maree

Meall Lochan a' Chleirich

see diagram p57

kilometre

0   1

N

An Groban

Sidhean Mor

Charlestown

P

To Gairloch

Loch Gairloch

B8056

A832

Loch Bad na Sgalag

Dubh Loch

Mullach nan Cadhaichean

Sidhean Mor

Fairy Loch

Diamond Loch

Shieldaig

see map p84

Loch Braigh Horrisdale

GAIRLOCH CRAGS

This section includes a number of crags which are within easy reach just south of Gairloch. The first group of crags, based around Raven's Crag, are sometimes known as the Thorsdale Crags and are about 6km to the south. The second group, based around An Groban, are approached from Charlestown, at the south end of Gairloch itself

Thorsdale Crags

RAVEN'S CRAG

(NG 797 712) Alt 120m   South-West to West facing   Maps p74, 84   Diagram p76

This pleasant low-level crag has more holds than the typical dome of gneiss, and is a good place for the lower grades. The rock is good and rough, and it dries quickly, although one can also climb it in the wet. Some of the routes are open to variation, particularly on the first pitch, so choose your preferred line.

Though admittedly a curiosity, the crag has been climbed in winter when higher areas were stormbound.

Approach: Just south of Gairloch take the B8056 to Badachro. After 2km, just before the Shieldaig Lodge Hotel (there is a big parking area just after it, but some folk park on the verge), walk up a track on the left (signposted) across a small ford. Ignore a track on the right after 100m, then ignore a small path on the left after another 50m, but continue up the main path till it opens out, then levels off and there are slabby crags close on the left. From here, the slabby right end of the crag is seen in profile about 300m away on the right; head direct to it, 30mins.

Descent: At either end of the crag.

The climbs are described from right to left.

1. Bright Star   50m   II   (1995)
Climb the slabs and grooves at the extreme east end of the crag. The entire end of the crag was under snow and ice and several variations were possible.

2 Bunny Slabs   50m   Difficult   (1997)
Start on a heather slope just round the right edge of the main face at a large pointed block. Climb slabs trending rightwards (choice of lines) to gain the pale smooth rib forming the crest. Follow this, stepping onto a nose on the right and on up to the top.

3 Constabulary Slab   65m   III   (1995)
Start at the right end of the crag, just left of a large flake. Go up and right to the flake. Climb this on the left to easier slabs, then up the corners and grooves to the top (choice of corners to finish).

4 Hydro Hek   50m   Hard Severe *   (1982)
Start at the right end of the crag, just left of the large flake and beneath a clean plaque of slab on the upper wall.
1. 20m Climb clean brown slabs to the base of the plaque.
2. 30m 4a From the right side traverse up left across the plaque and continue up leftwards towards the top.

5 Badachro   50m   Severe   (1982)
Left of the plaque of Hydro Hek is a wall with a diagonal crack with a slot in it. The crack continues down the lower wall as a series of thin cracks.
1. 20m Start up whitish broken rock and climb by the line of thin cracks to the heather terrace.
2. 25m 4a Climb the diagonal crack past the slot and continue up easy walls to the top.

10. Rainbow Pink   VS 4c
11. Stage Fright   HVS **

12. Charlestone   Severe **
13. Lucy   Very Difficult **
13a. Gem   Very Difficult
14. Entasis   Very Difficult *
14a. Direct Finish   VS 4c
15. Crack Climb   HVS 5b
16. Groove Climb   VS 5a
17. Two Guns   Severe
17a. Variation Finish 4c

RAVEN'S CRAG

4. Hydro Hek   Hard Severe *
5. Badachro   Severe
7. Lonmore   Severe *
8. Ken's Joy   Severe

Andy Nisbet

6 Shield Direct 40m VS 4c   (1995)
A counter diagonal to Badachro. Something of an eliminate, but good climbing nevertheless. Start 5m left of Badachro and climb the brown slabby wall crossing the crack of Badachro, then trend right to the base of the shield crossed by Hydro Hek. Climb this directly to the top.

7 Lonmore 55m Severe *   (1983)
The middle of the wall is divided at about 15m by a heather terrace with a tree at its right end, from which two diagonal faults rise up left, the left one leading to another tree high up and with a triangular niche close up on its left. Quite vegetated but the climbing is good.
1. 15m Climb directly to the tree on the heather terrace.
2. 30m 4a Move up left to the diagonal fault. Climb this to the high tree and niche. Climb left out of the top of the niche to a ledge.
3. 10m Finish easily rightwards.

8 Ken's Joy 55m Severe   (1982)
Start about 10m left of Lonmore. The route crosses Lonmore to finish up the right-hand diagonal fault.
1. 25m Climb by heather and rocks to the mid-way terrace and belay as for Lonmore.
2. 30m 4a Climb up to a small tree on the right of the Lonmore fault and climb the parallel diagonal fault to the top.

9 The Morning After 50m HVS *   (1995)
The upper wall between Lonmore and Badachro, close on the right of the following route.
1. 20m Climb up to the tree belay of Lonmore by a short slab and walls to the left of Ken's Joy.
2. 30m 5a Climb the wall directly behind the tree to finish at the same point as Badachro.

10 Rainbow Pink 50m VS 4c   (1984)
Start a few metres left of Ken's Joy. Easy slabs and heather lead to moves leftwards and upwards across a wall to the big heather ledge. Take the wall above, crossing the diagonal lines of Lonmore and Ken's Joy.

11 Stage Fright 55m HVS **   (1985)
Takes the blank looking upper wall left of Lonmore. Start at the base of a heather break which leads up left under the blocks of Lucy.
1. 25m Climb a vague crest on the right side of a clean area of slab to reach the right end of a higher left section of heather terrace.
2. 30m 5a Climb steeply up the wall to join the final moves of Lonmore. A good variation is to move left from the middle of the wall. Continue easily to the top.

12 Charlestone 50m Severe **   (1981)
Takes a direct line up the centre of the crag, featuring a water worn scoop left of the clean wall of Stage Fright. Start 5m left of the base of the heather break.
1. 25m 4a Climb a convex slab to the break. Continue up a line of weakness composed of a shallow groove, a crack-line and a steeper wall to the higher left section of the terrace and below the scoop. Or climb the first pitch of Stage Fright, as good and slightly easier.
2. 25m 4a Climb straight up on good holds left of the scoop to an easier finish. Or swing right from a big hold into the water worn scoop and follow it up left to the same finish.

13 Lucy 60m Very Difficult **   (1984/1991)
A high and prominent rowan tree marks the line, also huge blocks at 15m. Start below the blocks. Take the cleanest line to the blocks and pass them immediately on the right to gain a left-slanting depression. Follow this up to a heather ledge on

Ian Davidson

Steve Chadwick on the first ascent of Lucy, Very Difficult, Raven's Crag

the left (the belay of Entasis). Go right to the tree. Abseil from the tree (45m) or finish rightwards.

Variations:

This is the best line on this central area of slab but the slab is climbable in many places at Very Difficult. The original line started as for Charlestone, then took a left-slanting line of weakness to the heather ledge. Another line **Gem**, (1984) started on the left, as for Entasis and took a counter diagonal past the huge blocks to the belay of Charlestone. Either traverse left to Lucy or finish up Charlestone (Severe).

At the left end of the crag there is a large grass ledge with a tree about 15m up, forming part of a left-slanting rake. Below and right of the tree on the grass ledge is a broken scoop in the lower rocks. Above and right of the tree are two right-slanting ramps, the lower being much wider.

14 Entasis   60m   Very Difficult *   *(1986)*

Start just right of the broken scoop at a small red ramp.

1. 35m Start up the ramp, then climb directly up slabs to reach a heather ledge at the top of the wider rocky ramp running up right from the tree (belay as for Lucy).
2. 25m Finish rightwards to the tree, as for Lucy.
Variation Pitch 2: **25m   4c**   *(1986)*
Climb a left-slanting line to the smaller ramp and continue above, about 5m left of the tree and on good clean rock.

The following two routes climb the steep wall above the grass ledge and tree, gained most easily by traversing in from the left above the Dark Slab. The routes therefore combine well with a Dark Slab route.

15 Crack Climb   20m   HVS 5b   *(1997)*
Start 5m up the smaller ramp. Step left under a roof and up a crack to the base of an easier vegetated groove. Step right on to a clean steep wall and climb it.

16 Groove Climb   20m   VS 5a   *(1986)*
Start directly behind the tree at the base of the smaller ramp. Climb a short right-facing corner and steep cracks to finish.

17 Two Guns   50m   Severe   *(1991)*
Start under a small rounded hood of overhangs at the left end of the frontal face.
1. 30m 4a Climb up to and over the overhangs, then up a whaleback to the grass ledge.
2. 20m 4a Climb the left-slanting groove system towards the left end of the wall, finishing up a short shallow chimney.
Variation Pitch 2: **20m   4c**
Climb the crack-line just to its left.
Variation Pitch 2: **20m   4c**
Climb the left crest, passing a small roof on its left.

DARK SLAB

Diagram p80
Round the left end of the crag is a dark west facing slab of clean rough rock, which provides some good short routes. An abseil rope allows all the routes to be done quickly; otherwise scramble off left to descend.

18 Jutting Blocks   20m   Very Difficult *   *(1991)*
At the right side of the dark rough slab are prominent jutting blocks. Climb to and pass the blocks on the right (or slightly harder on the left), then continue to the top.

19 Leac McCac   20m   VS 4c **   *(1982)*
Start left of the jutting blocks and climb the smoothest and cleanest section of slab direct. Hardest at the start but limited protection in the middle.

20 Ricicles   20m   Severe 4a *   *(1982)*
Climb the slab direct keeping just left of its smoothest section and trending right towards the top.

21 Special K   20m   Severe *   *(1982)*
Climb the slab by a right-slanting line, crossing Leac McCac and Ricicles. Low in the grade.

22 Flakes   20m   Very Difficult   *(1982)*
Climb the corner forming the left side of the slab, passing obvious flakes on the right, then trending right.

23 Far Post   25m   Very Difficult   *(1982)*
Climb the rib on the left of the dark slab and finish up a groove. Slippery in the wet.

Andy Nisbet

RAVEN'S CRAG - Dark Slab

18. Jutting Blocks	Very Difficult *	21. Special K	Severe *
19. Leac McCac	VS 4c **	22. Flakes	Very Difficult
20. Ricicles	Severe 4a *	23. Far Post	Very Difficult

FRUITY CRAG

(NG 794 714)   Alt 120m   South-West facing   Map p84

This small crag 150m north-west of Raven's Crag and seen in profile from the left end of Raven's Crag offers some short steep routes as a contrast to Raven's. This is the first of several crags hereabouts, approached via Raven's Crag and easily visited as an alternative route back to the road from it.

Apples   10m   Very Difficult   (1991)
There is a slab up and left of the left end of the main wall. Climb a central crack.

Pears   10m   Severe 4a   (1991)
Climb a crack-line on the right edge of the slab.

Lemon   8m   Severe 4a   (1991)
At the left end of the crag is a pillar forming a chimney on its right and a crack on its left. Climb the crack and finish right over the top of the pillar.

Passion Fruit   10m   E4 6a *   (1998)
Climbs directly up the front face of the pillar. Excellent fingery climbing, but bold.

Fruit Chimney   10m   Very Difficult   (1991)
The chimney right of the pillar.

Banana Cake Conspiracy   10m   E3 6a   *(2002)*
A groove and arete forming the left edge of the smooth pillar right of Fruit Chimney. Very artificial.

Swapped   10m   VS 5a *   *(1991)*
The fine crack bounding the right side of this smooth pillar.

Starfruit   10m   VS 5a   *(1998)*
Just right of Swapped. Climb a short left-facing corner to a heather ledge, then a crack to a heathery ramp.

Pineapple   12m   Moderate
A useful descent route. Follows the obvious left-trending fault.

Mulled   10m   HVS 5a *   *(2001)*
The leftmost crack-line in the wall right of Pineapple, finishing left past a flake.

Paw-paw   10m   E4 6a **   *(1998)*
A great fingery little route taking the left-facing shallow corner in the smooth wall right of Pineapple, starting just to its left. Micro-wires useful.

Fruit-case   10m   E2 5c   *(2001)*
Climb the centre of a slender wall right of the shallow corner. Good moves but an eliminate. Side runners necessary at the grade.

Shrot   10m   HVS 5a   *(2001)*
A right-curving flake come corner-line, breaking left through its final roof. A slightly harder line breaks out of the flake-line earlier.

Blaeberry   10m   Hard Severe 4b   *(2000)*
A white speckled wall between the flake-line and another to the right. Climb the wall, starting at its right edge and finishing in the centre. A harder version climbs the centre throughout (VS 4c).

Plump   10m   VS 4b   *(2001)*
The left-facing flake-line. Low in the grade.

Cloudberries   10m   VS 4c *   *(2001)*
A thin crack in the wall right of the right-hand flake-line, starting through a low V niche.

Orange   8m   Severe 4a   *(1996)*
Near the right end of the crag is a crack with a holly tree. The full height corner-crack about 8m to the left of the holly.

Raspberries   8m   VS 4c   *(2001)*
A thin crack-line 1m right of Orange.

Jam   8m   VS 4c   *(2001)*
A right-slanting thin crack 1m to the right again.

Mango   8m   Severe 4a   *(1996)*
A slightly left-slanting wider crack-line about 3m left of the holly.

Bananas   8m   Severe 4a   *(2001)*
Climb the crack and ledges just left of the holly.

Lime   8m   Very Difficult *   *(1996)*
The corner just to the right of the holly.

Passion Fruit, E4, Fruity Crag. Climbers Paul Tattersall and Jim Buchanan

Angela Tattersall

There are three boulder problems on the shorter smooth wall to the right of the Lime corner. Keeping close to the right arete of the corner is 5a. A crack leading into a small left-facing corner is 5b. A crack 3m to the right, leading past a tiny roof, is 5a.

SNEAKY CRAG

(NG 792 713)   Alt 100m   South-West facing   Map p84

Approach: The crag is below Fruity Crag and towards the river, approached from Raven's Crag by starting towards Fruity but descending diagonally towards the river.

The crag has a pale overhanging wall towards its left end. Right of this is a roof at mid-height, then easier angled walls to the right.

Screwy Louis   12m   E4 6a   *(2001)*
Climb the centre of the pale overhanging wall to reach a crack. Go up this and move left to reach easier ground.

Bad Bob   12m   E2 6a   *(2001)*
Either start directly below the roof and climb the wall to a crack-line through the

roof, or start up a right-curving flake-line on the left to gain the same crack.

Mad John   12m   VS 4c   *(2001)*
Start right of the roof where there are good holds and climb direct to the top.

Dave the Miller   12m   Hard Severe 4b   *(2001)*
Starting where the angle eases, climb a crack and shallow right-facing corner.

Mighty Mo   12m   Hard Severe 4b   *(2001)*
Climb the left side of a smooth slabby wall, about 3m right of Dave the Miller.

Dog Pete   12m   Very Difficult   *(2001)*
Trend right to climb the right edge of the slabby wall.

DRUID ROCK

(NG 793 716)   Alt 120m   South-West facing   Maps p74, 84

A good crag for VS and HVS, but there are some hollow flakes.

Approach: From Raven's Crag, go over the rise beyond Fruity Crag and the crag is obvious on the far side of a shallow grassy gully. Or descend westwards about 200m from Vegie Crag.

Descent: From the top (the 30m routes finish here), go up and right, then down into the grassy gully for an easy descent. From the heather ledge above the smooth lower section (the 20m routes finish here), scramble down rightwards (facing down, north-west).

The crag has a smooth left-hand section facing downhill and a right-hand buttress facing the gully. There are also two walls directly downhill but facing away (the same direction as the main crag).

Burnt Offering   20m   HVS 5a *   *(2001)*
At the left-hand end of the main crag. Climb boldly up the centre of a russet coloured wall forming a small pillar to a ledge (with a rowan sapling on the left). Now climb the steep crack and groove above.

Alchemy   20m   VS 4c   *(2001)*
Start easily up the crack forming the right side of the russet coloured wall to a good spike runner. Step right and climb a fine flake-crack.

Shaman   20m   HVS 5a   *(2001)*
Right of Alchemy is an obvious stepped roof. Climb directly up to and over a break in the roof, trending rightwards on the wall above.

Healing Touch   20m   VS 4c *   *(2001)*
Start mid-way between Shaman and Totem. Climb boldly up the initial wall direct (or more easily via the stepped flake on the right) to a triangular roof which is at the top right end of the stepped roof system. Surmount this on good holds to finish by a huge flake.

Totem   30m   VS 4c *   *(2001)*
Climb the central open corner, then a thin crack over a small roof to a heather ledge. Finish up a slim groove in the upper section.

Sundance   30m   VS 5a *   *(2001)*
Fine climbing up the wall right of Totem. Climb the wall directly by a fairly obvious line of weakness to a rock ledge, then either up slightly left to a holly bush or (harder) step right and up the stepped overlaps to a heathery ledge (possible belay, 20m). Finish direct up the steep wall behind (technical crux).

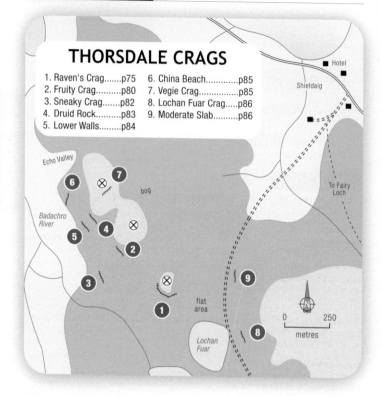

THORSDALE CRAGS

Taboo   20m   VS 4c   *(2001)*
Climb up the front of a pillar lying on the slabby wall, then a thin curving crack to
the heather ledge.

Voodubh   20m   Hard Severe 4b   *(2001)*
Climb a big flake forming the right side of the pillar and a steeper wall to the
heather ledge.

Acorn Slab   30m   VS 4b *   *(2001)*
Climb the centre of the slab formed where the wall turns towards the gully to reach
the heather ledge. Keep right of a pillar of stacked rocks and finish up rounded
walls (or over a smooth bulge on the right via a thin flake-crack - 5a).

Prophet and Loss   30m   Severe 4a   *(2001)*
On the right-hand buttress, right of a heathery gully. Start at the left end of a big
low roof. Climb a blocky corner to a ledge. Step out right, then up through a
heather ramp with a small tree to slabby walls on the right. Finish up these.

LOWER WALLS

Map p84

About 60m down and right (looking down) from the base of Druid Rock are two
smaller walls separated by a heather gully. The rock is less good.

Left-Hand Lower Wall

The holds are incut but there are hollow flakes.

Freeks and Mayonnaise   15m   Very Difficult   *(2001)*
Climbs the right-hand pillar. Start just left of centre. Pull through an overlap, then move right to a flake and climb the centre of the slabby wall above.

Poirot Woz Here   15m   Severe   *(2001)*
There are three crack-lines on the wall; the right-hand has a holly. Climb the central crack-line and the wall above.

Right-Hand Lower Wall

Sultan of Swing   20m   E2 5b   *(2001)*
Climb a short wall to an overlap which is above the left end of a pale rock patch. Pull through, then up a thin crack-line above.

Crooked Willie   20m   Severe 4a   *(2001)*
Climb a short wall to a ledge, go through the right end of the pale rock, then up a wall and through an open V-groove above.

CHINA BEACH

(NG 7924 7169)   Alt 75m   North-West facing   Map p84

A wall below those of Druid Rock. The map reference and altitude were taken by GPS and too late for checking.

Approach: From Druid Rock, walk west-north-west beyond and below the lower tiers to where a tree-filled gully begins to descend over boulders towards the flat grassy floor of the valley below (Echo Valley). At the bottom right of the gully is this slab, its base hidden in birch trees.

Sha Gua (Stupid Melon)   25m   Very Difficult   *(1990s)*
Climb the groove at the left of the slab moving right at the top to avoid grass.

Hong Qiang (Red Slab)   25m   Severe *   *(1990s)*
Climb the centre of the russet coloured slab and follow a thin crack to the terrace.

Xiao Long (Little Dragon)   25m   VS 4b   *(1990s)*
At the right edge of the slab there is an obvious crack sporting an insecure looking flake. Climb this crack to the terrace.

Two routes of about Severe have been climbed on a reddish slab on the gully wall to the right.

VEGIE CRAG

(NG 795 716)   Alt 150m   South facing   Map p84

Approach: From the foot of Fruity Crag, walk left (facing the crag) and head diagonally left up the hillside heading for the col between Point 179m and the hill to the north. The crag is on the north side of the boggy col 5mins from Fruity Crag. If heading there from the car, it would be quicker to approach direct from the path.

Neep   10m   Hard Severe 4b   *(1998)*
The left-hand line of weakness out of a steep bay. Start at the left end of the highest part of the cliff. Continue up short slabs to the top.

Swede 12m VS 5a   *(1998)*
Climbs the centre of the steep bay. Start below a left-facing corner in the upper part
of the crag. Climb the bouldery start to join and climb the corner. Either finish up
it or go right on to a platform and finish up the top wall.

Sweet Potato 12m Severe 4b *   *(1998)*
The obvious left-slanting crack gives the best route here. Start up the short corner
to the left.

Turnip 10m Hard Severe 4b   *(1998)*
Climb the steep crack 4m right of Sweet Potato. Continue up the slab to finish up
the right edge of the upper wall.

North of Druid Rock is Echo Valley, a wide shallow valley with broken crags and
leading to an undercut south facing wall at NG 795 721. The undercut wall is
impressive but not attractive for climbing. On the east side of the valley at NG 794
718 is **Chough**; climb easy angled slabs to finish left (30m Very Difficult 1990s) or
right up an obvious clean-cut corner (Severe). **Bei Hu Zi** (White Tiger) is the white
slab low down on the east side at NG 794 720, its base hidden in trees (20m Severe
1990s). **Sha Bi Corner** (30m Very Difficult 1990s) is a white corner at NG 795 720,
grassy at its base but clean higher up. Over a col and on the hillside on the right is
a west facing slabby crag at NG 797 721, best approached from Leacnasaide. Its
left and highest side gives a 16m Severe (2005).

LOCHAN FUAR CRAG

(NG 800 709) Alt 110m South-West facing Map p84
A slab at NG 800 713 offers a pleasant 15m Moderate. This crag is a gneiss outcrop
close to the path. Continue past Raven's Crag until Lochan Fuar is reached. The crag
is a diagonal face with an overhang at half-height.

Hungover 10m VS 4c   *(1999)*
Start just left of centre and climb a slab to the overhang. Pull through and step left.

LOCH BRAIGH HORRISDALE CRAG

(NG 802 703) Alt 120m South-West facing
Continue further along the path to Loch Braigh Horrisdale. This gneiss crag is
situated 100m past a steep bridge crossing the burn. It has an obvious off-width
corner-crack formed by a massive detached block.

Burke and Hair 15m Severe   *(1999)*
Start directly below the corner-crack. Climb past a holly bush and ascend the crack.

Evil-hearted Ewe 15m E1 5a   *(1999)*
An exciting but scary pitch which climbs the right edge of the detached block. Start
right of Burke and Hair below the obvious flakes. Gain and climb these.

The following crags are increasingly far from the road, best suited as part of a day
in wild country (or for the bored fisherman) There are also two minor crags with
some short routes of up to 20m on Sidhean Mor, facing the Fairy Loch to its south.
They are situated at NG 810 716 and NG 812 715.

DIAMOND CRAG

(NG 814 700) Alt 170m North-West facing
A crag south of the Fairy Loch and near the Diamond Loch, named because of its
shape. There is no crag symbol on the 1:50,000 map. The Diamond Loch is best

reached by a fishermans' path which leaves the main Loch Braigh Horrisdale path immediately before the burn crossed by the wooden ramp at NG 802 705.

Heather Gem   30m   Hard Severe *(1993)*
Climb grooves and slabs from the toe of the buttress.

Solitaire   50m   Moderate *(2005)*
This is a prominent rib at NG 815 702, alt 200m, high above and pointing towards the Diamond Loch. There is a crag symbol. The rib gives a pleasant saunter and a panorama of the area.

BACK COUNTRY CRAG

(NG 816 699)   Alt 200m   South-West facing   Map p74

Another crag unmarked on the 1:50,000 map. It has a shallow heather gully with clean slabs either side. A steep but shorter wall of black rock lies further right.

Yokel   25m   Very Difficult *(2005)*
The slab left of the gully. Start close to the gully but take a line some 2m left.

Hillbilly   25m   Severe *(2005)*
Start 3m right of the gully. Climb the slab to a steeper wall. Climb this by a red vein on the right to an easier finish.

CADFAEL CRAG

(NG 824 691)   Alt 180 - 210m   South-East facing   Map p74

A long band of broken cliff, but with some substantial pieces.

Cloisters   40m   Hard Severe 4b *(2005)*
Lies on a steep black wall at NG 825 691, opposite a long spur. It takes a distinct line in the centre of the wall some 10m right of a vegetated corner which marks the left end of the wall. The line leads to a huge wedged (but safe) block under a capping overhang. Climb a large flake to reach the line, followed to the huge block. Move out left through the overhang and up to a terrace. Finish up easier slabs.

The east end of the significant cliff forms a dome at NG 829 693. This is directly opposite a well formed knoll in the flat ground in front of the cliff. On the dome are two broad ribs either side of a gully with a huge block at its base.

Stripey   40m   Very Difficult *(2005)*
The right rib. Climb stripey gneiss in the centre, then move right at a break to continue up the stripey gneiss.

Paradise   60m   Severe *(2005)*
The left rib is scrappy low down but with two clean walls above a terrace. Climb the lower heathery rib with an awkward move to reach the terrace. The first clean wall is excellent up its centre. Traverse right to the second wall, climbed up a slight scoop on the right.

BADACHRO CRAG

(NG 790 735)   Alt 60m   South-East facing   Map p74

A small but accessible crag clearly seen when driving west from Leacnasaide. A little lichenous, the routes could do with a quick brush. The obvious feature is a central corner capped by a roof and with large dubious wedged blocks at its base. The corner is 12m Severe, passing the roof on the right. The wall 3m to its right is VS 5a and the slab on its left is HVS 5a.

An Groban

AN GROBAN

(NG 837 752)   Alt 300m   West facing   Map p74

The hill An Groban (383m) holds the crag of the same name. It provides some pleasant climbs, particularly in the afternoon when it gets the sun.

Approach: Park at NG 810 752, next to the main road. No cars are allowed on the tarmac road to Flowerdale Mains, so walk and continue as signposted to Flowerdale Waterfall. Cross a substantial bridge and continue beside the stream, then cross a stile on the left and go up to a ruined building (marked on the map). Move right and up a wide gully between crags to its top, from where the crag is easily seen.

Descent: Scramble down broken ground right of the right-bounding gully (looking up). It may be easier to abseil; one abseil will get down from the top of the difficulties of all routes except Alleyway (from the abseil point to the top is scrambling common to all the routes, but it can be done after the last route).

The crag is defined by a gully on the right and grassy grooves on the left. About 15m right of these grooves is a large boulder which marks the start of Blackgang.

Alleyway   70m   Hard Severe 4b *   *(1994)*
This route takes a line parallel to the grassy grooves on the left. Climb slabby rock immediately to the right of the grassy grooves to reach and climb a left-facing corner at half-height. Exit left to emerge below a steep wall barring entry to a large recess. Move right and ascend via two jammed blocks, then move left into the recess (crux). Exit the recess by the left hand wall and crack; proceed to the top.

Slipway   60m   VS 4c   *(1973)*
A pleasant climb but the line is ill-defined with variation possible. Start 5m left of Blackgang (cairn). Climb a broad slabby rib first trending left then right to easier ground (50m, splitting the pitch will force a less direct line.). Scramble to the top.

Blackgang   60m   HVS **   *(1973)*
The central line on the crag. Start at a grassy crack 3m from the large boulder.
1. 30m 5a Climb the crack and wall above into a corner; continue up easy rock into a corner leading to a bulge which is taken on the right (or direct, good but slightly harder).
2. 30m 5a A short brutal chimney (avoidable) leads to easier rocks.

Hatman   60m   E1   *(1973)*
Start below a prominent overhang near the right side of the crag (cairn). Climb up to the first overhang, traverse left across a clump of vegetation in order to pass the overhang on the left and go up to a second overhang (5a). Traverse left and climb the crack above (5b). After 30m the climbing eases.
Variation:
A much cleaner start is up Blackgang, followed by a traverse right to the crux crack (certainly worth a star this way).

Growbag Grooves   60m   E1 5b *   *(1998)*
Start as for Hatman but climb rightwards up an inset slab to where it meets Straker. Step left and climb shallow grooves up the crest of the buttress (35m). Scramble to the top.

Straker   60m   Severe 4b **   *(1973)*
This is the obvious groove and spectacular ramp on the right edge of the main face. Start at the right corner of the crag at the foot of the gully (cairn). Climb the groove steeply (crux), step left at 7m and continue up the narrow ramp overlooking the gully. At its end, climb steeply up on jugs to an easy finish.

FLOWERDALE BASTION

Map p74

At the very top of Flowerdale, to the left of the river, stands this steep two-tiered crag. There are other crags around, but many are loose. The Lower Wall is much the more amenable, but the upper crag is vertical to slightly overhanging for 30m, with substantial roofs adding to its defences. The upper crag (The Bastion) possesses some very impressive unclimbed lines. The rock is gneiss, exposed along the bedding plane, which creates flaky, juggy holds in places, but also areas of less sound rock, with some calcification.

Approach: Park at NG 810 752, next to the main road. No cars are allowed on the tarmac road to Flowerdale Mains, so walk and continue as signposted to Flowerdale Waterfall. Continue beyond it and over a stile on the left, then by a rough track over the meadows to the top of the glen. The Bastion is clearly visible on the approach up the meadow but the lower wall is hidden, 1hr.

Descent: On the left for both tiers.

LOWER WALL

(NG 843 744)   Alt 230m   South-West facing

The Scaling Ladder   30m   VS *   *(2000)*
A pleasant route on mainly good rock. Just left of the lowest rocks is a tree. This climb starts up the rib to its right.
1. 20m 5a Climb the rib to a ledge. Go right along this to an undercut crack. Go up and left to gain easier ground and a ledge.
2. 10m 4b Go straight up rough slabs to finish direct by a small crack.

Ballista   30m   VS 4c   *(2000)*
To the right of The Scaling Ladder is a leftward-facing crack. Climb this, then continue by thin cracks on better rock slightly rightwards to small walls.

THE BASTION

(NG 843 745)   Alt 280m   West-South-West facing

Bastionard   30m   E2 5b **   *(2000)*
This steep and sustained climb takes the easiest line on the main part of The Bastion. It was cleaned on abseil but a few doubtful holds remain. Protection is mainly good, although strenuous to place. Start at the third spike right from a huge unclimbed diedre. Climb the right-hand of twin cracks up to a projecting block and hands-off rest below the crux. Continue up the crack into a left-facing groove, when a step right leads to an easier finish.

SIDHEAN MOR - NORTH FACE

Map p74

The upper face has five ribs facing the Flowerdale valley, the most continuous of which is in the middle of the face and is Very Difficult (2000). In general, the rock is rather discontinuous and the potential in relation to the amount of exposed rock is disappointing. But a two pitch HVS has been reported; its most likely position is a two-tiered rib just above the meadows at NG 836 744.

Gairloch North

Map p97

There are three smaller crags near the road north-east of Gairloch, heading towards Poolewe.

GAIRLOCH CRAGS

AZTEC TOWER

(NG 815 784)   Alt 110m   South-West facing   Map p97

A smooth wall, soon obvious on the left when driving north-east from Gairloch on the A832 and overlooking Lochan nam Breac. The rock is partially metamorphosed sandstone, so with more holds than normal.

Quickstep   20m   VS 4c   *(2001)*
The left side of the broken north-west face left of the main wall. Start below a holly tree. Climb a short arete, step right and climb straight up the middle of the wall finishing up a ragged crack.

Horse Feather   15m   HVS 4c   *(1997)*
A bold route up the centre of the broken north-west face, just right of Quickstep.

Astriding Edge   15m   Very Difficult
The right end of this north-west face forms an arete.

Rough Voyage   15m   Difficult
The vegetated corner left of the main face, finishing out right.

Conquistador   15m   E1 5a   *(1997)*
Climb directly up the left arete of the main face. Minimal protection.

Human Sacrifice   15m   HVS 5a **   *(1997)*
The crack-line 2m right of the arete.

Warrior God   15m   VS 4c *   *(1997)*
In the centre of the face. Climb a central crack-line past a tiny tree to the left end of a ledge. Climb the wall directly above to finish up a left-slanting crack.

Torn Heart   12m   VS 5a   *(1996)*
A crack-line towards the right side of the wall. One hard move just above the ledge and a tiny roof.

Cortes   12m   VS 4b   *(1996)*
A more broken crack-line 3m to the right. Low in the grade.

Sun God   12m   VS 4c   *(1998)*
A pleasant route up the wall to the right of Cortes. Climb up a short groove which cuts a bulge to a heather ledge. Continue up the middle of the clean wall between a small tree on the left and a dirty crack on the right.

Infanta   8m   Severe 4a   *(1998)*
Near the right end of the crag is a short overhang of blocks. Climb through these and gain the top wall.

Two Step   10m   Difficult   *(2001)*
At the right end of the crag. Climb the centre of a short pillar, then a left-facing corner.

SUNSET CRAG

(NG 815 783)   Alt 110m   South-West facing

The next small crag towards the road in the same escarpment as Aztec Tower. It has two sectors; the left is split by a grassy ledge at half-height. Cracks near the left edge of the left sector are Severe; further right, a right-slanting lower crack and upper twin cracks are Hard Severe 4b. The following routes are on the right sector.

Evening Breeze   10m   Hard Severe 4b   *(2005)*
Climb the left end of the wall, then the slab on the left to finish up the arete.

April Showers   10m   VS 4c   *(2005)*
A prominent right-slanting crack in the centre, stepping right at the top (harder straight up). Alternatively, finish left to the arete of Evening Breeze.

Monsoon   10m   Severe 4a   *(2005)*
A less obvious right-slanting crack on the right side of the wall.

GRASS CRAG - A' CHREAG FHEOIR

(817 790)   Alt 150m   South-West facing

A small sport crag, originally developed as a winter venue because of its sunny aspect and being very quick drying. The rock is gneiss, slightly brittle and with very limited natural protection, so offering little to the traditional climber. The descents are all lower-offs.

Approach: Park at NG 822 781. Approach fairly directly across rough and boggy ground, passing east of a lochan at NG 818 784. 20mins.

RIGHT SECTOR - THE RED CRAG

This is 8m high and of reddish rock, with steep moves off the ground. Listed left to right.
The Joint Account (6a) and **Invest Wisely** (6a) lead to a shared lower-off.
The Thinker (6a+) and **Constipated Miser** (6b+) lead to a shared lower-off.
The Dump (6c) has its own lower-off.
Pants on Fire (7a) and **All the Arts** (6c) lead to a shared lower-off.
Third and Final (5) has its own lower-off.

LEFT SECTOR

This is 12m high and of better pale rock. More routes will appear soon if a large dangerous block on a ledge above can be removed.
Like it Hot? (7a) has 5 bolts.
Waiting for the Man (6a+) also has 5 bolts.

CREAG BHADAN AN AISC

(NG 826 782)   Alt 120m   South facing   Map p97

This crag stands on the west side of the main A832 from Gairloch to Poolewe, about 50m from the road. It has a slabby left-hand section, where the first described routes lie, along with a mainly overhanging right-hand wall. The rock on the slabs is good rough Lewisian Gneiss, less good on the steeper section. The old dry stonework below the steep section may be the grave of two young Mackenzie heirs horribly murdered in the 15th century; hence the name of the crag, "The Crag of the Place of the Burial".

Approach: There is a good parking place 200m down from the crag. One car can squeeze off the road opposite Curtain Wall.

BLONDE BITCH'S BUTTRESS

This is the slabby left-hand part of the crag, about 25m high and separated from the overhanging crag by a grassy descent gully. The only belay is on a large boulder some 15m back from the top of the crag.

Dark Roots   20m   Hard Severe 4b   (2005)
Start at a recess on the left of the crag, just right of some ivy and behind a tree. Immediately right of the ivy, climb flakes over a bulge and finish up the left side of an upper slab.

Handbagged   20m   Hard Severe 4b *   (2000)
Start in the recess right of the ivy. Go steeply up a wall, then delicately to the top break. Go slightly left between two cracks to finish.

Blondes Don't Reverse   22m   VS 4c   (2000)
Climb the obvious and well protected central rib, with a delicate step where the crack steepens.

5.10 Stilettos   22m   VS 4c   (2000)
There is an obvious flaky line to the right of the central rib. Climb this, with some delicate moves where the flakes run out. Move right, then straight up through the break to finish.

Lip Gloss   22m   Hard Severe 4b   (2000)
The rough slabs to the right of the flake-line give good, though somewhat artificial climbing on excellent rough rock.

A small buttress 15m right has been climbed at Hard Severe 4b.

CURTAIN WALL
This is the overhanging right-hand sector of the crag.

Curtain Wall   12m   E3 5c *   (2001)
At the left-hand end of the crag is a groove and overhanging crack. This is the route.

Windhover   12m   E2 5b   (2002)
Right of Curtain Wall is a smooth headwall with a thin crack. Further right, climb directly up to an alcove with a small tree; make a heathery exit.

Ante Naval Base   12m   E1 5b   (2005)
Start midway between Windhover and Tired of Creation at a shallow open groove. Climb the groove to reach a large spike on the right wall at one-third height. Make some bold moves up the steep groove to a rest, then continue by a ledge and small tree.

Tired of Creation   10m   E5 6b   (2003)
A central line, finishing by a hanging groove. Climb the wall, stretch right to reach and climb the slim hanging groove.

Hobbyhorse   12m   E3 5c   (2002)
A bottomless wide crack-line (second from the right).

The Crack   12m   E2 5b   (2001)
At the far right end of the crag is a prominent off-width crack. The climb uses the crack and the wall to its right.

Rubha Reidh

The coastline north of Gairloch provides a playground for those seeking to explore the vast array of sea-stacks, arches and caves. There are three main areas that have been climbed; the cliffs and stacks to the north and south of Port Erradale and the stacks to the east of the lighthouse at Rubha Reidh.

RUBHA REIDH STACKS

(NG 7490 9195)

Four stacks lie within 300m of each other. Two are marked on the map. The most westerly, A' Staca Dubh, is flat topped and can easily be ascended from the north side to a large grass covered top. The second, A' Staca Buidhe, is 30m high with a large grass covered top and has a narrow arch that cuts through it. The other two stacks lie south-east of this.

The first is Stac 'n Iolaire (Stack of the Eagle) and its shape is likened to a half bottle of whisky with two shoulders and a neck. The base of this 40m stack is accessible at most states of the tide and is rarely completely surrounded by the sea. A smaller stack, A' Staca Biorach, lies to the south east of this and is 20m high with a vertical north face and a narrow arch. The precarious state of rock on the stacks has seen only one route recorded to date.

Approach: Park near the lighthouse (NG 7500 9185) and follow a track to the east past the small harbour for 750m. Access to A' Staca Buidhe, Stac 'n Iolaire and A' Staca Biorach is gained by scrambling down a steep gully opposite Stac 'n Iolaire.

STAC 'N IOLAIRE

(NG 7490 9195)   Tidal

The Levitant   50m   E1 4c   *(2005)*
This route climbs the west face before traversing on to the east face for the final moves. Ten to 15m of rope is required to wrap around the summit for the belay and descent abseil. A further 6m of rope is useful as a sling around the lump of rock on the left of the gully on the second pitch.
1. 35m 4c Start from a raised terrace 5m right of the north arete. Climb a steep right-slanting cracked ramp for 20m. Traverse up and rightwards for 3m on a grassy ledge. Climb up to a ledge right of a vegetated gully.
2. 15m 4b Step left and ascend the gully with care to a col between a lump of rock on the left and the summit on the right. Traverse carefully around the summit pinnacle for 3m. Climb the steep vegetated rock direct to the top.

PORT ERRADALE

Park by the T-junction in North Erradale (NG 7420 8107). Port Erradale is the bay to the west of here. The first stacks are north of Port Erradale. Follow the road north for 250m and then head west along the side of a fence. Follow this to a sheep pen and then north-west for 450m to the second grassy bay that looks out to Camas an Arbhair.

STAC 'N ARBHAIR

(NG 7363 8154)   Tidal

This consists of three stacks. A large 20m stack is climbed by a ramp on the landward face and scramble to the top (Moderate). A small 8m stack is found on the east corner and a long 10m rib of rock to the north-west which is climbed by a small corner on the left of the landward face (Difficult), or more easily by a corner to the right of the landward face.

To the north of Camas an Arbhair is a striking arete on a flying buttress of rock with an arch through it and two more stacks.

SOUTH STACK

(NG 7355 8160)   Tidal

This 15m stack is accessible one hour either side of low tide by climbing the north-west side to the seaward platform and then a broken stepped ramp to the top (Moderate).

NORTH STACK

(NG 7352 8161)   Tidal

A 20m stack which is accessible 2hrs either side of low tide.

Landward Face   20m   Difficult   *(2005)*
Start beneath a loose wall and traverse up and leftwards on good rock to a left-facing corner and climb this to the top. Descend by simultaneous abseil.

The arete overlooking the stacks has one route.

The Watchman   20m   VS 4b   *(2005)*
Climb the wall to the left of the arete for 10m before stepping on to the sloping wall right of the arete. Ascend this for 3m and the arete direct to the top.

To the north of Camas an Arbhair is the promontory of Rubh' Erradale. The north of this is defined by a geo with a 12m stack which is accessible two hours either side of low tide.

A' STACA GOCAMAN

(NG 7352 8172) Tidal

Access the bay by scrambling down a grassy bank in the east end of the geo.

The Sleeping Sentinel   9m   Very Difficult   *(2005)*
Fine climbing up a right-facing corner come ramp. Descent is by down climbing the stepped ramp to the left of the route (Easy).

Beaten by the Tide   20m   Difficult   *(2005)*
The right-facing stepped corner on the wall of the geo south of the stack.

Further north is the larger bay of Camas an Rubha. To the north of a small burn is another bay with a stack.

A' STACA GHIBNICH

(NG 7354 8197)   Tidal

Access to the bay is by abseil or down climbing a 10m west facing wall just south of the bay at the lowest point of the cliff (Moderate). The stack is accessible two hours either side of low tide and is climbed by a short right-facing corner on the south face (Difficult), then a scramble up the seaward face.

North of this bay is Camas Glac an Rubha, which holds a flatter and more lumpy stack climbed by an easy scramble up a south ramp at low tide.

The following stacks are south of Port Erradale. This area is a hidden gem of beautiful small bays, arches and caves and two fine stacks. Follow the road south 150m to a turning area, then head west to the cliff-top along a fence. A' Staca Chaistel, a 20m stack with a large arch, can be seen from the cliff-top 50m south of the fence. A' Staca Beag, a 10m stack with a smaller arch, is tucked in close to the wall of one of the bays and is characterised by a narrow fin on its north end. Access the beach by continuing 100m further south to an easy descent to the beach.

A' STACA CHAISTEL

(NG 7364 8085) Tidal

The south face of the stack has a large ramp that slopes up to half-height and a prominent open book corner system in the middle of the wall. Descend by scrambling down the seaward side, then down climb the short wall at the lower end of the large ramp.

The Storyteller 12m Hard Severe 4c   *(2005)*
Climb a line 5m to the left of the open book corner.

The Book 10m Hard Severe 4b   *(2005)*
Climb the prominent open book corner.

The Calm Sea 20m VS 4c   *(2005)*
This climbs the right-facing corner to the left of the arch on the landward face and only accessible for an hour either side of low tide. Climb the corner to where this joins the large ramp on the south face. Pull up and right on to the short wall and climb this to the top (crux).

A' STACA BEAG

(NG 7366 8078) Tidal

Descend by scrambling down the fatter south end of the stack.

The Ogre Within 10m HVS 5a *   *(2005)*
Climb the face just left of an arch for 4m. Step right and climb the wall above the arch.

Hidden Story 10m VS 4c   *(2005)*
Climb the left-facing corner 3m left of the arch.

Silent Wisdom 10m HVS 5a *   *(2006)*
The stepped shallow corner 2m left of the arch on the landward face.

A' STACA EILAN AN AIR

(NG 7360 8905) Tidal
Descent is by simultaneous abseil.

South Face 15m Hard Severe 4a   *(2006)*
Climb the corner right of a large flake and pull on to a ledge. Climb a rising leftward traverse to the top.

POOLEWE & TOLLAIDH CRAGS

There are many gneiss crags near Poolewe, including many of the best and most accessible in this guide. A group of crags around Loch Tollaidh are 3km south of Poolewe although only 5km from Gairloch. Slightly nearer Poolewe is the 343m hill of Creag Mhor Thollaidh, surrounded by crags, of which Creag Mhor Thollaidh itself is the best known. Finally there are some recently developed but smaller crags east of Poolewe.

Loch Tollaidh Crags
Maps p97, 99

This is the collection of gneiss crags overlooking Loch Tollaidh, just off the road and clearly seen on the south side of the Gairloch to Poolewe road. The hillside is named on the OS Map as Creagan Dubha but the crags are usually referred to as the Loch Tollaidh Crags. Many of the climbs are steep slabs typical of gneiss and, facing west or north-west, get the sun in the afternoon. The altitudes are between 130m (Raven's Nest) and 180m (Fraggle Rock). One can move around easily from crag to crag according to fancy. The nearest crags are reached by a 15 minute walk across boggy ground passing the northern end of Loch Tollaidh where there are stepping stones across the outflow, the Tollie Burn. Wellies may be useful after wet weather. There are a number of places to park just off the road at the northern end of the loch.

From the road, three main bands of crags can be seen running diagonally south-westwards (left to right) up the slope, away from the road. This becomes more obvious when the crags are reached. The Lower Tier is closest to the road, with the Middle lying just behind. The Upper Tier is behind again but its climbing is well to the left, behind and left of the left end of the Middle Tier. To the right of The Lower Tier, there is a collection of crags, The Inlet Area, grouped close to a narrow inlet on the loch. Another group of crags further right has no climbing.

LOWER TIER

Closest to the road, this is the main band of crags. It runs from the first crag, Raven's Nest, some way up rightwards to Fraggle Rock on the skyline, identifiable by a large block just out from its base.

RAVEN'S NEST

(NG 849 783)   Map p99   Diagram p101

This is the first crag reached after crossing the outflow from the loch and walking across the flat boggy ground. Unfortunately there is a rather large eyrie sitting in the middle of the crag blocking one of the main lines and thereby preventing development of the central section. The right edge of the crag is formed by a fine 40m slab. A metal stake at the top of the slab indicates an old abseiling site.

Flag Wall

The overhung short wall just past the left end of the crag has three routes.

Deliver Me   12m   E1 5a   *(2001)*
Climb to a ledge left of the left arete of the main wall. Continue up just left of the arete via shallow grooves.

Crossroads   10m   E5 6b *   *(1998)*
The wall has an interesting cross intrusion feature. Climb the wall through the left half of the cross to gain a thin crack (Rock 3 at its base) through a bulge. Hard, well protected moves lead to a short hanging groove and easier ground.

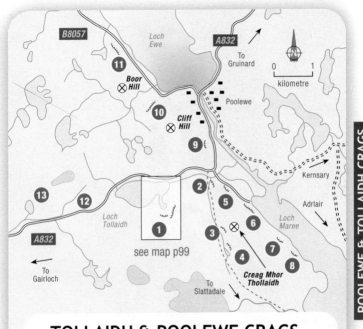

TOLLAIDH & POOLEWE CRAGS

Path   8m   E1 5b   (1998)
The crack on the right, avoiding the temptation to step back at half-height.

The following seven routes are tightly packed together at the left-hand end of Raven's Nest, up the slope, left of the eyrie.

Rushed-up   20m   HVS 5a   (1992)
The flaky groove at the left side of the wall.

Slowed-down   20m   E2 5b *   (1996)
Immediately right of the groove, climb the edge and continue up this to some protection before pulling round right and continuing to a thin crack which leads to the top.

Squeezed-in   20m   E3 5c   (1996)
Eliminate in the upper part and bold in the lower section. Start in a shallow recess with a crack, climb up, step right, then go up a thin crack to the jug on Boldered-

Semi-Automatic, E4, Raven's Nest, Loch Tollaidh Crags. Climber Rab Anderson

Cubby Images

out. Climb directly up a vague crack-line between the routes on either side with good gear in Slowed-down.

Boldered-out   20m   E3 5c *   *(1996)*
The thin crack up the right side of the wall. Boulder directly to the crack at 5m, then climb this to the top.

Blast Off   20m   E5 6a   *(2000)*
Climb the steep wall to reach the base of a short vegetated corner, place a runner and tackle the bulge on the right to finish.

Blow-out   20m   E5 6b *   *(1997)*
Start 3m right of Boldered-out at the left end of a very overhanging section of wall. Climb the overhanging wall to a flake, then up a short crack to finish up a gangway.

BaBa   18m   E6 6b   *(2002)*
Climbs a direct weakness up the overhanging wall. Well protected and strenuous. Start 2m right of Blow-out. Go up to some good gear at 4m, span left to a right-trending flake, then climb this to finish by Blow-out.

On the section of cliff right of the eyrie there are two short, right to left-slanting

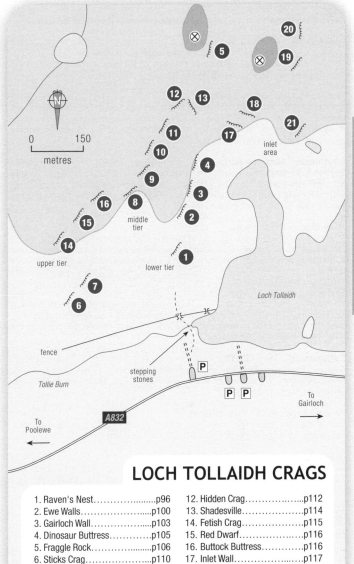

0 —— 150
metres

inlet
area

Loch Tollaidh

middle
tier

upper tier

lower tier

fence

stepping
stones

Tollie Burn

A832

To
Poolewe

To
Gairloch

LOCH TOLLAIDH CRAGS

cracks starting at ground level, then two grooves just before the fine 40m slab marking the right end of the cliff. Use the stake belay at the top of the slab.

Super Sleuth 40m E2 5b   *(1996)*
Climb the short left-hand crack, then step right and follow the ramp of Semi-Automatic all the way up right on to the edge of the crag. A slim groove on the crest leads to heathery ground, then the top.

Semi-Automatic 40m E4 6b **   *(1996)*
The right-hand crack. Start at the base of the left-hand crack and climb boldly up to the right-hand crack. Follow the crack to the ramp and go up this to near its top. Move left to breach the bulge and continue directly above to reach heathery ground on the crest which leads to the top.

MacDonald 40m E4 6a *   *(1999)*
Start up Semi-Automatic to reach the diagonal crack which that route now follows left. Pull over a small roof and step right into a groove. At the top of this, climb slightly right to reach better holds. Swing back left on jugs before climbing up to the big slab. Climb its left edge to the top.

Ming Mong 35m E5 6a   *(2002)*
Start up MacDonald to the left end of the diagonal overlap. Place a good nut on the left and make a long move straight over. Follow the overlap rightwards using holds below and above to join, then finish up Feathering the Nest. Micro-wires are useful.

Feathering the Nest 40m E4 6a *   *(1996)*
This route climbs the groove just left of a short groove leading on to the slab marking the right side of the crag. Climb to the bulge, pull up on to the right wall, then move up into the short groove. Step left and climb the second groove to the slab, which leads easily to the top.

Smokescreen 35m E1 5b   *(1997)*
Climb a shallow right-facing groove further right with a few athletic moves leftwards before pulling over on to the slab (about 10m). Go up this to the belay stakes (via Raven's Edge).

Raven's Edge 40m Very Difficult **   *('40s)*
Start at the right edge of the steep wall, where it turns round into a big clean slab. Follow the left edge of the slab throughout. The top is less clean.

Assault Slab 40m Very Difficult ***   *('40s)*
Clean rough rock and good protection; the start is the crux. Follow the same first 5m as Raven's Edge, then trend right up the centre of the slab, passing the right side of a curving corner. Other variations are possible.

EWE WALLS

(NG 849 782) Map p99

An area of slabs and walls just to the right of Raven's Nest, before the slope rises to Gairloch Wall. The first impression is of a very mossy wall. From the top of the routes a heathery ramp leads back down rightwards to the base of Gairloch Wall.

Ewephoria 30m VS 4b **   *(1982)*
The fine, dark coloured, narrow slab at the left side of the crag is climbed by a central line, poorly protected.

Ewe Tree Slab 25m VS 4c *   *(2001)*
The slab to the right, just left of the moss. Better than it looks.

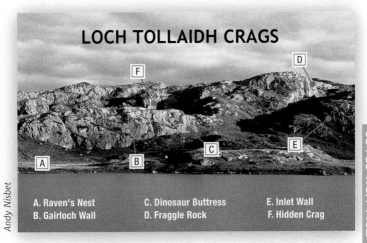

LOCH TOLLAIDH CRAGS

A. Raven's Nest   C. Dinosaur Buttress   E. Inlet Wall
B. Gairloch Wall   D. Fraggle Rock   F. Hidden Crag

Andy Nisbet

Foot in Mouth   20m   E2 5b *(2001)*
Start just right of some fallen debris. Make a steep start, then move right into a hanging scoop. Go directly up on blind but good holds, then easily to a rather rounded finish.

Incisor   30m   HVS 5a * *(2000)*
Climbs the arete and overhanging corner to the left of Ewereka. Start directly below the overhanging corner. Pull through a strenuous overhang into the cracked corner.

Peweky   20m   E2 5b * *(2002)*
Climbs the right side of the arete between Incisor and Ewereka.

Ewereka   25m   E1 5c *(1996)*
Around to the right is a corner with a small holly tree part way up it. This route climbs the thin crack which springs from above a small roof at the start, passing just left of the holly.

Right of the corner and holly is a slab with the first route, then a grassy recess and a short vertical wall with the following four routes.

U2   15m   Severe *(2005)*
Climb the slab right of the corner and holly.

Left Out   15m   E1 5b *(2002)*
A left-slanting crack-line in the vertical wall.

Right On   15m   HVS 5b *(2002)*
Just to the right of Left Out, climb a thin crack to a wide crack, then swing out right and climb directly to the top.

New Horizons   15m   VS 4c *(2000)*
Start 20m to the right of Ewereka below a bottomless grass choked corner. Climb directly towards the base of the corner, step left into a triangular niche and take the overhanging groove line above.

Frozen in Time   20m   E2 5b *(2002)*
Start as for New Horizons into the base of the corner. Make a hard pull right round the right arete and finish up a bottomless groove.

GAIRLOCH WALL

1. Balding Oldie   E6 6b **
2. El Passe   E6 6a ***
3. Old El Pastis   E6 6b ***

4. Conquistador   E7 7a **
5. Ageing Bull   E3 6a *
6. Steer Clear   E5 6b

8. The Imposter   E3 5c *
9. Avoidance   HVS 5a
10. Zig-Zag   HVS 5a
11. Rough Slab   VS 4c

Andy Nisbet

GAIRLOCH WALL

(NG 849 782)   Map p99   Diagrams p101, 102

Lying just to the right, this wall is located above a slight rise in the slope, just above some large boulders. Undercut at its base, the cliff has a vertical wall at its left side and a ramp slanting up rightwards from beneath the undercut section. The base of the crag is sheltered from the elements.

1 Balding Oldie   35m   E6 6b **   (1996)
The left-hand line on the vertical wall at the left side of the cliff. A bold route with the crux at the top. Small cams and small wires required, but hard to place. A flake-line springs from a slanting break at half-height. Stand on an embedded flake and climb to a good but hollow sounding hold. Stand on the hold and continue directly to the break. Gain the flake-line, then make a hard move to reach a crucial nut placement in the base of a small undercut directly above. Continue directly up the thin crack to pull over on to easier ground leading to a belay just below the top.

2 El Passe   35m   E6 6a ***   (1996)
The obvious crack-line up the right side of the vertical wall, where a slime streak springs from a niche at the start. Swing right into the niche from good holds and continue up the unobvious wall to reach a break and protection. Step right and climb the fine overhanging crack to easier ground and a belay just short of the top.

3 Old El Pastis   35m   E6 6b ***   (1996)
The obvious undercut crack-line up the middle of the leaning wall. Pull into the crack and awkwardly place a crucial Rock 6 above the obvious slot, then continue to a point at mid-height where a span across left gains a jug. Pull up right, then climb the crack to the top.

4 Conquistador   25m   E7 7a **   (1996)
The vague crack-line immediately to the right of Old El Pastis. Preclip gear on the lip (a peg was originally stick-clipped) and boulder up the shallow prow to it. Continue up and right to a good shake-out. Tackle the impending wall above, which gets progressively more difficult, culminating in a second crux move going right to a bulge near the top. Finish on improving holds and the return of better protection.

5 Ageing Bull   35m   E3 6a *   (1996)
The thin crack which cuts through the bulge above the start of the slanting ramp. Gain the crack after a bouldery start, then follow this through the bulge and on up the groove to easy ground. Perhaps 6b.

6 Steer Clear   15m   E5 6b   (2002)
The rib between Ageing Bull and The Imposter with a boulder problem start. Eliminate.

7 The Ramp   35m   E2 6a   (1994)
The same boulder problem start as Ageing Bull gains the ramp which is followed more easily rightwards to finish.

8 The Imposter   35m   E3 5c *   (1996)
Just right of Ageing Bull is a short hanging groove in the lower wall leading to the ramp and a thin crack in the headwall. Bouldery moves gain the groove and then the ramp. Move up the ramp a short way, step left on to the wall and climb to easy ground. The thin crack provides some protection but the holds are on the wall to the right.

9 Avoidance   35m   HVS 5a   (1996)
Start immediately to the right of The Imposter below some jugs. Gain the jugs by

DINOSAUR BUTTRESS

1. Crack Bush Chimney Route	VS 4c	6. Red Faced	E1 5b
2. Reeperbahn	E4 6b *	7. Rouged-up	E2 5b *
3. Scarlatina	E2 5b	8. Flushed-out	HVS 5a **
4. In the Pink	HVS 5b **		

Andy Nisbet

bouldery moves, then move up right into the niche of Zig-Zag. Move up and left around the roof, then go right onto the edge, avoiding the block above, and climb directly to the top.

10 Zig-Zag   35m   HVS 5a   *(1994)*
The right end of the crag is formed by a pleasant looking rough slab; this route takes a line immediately to the left. Climb a short corner up left to a niche, move right around the roof, then move left onto the edge and climb to the top.

11 Rough Slab   35m   VS 4c *
The slab of lovely brown rock forming a sidewall at the right end of the crag. A left finish has also been climbed.

CURRA WALL

(NG 849 781)

The extension of Gairloch Wall is a low band of steep rock which is useful for bouldering. There is a slabby upper tier.

Eight Below   30m   Hard Severe 4a   *(1992)*
Start as for Rough Slab at a big heathery V-groove. Climb the slab on the right side of the groove (15m). Continue up the cracked rib directly above (15m). Poorly protected. The lower wall to the right has been soloed at 5b.

Mint   30m   E1 5b   *(1994)*
A central line on the lower wall, then boldly up a small open corner and vague crack-line.

Eights and Reel   25m   HVS 5a   *(1999)*
Boulder up the lower wall, then climb the smooth central corner on the upper tier.

Eighted   30m   VS 5a   *(1994)*
Start towards the right side of the low band and climb it by hard moves up via a flake. Go to the upper tier and climb just right of the smooth corner, then the left side of the slabby rib of After Eight.

After Eight   30m   Severe *   *(1994)*
Climb easily up the right edge of the lower band to the upper tier, where a slabby rib comes down lowest at its right end. Climb the rib.

Pieces of Eight   10m   Very Difficult   *(1999)*
Start just right of the rib of After Eight and climb up and right into a short steep left-facing corner.

DINOSAUR BUTTRESS

(NG 848 781)   Map p99   Diagrams p101, 104
Immediately right of Curra Wall is an area of fine reddish rock, beyond which the crag merges into the hillside before rising up towards Fraggle Rock. The base of the crag is flat and boggy.

1 Crack Bush Chimney Route   30m   VS 4c   *(1995)*
A crack and chimney at the left end of the crag, passing a holly.

2 Reeperbahn   20m   E4 6b *   *(2002)*
The wall and hanging groove left of Scarlatina.

3 Scarlatina   30m   E2 5b   *(1995)*
Bouldery moves lead directly on to a ledge just right of Crack Bush Chimney Route. Move right, then up and left to the roof. Continue up the crack above. High in the grade.

4 In the Pink   30m   HVS 5b **   *(1981)*
The obvious crack in the middle of the crag, strenuous at the start above wet ground.

5 Off the Bone   20m   HVS 5b   *(2002)*
Swing rightwards above the roof a short way up In the Pink and climb directly to the top. Eliminate.

6 Red Faced   30m   E1 5b   *(1992)*
The next crack just around the edge to the right leads to a finish up an easy corner.

7 Rouged-up   30m   E2 5b *   *(1995)*
A direct line up the centre of the wall immediately right of the crack (better but E3 without a runner in Red Faced), finishing by an easy arete and slab.

8 Flushed-out   30m   HVS 5a ** *(1992)*
The crack and shallow groove at the right end of the crag.

9 Chitin   8m   VS 5a *(1999)*
The small buttress about 20m right and slightly up from Dinosaur Wall. Climb the crack in the nose direct.

FRAGGLE ROCK

(NG 848 778)   Map p99   Diagram p101

This crag, visible in profile from the road, lies higher up at the far right end of the Lower Tier, beyond where Dinosaur Buttress merges into the hillside. A huge shattered block lies just out from the base of the crag. The left and lower end of the crag is split into two smaller tiers and the climbs are described from this end, the lower tier first, then the upper, then full height routes moving right.

Lower Tier

Fozzy Bear   10m   VS 4c *(1992)*
On the front face (left end) of the lower tier is a clean red wall with a crack just right of a small right-facing corner. Climb a short wall, cross a heather ledge, then follow the thin crack and wall above. Low in the grade.

The right end of the lower tier is a defined rib **Scooter**, (Very Difficult 1992). Left of this is another rib (Moderate, finishing left up a ramp). A parallel ramp lower down gained past a small black and white striped patch (4c) or further left (5a) is **Gonzo** (1992). A third rib, ending up a steep wall with a right-slanting crack, is **Low** (VS 4c 2001).

Upper Tier

The Upper Tier consists of two walls separated by a heathery break. The first three routes are on the left-hand wall, which has a slight crest.

Arctic Dreams   20m   E2 5b * *(2001)*
Start well left of the crest and climb a right-slanting intermittent crack-line. Where this ends, make a difficult move right to a ledge and finish direct.

Deathmarch   20m   E3 5b * *(2001)*
Climb the prow direct.

Dr Beaker   15m   E2 5b * *(1992)*
Start immediately right of the prow and climb a slight groove to a right-trending line leading into heather. Go up a steep wall to a prominent right diagonal crack and finish up this.

A small pillar finishing in a heathery top just right of the heather on Dr Beaker and 3m below the cliff-top is **Sam** (Hard Severe), the main interest being the descent.

The following two routes are on the right-hand wall.

Nippy Heed   10m   E3 5b *(2002)*
Climb the centre of the wall going up, then slightly right passing a thread (wire) near the top. Worthless protection although the climbing does ease a bit towards the top.

Itty Bitty Gritty   10m   E1 5a *(2002)*
A right-trending line immediately right of Nippy Heed leads to a ledge, then up the groove above.

Main Wall

Diagram p108

The following routes climb the full height of the cliff.

1 Miss Piggy   25m   Difficult   *(1992)*
Left of the steep section of cliff and left of a horizontal cave at mid-height is a
gently left-sloping ramp. Climb this, then clean rock straight up.

2 Animal   20m   HVS 5a   *(1992)*
Start at the base of Miss Piggy ramp. Move out right and climb a rib to the big
horizontal cave. Traverse left and climb the steep groove which springs from the left
end of the cave. Starting further right would reduce the grade to VS. Climbing
direct from the start of the ramp is harder.

3 Animal Instinct   20m   E1 5a   *(2005)*
Start as for Animal to the cave. Pull up into a small groove above the cave and
climb the wall direct to the top.

Right of the horizontal cave and nearly opposite the huge shattered block is a big
corner, rather vegetated. The base of the right wall of the corner holds a slab
leading to two roofs near the right arete.

**4 Kermit   25m   E1 5b ** **   *(1992)*
Climbs the right wall of the big corner. Gear is spaced but perhaps only 5a. Start
near the corner at the left edge of the slab, then trend right up the middle of the
wall. An original line climbed the corner itself (vegetated).

5 Sprocket   25m   E2 5b ** *   *(1992/1995)*
Climb the centre of the slab (poorly protected) to the roof, move right, then pull
left through the right end of the roof and go up to the next roof. Move out right
and climb cracks to the top. The original ascent was less direct.

The following routes lie just to the right of the big corner. Opposite the huge
shattered block is a small alcove occupied by a split boulder.

**6 Tall in the Saddle   25m   E6 6b ** *   *(2002)*
The white wall above the split block.

**7 Heave-ho   25m   E4 6a ** *   *(1995)*
Climb a thin crack just right of the split block, pull through the roof and continue
up the crack to the top.

8 Lean-to   25m   E3 5c   *(1995)*
A leaning, cracked groove immediately right of Heave-ho is climbed steeply to
easier ground and a deep crack leading to the top.

**9 Fraggle Roll   25m   HVS 5a ** *   *(1995)*
Just right of Lean-to is a short leaning crack whose right side forms a pedestal.
Climb the crack to the left end of the holly bush, then a corner left to the pedestal
and an overhanging corner above. A hanging crack-line leading direct to the corner
is E1 5b.
Variation: **Roll Up   E3 5c** *   *(2001)*
A direct finish. Climb through the holly and up the groove and crack above.

10 Barking Shark   30m   E2 5b   *(2001)*
Start below a small roof. A broken crack-line leads to easy ground which is followed
leftwards to an obvious finishing flake-crack.

The following routes lie a short way further right and break through a roof system.

FRAGGLE ROCK - Main Wall

1. Miss Piggy — Difficult
2. Animal — HVS 5a
3. Animal Instinct — E1 5a
4. Kermit — E1 5b **

5. Sprocket — E2 5b ***
6. Tall in the Saddle — E6 6b *
7. Heave-ho — E4 6a *
8. Lean-to — E3 5c

9. Fraggle Roll — HVS 5a *
10. Barking Shark — E2 5b
11. Welcome Home — E3 5c
12. Joyful Departure — E3 6a *

13. Peek Practice — E4 6a *
14. Waldorf — HVS 5a
15. Alien Spacemen — HVS 5b
16. They Think it's all Overhang — HVS 5a
17. The Snapper — HVS 5a
18. The Bulge — HVS 5a

Andy Nisbet

11 Welcome Home   30m   E3 5c   *(2000)*
A crack-line through the left side of the roof.

12 Joyful Departure   15m   E3 6a *   *(1998)*
A crack-line towards the right-hand end of the roof (Friend 4 at the lip).

13 Peek Practice   25m   E4 6a *   *(1995)*
This route climbs the right side of the smooth wall right of the roof system. Climb a groove to a recess, then move left and go up a shallow groove with difficulty to easier ground. Go a short way up a slabby groove, climb to a recess under a roof, then pull out left through the top of this and continue to the top.

14 Waldorf   25m   HVS 5a   *(1992)*
Immediately to the right of Peek Practice is a reddish coloured intrusion of unusual rock running up the wall. Climb this past a recent rockfall and straight up to easier slabby ground.

15 Alien Spacemen   25m   HVS 5b   *(1998)*
Right of Waldorf is a downward-slanting crack about 5m up and containing an obvious wedged block near its right end. This takes a direct line past the wedged block.

16 They Think it's all Overhang   25m   HVS 5a   *(2000)*
Right of the end of the crack with the wedged block are three grooves. This starts at the end of the crack and has an overhang higher up. Climb straight up to the overhang and through it leftwards on good holds. Finish direct via a left-facing corner.

17 The Snapper   20m   HVS 5a   *(1999)*
The takes the central and best defined of the grooves right of the wedged block. Climb up into and up the groove to a block, pass this and go to a roof. Trend up and right naturally to finish.

18 The Bulge   20m   HVS 5a   *(1999)*
The right groove, about 3m right of the central. Climb up to a small niche, then steeply over the bulge on good holds. Finish direct via grooves, cracks and ribs.

19 Cookie Monster   25m   VS 5a   *(1993)*
About 10m from the right end of the wall is this heathery crack with an undercut start.

20 Reddy Ribbed   25m   VS 5a *   *(1995)*
Just right of the heathery crack is a short V-groove. Gain and climb the groove, then pull out left and climb a clean rib to easier ground and the top.

21 The Rub   25m   HVS 5a   *(2006)*
Start below the left-hand end of the Doozer Slab. Climb a short ramp leftwards to below a steep groove (close to Reddy Ribbed but separate). Climb the groove to easier climbing, following a line right of Reddy Ribbed to the top.

22 Doozer   20m   Very Difficult *   *(1992)*
A clean slab, the furthest right climb on the crag. Climb the slab to its top right corner, cross a heather break and climb a small rib to the top.

BOG CRAG

(NG 848 777)

This lies 100m beyond Fraggle Rock on the same tier. The approach is very wet underfoot, hence the name, wellies recommended. The crag has four main cracks. The deep one furthest left contains a small holly and a Scots pine while the furthest right is more like a deep recess. Descend at either end.

Out of the Mire 15m Hard Severe 4b   *(2006)*
The left-hand of the two central crack-lines. Start from an island of turf amongst the wet ground or traverse in from eother side. Good holds lead to the fine upper flake-crack.

Bog Bean 15m VS 4c   *(2006)*
The right-hand of the two central crack-lines.

Bog Trot 15m Difficult   *(2006)*
An obvious ramp line leading out rightwards from the recess on the right side of the crag. An airy move near the top of the ramp leads to easy ground.

Bog Trot Direct 15m Very Difficult   *(2006)*
After a few moves up the ramp, climb straight up on good holds through a break below a prominent nose of rock.

MIDDLE TIER

The line of crags running parallel to and about 100m behind the main band of crags, overlooking a flat boggy area; The Meadow. They can either be reached from the left side of Raven's Nest, or from the right side of Dinosaur Buttress. There is also a smaller continuation about 400m nearer the road and seen well to the left from the road, described first.

STICKS CRAG

(NG 853 785) Map p99

The left-hand of the two crags nearer the road.

Strongbow 20m VS 4c   *(2000)*
This is the central of three right-curving cracks.

Rosie 15m Hard Severe 4b   *(2000)*
The right-hand right-curving crack, set in a corner.

STONES CRAG

(NG 852 785) Map p99

These routes lie on the right-hand crag, with excellent red rock on the lower part and more lichenous grey rock above.

Bluenote 20m VS 4c   *(2000)*
Climb directly up the centre of the buttress.

The Dreamcoat 20m HVS 5a   *(2000)*
Start up a crack, then make delicate moves left into the middle of the wall. The upper slab is easier, but unprotected.

SIREN SLAB

(NG 851 782) Map p99

This is the obvious large steep slab which lies at the left-hand side of this band, set back and a little higher than the rest of the crags. Buttock Buttress on the Upper Tier lies just behind it.

Hypocrites and Bastards 15m E1 5a   *(2004)*
Take the left-slanting crack-line left of The Snake to just before the arete, then break right to finish up a right-trending line of holds.

The Snake   20m   E1 5a   *(1997)*
The snaking shallow slot, quite mossy, on the left side of the slab. Poorly protected in the middle.

Lorelei   35m   E4 5c *   *(1996)*
A line up the middle of the slab. Good climbing but somewhat marred by having to search for gear. Start at the lowest rocks and climb up, then left to a heathery ledge beneath a short groove in the middle of the wall. Climb the groove, step leftwards, then go straight up the wall passing left of a small roof to reach a left-slanting diagonal crack. Finish directly from this.
Variation: **Alternate Finish   5c**
From the start of the diagonal crack near the top, step right and climb straight up passing some thin horizontal breaks.

Strip-teaser   35m   E4 5c **   *(1996)*
The very thin right-slanting crack, right of centre on the slab. Sustained and thin, the gear is good but spaced, therefore just E4. Start at the lowest rocks and climb straight up to the right end of a heather ledge below a shallow groove just right of Lorelei. Climb the groove, then go up and around the left side of the obvious overlap to reach the thin crack which leads to a bulge just below the top. Pull out left to finish more easily.

Temptress   35m   HVS 5a   *(1996)*
The right-slanting crack-line which leads to the right edge of the slab. Start as for Strip-teaser but climb up right to reach and climb a right-slanting corner and the crack-line. Finish up the easy edge of the slab.

CLOICHE WALL

(NG 851 782)   Map p99
The wall some 50m to the right of Siren Slab, from which it is set slightly further forward and lower down. The crag appears to incline to the right with slanting faults either side of it.

May Election   25m   VS 4b   *(1999)*
At the left end of the crag and to the left of Someone Else's Dream is a curving pillar. Climb an obvious cracked groove, trending up right to a difficult move right into finishing cracks in the upper pillar. Low in the grade.

Someone Else's Dream   25m   E2 5b **   *(1991)*
A fine strenuous route taking the obvious groove and crack which slant up rightwards. High in the grade. Always wet at the base.

Distraction   25m   E4 5c   *(1998)*
Halfway between Someone Else's Dream and White Fright is a shallow groove which ends at about 3m height. Climb the groove and the line above, trending slightly right to reach another left-facing groove. The wall on its right is climbed to join Someone Else's Dream.

White Fright   25m   E3 5c *   *(1996)*
The shallow quartzy groove just to the right. Move up and boldly right into the base of the groove which leads with interest to easier ground.

BOOR BUTTRESSES

(NG 851 781)   Map p99
Two small but steep buttresses down the slope a short way right.

Sage Bush Rider   10m   E2 6a *(1991)*
On the left buttress. Climb the thin crack through the middle of the steep wall above a small holly tree, passing right of an obvious square block at about half-height.

Gutbuster   10m   E3 5c *(2001)*
The central thin crack-line on the right buttress.

FEOIR BUTTRESS

(NG 850 781)   Map p99

The bigger buttress a little further right, steep at the bottom and slabby above. The steep lower face is split by two obvious crack-lines which finish beside each other.

Rock Bottom   25m   E3 5c *(1996)*
The left-hand crack which springs from above a wet streak. Finish up the slabby rib of Zeazy Top.

Zeazy Top   25m   E3 6a * *(1996)*
The right-hand, Z shaped crack, then the slabby rib above.

HIDDEN CRAG

(NG 850 780)   Map p99   Diagrams p101, 113

This crag sits at the right-hand end of this line of crags and is hidden from the road. It lies just behind Dinosaur Buttress and is best reached by crossing the slope just beyond that crag and cutting across The Meadow to it. A tall, reddish coloured wall is cut by a number of prominent crack-lines. There is a smaller crag to the left of the main wall, called The Real Hidden Crag.

Real Hidden Crag

Tasty Little Number   15m   VS 4c *(2000)*
The wall at the left-hand end of this smaller crag, leading to a mantelshelf finish.

Mother Earth   15m   E1 5b *(2000)*
An obvious crack just right of a slight crest, gained by a short wall.

Bradan   15m   HVS 5a *(2000)*
The left-hand of twin crack-lines 1m apart, right of Mother Earth.

Breac   15m   HVS 5a *(2000)*
The right-hand crack.

Rockspawn   12m   VS 4c *(2000)*
The obvious line up the middle of the wall to the right, right of a grass patch.

Horny Handed   15m   HVS 5a *(2000)*
Go up towards a small roof, then keep left following the cleaned line to finish as for Rockspawn.

Mud Wrestler   15m   HVS 5a *(1999)*
Climbs near the right end of the wall. Move up to a series of left-curving cracks leading on to the ledge.

Main Crag

1 Social Club   35m   E2 5b *(2000)*

HIDDEN CRAG

Andy Nisbet

1. Social Club	E2 5b	5. Malpasso	E3 5b **
2. Wild Iris	E4 5c *	6. Monte Cristo	E3 5b *
3. Water Lily	E2 5c **	7. Shotgun Wedding	E3 5c *
4. Buena Vista	E2 5b ***	8. Frog Dance	E5 6a

Just right of the left edge of the main crag, a short flake leads to a shallow scoop, a wall and then easier but sparsely protected climbing.

2 Wild Iris   35m   E4 5c *   *(2000)*
Climbs the wall to the left of Water Lily. Start up a hollow pillar and boldly tackle the wall above to finish as for Social Club.

3 Water Lily   40m   E2 5c **   *(1994)*
A well protected crack-line that runs up and slightly left from a series of soggy sods of turf. The start is usually wet but on jugs. The finish is thin but try not to escape right to Buena Vista.

4 Buena Vista   40m   E2 5b ***   *(1994)*
The vertical crack-line which lies immediately right of the wet sods. Sustained and well protected.

5 Malpasso 40m E3 5b ★★ *(1994)*
Gain a ledge just up and right of Buena Vista and boldly climb the short initial wall to better holds and protection. Climb a vague crack in the wall, step right to another crack and continue to the top.

6 Monte Cristo 35m E3 5b ★ *(2002)*
A thin crack-line immediately right of Malpasso and just left of the corner. Climb as for Malpasso to above the grass ledges, then move up right to a steepening and the crack.

7 Shotgun Wedding 25m E3 5c ★ *(2001)*
To the right of Malpasso is an upper heather terrace with this crack-line starting from it. The finishing slab is easy but unprotected.

8 Frog Dance 20m E5 6a *(1999)*
A vague crack-line about 8m to the right, passing a small roof.

9 Back to Business 15m E1 5b *(2003)*
A blocky looking line through the bulge at the right end of the wall, then directly to the top.

SHADESVILLE

Map p99

A wall right of and at right-angles to Hidden Crag. There are two routes on the clean section at its right end.

Bitches from Hell 10m E3 6a *(2001)*
Follow the left crack-line to a break. Step left and climb a short wall on good holds to the top.

Unrepeatable 10m E2 5c *(2001)*
The more obvious right crack-line.

There is a pink wedge shaped buttress behind Hidden Crag, best seen from in front of the Real Hidden Crag. There is one route on good rock.

Wedgie 15m Hard Severe 4b *(2001)*
Climb the lower section just right of a heather fault to the ledge. Climb the middle of the wall with a steep start.

UPPER CRAG

A small crag of fine compact rock, just left of and set back from the top of Hidden Crag. At the highest point at the base of the crag an obvious wide crack provides a break in the small lower section of the cliff, with an obvious heathery fault slanting up leftwards just to its left. The routes start here.

The Crackline 15m HVS 5a *(2002)*
Climb the small lower section to a ledge, then up the obvious crackline to just below a recess at the top, then swing out left and go up and over blocks to finish. Probably climbed before.

The Walline 10m E2 5a/b ★ *(2002)*
The centre of the wall immediately left of the crack-line, passing a small rock scar.

The Nextline 15m E1 5a *(2002)*
Immediately left of The Walline. Climb the initial wall and make a few moves

leftwards up the heathery fault to a tiny roof, then swing out right and climb the
wall to the top.

UPPER TIER

This is the highest level of crags, on the left. Viewed from the road, the tops of the
crags form the left-hand skyline.

FETISH CRAG

Map p99

Left of the more obvious Red Dwarf (see below) is an area of steep walls and
overhangs. The leftmost section of wall has a big roof with a groove through it.
Further right are two sections of wall separated by a steep vegetated fault with a
thin tree high up.

Left Section

Bound and Gagged   30m   VS 4c   *(2001)*
Start up a cracked corner towards the left end of this section and reach a diagonal
crack. Go left round a small roof to a heathery finish.

Silky Smooth   25m   E3 5c   *(2001)*
Climb the wall right of the corner to a break in the roof. Step right to surmount the
roof.

Rubberist   25m   E3 6a   *(2001)*
A line close on the left of the vegetated fault. Climb a shallow corner left of the
fault, then swing left on to the wall and go up cracks and a break to easier ground.

Right Section

The cleaner right section of wall has a curving left-trending crack breaking through
a long roof at a niche. Right of this and low down is a big down-pointing flake.

Stiff Egg White   25m   E2 5c   *(2000)*
Start up the middle of the wall left of the crack. Cross the crack close to the roof
and break through above.

Brewer's Droop   25m   E2 5b **   *(2000)*
The prominent left-curving crack, finishing through the niche in the roof.

Viagra Falls   25m   E1 5b   *(2000)*
Climb the left side of the down-pointing flake and the crack above.

Lewd Behaviour   25m   VS 4c   *(2000)*
The down-pointing flake continues right to form a roof. Climb the pink wall
immediately right of the roof, then a groove to a short upper wall.

Prickly Pair   25m   VS 4c   *(2000)*
Start 1m right of Lewd Behaviour. Climb the pink wall and finish up the groove
above the small holly bush.

Large Libido   25m   VS 4c   *(2001)*
A parallel line just on the right of Prickly Pair and passing just left of a big heather
patch. Climb a corner and wall to a diagonal crack. Go left round a small roof to a
heathery finish.

POOLEWE & TOLLAIDH CRAGS

The following three lines are on the wall to the right of the heather patch.

Gaugely   15m   VS 4b   *(2001)*
This follows a curving crack to finish straight up whitish rock.

Babyface   15m   HVS 5a   *(2001)*
Climb directly up from the toe of the wall to a crack leading to the top end of a
ramp and flake holds to finish.

The Upsetter   15m   VS 4b   *(2001)*
The groove line at the right end of the wall. Move left at 10m up the ramp to
finishing flake holds.

RED DWARF

Map p99

Perhaps the most obvious crag and clearly seen from the car park is a small slab of
bright red rock split into two parts by a central crack.

Sunspot   10m   Severe 4a
Climb the left side of the left slab via a small right-facing corner.

Cheeky Slab   10m   VS 4c
Climb the left slab keeping just left of the central crack.

Supernova   10m   VS 4c
Climb the right slab keeping just right of the central crack.

Switch   10m   Severe 4a
A combination of 2. and 3. has been made, based on the central crack.

Black Hole   10m   Very Difficult
Start 3m right of the central crack and immediately left of a step in the base. Climb
the slab trending slightly right and back left.

BUTTOCK BUTTRESS

(NG 852 782)   Map p99

This is the rightmost crag on this band, lying just below the highest point on the
left-hand skyline (point 208m). It is best reached from Siren Slab, which it lies just
above and behind. Smallish looking but clean, the crag is split into two halves by
a diagonal fault, a steeper left half and a less steep right half.

Yabugga   20m   E1 5b   *(2001)*
The crack-line at the left edge of the crag, moving left at a small bulge (moving
right at the bulge with a high side runner is E2 6a).

The Drying Game   20m   E2 5b *   *(1996)*
The shallow, chocolate coloured groove at the left side of the crag.

Inclement Proposal   20m   E2 5b *   *(1996)*
The thin cracks in the wall immediately right of The Drying Game, leading to a thin
slanting crack, passed on the left, at the top of the crag.

Dangerous Lesions   20m   E5 6a **   *(1996)*
A line straight up the middle of the wall. Start at the foot of the fault. Pull left on
to the wall, then gain a break beneath the left side of a small roof and pull around
this to enter a shallow groove. From the top of the groove, place awkward

protection and continue up, then right to good but hollow sounding holds. Go up to a small triangular feature, then reach rightwards to finishing moves. Small wires for protection.

Balls of Fire   20m   E2 5c   *(2001)*
On the right cheek. The steep wall just right of the arete leads to an easy finish.

Yabbandit   20m   VS 5a   *(2000)*
Climbs the steep wall right of Balls of Fire, finishing easily up slabs and exiting left.

INLET AREA

These are the crags grouped around the head of a narrow inlet on the loch. From the parking place, an extensive craggy area is visible on the front slopes of a triangular hill (which is right of Fraggle Rock, also on the skyline). Most of the crags are broken but two steep walls face directly toward the road. Wee Lochan Crag can be seen in profile as a separate (and small) crag to the right.

INLET WALL

(NG 848 780)   Map p99   Diagram p101

This is the impressive crag situated at the head of the inlet on the shore of the loch.

For Schny Dung   15m   E2 5c   *(2001)*
The dirty left-leaning corner at the left end of the main wall.

Fill An Der   25m   E3 5c   *(2001)*
Near the right arete of the corner. Climb the steep lower wall to a ledge of sorts where a swing right over a small roof attains a line of flakes and jugs that lead rightwards, then up to a heathery finish.

Lifeline   30m   E3 5c ***   *(2000)*
The route follows the obvious crack-line, with a cleaned ledge part way up.

Chopsticks   25m   E3 5b   *(2001)*
Start at the base of the wall, about 5m right of Lifeline. Go up to hollow flakes, then up and slightly leftwards to reach a horizontal break. Finish up a short groove above (crux). Sparse on gear low down.

RECESSED WALL

(NG 847 779)   Map p99

The upper and right-hand of two smooth vertical walls above the inlet and facing the car park. The nearer and left-hand is the unclimbed Inlet Wall. Although it can be reached by scrambling rightwards up deep heather from beneath that crag, it is best reached by following the path up towards Fraggle Rock, then heading away right from the lowest part of Fraggle, slightly rising until overlooking a grassy basin. From here the "wee lochan" is clearly seen. Descend into the basin and go down a ramp towards the inlet until the crag is obvious.

The first route climbs a slabby rib passed on the descent and the right-hand of two well defined ribs up the ramp from the main wall.

Descent Gully Rib   20m   Severe 4a   *(1996)*
Climb a shallow groove in the lower buttress, then climb the slabby rib to the top.

The next three routes take lines up the centre of the fine wall. A large boulder lies at the base of the wall.

**Hollow Heart   25m   E3 5c ** *(1996)*
The obvious central line, starting at the boulder. Make a move up a thin crack, then pull out left to flake holds and continue up to reach the left side of a ledge girdling the wall at one-third height. Move up, then right to the base of a line of flaky holds and follow these to the top.

Simple Mind   25m   E3 5c * *(1996)*
Start as for Hollow Heart but climb straight up the thin crack to gain the girdling ledge. Move right, then up to a junction with Hollow Heart. Move up right and climb the obvious line just right of Hollow Heart.

Tortured Soul   25m   E3 5c * *(1996)*
Start to the right of Simple Mind where a diagonal crack slants up right at the base of the crag, and a black streak comes out of a small hole above. Climb to the hole and climb the wall just to its right to reach the girdling ledge. Step left, then pull up right and climb up to the right side of a block type feature at the top of the wall just right of Simple Mind. Finish up the edge of the wall.

Recessed Groove   20m   E2 5b * *(2001)*
A climb up the right side of the wall with a difficult start which is sometimes wet. Climb to the first good break near a bush, move slightly left and up into the groove. Climb to the block on Tortured Soul and finish direct.

Primrose Slab   25m   VS 4c *(2002)*
At the far right end of the crag, overlooking Recessed Wall is a clean slab of fine rough rock. Gain the easy angled slab by a steeper start and climb this more easily, finishing up the central heather crack.

HALF DOME

(NG 845 778)   Map p99

Behind (above) Wee Lochan Crag, on a flat area of ground, is a pink dome shaped wall some 15m high at its tip. The resemblance to its namesake is optimistic, but it gives small routes described right to left.

Route 1   10m   Very Difficult
A left-slanting crack near the right end.

Route 2   10m   Severe 4a
Straight up the centre of the right-hand pink wall.

Route 3   10m   Very Difficult
A straight heathery crack-line between the two pink walls.

Route 4   12m   Severe 4a
The left-hand pink wall.

Route 5   12m   HVS 5a *
The steep wall at the highest point of the crag.

Route 6   15m   VS 4c
A shallow scoop forming the left side of the steepest section and finishing up a short corner.

Route 7   15m   Very Difficult
A direct line about 3m to the left and finishing up an open groove.

Route 8   15m   Severe 4a
A right-slanting crack-line which curves and follows the wall above.

Route 9   15m   Severe 4a
A pink scoop and the wall above.

Route 10   15m   Difficult
A crack-line and wall where the face starts to form more holds on the left.

POSSE CRAG
(NG 845 777)   Map p99

A compact chunk of rock about 150m right and slightly uphill from Half Dome. It has a blunt arete with a large spike boulder at its start, diagonal plates of rock on its steeper right side and a slabbier left side. Not to be confused with another arete further left (above Half Dome), which also has a spike boulder at its start.

Mary, Mary   15m   VS 4c   *(2001)*
This takes the clean crack and groove to the left of the arete. Just before the crack peters out, step right on to the slabby wall and climb it, delicately at first, to the top.

Molly Moo's Posse   15m   HVS 4c   *(2001)*
Climb the grooved arete, with an awkward start and some interesting moves to finish. Sparsely protected; RPs advisable.

The Wild Bunch   15m   E1 5b   *(2002)*
Start right of the arete. Climb straight up to a pale recess. Pull rightwards and up to finish.

WEE LOCHAN CRAG
(NG 845 780)   Map p99

This small separate crag lies low down, just beyond the small inlet on Loch Tollaidh. Neither it nor the lochan are seen from the parking place. After crossing the river, trend rightwards across boggy ground and around the head of the distinct inlet. Go up a short slope on to the promontory which forms the right side of the inlet to where the crag becomes visible around the corner. The crag is in two sections, with the right portion set back about 1m by a corner with embedded blocks at its base. A lochan, a definitive feature but not quite big enough to be marked on the 1:50000 map, lies about 100m out from the base of the crag.

Left-hand Section

Three boulder problems occupy the left-hand side of the crag. A crack splitting an upper block at the far left end (4c), the pink wall direct (5a) and shallow scoops up and right (4c).

The Arrow   8m   HVS 5c
From the base of a flake-line left of centre, go up to an arrow shaped niche and thin crack above.

Solo   8m   VS 5a
The flake-line, or its front.

Duet   8m   HVS 5a *
The centre of the steep wall just to the right of the flake-line.

Om   8m   HVS 5a
The left-hand of two flake-lines facing each other, either approached direct or layback in from the left.

Namestain, E3, Wee Lochan Crag, Loch Tollaidh Crags. Climber Andy Cunningham

Allen Fyffe

Chant   8m   Hard Severe 4a
The right-hand of the two flake-lines.

Trio   10m   Difficult
Just right of the flake-line of Chant, easy rock slants up right, before the crag turns the corner. Climb this a short way then go straight to the top.

Namestain   10m   E3 5c
At the far right end is an arete with a hanging groove, just left of the embedded boulders. Begin up the front face, keeping just left of the start of the hanging groove higher up.

Right-hand Section

This is in two parts, a left and a right, with the central area being heathery and less high. The first four routes lie on the left side of this section, all climbing to the highest point.

First Amendment   15m   VS 4c   *(1996)*
Start just right of the embedded boulders at the foot of the corner. Climb thin cracks just right of the corner, then slant up and right to the top.

**Second Charge   15m   E2 5b ** **   *(1996)*
Start in the centre of the wall beneath a small curving overlap. Climb to the overlap and gain a short left-slanting crack. Move left up the crack a short way, then climb directly to the top.
Variation: **Direct   E2 5c**   *(2000)*
Climb direct from the overlap to the top.

Third Degree   15m   E1 5a   *(1996)*
Just right of the previous route, climb past the left side of a right-slanting crack to a blunt spike, then up a thin crack. Move up left to a jutting block type feature and climb straight to the top.

Fourth Dimension   15m   HVS 5a *   *(1996)*
Climb the right-slanting crack to gain a spike, then up a short, shallow right-facing corner and on directly to the top.

Fifth Wave   HVS 5a   *(2000)*
The wavy red wall, starting by a crack.

Underneath the Arches   15m   VS 4b   *(2000)*
Start at the left end of a curving overlap. Move up and right underneath the overlap to its end, then finish direct. Climbing direct to the right end of the overlap is the same grade.

Pullover   15m   VS 5a   *(2000)*
On the right is a small arch with black seepage underneath. Make reachy moves on good jugs through the roofed arch. Follow flakes leftwards to finish direct.

One Up   12m   HVS 4c   *(1996)*
Start in line with the crack in the headwall. Climb a dark streak with flaky holds for 3m, step right and continue over a small overlap and on directly to the top using the crack.

**Two Down   12m   HVS 5a ** **   *(1996)*
Climb straight up the middle of the wall, excellent and well protected.

Three Across   12m   HVS 4c   *(1996)*
Gain a small overlap, pull left around this, then up and slightly left and on directly to the top.

Creag Mhor Thollaidh

(NG 864 776)   Map p97

Overlooking the shore at the western end of Loch Maree, this rugged lump of Lewisian gneiss has numerous crags dotted about it on all sides.

POOLEWE & TOLLAIDH CRAGS

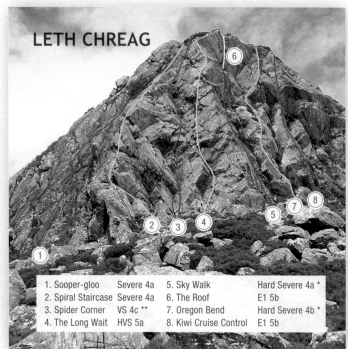

LETH CHREAG

1. Sooper-gloo	Severe 4a	5. Sky Walk	Hard Severe 4a *
2. Spiral Staircase	Severe 4a	6. The Roof	E1 5b
3. Spider Corner	VS 4c **	7. Oregon Bend	Hard Severe 4b *
4. The Long Wait	HVS 5a	8. Kiwi Cruise Control	E1 5b

Andy Nisbet

LETH CHREAG

(NG 859 785)   Alt 100m   South-West facing   Map p97   Diagram p112

The crag is a prominent prow, well seen from the road. It offers pleasant routes without a serious feel, although there are a few hollow blocks. Its prominence, aspect and the faulting of the rock means that it dries very quickly and catches any midge-repelling breezes. It was first used by the Field Craft Training Centre during World War 2 as an abseil practice cliff, hence the legacy of the steel spike driven into its summit (belays for all the routes).

Approach: Either go about 200m down the Tollie farm track (park here) and walk up the stream for 250m to the crag, or follow the Tollie to Slatterdale path for 500m until it crosses the stream below the crag.

The left side of the crag consists of a somewhat scrappy slab which can be climbed anywhere at about Severe, although protection is scarce. Of three lines, the central and best is:

1 Sooper-gloo   20m   Severe 4a   *(1992)*
Climb the centre of the slab, curving right below the top.

2 Spiral Staircase   25m   Severe 4a   *(early '80s)*
The main climbing is on the right-hand face, beginning at the left-hand arete. Start right of the arete. Move up left over broken flakes to the arete and follow this to the top. A nice start but a disappointing finish.

Variation Start: **Hard Severe 4b** *(1992)*
Start at the same place but go straight up into a bottomless flake-corner, climbed to the arete.

**3 Spider Corner 25m VS 4c ** *(1985)*
Follows the main corner between the two aretes. Go straight up the corner passing a couple of overlaps. The holds appear just when the going gets tough.

4 The Long Wait 25m HVS 5a *(2005)*
A crack-line just right of Spider Corner is rather squeezed in. Follow the wide crack-line to overhanging flakes and blocks. Climb over these on to a steep wall, joining Sky Walk Direct. Go right on to the arete to finish as for that route.

5 Sky Walk 25m Hard Severe 4a * *(1980)*
Based on the prominent arete right of Spider Corner. Climb the slab right of the arete to an overhang. Turn this on the right and return left to the crest with delicate moves round the top overhang in a fine exposed position.
Variation: **Direct Line HVS 5a** *(1997)*
Keep as close to the arete as is sensible, to the overhang. Move left and back right on the crest to the same finish.

6 The Roof 20m E1 5b *(1995)*
Start as for Sky Walk but climb direct through the capping roof at a block in the base of a V-slot on its lip.

The two groove lines to the right contain shrubbery but the routes keep to the ribs on their right. The rib between the grooves has a bend right above an overhang (Oregon Bend). The right rib ends below a V-slot in a roof system (Kiwi Cruise Control).

7 Oregon Bend 25m Hard Severe 4b * *(1992)*
Climbs the central rib. Start on the right and traverse left across the groove to gain and climb the rib. A corner leads through the overhang, then step right on to a prow in a fine position. Finish just left of a large jutting flake.

8 Kiwi Cruise Control 20m E1 5b *(1992)*
The right rib and roof. Start on the right side of the rib and traverse left to its crest. Climb the rib and roof above at the V-slot. Trend right to finish.

CREAG FHADA

(NG 862 776) Alt 250m South-West facing Map p97

A cliff of white gneiss lying 1.5km along the Tollie to Slattadale path. The crag is on a broad whaleback of slabby rock with overhangs at its base and set back in a slight widening of the valley, 80m above and east of the path. It consists on the left of two rounded ribs undercut by overhanging walls and lower down on the right by a slabby wall again undercut by short overhanging walls. The first four routes are on the right section and are described right to left. They can be combined with a route on the left section, which don't include the overhanging wall at the base, by a descending scramble. The routes are pleasant but nothing special and haven't been given any stars.

The Great White Whale 80m Very Difficult *(1989)*
The precise line is unsure but the route climbed "the middle of a slab, then an upper slab".

Toe Route 20m Severe *(1992)*
Start at the lowest part of the buttress and climb broken rock and slabs.

Break In   20m   HVS 5a   *(1992)*
Start 4m left of Toe Route. Climb the bulging wall just right of the first overhang and continue more easily up slabs to join Toe Route.

Break Out   20m   VS 5a   *(1992)*
Start left of Break In. Climb a steep crack between two overhangs and slabs to the top of the lower buttress.

Midsummer Wallpaper   15m   VS 5a   *(1992)*
Start left of the second overhang. Gain the wall with difficulty and follow a groove rightwards to a large heather depression.

The next three routes climb the upper left-hand wall and are best reached after doing a route on the right section.

Sunday Lies   30m   Hard Severe   *(1992)*
Climb out right to join a diagonal overlap. Follow this to climb a bulge on the right and follow a slab to the top of the wall. Up and right is a further wall. Climb this direct to finish by a right to left crack.

Gneiss Groove   40m   Severe   *(1992)*
Climbs the central groove until vegetation and a search for interesting climbing forces an exit on to the left wall and up a corner. Finish up a slab behind and right.

Route 66   35m   Severe   *(1992)*
Make a move up the Gneiss Groove, then go out left from the groove and climb the blunt buttress on its left, finishing by a contorted block of rock.

CREAG A' MHIC TALLA

(NG 862 771)   Alt 220m   South-West facing   Map p97

A very steep and impressive crag which would be improved by more cleaning.

Bowel Crusher   25m   E2 5b   *(1999)*
At the left-hand end of the crag is an obvious black corner which leads into a crack to finish.

Felso Belsik   25m   E2 5b   *(1999)*
The rightmost crack-line, starting up a short right-facing corner and finishing up slabby ground.

Further east along the path at NG 864 768, beyond Creag a' Mhic Talla, there is a pleasant narrow red slab (25m Severe, poorly protected).

CREAG NAN LUCH

A crag recently bolted to provide sport climbs. This is now one of the best sport climbing venues in Scotland, particularly in the middle grades, although harder routes are being developed. Seek local information about the latest developments.

LOWER TIER

(NG 864 783)   Alt 70m   North-East facing   Map p97   Diagram p127

The main section. Because of its aspect, it can stay dry in showery westerly weather or if rain has just started. There is some seepage, so it is not good after prolonged rain. In summer it gets the sun until mid morning.

Approach: About 2km south of Poolewe, on the Gairloch road, a single track road

Andy Nisbet

Old Snapper, 6b+, Creag nan Luch. Climber Martin Moran

(signposted Tollie Bay) branches off. Follow this and park below the crag. Cross a stile and head direct, 5mins.

1 Old Snapper   15m   6b+ ** **
A groove line on the left. Step on to a hanging slab and move right into the groove.

2 Hairdubh   18m   6c+ *
The rib on the right to the same lower-off.

3 Superblue   20m   7b+   **

An obvious curving flake line and headwall above. Finish rightwards to the Astar lower-off.

4 Shottabeena   20m   7c

The steep wall on the right past five bolts to an alcove. Lower off from here or step right across Astar and climb past one more bolt to a lower-off.

5 Astar   20m   6a+   **

A shallow corner, then trend left across Shottabeena to finish up a flake-line in the steeper wall wall above. The first bolt is common with Ni Dubh.

6 Ni Dubh   20m   6b   **

Start as for Astar and take a more or less direct line up the slabby wall to the right, then climb diagonally rightwards to finish at the Toss lower-off.

7 Toss   20m   6c+   ***

Start just right of Ni Dubh and head rightwards to clip the (high) first bolt, then directly up to a tricky crux at the first small overlap. Sustained but steady climbing then leads to the top.

8 Walkaway   20m   7a+   *

Just left of the central fault. The slabby upper wall offers a good technical exercise. Start up a rib. The easy climbing finishes abruptly at a thin crux sequence to finish at the Toss belay.

9 Psychopomp   18m   6b   *

The slabby wall right of the central fault.

10 Mr Smooth   15m   6c

Near the right end of the wall. Not to be confused with a partially bolted project which leads rightwards to the same lower-off.

UPPER TIER

(NG 864 782)   North-North-West facing   Alt 100m

An upper tier of blacker rock is sharply overhanging. The lower sections of the routes and some projects stay dry in most weather and can be climbed at 6b+/6c. It is situated 5mins walk directly above the Lower Tier (pass to its right) and sometimes catches a breeze when the lower tier is sheltered. There are left and right sections. Six routes have been climbed but there are also several projects.

Left Side

Highest and left is **Little Leaf** (12m 6c). Next is a partially bolted project. **King of the Swingers** (25m 7a) starts at the same point but goes diagonally right across a crack-line. The crack-line is **Big Knives** (20m 6c) and obviously crosses King of the Swingers. Next are two fully bolted hard projects, then **I'm a Tit, I Love Flying** (20m 7b+ ***), which is the pink flake-line and black right-facing groove at the right side of the crag.

Right Side

This has three partially bolted projects on its left side, the first two with the same start and the third which starts as for the following route but leaves after 3m. Next is **The Power of Tears** (25m 7b), which starts near the projects and moves right to an apex before climbing the wall centrally. On the right is **Swingers** (20m 7b), which starts near the base of a right diagonal fault but climbs direct into a reddish groove, then slightly left and up.

Andy Nisbet

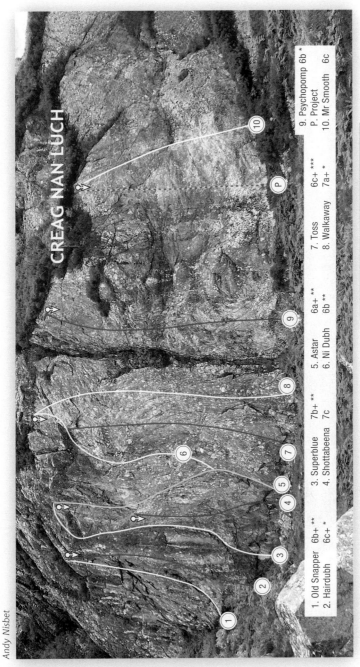

CREAG NAN LUCH

1. Old Snapper	6b+ **	5. Astar	6a+ ***
2. Hairdubh	6c+ *	6. Ni Dubh	6b **
3. Superblue	7b+ **	7. Toss	6c+ ***
4. Shottabeena	7c	8. Walkaway	7a+ *

9. Psychopomp 6b *	
P. Project	
10. Mr Smooth	6c

POOLEWE & TOLLAIDH CRAGS

Allen Fyffe

Hamilton's Groove and Arete, E3, Lower Tollie Crag, Creag Mhor Thollaidh. Climber Andy Cunningham

CREAG MHOR THOLLAIDH

Map p97

Set amidst picturesque surroundings, the crags have an atmosphere akin to the Lake District and offer a variety of fine, easily accessible routes on excellent rock.

Although the biggest crag in the area with some marvellous multi-pitch routes, it has never gained the popularity of (say) Diabaig because of its jungle surroundings, midge rating and vegetation on some routes. The area has been climbed since the 1960s, but exploration has been slow, although over the years a number of notables have contributed to its development. The crags catch the early morning sun and are fairly quick to dry. Their sheltered position produces a serious midge problem, particularly in the trees at the base of the Lower Crag, and spring is undoubtedly the best time for a visit. The Upper Crag is more open and can be clear on a breezy day.

Approach: About 2km south of Poolewe, on the Gairloch road, a single track road (signposted Tollie Bay) branches off to run past Tollie Farm and ends at a small car park close to the water's edge. There are limited spots for camping near the car park. Permission should be sought first from the farm. There is a campsite at Poolewe, with sea breezes to keep the midges at bay. For access from the car park and descent, see each crag individually.

There are three principal crags. Lower Tollie Crag is the nearest to the car park, Upper Tollie Crag is its continuation while Gully Crag is up and to the right.

LOWER TOLLIE CRAG

(NG 869 779)   Alt 30-60m   East facing   Diagram p131

Easily seen from the car park, the crag is only a few minutes walk away. Head direct for its right end through trees. On arrival a two grooved arete, overhanging at its base, marks the right end of the lower right section of the crag. The routes are described from right to left.

Descent: From climbs at the right end of the crag either abseil from small trees or scramble up right through heather to gain a shallow gully filled with jungle which runs down the side of the crag past Fatg (the first route). From the main central wall traverse right through deep heather to reach the descent gully. From the left end of the crag it is best to abseil from a tree just right of the top corner of Stoney Broke (when looking up, the largest and nearest tree on the cliff-top left of Stoney Broke).

1 Fatg   20m   E2 5c *   (1999)
The route is on the sidewall at the far right of crag, up from Hamilton's Groove and Arete. Start below a cave and follow a crack and slabby wall on positive holds to finish up a steep wall to grassy ledge. Probably E3 6a without stepping back on to the roof of the boulder at 5m.

2 Hamilton's Groove and Arete   25m   E3 6a *   (1983)
A 2m shallow chimney and overhanging crack a short way round to the right of the arete. Step left and climb a finger crack in the wall above.

3 Trick of the Light   30m   E3 6a   (1985)
Immediately right of the lowest rock of the arete is a short overhanging corner topped by a block. Climb this, then a flaky groove on the left to a ledge with a big flake. Go up left on flakes to the crest and finish by returning right around the arete. A direct finish would be better but needs cleaning. The original finish was a traverse left to finish as for Cloud Cuckoo Land.

4 Cloud Cuckoo Land   25m   HVS 5b *   (1987)
The obvious crack-line through the break in the steep lower wall starting 12m left of the arete. Climb a short corner, pull through the roof at a block jammed in the crack and follow the continuation crack to step up left and finish by a corner-crack.

5 Hostile Witness   25m   E2 5c   (1993)
Climbs the wall left of Cloud Cuckoo Land, finishing up the fine flake-crack at the top of the wall. Start at the top of the diagonal grass ledge and climb a set of

grooves up the left edge of the wall to gain then follow the flake-crack up and right. Move right and finish as for Cloud Cuckoo Land.

6 Sailing to Byzantium   20m   E2 5c   *(1985)*
Climbs the obvious overhanging wide crack in the inset wall bounding the left side of the wall with the previous two routes and at the top of a grassy ramp. Start up the black corner below the ramp, then the strenuous crack.

7 Second Coast   30m   E2 *   *(1987)*
Start at a shallow cracked corner-groove just left of the bigger corner system with its prominent crack (Sailing to Byzantium), where a grassy tree-lined ledge slants up left.
1. 10m 5a Climb the corner-groove to a ledge.
2. 20m 5b Move up right, climb a crack in the leaning wall and continue up, crossing a small overlap, to finish by a short tricky slab.

8 Home Start   20m   E1 5c   *(1988)*
Start from the grassy tree-lined ledge, where a flake-crack slants up right. Climb the crack, move right then up into a niche below a steep crack. Up this past an ancient wooden wedge.

9 Loctite   35m   E3 *   *(1987)*
A good route which starts below the tree-lined ledge at a short undercut crack, just right of the corner of Rumple Fyke. The first pitch is now unclimbable due to dirt and vegetation, but it is possible to scramble to the start of the second pitch.
1. 10m 5c Gain the crack and follow it to the ledge.
2. 25m 6a Climb the flake-crack as for Home Start, pull left and follow a thin crack up the wall and move left just below the top.

10 Uhu   20m   E1 5b   *(1987)*
Start from the tree-lined ledge. Climb the crack left of Loctite directly, to finish up the last few moves of Rumple Fyke.

11 Rumple Fyke   60m   VS †   *(1967)*
Start below the obvious, steep and often slimy corner marking the left edge of this section of crag. The first pitch is the crux and VS 5a has been suggested.
1. 15m Climb the corner to the grassy ledge and the foot of a right-slanting flake-crack.
2. 20m Climb the crack.
3. 25m Go up the slab above the belay to an overhang, then move left to finish up steep grooves.

12 Friday the Thirteenth   65m   E1   *(1975)*
Takes the obvious corner capped by an overhang, starting as for Rumple Fyke.
1. 20m Climb the corner and follow a grassy ramp left to the foot of the continuation corner.
2. 45m 5b Follow the corner to a roof, traverse out right to the lip of the overhang and climb the large crack above to join Rumple Fyke at the steep groove.

Moving left, the crag now reaches its maximum height. The next few routes virtually share a common start.

13 North-West Orient   60m   E4 *   *(1991)*
A good line which takes the right arete of the wall. Start to the right of the tree start of Gudgeon beneath a short crack springing from a niche with a holly on the left and a small tree on the right.
1. 25m 5b A flake-crack leads to the niche, then climb the short crack and to a horizontal handrail. Traverse right for 5m, climb the wall past a crack to reach a left-slanting ramp, then move up to belay as for Gudgeon.

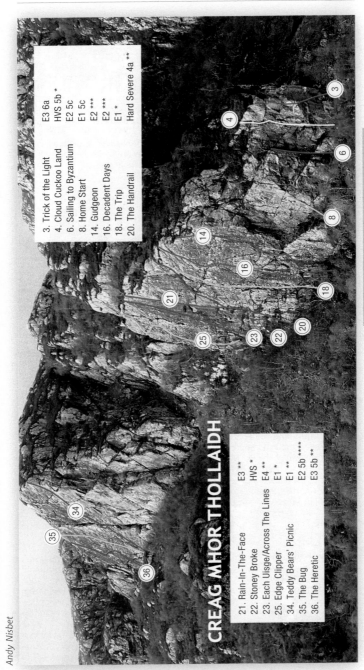

Andy Nisbet

131

POOLEWE & TOLLAIDH CRAGS

3. Trick of the Light	E3 6a
4. Cloud Cuckoo Land	HVS 5b *
6. Sailing to Byzantium	E2 5c
8. Home Start	E1 5c
14. Gudgeon	E2 ***
16. Decadent Days	E2 ***
18. The Trip	E1 *
20. The Handrail	Hard Severe 4a **

CREAG MHOR THOLLAIDH

21. Rain-In-The-Face	E3 **
22. Stoney Broke	HVS *
23. Each Uisge/Across The Lines	E4 **
25. Edge Clipper	E1 *
34. Teddy Bears' Picnic	E1 **
35. The Bug	E2 5b ****
36. The Heretic	E3 5b **

2. 35m 6a Climb the groove to a flake then step up right to a thin crack (as for Gudgeon). Place a high runner, then traverse right to a peg and climb the arete and cracks to the top.

14 Gudgeon   70m   E2 ***   (1971/1988)

A good route with an excellent second pitch taking the thin crack up the right edge of the crag. Start at a tree right of the obvious fault of The Trip, at a recess. This is about 10m up from the lowest rocks.

1. 20m 5b Climb the tree and step up left to climb a short corner. Move right, climb a groove then go right below the roofs to a stance on the edge where a grassy ramp comes in from the right.
2. 30m 5c Step left to climb the corner-crack to a horizontal break, then step across right and climb a thin crack-line in the wall to a belay on the left of a large flake.
3. 20m 5a Climb the flake, step right then climb cracks to the top.

15 Catastasis   90m   E2   (1968)

Takes the obvious diagonal crack slanting left across the face.

1. 20m 5b Pitch 1 of Gudgeon.
2. 25m 5b Climb the corner-crack to the horizontal break (as for Gudgeon) then move left to gain the diagonal crack and climb this to a small stance.
3. 15m 5c Continue up the diagonal crack to a footledge. Go up and left to the upper stance on The Trip.
4. 30m 4b Move up then left and across to trees, then climb the large flake on the right to the top.

Variation: Toady   (1971)

2a. Traverse left to a rising diagonal rake blocked by a large wedged boulder. Climb the rake to where it is crossed by a vertical crack (Decadent Days) which is then followed to the small stance at the diagonal crack.

16 Decadent Days   70m   E2 ***   (1983)

A superb route following a thin crack-line directly up the crag. Start as for the previous routes at the tree.

1. 40m 5c Climb the tree and step up left to climb the short corner until it is possible to step left on to the lip of the roof to reach the thin crack-line. Follow the crack to belay as for Catastasis at the diagonal crack.
2. 30m 5c Step up left to the diagonal crack then move right to gain thin cracks which are climbed to the top.

17 Sarah'n'Dipity and the Forgotten Pill   55m   E3 **   (1998)

An excellent climb in an impressive situation, taking the fine shallow groove in the centre of the wall, between The Trip and Decadent Days.

1. 15m 4c As for The Trip to the large oak.
2. 25m 5c Continue 6m up until it is possible to step right past a perched block. Move up and right to gain good holds at the base of a shallow groove. Follow this over a slight bulge to a junction with Catastasis; follow this diagonally left to a niche and old peg belay.
3. 15m 4a Pull out of the top of the niche into a slanting crack. Follow this to finish easily.

18 The Trip   85m   E1 *   (1967)

This good route takes the obvious shallow groove and crack in the left section of the highest part of the crag. A superb line which would be a *** HVS with a good clean, but there is heather in many of the cracks. Start at the base of the broken groove.

1. 35m 5a Climb the groove to an oak tree. Continue up the groove (crux) and up a small chimney.
2. 25m 5a Continue in the same line, initially over perched blocks to the base of a large flake. Go up for 4m, then traverse right to a niche.
3. 25m 4c Climb the right-slanting crack behind the stance for 4m, step left to

avoid an unpleasant heathery rake and continue up in almost a straight line, following the zigzag cracks leading to a heathery shoulder.

19 Gulf Coast Highway 75m E3 ** (1988)
An excellent route which initially takes a line between The Trip and The Handrail, crossing through the latter to climb a fine crack in the headwall just right of Rain-In-The-Face. Start about 10m left of The Trip.
1. 25m 5a Move up and traverse right to blocks to gain an obvious left-slanting crack, which is climbed to a tiny sapling. Step right and climb the edge of the corner to belay beside a large flake just left of The Trip.
2. 25m 5c Start in the groove on the left and climb to a roof, pull round left and move up to gain a good jug on the right. Move up left to the edge of the buttress, then back right to surmount a roof and continue up to a tree belay on The Handrail.
3. 25m 6a Move up then left to gain a quartz patch, then go up to the base of the thin right-leaning crack which is climbed to the top.

20 The Handrail 80m Hard Severe 4a ** (1966)
The left margin of the highest part of the crag is marked by the obvious right-angled corner of Stoney Broke. Below this is a heathery depression from which a well defined vegetated fault-line slants up right onto the main face. The route gives two fine pitches with good exposure.

21 Rain-In-The-Face 75m E3 ** (1987)
A superb pitch up the obvious blunt arete right of Stoney Broke, gained from The Handrail.
1. 40m 5a Climb the vegetated fault of The Handrail to beneath the roofs. Hand traverse a big jagged block to a hanging belay at the foot of the arete.
2. 35m 6a Make awkward moves out to the arete to a slim groove (hidden peg runner). Climb the groove to the roof and move right to gain a thin crack-line, which springs from the end of the roof and is climbed in a fine position, close to the arete, to easier ground.

22 Stoney Broke 70m HVS * (1970)
The large right-angled corner marking the left edge of the highest section of the face. Start 12m left of The Handrail on a grassy terrace.
1. 40m 5b Climb a short wall to a heather patch, then go up diagonally right to climb a sloping ramp leading towards the corner. A small ledge is gained after a struggle with some bushes and the corner is then climbed to an overhang where a move onto the right wall and up gains a ledge and tree belays.
2. 30m 5a Continue in the corner with occasional detours onto the left wall and wide bridging to avoid some heather.

23 Each Uisge/Across The Lines 50m E4 ** (1987/88)
This combination of the original route and its direct start provides an excellent sustained route up the steep slab left of Stoney Broke. Scramble to a belay beneath the obvious direct entry crack to Shazam.
1. 25m 6a Immediately right of the direct entry to Shazam move up to small wedged blocks and a short thin crack, then step right and gain the horizontal break above. Continue to the next break, then climb directly to another break beneath a roof; step up left then up to holds at the next break and easier ground. Continue to a horizontal break, step up left then go up right to another break and peg belay.
2. 25m 6a Climb slabs up right then straight up to another horizontal break, peg runner. Step right and climb a thin crack with difficulty to the abseil tree.

24 Shazam 70m VS (1969)
The wall and obvious wide heathery crack in the steep slab left of the corner of Stoney Broke. Start by some oak trees. (The obvious direct start was climbed on the first ascent of Each Uisge, 5b).

1. 25m Break through the overhangs through the trees and climb the wall trending right to a prominent tree halfway up the main crack.
2. 25m Follow the crack to the ledge at the top.
3. 20m Continue up the wall above by a steep crack.
Variation: **An Alien Heat   25m   HVS 5a ***   *(1985)*
2a. 25m An alternative finish from the prominent tree, climb a right-slanting scoop to the abseil tree. Fine clean rock but poorly protected.

25 Edge Clipper   50m   E1 *   *(1985)*
Climbs the big slab left of Shazam keeping as near to the arete as you dare. Fine positions but the rock is a bit lichenous (similar to Murray's Arete). Start in the oak trees at the same place as Shazam.
1. 20m 5a Climb directly up on hollow blocks and climb the slab about 3m right of the arete (but on the arete for one big foothold) to a small ledge below a prominent old leeper.
2. 30m 5b Climb a right-slanting ramp until a break leads left across the wall to gain a higher ramp, followed by a small tree near Shazam. Step left to climb a final ramp to a tiny col on the finishing arete.
Variation: **Optional Finish   20m   5b**
Instead of walking over to the abseil tree, climb the left edge of the wall above.

26 Murray's Arete   45m   E4 5c *   *(1983)*
The obvious sharp arete marking the left end of the crag gives a serious pitch. Perhaps E3 if brushed clean.

MIDDLE TOLLIE CRAG

Moving up left two big messy gullies divide the Upper and Lower crags. The next route lies on the buttress between these gullies.

27 King Prawn   130m   Severe   *(1969)*
Start in a little grassy bay at the foot of the leftmost of the two gullies, below a slab.
1. 20m Go straight up the slab to a short heather ledge.
2. 20m Continue up the wall above to another heather ledge.
3. 10m Go up for 3m then left along the ledge to belay.
4. 15m Move up then slant leftwards to a holly tree.
5. 20m Go left to a white birch, then continue to a ledge.
6. 20m Ascend the wall above to belay well back.
7. 25m Climb a black crack in the wall behind to finish.

UPPER TOLLIE CRAG

(NG 870 777)   Alt 120m   East facing   Diagram p131

This lies a few minutes walk beyond and uphill from Lower Tollie Crag (walk along its base and continue) and has a much more open aspect. A huge V-groove with trees in front and beyond is the main face. The most obvious features are the prominent tree-filled chimney fault of Knickerbocker Glory and on its right the crack of Cocaine. On its left is an intermittent crack-line in a smooth slabby wall (The Bug).

Descent: By the easy slopes on the left.

28 The Ugly Duckling   130m   Scottish VS   *(1967)*
This follows the right edge of the crag and is harder than it appears. Start at the lowest rocks immediately left of an obvious gully.
1. 45m Climb the black wall (crux) then go left past a small tree and up a good crack, moving left at its top to trees.
2. 40m Go left into a corner, climb the lower crack then go right to a tree and diagonally up right to mantelshelf on to the arete. Continue up thin slabs to belay.

3. 45m Climb the crack direct to the top.

29 Siren   70m   Scottish VS   (1968)
Takes an obvious line of cracks in a corner on the right side of the buttress left of
The Ugly Duckling.
1. 30m Climb cracks past a tree to gain a ledge.
2. 20m The fierce corner above provides the crux and leads to a belay on the left.
3. 20m A short groove and slabs lead to easier rock and the top.

30 Love is the Drug   90m   E2   (1988)
Climbs the wall right of Cocaine, starting right of that route below left-slanting twin
cracks, directly below small holly and oak trees.
1. 25m 5b Climb twin cracks to a holly bush. Go up right to steep twin cracks
which lead to easier climbing over huge blocks to a belay on the right.
2. 15m 5a Traverse left over the top of the blocks to a small ledge. Gain a small
ledge above then a second ledge before moving left to the line of Cocaine. Climb
up for 4m and belay at the right side of the huge flake.
3. 20m 5b Leave the belay on the right and climb the obvious cracks to a roof.
Pull out left and struggle up the crack above to a peg belay on a small ledge on
Cocaine.
4. 30m 5a Follow pitch 3 of Teddy Bears' Picnic.

31 Cocaine   80m   HVS   (1968)
The obvious crack-line in the wall right of the chimney-fault of Knickerbocker Glory.
Although the crack is good the remainder of the route is a bit scrappy and would
benefit from some gardening. Start at the foot of the chimney-fault.
1. 25m 5a Climb a right-slanting ramp, then move up to trees at the base of a
huge flake. Move right to climb its right edge and squeeze through to belay on its
top.
1a. 25m Or, follow Knickerbocker Glory for 10m then go right up a crack and
chimney to belay on the top of the flake.
2. 18m 5b Follow the crack above the flake to a horizontal break and step up right
to belay.
3. 40m 5a/b Move right, then hand traverse back left for 12m to gain a slabby
ramp slanting back right to the edge.
3a. 30m 5a Alternatively and better, follow Big Toe, pitch 3.

32 Knickerbocker Glory   90m   E1   (1966)
The obvious tree filled chimney-fault with an excursion onto the left wall to avoid
a bottleneck occupied by a holly tree.
1. 30m 5b Climb the loose chimney to the bottleneck. Move left, climb a thin
crack to easier ground, then regain the chimney,
2. 60m Continue in the chimney to the top.

33 Big Toe   75m   E1 *   (1987)
An alternative start to Teddy Bears' Picnic, climbed unaware that it joined it and an
alternative (albeit eliminate) may be available. Start immediately right of Teddy
Bears Picnic.
1. 25m 5b Climb a slabby wall up and right to reach the crack of Knickerbocker
Glory. Follow this to a tree belay in the chimney.
2. and 3. Finish as for Teddy Bears' Picnic (or abseil off).

34 Teddy Bears' Picnic   75m   E1 **   (1967/85/88)
A good route which cuts through Knickerbocker Glory and Cocaine, but by a natural
line.
1. 25m 5b Climb the obvious right-slanting corner come ramp over a roof towards
Knickerbocker Glory, step up left to gain a horizontal break, then pull up to holds
and climb a short crack to reach a tree belay in the chimney. The original route
followed the ramp all the way into and up the chimney.

2. 20m 5b Step down to gain and follow a right-rising crack-line across the wall to belay on Cocaine beside a perched block.

3. 30m 5a Traverse right to climb a crack leading up to the right edge, step right and continue up easier rock to the top.

35 The Bug 50m E2 5b ****   (1974)

A tremendous route taking the intermittent thin crack-line in the wall left of Teddy Bears' Picnic. A similar atmosphere and standard to Diabaig Pillar. Climb the crack over a small bulge to a ramp. Follow this briefly rightwards then step back left and go up to another bulge. Climb this on good holds (or easier via the ramp on the right) to reach delightful, delicate and occasionally run-out thin cracks in the slabby wall. Unfortunately, all good things come to an end. Belay where the angle eases. Scramble up slightly right to the top. The best descent is down heather to the left.

36 The Heretic 55m E3 **   (1987)

Good though sparsely protected climbing up the wall between The Bug and Pokey Hat. It takes the main feature of the face left of The Bug, a huge right-leaning shallow scoop.

1. 45m 5b Start as for Pokey Hat. Stand on the two blocks and step right to a shallow slabby groove. Climb this (poor protection) to gain a ramp (runner placement in the Bug up right). From a good hold at the base of the ramp, move up then left to the start of a diagonal crack which is climbed past a shallow scoop. Stand in the crack where it becomes horizontal and continue above, first right then left, to a diagonal break. Move up to another diagonal break and pull over onto a slabby ledge.

2. 10m Go easily up right, then up and off left.

Variation: **Original Start** 5c   (1985)
This probably started up The Bug and went left at its first bulge.

Variation: **Heresy** 5c (or 6a truly direct)
A direct start over the initial bulge and up to join the normal route (unprotected).

37 Pokey Hat 70m Scottish VS   (1970)

Start 3m right of the obvious chimney at the left of the crag.

1. 35m Climb up right to two blocks and join a wide left-slanting flake-crack. Move slightly left, then climb a thin right-slanting groove for about 9m before moving left to a wide crack which leads to heather ledges. This pitch appears to be poorly protected.

2. 35m Climb slabs and grooves crossing Knickerbocker Glory to finish.

38 Soft Option 75m Severe   (1969)

The right-hand of two black chimneys at the left end of the crag.

1. 30m Follow the loose chimney for 25m, then move right onto a big slab. Belay in the obvious shallow right-trending scoop come ramp.

2. 45m Do not follow the scoop. Instead, climb cracks in the steep slab above and eventually cross Knickerbocker Glory and finish up a short slab.

Moving left level with this crag and a few minutes walk away are two ridges. **Minute**, (45m Severe 1975), climbs the first ridge, and **Second** (50m Severe 1975), the second (which is about 30m left of the first ridge).

GULLY CRAG

(NG 864 778)

This lies up and right of Lower Tollie Crag. There is a smooth diamond shaped crag on the right wall of the gully which starts from the road about 200m short of the car park.

Anti Gravity 65m Scottish VS   (1966)

Start in the centre of the cliff between two cracks at an arrow.

1. 35m Climb straight up, first into a groove, then on good holds to a peg belay.
2. 30m Continue up a thin crack, above and left of the belay, then left of a grassy line to trees.

WHITE WALL CRAG

(NG 875 772) Alt 100m North-East facing Map p97

This is the obvious white wall situated mid-way between Tollie Crag and Loch Maree Crag. The central fault is full of trees, and the right side is crossed by several diagonal cracks. The clean left side is split at mid-height by a diagonal crack.

Approach: From the parking place, go down and follow the shore, mostly on the pebbles if the loch is low. But in the spring, before the bracken has grown, an old path above the shore is better. Leave the shore when the slope above becomes less steep. The crag is immediately seen; go up through the trees to it, 30mins.

Descent: By abseil.

The Left Arete 40m VS 4c   *(1968)*
Climb the slabby left arete of the left side of the crag, keeping close to the edge all the way. The crux is at the top and is protected with RPs.

The Shimmer 30m E4 6a **   *(1992)*
This gives superb face climbing up the clean left side of the wall, sustained and with good protection for the hard sections. Start 5m from the left edge at a thin wiggly crack leading to a patch of black rock below a small ledge at 6m. Climb the crack to the ledge. Step left, then follow the line up and right to a small flake. Traverse right and gain the diagonal crack, then follow this left with surprising difficulty to near its end. Step back right, then go diagonally up and right (again with difficulty) to gain a thin crack to finish at a tree.

LOCH MAREE CRAG

(NG 879 789) Alt 60m North facing Map p97 Diagram p138

This is one of Scotland's most impressive crags, an awesome wall but with good holds, ideal for those with stamina. The routes have been upgraded since the last guide and are unusually long and sustained; an extra large rack is recommended. A prominent overhanging arete is the crag's most striking feature; the climbs take the gently impending wall to its left. The wall has a right-rising diagonal fault with a big holly near its top and a holly forest at its very top. The diagonal fault has been climbed throughout at E3 5b, 5b (1997).

Approach: From the parking place, go down and follow the shore, mostly on the pebbles if the loch is low. There are a couple of places where you are best to leave the shore briefly, one quite soon and one near the access to White Wall Crag. But in the spring, before the bracken has grown, an old path above the shore is better. The going in general is rough and it may take an hour to reach the crag, but 45mins in the spring or if the loch is low.

Descent: By abseil, using in-situ gear. There are slings and krab in the holly forest.

1 Hoax 80m VS †   *(1967)*
This route takes an obvious groove just right of the prominent arete. The description was supplied by the second ascentionists, who thought the original description somewhat lacking, bearing in mind the name!
1. 25m Climb the groove for 20m, move right across a steep wall, then go up and left to an obvious large nest.
2. 15m A steep wall and groove lead to a step left and loose blocks. Climb up to a ledge and tree.
3. 20m Make a remarkably ungardened traverse left across a steep wall to a groove above a grass ledge. Gain terraces above the tree belay on the right.

LOCH MAREE CRAG

1. Hoax	VS †	
2. Spirit Air	E5 6a	***
3. Destitution Man	E4 5c/6a	**
2/3a. Easier Option		
4. Arial	E3 5c	***
5. Pagan Love Song	E4	**
6. Blasad Den Iar	E4 5c	**
7. Jarldom Reach	E6 6b	***

Andy Nisbet

4. 20m Climb a wall on excellent rough rock diagonally left to a final short wall.

1 Spirit Air   50m   E5 6a * **   *(1987)*

A stunning route, unremittingly sustained and strenuous, which takes the crack up the left side of the impressive arete. Start at the base of the arete. Go up an easy groove and where this ends pull directly up the wall to gain the crack, which is followed in a mind blowing situation with continual interest until it fades out. Move up to reach and follow a line of good holds leading diagonally leftwards to a white shield of rock (not particularly obvious from the base). Here a diagonal crack continues across its base to join Ariel (an option for those running out of steam). Instead, climb the right side of the shield to reach up right for good holds and follow them diagonally left to below the holly forest at the cliff-top.

Variation:
To make the route E4, split the route into two 25m 6a pitches by sneaking round the arete to the right after about 25m. There is a fine airy nook which gives a good belay stance, not hanging.

2 Destitution Man   50m   E4 5c/6a **   (1987)
The first crack-line left of Spirit Air, steep and strenuous in its lower half. Start below the crack with a bushy sapling at 5m. Climb the crack through the bulges, trending right past blocks to follow the right-hand cracks diagonally up right, with brief excursions onto the right wall. Join Spirit Air at the white shield and finish up this, 6a (or take the diagonal crack going left to join Arial - 5c).

3 Arial   50m   E3 5c ***   (1992)
An excellent route which gives sustained and strenuous climbing up the fine crack-line up the centre of the wall immediately below the abseil point. Start as for Destitution Man. Climb the crack past the sapling and through a bulge, then continue directly. The crack-line becomes more defined, then bends right into a jagged flake-crack. Continue in the same direct line, up a shallow groove in the centre of the face, passing just right of the big holly in the diagonal fault to the holly forest at the top.

4 Pagan Love Song   55m   E4 **   (1992)
This climbs the right-hand of the twin cracks left of Arial, then breaks out left to finish up the upper wall. Good climbing but the start is often wet and some ivy has regrown.
1. 30m 5c Pull into the corner and make tricky moves up and right to a small flake, which leads to a ledge. Follow the right-hand of twin cracks over several bulges to gain an obvious large niche. Continue directly up the crack above, then follow a flake bending slightly right until above an obvious moss covered rock boss in the fault on the left (5m below the tree). Traverse left to stand and belay on the boss.
2. 25m 6a Pull out left from the belay using an obvious horizontal line. Go up to a horizontal crack, then gain and climb the flake up and right. At its top, traverse left with increasing difficulty to join the slabby scoop of Blasad Den Iar. Climb this for 3m, until the right side bulges. Traverse out right at the level of a small slot, then move diagonally up right to the top. Belay 5m up and left.

5 Blasad Den Iar   50m   E4 5c **   (1987)
A direct line through the centre of the diagonal fault, starting about 15m up the gully from Spirit Air, where it closes to form a wide chimney. Climb a seepage of white calcite, then take the crack above to the left end of a ramp, which is followed right to below a short hanging corner. Pull steeply through an overlap on jugs to ascend the left side of the corner, then trend right to gain thin cracks leading to the large diagonal fault. Pull out of the fault via the flake and climb directly to a horizontal crack where thin climbing up an intermittent crack enables a good flat hold to be gained, runner above. A traverse right gains a shallow groove which is followed until it forms a slight ramp; break up the wall above to a large perched block on the lip and a belay on the right.

6 Jarldom Reach   50m   E6 6b ***   (1987)
Another excellent route which starts as for Blasad Den Iar then breaks left to go directly up the wall above the diagonal fault via two scoops. Follow Blasad Den Iar to the ramp, then go up and left to cracks leading steeply to blocks at the left end of the fault. Follow the fault right just beyond a large wedged block (possible belay). Pull out of break using a flake, then follow this to another flake. Step left into a scoop, then take a slim groove on its right to a jug at its top. Pull up left with hard moves through a white bulge to a second scoop. Traverse right to a slim groove which is followed with hard moves near its top reaching right for jugs. Finish at the perched block of Blasad Den Iar.

Poolewe Crags

Map p97

There are a number of small crags on the hillside overlooking Poolewe and Boor.

CROFT CRAG

(NG 859 795) Alt 60m East facing Map p97

A wall on Croft Hill and easily seen from the road below. It is easier to park at NG 860 790 and traverse the hillside north to the crag.

The Gay Waiver 12m E4 6a   *(2003)*
A central line up the wall.

CLIFF HILL - THEATRE OF DREAMS

Map p97

An amphitheatre of gneiss crags not far from the road but facing away from civilisation.

Approach: Park in a large space on the left just after a sharp bend (NG 847 819). Walk up the hill and through a tied gate in a fence. Continue up to a flat area, then along and up to the amphitheatre. 10 to 15mins.

BOSOM BUTTRESS

(NG 844 807) Alt 120m South-West facing

This is the first wall reached. It has a sunny aspect and therefore clean rock.

Memory Gland 15m Very Difficult   *(2003)*
The slabby buttress at the left and lower end of the crag.

Silicon Implant 15m VS 4c   *(2003)*
Start from a raised heather ledge and climb broken walls.

Left It 15m E4 5c   *(2003)*
Climb the right side of a smooth pillar up quartz intrusions.

Cleavage 15m HVS 5a   *(2003)*
Climb just right of Left It into a capped V-groove. Pull out left and finish above.

Full Frontal 15m HVS 5a *   *(2003)*
Start at the lowest point of the largest section of rock. Climb a thin crack up a scoop, move right and finish up cracks above.

34D 15m HVS 5a *   *(2003)*
Start on a raised heather ledge at the right side of this section. Climb the slabby wall direct.

Pair Shaped 10m Severe 4a   *(2003)*
Start left of a pillar left of a big holly. Climb a groove and up walls above the pillar.

DELUSION WALL

(NG 846 806) Alt 150m North-West facing

A wall with an undercut base at the top left corner of the amphitheatre.

Colin Meek

Cleavage, HVS, Bosom Buttress, Theatre of Dreams. Climbers Jim Buchanan and Alan Gorman

Bats the Size of Woodcocks   10m   E2 5b/c   *(2003)*
The groove line at the left end of the undercut, on the left side of the crag.

Wishful Thinking   10m   E2 5b   *(2003)*
Climb the wall right of a holly and up the crack above.

The Outwit 10m E4 6a *   *(2003)*
A thin crack-line in two stages and with a bouldery start 2m right of the alcove.

Ship of Fools 8m E2 5b   *(2003)*
A thin crack-line just right of the end of the undercut base.

Disillusion Crack 8m E1 5b   *(2003)*
A thuggish crack-line right of a small rib. Slow to dry.

Glassbeads 8m E2 5c   *(2003)*
Boulder to the left end of a shelf at 3m, then go boldly up the wall above on improving holds.

The Learning Curve 10m E1 5b *   *(2003)*
A right-trending crack-line through the shelf and wall above.

Out of Control 8m E1 5b   *(2003)*
The crack-line at the right end of the wall.

LOBSTER CRAG

(NG 845 805)   Alt 150m   North-West and South-West facing

A crag of darker rock to the right, with a big heathery groove in its north-west face and a steep south-west facing wall which is hidden on the approach.

The Pillar 20m HVS 5a   *(2003)*
Climb the pillar left of the big heathery groove by coming in from the right.

Zap the PRAM 20m VS 4c   *(2003)*
Start at a flaky recess at the base of the change of aspect. Climb the flakes up left to finish up the wall right of a groove.

Alien Skin 20m VS 4c   *(2003)*
Start at the same point but move right below overhangs on to the south-west facing side and finish up the crest.

Itchy Trigger Fingers 12m E3 5c *   *(2003)*
Climb thin cracks up the centre of the south-west facing wall.

CYCLOPS CRAG

(NG 844 805)   Alt 140m   North-West facing

This is a wall at the back of a more recessed bay 50m to the right. It is easily identified by a prominent capped groove.

Erebus 20m E2 5b   *(2003)*
The groove.

LOCH CHRIOSTINA CRAGS

(NG 837 821)   Map p97

Two tiers of crag overlook the road and parking place, although much of the lower tier is hidden. Two pillars separated by a gully on the upper tier are easily seen. The crags required cleaning and some routes are not fully clean, particularly on the upper tier. The rock is good quality gneiss.

Approach: Park opposite the crags by an old gun emplacement (NG 837 823). Head straight up the hill. 5mins.

LOWER TIER

Alt 70m   North-East facing

Rainbow Alliance   10m   Severe   *(1997)*
The leftmost scooped slabby wall separated from the bigger crags to the right by a grass apron. Climb the cracks on the right side of the scoop.

Candle Buttress   12m   VS 5a   *(1998)*
The slender buttress on the left flank of the two biggest ones. Pleasant climbing leads directly up the 'candle'.

Boor Constrictor   18m   E3 5c *   *(1999)*
The left-hand of the two central buttresses gives a thin and sustained climb with awkward protection. Start centrally and gain the first horizontal break above the overlap. Move up in the same line the to the next break and step right to a big foothold, then finish more easily.

The Scorcher   18m   E2 5b **   *(1997)*
The left of two fine crack-lines on the right-hand central buttress. The crack is awkward to start, with limited protection, but holds and gear improve rapidly as the upper layback crack is gained.

Blinding Crack   18m   E1 5a **   *(2000)*
The excellent right-hand crack. An awkward start leads to better holds in the flake-cracks above. Sustained, strenuous climbing.

UPPER TIER

Alt 90m   North-East facing

The left side of the top tier has a slabby buttress (Mission Crag), steeper than it appears from below.

Left Crack   25m   VS 4c   *(1999)*
The left side of the top tier has a slabby buttress steeper than it appears from below. This line takes a slanting crack on the left with the hardest moves in the first half; well protected.

The Mission   25m   HVS 5a   *(1999)*
A route with entertaining climbing up the steep slabby wall to the right of the crack. Climb up to a hanging flake with interest and continue direct to the top on hidden holds.

The next buttress, Pillar Crag, lies about 50m right and a little higher than Mission Crag. It lies to the right of the gully seen from the car park.

Isle of Ewe Pillar   22m   HVS 5a *   *(2001)*
Takes the obvious cleaned pillar to the right of the gully. Start at a groove on the right, then step left towards the main crack-line, which is followed, steadily steepening, to the top. Finely situated, with good rock

One for Angus   18m   E1 5a   *(2001)*
On the right-hand and highest of three sections of the crag is an obvious cleaned slabby line. Step left on to the rock, then follow a groove above, with a crux moving right into an upper groove. Protection is poor.

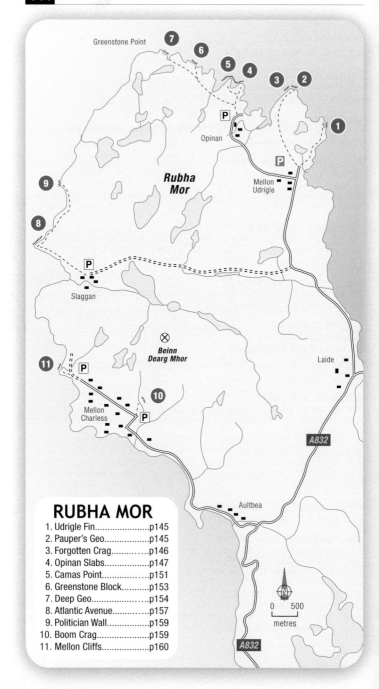

RUBHA MOR

RUBHA MOR

Rubha Mor is the peninsula between Gruinard Bay and Loch Ewe, and although not as extensive as its namesake near Reiff to the north, it nonetheless offers some good climbing and bouldering mainly on similar small Torridonian sandstone sea-cliffs. Its northern tip is called Greenstone Point. As a bonus, the views are stunning, particularly to the north and inland to the Great Wilderness and Torridon mountains. The peninsula may also enjoy fine weather whilst it can be wet inland. A word of warning though; this headland suffers from ocean swells and consequently may limit your climbing even on a fine calm day!

Most of the climbing is on the north coast and accessed by turning off the A832 at Laide and parking at Mellon Udrigle or Opinan. There is one area of climbing on the west coast at Slaggan and two crags near Mellon Charles on the south side of the peninsula.

The area has all the usual West Highland amenities (Aultbea and Laide) which includes a campsite at Laide with good facilities and a rough campsite at Mellon Udrigle by the lovely Camas a' Charraig.

Mellon Udrigle

UDRIGLE FIN - LEAC AN FHAOBHAIR

(NG 897 968)   Partially Tidal   West facing

This is a narrow sea-stack lying just off the middle of three slabby promontories. It has a steep west face with a boulder choke at its base and an obvious jam crack near the centre, Huckleberry Fin. The left side of the face is tidal. The climbing is unusual, mostly on large scalloped holds, but marred by some suspect rock at mid-height.

Approach: From the beach car park at Mellon Udrigle (NG 890 959), walk to the end of the road and follow a good path along the coast to the crag, 15mins.

Descent: Descend at the back of the geo and boulder hop and or traverse the foot of the slab to gain access to the boulder choke. From the top of the fin and in-situ thread, abseil down the line of Huckleberry Fin.

The climbs are described from right to left.

Sitting Duck   10m   HVS 5b   (2003)
Start by the right side and boldly gain the edge and up to a good ledge. Move left on to the face and go up on big scalloped holds and a crack to the top.

Huckleberry Fin   10m   VS 4c *   (1990s)
The obvious steep jam crack.

Decoy Cafe   10m   E1 5b   (2003)
Start 2m left of the jam crack of Huckleberry Fin and climb direct to an overlap. Move left and up to cracks leading to the capping roof. Finish leftwards below the roof.

PAUPER'S GEO - CREAG AN EILEIN

(NG 890 976)   Tidal   West and North facing

Pauper's Geo is a narrow boulder filled inlet on the headland north of Mellon Udrigle which features a fine wall on the east side, a steep backwall undercut by a low cave and a low angled slab on the west side. There are belay stakes in place.

Approach: The best approach is from the beach car park at Mellon Udrigle (NG 890 959) and follow the old croft track (marked on the OS 1:50000 map) north-west towards the coast. Go round the hill to spot height 56m and descend to the geo, 20 to 25mins.

Descent: At low tides, descend the easy slab and cross the tidal boulders to gain the climbs. At high tides, it is possible to abseil (use a separate abseil rope) on to a convenient ledge system below the routes.

The climbs are described firstly on the east wall from left to right as height increases.

A Blip in a Sea of Mediocrity **12m** **VS 4c** * *(2003)*
Walk towards the end of the promontory and scramble or abseil down to grey ledges a few metres above the high tide mark. From the right end of the grey ledge, swing down and move right into a narrow niche on the black slab. Climb direct to finish up an open groove.

Salary Man **15m** **HVS 5a** ** *(2003)*
Start at the left end of the main ledge system below a black flake-crack. Climb the crack to a ledge and a good horizontal break above. Traverse the break leftwards and at its end, move up to another good break. Finish direct past a third break on pleasantly good holds.

Same Old Song **15m** **E3 5c** * *(2003)*
Start a few metres right of Salary Man at the next line of weakness. Climb a groove to the first break, move left and climb more or less direct via breaks and edges to good holds below the top blank looking section. Steady bold climbing leads to the top by twin short corners.

Hard Up **15m** **HVS 5b** *(2003)*
Near the centre of the east wall is a prominent corner fault-line with a short chimney at the base. Climb by the chimney, pull right round a roof and finish up the corner on the right.

Skint **20m** **E1 5b** * *(2003)*
This climbs the first obvious line a few metres right of the corner of Hard Up. Climb initially via twin black cracks and follow a slightly right-trending line to the top.

Pauper's Corner **25m** **E1 5b** * *(2003)*
The fine corner at the right end of the wall.

Lightning Cracks **15m** **E1 5b** * *(2003)*
The dog-leg cracks in the wall at the right side of the cave and crag.

FORGOTTEN CRAG

(NG 889 976) **Tidal** **North facing** **Map p144**

This is a small crag on the coast about 200m south-west of Pauper's Geo.

Approach: As for Pauper's Geo.

Descent: To the left.

There is an easy low angled slab bounding the left (east) side of the crag. The crag rises from black slabby rock on the right side to a higher steeper left side with a series of orange roofs. Described from right to left.

Black Rib **8m** **Difficult** *(1997)*
Climb the black blocky rib bounding the right side of the face.

Calum's Corner **10m** **Hard Severe 4b** *(1997)*
The left-facing black corner bounding the left side of Black Rib, with a move left and back right at half-height.

First Born **12m** **HVS 5a/b** *(1997)*
Start at a small triangular niche 3m left of Calum's Corner. Climb up to and follow

a thin crack in the steep black slab and finish direct.

Pampers Groove   15m   VS 4c   *(1997)*
The obvious groove in the middle of the crag. Start by the triangular niche as for
First Born and follow a left diagonal crack leading above a recess into the groove.
Climb the groove and finish out right below the orange headwall.

Frontpack   20m   E1 5b   *(1997)*
Start under the roofs at a short groove at the base of the descent slab. Climb left
round the overhangs to the top pockmarked roof. Traverse right under this and
finish straight up at its right end.

OPINAN SLABS

(NG 879 978)   Partially Tidal   North-West facing   Map p144
This is a long low escarpment on the eastern of two small headlands due north of
Opinan and east of Camas an Lochain. The escarpment runs on the west side of the
headland and forms a fine cracked slab at its seaward end. There is a narrow semi-
tidal platform at the base of this slab.

Approach: Park at Opinan (NG 877 970) and walk direct to the crag. 15mins.

Descent: There are two cairns marking the headland. Directly west of and below
the cairns is a wide flat area and is a good place to gear up. Duck through a hole
created by a boulder on to another ledge overlooking a short slab (Lower Slab) and
descend to the right via a prominent stepped fault-line leading to the wider right
end of the semi-tidal platform. This end of the platform is below a bulging section.
There is also a chimney crevasse with a chockstone below the bulging wall.

The climbs are described from right to left starting at the right side of the bulging
section. The original ascents started from the semi-tidal platform and climbed the
chimney crevasse to start. However, the routes are described by starting from the
step level with the top of the crevasse.

Consolation Corner   6m   Very Difficult   *(1999)*
Start at the right end of the first step and climb a short layback corner-crack to a
walk-off ledge. Climb direct up the top wall.

Blasted Wall   8m   VS 4c *   *(1999)*
The right-hand of three short steep crack-lines. Step across the chockstone with an
awkward start on to a ledge at 2m.

Torpedo   8m   HVS 5a *   *(1999)*
The central crack. Step across the crevasse and climb up to the overhang and turn
it on the right.

Depth Charge   8m   HVS 5b *   *(1999)*
Step across the mouth of the crevasse and climb the left-hand crack.

The next routes start from the wide right end of the semi-tidal platform. A low
right-trending narrow black ramp runs from below the right end of the slab across
into the middle of the bulging wall. The ramp gives the start to four routes.

Mexican Wave   15m   VS 4b   *(1997)*
Climb along the ramp to its end. Pull up on to the slab above and climb this up
and right to finish at the top of the crack of Depth Charge.

Sea Monster   12m   HVS 5a *   *(1999)*
Follow Mexican Wave to near the end of the ramp and climb via thin cracks 1m
right of the edge to a horizontal break. Finish up right.

Two Shakes 12m Severe *(1997)*
From halfway along the ramp, pull into a wide scoop and climb up right to finish by a steep corner-crack.

Six Different Ways 12m Very Difficult *(2003)*
Climb Two Shakes into the wide scoop and finish direct via a vague crack.

A steep start may be made on to the ramp at holds about 6m left of the crevasse (5b), or small edges just left of the crevasse (6a), or it can be climbed from near its left end at a break with a 1m high C shaped crack.

The next routes are on the slab. The slab may be climbed anywhere but there are a number of obvious lines giving pleasant easier climbs. The slab is cut at its right side by a broken ramp descending from right to left which may be used as a descent.

Wrack and Tangle 15m Severe *(1999)*
Start at the break with a 1m high C shaped crack as for the above routes. Pull up by the C shaped crack and up to the slab. Climb the smooth slab on the left, passing left of a huge slot.

Precision Decision 15m Hard Severe 4b * *(1999)*
Start from the platform a few metres left of Wrack and Tangle's top slab below the middle of the smoothest section of slab. Climb the slab direct to the top.

Mermaid's Slab 15m Hard Severe *(1999)*
A few metres left of Precision Decision is a very shallow groove. Climb direct to the groove and up this to finish.

Next left is a wide shallow recess with a black and tan streak in the middle and bounded at the left side by a right-facing flowery corner at half-height (Opinan Corner).

Old Salt 15m Very Difficult * *(1999)*
Start below the right side of the wide recess and climb by cracks and breaks direct to the top.

Opinan Corner 15m Difficult *(1999)*
Start from the platform and climb to the corner, then follow a pair of cracks on the right.

A Good First 15m Difficult *(1997)*
Climb wide cracks just left of Opinan Corner.

Poor Second 15m Difficult *(1997)*
Start at the end of the platform and climb wide cracks passing a huge niche.

Third Class 15m Very Difficult * *(1997)*
An eliminate direct line between the wide cracks of A Good First and Poor Second.

The left end of the platform is tidal and is blocked by a 4m pedestal.

An Ill Wind 15m Difficult *(2003)*
Climb to the top of the pedestal and follow the pair of wide cracks immediately left of the cracks of Third Class.

Westward Ho! 18m Very Difficult * *(1999)*
From the top of the pedestal, climb a left-slanting crack to its end and finish via a wide crack.

John Mackenzie

Mermaid's Slab, Hard Severe, Opinan Slabs. Climber Rosie Goolden

The routes at the left end of the slab are best accessed from the left by scrambling down at the far west end of the slab and then traversing down left (looking out) to a recessed triangular ledge.

Gung Ho! 20m Severe *(1999)*
Traverse 8m right from the triangular ledge to the left side of the pedestal and climb up, crossing the slanting crack of Westward Ho! to reach the blankish upper slab left of the cracks of Cracked by Time. Climb this direct avoiding the lichenous crack on the right.

What Not 18m Severe *(2003)*
Traverse 4m right of the triangular ledge and climb via double left-facing very shallow grooves, crossing the diagonal crack of Westward Ho!

Why Not? 15m Very Difficult *(2003)*
From the triangular ledge, climb rightwards to a niche and climb a wide crack to join the final crack of Westward Ho!, or finish up the thinner crack on the left.

What Ho! 15m Hard Severe 4b *(1999)*
Climb via the right-hand crack out of the triangular ledge steeply on to the slab. Climb the slab centrally between the cracks of Why Not? and Carapace Crack.

Carapace Crack   15m   Hard Severe *   *(1999)*
The crack near the left edge of the slab. Take the left-hand crack out of the recessed triangular ledge up the steep lower wall to gain the easier upper crack on the slab.

To the left of the slab and set back is a two tiered leaning wall above a sloping platform that dips to the left to sea-level. This end of the platform is tidal.

Friendly Fire   8m   E2 5b *   *(2003)*
Start about 3m right of the left edge and climb a steep black shattered crack to an easing. Turn the roof on the right.

Collateral Damage   8m   E2 5b/c *   *(2003)*
The crack-line near the middle of the steep lower wall 4m right of Friendly Fire. Climb to the easing and finish by the slot on the left side of the block.

Minister of Information   8m   VS 5a *   *(2003)*
The right-hand line is characterised by a short curving crack low down. Climb the short lower crack and finish up the right side of the block.

LOWER SLAB

This is a short 30m long slab above a platform with a jumble of huge boulders. The left end of the slab lies directly below the fault-line descent to the main slab.

Approach: Access is either from the wide right end of the semi-tidal platform (at low tide), or walk along the ledge above the slab and descend a grotty corner at the right end of the slab.

The slab can be climbed anywhere but the following lines have been recorded. The climbs are described from right to left. Towards the right end is a left-facing corner with a grassy ledge at half-height.

No More Tears   8m   Hard Severe   *(2003)*
Start beside the boulder and climb direct passing the left end of the grassy ledge.

Balancing Act   8m   VS 4b *   *(1998)*
Start 2m left of the boulder and climb direct passing a slot at half-height.

Fat Man's Fingers   8m   Hard Severe   *(2003)*
Start half-way between the two boulders about 2m left of Balancing Act and climb straight up on small ledges.

Above the next boulder on the left is a vague wide blunt rib.

Nut Juggler   8m   Severe *   *(1999)*
Start by the boulder and take the line of least resistance up the blunt rib, moving left and up to finish. Finishing direct is the same grade.

A Long Way Off   6m   Severe   *(2003)*
Start off the middle of the long boulder and climb direct up the left side of the blunt rib to finish near Nut Juggler.

On the Fringes   8m   Very Difficult *   *(2003)*
Climb via a wide black streak starting between two boulders.

Funfest   6m   Very Difficult   *(2003)*
Start off the next boulder to the left and climb via a thin black streak in a shallow depression.

The left side of the slab, past the boulders, is semi-tidal and characterised by a huge right diagonal break starting at half-height near the left edge of the slab.

Ambling Gambler   8m   Severe   *(1998)*
The blunt nose on the left is reached via a flake then straight up to finish.

Glabrous Crack   8m   Very Difficult   *(2003)*
Climb direct to and up the thin lichenous crack where the slab heightens near the left edge.

Round to the right of the Lower Slab, past the boulders, is a short broken area of rock. It offers limited climbing on a cracked vegetated wall.

Left Crack   8m   Very Difficult   *(1999)*
Climb the left-hand crack near the left edge of the wall.

Jugs Galore   8m   Difficult   *(1999)*
Climb the right section of the wall up flakes.

RED WALL

This is the last area of rock at the back of the bay and about 50m right of the short Lower Slab. It is a leaning wall with conspicuous orange-red rock and topped by a slab. Scramble up to a grassy ledge below the routes. Belay stakes are in place above the middle of the wall.

Held to Account   8m   E2 5c *   *(2003)*
A steep crack-line near the right end of the leaning wall leads into a short right-facing corner.

CAMAS POINT

(NG 876 978)   Partially Tidal   North-West & North to East facing   Map p144
This is the small headland on the other side of the bay from Opinan Slabs, on the east side of the larger bay Camas an Lochain. A platform dips seaward under the cliff and into a tidal area below the nose of the promontory. There is also a bouldery tidal slot under the cliff on the east side. The whole area may be traversed at low tides.

Approach: As for Opinan Slabs, 15mins.

Descent: On the west side descend easy slabs on to a platform.

The climbs are described from right to left as approached from the slab descent. Firstly, there is a short steep area of black streaked rock bounding the left end of the easy slab and where the platform widens.

Black Ice   8m   Very Difficult   *(2003)*
Start near the right side of the wall and climb via small ledges and crack above.

Skid   8m   Severe   *(2003)*
Start at a short shallow left-facing corner at head height 3m left of Black Ice. Climb direct.

Next left is a low stepped roof.

Icicle Works   8m   Severe   *(2003)*
Start at the lower right end of the stepped roof and climb direct up a crack and niche to ledges and the top.

Baltic   8m   HVS 5c *   *(2003)*
Start under the left end of the stepped roof and pull into the hanging corner exiting right on to a ledge. Finish direct up the front face via big breaks and long reaches.

Numb Nuts   8m   Severe   *(2003)*
Start 3m left of the stepped roof of Baltic at a series of holds. Climb these to the
big ledge and finish by the wide corner-crack on the right.

Mr Freeze   8m   Very Difficult 4a   *(2003)*
Just left of Numb Nuts is a shallow right-facing corner. Climb this to the big ledge
and finish up the steep wide crack directly above.

Winter Break   8m   Difficult *   *(2003)*
Start by the blunt edge of the wall before it runs into a wide stepped groove. Climb
a crack and groove to the big ledge and finish by the slabby groove on the right.

Traction Control   8m   Hard Severe 4b   *(2003)*
Start just left of the blunt edge at a very thin crack. Climb by thin cracks and horizontal breaks to a ledge and finish by the short steep wall.

The big stepped groove is Moderate and can be used as a descent.

To Infinity and Beyond   8m   Very Difficult   *(2003)*
Climb the nose and top wall on the left edge of the wide stepped groove.

Cranreuch Cauld   8m   Difficult   *(2003)*
Start at steps at the middle of the ledgy buttress left of the wide stepped groove.
Climb up and left and up on to a ledge. Finish up the wall above.

Next left is a fine steep wall with a shallow cave near the right side and a black
open groove above. The left side of this wall is tidal.

Chrome Melons   8m   HVS 5a *   *(1998)*
Start at the right end of the cave and pull right on to a ledge. Climb the slanting
left-facing corner-line above. Alternatively, traverse left into the top of Am I a
Woman? (VS 4c).

Am I a Woman?   8m   E2 5b *   *(2003)*
Start in the middle of the cave. Pull through the overhangs with much determina-
tion (bold) and finish up the black open groove above.

Heather's a Blether   10m   E1 5b **   *(1998)*
Start at the left end of the cave at a slight pillar. Move up and left and pull through
the bulge to a good break. Climb the slim orange groove on the right. A sweet
climb, low in the grade.

Buzz Lightyear   10m   E1 5b **   *(2003)*
Start as for Heather's a Blether and climb to the break. Climb direct via thin cracks
and good horizontal breaks up the steep wall.

Green Goblin   12m   E4 6b ***   *(2003)*
A fine steep climb through the roofs at the left end of the wall. Start below the
biggest roof. Climb to the roof, traverse right and pull up via a flake to the next roof.
Pull into the short hanging corner above (crux). Move right on a break and finish
up a slabby groove.

Immediately left of the steep wall, a wide open black groove leads to a capping roof.

Lost Friends   12m   Difficult *   *(2003)*
Climb the groove to the roof and escape leftwards.

Zurg   12m   VS 4c *   *(2003)*
Move up to the ledge at the base of the black open groove of Lost Friends and
climb the hanging stepped corner on the right.

Moving round to the left, a more broken tidal wall faces the open sea. At its far left side there is a short overhanging wall, The Prow.

**Melons in a Muddle   8m   E1 5b ** **   (1998)
Start near the left edge and climb a short steep groove to gain a right-trending break. Go along this a short distance, then pull up and left to a finish on the left arete.

Nice Melons!   12m   E1 5a *   (2003)
Climb to the break as for Melons in a Muddle and continue traversing the break strenuously to the right edge. Go up this to finish via a short corner.

To the left of The Prow is a bouldery tidal inlet with a steep south-east facing lower wall with a less steep top section.

Slotted Pig   15m   Very Difficult   (2003)
Bounding the left side of The Prow is a deep slot. Climb this with an awkward squeeze at the top.

The Snout   15m   Severe   (2003)
Left of the slot, the crag changes aspect. On the edge is a deep stepped corner starting at half-height. Climb to a ledge and up to a roof on the left. Swing right round the nose and finish up the easier stepped corner.

Slinky   15m   HVS 5b   (2003)
Climb the first groove line left of the edge to the top roof with a protruding horn like flake. Pull up to the roof and move awkwardly right to finish.

Time and Tide   18m   VS 4c   (2003)
Left of Slinky and bounding the right side of the overhanging lower wall is a short hanging corner at 4m. Climb into the corner with difficulty and up to easier ground. Move left to finish up some convoluted features, avoiding more dubious rock in the direct line.

The Stamp of Australia   15m   HVS 5a   (2003)
Start at the left end of the overhanging lower wall near the back of the inlet, beside an off-width crack with jammed buoys. Climb steeply via thin cracks to an easing and finish up a vague rib above. Climbing the off-width crack to a ledge and moving right to gain the vague rib reduces the grade to Hard Severe.

Next left is a steep smooth slab.

A New Day Yesterday   10m   HVS 5b   (2003)
Scramble up to a bouldery gutter and start below the middle of the slab. Climb the slab centrally via two horizontal breaks and a long reach for the top.

GREENSTONE BLOCK

(NG 870 982)   Mostly Non-tidal   Various Aspects   Map p144

This is a 10m high detached block on the coast below Druim an Fhasdaidh, with some reasonable climbing and great views to the north. The climbing is mainly on the seaward north-east aspect above a non-tidal slab.

Approach: Park in Opinan as for Opinan Slab and Camas Point and walk direct to the block, 20mins.

Descent: Step across the gap and spiral down on the north-west (left) side.

There is one route on the lower north-west side. It climbs a prominent corner at the landward end and finishes on the yellow lichenous ledge;

RUBHA MOR

Shagger's Route 8m Hard Severe 4b *   *(1994)*
Start in the tidal boulders near the entrance to the slot behind the block and climb the fine corner. Approach at low tide from the west across a tidal inlet.

The next four routes are on the north-east side. The crag heightens from right to left; the first obvious feature at the right end is a niche with a wide crack crevasse running through the cliff.

Coach's Climb 8m Difficult   *(1994)*
Climb the slim buttress 1m left of the crevassed niche.

Anuna 10m Hard Severe 4b *   *(1994)*
Just left of the slim buttress of Coach's Climb is a recessed fault-line. Climb by the right side of the fault.

Look Left 10m HVS 5b   *(1994)*
To the left of Anuna is a sharp arete. Climb the crack just left of the arete up to a niche. Pull up direct to finish.

Hourglass Cracks 12m Severe *   *(1994)*
At the left end of the crag is a wide slot with cracks leading to a ledge. Climb to the ledge and finish up the cracks above.

The Gentleman Adventurer 12m E2 5c **   *(1994)*
The south-east face is a steep slab with horizontal breaks. Start about 2m from the right edge at barnacle level. Climb to a ledge and follow steep thin cracks to the first horizontal break. Move slightly right and follow more thin cracks past horizontal breaks to the top.

SANDPAPER SLAB
(NG 868 983) Tidal North-West facing

This is the inlet 250m north-west of the Greenstone Block. It has a low angled slab, accessible at low tide, with the following route.

Sandpaper 20m Very Difficult   *(2000)*
Climb the slab centrally, left of a corner-crack.

DEEP GEO - SRON AN DUN-CHAIRN
(NG 864 984) Partially Tidal South-East facing Map p144

About 500m west of Sandpaper Slab is a long geo with a stone dyke at the back. There are steep walls lining both sides of the geo with the best rock toward the seaward ends.

Approach: As for the Greenstone Block; about 25mins walk from Opinan.
The first climbs are on the seaward end of the east side of the geo. Seen on the approach to the head of Deep Geo are short crags on the right with a prominent springboard block (Spit and Polish) at the top. The first climbs are near here.

Descent: Walk down toward the springboard and descend a final bouldery slot on to a wide platform on the left. There is a short narrow orange and black wall (Black Hearted Bitch) by the wide platform with a small low angled slab bounding its left side (Fair Lady Slab). The platform narrows round the edge from the orange and black wall, leading towards the geo and an awkward scramble out.

Spit and Polish 10m VS 4c   *(2003)*
A climb on the right side of the bouldery slot descent. Step across the slot and climb a vague pillar to the roof springboard. Traverse left underneath and pull on

to the slab above to finish.

Fair Lady Slab   10m   Moderate *(2000)*
Climb the slab corner bounding the left side of the steep wall above the wider platform.

Black Hearted Bitch   10m   E2 6a * *(2000)*
The centre of the wall is cut by a slender corner. Climb the crack and pod into the awkward corner.

Wandering Wifie   12m   Hard Severe 4a *(2000)*
From the start of Black Hearted Bitch, climb the right edge of the black rock rightwards to a shelf. Finish up the shallow corner above.

Lady Luck   10m   Hard Severe 4b *(2003)*
Take the green slab at the right side of the wall to a ledge. Climb direct up the steep wall and short corner to the top.

Round the edge the platform narrows, is tidal and has a large pool below an undercut slab.

Femme Fatale   20m   HVS 5a ** *(2000)*
Near the right end of the platform is a fine left-trending slabby corner below a steep wall. Climb into the corner and follow this up left to finish up a notch.

The following climb is on the short vertical crag by the stone dyke at the head of the geo.

Damp Start   15m   HVS 5b *(2004)*
Climb the vague crack and breaks at the left end of the crag. Turn the capping roof on the left and finish up a corner.

The next three climbs are on the end of the promontory at the west side of the geo. Cross the head of the geo by the dyke and walk out to the end. A scrambling descent to the left gains access to a sloping tidal platform below the climbs. From right to left.

Scabious   8m   Severe *(2003)*
Near the right side, climb steeply into a left-facing corner-crack.

Scurvy   10m   VS 4c *(2003)*
Climb leftwards into an awkward right-facing slabby corner.

Terms and Conditions   10m   E1 5b * *(2003)*
Climb a thin steep crack-line leading into an easier corner to finish.

The Contract   10m   E2 5c * *(2004)*
Climb via the centre of the wall left of Terms and Conditions to finish by the steep groove.

Slaggan

(NG 835 947)   Non-tidal   North-West Facing

Halfway between Laide and Mellon Udrigle, turn through a gate and down a well defined track to Slaggan. Although the track is signed suitable only for 'rough terrain' vehicles, an average clearance motor will make the 5km. Otherwise, park your Ferrari or Porsche and walk!

Slaggan is ideal for an afternoon with the family; ditch the kids with granny on the beach, shoulder your bouldering mat and check out the crags. There is much

good bouldering hidden in numerous nooks and crannies along the coast.
An easy 15min walk along the coastline from the ruined croft at Slaggan lead to the climbing on short sandstone cliffs up to 15m in height, running north-east from Gob a' Gheodha to Gob a' Chuaille.

GOB A' GHEODHA - GOB GEO

Descend to the geo from a solitary post by the path on the headland. There is a huge jammed block at the back of the geo with an access through route. The climbs are on the right wall, mostly slabby, all worthwhile and described right to left from the back of the geo. It is a sea filled geo!

Tat's Route   10m   VS 4b   *(1999)*
Start below the outside edge of the block and ascend direct, through a short curving crack to finish by the left diagonal fault.

Cacofonix   10m   Hard Severe 4b *   *(1999)*
The first obvious crack-line left of the block.

Asterix   10m   VS 4b *   *(1999)*
The second crack-line and about 6m left of the block. It thins out at the top.

Head Games   10m   VS 4b *   *(1999)*
Start off a jammed boulder and climb direct through an obvious hole with a bold top section.

Towards the left end of the wall are two right diagonal crack-lines, accessed by a traverse left from the jammed boulder.

Getafix   10m   Hard Severe *   *(1999)*
The right-hand of the two diagonal crack-lines.

Obelix   10m   Severe   *(1999)*
Takes the left-hand diagonal crack-line.

Past a broken section, the crag steepens again; perfect Deep Water Soloing! The climbs are best accessed by descending the fault on the right side.

Dogmatix   6m   VS 5b *   *(1999)*
Start at the right end of the wall by the right diagonal fault and climb out left above the cave and up.

Vitalstatistix   5m   VS 5b *   *(1999)*
The crack-line in the middle of the wall.

Cleverdix   4m   VS 5a   *(1999)*
Start halfway between the central crack-line of Vitalstatistix and the left edge and climb direct via a crack and horizontal breaks.

NEPTUNE'S WALL

Descend from the post as for Gob Geo, walk along a rocky shelf above the climbs of Gob Geo and turn right to a non-tidal rocky amphitheatre. The climbs are located on the higher left end of the wall with reasonable bouldering at the left side. From right to left.

Gutbuster   8m   Difficult   *(1980s)*
Start about 6m right of the smooth section, pull over a bulge and ascend via cracks by the right-hand black streak.

Head Case 8m Very Difficult   *(1980s)*
Just left of Gutbuster at the left end of the low bulge, climb the slab and pass the right end of an upper bulge.

Beer Belly 8m Severe   *(1980s)*
Climb the slab and pull through the middle of the bulge.

Intimate Ending 10m Severe *   *(1980s)*
Climb the obvious groove and crack bounding the right side of the smooth section.

Birthday Treat 12m VS 4c *   *(1980s)*
Start at the groove of Intimate Ending and climb direct, passing the left end of the high horizontal break.

Climb and Enjoy, Fatboy 12m E1 5b *   *(1998)*
Climb the centre of the wall, between Birthday Treat and the left edge.

Jagged Edge 15m Difficult   *(1980s)*
Climb the right-curving slabby groove left of the edge.

ATLANTIC AVENUE

Map p144

This area is about 200m along the coast from Neptune's Wall. Drop off the grass top path to the head of a bouldery geo. On the left side of the geo are a number of short walls and some good bouldering. The two prominent short right diagonal cracks are **Cheech** (Hard Severe) and **Chong** (Severe).

The main climbs are reached by a scramble round right of the geo to some good non-tidal short walls and an obvious square-cut pillar. The climbs are described right to left from the pillar:

O La La 12m E1 5b *   *(1998)*
Up the middle of the right sidewall of the pillar, starting up a short flaky crack.

Wild Sex 12m E1 5b/c *   *(1998)*
The right edge of the front face. The true edge of the lower wall is hard, otherwise take the wide crack on the right.

Walk on the Wild Side 12m E1 5b **   *(1980s)*
Climb the middle of the front face including the hard lower wall. The original route started up the wide crack of Wild Sex and moved left on the break to the upper front face (HVS 5a**).

Wild Thing 12m VS 4c   *(1980s)*
Climb the corner bounding the left side of the pillar and finish up the pillar wall on the right via a groove line. Continuing up the crack-line is Severe.

The next three climbs are on the broken ground to the left of the pillar.

Munich Man 12m Very Difficult   *(1980s)*
The wide crack-line to the left starting low down and finishing direct or to the left.

Heron Crack 12m Severe   *(1980s)*
Climb the corner-crack in the angle of the wall and finish leftwards.

Lunar Dance 12m Severe   *(1980s)*
Start by the corner of Heron Crack and move out left to the edge above a low prow. Finish up the edge.

The next routes are on the front face.

Nuptial Flight   12m   Severe *   *(1980s)*
Climb a short crack in the slab up and left of the low prow, step right on to a ledge and finish direct through higher ledges. The overhanging left side of The Prow has been top-roped at 6a/b.

Twinkle Toes   12m   Severe *   *(1980s)*
Climb thin cracks left of Nuptial Flight and up to a niche. Finish direct.

Trench Foot   12m   Hard Severe   *(1980s)*
Takes thin cracks just right of the wide crack of The Gash on to a slab. Finish easily.

The Gash   12m   Difficult *   *(1980s)*
Climb by the wide crack and fault-line direct.

Bum Thrust   15m   Severe *   *(1980s)*
Start up the awkward chimney, or its left edge and finish up leftwards via a slabby corner. Finishing direct up the steep off-width is VS 4c.

The next routes start by stepping across a crevasse, or it may be started from a higher platform.

The Pit   12m   VS 4c *   *(1980s)*
The true start is by a jump across the crevasse pit to a good hold and climb to the platform. Continue up a crack to the edge and finish up the top of Bum Thrust.

Writer's Block   12m   E4 6a *   *(1998)*
Climb the steep wall a few metres left of The Pit. Use runners left and right in the top break.

Malignant Tumour   12m   VS 4c *   *(1980s)*
Climb the crack-line near the middle of the wall throughout finishing via a well positioned embedded stone.

Boundless   12m   HVS 5a   *(1998)*
Start just right of Malignant Tumour and climb by thin cracks, crossing that route to finish out left.

Wide Eyes   12m   VS 5a   *(1998)*
Start down in the tidal pit below the fault at the left end of the wall. Climb the wide lower break and finish up the steep crack-line on the right.

Endless   10m   Very Difficult   *(1980s)*
Climb the fault-line out left. Hard start.

HAMMERHEAD ROCK

This is an interesting rock formation about 200m further north, sporting several small climbs. It is an overhanging prow situated well above sea-level and by the burn that drains the lochan above the path.

Birthday Hangover   6m   Severe   *(1980s)*
Climb up the right edge pulling over the bulge to finish.

To the left of Birthday Hangover are two strenuous problems over a slightly over-hanging wall; **The Dog** and **The Seal** (both 4m VS 5a 1980s).

GOB A' CHUAILLE

The highest and most extensive cliffs are found a further 15mins along the coast and easily visible from the climbs of Gob Geo. Follow the sheep track passing a stoney beach and descend on to wide rocky terraces.

POLITICIAN WALL

Map p144

This is the prominent wall bounding the north side of the bay and obvious from the path. It is a fold in the rock and looks like a piece of jigsaw puzzle. Access is down the slab opposite.

SNP   10m   VS 4c   *(1980s)*
Climb the corner near the left edge.

Labour   10m   Very Difficult   *(1980s)*
The left-hand crack of the jigsaw puzzle.

Lib/Dem   10m   Very Difficult   *(1980s)*
The right-hand crack.

Tory   8m   Severe   *(1980s)*
The awkward undercut corner on the right - often wet.

SEAL WALL

There are short walls and corners, mostly broken, about 150m towards the headland of Gob a' Chuaille. The crags gain in height and quality further left. Seal Wall is in this area and there are four recorded climbs:

Cavity Corner   Severe   *(1980s)*
Climb the most obvious big crack.

Drilling the Nerve   VS 4c   *(1980s)*
A hard start, particularly for the vertically challenged, steps across the undercut and up to a small ledge. Pull on to a shelf above and finish by the right-hand crack.

Laughing Gas   Severe   *(1980s)*
Climb the corner to the left of the previous route and finish up the slab.

Painkiller   Severe   *(1980s)*
Climb up about 5m left of Laughing Gas.

Mellon Charles

BOOM CRAG - CREAG AN FHITHICH MOR

(NG 850 919)   Alt 80m   West facing   Map p144

This is a fine grained sandstone crag on the hillside above Mellon Charles. The routes are quite broken and mostly slabby but promises good views and a nice breeze in the evening. In the past, the military and mountain rescue teams used the crag for training purposes, hence the occasional stake at the top.

Approach: Park sensitively at a long passing place at the crossroads by the garage at NG 847 916. Walk up the smokehouse road and direct to the crag, 10mins.

Descent: To the left.

The crag is divided into three buttresses, split by heathery faults. The climbs recorded are on the middle and left-hand buttress, the right-hand buttress being a broken low-angled slab. From right to left.

RUBHA MOR

Call Out   18m   HVS 5a   *(2003)*
Climbs the steep right-hand sidewall of the middle buttress. Climb rock just left of
the heather fault to pass the square roof on the right and take the middle of the
sidewall direct.

The next two routes take the main slab of the middle buttress.

Sore Finger   20m   Severe *   *(1996)*
Start at the right side of the lower slab. Climb cracks to cross a heather ledge and
take the orange right-hand of two crack-lines, cross a wide heather break and take
the top slab finishing right of an overlap.

Sore Thumb   20m   Severe   *(1996)*
Climb the lower slab to the heather ledge and take the left-hand of the two crack-
lines. Cross the upper heather break and finish direct over bulges.

The remaining routes are on the left-hand buttress.

Nato Crack   18m   VS 4c   *(2003)*
Takes the steep sidewall of the buttress. Climb left of the heather fault and up into
a groove crack just right of the prow. Move right on a ledge to climb the buttress
via a steep crack-line, taking the first of three triangular roofs direct, and bypassing
the top two on the right.

Just to the left is a grassy bay with a vegetated fault-line above shattered blocks.

Battle Stations   15m   HVS 5a   *(2003)*
Start a few metres up left of the toe of the buttress and climb a dirty left-facing
corner to the heather ledge. Continue up to the overlap on the right, pull through
this and climb direct to the top.

MELLON CLIFFS - LEACAN DONNA

(NG 838 923)   Non-tidal   West facing   Map p144

A short bouldery crag, great for a few hours particularly in the evening! Drive
through Mellon Charles to the end of the road and park sensibly near the turning
place.

Approach: Continue through the gate and along the track passing an old pill box
on the headland, and follow the coast crossing a stream and above the crag to
descend steeply at the far end onto angular boulders, 5mins.

Descent: Either side depending on tide levels.

Starting at a black streaked short steep wall on the left:

Surf's Out   5m   Severe   *(1998)*
Start by the right-hand black streak and climb leftwards via cracks.

Surf Direct   5m   VS 5a/b   *(2004)*
Start as for Surf's Out and climb direct just right of the right-hand black streak.

Aquanox   5m   E1 5b *   *(1998)*
Climb direct via the obvious crack, starting mid-way between Surf's Out and the
right edge.

Flotsam   5m   Severe   *(1998)*
Climb via steps left of the corner.

Jetsam   6m   Severe   *(1998)*
Climb the corner-crack.

Neptune's Ladder   7m   E2 5b *   *(1998)*
Take the middle of the steep wall on the right via horizontal breaks.

Rungs Missing   7m   VS 5a   *(2004)*
Start under the high arete and climb to a ledge, finishing up the right side of the arete.

Drunken Sailor   7m   Very Difficult   *(1998)*
The stepped corner on the right.

The watery channel at the base of the crag widens to a pool further right.

Meloncholy   6m   HVS 5b *   *(2003)*
Start by the right edge of the wall right of the corner and take a left-trending thin crack-line.

Mileage   5m   VS 5a   *(2003)*
Start by the edge as for Meloncholy and climb just right of the edge via thin cracks.

Witz   4m   Hard Severe 4c   *(2003)*
Climb the middle of the short wall just to the right and above the pool.

The crag gains in height again a few metres to the right above a grass platform. At the right end of the grass is a smooth plaque of rock at half-height.

MC's Chicken   7m   E2 5b *   *(1998)*
Climb a left-diagonal crack-line passing the left side of the smooth rock.

Mother Carey   7m   E3 5c *   *(1998)*
Start up MC's Chicken and climb up the centre of the smooth plaque.

Melodrama   6m   HVS 5b *   *(2003)*
Climb through bulges to a crack bounding the right side of the smooth plaque of rock.

Continue about 20m to the right round an edge to an inset area of rock with a vegetated right-facing corner.

Squid   8m   Severe   *(1998)*
Start in the middle of the wall right of the corner and climb leftwards to finish up the top of the corner. A steep start may be made up the corner.

Fishnet   8m   HVS 5b   *(2004)*
Start just right of Squid and climb direct up the thin crack, finishing right of the triangular roof.

Barnacle   8m   Hard Severe   *(1998)*
Just right of Fishnet is a chockstoned fault. Take the crack-line with a jutting block just right of the fault.

Shark's Fin   8m   Hard Severe   *(1998)*
Climb via crack-lines just right of Barnacle.

The right end of the crag is tidal and there is bouldering centred around a hanging corner, a short steep wall and an undercut arete.

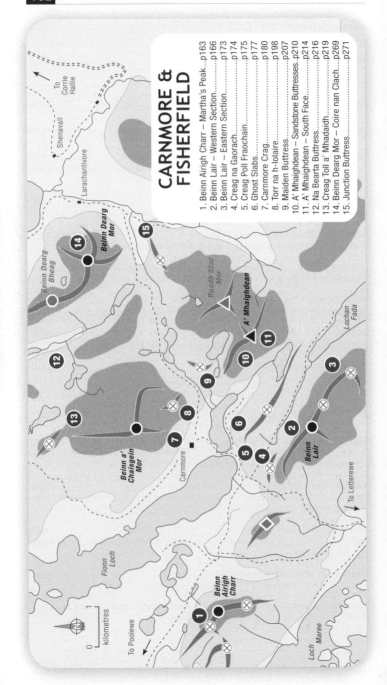

CARNMORE & FISHERFIELD

To Corrie Hallie

Shenavall

Larachantivore

Beinn Dearg Bheag

Beinn Dearg Mor

Ruadh Stac Mor

A' Mhaighdean

Lochan Fada

Beinn a' Chaisgein Mor

Carnmore

Beinn Lair

To Letterewe

Fionn Loch

Beinn Airigh Charr

To Poolewe

Loch Maree

kilometres
0   1

CARNMORE & FISHERFIELD

This area has some of the best climbing and wild walking in the Northern Highlands. The distances can be quite large; indeed, A' Mhaighdean is frequently cited as being the most remote Munro summit. A good approach is to plan a trip lasting a few days, thus enabling visits to several of the excellent crags. The owner likes climbers to visit his estate but restrictions may be found during the stalking season ("15th September to 15th November, except weekends", quoted in 2005). The owners have recently renovated the barn at Carnmore with a new roof, and there is a sign stating "Walkers and climbers are welcome to use the barn".

Approach: The usual approach to the barn is from Poolewe via Kernsary, a walk of about 4hrs, and unless obvious, access to the different crags is described from this route (see each crag). A quicker approach is by boat across Loch Maree and over the Bealach Mheinnidh. Another longer but attractive approach is from Dundonnell via Shenavall.

The Poolewe approach is shorter if one starts by cycling to Kernsary and along the vehicle tracks beyond it. Go past Kernsary and soon take a right turn by a plantation. This is less obvious than straight on, therefore easy to miss. Go through the plantation for just over 1km to where a path leaves on the right (cairns). Follow this path to the edge of the plantation and on across moorland above the Allt na Creige. This is a new path, at a higher level than that shown on the current map and provides easy walking on a largely hard surface all the way to Carnmore. Continue along the path south-east to the foot of Srathan Buidhe and cross the stream in this narrow glen to follow the path as it drops below the north-east face of Meall Mheinnidh towards Fionn Loch. Cross the causeway to Carnmore.

BEINN AIRIGH CHARR - MARTHA'S PEAK

(NG 931 764)   Alt 350m   North-East facing

This is the most accessible of the mountains north of Loch Maree. Like Beinn Lair, the cliffs are of hornblende schist, providing good incut holds but treacherous when wet. Despite their imposing appearance, the climbing on the main cliffs is primarily in the nature of Alpine scrambling, but most enjoyable all the same. There are shorter, steeper climbs towards the left (south-east) end of the cliffs, whose sensational overhanging profile is seen soon after leaving Kernsary. The climbs are described from right to left, as one would normally approach from Kernsary, and the heights of the older routes are measured as vertical height.

Approach: Coming from Poolewe, the path from Kernsary to Carnmore passes close under the large north-east facing cliffs of Martha's Peak, which is the north top of the mountain.

Descent: Normally climb with sacks and walk off. The easiest descent to the cliff base is by Coire na Laoigh to the west. It is also possible to start down scree in Coire na Laoigh and then gain a prominent rake which cuts diagonally rightwards down the main face. Cross Staircase Gully and from the top of Lower Buttress, traverse right (east) to avoid difficulties below.

Walker's Route   250m   Very Difficult   (1910)

This route follows as nearly as possible the centre of the curve of the buttress between the main face and the corrie to its west. The first two-thirds are relatively straightforward. From a ledge at the top of the diagonal rake which crosses the main face, follow a small chimney direct to the summit.

Comic Relief   250m   III   (1988)

This climbs up the face overlooking the corrie above the north-west end of Loch an Doire Crionaich, right of the main cliffs of Martha's Peak and may well be a winter ascent of the upper part of Walker's Route. The climbing starts at an altitude of about 500m below this north-west facing section of cliff which lies below the main summit of Beinn Airigh Charr. Follow the distinct gully come chimney-line splitting the centre of the face, taking the right fork at mid-height. Near the top it is possible to finish more easily to the right or follow the natural line up a narrow chimney.

Face Route   330m   Difficult *   (1910)
The main face of Martha's Peak rises directly above Loch an Doire Crionaich and provides a fine mountaineering route to the summit of the hill. There are two lower buttresses on either side, somewhat like the parts of an arrowhead with the head formed by the main face. Go up screes and easy ground between the two lower buttresses to the foot of the main face. Thread heather ledges and easy rocks up and right until below the steep upper part of the face. Climb some way right of the steepest section, which forms a vague nose. From a platform halfway up the upper crags a wide choice of routes leads to the top. Ling's original party followed a narrow, well defined but grassy chimney, with scant holds.
Winter: **IV,5** ***   (1999)
Follow Ling's original line including the fine chimney in the upper buttress. A magnificent route in a remote setting, assuming at least the upper buttress is well frozen, which is rare.

2003 Route   380m   III   (2003)
This route zigzags up a series of ramps and shelves on the main face of Martha's Peak. Initially the 2003 Route follows a line left of the 1910 Face Route. At the "platform halfway up the upper crags" it crosses Original Route and finishes up an easier chimney-line to the right.
   Start near the bottom left corner of the main face and follow an obvious ramp line up and left. This leads to a platform overlooking Staircase Gully. From the platform a large shelf leads easily up and right to beneath a deep chimney slot (obvious from the base of the crag). From beneath the slot a short rock band needs to be climbed up and left to gain access to another left-trending ramp-line. This leads to a shallow gully which is followed back right up to the "platform halfway up the upper crags". The well-defined chimney of the 1910 Route could be climbed from here but, instead, a separate chimney-line further to the right was climbed in two pitches, finishing just beneath the summit.

Staircase Gully   360m   Severe   (1964)
This is the gully separating the main tower of Martha's Peak from the lower cliffs to the left. The climbing is about Very Difficult except for the crux pitch. There is much loose scree between pitches. Begin by climbing the left wall of the gully. After 60m the second pitch follows a groove left of a chockstone (20m). After another 45m, climb in the right corner of another huge chockstone (20m). Easy ground follows, then a steep, rotten section (20m). Above this a slimy part of the gully is avoided by two pitches on the left (45m). An overhanging chimney above gives the crux (12m), followed by 90m of easy ground to the top of the gully.

Bell's Route   350m   Difficult *   (1928)
This route starts up the left-hand Lower Buttress above the south-east end of Loch an Doire Crionaich, and eventually finishes up the top of the main face. It is mainly scrambling with only one Difficult pitch. Climb the clean rocky crest at the right side of the Lower Buttress and continue to a steep wall which sweeps across the buttress at about 120m. Breach this by a 15m pitch (crux) to reach the top of the Lower Buttress. Cross easy ground and ascend a series of delightful slabby buttresses to reach easier upper slopes. Descend slightly rightwards across the top of Staircase Gully. Climb the main cliff to the right up a rib of good rock and traverse right to a grassy ledge. A sensationally exposed finish leads to the summit.

Lower Buttress Direct   150m   Severe   (1951)
Start at the lowest rocks and go left up a rake on loose, flaky rock. Continue for 90m up easy grass and rock to boiler-plate slabs and then a steep 30m wall, with a crack in its upper part near the centre. Below and left is a 5m sentry-box with a grass ledge on the right. Climb with difficulty over the nose of the sentry box and

continue right on a narrow ledge with good holds, then back over slabs higher up. Easy rocks lead to the top of the Lower Buttress, from where a choice of lines may be taken up the upper face.

Original Route   300m   Moderate   *(1909)*
Start near the left end of Lower Buttress and bypass most of its difficulties to reach a gully on the left of the continuation buttress. Start up this but soon move out on to the continuation buttress and reach its top. Scramble to the summit (up the "easier upper slopes" avoided by Bell's Route).

A little way left from Lower Buttress there is a jumble of monstrous boulders below a big wet overhanging wall, which has, as yet, no routes. Below and left of this is a very prominent clean arete with a slabby face on its right.

The Roc   90m   Scottish VS   *(1974)*
Start 25m up and right from the base of the clean arete of The Beanstalk.
1. 40m   Climb diagonally left up steep rock to overcome a lower bulge, then traverse back right to belay below a groove.
2. 35m Climb the groove to a stance on the right.
3. 15m Finish up a deep groove.

The Beanstalk   100m   HVS ★★   *(1971)*
The clean arete gives a fairly serious climb in fine position.
1. 35m 4c Climb on the left of the arete, with an awkward move left at about 20m, and continue to a good ledge.
2. 35m 4c Start on the left and move up and right towards the arete. An awkward move left past a bulge leads to easier climbing and a belay on the left.
3. 30m 4a Climb the left wall to the top.

Square Buttress   120m   Difficult ★   *(1951)*
This is the next prominent buttress, well left of The Beanstalk (at NG 938 705, near a small lochan unnamed on the 1:50000 map). The main feature of the buttress is on its left flank, but to the right of the buttress is an obvious black crack (50m Very Difficult). Start at a gangway slanting left from the bottom right-hand corner, leading to a ledge which is followed right for 6m. The wall above is steep, then slabby. A further 18m pitch ends the lower half of the buttress. The upper half is easy but interesting.

MEALL MHEINNIDH

(NG 955 748)   Alt 720m

This is the next hill south-east of Beinn Airigh Charr. It has one recorded route, **Glasgow Ridge** (150m Very Difficult 1947) takes the central rise, starting below an obvious slanting terrace.

BEINN LAIR

(NG 982 733)   860m

NORTH-EAST FACE

**Alt 450-500m   North-North-West to North-East facing   Map p162
Diagrams p169, 172**
This long face of Beinn Lair has the greatest escarpment of hornblende schist in the country. It offers a number of interesting climbs in the lower grades, both summer and winter. The greenish hornblende schist, with its sharp holds, offers an unusual and quite characteristic type of climbing. It tends to be very greasy when wet and not good for protection; however the steeper parts are less vegetated than might be expected. The Wisdom Buttress end of the face catches the sun before 9am and

CARNMORE & FISHERFIELD

after 5pm in mid-summer. The larger central and east section of cliff is in the sun all morning.

Approach: The approach is usually from Carnmore or directly from Poolewe. From the path junction at the south end of Fionn Loch it is possible to climb up the Letterewe path towards Bealach Mheinnidh then strike off left and climb up to Bealach a' Chuirn, bringing one out below the highest cliffs at the right end of the face. A slightly more interesting variant is to go from the path junction directly up the narrow valley below Creag na Gaorach (see below), which brings one out opposite Butterfly Buttress. For the climbs at the south-east end of the face above Lochan Fada the Carnmore based climber may possibly prefer an approach via Dubh Loch and Beinn Tharsuinn Chaol. Although this involves more ascent and descent, it offers a remarkable view of the face as a whole. Lochan Fada can also be reached from Kinlochewe via Gleann Bianasdail.

Descent: Probably climb with sacks and descend to Bealach Mheinnidh.

The climbs are described from right to left (west to east), and the individual buttresses may be identified from the diagram. The slender, cigar-shaped Wisdom Buttress is easily recognised, with the vertical slot of Bat's Gash on its left. The buttress to its right is called The Tooth and right again is an area of indefinite cliff ending in a deep-cut gully. The first climb is on the buttress right of this. Stars have been assigned with limited information, so some good routes may be unstarred.

1 Excalibur   120m   Very Difficult   (1952)
This lies on the clean mass of rock right of the main crags. There is a deep gully on the left and a buttress with overhangs on the right. Start at the side of the gully. The climbing is initially Moderate, becoming steeper. Negotiate some minor overhangs with good holds to reach a capacious ledge, below a steep slab ending in an overhang. Cross the slab diagonally left, then traverse right below the overhang. Climb easily to the top.

2 West Chimney Route   180m   Very Difficult   (1951)
Climbs the right side of the buttress right of The Tooth. The details may be hard to follow. Start about 30m left of the 'nose' of the buttress. Climb a moist groove leftwards over steep, discontinuous rock to a large grass terrace, below a steeper wall (120m). Climb the wall by a wet chimney in the left corner to a stance. Enter a gully leading to a cave above. Climb a steep rib of good rock up to the right. Continue easily to the top.

3 The Tooth   200m   Difficult **   (1951)
Start near the middle of the buttress right of Wisdom Buttress. Climb directly up until at about half-height the route joins the left crest of the buttress. Continue to the top by a delightful series of short, exposed pitches.

4 Cavity Chimney and Wisdom Wall   215m   Very Difficult   (1951)
Cavity Chimney is the short chimney to the right of the foot of Wisdom Buttress. This is followed by a long crack, grassy and easy, to a fork. The buttress between the arms of the fork is The Fang, and to its left, separated by a crack, is Wisdom Wall (on the right side of the upper half of Wisdom Buttress). Follow the crack for 30m, then climb up and across the exposed wall on the left (30m, poor belays). It is possible to move left onto Wisdom Buttress, but a better finish is to traverse back right to the crack and follow it to the top.

5 Dragon's Lair   240m   V,6 *   (1997)
The first obvious line right of Wisdom Buttress gives a good winter climb. Climb Cavity Chimney to the large snow bay; Wisdom Wall takes the left fork. Climb the right fork in three sustained pitches, a narrow off-width section and an overhanging chockstone were avoided by moves on the right wall. Exit right at the chimney's conclusion finishing up an easy snow ridge.

6 Wisdom Buttress   220m   Severe *** *(1951)*

The obvious, slender, cigar-shaped buttress gives the most popular climb on the mountain, exposed and sustained, low in the grade. Start at the bottom right corner of the buttress.

1. and 2. 75m Climb diagonally left, above a lower overhang, then up right to a small platform. Take an obvious line of weakness to a diminutive stance below a small overhang.

3. 25m Traverse left and evade the overhang by a slab on the left.

4. 30m Continue straight up slabs on the left, then traverse right along a ledge to the centre of the buttress.

5. 30m Climb the nose above by an excursion on the right wall, steep and with sloping holds, and return to the crest.

6. and 7. 60m Continue up the steep nose above, then follow the crest of the buttress to the top.

7 Bat's Gash   220m   Very Difficult *(1951)*

This is a route of maintained interest with impressive cave scenery in the middle section. Start at the foot of the deep-cut chimney immediately left of Wisdom Buttress. About 30m up there is a chimney pitch with a narrow exit, leading to a couch of blaeberries. At about 140m there is a two-tiered chimney, followed by a four-tiered one, the last of which overhangs. This is avoided on the right and the chimney rejoined above the overhang. Continue in the chimney to the top, only one pitch having any difficulty.

Winter: **220m   V,6 ***** *(1997)*

Follow the summer route. Two through routes were used, the first requiring a partial undressing. Passing the chockstones on the third pitch constituted the crux (well protected). A route of great character, although some of the sections are so recessed they hold little snow.

The buttress left of Bat's Gash is Angel's Buttress. In its upper half there is an obvious bar of overhangs, split towards the right by a deep chimney which continues below as a minor gully, which divides the lower part of the buttress into separate noses.

8 Ordinary Route   240m   Difficult *(1951)*

Start just left of Bat's Gash. Take the line of least resistance, diagonally left following grooves across steep slabs, to gain the deep chimney. Follow the chimney through the overhangs, the most difficult section being the second chimney pitch. Continue directly to the top.

Variations:

There are two possible variations. The first avoids the chimney by going up the right side of the buttress, passing the overhangs on the right. Wrangham's Variation starts at the foot of the minor gully that leads to the deep chimney and follows this to join the Ordinary Route. Both are Difficult.

Winter: **IV,5 *** *(1998)*

The summer line was followed using Wrangham's Variation. The main challenges were a series of chockstone pitches in the chimneys, one of which offers a through route for the most slender of leaders!

9 Pilgrim's Progress   240m   Severe * *(1951)*

This is the best route on Angel's Buttress. Start from a scoop in the screes at the lowest point of the rocks, up a large triangle of slab which leads to the main slabby face on the right of the buttress. Go straight up this until the grooves of the Ordinary Route are joined just short of the deep chimney (110m). Cross the chimney and climb the slab on the left to the foot of the great overhangs. Traverse left to the edge of the buttress (40m). Two short pitches up the edge lead to the crux, a very exposed wall with the hardest move at the top. Follow the crest to the top of the buttress.

The broad buttress left of Angel's Buttress is Molar Buttress. The two are separated by Y-Gully, which encloses **Y-Buttress** between its upper arms. This has a messy and vegetated route (120m Difficult 1951). Molar Buttress has five routes recorded in 1951, by two separate parties, but some of these are not easy to distinguish.

10 Y Gully, Left Fork   250m   III *   *(1998)*
The first ascent was in thin conditions, when a large chockstone in the fork section provided the main obstacle. Fine rock scenery.

11 Right-Hand Route   210m   Very Difficult   *(1951)*
Start up easy-angled slabs at the right side of the buttress, aiming left to join a system of cracks which runs up the side. Follow these for about 45m, then up steep walls slightly to the left to a scoop below an overhang of the steep band of rock which crosses the buttress in the upper half. Above and right is a break in the form of an open corner, the most westerly of the breaks in the steep band. Make an upward traverse right into the corner and climb it, with an exit left. Easier climbing to the top.

A route up the centre of the buttress was made by an Oxford party **Damocles Cracks** (Severe), but no details are available.

12 Left-Hand Route   190m   Difficult   *(1951)*
This follows the left edge of the buttress all the way. Start at the foot of the buttress, just left of a conspicuous short black chimney. Climb up broken rocks and vegetation, making for the foot of the chimney above. This has three pitches, the second being easier than it looks. Above, the climbing is undistinguished, keeping to the left but on the front face of the buttress. Two steeper walls intervene, the first being climbed on good holds, the second being traversed to the right. After this the angle eases.

13 Route 1   210m   Very Difficult   *(1951)*
This is thought to start left of Left-Hand Route and cross it higher up, but the routes may have parts in common. Start up an easy gully (with a short difficult chimney) towards the left of the buttress. From a terrace at the top of the gully traverse right towards the main mass of the buttress. Climb on the right of the crest for 30m to a large ledge. Make a hard traverse right to a sloping stance. Climb the steep wall on the right, then a shattered chimney, and finally a steep nose to regain the crest. Scramble easily to the top.

14 Rose Route   210m   Moderate   *(1951)*
Follows the far left side of Molar Buttress overlooking a large gully on the left (the Amphitheatre). The gully is suitable for descent.

Left of the Amphitheatre is a large mass of rock, Butterfly Buttress, which is actually composed of four separate buttresses, the two outside ones (the wings) running the full height of the cliff, with the two smaller ones (the head and tail) inserted between them at top and bottom. To the right of the right wing, and left of the Amphitheatre, are two prominent gullies splitting the full length of the cliff.

15 Cabbage White   300m   IV,4   *(1978)*
This is the first gully left of the Amphitheatre. A prominent, short ice step marks the start of the difficulties. Above this move right, then back left into the main line. Near the top the gully branches. On the first ascent the right fork was taken.

16 Butterfly Gully   300m   II   *(1978)*
The long couloir left of Cabbage White; prominent from Carnmore. It forks about 150m below the plateau. On the first ascent the more interesting looking left fork was taken.

Andy Nisbet

BEINN LAIR West

A. Angel's Buttress
B. Molar Buttress
C. The Amphitheatre
D. Butterfly Buttress

3. The Tooth	Difficult **
4. Cavity Chimney & Wisdom Wall	Very Difficult
6. Wisdom Buttress	Severe ***
7. Bat's Gash	Very Difficult
8. Ordinary Route	Difficult

8a. First Variation	
8b. Wrangham's Variation	
9. Pilgrim's Progress	Severe *
10. Y Gully, Left Fork	III *
11. Right-Hand Route	Very Difficult

12. Left-Hand Route	Difficult
14. Rose Route	Moderate
15. Cabbage White	IV,4

17 Right Wing, Butterfly Buttress   300m   Very Difficult   (1953)
Start just right of the foot of the rocks.
1. 25m Take a ledge slanting left to the centre of the buttress and go up to a ledge with a birch tree.
2. 20m Go round the right corner of the steep wall and then up and back left. Climb about 9m to a belay under a steep wall.
3. 45m Take a shallow crack on the right which develops into a ledge curving left under an overhang. Follow this to its end, then go up the higher of two grass ledges.
4. etc. 200m Continue, keeping to the left for about 75m, then follow the indefinite crest to the top.
Winter: **600m   III**   (2005)
Start at the lowest rocks, just left of the summer start, uphill from a huge rectangular boulder and directly below a pointed top (point 830m on the 1:25000 map) of the buttress. Climb more or less directly upwards following grooves, chimneys, aretes and with a zigzag on open snow slopes between one-quarter and one-third height. Finish just right of the summit with a belay on the cairn.

18 Left Wing, Butterfly Buttress   300m   Moderate   (1967)
Start up slabs on the right, then move left to join and follow the crest.
Winter: **III** *   (1988)
An interesting climb following the crest of the buttress.

Left of Butterfly Buttress is a cone-shaped buttress of enormous bulk that falls from the north-west summit of Beinn Lair. From here leftwards is the highest section of cliff leading across to Marathon Ridge, the equivalent buttress leading down from the main summit.

19 North Summit Buttress   350m   Moderate *   (1957)
Really the north-west summit. Start at the bottom left corner of the rocks, where a stream emerges from the left-bounding gully. Climb easily up the left edge of the buttress for about 100m. Cross a minor gully that comes up from the left and go across a slab to a small nick on the extreme left edge. Continue with more difficulty for about 50m up the rib above and then by easy ground to the foot of a steep wall with several turfy chimneys. Pass this by a long traverse right, then climb a small ridge to easier ground. Scramble to rejoin the left edge of the buttress, now a sharp ridge. Follow this until it merges with the steeper upper buttress. Climb this by a zigzag line near the edge to emerge close to the summit cairn.
Variation:
More direct and slightly harder. Start below stepped overhangs in the centre of the buttress. Pass these on the left, then work up left to the sharp ridge.
Winter: **III** **   (1978)
An excellent climb with enjoyable route finding. Start up an ice runnel, probably right of the summer routes, then trend generally left.

20 Tower Ridge   350m   Difficult *   (1980)
The next ridge to the left. Start at the bottom right. At two-thirds height is a steep step, then the ridge narrows to three small pinnacles. Pass the last one on the right.

21 Geodha Ban   350m   IV,4 *   (1969)
Close on the left of North Summit Buttress are two parallel gullies, possibly the gullies either side of Tower Ridge. The start is described as being 'some 200 yards left of a large prominent standing block halfway along the main crag. Looking up there are two obvious deeply-cut parallel gullies.' The climb follows the left-hand gully. Short pitches lead to a chockstone, climbed on the left. A long snow section then leads to a 90m icefall, started by a corner on the left. Chimneys above lead to the top.

22 Marathon Ridge   400m   Difficult *   (1951)
Finishing at NG 983 735, this is almost the nearest ridge to the summit of the

Andy Nisbet

North Summit Buttress, III, Beinn Lair North-east Face. Climber Jim Unwin

mountain. It sends down a long cleanish nose with a distinctive tapering base. The ridge has a subsidiary top just below the true top, and is joined to the summit plateau by a grassy neck. The route is mostly scrambling but has a short, sharp crux. Start below a 60m nose. Climb by a succession of walls and ledges, in roughly 30m steps, to where the ridge steepens before it joins the left-hand ridge, from which it is separated by steep narrow chimney (250m). Climb the chimney, which has a steep crux section (30m). Continue up to the grassy neck on the main buttress below the final tower (60m). The face is broad for 45m then narrows, the final climbing being by a thin fissure on the crest. Scrambling leads to a grassy pinnacle at the top (60m).

23 Olympus 150m Difficult *(1953)*
On the immediate left of Marathon Ridge is a rather thin buttress, starting a good deal higher up. Scramble up this until a gully cuts sharply across the buttress, which now steepens. Continue up, keeping as possible to the left edge.

BEINN LAIR Central

18. Left Wing, Butterfly Buttress	Moderate
19. North Summit Buttress	Moderate *
19a. Direct Variation	
20. Tower Ridge	Difficult *
21. Geodha Ban	IV,4 *
22. Marathon Ridge	Difficult *
23. Olympus	Difficult
24. Easachan	III

Andy Nisbet

24 Easachan 300m III   *(1969)*
The main section of crag ends at easier ground below the bealach between the main summit and Sgurr Dubh. Right of this, the last buttress of the main section of crag, is a rounded slabby buttress (NG 987 735). This gully is on its right. A huge chockstone is climbed on the left, and a bulging ice pitch near the top is climbed direct.

The following climbs lie on the eastern part of the Beinn Lair massif, near Lochan Fada. Stag Buttress is upstream of the loch, the remaining routes are more or less above the head of the loch.

25 Stag Buttress   130m Severe   *(1951)*
This is the highest buttress visible from the head of Lochan Fada. It has a large steep ridge running up its left side in the upper section. Scramble easily up to the foot of the ridge (120m). Start about 30m up the gully on the left.
1. 25m Climb a corner to a moss ledge.
2. 25m Follow the arete, keeping to the edge of the gully.
3. 25m Continue up the edge to a large mossy patch, then straight up to below steeper rock.
4. 25m Avoid the first overhang by a steep corner on the left, overlooking the gully, then move back right onto the arete and go straight up to a small stance.
5. 30m Climb a small overhang and follow the edge of the buttress to the top.

26 Falstaff 120m VS *   *(1951)*
This is the right of the two clean buttresses near the head of Lochan Fada. Start at the lowest point of the rocks.
1. 20m Climb directly up to a ledge under a large overhang.
2. 10m Climb steep, broken rock slanting right to a ledge.
3. 20m Traverse delicately left onto the face and go straight up past a large ledge to a belay at a block in a groove on the left.
4. 20m Traverse back to the middle of the face and up to a belay in the groove on the left.
5. 20m Traverse right onto the main face and climb straight up.
6. 30m Continue up the central rib on easier rock to the top.

27 Sesame Buttress 140m Severe *   *(1951)*
Start at the lowest point of the buttress to the left of Falstaff, to the right of a prominent crack.
1. 10m Climb the wall and move left to a heather ledge.
2. 25m From the right end of the ledge traverse left onto the arete (overlooking the crack) and climb it past a small overhang until level with a distinctive block in the crack.
3. 25m Cross the crack to a mossy ledge, then climb the arete on its left side to a prominent poised block. Continue up the arete to a grassy groove on the left.
4. 25m Move left onto an arete, then straight up to the beginning of the next arete on the left.
5. 25m Climb the arete and belay above a steep section.
6. 30m Continue straight up to easier ground.

On the hillside above and left of the last two climbs is a rock tower known as The Keep. It appears as a steep-sided wedge of clean looking rock. Its right (west) face is smaller, but cleaner and continuous and contains Rainbow Wall. Central Route goes straight up the nose. The east face is about 120m high at the centre, but tapers to about 30m and is more broken.

28 Rainbow Wall 105m Severe *   *(1951)*
Some way up the gully on the right of The Keep there is a fork and a spring. On the left is a wall bounded by a left-trending groove and on the right an incipient crack. Start below a ledge with two poised blocks.

CARNMORE & FISHERFIELD

1. 20m Traverse left for a short distance then climb the wall to a large sloping ledge.
2. 20m Traverse up and left to the skyline below a small roof.
3. 20m Go straight up to a shattered ledge.
4. 10m Climb the twisting arete to a large ledge (spike belay).
5. 35m Climb another twisting arete to the top.

29 Central Route   220m   Severe   (1951)
Start at the lowest point of the buttress. The route stays on the central line, but variations can be made to reduce the standard to Very Difficult.
1. 25m Climb initially up to a large sloping heather ledge.
2. 20m Climb an awkward corner at the left end of the ledge, then go up a rib to another heather ledge and block belay.
3. 25m Ascend the wall above, then a groove on the right of an overhang until a left traverse can be made onto the central rib.
4. 20m Take the most central line to steeper ground.
5. 20m Climb the overhang on good holds and continue up the rib to a large ledge.
6. 20m Climb the nose above to the foot of a prominent arete.
7. 20m Climb the arete, turning the steep part on the left, and continue to a broken ledge.
8. 20m Climb the nose, then easier rock and moss to a low wall.
9. 30m Climb the wall on the left and easier rock to the top.

CREAG NA GAORACH

(NG 974 747)   Alt 340m   North facing   Map p162

A band of cliffs between the west end of Beinn Lair and lower cliffs around Fionn Loch and Dubh Loch.

Approach: These pleasant buttresses are reached by following the stream from the junction of the Kernsary and Letterewe paths at the south-east end of Fionn Loch. The stream leads into a narrow defile with three principal buttresses on the right (south) side, and another small buttress just below the col at its head.

Jealousy   200m   Very Difficult   (1957)
This lies on the first (west) buttress. Start a few metres left of where the stream washes against the foot of the rocks.
1. 30m Climb a steep slab slightly left.
2. 25m Climb a slabby rib left of a wet corner-crack.
3. 25m Climb up to an overhung ledge.
4. 30m Go over the lip of the overhang and straight up to a ledge; then left and up to perched blocks.
5. 25m Go diagonally right up the ledge and then up a bulbous grey slab to a small ledge.
6. and 7. 65m Follow the blunt rib and continue to the top.

The middle buttress is characterised by a large reddish slab at the bottom leading up to a prominent overhang. **Denizen** (135m VS 1978) trends left up the lower slab and bypasses the steep central barrier on the left. The exact details are uncertain; see SMCJ 1980.

Zebra Slabs   135m   Very Difficult **   (1957)
This excellent climb lies on the third (east) buttress, also known as Nanny Goat Buttress. Start at the centre of the buttress behind some fallen blocks, just left of a sapling.
1. 25m Climb the steep rib, which is hard to start but soon eases, and follow it to a belay below a little lip on the left.
2. 25m Return right and gain a narrow ramp of slab leading into a crack on the

left. Climb this then return to the crest of the rib at the top. Pass a small turf ledge and climb the slab above to belay in a shallow chimney on the right.
3. 35m Traverse left and climb a blunt rib to large turf ledges.
4. 15m Directly above is a block overhang on the skyline, with other overhangs on the right. Climb up to gain a slab rib which slants up left of the block overhang.
5. 35m Follow the rib to the top.

Rainbow's End   130m   VS   (1967)
This follows the rib forming the left edge of the buttress. The difficulties ease after the first two pitches. Start about 15m left of Zebra Slabs, just right of a gully.
1. 25m Go up the rib to a heathery stance at the foot of a corner-groove below overhangs.
2. 20m Climb a short way up the steep rib and step round onto the left wall; move left and up by a crack, then back right to meet a diagonal fault going back left. Move up to a small roof and traverse blindly right round the nose above an overhang to reach easier slabs which lead to a grass ledge.
3. 40m Go up the slabby rib on the left, keeping left of a projecting block at 15m, and continue to a terrace.
4. 10m Trend left to a groove below the attractive skyline rib.
5. 25m Climb a slabby rib to a ledge and a small nose on the left to the top.

The following routes lie on the small buttress just below the col to the east of the large east (third) buttress (containing Zebra Slabs).

Ugly Duckling   50m   Very Difficult   (1994)
Climbs the rib at the right side of the buttress starting at a quartz studded overhang. Trend up and leftwards from a small grassy bay at half-height. The rock to the right of this route was climbed in 1967 at Difficult.

The Little Mermaid   45m   VS 4b   (1994)
Start up a small rib 5m left of Ugly Duckling, just right of a damp groove. Climb to a roof at 10m, then traverse hard left into a short corner containing a prominent flake. Go up the corner, then trend up and slightly left to a corner-crack. Finish up the corner and easy slabs above.

Red Shoes   45m   VS 4c *   (1994)
Start up a black wall at the left end of the lower roof running across the middle section of the crag. Climb flakes to the next roof, then traverse 2m right to the foot of an obvious scoop in the centre. Pull into the scoop, then make a short traverse right to a prominent crack. Go up cracks, pull out left at the top and finish up easy slabs. A later ascent thought Severe.

Below Meall Mheinnidh the Carnmore path descends towards Fionn Loch where it is joined by the path from Letterewe. The path continues below Creag Poll Fraochain, past some delightful sandy strands at the head of the loch and over the causeway.

CREAG POLL FRAOCHAIN

(NG 970 753)   Alt 200m   North-West facing   Map p162
This crag lies directly above the junction of the Kernsary and Letterewe paths at the south-east end of Fionn Loch. Named Creag Beag in the 1993 guide.

Little Big-Horn   60m   E5 **   (1988)
There is a prominent jutting roof halfway up the main left-hand dome of the crag. This route takes a prominent line of bulging grooves which skirt the great roof on the right. It is a very good climb with impressive situations. Start just left of an obvious corner flanking a tree-filled bay.
1. 15m 4c Climb straight up orange rock, where there is a quartz intrusion, to

reach a curving flake-fault. Move right and up two detached flakes to traverse round right into the top of the tree-filled bay.

2. 25m 5c Move back round left and up right onto the nose. Climb the wall and bulge above into a slabby corner. Move up to the roof and traverse the slab left to the top of a creaking flake above the great roof.

3. 20m 6b Move up a little rib to surmount the big roof above and gain a leg-jam rest in the overhanging groove. Finish up this to a rest at a wobbly spike. Move up grassy ground past a loose tree to belay.

Temerity   85m   HVS **   (1957)
A little to the right of the great central break that splits the crag is a nose, slightly undercut at its base and with a steep groove on the right. The climb is enjoyable for the first two pitches but disappointing above; it is easy to abseil from a tree whereas including the last pitch incurs a long descent. Start just left of the nose at an indefinite groove.

1. 30m 5a Go up the left wall of the groove, traverse right and pull up. Continue up for 3m and go right into a shallow groove. Ascend 3m and go right again, then climb a 5m wall and continue more easily to a stance below a smooth wall.

2. 20m 5a Traverse right to a corner-crack and climb this to a large terrace.

3. 35m Above the terrace the upper part of the crag is more broken. Climb a wall for 8m to a pulpit, then go right then left to an ash tree and finish up a steep wall.

Central Groove   80m   VS 5a *   (1972)
The groove leading directly up to the corner-crack on the second pitch of Temerity gives an enjoyable route. Approach the groove from the right by a tricky move, then climb it and steep slabs above to reach the terrace close to Temerity. A finish independent of Temerity should be possible, or abseil.

Right of Central Groove are two cracks; the left one is 40m E2 5b (1994) and the right one is 40m E2 5b (1994). The rib at the right end of the crag is 75m Very Difficult (1958).

Into the Valley   45m   E5 6b   (1994)
This route climbs left of the left-hand crack mentioned above. A scoop leads up into a short awkward wall and groove. Move left round an edge before following a fine crack in the headwall.

HANGING CRAG

(NG 976 751)   Alt 400m   North-West facing
This crag, clearly seen from the causeway, lies high on the hillside between Creag Poll Fraochain and Ghost Slabs. It can easily be recognised by its smooth slabby top.

Approach: The ground below the crag is steep and broken, so it is best to approach along the ridge which extends west-north-west from the right end of the cliff towards Creag Poll Fraochain. This leads to the foot of the west face, which has a steep, grey pocketed wall to the left, with corners and overhangs to the right. The largest (leftmost) overhang is near the middle of the face, with a large right-slanting corner above and to the right. Below this overhang are two grooves. The right-hand groove leads to the foot of the aforementioned corner; the left-hand groove contains a large detached flake and peters out just below the overhang.

Causeway Corner   50m   Hard Severe   (1988)
This route climbs the right-hand groove and the large corner.

1. 25m Climb the groove, moving slightly right at the top into grass at the foot of the corner.

2. 25m Climb the right wall of the corner to the top.

Changing Face   70m   HVS *   *(1988)*
An exposed and exciting climb.
1. 10m Gain a turf ledge at the foot of the left-hand groove.
2. 30m 5a Climb up the groove, passing right of a detached flake, then traverse
back left to good holds below the overhang. Follow a rising traverse left on pockets
out onto a steep undercut wall, and around a blunt rib to easier rock. Trend up and
right to a grassy stance and small spike under an overhang.
3. 30m Finish leftwards up the top part of the wall towards an obvious ledge on
the skyline. Easy slabs above lead to the top.

GHOST SLABS

(NG 978 755)   Alt 230m   North-West facing   Map p162

These are the strikingly pale slabs running down towards the south end of the
causeway between Fionn Loch and Dubh Loch. They descend in two distinct
sweeps, overshadowed by darker headwalls. High, wandering ramparts and dead-
end terraces run underneath these walls, overgrown with lush vegetation and
stunted birches. The slabs are of excellent white quartzitic gneiss. Easings of angle
make for more broken and easy sections in places, which is a pity because at its
steepest and most sustained the climbing is very fine. No stars have been assigned
due to insufficient information but the routes are good.

Approach: Walk easily up from the causeway.

Descent: Walk off to the west.

LEFT WING

There are three routes on this sector, two older routes to either side of a prominent
central overlap and a recent route up the centre. The older routes are open to a
great deal of variation, but have some good pitches (quality unknown). The
finishing funnel was previously described as "easy" but the recent ascent found it
serious and VS (see the description of Spirit of Letterewe). The mystery remains.

Left-Hand Route   270m   Scottish VS   *(1958)*
Climbs the cleanest sheets of slab on the left side. From the high terrace finish
directly up scrappy walls, or traverse away right to finish up a central funnel.

Spirit of Letterewe   370m   E3   *(2001)*
A fine but bold line taking the centre of the slabs via the two overlaps. There are
sections where the leader (and possibly second) 'must not fall'. Start at a boulder
above the loch.
1. 50m Climb the easy slab aiming for a tree below a corner up left.
2. 45m Continue in the same line up black juggy rock, moving left to belay.
3. 25m Continue up a black slab to a tree.
4. 40m 5b Move left to a steep rib overlooking a corner and climb this direct with
poor protection to step left to a crack. Continue straight up the slab to below the
left end of the first overlap.
5. 50m 5a Climb a steep groove (last protection) to step right on to the lip of the
overlap. Traverse right in an exposed position, then go straight up the middle of
the excellent slab to a small groove on the left.
6. 50m 4c Climb up the slab to the second overlap (often wet) and traverse left
under it to a hidden chimney. Climb the steep juggy chimney to exit right on to a
narrow ledge. Traverse to its right end and a diagonal crack (poor belays).
7. 40m 5a Climb above to a fine slab, unprotected and climbed centrally to a
heather cornice and ledge above. Climb the final short slab to grass and trees
below the funnel.
8. 50m 4c The funnel starts with wet and goat-trodden chimneys, soon steepening
to an overhanging black chimney. Move left and climb a fine but bold groove to

an easing, move right into a short chimney, then back left up pleasant slabs to where the funnel opens out.

9. 20m Move back right into the exit chimney climbed on huge spike holds.

Right-Hand Route   270m   Scottish VS   *(1958)*
Nice climbing up the right side of the slabs. Finish up the central funnel, or take to the rocks to left or right.

RIGHT WING

The routes described start up the clean sheet of slab on the left side. The vertiginous headwall adds atmosphere to the location and variety to the climbing. The main part of the slab is spoiled by islands of heather and birch. At least one route has been made up the cleanest area, avoiding the islands as much as possible. The climbing is good, but poorly protected and obviously artificial. However, this area dries more quickly than the routes described hereafter. The impressive headwall is turned by traversing the terraces right and climbing a good pitch up and right round an exposed nose to escape. The 1967 routes have been given their original grades, but have not been checked. Peg belays were used in places.

Doodle   165m   Scottish VS   *(1967)*
Climbs the white whaleback on the left side of the slab. The pioneers climbed up to the island with a tree belay, on the right, but it is far better to start up the whaleback direct.

1. 45m 4c Scramble up to the last grass patch below the whaleback. Climb straight up the clean slab to the whaleback and on up this to belay on small wires.
2. 35m Continue directly up and right of a watercourse to climb a broken rib to a flake.
3. 30m Climb direct above the flake to belay on the sloping slabs to the right of an overhung recess.
4. 20m Turn the overhang on the right, then go back left and up to a ledge.
5. 35m Climb straight up the slab trending slightly left to a ledge to the right of the waterslide. Then go left under the roof and up the waterslide to finish.

Moby Dick   170m   HVS   *(1988)*
A long variation to Doodle, breaking left instead of right.

1. 45m 4c Doodle, pitch 1.
2. 45m 4c Start up the second pitch of Doodle, but then traverse left across the watercourse and work up left to the left end of a big roof.
3. 35m 5a Climb the roof by the flakes above the belay, then go up to a grass ledge with a dead tree. From the left end of this go up onto a ramp and follow this right immediately under the next roof, to a point just below a rowan tree. To avoid the vilest vegetation, break left through the roof. Belay on the lip.
4. 45m 4c Climb directly up steep slabs, becoming scrappy, to belay on a small tree. Finish up the vegetated fault on the right. (In dry conditions it would be better to avoid this scrappy upper section and to veer right and straight up the watercourse.)

Leviathan   275m   Scottish VS   *(1967)*
This looks an interesting route with fine situations. Start at the foot of a smooth water streaked slab where a small burn starts. This lies below and right of the island with trees.

1. 20m Climb up the middle of the slab, passing a divot at 12m, to the left side of a grass ledge.
2. 25m From the left edge of the ledge climb straight up (peg runner used) to below a jutting flake. Traverse right and climb the slab to a good thread.
3. 45m Go straight up the slab above to a peg belay beneath a small triangular overhang.
4. 35m Climb the wall immediately on the right to a large ledge. Go up the rib on

the right to a flake belay.

5. 30m Continue up the steep wall to birch trees below the first big overlap.

6. 20m Traverse right along the grass ledge to a prominent break in the overlap and climb this to a holly tree.

7. 20m Go up the corner above to gain the arete on the right. Continue up this and traverse right to a tree at the right edge of a big grass ledge.

8. 20m Above is a green mossy wall with an overhanging corner-crack at its left edge. Climb up the wall rightwards then straight up to beneath a dangerous looking flake; move right then up to a ledge, traverse right to a cracked overhang and surmount this using a nut for aid (dangerously loose above). Continue up, slightly right, to a peg belay beneath an enormous roof.

9. 25m Traverse left under the roof to a thread below large blocks.

10. 35m Take the obvious traverse line on the right leading to an arete above the roof. Climb this to belay well back.

CREAG DUBHDEARG

(NG 983 756) Alt 300m North-West facing

There is a big amphitheatre, or shallow corrie, left of Ghost Slabs. Creag Dubhdearg is the name suggested for the steep wall at the top of this atmospheric place. A waterfall drops down the centre of the crag, easily seen from as far away as Carnmore barn. A lengthy dry spell is needed for it to dry up, and the two existing routes take the black stained rocks of the fall.

Approach: Walk up from the causeway.

Descent: From the cliff top it is possible to descend by walking across to the northerly nose of the hill, then cutting back down a big diagonal terrace-system.

Black Rain   105m   Hard Severe ✱✱   (1988)

Takes the main line of the waterfall. A remarkably steep and impressive route for its grade. Recommended (when dry). The lower VS tier can be avoided on the right.

1. 25m 4c There are three grooves in the initial tier. Climb the one on the right. Above, climb a chimney behind a huge block, or avoid it by a detour right and back.

2. 15m Climb the obvious chimney-line up the main wall, using the left rib.

3. 30m Continue left up a ramp to a ledge, then go straight up in the same fault-line to a ledge.

4. 35m Go up the wall above, slightly right at the start, to an easy funnel. Scramble to the top.

Tannasg Dubh   85m   E2   (1988)

Climbs grooves up the right side of the fall. Start about 10m right of Black Rain's chimney.

1. 25m Climb the wall on good holds, then move right and up a left-facing curving corner (heathery) to a ledge.

2. 25m 5b Climb a crack trending left up brown rock to a very steep groove, and up this to a ledge. Now surmount the overhang above directly (sensational, but an option to the right looks easier).

3. 35m Finish straight up juggy walls to easy ground.

BEINN A' CHAISGEAN MOR

(NG 983 786)   857m

The outlying shoulders of this flat topped hill drop away steeply to provide two climbing crags which offer a host of varied routes, some of which must rank amongst the best in Britain. The twin southerly knolls, Sgurr na Laocainn and Carn Mor, present an unexpected grandeur in an idyllic setting. Indeed, the very isolation of the crags adds an extra ingredient to any visit.

Torr na h' Iolaire is the huge terraced tower above Carnmore Lodge (NG 980 768). Just west, and separated by a grass sloped ravine, sits Carnmore. Unimpressive from a distance, its scale and ferocity only grow apparent to the climber drawing near to the Lodge.

CARNMORE CRAG

(NG 980 775)   Alt 350m   South-West facing   Map p162   Diagram p188

This is the great crag above the barn. It is one of the few major Scottish crags to catch the sun for most of the day, and generally dries quickly after rain. The cliff is basically of solid pale gneiss – rough and gnarled, and, at its most accommodating, eroded into pockets, buckets, and letter box slots. Nevertheless the character of the rock varies over the crag and the climber is just as likely to come across loose rock here as on most other crags. The most popular routes are Fionn Buttress, Dragon, and Gob, and it is worth bearing in mind that all three contain very exposed traverses and are not recommended for inexperienced seconds.

Approach: Walk easily up to the base. For a direct approach to the Upper Wall, see that section.

Descent: Either to the east or west. The west descent is probably the least knee jarring. There will usually be short damp sections except during a dry spell. Traverse well over from the top of the crag and descend an easy gully system to grass slopes. It is important not to start descending too soon. The east descent lies down the grassy slopes of the ravine. A big gully compels a slight ascent from the top of the crag, over a couple of rocky crests, before descent of vague paths overlooking the ravine. Lower down either cut back west to the base of the crag, or continue down into the lower reaches of the ravine.

The crag is roughly 'C' shaped, the Lower Wall and Upper Wall being divided by the grassy Central Bay, with Fionn Buttress forming the left-hand upright.

Left Wing

This is the extensive, but little frequented, area of rock left of Fionn Buttress.

1 Thrutch   90m   Very Difficult   *(1956)*
Start at the extreme left of the crag below two gullies. The route takes the one on the right, a grassy groove followed by a narrow chimney.

2 Claymore   90m   HVS   *(1976)*
Right of Thrutch is a prominent groove capped by an overhang. Claymore takes a direct line to the foot of the groove and then climbs it. Start by traversing grassy slopes to below a steep wall and belay below the right-hand of two recesses, (or reach the same point by climbing the slabs below).
1. 25m Climb the recess and a steep corner-crack. Continue by the crack above then move right to belay.
2. 25m Climb a cracked wall, past a prominent hanging flake at 12m, then the groove above to a ledge near an embedded flake.
3. 20m Move down the ledge and round onto a rib. Follow this to below the final overhung groove.
4. 20m Climb the corner to the overhang, traverse right and up the groove to the top.

3 Happy Wanderer   150m   VS   *(1956)*
This route lies right of Claymore and avoids the final steep tier by traversing right along an obvious grass rake (the Goat Walk).
1. 30m Start up heather and slabs to gain a huge spike embedded in turf in a little

recess at the foot of a prominent purple coloured wall.

2. 15m Traverse left and up slightly into a slabby corner. Continue the traverse and gain a badly overhung recess with a little tree.

3. 20m Climb the vertical right wall by a crack, finishing at a poor stance in another slab floored recess with steep walls.

4. 15m Escape by a left traverse below the belay, across a very steep wall. Ascend grooves and a slab beyond to turf ledges.

5. 20m Climb up to the overhang and the Goat Walk traverse.

6. 50m Continue the traverse to easier ground. A finish can also be made up the wall on the left.

4 Purple Wall   170m   HVS   (1974)

1. 30m Happy Wanderer, pitch 1.

2. 20m Climb the groove above the embedded spike to a stance where the groove widens.

3. 45m 5a Descend the groove for a few feet and traverse right onto the wall. Continuing right would lead to easy ground, so climb half left, taking the easiest line, until roughly above the stance; go straight up to the Goat Walk. A sustained and poorly protected pitch.

4. etc. 75m Finish along the Goat Walk.

5 Tinkerbell   290m   VS   (1957)

The obvious fault bordering Fionn Buttress on the left is the Great Chimney. Lower down it peters out into vegetated grooves. Tinkerbell starts at the lowest point of the heathery slabs, left of the line of the Great Chimney, where a number of fallen blocks lie on the grass. Higher up it passes a prominent cluster of roofs on the left.

1. 40m There is a prominent block lying against the face above and slightly left of the fallen blocks. Climb easy slabs just to its right to belay to the left of its top high above a ledge.

2. 25m Climb the slab directly above the block, cross a little lip and continue until a 12m traverse left becomes desirable. Belay at a slightly overhung turf ledge well out to the left.

3. 45m Traverse left and gain a heather rake. Follow this back to the right until rocks start again.

4. 35m From some perched blocks climb directly and easily up slabs to a slab floored corner. Climb the rib on the right, and belay above the corner at perched blocks.

5. 35m Continue up pock marked slabs, slightly to the right after an initial crack. Belay at a bedded spike on a ledge above to the left.

6. 25m Aim for the right centre of the base of the great block of roofs. Huge flake belay.

7. 10m A short wall behind the flake leads to an easy narrow slab which goes through the overhangs.

8. 30m Continue left over easy slabs, then follow heather to the Goat Walk. Belay in a corner at the foot of a prominent break in the overhangs above, below a minor overhang.

9. 30m Traverse about 8m left along the rake to the last likely point at which lodgement can be made on the wall above. Climb back to the right and up into a steep heathery recess below a steep corner.

10. 15m Traverse left onto the steep wall, then ascend directly to gain an obvious ledge on the left. Easy to the top.

6 Poachers Route   210m   Very Difficult   (1954)

Starting right of Tinkerbell, this route climbs directly up slabs to share a belay at the huge flake under the great block of roofs. Some of the climbing to this point is probably common to Tinkerbell. Poachers Route then traverses right and up slabs and walls to join the Great Chimney which is followed to the top. Start just to the left of the fall line of the Great Chimney, and left of a 30m pinnacle leaning against the face, as seen from the right. Apparently this is a poor and vegetated climb.

Fionn Buttress

This is the massive nose forming the most continuous piece of rock on the crag. It is climbed by the following superb long route.

7 Fionn Buttress   240m   VS ***   (1957)
Although initially vegetated, this route unfolds to give an exposed and varied climb on perfect rock. Harder climbers may be disappointed because the pitches don't match Dragon or Gob but a great mountaineering experience for the VS leader. Start from the highest point of the heather in a bay under the Great Chimney, at the base of a steep, clean slabby wall capped by a prominent roof.

1. 30m 4b Start up the right of the slabby wall for a metre. Traverse right into a corner, climb its right wall and go round onto a ledge. Climb the crack in the wall on the right for 3m then step right onto a slab. Cross this to a chockstone in the chimney beyond.
2. 25m 4a Go up the right wall and then grass trending right. Climb a flake leaning against grey slabs to its top.
3. 15m 4c Climb the slab, then left to a ledge and back right as high as possible for 2m. Then go up to an overhung ledge.
4. 25m 4c Go left to a recess (usually wet) with large bollards. Go up the wet red corner above to a grass recess.
5. 25m 5a Go up corners or walls above to reach the prominent overhang which is surmounted by sensational moves 3m from its right end. Move right above to a stance.
6. 25m 4b Traverse right across the face to a stance on the true nose of the buttress.
7. 20m 4b Gain a flake up on the left by a steep groove above the belay. Above it move a little left, then go up right.
8. 20m 4a Follow the slabs above on the crest to reach a niche.
9. 20m 4a Go up the crest to a heather ledge and perched blocks below an overhanging slab.
10. 20m 4b Climb over the blocks and go up the slab on to a shelf. Move right to its top corner.
11. 20m 4a Finish up the wall above and then left to the top.

8 Fionn Castle   215m   VS *   (1957)
A long variation finish to Fionn Buttress, climbing directly up the face of the buttress, rather than traversing to the right edge. Although the climbing is good this line lacks the fine situations of the normal route. Start from the belay at the end of pitch 5 of Fionn Buttress.

6. 20m From the platform above the overhang climb a groove directly above the belay. Exit left to a perched block.
7. 25m Follow further grooves above.
8. 15m Continue in grooves to a narrow ledge.
9. 35m Move right a little, then go left up the wall onto a slab (hard). Go up this and a slab-ramp on the wall above, across the overhang. Follow this into a corner and climb its right wall to the top.

9 Original Route   200m   VS   (1956)
This is the original line up the buttress. It is vegetated and not as good as its successor, but worthwhile cleaner variations have been made. The fine upper pitches are used by Fionn Buttress. Start at a 10m plinth which lies about 20m left of a prominent curving fault - the Red Scar. This is well below and right from the highest heather bay where Fionn Buttress starts. The route takes the easiest looking groove above the plinth, vegetated in parts, and just left of a steep broad rib.

1. 35m Climb the plinth to a steep wall. Go up the wall to gain a deep groove to the left. Follow this to a steep section.

Fionn Buttress, VS, Carnmore Crag, Beinn a' Chaisgean Mor. Climber Pete Gwatkin (photo Fran Pothecary)

2. 40m Now either follow Achilles, up the steep clean rib using a shallow groove followed by slabs, or climb turfy grooves and chimneys to an overhung niche, followed by turf to the right, then up right over slabs to the foot of a steep wall. By either line head for a niche with two stairs below a short steep corner-crack.

3. 30m Climb the crack and traverse hard left and up to a grassy ramp. From here it is best to take a fairly direct line past a nose of cracked blocks, and so up steep and exposed rock to the traverse ledge and belays at a junction with Fionn Buttress. (Several variants have been made on the section. The original line goes up turf to the bottom corner of the grassy Central Bay, then directly up to an obvious traverse left to reach the same point, 75m.)

4. etc. 95m Finish as for Fionn Buttress up the crest.

10 Achilles 160m VS *   (1975)

A direct version of Original Route, with some good pitches. It crosses Original at the belay niche and short, steep corner-crack. Start at the same point as Original Route at the 10m plinth. The climb heads for the steep broad rib above, on the left side of a steep black streaked wall.

1. 40m Climb the plinth and enter the chimney on the right. Climb the chimney to a wall, past an old peg, and up to a grass ledge in a groove. (Original now continues up the vegetated groove on the left.) Step right onto the crest of the rib and climb a shallow groove to a small ledge.

2. 45m Continue directly up pleasant slabs to beneath a steep wall. Belay in a niche with two stairs below a short steep corner-crack.

3. 40m Climb the crack, traverse hard left then move back right and up to reach a grassy ramp. A few metres up the ramp climb a short crack then finger traverse left for 6m to a grass ledge. Climb a lichenous wall to an overhung grassy bay with an abandoned eyrie.

4. 35m Leave the eyrie on the right and climb an overhung ramp to a shelf. Move left outside some perched blocks to an exposed pulpit stance. Climb up a shallow rib and under an oblique overhang emerging on the right at the end of the long traverse ledge of Fionn Buttress. Several variants have been made in the vicinity of the eagle's eyrie.

5. etc. The pioneers continued up Connie-Onnie, took a slightly descending traverse line across the left wall of Green Corner, then finished up Dragon slab, Abomination crack, and the finish of Dragon! However the natural finish is up pitches 7-11 of Fionn Buttress.

Lower Wall

This is the extensive band of rock below the level of the Central Bay, and includes all the rock to the right of Fionn Buttress. The main landmarks are two broad ribs, the First and Second Ribs. Both are prominent in the morning light and both merge into slabs higher up. The First (left-hand) Rib is bounded on the left by a prominent curving red fault, The Red Scar. The Second Rib has a prominent yellow scar right of its base, bounded on the right by the very steep and obvious recess of Balaton. This has a prominent vertical black streak on its right wall. Right of this is a more vegetated area, the location of Botanists' Boulevard, and right again the distinct shield of overlapping slab and wall is taken by Penny Lane and Strawberry Fields. The Lower Wall routes generally boast some good steep climbing, followed by pleasant slabs which peter out in the Central Bay.

11 Kaleidoscope 115m HVS *   (1967)

Left of the Red Scar fault lies a steep black streaked wall. Kaleidoscope takes the left bordering groove (the right side of the Achilles rib). Start on the right of the 10m plinth of Original Route, some 20m left of the Red Scar fault.

1. 35m 5b Go up slabs to a point below and left of the groove. Climb the groove via a small slab on the right, past a large jammed block. (The groove looks climbable direct but may be wet.)

2. 35m Trend right up slabs towards an overhang on the skyline. Junction with Initiation.

3. 45m Climb the overhang on its right to finish up ribs .

12 Quagga   110m   E1 *   (1988)
This is the obvious right-bordering groove of the black streaked wall. It angles right higher up. Like Kaleidoscope, a good main pitch. Start at a belay just left of the grassy fault running up to the Red Scar.
1. 40m 5b Climb the brown rib just left of a recess, starting on the left side, then move into an obvious groove on the rib's left. Climb up to another groove slanting right, and bulging at the bottom. Climb it to a belay above.
2. 30m Follow the rib on the right, climbing close to the Red Scar, to join Initiation. Go up to belay under an overhang.
3. 45m Finish up ribs to grass.

13 Initiation   140m   Hard Severe   (1957)
This route starts up the approximate line of the Red Scar, then climbs the wall and slabs directly above.
1. 40m Start up the grassy initial fault of the Red Scar, then climb right of the Scar to a belay above a gangway on Red Scar Entry, just short of the Red Scar.
2. 40m Go up left for a few feet, then make an ascending traverse right across the steep red wall above to regain the crest of the rib. Go up this then right past a detached block, and so up a groove on the left. At its top traverse a ledge to the right, and go up to a ledge below a steeper wall. Move left into the Red Scar. Climb the diagonal chimney-crack to a shelf, and then to a niche and chockstone belay. Red Scar Entry trends right here.
3. 30m Climb the wall on the left and go up to a sloping ledge, then briefly up a steep corner. Move right and up to a heather ledge.
4. 30m Go up the boiler-plate wall on the left and traverse right to an overhang which is passed on the left. 45m of easy climbing leads to the Central Bay.

14 Red Scar Entry   150m   VS   (1956)
Starts up the First Rib, right of the fault of the Red Scar, then climbs mainly right of the Scar. Not as good as it was once thought to be. Start at the foot of the First Rib from a slightly overhung recess.
1. 20m Climb a crack on the left for about 4m, then traverse right and up to a slab, returning diagonally left near the top. Belay at an overhung ledge.
2. 15m Evade the overhang by a left traverse. Go up a gangway to a stance just short of the Red Scar.
3. 40m As for Initiation, pitch 2.
4. 15m Climb across the right wall below the overhanging scar. Belay in a niche.
5. 30m Continue the traverse to grassy ledges. Follow these to a good belay high on the wall.
6. 30m Climb the wall going up and left to the forest of perched blocks.

15 Black Magic   120m   VS   (1982)
Between the First and Second Ribs is a recessed area of cliff with a heathery bay. Start up the left corner of the bay.
1. 35m Ascend the left-hand short black corner. Before it finishes exit right onto a gangway. Ascend this and the parallel cracks above, passing through two bulges, to belay underneath the obvious large overhang.
2. 30m Traverse horizontally right for about 6m and climb the obvious right-trending crack system behind the vestigial tree.
3. etc. 55m Continue to the Central Bay.

16 Black Mischief   130m   VS **   (1966)
An enjoyable climb and a useful preamble to Gob. Start at the foot of an obvious black groove at the top right corner of the heather bay. This groove is capped on the right by a conspicuous square-cut overhang. An alternative, more direct, line has also been climbed above pitch 1.
1. 25m 4c Ascend easily to the first bulge in the groove proper and surmount this on the right. Continue up the groove past another bulge and exit left to a stance.

2. 25m 4b Climb up right where the groove steepens at 6m; good spike. Move delicately right under a bulge onto a slab. Traverse diagonally across this to a conspicuous ledge on the skyline. Climb the crack above and exit right with difficulty onto a grass ledge level with and to the right of the square-cut overhang.
3. 20m 4c Climb the cracked wall above (hard above a good ledge at half-height on the right). Continue more easily to large ledges.
4. etc. 60m Easier climbing leads to the Central Bay.

17 Diagonal Route 250m Severe   (1952)
The original climb on the crag. It continues out by the top right corner of the Central Bay to exit onto easy ground by a slabby gangway on the right margin of the Upper Wall. The lower half gives a pleasant approach to the Upper Wall routes. Start on the right side of the heather bay, left of the Second Rib (down and left from the Balaton recess).
1. 25m Go up and traverse right onto a line of ribs slanting right. Continue in this line to a quartzite belay.
2. 20m Step left onto a slab, climb it using a corner-crack and move right round a corner and gain a stance.
3. 10m Go straight up on good holds until it is possible to traverse left and up to a perched block.
4. etc. 195m Easier climbing leads to the slabs and heather of the Central Bay. Traverse up and right to the foot of the ramp of slabs to the right of Carnmore Corner. Climb the slabs to scrambling ground.

18 Yogi 120m HVS   (1962)
Climbs directly onto the crest of the Second Rib and then keeps to its right side. A bit artificial above the steep lower section. Start at the left extremity of Balaton recess, under the Yellow Scar.
1. 35m 5b Start up two great red flakes in the left rib, then climb the crack-line straight above, avoiding a hard bit on the immediate left.
2. 45m Continue up the arete by shallow grooves.
3. 40m Finish up slabs to the Central Bay.

19 999 120m E2 *   (1984)
Climbs the corner on the left side of the Yellow Scar, just right of the great flakes of Yogi. Above this the line is distinctly contrived, keeping to the edge of the rib, right of Yogi, but the climbing is good.
1. 35m 5c Climb the corner to the large roof. Turn this on the left and climb the crack above. Easier climbing leads to a belay.
2. 40m 4c Traverse right to a rib overlooking the recess of Balaton. Climb the rib and finish up the obvious hanging curved groove (common to Dandelion Days).
3. 45m Continue easily to the Central Bay.

20 Dandelion Days 120m E3 *   (1982)
Takes a fierce line up the left side of Balaton recess. Start at the foot of the left-hand corner.
1. 35m 5c Climb the corner-groove for about 25m, then, when over the band of overhangs and slightly below the second stance on Balaton, traverse left across the wall and ascend into the obvious niched overlap. Surmount this and go up the crack to belay on the pinnacled arete.
2. 30m Climb the rib and pull over the overlap to finish up the obvious hanging curved groove.
3. 50m Continue easily to the Central Bay.

21 Balaton 105m HVS **   (1966)
Takes the very steep crack at the right side of the recess, then traverses left under a roof to climb the obvious big corner-line at the back of the recess. This is the best line on the lower Wall, and one of the best routes on the crag, making a fine combination with Dragon with which it is a similar standard.

1. 25m 5a Climb the crack to a belay on the right.
2. 10m 5b Descend a little, step across a crack, and traverse a steep band of slab to the foot of the large corner.
3. 35m 4c Climb the corner to a slab, traverse right, turn an overhang, then move up left to below a big roof. Break out right, then go up to a stance.
4. 45m Move up and left of a rib on the skyline, then continue by slabs to the Central Bay.
Variation Pitch 3: **35m E1 5b**
Provides a more sustained route and still of good quality. Where the route goes right, continue direct up the groove, then join the original route below the big roof.

22 Running Bear   95m   E3   (1981/1988)
Climbs the rib right of Balaton, direct, just right of the broad black streak, then continues straight up the groove above. (The rib was originally climbed with a detour into Boo-Boo at half-height (E2 5b) but this is much inferior). Protection is poor on the lower half of the rib, but good on the hard moves higher up.
1. 25m 6a Start up a tall block (just left of Boo-Boo). Move left over a bulge and climb straight up the crest of the rib. Surmount the top bulge direct via a big jug and a fragile looking sidepull on the left, to belay at the top of a crevasse.
2. 25m 5a Climb the bulge above and go up left into the groove. Climb this to slabs.
3. 45m 5a More slabs lead to the Central Bay.

23 Boo-Boo   105m   HVS   (1966)
Climbs obvious grooves right of the Running Bear rib. Start just right of the tall block of Running Bear.
1. 30m 5a Climb a crack which splits a triangular overhang at 7m. The bulge is most easily climbed on the right; move up a wall slightly rightwards and climb a corner to a ledge and belay left of a larger overhang.
2. 35m Traverse left 3m then back right to a point above the belay. Climb a corner to a ledge, go up the right edge of the wall, then move left and up a slab.
3. 45m Go up the slabs above to the Central Bay.

24 Naughty Alien   105m   HVS   (1981)
A direct line through the break in the roof right of Boo-Boo.
1. 20m 4b Start at the foot of Boo-Boo. Move right up slabs and under an overhang. Work upwards by fluted slabs to belay under the roof.
2. 15m 5a Traverse left and climb through the break in the roof to gain a groove. Climb this to vegetatious slabs.
3. etc. 70m Probably the best finish is to gain the rib of Boo-Boo on the left as soon as possible and climb this to finish.

25 Botanists' Boulevard   135m   Severe   (1956)
Lies up the recessed and vegetated area right of the Balaton recess, leading into the lower right corner of the Central Bay. The original description mentions belaying round a turf pinnacle at one point.
1. 30m Start about 18m right of Running Bear rib, on a heather topped plinth. From the left edge of the plinth ascend into a scoop, then climb up the rib on the right to the top of the scoop. Belay below a small roof.
2. 25m Traverse right, go up a short wall and back above the small roof to a grassy bay.
3. 30m Exit over the left wall and climb up to an undercut slab. Climb this and go left into a steep corner at 20m. Move right over a bush, cross a steep red wall and go up a grassy rake.
4. 50m Go straight up the wall, then steep vegetation, going left when in doubt, to an ash tree in the bottom right corner of the Bay.

The remaining two routes on the Lower Wall lie on a distinctive pale shield of overlapping wall and slab. This is separated from the scrappy Botanists' Boulevard area by a grassy rake which curves up left as a steep fault.

CARNMORE CRAG

7. Fionn Buttress	VS ***	20. Dandelion Days	E3 *
8. Fionn Castle	VS *	21. Balaton	HVS **
11. Kaleidoscope	HVS *	22. Running Bear	E3
14. Red Scar Entry	VS	23. Boo-Boo	HVS
15. Black Magic	VS	25. Botanists' Boulevard	Severe
16. Black Mischief	VS **	26. Penny Lane	HVS **
17. Diagonal Route	Severe	27. Strawberry Fields	HVS *
19. 999	E2 *	28. Connie-Onnie	VS

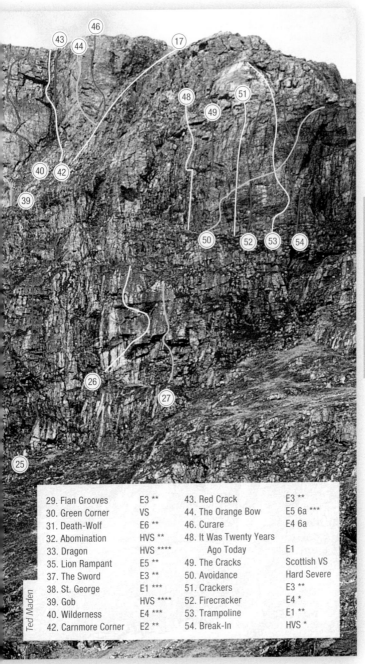

CARNMORE & FISHERFIELD

Ted Maden

29. Fian Grooves	E3 **	43. Red Crack	E3 **
30. Green Corner	VS	44. The Orange Bow	E5 6a ***
31. Death-Wolf	E6 **	46. Curare	E4 6a
32. Abomination	HVS **	48. It Was Twenty Years	
33. Dragon	HVS ****	Ago Today	E1
35. Lion Rampant	E5 **	49. The Cracks	Scottish VS
37. The Sword	E3 **	50. Avoidance	Hard Severe
38. St. George	E1 ***	51. Crackers	E3 **
39. Gob	HVS ****	52. Firecracker	E4 *
40. Wilderness	E4 ***	53. Trampoline	E1 **
42. Carnmore Corner	E2 **	54. Break-In	HVS *

**26 Penny Lane   70m   HVS **   *(1967)*
Gain the grass rake by grassy slabs or an easy traverse from the right. Belay up at the left end of the rake. The route traverses right along the steep wall under a roof.
1. 30m 5a Traverse right along a big flake and continue traversing above a lower roof to go round the corner into the central groove.
2. 25m 4b Go diagonally left under the top overlap and climb over it into a groove.
3. 15m Finish right up slabs to the grassy Gangway.

**27 Strawberry Fields   45m   HVS *   *(1967)*
Start near the right end of the grass rake below a black corner going up to a large roof.
1. 25m 5a Climb the wall on the left of the corner for a few metres, traverse into the corner and climb up to the roof. Move left and go up on quartz to a second smaller roof. Step right onto the arete and go up to a stance.
2. 25m 4b Climb the slabs above trending left to a bulge. Climb this into a grassy crack and go up slabs to easy ground.

Upper Wall

This is the very steep upper band of crag, providing fine climbing with considerable exposure. It lies above the Central Bay, an area of heathery slopes and scraps of slab. Great care is needed in wet conditions.

Approach: Apart from approaches via one of the Lower Wall routes, access or exit can be most easily made either by the Gangway (a series of exposed ledges and steps running from the right, passing above the pale shield of rock containing Penny Lane). Access for a second route on the Upper Wall is possible by descending broken ground to the right of the top slab of Diagonal Route. This is exposed and rather loose (Moderate), but the quickest climbing way back into the Bay from the cliff top. An alternative is to make a largely free 50m abseil down the line of Red Crack (the top of Carnmore Corner is easily found from above on account of the springs) landing on slabs just right of the easy traverse left on pitch 1 of Gob. From here it is 20m of easy down-climbing to the true start of Gob and access to other routes.

The left end of the Upper Wall is bounded by the out thrust nose of Fionn Buttress. To the right its height gradually dwindles. The most obvious features are:
1. A pale easy-angled slab at bottom left. Dragon climbs the slab to the top right corner then takes cracks up the wall above, to the right of a towering corner system.
2. A great roof roughly halfway up the central wall and descending slightly from left to right. Gob climbs up to traverse under this roof from right to left.
3. The unmistakable Carnmore Corner, to the right. There are twin cracks in the back and it is usually wet. Its scale is diminished by a tongue of scrappy terrain extending up from the Bay. The jutting right arete is taken by The Orange Bow.

**28 Connie-Onnie   100m   VS   *(1967)*
A minor climb linking the Bay with the upper part of Fionn Buttress. The left side of the slab at the foot of Dragon is bounded on the left by a big corner – Green Corner. Left of this is a smaller corner. The route climbs this and the slab above.
1. 40m 4c Climb the corner passing loose blocks at the top.
2. 15m Climb the slab to a ledge at the top of Green Corner.
3. 45m Climb slabs on the left and a steep V-chimney, then more slabs to the top. This section is the same as Fionn Buttress.

**29 Fian Grooves   110m   E3 **   *(2000)*
An excellent route based on the bulging arete immediately left of Green Corner. Start as for that route.

1. 45m 5c Go left into an obvious clean groove and follow this to an overhang. Swing out left along a handrail and pull round the left end of the overhang into another groove. Move up the wall on the left, then back right to a crack which is followed to an awkward mantelshelf. Continue straight up the crest to the base of a corner. A fantastic pitch.

2. 20m 4b Climb the corner with surprising ease to a terrace and junction with Green Corner.

3. 20m 5c Above is a shallow leaning groove. Gain this from the left, then follow it to step left.

4. 25m 5a Go directly across a ramp behind to enter and climb a constricted groove to easier ground.

30 Green Corner 85m VS   (1963/1967)
The big corner running up to the great roof above the Dragon Slab. A good main pitch. Start at the base of the corner.

1. 15m Up grassy rocks to a ledge.

2. 20m 4c Continue up the slab and chimney to the roof. Traverse left under it on good holds to a big ledge.

3. 50m Move left and climb the wall above, joining and finishing up Fionn Buttress.

31 Death-Wolf 110m E6 **   (1986)
There are two flake gangways cutting through the great roof above Dragon Slab. This route takes the right-hand one, then climbs the steep wall above, trending right then left. A very strenuous undertaking.

1. 40m Climb the Dragon slab to its top, then traverse 10m left from the left end of the narrow ledge to a peg belay under the gangway. (This could be reached by a direct ascent of the slab).

2. 30m 6b There is no rest on this pitch until 10m above the roof. (The gangway is often wet lower down but this can be avoided on the outside). Climb the gangway out over the lip of the roof, into a little scoop with a hidden sidepull in a crack. Go straight up the wall to a flaky jug then move right and up onto a resting ledge. Climb the little arete and groove above to a belay ledge close to the right arete.

3. 25m 6a From the right end of the ledge move up and across left, then up left to gain isolated knobbles. Traverse right by a thin horizontal crack to gain better holds and pull out right to easy ground. Move up left to the left end of a big heather ledge.

4. 15m 5c Climb the wall above the belay (unprotected for some distance), veering left under an obvious scooped groove and up the wall to the top.

32 Abomination 100m HVS **   (1966)
A towering corner system is formed where the bulging wall of Death-Wolf thrusts out from the main wall. Abomination takes the obvious plummeting groove in the undercut sidewall. Although intimidating, it is not as hard as it looks. A fine climb.

1. 35m Climb the Dragon slab rightwards to its top.

2. 35m 5b From the ledge climb the right-hand groove for a few metres, then step left and climb the hanging crack for 20m to a ledge. Climb the crack on the right with increasing difficulty to a sloping ledge.

3. 30m 4c Continue up the groove to a ledge; climb a chimney to below a square-cut roof; move right and up a slab on loose flakes to the top.

33 Dragon 95m HVS ****   (1957)
The classic original route on the Upper Wall, high in its grade and much harder than Gob. Superbly exposed, it takes an improbable line and is not for nervous seconds. Above and right of the big corner system is a huge jutting triangular roof. Dragon takes obvious cracks right of the main corners to turn the roof on the left. Start at the base of the pale grey slab.

1. 35m 4b Climb to a grass patch then trend right up the slab to belay on a narrow

ledge under the main wall. (Alternatively, the slab can be missed out by climbing a short chossy groove at the top of the right retaining wall).

2. 35m 4c Climb a groove for 5m, passing the small roof which fills it, on the right. Traverse left out of the cracks a short distance above the roof to gain easier grooves. Pedestal belay 9m up on the right.

3. 15m 5a Climb a steep short wall to reach a yellow chimney up on the left. Climb this and exit left at the top to a tiny perch under the great roof. Traverse the steep wall on the left to belay in a little bay. (Seconds falling from the traverse might have to prussik!).

4. 10m Traverse round left and up to the top.

34 Beastmaster 50m E4   (1986)
This climbs the corners just left of Dragon. Escape is possible back into Dragon in places, but the climbing is good. Start from the ledge above Dragon Slab.

1. 20m 5b Climb the obvious crack just left of the start of Dragon, going past the left side of the small roof. Go up an easy section of Dragon to belay under the bulge at the base of the corners.

2. 20m 6a Climb the awkward bulge up left to enter the first corner. Climb this and two succeeding corners direct to the belay in the little bay left of the Dragon traverse.

3. 10m 5b Finish directly up the flake-choked corner above.

There are two routes, of which Lion Rampant is the better, up the fine wall right of Dragon. They take minor breaks through the main roof on either side of the main break taken by Gob.

35 Lion Rampant 85m E5 **   (1986)
1. 20m 6b A crack in the steep right-bounding wall of the Dragon Slab provides a good introductory pitch. Climb the strenuous crack and go up to the ledge under the main wall.

2. 35m 6a A serious pitch. Climb the wall past a spike at 10m to an expanding block. Pull straight over the bulge and move up right to small ledges at the foot of a great scoop in the wall. Go up left then right and up to an expanding flake. Move left to another flake and pull onto the left-slanting ledge above. Continue directly up the unprotected wall above, just beside the arete overlooking the groove of The Sword, past a poor peg runner, to gain a ledge. Go left along this to belay at the right side of great detached blocks.

3. 15m 6a Climb the wall right of the belay to gain the traverse of Gob, under the roof. Climb the bulge up into a small corner then pull out right on layaways to reach slabs and belay above.

4. 15m 5c Climb straight up to the roof above. Traverse left and pull over the roof, using a jug to swing up and right to blocks. Veer left and up the steep wall to an overhanging finish on big flakes.

36 Ride of the Valkyrie 65m E5   (1986)
Another serious line up the Dragon wall, rather artificial but more direct than Lion Rampant. Start from the ledge above Dragon Slab.

1. 30m 6a Follow Lion Rampant (pitch 2) to the expanding block, then step left to surmount the bulge at a thin crack. Climb up slightly left to a peg runner. Step left and go up to gain a good horizontal flake running across the wall. Step up right then back left and straight up the wall to gain a left-pointing jug. Go up and left to ledges on Dragon and a belay on top of the pedestal.

2. 35m 6a Climb the cracks up the wall above, then move right and up Gob for a few metres, below the big break in the roofs. Move up left and go rightwards up a bulge to gain undercut slabs under the main roof. Traverse rightwards up under the roof and pull out right using undercuts under a nose to gain easier ground. Finish obviously as for Gob.

37 The Sword 80m E3 ** (1967)

An atmospheric and very direct route taking the big groove above the cave right of the Dragon Wall. One of the best natural lines at Carnmore, but with some poor rock. Start at the right end of the ledge above Dragon Slab.

1. 35m 5c Traverse right for about 3m on the lip of the overhang, then climb up and right to gain the main groove. Climb the groove to a small stance at the Swallow's Nest of Gob. Alternatively, use the original start (5c): Climb the wall for about 5m then traverse right to the arete. Continue delicately down and right across a steep slab, then right and up to reach the main groove.
2. 20m 6a Climb up and right through the steep break in the roof (therefore crossing Gob) to gain the rib and go up to a stance.
3. 25m Climb the shallow groove above to the top, the original finish of Gob.

38 St. George 90m E1 *** (1967)

This route takes the fine steep crack-line in the wall right of the cave of Sword.

1. 20m 5b Climb a short wall to the foot of the crack, which has an overhang at 8m. Climb the groove to the overhang. Pull round this into a sentry box and climb the wall on the left to a superb stance on top of a big doubtful flake.
2. 40m 5a Climb the groove for 6m, then traverse left to another obvious groove. Go up this for 8m, traverse left round the arete to join The Sword, and climb up to the Swallow's Nest under the roof. Now joining Gob, move left to a pulpit belay.
3. 35m 4c Take the obvious break right through the roof. Finish direct up the left-slanting fault.

39 Gob 110m HVS **** (1960)

The line of least resistance on the Upper Wall, snaking left under the main roof to find its main break. A classic, with all the best that Carnmore has to offer, huge holds and tremendous exposure. VS climbing in an impressive position and comparable in difficulty to Dream of White Horses at Gogarth. Start at the right end of the main face, where the Central Bay begins to rise up into the base of Carnmore Corner.

1. 30m 4c Traverse left along an overhung ledge to a break in the overhang; go up right and climb a shallow corner to a belay.
2. 45m 4c Traverse away left by the easiest line under the great roof to negotiate an out-thrust shield of rock (the Swallow's Nest) where The Sword and St. George come up from below. Continue the traverse to a good pulpit not far right from Dragon's pedestal.
3. 35m 4c Take the obvious break up and right through the roof. Finish direct up the left-slanting fault.

Variation: **The Original Finish 45m 4c**
After going right through the roof traverse away right to finish up a steep corner.

40 Wilderness 80m E4 *** (1980)

A diagonal crack-line (unclimbed) cuts across both walls of Carnmore Corner. Jivaro Crack is the thinner crack running vertically above the diagonal one on the left wall; this route climbs the wall to its left on immaculate rock. It was climbed on-sight and has had few repeat ascents. Start by scrambling up to an obvious diagonal break running up left.

1. 20m 5c Climb the break, which has an awkward bulging start.
2. 35m 6a Go up the diagonal crack a short way, then traverse horizontally left on jugs to the base of a thin crack. Climb this, then go straight up into a groove system which is followed out left to a scoop. Step across the scoop on to the arete and follow this past twin cracks to a ledge at the base of a corner.
3. 25m 5a Climb the corner, right of the original finish of Gob.

41 Jivaro Crack 60m E4 * (1987)

A well protected climb apart from a bold bit leaving the diagonal crack. Start as for Wilderness.

1. 20m 5c Wilderness, pitch 1.
2. 20m 6b Move right up the wide diagonal crack, then climb a blind crack-line to a rest at a bucket. (The crack splits before rejoining; the thin right fork was taken on the first ascent). Pull up over the top into an obvious slabby groove and go up this to move up right to beside a detached block.
3. 20m 5c Step left from the block and go up a small hanging corner to pull over the bulge to good holds. Join the original finish of Gob about 10m below the top.

42 Carnmore Corner 65m E2 ** _(1968)_

There is a spring in the hollow at the top of this climb so a lengthy spell of good weather is needed for it to dry up. Although relatively short, the Corner is a route of some character; steep and intimidating. The obvious direct start is nearly always wet and slimy so the route starts to the right before moving left into the corner. A curving fault with two recesses undercuts the right wall. Start below and left of the lower one.
1. 40m 5b Climb slabby rocks up and left, then go up steeply into a niche just up left from the second recess (old pegs). Go straight up for a short way, then quit the crack-line to follow a diagonal line, starting as a small ramp leading up left into the corner. Belay below the big overhang.
2. 25m 5a Move left, up and delicately back right and finish up an easier crack.
Variation: **Direct Start 50m E3 5c** _(1997)_
A brilliant varied pitch, though one of the last routes to dry on the cliff. Start at some horizontal pockets high on the slab, about 8m above the start of Wilderness. Climb the corner and hand traverse right on a large block at its top to gain the normal route. Continue up this, then direct up an awkward hand crack (wet) to finish up the easier final corner.

43 Red Crack 65m E3 ** _(1988)_

Climbs the right-hand crack-line all the way. It is quicker drying than the corner.
1. 20m 5a Climb Carnmore Corner to a belay in the niche.
2. 45m 6a Continue straight up the crack-line to a resting place at a niche under a big bulge. Climb the bulge (crux) and follow the easier fault to the top.

44 The Orange Bow 35m E5 6a *** _(1985)_

The impressive arete right of Carnmore Corner. Start at ledges up on the right, 10m above the last slab of Diagonal Route. Traverse out left along a slabby shelf and negotiate a tricky bulge to move up left to big footholds under the bulging edge. Swing out left on flakes and climb a vague intermittent crack-line up the overhanging wall for 10m to good runners before the crack peters out. Traverse right and up slightly for 5m to gain the edge and a rest. Climb up the edge, as the angle eases, and finish up the left-slanting crack.

45 Left-Hand Start 25m E5 6b ** _(1988)_

This good pitch gives the route some length, but is probably harder than the edge itself. Start below and left of the first recess of the curving fault undercutting the right wall of the Corner. Move up to the recess and swing up right onto a platform. Go up on to a bulging wall, swing left and up to a resting place. Peg runner on the right. Pull up to a good pocket, move up left to a flake, then make a hard move across right to jugs. Poor peg runner. Climb straight up the wall to gain a horizontal fault and a resting place. Traverse right and slightly down to a flake-crack and hanging belay (peg above) under the "vague crack" of the edge pitch.

46 Curare 30m E4 6a _(1985)_

The obvious crack-line on the right wall of the Orange Bow prow. Start at the same belay ledges above the slab of Diagonal. Climb a jam crack slanting up right, then traverse across left and up to an awkward niche under a layback crack. Climb this strenuously to a ledge and finish up the crack-line over a roof.

Gob, HVS, Carnmore Crag, Beinn a' Chaisgean Mor. Climber Paul Winder
(photo Will Herman)

Grey Wall

This is the wall right of the Central Bay, just above the Gangway approach.

47 The Kady   60m   Scottish VS   *(1966)*
Start from the Gangway, left from the Grey Wall proper. The route follows a break in the overhanging wall running into a hanging corner capped by an overhang which is obvious from below.
1. 45m Climb a heathery groove to beneath the overhanging wall.
2. 45m Climb the break in the wall trending right to the corner. Climb the corner until forced right onto a slab which is followed to a belay.

48 It Was Twenty Years Ago Today   50m   E1   *(1987)*
Well right of The Kady, on the left side of the Grey Wall proper, is a prominent red diedre. This is the line.
1. 25m 4c Climb up to the diedre, then climb it to a stance.
2. 25m 5a Hand traverse a few feet left to two spikes, then up by the line of least resistance. Poorly protected at first.

49 The Cracks   40m   Scottish VS   *(1967)*
1. 20m Climb cracks just right of the prominent red diedre to a ledge on the right.
2. 20m Go up the crack above to ledges.

50 Avoidance   65m   Hard Severe   *(1957)*
A devious line which goes rightwards across the Grey Wall. Start just right of The Cracks.
1. 30m 4c Traverse right along an ascending ledge for 15m, then climb a very steep crack and go up left to a ledge. Climb a short groove on the right to a ledge running right.
2. 20m Traverse right, climb up a rib in the corner and traverse right again to ledges below the steep upper wall.
3. 15m Continue traversing around the rib on the right and step across a groove to more broken ground. Scrambling to the top.

51 Crackers   70m   E3 **   *(1985)*
The central parallel cracks on the Grey Wall. Start 15m right of The Cracks.
1. 25m 5c Climb a steep crack.
2. 45m 5a Continue up cracks. Easier to finish.

52 Firecracker   70m   E4 *   *(2000)*
Another fine route with a strenuous first pitch taking the obvious crack-line immediately right of and parallel to Crackers. Start at a huge block.
1. 20m 6a Climb a steep jam crack on the front of the block to the base of the crack proper, then forge up this to an evil stretch (crux).
2. 50m 5c Continue directly up the groove over a bulge to easier ground below a scoop. Pull up left into the scoop, then continue steeply trending slightly right to the top.

53 Trampoline   100m   E1 **   *(1967)*
A good climb previously graded HVS 5a, so there may be an easier line. Some 12m left of the right-hand chimney of the Grey Wall there is a traverse line across the steep wall. Start below a niche a few metres along this line.
1. 25m 5a Climb into the niche and traverse right until the angle eases. Climb the wall above by twin cracks and go up to a good stance beneath an obvious deep crack.
2. 35m 5c Climb slabs on the left to below the crack. Gain the steep crack from the right and climb it to easy slabs which lead to blocks.
3. 40m Finish up slabs.

Variation: **The Proprietor   35m   E2 5c**   *(1997)*
A well protected direct finish to The Trampoline. Follow that route to beneath steep
twin cracks in the headwall. Climb the left crack, moving into the deeper right crack
with difficulty. Up this past a dubious looking block near its top, then more easily
up slabs above to a large block at the top.

54 Break-In   65m   HVS *   *(1984)*
Start at the prominent chimney at the right end of the Grey Wall.
1. 30m 4c   Climb the chimney for 7m, then break out left onto the wall by a short
hand-traverse. Climb the wall above and trend left to a good stance below a
leftward-sloping groove.
2. 35m 5a   Leave the stance on the right and climb cracks to reach a V-groove.
Climb the groove, breaking out left to finish up the crack above.

There is one remaining route lying up the left side of the gully across right from the
Grey Wall. It is not very good, but is the easiest route on the crag.

55 Needle   170m   Difficult   *(1957)*
Start just left of the gully, at the foot of some pale easy slabs a metre left of a
detached block.
1. 35m   Climb the slabs for 30m, then traverse left across a turfy groove and up
another slab to below a small lip.
2. 35m   Climb the lip and continue directly above to belay at the foot of a steep
wall below a conspicuous overhang.
3. 20m   Climb the wall to the overhang, escaping on the left.
4. 30m   Continue directly above, aiming for the conspicuous 'needle's eye' above.
5. 15m   Up a blunt rib just left of the gully.
6. 20m   Ignore the easier ground to the right and climb the red wall on the left,
then another short wall and finally a short slab to reach the foot of the 'needle's
eye'.
7. 15m   Climb the chimney-crack and surmount the eye. Easy ground leads to the
top.

Girdle Traverses

There are two girdle traverses of the Upper Wall, from left to right. A third traverse,
of the Lower Wall from right to left, uses Achilles and Fionn Buttress to link with
either of the upper traverses to make a huge 'C' shaped expedition. This is Ulysses.
Only key sections are described in detail, since much variation is possible, and the
route finding provides half the attraction of these adventurous wanderings. There
are some marvellous pitches but allocation of stars is up to yourself.

56 Odyssey   550m   HVS   *(1974)*
Start high up on the left of the crag under the Left Wing. Use Purple Wall to gain
the Goat Walk (probably the hardest part of the girdle), or start up Happy
Wanderer. Continue easily along the Goat Walk then reverse a section of Tinkerbell
down right to reach a grass terrace below the great block of stepped overhangs.
Climb diagonally up right in two pitches to gain the fault-line of the Great Chimney.
From a stance here the pioneers descended the fault for a metre to make
lodgement on the right wall. The edge above was climbed for 6m and then a
diagonal traverse made up right across Fionn Castle aiming for a small col on the
far side, overlooking the D-shaped slab. Descend easily over perched blocks to a
stance at the top of Green Corner (6m). Reverse the main pitch of Green Corner,
traverse across the slab and go up to the ledge under the main wall, as for Dragon.
Climb Dragon to the Pedestal belay. A choice of lines leads across and up right to
the Pulpit of Gob. Follow Gob through the overhang and take the original line of
Gob away right above the great roof. Finish up the corner-line of Gob original, or
continue right into Carnmore Corner, as for Ring of Bright Water.

57 Ring of Bright Water   350m   HVS   *(1974)*
This takes a higher traverse line than Odyssey, starting up Fionn Buttress. Follow
Fionn Buttress, with the option of including Connie-Onnie, to the ledge at the top
of Green Corner (200m). Continue up Fionn Buttress to a shelf and move right into
a corner (20m). A grassy ledge leads to a small col and thence down easily to join
the top pitch of Abomination (10m). Continue up Abomination and traverse right
to the top pitch of Dragon. Belay in the little bay beside the crucial traverse (10m).
Reverse the Dragon traverse and descend the yellow overhanging chimney to cross
right to the Pulpit on Gob (25m). Follow Gob through the overhang and away right
above the great roof. Belay at loose blocks on a shattered pillar (40m). Continue
traversing below a bulging wall to the stance among the overhangs of Carnmore
Corner, a pitch similar in outlook and difficulty to the Fionn Buttress traverse (25m).
Continue up the second pitch of the Corner (strenuous) and delicately across the
slabby upper section of the right wall (30m).

58 Ulysses   600m   HVS   *(1975)*
A unique 'C' shaped traverse providing some 600m of continuously enjoyable
climbing. The Lower Wall is traversed from right to left, the easiest start being by
Botanists' Boulevard, to traverse left into Balaton at the stance above pitch 1. The
pioneers continued by the second pitch of Balaton but narrowly failed to cross the
left rib directly. Instead a groove with overlaps was climbed to gain the crest of the
rib and a 15m descent made via Yogi or Diagonall. From Diagonal the traverse was
continued and part of the second pitch of Black Mischief reversed to the stance at
the top of pitch 1. A direct ascent was made for 6m to traverse across left into the
Black Scar, and so to join the Red Scar. From Red Scar find a way across left and up
into the eagle's eyrie of Achilles, ultimately to link up with Fionn Buttress, and one
of the upper traverses.

TORR NA H-IOLAIRE

**(NG 985 772)   Alt 350-500m   South-West to West facing   Map p162
Diagram p200**

This is the great rocky tower directly above Carnmore Lodge, leading to the summit
of Sgurr na Laocainn. As with Carnmore Crag the rock is excellent and the aspect
sunny. However the crag is broken by terraces into several tiers and although many
climbers will prefer to join routes together to give one long climb, it is easier to
describe the tiers separately. The main features are as follows:
1. The Lower Wall, which slants down from left to right, with two prominent ribs
at the left end, below a huge perched block. Well round to the right is South Gully.
2. Harlequin Wall, which is the short steep 40m wall immediately above the
perched block.
3. Above and left of Harlequin Wall is a steep 60m wall with some prominent
clean-cut corners and ribs. This is Carcase Wall, which has the hardest routes on the
Torr.
4. Above and right of Carcase Wall is an area of broken grey rock, the Lower
Summit Buttress.
5. Below the summit of the hill is a long wall of steep clean rock with twin chimneys
at the left and a huge right-angled recess at the right. This is Upper Summit
Buttress.
6. Coming down and left from Upper Summit Buttress is a fine crag facing more
towards the col on the north side of Sgurr na Laocainn. This is the West face of
Upper Summit Buttress which has some of the best climbs on the Torr.

Descent: From most of the climbs descent on the left is easiest. However, from the
east side of the terrace below Summit Buttress a goat track crosses South Gully,
threads a way through very steep ground and then descends the next grassy spur
to the east. This track is also useful for direct access to climbs such as Rainbow
Corner.

Lower Wall

1 Rose Rib   65m   Very Difficult   *(1957)*
This route takes the left-hand of the two red ribs below the huge perched block.
Start at the foot of the rib, which is undercut.
1. 30m Use a spike to gain the wall. Climb a short overhang, then the short wall
to a pleasant slab leading to a narrow turf terrace. Continue up the rib to a turf
ledge.
2. 35m Climb slabs and grooves just left of the crest to reach the great perched
block.

2 The Long Reach   80m   VS   *(1957)*
This takes the right-hand red rib. Start at a black greasy recess at the foot of the rib.
Climb 6m to a steep grassy bay. Traverse right onto the rib and ascend 12m to a
slight overhang. Step left and climb grooves to easier ground. Follow the rib easily
and the rocks above to the great perched block.

3 The Eyrie   70m   VS   *(1978)*
Start below and right of The Long Reach at a large boulder where a traverse line
leads across right to a hanging corner.
1. 40m Climb right and up for 15m; traverse right and up a short groove; at the
top move left onto a slab under the prominent overhang. Follow the slab to the
ledge on the left.
2. 30m Climb up for 3m, then left into a corner; climb this and the easy slabs
above.

4 Sickle   60m   VS   *(1966)*
Start, as for The Eyrie, at a large boulder, where a traverse line leads across right to
a hanging corner.
1. 25m Traverse diagonally right across the steep wall to just beyond the foot of
the hanging corner.
2. 35m Go right for 6m across an easy ledge into another corner and climb this to
a large grass ledge. Step back left onto the steep wall and climb it by the line of
least resistance. Continue up steep rock and grass to the top.

5 Ipswich Rib, Lower Part   70m   Very Difficult   *(1956)*
Start at the foot of a little rib below and at the right end of the Lower Wall. This is
the lowest point of the rocks.
1. 30m Follow the crest of the rib to where it joins the steeper wall at the foot of
a crack.
2. 20m Climb a few metres, traverse right and continue into a niche below a
bulging overhang.
3. 20m Step down to a ledge below the right wall of the niche, then up for 5m
and traverse a slab into an overhanging chimney; climb this to easy ground.
The route can be continued by easy scrambling for about 250m to the Upper
Summit Buttress. Keep near the crest of the vague rib and aim for the great slab
recess on the right of Upper Summit Buttress. The upper part of the climb is
described below.

Harlequin Wall

6 Intimidation   35m   HVS   *(1957)*
Loose rock makes this a serious climb. Start at the foot of the wall, right of the huge
perched block. An obvious crack slants up right. Gain the top of an initial 10m
pinnacle by easy grooves on its right. Follow cracks with increasing difficulty on
decreasingly stable rock, over a bulge at 20m, to the crux at 25m. Easier ground
above leads to the terrace.

TORR NA H-IOLAIRE

1. Rose Rib	Very Difficult	15. Cleopatra	E2 5c *
2. The Long Reach	VS	16. Frogmarch	Difficult
6. Intimidation	HVS	17. Toad Hall	HVS 5a
7. Holly Tree Wall	VS	20. Juniper Groove	Severe
8. Skeleton Corner	VS	21. Ipswich Rib, Upper Part	Difficult **
9. Skull	E1 **	22. Rainbow Corner	VS
11. Cadaverous Crack	E1	23. Sunday Climb	Severe
12. Wishbone Rib	HVS *	27. Red Admiral	VS
13. Hyena Corner	HVS *	29. Hieroglyphics	VS **
14. Sarcophagus	VS **	30. Tiger Lily	VS **

Andy Nisbet

7 Holly Tree Wall   45m   VS *(1978)*
This lies below and left of Harlequin Wall, on a black wall of better rock with a holly tree. Climb up to the tree, step right and follow a crack for 5m. Traverse left across a slab and back right under a huge block into a chimney forming the right side of the block. Climb the chimney and belay on top of the block. Traverse right for 5m and climb the wall just left of an unpleasant gully.

Carcase Wall

8 Skeleton Corner   65m   VS *(1967)*
The big right-angled corner with a smooth right wall at the left end of Carcase Wall.
1. 35m Climb the steep wall directly below the start of the corner, and follow the corner by walls and ledges to beneath an overhang where the corner steepens.
2. 30m Continue up the corner on the right to the top.

9 Skull   55m   E1 ** *(1967)*
This takes the rib on the right of Skeleton Corner, the prominent feature of which is a steep red slab split by a thin crack.
1. 35m 5b Climb a groove just right of Skeleton Corner to the bottom left edge of the steep red slab. Traverse right across the slab, and climb its overhanging right edge to a ledge. Climb the fault above, trending slightly right to a large ledge beneath a corner.
2. 20m Go up the corner until a move right can be made. Continue up right to the crest and back left to finish.

10 Carnivorous Crack   45m   E2 * *(1988)*
The large recess right of Skull contains two cracks; this takes the left-hand one.
1. 25m 5c Climb the crack, bulging at the top, and move right into the main recess.
2. 20m 4c Finish up the left-hand blocky fault.

11 Cadaverous Crack   50m   E1 *(1978)*
1. 30m 5b Climb the right-hand crack in the recess past three overhangs to a ledge.
2. 20m 4c Climb the dank, vegetated chimney above, then step left to finish.

12 Wishbone Rib   45m   HVS * *(1967)*
Start at the bottom left of the rib right of Cadaverous Crack.
1. 30m Surmount a bulge. Climb up, then left, to gain a ledge which slopes up right. Go along this to the crest and then straight up to a bay.
2. 15m Climb up right, then steeply to finish.

13 Hyena Corner   40m   HVS * *(1988)*
The corner right of Wishbone Rib (often wet).
1. 15m 4b Climb a wall by the easiest line to reach a ledge in the main recess.
2. 25m 5a Climb the right-hand crack, and so to the top of the corner. Easier rocks to the top.

Lower Summit Buttress

This is the area of rock between the top of Carcase Wall and the terrace below the central part of Upper Summit Buttress. **Skyline Route** (60m Very Difficult 1951) follows the left side and is naturally combined with one of the routes on the Upper Buttress.

Upper Summit Buttress

The obvious feature of the twin chimneys at the left of Upper Summit Buttress makes a convenient starting point for description. The climbs are described from left to right from here, then (perhaps rather illogically) the climbs on the West Face of Upper Summit Buttress are described.

CARNMORE & FISHERFIELD

Alec Keith

Ipswich Rib, Upper Part, Difficult, Torr na h-Iolaire, Beinn a' Chaisgean Mor. Climber Susan Blackwood

**14 Sarcophagus 60m VS ** *(1957)*
This takes the rocks left of the left twin chimney via an enormous flake. It is a good climb, steep and exposed.
1. 15m   Start up a vertical wall, then an obvious chimney above to reach chockstones at an overhung ledge.
2. 35m 4c Move up and right to the foot of an overhung groove with a corner-crack. Climb this and traverse left to the foot of more grooves that lead to the base of the great flake. Climb the flake by the left-hand chimney (loose blocks) and go up to a large ledge.
3. 10m Ascend the slab above to a large block on the skyline.

15 Cleopatra 45m E2 5c * *(1988)*
Left of Sarcophagus is a steep nose. This route takes the crack-line just to the left, well seen from the top of Carnmore Crag. Start up on the right. The initial bulge is the crux.

16 Frogmarch 55m Difficult *(1957)*
This is the left-hand of the twin chimneys, wet and unpleasant.
1. 20m Start from the terrace below and climb steep rock and vegetation to the foot of the chimney.
2. 25m Climb the chimney to a small cave, then climb the right wall to a stance and belay on a rib.
3. 10m Move left and continue to the top.

17 Toad Hall 45m HVS 5a *(1988)*
The right-hand chimney, though dark and messy, gives a good old fashioned route.

18 Sapros 60m VS *(1966)*
To the right of the twin chimneys are a nose and then a steep corner-groove. This climb attempts to follow the wall right of the groove. The rock is doubtful.

1. 35m Start about 10m right of the groove. A line of weakness leads up left for 15m. Just short of an insecure grass ledge break right and make an ascending traverse right above the lip of an overhang.

2. 25m Ascend right across a steep slab to easy ground (junction with Tantivy Tower). Continue to the top.

19 Tantivy Tower   65m   Difficult   *(1951)*
This takes the true nose of the Upper Summit Buttress. Start near an overhung recess at the foot of the frontal wall.

1. 15m Go up a short wall, then to the foot of a steeper wall.

2. 25m Climb the wall, moving left then up the edge to large perched blocks on the shelf above.

3. 25m Go up the blocks to the right and rightwards to a shelf below the final short tier. Reach a small recess at waist height in the wall above and climb to the top.

20 Juniper Groove   60m   Severe   *(1957)*
Start about 20m right of Tantivy Tower at the bottom right-hand corner of a large slab. On the left is a corner and a rib which juts out a little from the face.

1. 30m Go diagonally left up the slab to gain grooves in the corner and climb these to a platform.

2. 20m Climb the grooves to the terrace below the final tier.

3. 10m Climb this to the top.

The next few climbs start at a somewhat lower level, which can be reached by following a lower terrace round to the right.

**21 Ipswich Rib, Upper Part   60m   Difficult ** **   *(1956)*
This is the continuation of the lower part of Ipswich Rib. Traditionally the routes are combined to give a long and enjoyable climb. Start below a rib running up the left edge of the great slab recess that lies towards the right of Upper Summit Buttress.

1. 20m Climb a chimney just right of the rib and go up slabs to the foot of a steep crack.

2. 15m Traverse right to a platform below the diedre in the slab recess. Mantelshelf and traverse left to the top of the crack.

3. 25m Climb a chimney behind a flake and follow slabs to the top, keeping close to the crest.

The next two climbs start at a somewhat lower level, which can be reached by scrambling down to a lower terrace.

22 Rainbow Corner   65m   VS   *(1957)*
This is the diedre above the great slab recess. Start a little right of a point directly below the corner, at a shallow V-groove.

1. 40m Climb the groove and continue more or less directly by further grooves to a small bay. Leave this at the back and gain the foot of the main corner.

2. 25m 4c Climb the corner and finish up the easier groove.

23 Sunday Climb   60m   Severe   *(1957)*
Start 15m right of Rainbow Corner, below a prominent partly detached flake.

1. 35m Climb a series of corners and slabs to the lower right corner of the slab recess below Rainbow Corner.

2. 25m Climb a slab to below the right end of a large roof. Traverse right to the edge, then go up ledges. From here it is possible to traverse right into South Gully, or climb short walls and ledges to the top.

24 Goats' Groove   85m   Very Difficult   *(1957)*
Start at the lowest south-west point of Upper Summit Buttress, slightly up the right-bounding gully.

1. 10m Climb a steep groove that is awkward to start.

2. 20m Cross heathery rock leftwards to perched blocks.
3. 25m Go up and left to a slabby rib, climb this and continue to a ledge with a chimney at the back.
4. 20m Climb the chimney to a ledge; belay on the left at a fallen block.
5. 10m Step from the top of the block onto the wall behind and ascend the rocks above to the top.

West Face

The climbs here are described from left to right, starting with the routes nearest the col on the north side of Sgurr na Laocainn and finishing with routes just below Sarcophagus. An obvious feature of the West Face is the large red streaked slab of Hieroglyphics. Right of this a grassy ramp slants up to the right while left of the slab is a deep T shaped chimney. Left again is another big striped slab, Red Admiral.

25 Wester 105m Very Difficult (1957)

Start near the left end of the face, about 10m right of a deep-cut grassy gully leading to a cave, at a boulder below a striated rib.
1. 30m Go up an obvious line from the boulder, over a perched block, to the foot of the striated rib. Move left over a flake, and up to reach a small grassy ledge above the gully on the left.
2. 25m Climb behind a narrow boulder on the right, step left onto a rib, then up to a narrow ledge below an overhang. Pass this on the right and go straight up to a wide grass ledge.
3. 20m Climb a narrow wet chimney to another ledge.
4. 30m Traverse left and go up easier rocks to the top.

26 Suspension 90m Severe (1959)

Start 2m right of Wester, up slabs leaning at right-angles to the cliff. Follow a ledge rising to the right. Avoid an overhang on the right and climb 30m to a ledge and belay. Climb easier rock to a broad rake. Ascend a right-trending crack to a notch in the overhangs above. Climb the notch to a ledge above, just left of a prominent chimney. Climb a steep wall for 15m on the left of the chimney and finish up easier rocks.

27 Red Admiral 125m VS (1957)

A pleasant if somewhat scrappy route, not as good as the appearance of the first pitch might suggest. Start some way left of the T shaped chimney, at the foot of a narrow wedge of red and black striped slab.
1. 45m 4c Go up the corner on the right of the slab for 10m, then go diagonally left across the slab to the edge. Make a tricky move up, then climb the easing slab to the top.
1a. Original Line. Not as dramatic, but easier. Start up the corner as before, but continue up the slab just left of the corner (40m). Continue to the rake and gully (20m).
2. 20m Climb broken ground trending right to reach a left-rising rake.
3. 20m 4a Climb a rib on the right of a conspicuous gully.
4. 40m 4b Continue up the rib to the top. Difficulties are avoidable.

28 Eryr 135m Severe (1970)

1. 20m Climb the deep T shaped chimney to a line of overhangs.
2. 45m Traverse left along the overhung ledge for 5m to gain and follow a bottomless groove.
3. and 4. 70m Climb right, then left along a rake and right to the foot of an open chimney, which is followed to the top.

An earlier climb, **West Face Ledge Route** (Difficult 1952), traverses further left from the bottomless groove, and then breaks through and takes the line of least resistance, leftwards, to the top.

29 Hieroglyphics 130m VS ** * (1957)*

This well named route gives an excellent first pitch, possibly only Hard Severe, but is easier and not as good thereafter. Start immediately right of the deep T shaped chimney, at the diamond-shaped slab streaked in green and red.

1. 35m 4b Climb direct to ledges at 5m, then diagonally left to a green slab near the edge at 20m. Easier climbing leads to a large grass ledge above and belay at the foot of a short overhanging corner.

2. 35m Climb the corner, then go directly up by a rib just right of wet grooves. Belay at the foot of a steeper wall where a prominent forefinger of rock guards the foot of a deep groove.

3. 20m Climb the groove until above a short overhanging section.

4. 35m Climb a rib on the left, then scramble to the top.

30 Tiger Lily 120m VS ** * (2001)*

A route designed to keep to the cleanest rock. Start about 10m right of Hieroglyphics, at the right end of the level base of the slab.

1. 45m 4b Climb the main slab trending slightly left to reach and climb a right-facing corner near the top. Continue up and slightly right to a pedestal which is at the right end of the grass ledge of Hieroglyphics.

2. 45m 4b Climb the steep wall behind the pedestal on big holds, then continue slightly right on equally big holds, keeping to the best rock, until grassy ground is found on the right.

3. 30m Climb leftwards up a vague rib to the top.

31 Sigma 55m VS *(1957)*

A grass rake runs up rightwards below the Upper Summit Buttress from Hieroglyphics. About 60m up this is a Cioch like pinnacle on the right and just above this an obvious line of weakness runs across the wall on the left towards a short V-chimney.

1. 15m Follow the line of weakness and belay on top of the pinnacle forming the outside of the chimney.

2. 40m Climb the black corner above for 5m, step out left to the crest, move up and back right. Surmount an overhang on good holds, move right and climb up to easier ground.

32 Baird's Route 120m Very Difficult *(1933)*

To the right of the start of Sigma a ridge runs up to the left from the grass rake. Start just below this, where a shelf slopes up into a vertical crack. Climb the shelf and crack, avoiding the top overhang by the wall on the right. Go up the arete and into a gully flanked on the right by a steep wall. A crack in this gives a good pitch; continue easily to the top.

CARNAN BAN

(NG 999 764) 652m

PRACTICE PRECIPICE

(NG 996 767) Alt 430m West facing

This is a small outcrop just across the stream from the Carnmore to Shenavall path, about 60m above the zigzags above the Dubh Loch. A steep wall lies to the left of three easier angled ribs. Pleasant 40m Difficult or Very Difficult routes may be found up the ribs.

BARNDANCE SLABS

(NG 998 765) Alt 500m West facing

This is the slabby mass of gneiss on the western slope of Carnan Ban. It overlooks the burn that flows out of Fuar Loch Beag. The approach from Carnmore to Maiden

Buttress passes close underneath; if a climb is first undertaken on the slabs, from the top a short traverse across the hillside and diagonal descent along a grass rake leads to Maiden Buttress. The main features of Barndance Slabs from below are two turfy rakes, one slanting up from left to right, the other from bottom right steeply up to cross the first. These isolate a triangle of clean grey slab between them, with a steep base and an overhanging nose at the lower right corner. Above the left rake the slabs continue upwards before becoming lost in the hillside. To the right of the right-hand rake there is a strip of steep and often wet slab.

Barndance 115m Difficult * (1956)
An entertaining climb. Start at the lower right corner of the triangle of slabs, below the overhanging nose.
1. 10m Climb up to the overhang, either via the slab or a corner, and belay on the right.
2. 15m Move right to the edge of the grassy chimney then up for 2m before traversing back left along an overhung ledge. From the left end move into grooves running up and left.
3, etc. 90m Follow the grooves for 60m to the left-hand rake, then continue in the same line for 30m until interest wanes.

The following two routes are on the slabs to the left of Barndance. The rock is excellent.

Strider 110m Severe * (1967)
Above a large pointed pinnacle in a gully is a leaning rectangular block. Start just left of the block.
1. 25m Climb slabs to a triangular recess. Go right and up to a sloping rock shelf.
2. 25m Follow the obvious gangway on the left, steepening at 10m, under an overlap. From the left end go up past a detached pinnacle to a narrow grass ledge. Move 5m left to a pinnacle.
3. 40m Step right and go up a short crack and bulges, then follow a reddish slab corner. Break out left when this becomes wet and move up to a shelf with a loose flake. Continue straight up behind the flake and climb a bulge using a right-trending crack to a shelf.
4. 20m Scramble up slabs to the top.

Balrog 105m Severe (1967)
Start as for Strider.
1. 25m Follow the obvious right-slanting crack easily to a grass niche. Go up the curving crack above to a small heather ledge.
2. 20m Climb the crack trending left up the wall above, over the crux bulge. Belay in the fine slanting niche above.
3. 40m Follow the crack then the slabby wall to a grass ledge.
4. 20m Scrambling above.

The following is two linked routes on the crest between the slopes with Barndance Slabs and Maiden Buttress. No great quality but arrives at the top of the descent ramp leading to Maiden Buttress.

Blind Date 100m + walking Hard Severe 4b/Very Difficult (2001)
Low down on the crest is a clean patch of slab. Start at its base where there are cracked blocks in a steep wall. Climb the wall on surprising holds to reach a slabby ramp leading up left. Go up this until a crack leads up (crux) to a higher and thinner ramp. Go up this until the wall above can be climbed right of a recess. Finish up padding slabs (40m). Walk up to the prominent rocky nose above. There are several ribs which look possible on its left side but the longest and easiest rib was chosen. Start at the lowest rib on the left. Climb this, leading into a scoop. Go up the scoop and move right to finish up a blocky rib (60m). The right rib, finishing by the left-hand of two cracks, is also Very Difficult.

MAIDEN BUTTRESS

4. Dishonour   Very Difficult **
5. Tweedledum Severe *
6. Modesty   Very Difficult
7. Tweedledee   Severe

1. Strewth   VS
2. Ecstasy   Severe ***
3. Sleeping Beauty VS **

Andy Nisbet

MAIDEN BUTTRESS

(NH 001 762) Alt 500m South-West facing Map p162

This is a small but well formed mass of rock on the south-east side of Carnan Ban. It is visible from the Dubh Loch causeway, but is more or less concealed in the small basin that holds Fuar Loch Beag. It is well seen from the lower part of the north-west ridge of A' Mhaighdean, on the opposite shore of the lochan. Climbing on the buttress is pleasant due to immaculate rock and a sunny aspect. Most of the climbs have one or two difficult pitches at the start then become comparatively easy. The rock is good clean gneiss.

Approach: Access is easy from Carnmore by the Shenavall path to just beyond the zigzag, then across the ravine and up to the col, passing beneath the Barndance Slabs. The buttress is visible across the lochan from this col. From the Shenavall direction, take the side path which leads up into the corrie of Fuar Loch Mor. Follow it for about 800m or so then cut over to the right to a large perched boulder on a rocky knoll. This is the top of the buttress.

Descent: On the north-west side.

1 Strewth 75m VS   *(1955)*
Start from the grass slope at the foot of the second rib left of the bottom left of the buttress. This is about 40m above the start of Dishonour, and 10m above the start of Ecstasy.
1. 10m Climb a wall below the start of the rib and continue up the rib to a ledge.
2. 25m Climb the wall behind to gain a corner-crack with a narrow slab on its left. Climb this until it begins to overhang, then take an easy crack on the left.

Ecstacy, Severe, Maiden Buttress, Carnan Ban. Climber Mark Gear

Mark Gear collection

3. 20m Continue up easy slabs on the left of the buttress, passing a big ledge on the left wall and belaying on another ledge at the foot of the steeper wall, also on the left.

4. 20m Climb the wall on the right and follow the edge of the buttress to easy ground.

2 Ecstasy 95m Severe ***　　　　　　　　　　　　　　　　　　　(1955)

A climb of particular quality. Start at the foot of the first rib to the left of the bottom left corner of the buttress. The rib widens rapidly upwards into a V of slab bounded by vertical walls.

1. 30m Go up the left edge of the slab for 14m, well past an obvious right-slanting finger-crack, then swing out right on to an ascending hand-traverse. Follow it past an obvious niche above, go round a rib, then climb a small slab and corner to gain a large ledge and block. The original line (as shown in the photo above) followed the obvious right-slanting finger-crack, then steped down under an overhang before climbing the corner on the right to rejoin the route at the small slab. There is debate as to which line is better.

2. 15m Go up the slab above, first right then back left above an overhang to reach and climb a groove.

3. 30m Continue easily up the buttress edge to below a steeper slab.
4. 20m Climb the slab, first delicately right, then left and up the edge.

3 Sleeping Beauty   110m   VS ** (2001)
Right of the prominent V-slab of Ecstasy is a recessed inverted V. This route climbs the right corner of the V, then the crack-line above. Start from the first platform left of the bottom left corner of the buttress.
1. 25m 4b Climb the corner to a ledge below a vertical section with a small overhang.
2. 20m 4c Climb this vertical section leading to the top of the V, then the crack-line above to a big ledge.
3. 20m 4b Climb the crack above, initially overhanging.
4. 45m 4a Continue up the crack over two steep sections.

4 Dishonour   115m   Very Difficult ** (1955)
A close second to Ecstasy. Start at the foot of the left edge of the front face of the buttress.
1. 20m Climb the slab up the left edge to a steeper wall. Belay to the right.
2. 20m Move around the edge onto a large flake, then step back right onto the front face and climb to a small ledge in a niche. (A harder alternative is to climb the wall direct.) Continue straight up the slab to a ledge with a large perched block.
3. 25m Move up right into an easy chimney; climb this then go diagonally left to a ledge under an overhang.
4. 25m Go up right then back left above the overhang, then straight up a narrowing groove to a ledge. Take a groove on the right to reach a large terrace.
5. 25m Climb just right of twin cracks in the wall above and up a second wall by a crack to easy ground.

5 Tweedledum   115m   Severe * (1955)
Start 5m right of Dishonour.
1. 20m Climb the slab between two vegetated cracks and belay on the left below a steeper wall.
2. 10m Move right to the overhang and climb it on the right. Belay in a niche on the left.
3. 20m Climb the rib on the right then a chimney on its right.
4. 20m Continue up the chimney.
5. 20m Traverse left on ledges above overhangs, then go up the broad scoop. Climb a short V-groove to a large terrace.
5. 25m Climb easily on the left of the central turfy gully, finishing up a steep 'boulder problem' wall on good holds.

6 Modesty   115m   Very Difficult (1955)
Start immediately right of a line of turfy cracks, at the centre front of the buttress, about 5m right of Tweedledum.
1. 15m Climb the left of the slab. The cracks in the middle are harder.
2. 25m Climb the wall on the right of the vegetated fault. Continue up the fault and step left to ledges.
3. 25m Continue up the fault and the chimney above.
4. 25m Climb easily up slabs to large terraces.
5. 25m Layback up the flake in the centre of the wall, then continue leftwards to the top.

7 Tweedledee   115m   Severe (1955)
Start towards the right of the buttress at a line of cracks which pass just left of the great overhangs as a wide shallow chimney.
1. 30m Go up the slab, or the crack, to the foot of the chimney. Climb the chimney passing the first bulge on the right and the others on the left.
2. 30m Follow the cracks for a short distance and then go out up the left wall to blocks on a terrace.

3. 25m Go right up a big corner-crack.

4. 15m Ignore an easy escape to the right and climb the wall on the left by a diagonal crack.

5. 15m Climb the right edge of the small overhang above and continue to the top.

8 Cakewalk   80m   Difficult *   (1955)

Start at the base of the third narrow (red) slab right of the big overhang and immediately below a small overlap.

1. 30m Climb by cracks just right of the overlap, then follow the outside edge of the slab to belays below steeper ground.

2. 20m Follow a gangway on the right, pass loose blocks and climb a thin crack above. Belay on the shelf.

3. 30m Take a prominent crack in the wall on the left (definite crux) to a platform, then go easily up the slabs above.

9 Eastern Wall   50m   E1   (1994)

Start from a grassy bay on the south-east side of the buttress (presumably inside the gully right of Cakewalk).

1. 15m 5a Climb the dark wall towards overlapping rock tiles and a belay to the left of a prominent hanging water stained groove (seen from below as the main feature of the route).

2. 35m 5b Step right from the belay to reach the foot of the steep groove. Climb the groove and exit with difficulty (crux) on to clean compact rock, leading with continuing interest to the top of the buttress.

Immediately to the right of Maiden Buttress is an easy angled broken buttress, climbed easily by **Doddle** (75m Moderate 1956).

A' MHAIGHDEAN

(NH 008 749)   967m   Map p162

A graceful mountain lying in the heart of this magnificent wilderness and often reckoned to be the most remote of the Munros. The bulk of the mountain is composed of Lewisian gneiss, the summit being the highest point at which this rock outcrops in Scotland. However much of the climbing is concentrated on a series of sandstone buttresses that flank the south-west side of the north-west ridge. The rock is a coarser sandstone than in most other crags, quite akin to gritstone. The Pillar Buttress and the face to its east are gneissose.

Approach: The best approach to the majority of the cliffs is via the north-west ridge, easily reached from Carnmore by following the approach to Maiden Buttress as far as Fuar Loch Beag. Cross the outflow of the loch to reach the ridge. If aiming for the Pillar Buttress area it is best to walk over the summit. From Shenavall the best approach is via the path to Carnmore as far as Lochan Feith Mhic-illean. Just past the lochan take the branch track that crosses the Allt Bruthach an Easain. If heading for the Sandstone Buttresses, follow this path for 800m or so, then cut over to the right towards the west end of the Fuar Loch Mor and thence onto the north-west ridge of A' Mhaighdean. On the map the track is shown as stopping underneath Ruadh Stac Mor, but in fact it continues right up to and over the saddle between the two mountains and gives good walking. The summit of A' Mhaighdean is easily reached from the col. Some of the longer climbs on the south-west face are more easily reached by walking up from the Dubh Loch.

SANDSTONE BUTTRESSES

(NH 002 755)   Alt 700 to 740m   South-West facing   Map p162   Diagram p212

The sandstone buttresses lie on the long north-west ridge of A' Mhaighdean. They sit on a fault dividing them from gneiss below and some melting along the fault has made the sandstone more solid as well as including some small gneiss rocks which make the cliff base appear conglomerate.

Approach: Follow the north-west ridge to a big perched boulder at 610m and clearly seen from Fuar Loch Beag. Continue up the ridge to a level section at 690m from where sandstone is visible at the top of the slope on the right. A short traverse on sections of goat track reaches the start of the cliff. There are four buttresses described from left to right. The cliff base is very steep but there is a surprisingly easy line at the very base of the cliff, the boundary between gneiss and sandstone. The first non-descript buttress is quite long but has no routes. When reaching some rock that appears worth climbing, this is the second, Breccia Buttress. The Red Slab is the third buttress and suitably named. The continuing traverse from here has the only section of scrambling and reaches the fourth, the unmistakeable Gritstone Buttress. The slope below it is more open.

Breccia Buttress

1 Conglomerate Arete   90m   Very Difficult   *(1957)*
Start at the bottom right corner of the buttress, at the foot of an obvious arete between the broken frontal face and the vertical right wall. Rather artificial in parts.
1. 20m Go up a groove onto the crest of the rib and climb an overhanging nose to a little platform. Continue up the step above by a narrow crack on the edge.
2. 35m Follow the arete over several short steps keeping near the edge.
3. 35m Scramble up easy rocks in the same line to the top.

Red Slab

This is the third buttress, terminated on the right by a steep wall and the bottom right corner is severely cut away. There is a subsidiary pinnacle like buttress on the left. An easy descent can be made down the gully between this buttress and Breccia Buttress.

2 Doe Crack   70m   Very Difficult *   *(1957)*
Takes a direct line up the slab. Start in the corner between the subsidiary buttress and the slab, at the farthest right point at which an easy access to the slab is available.
1. 25m Climb the slab, about 3m to the right of the corner between the slab and subsidiary buttress, to a terrace.
2. 10m Climb a zigzag crack to the foot of a V-chimney.
3. 25m Go up the chimney, then follow cracks to a terrace. Cross this to the foot of the final wall.
4. 10m Go up the left-hand crack in the wall.

3 Red Slab   90m   Difficult **   *(1957)*
An enjoyable exposed climb. Start from the point of easiest access to the slab, at approximately the same position as the previous route.
1. 35m Go up 10m to a ledge. Traverse this right to the edge. Go up to another small ledge and up the slab above to a terrace. Belay at blocks 5m up on the left.
2. 20m Diagonally right is an obvious block on the edge. Gain the outer edge of the slab a few metres above this. Climb the slab above, keeping as close as possible to the edge, to a platform and a large perched block.
3. 15m Continue to a terrace.
4. 20m Go easily to the foot of a final 9m wall. Climb the wall to the top.

Gritstone Buttress

This is the fourth and steepest buttress. Its fine central wall is split by the distinctive deep chimney feature of The Cave. The gully right of the buttress can be used for descent.

A'MHAIGHDEAN – Sandstone Buttresses

1. Conglomerate Arete	Very Difficult	6. The Cave	Hard Severe
2. Doe Crack	Very Difficult *	7. The Cave-Mouth	VS 4c *
3. Red Slab	Difficult **	9. Mossy Bower	Hard Severe
4. Kraken	Severe	10. Gearradh	HVS 5a
5. Purity	HVS *	11. Windslab	Severe

Andy Nisbet

4 Kraken   70m   Severe   *(1965)*
This takes a hidden internal corner round the left side of the buttress.
1. 25m Traverse left from the central cave over broken ground, round a corner and up to the foot of a prominent vertical corner, partially concealed in the fault which defines the left edge of the buttress.
2. Climb the crack in the corner, finishing in a short chimney to the lower of two overhangs.
3. Make an exposed traverse to the left for 6m to gain a short chimney and climb this to easy ground.

5 Purity   50m   HVS 5a *   *(1988)*
This is the fine corner-line left of the cave. An excellent pitch. Climb the corner negotiating a bulge (crux) and so to belay on slabs. Finish out left by big blocks.

6 The Cave   60m   Hard Severe   *(1988)*
An unusual subterranean climb. Go right to the back of the cave. Climb up and out then head for the obvious narrow through route. Thread this and follow the open chimney to the top.

7 The Cave-Mouth   50m   VS 4c *   *(1988)*
From inside the entrance climb out on the right wall (looking out), then back and foot and bridge up until the chimney narrows. Climb the chimney to the top.

8 Compensation   55m   Severe   *(1967)*
This climb was done before the direct ascents of the Cave. Climb the corner of Purity for about 12m, then traverse right on ledges to enter the chimney. Climb the chimney to the top.

9 Mossy Bower   50m   Hard Severe   *(1988)*
This is the obvious right-slanting fault to the right of the Cave. Dank and mossy. The fault leads to a ledge system on the right side of the buttress. Finish out right.

10 Gearradh   50m   HVS 5a   *(1988)*
The obvious straight crack-line in the column just right of the previous route. Climb it to join the ledge system.

11 Windslab   55m   Severe   *(1957)*
Takes the slab and corner right of the Gearradh column.
1. 10m Go up blocks on the right, then traverse left into the corner to threads.
2. 25m Climb the vertical crack above, then take to the centre of the slab for pleasant climbing to a ledge and block belay.
3. 20m Continue up the centre of the slab to the top.

Octave Ribs

These are obvious on the upper of the two bands of coarsely crystalline gneiss that slant across the Dubh Loch face, underneath the sandstone cliffs. Fahrenheit is the fourth rib from the left, immediately right of a very obvious red rib.

Fahrenheit   60m   Scottish VS   *(1959)*
A sustained and exposed climb. Climb the edge for 12m then traverse left into a grassy groove and climb this to a belay. Rejoin the rib crest and climb it for 30m to a stance and belay. Continue up the crest to an overhang, take this directly and finish up short slabs.

Soh What?   35m   Very Difficult   *(1959)*
The fifth rib, just right of Fahrenheit. Follow the rib crest until a ledge is reached. Continue over a small bulge and follow the steep left wall of the groove above.

WEST FACE

(NH 007 751)   Alt 700m   North-West facing

The section of cliff which faces Carnmore from the summit of A' Mhaighdean. Routes are described right to left.

Whitbread's Aiguille   270m   Severe   *(1957)*
This climb is best approached by walking up from the Dubh Loch. Start at the foot of the easy angled buttress which forms the left side of the gully below the West Face of A' Mhaighdean, the West Gully. This buttress rises from a broad base to a small pinnacle, about 60m below the north-west ridge. At the bottom left, a huge pinnacle leans against the face. A detailed description was given in the 1993 guide, but on a subsequent ascent it was found that few of the features were easily identified. Some variation is possible and quite a hard pitch may be found low down. It is a good traditional route, suitable for those who enjoy an exploratory approach.

Vole Buttress   270m   Very Difficult   *(1957)*
This is the indefinite buttress left of Whitbread's Aiguille. Start at the foot of a prominent V-groove with a slab for its left wall, towards the left of the buttress. Climb this in a series of quite hard pitches for 120m, after which the difficulty relents.

Ermine Gully   300m   III   *(1978)*
This is the most prominent, long gully left of West Gully, just left of Vole Buttress, and well right of the Sandstone Buttresses. On the first ascent two pitches were encountered low down.

West Face   240m   Severe   *(1951)*
The large and indefinite West Face of A' Mhaighdean overlooks the Dubh Loch. One climb has been recorded, starting from a grass slope below the tapering southern extension of the face. The description is very vague (SMCJ Vol. 25).

SOUTH FACE

(NH 008 748)   Alt 800m   South to South-West facing   Map p162

The south face of A' Mhaighdean consists of two main buttresses, Pillar Buttress situated directly under the summit and Goats' Ridge to its right (south-east). Between the two is Trident Gully with the smaller Trident Gully Buttress between its central and east forks. Right of Goats' Ridge is Pinnacle Gully, near the end of the cliff.

Pillar Buttress

Approach: Direct access to the base of the crag is rather laborious from the west owing to the lie of the lower cliffs. The best approach from the west is to traverse the summit and descend the nearby big grassy gully (Trident West Gully) that leads towards the mouth of Gorm Loch Mor. After descending about 200m, traverse right (west) to the foot of the buttress. Alternatively the crag may be reached from Gorm Loch Mor, which is a pleasant walk from Carnmore.

Eagle Grooves   110m   Severe *   *(1957)*
This climb lies on the west (left) face of Pillar Buttress and gives a classic climb in fine position. From further down the north-west ridge of A' Mhaighdean a prominent clean looking rib of grey rock can be seen that starts at the same level as Pillar Buttress and immediately west of it. The start is gained by a left traverse along a turfy ledge from the boulders at the top of the first pitches of Pillar Buttress or Triple Cracks Route. Traverse the obvious ledge for 40m to below an indefinite

rib of clean grey rock. To the left are turfy grooves and a rib culminating in overhangs.

1. 35m Climb by slabs and grooves to a tiny platform on top of a large grey flake. Some 6m above is a small niche.

2. 25m Above and slanting left is a prominent crack in steeper rocks. Climb this to grooves and a spike beyond.

3. 30m Continue leftwards up the groove to a turfy ledge.

4. 20m Climb the slab above, then by a corner until it is possible to break out right onto easy ground near the top.

Pillar Buttress   150m   Very Difficult *   (1950)

The true nose of the buttress gives an enjoyable climb that finishes at the summit cairn. Start at the foot of the rib. Easy rocks lead in 25m to a platform. The obvious line up grooves to the right is Triple Cracks Route. Continue up slabs and walls slanting right of the true crest of the buttress, climbing a steep slab by parallel cracks. Easy rocks, a difficult crack, then 6m of difficult slab lead to an impasse requiring an awkward traverse to a huge crack full of chockstones. Climb this to finish.

A direct start to this climb has been made, commencing from a point to the right of the original line, and joining it after three pitches (**Leeds Variation**; SMCJ Vol.25).

A previous route recorded in 1933 (**Baird, Crofton and Leslie's Route**; SMCJ Vol.20) probably follows roughly the same line. Another variation traverses left after the first pitch and climbs grooves for two exposed pitches (VS).

Triple Cracks Route   120m   Severe *   (1951)

Follows the slot-like chimney several metres right of Pillar Buttress. Climb the chimney and follow the fault directly up the buttress to finish by the boulder-choked chimney of Pillar Buttress. Below the final chimney is the Triple Cracks pitch, which is the crux.

A Ridge Too Far   300m   IV,4   (2000)

"The next ridge east of Pillar Buttress." Climbed in mistake for Pillar Buttress in nil visibility, possibly Goats Ridge (see below)?

Goats' Ridge Area

Right (east) of Pillar Buttress is a broad gully which splits into three branches some 150m below the top. This is Trident Gully. The west and centre forks are easy, but the east fork rises to a damp recess below vertical rock walls some 75m below the top. The main feature of the flank of Pillar Buttress overlooking West Trident Gully is a blank red wall defined on the left by the slot of Triple Cracks Route. Between the west and central forks is a narrow rib of steep rock and grass that nowhere rises much above the floor of the gully. A more substantial ridge lies between the central and east forks, giving Trident Gully Buttress.

Approach: The climbs are best approached by descending Pinnacle Gully on the right (south-east) side of the crag (see below). Goats Ridge can then be crossed to reach the Trident Gully area.

Trident Gully Buttress   130m   VS   (1967)

The lowest rock rib is gained from the right, just above the overhanging base. A mossy slab leads to some grass and then, following the crest as closely as possible, pleasant climbing leads to a broad ledge below the final tower. The main feature is a central corner-groove leading up to an overhang at the top. An overhanging wall bars direct entry into the groove, which is gained by climbing the detached rib on the right of the ledge and pulling across left into the bottom of the groove. This is climbed up to the roof, with an excursion at half-height onto the left to climb a steep 3m wall on good holds. At the top of the groove, undercut holds under the overhang allow an escape left to the foot of a narrow ramp which leads awkwardly up the west wall to the top.

Right of East Trident Gully is a broad ridge, **Goats' Ridge**, which descends almost as low as Pillar Buttress. It has two steeper rock sections in its lower and upper parts with an easy-angled stretch in between (150m Difficult).
    East of Goats' Ridge is a wide, easy gully, **Pinnacle Gully**, leading down to an amphitheatre below a big sweep of light coloured slabs, forming the right flank of the upper part of Goats Ridge.

Gladiator   100m   Severe *   (1966)
Start at the lowest point of the slabs and trend slightly leftwards to reach the grassy corner and blocks below a V-chimney in 60m. A spike is passed at 20m and the foot of a thin grassy groove and quartz streaks are then followed. A prominent steep chimney-crack on the final tower above is climbed to a capping roof, where an escape is made by a left traverse. Scramble to the top.

In Pinnacle Gully, below the level of the slabs can be found **Hodge's Pinnacle**. Its short upper side gives a 10m climb (Difficult). On the west face is a slightly longer and harder crack. The long south ridge gives a good Severe climb of 45m, starting up the huge boulders below. East of Pinnacle Gully is a broken ridge, **Kids' Ridge,** giving pleasant scrambling, perhaps Difficult in its lower reaches.

STAC A' CHAORRUINN

(NH 023 744)   Alt 500m   East facing

This 'small' crag (perhaps 150m high) is the eastern bluff of A' Mhaighdean. It is possibly also the bluff of the first (and probably last) persons to climb here in 1909, that unstoppable pair Ling and Glover. The pioneers were prevented from making a full investigation by the weather, but they did make a long rightwards traverse along the large lower terrace. This led them to rocks overlooking a large gully (noted for its winter potential). They then turned up leftwards, following the edge of the gully to the flat top of the bluff. The possibilities for a good direct climb were noted (SMCJ Vol.12, p.29).

NA BEARTA BUTTRESS

(NH 004 808)   Alt 350m   East-North-East facing   Map p162

This is the considerable mass of rock which outcrops on the west side of Strath Beinn Dearg, just north of the burn that flows out of Lochan na Bearta. It lies in a remote place that is little visited, an exquisite setting despite the recently built estate chalet which presumably involved a helicopter in its construction. The rock is Lewisian gneiss interbanded with hornblende schist, and as usual provides clean rough slabs. Despite the north-east aspect, the slabby angle allows the sun until early afternoon.

Approach: The most direct approach is from Gruinard Bay, following the estate track that leads to Loch na Sealga. Leave the public road at NG 961 911 (locked gate) and follow the track for 7km, probably by mountain bike, until it crosses the Allt Loch Ghiubhsachain. Follow the Allt on varying sides but avoiding an initial gorge section on the hillside to the east, and reach the cliff after 5km of rough going. Dry conditions recommended to limit the bogs and to allow easy crossing of the Allt. 3hrs.
    Alternatively, from Carnmore follow the Shenavall path as far as Lochan Feith Mhic'-illean then cut north over the moor, past Lochan Cnapach, to Lochan na Bearta. From Carnmore take the Carnmore path up Gleann na Muice Beag and branch off past Loch Beinn Dearg and so down Strath Beinn Dearg.

Descent from left half: Easy down grassy slopes south of the cliff.

Descent from right half: There is an easy grassy slope to the north of the cliff but one has to go quite high above the end of the routes to gain its top.

The crag is split into two halves, the right being larger, by a central gully. The left half is topped by a clean 70m wall with slabby rock and several terraces below. The right side of the right half is clean rock for the full height and provides the best climbing, the two routes finishing either side of a shallow gully which runs down from the top and peters out into the slabs. The right edge of the slabs curves round into a north-facing wall of decreasing height.

LEFT HALF

The first two routes are on the clean slabby wall which forms the upper tier. This clean wall is reached by traversing in from the left.

Crucifer   60m   VS 4b *   (2000)
A route up cracks towards the left end of the wall. The base of the central section of the wall is crackless until just left of a long roof where there is a deep wide crack. Climb this crack until it becomes heathery, then make a thin traverse left into another crack. Climb this for about 10m until possible to return right to a crack (which may not be the original). Climb this until it bends away left, then finish up pleasant ribs.

My Fair Lady   70m   Severe *   (2000)
This would make a logical finish to Wallflower but was climbed in its own right. Start near the right end of the wall. Climb a short corner, then cracks in the slabby wall until the slab angle eases on the left and a left-trending line was taken below a heather patch into the centre of the wall. Here are crack-lines either side of a central scoop. Climb the crack left of the scoop to the top.

Wallflower   240m   Hard Severe   (1956)
Not a good climb but it has some good pitches, despite avoiding the upper tier. Start at the foot of the rocks left of the central gully and immediately right of a prominent gully-chimney with a cave on its right wall.
1. 30m Climb slabs to the foot of a detached layback flake. From here an obvious line leads up right to a prominent field and trees. Ignoring this, traverse left then up to a narrow turf ledge with small trees.
2. 25m Traverse the turf ledges to the right and climb the edge of the slab on good holds. Near the top turn left, crossing a small overhang. Belay at a turfy platform with trees.
3. 15m Go up a corner on the left to a ledge and climb the slab above. This leads to broken rocks below the first big terrace.
4. 60m Scramble to the terrace.
5. 15m Opposite the point of arrival on the terrace is an obvious groove and crack in the wall above. Climb the groove awkwardly, moving left at the top into a minor groove. One aid peg was used here because of vegetation.
6. 10m An easy slab on the right leads to another terrace at a huge block.
7. 10m The steep wall above was avoided, although My Fair Lady would be a logical finish. To the right the terrace falls away into a grassy scoop, the upper part of Central Gully. Level with the terrace, but across to the right on the edge of the gully, is a tree. Traverse "with carefully controlled breathing" along a ledge level with the tree.
8. 10m Above and on the left is a chimney. Gain its foot and belay 3m up on a ledge with blocks.
9. and 10. 60m Continue up the chimney and walls to the top.

RIGHT HALF

The main slabs are effectively split into two masses by a grassy crack and groove system running the full height of the buttress, to the left of a long terrace at 45m. The section of crag to the left of this is set back slightly and the base is higher up.

The lower section of this wall is seamed with cracks, of which there are three main systems leading to a horizontal break beneath a bulge/overlap. The following climb takes the central crack but shies away from the thin staggered crack in the centre of the slab (dampness, dirty cracks and midges).

Twice Bitten   185m   E3 *   (2000)
The central crack system. A great first pitch but the route is marred since it circumvents the crack above the bulge and the common finish is a little scrappy. The upper section is much easier than the lower and also take some drainage.
1. 30m 5c Climb the central crack-line to a shallow niche in the centre of the overlap.
2. 60m 5b Traverse 5m right to the first break, step up right, then go right again and climb the edge to a ledge at a wide, wet crack system. Go left to a crack-line in the slab, climb this and continue up leftwards into the centre and gain a heathery ledge. Climb a wide crack in the wall and continue to the top of the heather ledge above. Step up into the base of a groove with a spike on its left rib.
3. 55m 4c A choice of finishes lies above but on the first ascent, the quickest escape was taken. Pull on to the rib and continue up slabs to a steepening, move right and climb the side wall of a grassy groove, then step left on to the rib and climb clean rock to the foot of a wide crack with a small loose block at its base.
4. 40m Step right and climb a grassy groove to below a wide crack, traverse a ledge leftwards, climb the right side of the recess and step left across the top to flat ledges.
Easy walking up leftwards gains the top of the buttress.

Ricepaper   140m   Severe **   (1955)
A good climb which is easier than its blank appearance suggests and not spoilt by a little vegetation. Start at the lowest rocks below the middle of the clean right sheet of slabs, below the long terrace about 45m up.
1. 20m An artificial pitch leads up a vague rib to the foot of the main slabs (or walk round on the left).
2. 35m 4a Here is a slight scoop leading to a turf patch, with a second turf patch above and right. Start up the scoop, then follow cracks diagonally right under the first turf patch. Return left above the turf patch and continue left to gain the long terrace.
4. 35m 4a The line is 10m left of where pitch 2 arrives, a long grey groove which starts 10m above the terrace and runs out of sight on to the slabs above (the groove is better seen from a distance away). Climb up left of the base of the groove, then traverse right into it. Follow the groove (crux).
5. 20m Continue in the same line up cracks (or the slab on their right) towards a rib which is formed left of a shallow turfy gully. Move left under its steep base to a damp depression.
6. 30m Climb the depression for about 10m until the rib can be gained. Follow the rib to a big grass ledge. Scramble up rightwards for quite a distance to reach the descent.

Good Friday Slab   135m   VS 4b *   (1956)
Climbs the fine open slabs near the right end of the cliff. Several moves of 4b with runners and belays not obvious. Start at a low-angled white slab at the right corner of the face and immediately left of a shallow gully leading to an impressive flake-chimney.
1. 30m Climb the slab and a short groove to a small tree in a heathery recess. Step left on to the wall and climb cracks to a scoop.
2. 30m From the top of the scoop, take a diagonal traverse leading to the right edge of the slab and under an overhang. Traverse left to the right end of a ledge. Climb the wall above. Step left into a shallow groove and climb to a belay.
3. 25m Continue up a crack slightly to the left.
4. 20m The crack becomes a grassy gully. Take the slab on the left of the gully to a small belay below an undercut nose.

5. 15m Traverse under the nose to regain the gully at a tree.
6. 15m Finish up the gully.

**Good Friday Direct   130m   HVS ** *(1999)*
A direct line up the cleanest slab, but with limited protection providing a fine feeling of exposure.
1. 30m 4b As for the normal route. A crack in the wall to the left might be worth exploring.
2. 30m 4c Step left and climb a vague rib direct to the shallow groove of the normal route.
3. and 4. 70m 4c Start up the crack of the normal route, but soon step right and climb direct up slabs to join and follow a crack, then another which lies in the slab about 8m right of the grassy crack and groove system. Sustained climbing but the best belay position is unknown.

RIGHT-HAND BUTTRESS

Some 200m north of the main sweep of pale slabs is another darker smaller mass of slabs some 90m high. This climb takes the centre of the slab. Descend off the back and down the right side of the crag.

**Rough Bounds   95m   HVS ** *(2000)*
At the foot of the slab are two flat-topped boulders. Start some 3m left of these boulders at a short, shallow groove almost directly below the crack-line running up the centre of the slab to break through the small half-height roof left of centre. A fine climb on very good and interestingly featured rock.
1. 45m 4c/5a Climb directly to a diagonal ramp slanting up from left to right, make a move or so up this and pull back left over a short hollow section and continue up the cracks to a thread in a groove just below the roof.
2. 50m 5a Surmount the roof and continue up the cracks above finishing up a wide crack at the top. Continue to just below a fin of rock.

CREAG TOLL A' MHADAIDH

(NG 985 807)   Alt 450m   North-East facing   Map p162

This is a remote but disappointing mass of slabby rock above Loch Toll a' Mhadaidh. The rock is not of a quality to really justify the long journey, except for those wishing to guarantee seclusion in a wild setting. There is only one recorded route here, first (and last?) climbed by the indefatigable Mike O'Hara.

Approach: By bike up the Gruinard River (as for Na Bearta Buttress). Head south-eastwards up a stream in the hillside until near the north-east end of a stalkers path which comes from the Fionn Loch. Follow this to the Uisge Toll a' Mhadaidh, then the uisge (burn) to the loch and the crag.

Sanctuary Slabs   180m   Difficult *(1957)*
Start 50m left of the deep grassy gully in the middle of the crag, 25m left of and above the lowest rocks, where a grass rake slants up right. Take the right of two short ribs.
1. 35m Go up the rib to rock platforms. Continue by slabs to a turfy corner slightly to the right.
2. 10m Climb a slabby rib on the left to an obvious break.
3. 15m Follow a gangway steeply to the left past a crack and almost into the turfy grooves beyond before climbing past a cracked block to regain the crest of the rib.
4. 30m Follow the crest of the rib above. After 10m the angle eases and slabs lead to a grass terrace. Above, 90m of easy scrambling up the rib on the left leads to the top.

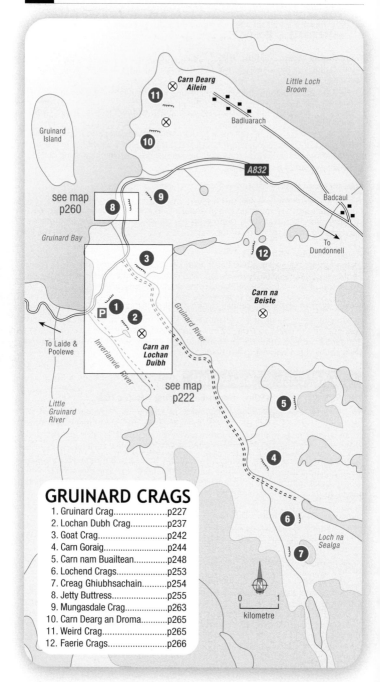

GRUINARD CRAGS

Little Loch Broom

Carn Dearg Ailein

Badluarach

Gruinard Island

A832

Badcaul

see map p260

Gruinard Bay

To Dundonnell

Carn na Beiste

To Laide & Poolewe

Inverianvie River

Gruinard River

Carn an Lochan Duibh

see map p222

Little Gruinard River

Loch na Sealga

0   1
kilometre

GRUINARD CRAGS

The numerous crags within the areas bounded by Gruinard Bay offer some excellent and easily accessible climbing. Unless already local, the north approach through Dundonnell is quicker because of faster roads. The rock is the typical gneiss, generally rough and with good protection cracks. Since many of the crags are on isolated summits, there is limited drainage and most routes dry quickly after rain; occasional wet holds tend not to affect the grade.

There are a number of crags grouped close to the Gruinard Bay car park and the Inverianvie River; these are described first. Just to the north is the Gruinard River, with Goat Crag near the road and Carn Goraig and other crags upstream. North again is the roadside Jetty Buttress and beyond this are other smaller crags.

Gruinard Bay Crags

Map p222

The view over the bay makes this a lovely place to climb. The routes above the Inverianvie River face south-west and receive sun for most of the day; the rest face approximately west and have the sun in the afternoon only. The crags will be described individually in order of increasing distance from the car park at Gruinard Bay (NG 953 899).

CAR PARK AREA

Map p222

There are a number of short routes within 5mins of the car park.

VERY DIFFICULT SLAB

(NG 954 898)   Alt 50m   South-West facing

This is the pink slab well seen on the hillside from the car park. It consists of a wall of slab with a vegetated break left of the central rib. The routes are easier than they look.

Two Minute Slab   20m   Very Difficult   *(1994)*
Climb the rib left of the vegetated break to blocks and continue straight up.

Small but Perfectly Formed   25m   Very Difficult *   *(1994)*
To the right of the break is a steep clean rib, giving the best route on the slab. Step off a boulder and climb the rib direct avoiding a heather patch. Step left and climb a steepening to the top.

Five Minute Crack   20m   Very Difficult   *(1994)*
This is the thin crack-line just right of the rib.

Flaky Wall   15m   Very Difficult   *(1994)*
A line of flakes lies right of the crack.

Gneiss Groove   10m   Very Difficult   *(1994)*
The fine wee groove which cuts up the slab near the right-hand end.

TRIANGULAR SLAB

(NG 954 898)   Alt 60m   South-West facing

This is just beyond and to the right of the crest of Very Difficult Slab in a hollow (not seen from the car park). There is a patch of heather in the centre and a crack rising from it. All the routes are good but undistinguished and harder than they look.

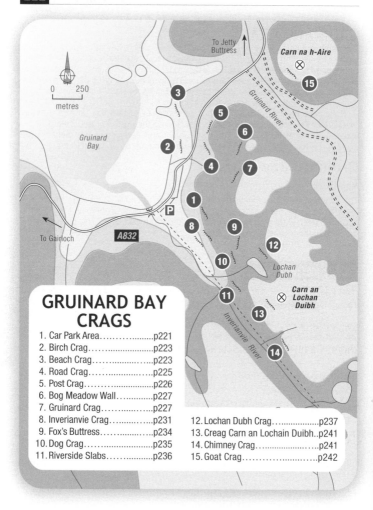

Gneiss 15m VS 4c * *(1994)*
Climb a water washed streak left of the crack, the more direct, the harder.

Gneisser 15m VS 4c *(1994)*
Pass the heather patch on the right and climb the central crack past a downward-pointing flake.

Gneissest 15m VS 4c * *(1994)*
The best of the routes (predictably!). Start right of the crack and climb up to an overlap; break through this at a notch and up to the top.

Not Bad 20m Very Difficult *(1994)*
Start as for Gneissest and climb up to where it steepens. Traverse right to a break and climb this to a smooth slab finish.

THE SIDE WALL

A steep line of crag running down right from Triangular Slab; west facing.

Atlantic Pillar   14m   Hard Severe 4b   *(1999)*
A well defined slabby rib with an undercut base is the first feature at the top left end. Climb it direct.

Staircase   12m   Very Difficult   *(1999)*
A black, diamond shaped wall 5m to the right is climbed first to the right, then to the left.

One Scoop or Two?   10m   VS 4c   *(1999)*
Well down to the right is a steep red wall. Climb its left side via a pair of scooped holds to a crack which leads up right to the top. Sustained.

MOLLY'S RIDGE

Molly's Ridge   15m   Difficult   *(1996)*
The blunt ridge above the Very Difficult Slab.

Mutt's Crack   8m   Severe   *(1996)*
The thin crack on the far right of the ridge's flank.

There are other short routes or boulder problems nearby. **Flake Buttress** lies right of and slightly below Very Difficult Slab and has a large flake at its right end. There are three routes 6 to 10m high near the flake; the crack on the front of the flake (VS 5a), the flake-chimney forming its left side (Very Difficult) and scoops and slabs on the left (Very Difficult). There is also a route at the top left end of the buttress, **Black Wall Special**; gain a diagonal crack and ramp, then climb the wall above - 10m Hard Severe 4b.

BIRCH CRAG

(NG 953 904) Alt 5m   West facing   Map p222

Somewhat hidden in trees just inland from the beach. Described right to left.

Approach: Walk along the beach to the crag, which is more easily seen when high tide forces a higher walk.

Hatrick for Patrick   25m   HVS 5a   *(2002)*
The central groove line over a capping bulge and into a clean short hanging groove to finish.

Panick Beach Teacher   20m   E1 5b   *(2005)*
The groove line just left of Hatrick for Patrick starting up that route and finishing directly above the small roof at the top.

50 Gallon Drum   20m   E4 6a   *(2005)*
Left again is a slightly right-trending discontinuous thin crack-line that leads past a horizontal slot (Camalot 2) to the easier flake-line above.

BEACH CRAG

(NG 953 907) Alt 5m   South-West facing   Map p222

This is the black wall at the far end of the main beach to the north of the car park (but not visible from the car park).

Approach: Walk along the beach to the crag. At high tide, walk back up the road and cut down onto the beach through a gate and follow a vague path.

Descent: Easily to the left or right.

There are two steeper areas of rock with the left-hand section forming a flat fronted tower with a crack up its centre and the right section again smooth faced but less steep.

Beach Groove Garden   20m   VS 4b *   (1998)
The V-groove at the left end of the crag. Take the left fork at the top.

Cowrie   20m   E1 5b *   (2005)
The left side of the tower. Go rightwards up a steep ramp passing some jutting blocks, then up the wall to a ledge. Step left and stay near the left edge to the top.

Armburger   20m   E2 5b **   (1998)
An increasingly steep and bold route up the crack in the front face of the tower, although escapable for rests and runners. Climb the crack using holds either side and working hard for good runners to the capping block and pull through this leftwards to finish.

Dechno   20m   E2 5b   (1998)
A line about 3m right of Armburger. Finish up cracks above the steep wall bordering the right side of the Armburger prow. Serious, loose rock.

Childs Play   20m   E2 5b *   (2005)
Start near the right side of the steep lower wall and climb leftwards to a tiny sapling in a break below a middle ledge. Move right and up to the ledge. Climb up the middle of the smooth looking upper wall.

Next right and immediately right of a broken vegetated area of rock is a steep scrappy looking wall with grooves higher up.

Family Fun   15m   HVS 4c   (2005)
Climb a cleaned blocky rib passing left of a small gnarly aspen tree to gain the steep upper grooves. Move into the bottom of the left-hand groove and up this to finish.

The next six routes are on the right-hand buttress, which has a big recess on its left side.

Aorta   20m   E2 5c *   (1999)
Start at an overhung groove at the right side of the big recess. Climb up the awkward groove to pull through the bulge at a crack at about 5m and on to the wall. Move slightly left and straight up the fine headwall to finish.

Adalat   20m   VS 4c   (1999)
Start as for Aorta and climb a right-slanting crack and edge round on to the front of the buttress. Move up and follow a right-trending crack-line near the right edge of the crag.

Capillary Wall   20m   HVS 5a *   (1998)
Start at the lowest rocks to the right of the recess. Climb the middle of the lower buttress, through the wide diagonal break, then continue trending leftwards, crossing Adalat and straight up the cracked buttress passing a niche near the top.

Voltarol   10m   Severe   (1999)
A route up the sidewall. Start under a short groove leading to a square roof. Climb steeply into the groove, move right at the roof on to the edge and finish straight up.

Armburger, E2, Beach Crag. Climber Paul Tattersall

Sheepless in Seattle   10m   E2 5b *   (2001)
To the right of Voltarol is a steep wall with a high bottomless crack on its left. Start at the base of a wide crack bounding the right side and climb diagonally left to join the crack. A high runner in the wide crack protects the first few moves.

Saga of Sewage   10m   E5 6a *   (2002)
Climb the bottomless crack of Sheepless in Seattle direct.

ROAD CRAG

(NG 955 903)   Alt 40m   South-West facing   Map p222

This is the reddish brown wall that lies just above the road, easily seen when driving up the hill northwards from the Gruinard car park. Descend by scrambling to the left, facing out and into a grassy gully. Routes are described from right to left. A rose bush near the right end makes a convenient landmark. A crack in an arete leading to slabby ground at the extreme right end is **Ataka** (4b 2000).

Celtic Ray   15m   VS 5a   (2000)
Start at the right end of the crag at a thin crack just right of the small rose bush. Climb up to a roof, place a runner in Ataka, then traverse left beneath the roof and climb directly above its left end to finish up cracks.

Trojan   20m   E2 6a **   (2000)
Start just down left of the rose bush, beneath a ledge in line with the left end of the roof. Gain the ledge (a high side runner can be used). Climb to the left end of the roof and where Celtic Ray goes straight up, continue up the diagonal crack-line to the top. Alternatively, finish leftwards from the ledge on excellent rough rock

Mongo   20m   E3 5c *   (2000)
Start down left of the rose bush and just left of Trojan. Climb up to and follow the diagonal break under the bulge and break through at a steep capped groove. Swing right, crux, and up via hidden holds, moving back left to finish near Trojan's left finish.

Raglan Road   20m   E2 5b **   (1999)
A fine line but a little bold. Start in the middle of the crag and under an obvious
crack in the headwall. Climb steeply up and left into the central scoop. Go up this
and exit rightwards into a crack leading to the big diagonal break. Finish up the
steep crack in the headwall.

On the Road to Baghdad   20m   E2 5c **   (2003)
A good eliminate between Raglan Road and the crack of Tom Jones. Start just left
of Raglan Road and climb to a small left-trending overlap. Move left to good holds
at the left end of the overlap and continue up and right to thin cracks. Use the
cracks to gain an obvious flake on the left and move up to the diagonal break.
Finish by the crack in the brown rock above.

Tom Jones   15m   E1 5b *   (2000)
Quite bold but low in the grade. A route on the slabby left side of the crag. Start
just left of On the Road to Baghdad and gain and climb a left-curving flake. Long
reaches for good hidden holds lead into the wide crack to finish.

Pockets of Resistance   15m   E1 5b *   (2003)
Start about 4m left of Tom Jones at a blunt nose. Climb to the diagonal break and
follow it to the right end of a roof. Climb a short crack and bulge to good holds on
the left and go up to the horizontal break. Move right to finish up the crack in the
brown rock.

Roadkill   15m   Hard Severe 4b   (2003)
Start below a groove leading to the roof on Pockets of Resistance. Climb to the left
side of the roof, pull over on big holds and go up to a heathery ledge with aspens.
Finish via cracks on the right.

POST CRAG

(NG 955 905)   Alt 80m   West-North-West facing   Map p222
This small but well formed crag of solid gneiss 5mins from the road. Park in a small
turn off on the west side just north of the crest of the hill. The crag is nearer the
car park on the opposite side of the road and well seen from the parking place. It
has a central orange smooth wall with characteristic breaks.

Post-it   12m   VS 4c   (2002)
The prominent blunt left edge of the smooth wall. Well protected but very
escapable.

Scoobie Dubh   12m   E4 6a **   (2000)
The immaculate central wall is quick drying.

Hate Mail   10m   E2 6a *   (2000)
To the right of the orange wall is a smooth slab with a pronounced left-slanting
crack-line near its right-hand end (Billet Dubh). This climbs the centre of the slab,
with a letterbox low down. Stand on the letterbox. Continue delicately up using a
triangular slot, then follow the broken crack to juggier rock at the top. A very thin
crux has a good runner.

Billet Dubh   12m   VS 4c   (2000)
The pronounced crack-line in the slab.

Instantly Forgettable   10m   VS 4c   (2002)
Start near the right end of the crag. Climb up steep blocky ground just left of a dirty
left-facing corner and finish awkwardly onto the terrace.

BOG MEADOW WALL

(NG 938 904)   Alt 110m   North-West facing   Map p222

A red leaning wall which lies behind Post Crag. When the sun comes around on to the crag at around 4pm it is transformed into a wonderful orange colour.

Approach: Park as for Post Crag. Head directly uphill and through a gate to a shallow valley. Break out right at its top to a plateau, then continue for about 200m to the line of crags overlooking a flat boggy meadow.

**Summer Breeze   15m   E5 6b ** **   *(2000)*
A superb and well protected climb up the central bottomless crack which starts just to the right of an obvious slanting overlap. Climb to ledges below the crack and move up to a horizontal break. Directly above is a 'plaque' - a thin crack in the left side of this takes a Camalot 0.1. Hard climbing gains the crack. Climb the crack with interest to the top.

Last Tango   12m   E1 5b   *(2000)*
The obvious C shaped crack up the right side of the central part of the wall. Climb to a holly tree, step up left on to a block and make a couple of scruffy moves to the base of the crack. Climb the fine crack to its top, pull out right then step up left on to a ledge and follow slabs up left.

Bloody Flake   10m   VS 5a   *(2002)*
The next crag right of the short right-hand section of Bog Meadow Wall is a narrow buttress split by flake-cracks. Climb the flake-corner right of the crest.

GRUINARD CRAG

(NG 957 900)   Alt 110m   North-West facing   Maps p220, 222   Diagram p228

One of the best crags in the guide, with steep positive climbing and good lines. The crag is well seen from the road 300m north of the car park but not from the car park itself. Not to be confused with Inverianvie Crag which is more easily seen and well to the right, nearer Inverianvie River.

Approach: It is best reached by skirting leftwards across the knoll directly behind the car park. Cross the fence at the left end of the car park and follow another fence up, then left. Where the fence runs horizontal, make a slightly rising traverse leftwards and the crag soon comes into view. 15mins. Lochan Dubh Crag can be easily reached from Gruinard Crag by curving up right from its base (the profile of Lochan Dubh Crag appears very soon) and following a flat area (marked on the map) south-eastwards.

Gruinard Crag is both bigger and better than it looks. The crag is in two diagonal tiers rising leftwards, the lower being a smaller smooth wall with a big flake on its left side, and the upper crag being higher and longer, with a prominent roof in the centre. The roof curves up at its left end to form a niche.

LOWER CRAG

**1 Halcyon Days   20m   VS 4c ** **   *(1994)*
The recessed break on the left has a prominent flake forming its right edge. Layback the flake to a large jug. Step right on to the blank looking wall which is covered in holds and either exit easily right up a heathery groove or, better but harder, finish up the steep slab on its left.

2 Who Shot JR   16m   HVS 5a *   *(1999)*
Start at the same place as Halcyon Days but follow a thin crack steeply up right. Traverse right across a pale streak (and Ueejit) into a small corner. Climb the corner to a heather ledge and up the crack above.

GRUINARD CRAGS

GRUINARD CRAG

1. Halcyon Days — VS 4c **
2. Who Shot JR — HVS 5a *
3. Breakpoint — E4 6a
4. Ueejit — E4 6a *
5. Utopia — HVS 5b *
6. Simple Perfections — Difficult **
7. Baywatch — E1
8. Paradise Regained — E1 **
9. Quick on the Draw — E5 6a **
10. Pistolero — E3 5c **
11. The Big C — HVS 5a *
12. Gunslinger — E2 5b *
13. Red John of the Battles — E2 5b ***
15. Overlord — E1 5a **
16. How the West was Won — E4 6a *
17. Stand and Deliver — E5 6a ***
18. Quail — Difficult

Andy Nisbet

3 Breakpoint   20m   E4 6a   *(1999)*
The slabby wall just right of Halcyon Days, a route barely separate from Ueejit.
Start as for Who Shot JR and gain a small ledge at the right end of a diagonal crack
(the middle crack), then move left up this to climb the wall and finish directly with
a reachy move. Perhaps 5c but thin and serious.

4 Ueejit   18m   E4 6a *   *(1997)*
Climb the right side of the reddish wall with three diagonal cracks between Halcyon
Days and Utopia, keeping just left of a pale streak and up a line of small flakes
leading from a small ledge at the right end of the middle crack to the topmost crack
(runners) and a hard move above it. Sustained, thin and serious in the middle
unless a runner is placed in Who Shot JR, when the route becomes E3.

5 Utopia   15m   HVS 5b *   *(1994)*
This is the thin vertical crack near the right edge. Climb the wall right of the lower
crack, trending left to join the crack at half-height and finish up it.

6 Simple Perfections   25m   Difficult **   *(1994)*
The right border of the wall is a slab, covered in jugs and the best line follows the
left edge.

UPPER CRAG

This lies above the Lower Crag and is very steep, but often easier than it looks and
generally well protected, therefore providing exhilarating climbing. Some of the
lines have a certain amount of heather higher up but this is a minor blemish.

Descent: The descent is unpleasant and abseiling might be preferred. Descend
diagonally rightwards (south) down a steep vegetated ramp until near the base,
then cut back left.

7 Baywatch   45m   E1   *(1994)*
A short sharp crux. Left of the holly tree of Paradise Regained is a slabby rib. Start
just left of Paradise Regained.
1. 25m 4c Climb up the rib then up the groove on the right to belay on the large
block.
2. 20m 5c Climb the blank red wall slightly left of the block and trend back right
higher up to finish left of Paradise Regained.
A good route of VS can be made by joining the first pitch of this route with the last
pitch of Paradise Regained (but started further right).

8 Paradise Regained   50m   E1 **   *(1994)*
The open chimney on the left side of the crag with a holly tree at its base. Sustained
but varied climbing with a bold section; high in the grade.
1. 30m 5b Climb the rib just left of the holly and step right into the groove above.
Climb the groove and short chimney to a hard mantelshelf onto the ledge on the
right. Step right and back left, climb a scoop to an easing. Move 2m left to a blunt
rib and climb a short crack, then continue slightly leftwards up the slab to a pair of
jammed blocks.
2. 20m 5a Climb the wall above the topmost block and follow rough rock to a nose
which is passed on the right.

9 Quick on the Draw   35m   E5 6a **   *(1997)*
The shallow corner-line immediately right of Paradise Regained. The crux is hard
6a and above gear. Start right of the holly at a left-facing corner. Climb the corner
and its shallow continuation to where it blanks out. Move up, then go out left to
the ledge of Paradise Regained. Move up and right and continue to a heathery
ledge. Either belay here and traverse right to descend or continue up the slab on
the left.

GRUINARD CRAGS

**10 Pistolero   25m   E3 5c ** *(1997)*
The intermittent cracks in the wall immediately right of Quick on the Draw, with better holds and protection than it looks. Low in the grade. Climb direct by a bold slab to the left end of the roof system. Alternatively, start up The Big C for 3m and move left or the short corner of Quick on the Draw and swing out right. Pull through the roof with difficulty; continue up the cracks above to a heather ledge. Traverse right to descend.

**11 The Big C   30m   HVS 5a ** *(1994)*
This is the central line taken through the niche. An atmospheric route with a big feel, but with a little heather. Start directly below the niche and climb a shallow corner to step left into the niche. Swing right on to the airy wall and follow the right-trending line to below a stunted holly (above and left of the more obvious holly at the top of Red John's crack). Climb up to the tree and step right. Climb a crack above and finish by a sporting mantel to its right.

**12 Gunslinger   25m   E2 5b ** *(2000)*
Climbs up to and over a protruding tongue of rock below the right end of the roof formed rightwards from Big C's niche. Climb the wall above to finish up the mantel of Big C.

13 Red John of the Battles   25m   E2 5b * *(1994)*
Right of The Big C is a straight crack running up an overhanging wall. Climb this strenuously with excellent holds and runners to gain a ledge and holly. Continue slightly left to finish by the "sporting mantel" of Big C.

**14 Coupe du Monde   25m   E3 5c * *(1998)*
Between Red John and Overlord is a groove and steep wall. The route climbs these, moving slightly right up steep flakes to a difficult finish in a small groove.

**15 Overlord   25m   E1 5a ** *(1994)*
To the right of Red John is an overhanging corner. Climb into the corner and up it to some blocks. The daunting wall above is climbed leftwards into a hidden crack and the climb finishes up a right-slanting ramp. Strenuous but very well protected.

**16 How the West was Won   25m   E4 6a ** *(1997)*
To the right of Overlord is a thin crack-line ending at hanging flake-blocks. Gain the start of the crack from a groove in the centre of the wall, pull out left onto a ledge then step right and climb the crack to where it stops. Move left, gain a ledge, then step right to climb the wall and a short slab.
Variation: **E5 6b ** *(1998)*
Go onto the flake-blocks and directly up the wall above on spaced holds and protection.

17 Stand and Deliver   25m   E5 6a * *(1997)*
The thin crack-line up the right side of the wall right of Overlord, just left of the fissure at the right end of the crag. Sustained and generally well protected but with a sting in the tail.

18 Quail   25m   Difficult *(1998)*
The obvious short fissure at the right end of the crag is climbed to a heather ledge, followed by a fine groove round the corner.

North Wall

Off-shore   25m   E3 5c *(2000)*
This route lies to the left of the main Upper Crag, about 100m ascending, then descending to the bottom of a long right-slanting narrow pillar (or approach direct from below; slightly higher than the main crags and about 150m left). Starting from

Cubby Images

GRUINARD CRAGS

Red John of the Battles, E2, Gruinard Crag. Climber Jo George

a short rightwards diagonal crack, go direct to a small flake. Traverse down right to a shallow groove line. Climb this (crux) to a left-trending line of better holds.

INVERIANVIE CRAG

Map p222

This contains a number of walls on the end of a flat knoll overlooking the start of the path up the Inverianvie River. The original crag, Bayview Wall, is seen in profile from the car park but the first crag, Yellow Wall, is the nearest crag and faces the car park.

YELLOW WALL

Predator   20m   E3 5c   *(2002)*

Start up a white groove, go right to the main groove line and finish right to a tree. Abseil descent.

Bloomsday   20m   E5 6a *   (2002)
A thin crack-line and wall leading to the tree and abseil descent.

Right of Yellow Wall, the walls are in two-tiers.

UPPER TIER

The Bayview Wall

(NG 955 896)   Alt 60m   South-West facing

The wall is seen in profile from the car park. The left continuation of the crag has a small forest below it, clearly seen on the approach. A huge wedged block in the centre of the wall is a distinctive feature. An intermittent sheep track rising from the car park leads up under the block to the right side of the upper face. Traverse left beneath the upper wall and along past the huge wedged block to a ledge beneath a wall with a fine crack.

Descent: Either climb down Chokestone Gully i.e. behind the block (subterranean Difficult), or by easy scrambling on the west (seaward) end. Walk right (west) along the cliff-top for 50 to 100m to reach a short scramble down to a lower ledge. Go left to a dead tree and scramble down here to the west end of the cliff base.

Routes are described left (Bayview Wall) to right (Optic Wall).

Perihelion   15m   Severe 4a   (2000)
At the furthest left of the ledge, cracks and flakes lead to a ledge, then a fine slab leads up left.

Shadow   15m   Severe   (1998)
A few metres right of Perihelion, a crack with some heather leads to a ledge. Continue up the cracked seaward facing wall on the right.

Between Shadow and Gneiss and Easy is a worthwhile eliminate (E1 5b).

Gneiss and Easy   15m   VS 4c *   (1990)
The cracked wall left of the heathery crack. Start 5m left of the crack up a wall on big holds, then move right and climb an upper crack.
Variation 1:
Starting as for Double Matured, go up into a left-slanting groove to join Gneiss and Easy before the upper right-slanting crack.
Variation 2: **The Pleasure Beach   Severe 4b** *   **(**1998)
From the point where Variation 1 joins, go straight up a superb whistle clean crack.

Double Matured   15m   VS 4c   (1990)
A heathery crack has a small tree at the bottom. Start up the wall immediately to its left and move into the crack above the tree. Not unpleasant, with bridging past the heather.

Cask Conditioned   15m   HVS 5a *   (1990)
The line just left of the crack and right of a heathery crack sporting a small tree. Climb to the roof and pull rightwards through this, then more easily to the top. Pulling leftwards through the roof makes it E1 5b.

Root Beer   15m   E2 5b **   (1995)
The obvious fine crack, with a strenuous start. Low in the grade.

Barrel of Fun   15m   E2 5c   (1995)
Climbs the wall just right of the crack to much better rock and protection. High in the grade.

Coffin Dodgers Eliminate   15m   HVS 5a   *(2001)*
A series of shelves in the wall right of Barrel of Fun.

Decommissioned Arms   20m   E1 5b   *(1998)*
A route up the middle of the slim buttress to the left of Chokestone Gully. Start by
climbing a thin undercut crack and move up a left diagonal crack until a swing right
leads to ledges. Easier up the middle of the buttress to finish. A less direct version
with a vegetated start to the left is Severe (1998).

Something Completely Different   12m   E1 5c   *(2000)*
A short but strenuous route up the front face of the chokestone of Chokestone
Gully. Climb the left side of the Gully and pull into the corner on the chokestone.
Climb this and go left to finish.

Chokestone Gully   15m   Difficult
The through route under the huge wedged block. Also a descent route.

Optic Wall

The long wall right of the huge block is less rough, yellow in tinge and composed
of less good rock.

Tuppenny Tipple   20m   VS 4b   *(2000)*
About 10m right of Chokestone Gully, there is a rib with a dirty crack on its right.
Go up, using the rib and the crack, to better protection and a traverse right below
a ledge, to finish just left of Slippery Nipple.

Slippery Nipple   20m   HVS 5a *   *(2000)*
Start 3m right of Tuppenny Tipple, aiming for the left-hand end of the M shaped
overhang. Climb the wall direct with thin protection, through the overlap and finish
up a small groove.

The Parting Glass   20m   E1 5b *   *(1998)*
From the lowest point, a rightwards-trending line is taken to breach the obvious
roof by a crack. On the first ascent, a lens fell from the second's spectacles.

Lock-in   15m   E1 5b   *(2003)*
Climb the slab between The Parting Glass and Gill to the widest section of the
overlap, pull through and then follow a faint groove trending slightly right.

Gill   25m   Severe 4a *   *(2000)*
There is a short left-facing corner 10m right of The Parting Glass. Go up this,
moving to an edge, then go up right on good rock to finish.

Synoptical   20m   VS 4b   *(2000)*
A few metres right of Gill is a large block. Start on this, using a right-curving crack,
but go directly up left on better rock to a thin crack, finishing at a large bollard.

Double Vision   20m   VS 4c   *(2000)*
Starting at the same point as The Dundee Dram, go straight up, then left with some
dubious holds, to a groove and good rock to finish.

The Dundee Dram   25m   VS 4c   *(1998)*
Climb the right edge of the wall up a cleaned crack, moving right to keep near the
edge and up to a heathery finish.

The Saloon of Life   15m   E2 5b **   *(2002)*
Right of the end of Optic Wall, the crag turns uphill into a sidewall. To the right of
a tree filled fault is a fine clean steep prow. This route climbs a crack-line splitting

the prow. Start up the slab below the prow and pull right onto it at a flake. Climb steeply into the crack and follow this line direct through bulges and all to the top.

LOWER TIER

Below Bayview Wall is a more broken section of rock, the Lower Tier. The first routes lie below the right end of the small forest.

Cerebral Harmer 15m E3 5b *   (2001)
The most obvious feature is a slightly tilted crest with a corner on it left. Climb the corner, with a bold start, just right of a rose bush.

Something Karma 15m Very Difficult   (2001)
Start just right of the crest up a ramp. Go up the face above and move left to finish.

Welly or Wonty 15m Hard Severe   (2001)
A left-slanting blocky crack-line just to the right.

Serial Farmer 15m VS 4c   (2001)
The centre of a slim buttress just to the right.

Farmer Giles 15m VS 4c   (2001)
This lies on a slabby buttress about 10m to the right and behind the left end of a buttress with ivy. Climb a crack-line, finishing direct or moving left where it steepens.

The following routes lies on the attractive buttress of gnarly rock characterised by ivy growing on its left side.

Winter Park 10m HVS 5b   (2001)
Climb directly up the left side of the wall right of the ivy.

Temporary Beauty 10m VS 5a *   (2000)
A good climb up interesting rock. Start just left of centre and climb steeply up to gain the prominent flakes. Take the natural line up and right and step left to finish.

The Wee Jumper 10m E3 5c   (2001)
The right arete, unprotected.

FOX'S BUTTRESS

(NG 958 895) Alt 90m West-North-West facing Map p222

This is the narrow buttress in the corner of the dome between Optic Wall and Dog Crag. It is characterised by a fine flat faced pillar of good rock with some deep red grooves on the right. These are of fine clean rock because they are prone to drainage.
Descent: Either by scrambling down the ramp leading right or down on the left of the main rocks (facing out in both cases).

Gone to Ground 10m HVS 5a   (2000)
On the left of the narrow buttress is a crack slanting right. Climb the crack and the wall on its right to finish.

Glacier Mint 15m E2 5c **   (2000)
Fine climbing up the front of the narrow pillar. Climb the front of the pillar using the obvious ledge and the thin diagonal crack on its left. Pull right into the scoop and finish straight up.

Foxtrot   15m   HVS 5a   *(2001)*
The arete right of Glacier Mint, finishing by a short crack.

Vulpine Groove   15m   HVS 5a *   *(2000)*
The deep red groove on the immediate right of the pillar is gained from the right
and followed steeply throughout.

Barking   15m   E1 5b *   *(2001)*
The steep crack just right of Vulpine Groove, slanting right to finish.

Earth Matters   15m   HVS 5a   *(2001)*
The leaning corner-crack right of Barking. There is a small aspen on the right a few
metres up. Well protected throughout.

Around 75m up and left of Fox's Buttress is quite a large diamond shaped slab.

Diamond Slab   20m   VS 4c   *(2001)*
Starting at the lowest point, climb the slab direct to a heathery ledge. Finish up a
short steep wall by a projecting block.

DOG CRAG

(NG 958 893)   Alt 70m   South-West facing   Map p222

This crag lies close to and downhill from Lochan Dubh Crag (although Lochan Dubh
Crag can only be seen from its top), just to the left of the stream which issues from
Lochan Dubh. The rock is variable in quality but mostly good.

Approach: Walk up the Inverianvie River from the main Gruinard Beach car park
for 1km, then strike up the hillside on the north-east side of the river. The crag is
clearly visible from the path as a small dome with a tree growing at its base and a
continuous terrace at two-thirds height.

Descent: On either side from the top or descending leftwards (looking up) along
the terrace.

A thin crack at the left end of the lower tier is 5a. A wider right-hand crack in two
steps is **Down Shep** (Hard Severe 4c 1990). The wall on the right gained via a
detached flake, the up via an obvious hold is 6a.

Lassie   8m   HVS 5a   *(1988)*
An undercut corner towards the left end of the lower tier. A reachy start and it's not
all over.

Cailleach   10m   E3 5c **   *(1990)*
A short nippy route up the red overhanging wall. Start mid-way between two large
flakes at the foot of the wall. Climb a slightly right-slanting flake-crack to reach a
flake on the right. Finish up a left-slanting crack and small corner. A right-hand start
is harder and more serious.

Tess   12m   VS 5a   *(1988)*
The obvious wide crack and big flake, with an overhanging start.

Dogged Persistence   20m   E3 5c   *(2000)*
Start 5m right of the wide crack of Tess. Climb into a vague pink scoop, move left
and gain the short but obvious crack. Climb the crack (crux) to the easing in angle
and finish up by the crack in the black rock above.

K9   30m   E1 *   *(1988/1995)*
A thin crack breaks the overhanging lower wall 5m left of the obvious feature of
Inverianvie Corner. It would be a two star route if the rock was perfect.

1. 20m 5b Climb the crack and wall, then continue in the same line to finish over the final bulge (or left, easier). Either traverse left along the terrace to descend or:
2. 10m 5a A short thin crack up the left side of the upper dome forces one out left into an easy angled groove after a few moves (or the groove throughout – 4b).

Inverianvie Corner   30m   E2 ** (1988/1995)
The big open corner towards the right side of the wall. The second pitch is optional but good. Start just left of the corner.
1. 20m 5b Make some thin moves up and left to reach a crack and small right-facing corner. Climb this and move right into the main corner. Either finish up the corner or move out left (harder).
2. 10m 5c The thin crack up the right side of the upper dome (hard).

Pig Monkey Bird   20m   E2 5b * (2000)
A bold start. Start up the corner itself to an easing in angle close to Inverianvie Corner. Go up a thin flake-line on the right, then rightwards to reach a darker finishing flake.

Slab Crack   25m   Severe * (1988)
To the right of Inverianvie Corner is an overhanging wall. Below and right again is a slabby wall. Climb its left side to reach a terrace level with the base of Inverianvie Corner. Continue up the crack behind, which widens into a small chimney.

Crab Slack   50m   Very Difficult (1999)
Start at the right corner between the base and the side wall. Climb a shallow scoop and subsequent left-slanting crack which runs just left of a broad rib.

Prospector's Rib   50m   Difficult (1996)
The broad rib formed between the front face and the right side wall, starting round on the side wall.

Wanderlust   30m   Very Difficult ** (1988)
Higher up on the right side wall of the crag is an area of slabby pinkish rock. Go up the centre of the slab to a steepening with some grooves. Go up the right side of the central groove, crossing a quartz vein and the continuation slab above.

Pluto   10m   Severe (1990)
Cracks in a vague slabby rib at the left end of the upper tier.

RIVERSIDE SLABS

(NG 958 891)   Alt 60m   South-West facing   Map p222
These slabs lie immediately above the Inverianvie river path, just past the turn off for Dog Crag and have an obvious holly tree at the right-hand end. The climbing is good but the quality is reduced by a degree of mossy rock. There is a left-hand section, a heather filled fault, a main central section followed by another heathery fault and a final rib on the right. Descend to the right.

Pipistrelle Crack   14m   HVS 5a (2002)
Climbs the left-hand buttress. Start at the lowest point and climb directly into a pod. Follow cracks left and up to a horizontal break. Move right, climb a short mossy crack and move right again to finish up the crack in the centre of the buttress.

The next routes are on the central section.

Blues Before Sunrise   15m   HVS 5a * (2002)
Start by a thin right diagonal crack at the left end of a low heather ledge. Climb direct to gain thin cracks leading to the base of a left-facing mossy corner. Finish by

the obvious left diagonal crack.

Passing Glance   15m   VS 4c *(2002)*
The obvious crack springing from a recess and lower left-facing dirty corner. Start left of the corner and heather patch and climb cracks in a vague rib to the base of the main crack. From its top move right and up to finish.

Blitzkrieg Bop   15m   E1 5b * *(2002)*
A right-trending line starting from the right end of the low heather ledge. Climb up and through a shallow slot to gain the right-slanting crack and up this to below the heather. Trend right and up to finish.

Sunlight Slab   20m   VS 4b * *(2002)*
This follows thin cracks in the slab split by a heather ledge. Start by some pale streaks and climb cracks to the ledge. Continue up the cracks heading right towards the edge and finish up a more obvious crack returning left. Low in the grade.

Autumn Rib   14m   Severe * *(2002)*
The rib right of the right-hand heather fault. Climb obvious clean cracks up the rib with a deviation on to the left edge at the top section.

Echolocation   10m   Hard Severe *(2002)*
The left arete of the block right of the holly tree. Start on the front face and follow the obvious crack over the arete to finish up its left side.

LOCHAN DUBH CRAG

(NG 960 894)   Alt 140m   South-West facing   Maps p220, 222   Diagram p238

This high quality crag is situated in a secluded spot overlooking Lochan Dubh. It is also known as Dome Crag, although Half Dome might be more accurate, since it is dominated by an awesome overhanging wall, flanked by more amenable ground.

Approach: From the car park follow the path up the Inverianvie River, then the stream up to Lochan Dubh. It can also be reached from the base of Gruinard Crag by a traverse curving up right and across a flat area south-eastwards to the crag which is soon seen in profile.

Descent: On the left (looking up).

The first two routes are on the left-hand sidewall.

1 The Crack   10m   Severe *(1989)*
Up the slope from Edgebiter is a smooth slab with a central line of holds leading to a groove, the platform and walk off.

2 Edged Out   40m   Very Difficult *(1995)*
The smooth slab has a crack up its right side. Climb the crack to the platform, step left and climb the blunt rib on rough rock with good holds.

3 Edgebiter   50m   Severe *(1994)*
This climbs the left edge of the crag. A little scrappy. Start at the left edge of the crag, at the first place where the rock is less than vertical.
1. 20m 4a Move up and immediately traverse right into a crack (or more direct into the crack, 4c). Climb straight up to a halfway platform (one can walk off left).
2. 30m Above is a broken corner and rib on the left edge. Climb the corner, then pull left onto the rib and follow this to the top.

4 The Recess   40m   HVS *(1996)*
The left end of the crag base is a bulging wall at the left edge of which is the crack of Edgebiter direct start. Start immediately right of this at a slight recess.

GRUINARD CRAGS

LOCHAN DUBH CRAG

4. The Recess	HVS
5. The Silk Road	E2 **
6. Flawed by Design	E4 **

7. Call of the Wild	E3 5c ***
8. Dead Calm	E6 ***
9. Major Domo	E6 ****
10. The Missing Link	E2 *
10a. Sunk Without Trace	E3 5c *
11. Nick the Niche	E1 5b **
12. Raid the Recess	VS 4c
13. Beat the Beak	VS 4c
14. Ducks with Attitude	E2 5c
15. Scrabble	Hard Severe

Alan Leary

1. 20m 5a Climbed the recess to the platform.
2. 20m 5a Climb a thin crack in the rib on the left.

**5 The Silk Road   50m   E2 ** **   (1994)
Left of the main overhanging wall is a short but prominent corner, which provides a fine technical problem as the second pitch. The first pitch is up the lower overhanging wall, starting on the right rib of The Recess.
1. 20m 5b Climb up steep orange rock to a bulge. Move right round the bulge and back left onto its top. Continue up easier rough rock to a smooth corner.
2. 10m 5c Climb the smooth corner to mantel on to the airy slab on the right.
3. 20m Pull over the bulge on the right and climb rough rock to the top.

**6 Flawed by Design   35m   E4 ** **   (1996)
Athletic climbing up the hanging flake in the sharply overhanging wall right of The Silk Road's corner (pitch 2). Left of the start to Call of the Wild a diagonal crack splits a red wall. Start just to the right.
1. 15m 5c Gain and climb the crack, then go right up easy ground to belay at the right end of the heather terrace and below a groove.
2. 20m 6b Follow the groove in the slab and climb the hanging flake, with a rounded finish.

7 Call of the Wild   50m   E3 * **   (1995)
Climbs the left-hand weakness of the central wall. A committing start but the technical crux through the roof is well protected.
1. 35m 5c From an ivy filled recess (well below the main ivy) pull over the roof to the right on a large loose looking flake, and climb the impending wall to a resting ledge. Layback through the flaked roof above, and swing left to easier ground.
2. 15m Easy scrambling to the top.
Variation Start: **E4 6a**   (1996)
Provides a very sustained route. Start up Dead Calm, then trend left above the low roof and up the wall to the rest ledge.

8 Dead Calm   50m   E6 * **   (1995)
The obvious discontinuous crack-line in the centre of the wall offers a stunning route.
1. 30m 6b Follow the line past a blankish section to an easing and continue up bulging rock above to easier ground where moves up, then left gain a large niche.
2. 20m 4c Climb up rightwards and follow the best line to the top.

9 Major Domo   50m   E6 ** **   (1995)
The striking niched crack-line up the right side of the overhanging wall provides a tremendous climb. Well protected with as many small wires as you can muster.
1. 25m 6b Climb the niched crack-line to a ledge.
2. 25m 5b An easy groove slants up left. Climb the buttress on the right via a central line which trends left and up to a ledge. Climb a juggy crack in the final short wall to reach a platform.

**10 The Missing Link   50m   E2 * **   (1990/1995)
Follows the right edge of the central wall with a deviation into the niche to the right. Start 5m left of Nick the Niche.
1. 20m 5b Climb cracked blocks and a wall to the roof, and make powerful moves to reach a handrail which leads right into the niche.
2. 30m 5b Traverse out left onto the steep face and gain a crack-line, then the groove on the left which leads to easier ground.
*Variation: **Sunk Without Trace**   **E3 5c *   (1996)
This direct version omits the deviation into the niche to give an independent but definitely harder route. Once on the handrail, place a runner in a diagonal crack and immediately pull left into the initially difficult slim groove and follow it to where the normal route comes in.

**11 Nick the Niche   45m   E1 5b ** *(1989)*

This excellent route follows the first line of weakness right of the overhanging wall. To the right of the overhanging wall is an easy angled corner topped by a large block. Start up the corner, step right and climb to a small ledge. The overhanging wall above is split by a thin twin cracks. Climb the wall immediately on their right and gain a large niche (possible belay). Climb the crack out of the top left corner of the niche (crux) to easier ground.

12 Raid the Recess   45m   VS 4c *(1989/1996)*

A wandering route through steep ground. Start just right of Nick the Niche and climb easy slabs rightwards to the projecting block on Beat the Beak. Gain the top of the block and traverse back left to enter the niche. Move up to the ledge behind and step right onto a shelf. Go up to a vegetated recess and climb the corner forming its right side. Finish up increasingly easy ground.

13 Beat the Beak   45m   VS 4c *(1989)*

Start at a pointed block near a tree growing from the loch shore. Scramble up the open chimney on the left to reach an easy shelf which is traversed to its far left end. Climb the hanging corner, which has a projecting block (the beak) on the left, to a slab. Left of the little tree is a pair of jam cracks; Climb these and step right over a block and slab to a rib. Climb the fine rib direct to easy ground.

14 Ducks with Attitude   45m   E2 5c *(2000)*

A much better line than its appearance might suggest. Start as for Beat the Beak.
1. 20m 5c Scramble up the chimney (or climb carefully past a wedged block on its right), then move left along the shelf to climb a crack up the left side of a short smooth rib and continue to the base of an obvious short corner. Climb the corner and its left wall.
2. 25m 4c As for Beat the Beak. Cracks in the rib lead to more pleasant rock and the top.

15 Scrabble   45m   Hard Severe 4b *(1994)*

On the right of the crag is a well defined corner. Start near the tree as for Beat the Beak. Climb the chimney and continue up a slight bulge to belay above a slab at the base of the corner. The corner is steeper than it looks and gives a traditional tussle with small trees and an overhanging finish.

16 Sunset Song   30m   E1 5b * *(2001)*

A nice pitch between the second pitches of Ducks with Attitude and Scrabble. Walk in to the start from the right. Climb a thin crack with difficult moves into a shallow groove. From a ledge climb more or less direct to the top.

THE APRON

A pleasant apron of easy angled slab on the next knoll to the north of Lochan Dubh Crag (this lies on the other side of the wide descent "gully" from Lochan Dubh Crag). The slab reaches the ground in two tongues with an inverted V of heather and turf between them.

Smashy   50m   Very Difficult * *(1996)*

Climbs the right-hand tongue which starts as a short pillar. The skyline block type feature is climbed by a thin diagonal crack leading to easier angled ground and a common belay with Gneissy.

Gneissy   50m   Difficult ** *(1996)*

A very pleasant route starting from the base of the left-hand tongue, climbing to a short corner on the skyline and continuing to the belay.

Mark Gear collection

Pink Streak, VS, Creag Carn an Lochain Dubh. Climber Mark Gear

CREAG CARN AN LOCHAIN DUIBH

(NG 961 888)   Alt 130m   South-West facing   Map p222

The craggy face of a dome overlooking the Inverianvie River. Walk up the path until shortly below the obvious waterfall from where the dome is well seen high on the left with its rocky face including a clean central section. Go straight up steepening grass and finally scrambling until below the clean section.

Pink Streak   45m   VS 4c *   *(1994)*

The clean rock gives fine open climbing, easier and better protected than it looks, although a little mossy. Start at the right end of a small vertical wall below the clean section. Gain the slab above, then climb the centre of the clean wall, passing just right of a heather ledge and finishing up a left-slanting crack. The smooth pink rock to the left and above the heather ledge is cleaner but harder.

CHIMNEY CRAG

(NG 962 884)   Alt 110m   South-West facing   Map p222

The crag is reached by walking up the Inverianvie River path past the big waterfall and a gorge section until it opens out into a distinct meadow. The crag is immediately above the footpath on the left and is split into three sections by two chimneys. The more prominent chimney is the one on the right side of the crag.

New Forest Gateaux   15m   VS 4c   *(2004)*
A crack-line up the centre of the left section, starting off a fallen block.

The Intrusion   15m   HVS 5a   *(2004)*
A red blocky intrusion.

Grunge   20m   E1 5b   *(1995)*
A mossy open groove between the two crack-lines on the left-hand portion of the crag.

The King's Hat   15m   HVS 5a   *(2004)*
The tricky left chimney-line.

Glam Rock   20m   E4 6a *   *(1995)*
A crack-line just left of the right chimney with moves out right to reach the wider upper crack.

Not in Vein   20m   Severe   *(2001)*
Found on a section of rock on the upper right side of the crag, reached by traversing in from the left along heather and rock ledges. The route climbs a quartz vein and slabs above.

Gruinard River Crags
Map p220

The larger Gruinard River runs parallel and north-east of the Inverianvie River. Goat Crag is near the road whereas Carn Goraig and Carn nam Buailtean lie well upstream, often approached by cycling. Creag Ghiubhsachain is further away, above the Allt Loch Ghiubhsachain, which flows into the upper Gruinard River. Na Bearta Buttress is 5km up the Allt Loch Ghiubhsachain and described in the Carnmore chapter (p162).

GOAT CRAG - CARN NA H-AIRE
(NG 965 911)   Alt 90m   South-West facing   Maps p220, 222

An impressive line of cliff overlooking the Gruinard River just upstream from the road bridge and clearly seen from the road. The cliff is in three sections; the central and largest is dominated by a smooth overhanging wall which is continuous along its base. Above this the crag is still steep but more broken. The left and right sections are much more broken but seem to have some good patches of rock. In particular, the right section has a very steep wall known as Am Fasgadh.

Approach: Park somewhere on the main road, walk into the fisherman's car park, cross a fence into jungle and fight your way up to the crag, 10mins.

Descent: 1. Down a heather ramp towards the right side of the central section; there are some short rock slabs but largely easy. From the finish of the difficulties of Liquidator or Barefoot in the Park, traverse left (looking down) with a slight descent to reach the ramp. From the summit of the knoll (Carn na h-Aire) head 50m towards the upstream river and take the first depression leading towards the cliff. This descends and curves left to become the descent ramp.

2. Down a ramp crossing the left section. From near the top of Tilted Slab Gully, go down rightwards (looking down) across the top of the left section until an easy heather ramp leads back left to the base of the cliff below a big groove (the most obvious feature).

3. It is also possible to descend the back of the knoll and return through heather at either end of the crag, but this is a long way in rock boots.

Missile   80m   Severe   *(1963)*
The route is situated at the left edge of the central section, formed by a rib just right

of its bounding gully (Tilted Slab Gully). A good line but with some fierce vegetation.

1. 10m 4a An awkward start at the foot of the rib leads to an easier angle and a spike.

2. 15m 4a Stand on the spike to gain and climb a crack with a jammed block, then through vegetation and up a groove.

3. 30m Go right below an overhanging block, through jungle and back left onto a nose. There are some good moves on the final block.

4. 25m Easier rock leads to scrambling.

Meridian 80m VS   *(1974)*
The route has some fine exposed moves but also a jungle section. Start below a vertical corner just right of the rib bounding the gully (Missile).

1. 10m 4b Climb the corner on big (but worrying) holds, then more easily up the rib to the spike.

2. 40m 4b Go up the crack in the rib with a jammed block to jungle (common to Missile). Go rightwards through the jungle into a vegetated groove, but go immediately on to the rib on the right and climb it on good exposed rock to easier ground.

3. 30m Finish easily, keeping to the good rock on the rib.

Commonsense 12m E4 6a *   *(2000)*
The crack-line on the short wall just right of the corner of Meridian. Abseil from a tree.

The following routes climb the overhanging wall right of another corner (which has been climbed at VS 4c). Above this is 50m of VS heather pulling. Alternatively, lower-off gargoyle and some other back-up stuff but no lower-off belay really exists.

Homosuperior 20m E5 6a **   *(2000)*
The second crack-line right of the corner (the first being too close to the corner), starting from a big fallen block.

Twilo Thunder 20m E6 6a ***   *(2000)*
The next line to the right going straight up to a scary looking gargoyle like fin of jammed rock to a heathery ledge. Low in the grade.

Freakshow 20m E5 6a **   *(2000)*
Start as for Twilo Thunder, then take an obvious curving flake-line out right, before going up to the right of the gargoyle.

Breach Route 70m Severe *   *(1966)*
There is an obvious break, a huge corner, in the centre of the lower overhangs.

1. 30m 4a Climb the break, moving out left at half-height.

2. 40m 4a Move briefly left (but ignoring the obvious escape out left), then return diagonally right across steep ground for about 15m until a line of weakness leads back left. A more direct second pitch would be better but probably VS.

Liquidator 70m E3 **   *(1971/1998)*
A white crack-line through the overhanging lower wall about 25m right of the obvious break taken by Central Route and passing right of a bay with a big raven's nest ('Liq' and 'VS' scratched on the rock). Calcified rock and a stubborn wet patch mar an otherwise 3 star first pitch. Some aid used originally.

1. 30m 5c Climb the crack increasingly steeply (Friend 4 useful) through a crux bulge near the top before moving out right.

2. 40m 5b Return left to finish up the vegetated continuation to a small tree. Move 5m left and climb up over a bulge to reach a left-slanting crack which passes steeply just left of a nose to reach a terrace. Slightly artificial but keeping to good

rock, since there are easier but less pleasant options both just left of this pitch and the direct finish to the first pitch.

Barefoot in the Park   80m   E2 *   (1974/1998)
An exposed route on the wall right of Liquidator, but with an occasional hollow block; low in the grade. The reported independent start 5m right of Liquidator looks unlikely, but Liquidator was graded HVS!
1. 40m 5b Climb Liquidator for 5m, then take an obvious line diagonally right past a small tree and a tricky bulge to a slab. Climb straight up a faint groove to below some rounded overhangs.
2. 40m 5b Traverse right on a small slab amidst the overhangs and climb through their right end. Finish straight up on good rock.

AM FASGADH

About 100m right of the descent rake (descent 2) is a steep wall which does not display its full height until viewed closely. There is a dry stone wall and other mysterious stonework below it. It is very sheltered and south facing. The crag has been used as a top roping and bouldering venue by local climbers for some time, but also by heroes of old for aid climbing, as the rusting pegs in the crack at the right end of the crag bear witness. Protection is very limited, so the wall has been set up for sport climbing. The crag is very much in the early stages of development, so things will change. This is a good winter venue, when there may be sun and no midges.

There are three lines on the left at **7b+, 7c and 7b+** (2002). Next is a pillar with 4 bolts (project). Next is a line at **7c** (2005). Then a central line starting off the wall is **7c** (2003). All unnamed.

The obvious steep crack at the right end of the crag was **Tatapult** (30m E6 6c 2000) with a boulder problem overhung start, then continuing up the unrelenting crack to a no hands rest. Continue up the crack. This has been equipped with three bolts but needs more. A right-hand start is **B Movie** (10m E4 6a/b 2000), joining at the no hands rest and third bolt.

CARN GORAIG

(NG 995 860)   Alt 100m   South-West facing   Map p220   Diagram p246

One of the best crags in the area, this is a three-tiered gneiss crag overlooking the Gruinard River not far from its source at Loch na Sealga. The upper tier is the largest and dominates the view on the approach.

Approach: Access is straightforward following a rough estate track for about 6km from the main road until opposite Carn Goraig; about 1hr 15min walk or 45mins on a mountain bike. Wade the river (knee depth on average, impossible in spate) and cross the boggy flats to the crag.

Descent: Descend to the cliff base on the left (north) down a steep scrambling rake that runs beneath a vertical wall. But there is no access to the base of the top tier, so to reach this, descend on the right (south) before scrambling in. It is equally possible to continue this descent further right to reach the base. Abseiling allows several top tier pitches to be climbed.

The crag is solid clean rough gneiss, the Top Tier offering generally slabby climbing with a steeper two-tiered lower section. The climbs usually follow crack-lines with good protection. Some of the routes are on the Top Tier only with access being on the right. The full height routes are described right to left across the lower tier (but the first starts on the middle tier), then single pitch routes right to left across the upper tier (mentioning the top pitches of those which have already been described).

1 Bootless Crow   55m   VS * *(2000)*
At the right end of the middle tier are two steep crack-lines. This route climbs the bottomless right-hand crack and Ramadan takes the left-hand crack. Start at a mossy groove bounding the right side of the second-tier.
1. 25m 5a Climb clean rock right of the moss and take an obvious left-trending line joining the main crack at an orange hole. Follow the cracks above on to the slabs and climb up to belay below and left of a wide blocky Y-crack in the upper tier.
2. 30m 4c Move right on to a huge block and climb the right branch of the Y over a bulge to a heather bay. Follow the line of vague cracks above (the best line is the same as Ramadan).

2 Ramadan   65m   E2 ** *(1995)*
1. 10m 4a Climb cracks on the right side of the lower tier to a belay by a large overhung recess (or walk round!).
2. 25m 5b Climb a steep widening crack out of the right side of the recess, strenuous but well protected, and up to a right-slanting flake-crack left of the blocky Y-crack of Bootless Crow.
3. 30m 4c Climb the crack, either reaching right into the left branch of the Y or continuing direct (5a). Finish up a pleasant shallow crack.

3 Slideline   15m   E3 6a *(2000)*
To the right of Whoopers is a shallow depression and short crack. A side runner in Whoopers is 'sensible'. Climb the scoop and crack where a hold on the left may be useful.

4 Whoopers   80m   E4 ** *(1998)*
The hardest route here, but it shares a lot with other routes. In the centre of the lower tier is a smooth looking scoop, split by some very thin cracks.
1. 20m 6a Climb the easy lower slab, then by a good crack which soon fades. Continue up the scoop, with a hard move to gain a thin horizontal break. Step up right and pull over the final bulge, using a good jug in the crack on the right.
2. 25m 5c Directly above is another smoother scoop. Start just left of this smooth scoop and reach an undercut flange and flake-crack; go strenuously up this to a foot traverse right across a small shelf. Layback into the crack and pull over onto the slab above. Scramble up to below the left-hand of three parallel cracks, the right-hand two being close together (Wailing Wall).
4. 35m 5c Climb the crack direct (see Call of the Muwazzin).

5 The Highland Cragsman   80m   E3 ** *(1998)*
An E3 version of climbing through the three-tiers, which gives some excellent sustained climbing on the lower two pitches with a more relaxed final pitch. Three stars if finished by Call of the Muwazzin, as originally intended before another team nipped in.
1. 20m 5c Start just left of the smooth scoop and climb to an arrow-shaped slot. Climb the crack above and step left then back right up a pair of thin cracks to the ledge (or direct at 6a).
2. 25m 5c As for Whoopers pitch 2 but a less direct finish. From just below the fine hanging crack, hand-traverse right to a heather patch below a steep crack. Climb the crack and continue up the slab and heather to belay at the base of the central scoop left of the three crack-lines.
3. 35m 5b Climb the rib between two rounded scoops left of the left-hand crack and join Whoopers or Call of the Muwazzin for a further 10m or so to a point where it is possible to do a thin traverse left to join another hidden crack above a grassy crack and scoop below. Continue up this crack on good holds until possible to step left to reach a prominent flange which is climbed to a rounded ledge and exit up the short top wall.

246

CARN GORAIG

1. Bootless Crow	VS *
2. Ramadan	E2 **
3. Slideline	E3 6a
4. Whoopers	E4 6a **
5. The Highland Cragsman	E3 **
6. Wailing Wall	E1 ***
7. Alba / Return to Mecca	E2 *
8. Olden Glory	VS **
9. Old Goats	E2 **
10. Crusader	HVS 5a *
11. Climbing with Heather	HVS 5a
12. The Wicked	E2 **
13. The Fatwa	HVS 5b *
14. Dispossessed	E1 5b **
15. Call of the Muwazzin	E2 5b ***

Andy Nisbet

6 Wailing Wall   70m   E1 **** *(1987)*
The best route here, being sustained and direct through the three-tiers. Pitch 2 is
the crux and close to E2 5c.
1. 20m 5a Start at the left side of the clean section, left of the smooth scoop (and
The Highland Cragsman). Climb a slab and gain a small scoop; exit via a crack on
the right to reach the terrace.
2. 25m 5b From just left of the scoop and the previous routes, climb steeply to
gain a shelf. Follow a left-trending fault and climb a rounded bulge and up to a
heather terrace. Belay below the obvious twin crack-lines, the closer right-hand two
of three parallel cracks (i.e. just right of the previous routes).
3. 35m 5a Climb the left-hand of the twin cracks initially until it steepens and step
right to gain the right crack at a bulge. Climb this and follow the crack over the top
bulge. Or climb the right-hand crack throughout.

7 Alba / Return to Mecca   80m   E2 * *(1998)*
The top pitch is definitely better than the lower one but the option is there for a
full height route.
1. 45m 4c On the left of the lower tier is a steep rib bottomed by reddish slabs.
Climb the slab direct to the rib which is climbed centrally to exit via a rightwards-
slanting crack. Scramble up broken ground to below a bowl shaped scoop on the
left side of the top tier.
2. 35m 5c Climb the crack on the left of the bowl to a bulging wall. Traverse 5m
left under the bulge to a hidden crack which is climbed strenuously, crux, to a slab
which is climbed up right to a wall. Move back left to a rightwards facing ramp
which is taken in a good position to the top. A good pitch; constantly varied and
interesting.

8 Olden Glory   85m   VS *** *(1998)*
The highlight is a fine pitch taking the easiest line up the top tier.
1. 35m 4b To the left of the steeper rib of Alba's lower pitch is a lesser one which
is climbed direct to slabs.
2. 15m Continue up pleasant slabs to a prominent short groove above.
3. 35m 4c Climb the awkward groove via cracks to a small tree. Move up left
round a shallow rib to a flanged crack which is climbed to a topmost bulge. Hand-
traverse below the bulge to a break and exit up this to the top.

9 Old Goats   65m   E2 *** *(2000)*
A direct line on clean rock throughout. It aims for the break at the left end of Olden
Glory's hand-traverse. The start lies to the left of the lower tier, on a heather rake
reached by a short crack. The base of a clean rib is marked by a large boulder
thread on its left and twin trees to its right. A small roof is visible some way up the
rib.
1. 30m 4b Climb the rib to the right of the roof and continue on excellent rock to
deep cracks at the left end of the upper terrace. Or climb pitch 1 of Crusader, the
original line.
2. 35m 5c Climb straight up to a cleaned ledge and up to thin left-trending cracks
(or step left from the ledge and climb the wall above before stepping back right to
the cracks). Climb the steepening cracks on improving holds to a ledge (passing
well left of an obvious triangular block). Step right and go up rust coloured slabs,
crossing the top bulge of Olden Glory to finish more easily.

10 Crusader   70m   HVS * *(2000)*
A pleasant climb. Start about 30m left of Olden Glory at the back of a large recess
with a smooth steep left wall.
1. 35m 4b Climb steeply out of the back left side of the recess and up to pass left
of a prominent triangular roof (left of a heathery aspen bay). Continue more or
less direct to belay as for Old Goats. Alternatively, start as for Old Goats but go
diagonally left past the roof and up slabs to the same belay (the original line).
2. 45m 5a Climb up to a left-trending ramp and climb its cracks and a flake. Step

rightwards into a groove, then continue up the fault, climbing a short wall on the right to reach a black groove and crack, a short distance left of the finish of Olden Glory.

Variation: **The Saracens** (2000)
Instead of stepping right on pitch two, continue in the same left-trending line, with a long span left to gain a good crack at one point. Finish up a short steep crack to a huge block.

11 Climbing with Heather   25m   HVS 5a (2000)
This lies on the wall above the descent ramp. Continue down the ramp to a chockstone and belay. Climb the overhung scoop and crack above to a steep slabby wall and a heathery crack which is climbed to a heathery ledge. Clean rock above leads to a massive flake and the fine rib which is climbed centrally to the top. Potentially good given a prune.

12 The Wicked   35m   E2 ** (1999)
At the base of the descent ramp is a steep wall split by a prominent crack below a shelf.
1. 15m 5b Climb the crack to the shelf.
2. 20m 5c Move right onto the arete, climbed on excellent rock in a fine situation to the top.

Top Tier

For direct access, scramble in from the right. Described right to left, mentioning the top pitches of longer routes which can be climbed alone.

13 The Fatwa   30m   HVS 5b * (1998)
A fine crack rising out of an obvious red groove. Follow the crack in the same line after the easing.

14 Dispossessed   30m   E1 5b ** (1998)
Start at The Fatwa and move left into a scooped line of cracks, small ledges and hidden holds to gain the easing by a small protruding spike. Climb in the same line via cracks and blocks to finish.

To the right lie the top pitches of Bootless Crow, Ramadan, and Wailing Wall.

15 Call of the Muwazzin   25m   E2 5b *** (1998)
A good pitch on the top tier, following the crack immediately left of the twin cracks of Wailing Wall — the left-hand of the three parallel cracks. Quite strenuous but well protected. Where the crack peters out at a half-height bulge, move right into the left-hand crack of Wailing Wall (where that route moves right) and move immediately back left into the original line after the bulge.

To the right lie the top pitches of Whoopers, The Highland Cragsman, Return to Mecca, Olden Glory, and Old Goats.

CARN NAM BUAILTEAN
(NG 002 876)   Alt 150 to 200m   West facing   Map p220

A series of generally slabby gneiss crags scattered about the hillside of Carn nam Buailtean provide some fine climbs in a remote setting. The rock is equally good quality but often not as clean as Carn Goraig.

Approach: As for Carn Goraig but skirt the western edge of this crag and continue for a kilometre or so to a line of clean pale crags that run along the hillside. In dry conditions it is slightly quicker to cross the Gruinard River at an island and head direct across boggy moor to the crags. A second shallow wade is required. About 1.5 km from the Gruinard River.

The crags of Carn nam Buailtean are clearly seen from the track near the island. The largest and cleanest buttress as seen from here is Sylph Buttress, the right-hand of three low down and in a horizontal line. Right of this buttress is a spur on the hillside with a smaller group of three arranged vertically (Terrace Crags). Left of the Sylph group is a broad boulder filled gully, somewhat central on the hillside. At mid-height on its left side is another obvious buttress, a well defined crest with a big roof on its right side; this is Golden Buttress. Further details are best picked out from closer up.

The very clean pale buttress, Sylph Buttress, can hopefully be picked out as the right-hand of three. The central one of the three is a less conspicuous brown coloured crag, Stealth Buttress. A broader slabby crag that starts lower down to its left and with a tree covered ledge low down is Blank Buttress. Above Blank Buttress is a slabby wall that rises from a tree covered balcony, Rock of Ages Buttress. To the left of this sector lies the broad gully and mid-way up on the left is Golden Buttress with its clean-cut slab on the left and roof on the right. At the foot of the gully on the left is the steep but less obvious Nose Buttress with characteristic black rock.

Beyond Nose Buttress to the left lie a line of slabby buttresses that stretch along the western frontage of Carn nam Buailtean at a much higher level. At the far end of the hill lies a steep nose, Beyond Buttress.

The routes and individual buttresses are approached and described from right to left.

TERRACE CRAGS

These three-tiered crags are of excellent rock with the middle tier providing the main climbing. The top and bottom tiers have been climbed by various lines, nowhere more than Severe.

**Shogun 20m E2 5c ** (2000)
An obvious roof marks the start of several fine cracks. Shogun takes the fifth crack right of the roof, following excellent rock. Difficult climbing leads to a break, then move left into the upper crack to finish.

Terrano 20m HVS 4c (2000)
This takes the third crack right of the roof, finishing up reddish rock.

Freelander 20m VS 5a (2000)
The second good crack right of the roof.

Terra Nova 20m HVS 5a (2000)
The first thin crack right of the roof, with a move right into the upper cracks.

SYLPH BUTTRESS

This is the obvious pale crag split into two halves by a thin heather rake. It is bounded on the right by a block filled gully which has an overhanging left wall. The rock is impeccable white gneiss save on the gully wall which has seen substantial rockfall and has a much less attractive darker fissile rock. Descents are down the gully to the south (right looking up) with a diversion left at a step.

Sylph 70m Very Severe * (1999)
This good climb takes the right edge of the buttress. Start on a shelf below a prominent dead tree.
1. 40m 4a Climb a short steep wall at its left end via cracks to a slab. Move left to an arete and climb this on superb rock to below the steep upper section which is split by a crack.
2. 30m 4b Climb the arete via the crack in an exposed and fine position, past the awkward crux and continue in the same line to the top. A lovely pitch.

Gossamer 100m VS *

(2000)

This good route begins left of Sylph and takes a diagonal line to reach it, then climbs a diagonal crack beneath and right of it. Start beside Nymph at the foot of a long slabby rib with an undercut right wall.

1. 50m 4c Move up and step right onto the rib and climb it. Go diagonally up right to climb cracks leading to a junction with Sylph. Follow this route to its belay below the blunt arete.

2. 50m 4c Step right and climb the crack that runs diagonally rightwards below Sylph.

Nymph 65m E1 **

(1999)

A route on superb rock with a hard but very well protected crux section. The climb follows a thin central crack-line over the two bulges on the left half of the buttress. Start at a lower tier which lies below a grass shelf. The first pitch is pleasant but optional.

1. 15m 4b Climb a steep narrow slab to the grass and below the central of three clean ribs.

2. 50m 5c Climb the narrow rib for a few metres until forced left to below to a bulge. Move up and right to arrive beneath the lower bulge at the central crack. Climb the bulge on generous holds and up the crack in the slab to the next bulge. A thin overhanging crack, crux, surmounts the bulge and the climb continues up the slab above to a slight terrace below a further bulge. Move right and climb the bulge to finish up a short slab.

Satyr 50m VS

(1999)

A pleasant route, taking a line left of Nymph. Start as for Nymph's second pitch.

1. 35m 5a Climb to the bulge and up a thin crack (crux, well protected) to the first overlap. Step up right and climb the slab to the next overlap, taken by the groove on the right, or the left, to a slab and belays by the left edge below an arete.

2. 15m 4a Climb into a groove and climb the clean arete to the top.

STEALTH BUTTRESS

This lies up a grassy ramp left of Sylph Buttress. The best descent is down the gully as for Sylph Buttress. There is a prominent nose on arrival with a large flake at its foot and to the left a steep reddish slab with a capping wall. The rock is perfect but protection can be rather skimpy.

Foxbat 80m VS

(1999)

Start at the large flake.

1. 35m 4c Climb the clean frontal slab direct to a short wall. Climb this directly, crux, to a ledge above.

2. 45m 4c Climb the clean nose above to a crack, step left and climb a thin slab to below a slab and headwall. Climb the slab to the wall which is turned by a 'hand-traverse' crack and slab above to finish.

Stealth Fighter 90m E2 *

(1999)

To the left of the last route is a steep reddish pock marked slab, noticeable by the absence of protection. This fine but serious route climbs the slab direct and takes the capping wall centrally. Start at the lowest point of the slab below some pock marks.

1. 25m 5c Climb up to a blank section; a scattering of small RP runners only. Step right and up the slab thinly to an obvious hold and up to some welcome protection under a small overlap. Continue thinly up the red slab on the left to a point where a delicate traverse right gains a heather groove.

2. 20m 5b Step right and up to the overhang and boldly through this on hidden holds and better protection to a grass ledge above.

3. 45m Climb the straightforward slab up and right to near the 'hand-traverse' of Foxbat but finish up the left-slanting groove.

BLANK BUTTRESS

This is the slabby buttress to the left of Stealth Buttress. It has a prominent tree covered ledge at one-third height and steep blank slabs above that lead to a short top tier. Descents are easiest by abseil from trees above the top tier. Fifty metres will reach the tree covered ledge and a scramble down to the left or a shorter abseil from the trees will reach the base. Continuing above the top tiers leads to steep heather with Rock of Ages Buttress on the right and a shorter steep crag on the left.

Point Blank   65m   HVS   *(1999)*
This route takes a roughly central line up the slabs to the right of the tree covered ledge. Some thin but not sustained climbing on excellent rock. Start near the grass rake up to the right at a pair of prominent grooves.
1. 25m 4c Climb these awkwardly past some heather. Continue on clean rock up right to a little niche.
2. 20m 5b The fine bald slab is now taken directly above the stance, initially via a crack which then blanks out. Some very tenuous moves, crux, are then made to the left to reach a groove which is quite bold and followed to a ledge.
3. 20m 5a Climb the steep bulge above which has a thin exit, poorly protected, to heather and a corner.

Blanked Out   60m   E2 **   *(2000)*
A good route with a tricky crux, very well protected. At the base of the crag is the lower wall leading to the tree covered ledge. Start at the base by a triangular flake.
1. 20m 4c Climb straight up the pleasant wall to the ledge.
2. 40m 5c Move right to a tree belay below the right-hand slabs which are capped by a cracked bulge. Climb the slab past a small tree and continue on excellent rock to a cosy niche below the bulge. The thin crack is well protected by small Friends and has a rounded exit on to the slab above (crux). Continue straight up the crack to a small ledge. Climb the wall above, first left then right to below another short wall. Climb this up a heathery funnel to the wall behind.

Step Dance   70m   HVS *   *(1999)*
To the left of the wall that supports the tree covered ledge the brown slabs form a clean tongue. This route is unfortunately often wet. Start 2m left of a vegetated groove.
1. 30m 5a Climb directly up excellent sustained rock with good protection, over the overlap and up to a ledge below a prominent curved crack.
2. 40m 5a Climb up a short distance, then traverse left to a scoop which is followed more easily to the short top tier, a slab, climbed centrally to the jungle above. Abseil descent from trees.

ROCK OF AGES BUTTRESS

Above Blank Buttress lies a superb wall, the lower and right of two walls and with a big tree in a gully to its right. It is best approached either by a route on Blank Buttress or by abseil from the level ground at its top (the buttress is visible from just to the north); scrambling approaches are quite unpleasant. The wall has a roof to the left and a steep slab to the right guarded by a short wall. To the right of this wall is a tree.

Eternal Cleft   30m   E2 5c ***   *(2000)*
A splendid route, full of character and well protected. Climb a corner to the roof and turn this subtly on the right to gain a thin crack (crux). Continue up the fine crack to join Rock of Ages to finish. Low in the grade.

Rock of Ages   35m   HVS 5a **   *(1999)*
An excellent well protected route. Start to the left of the tree and climb the short wall on sharp holds to a small ledge, then move left to the slab. Climb a thin crack

and its continuation to its end. Step thinly left and up to a suspect block in a groove. Climb the headwall above by the central thin crack in a great position to arrive at a sentry box right of a cracked block. Exit onto the final slab via a thin crack on the right.

GOLDEN BUTTRESS

This lies at the top left of the wide gully left of Blank Buttress. Very clean with strongly cut features, it is very prominent from below with an undercut slab on the front face, a widening ramp and a crack split wall with a large roof to the right. Descents are easiest to the north (left looking up).

Glistering Slab   55m   VS **   (1999)

A splendid climb on impeccable rock. The line follows the best part of the slab to the left of a deep crack. Start below the frontal slab on a grass shelf above broken grooves.
1. 35m 4c Traverse the slab rightwards below overhangs, usually a bit wet, to reach a narrow gangway that cuts above the right wall. Climb a groove on the left and emerge on the superb slab. Move left and follow a crack over all the obstacles en route, to reach a spacious stance below a scooped slab.
2. 20m 4b Climb the steep rib on the left to finish.

Golden October   60m   VS *   (1999)

This takes the crack-line to the right of Glistering Slab on excellent rock. Start below a steep groove with some vegetation which lies near the left end of the vertical retaining wall on the right of the crag.
1. 40m 4c Climb into the groove and go up this to the gangway. Move right along this to the crack just right of the shallow groove of Glistering Slab. Climb the crack onto the slab and continue up its right side to the ledge below the scooped slab.
2. 20m 4b Climb the slab up the middle to step left into a square-cut groove just below the top of the slab. Climb up the groove to finish.

Heart of Gold   60m   Hard Severe *   (1999)

This route takes the hanging corner on the upper right of the crag reached by the scooped wall below the roof. Some pleasant open climbing involving both walls and slabs. Reach this wall via a grassy ramp on the right of the crag that has a short rock step.
1. 30m 4a Climb the scooped wall from right to left on good holds via two ledges with perched blocks to exit below the hidden corner. Continue up the corner to a belay on the left.
2. 30m 4a Step right to a fine slab and climb this direct to a grass ledge (optional belay). Move left to the top tier and climb a concave slab to its crest; step left and easily up a broken wall to the top of the buttress.

HORIZON BUTTRESS

This is the small crag seen above Golden Buttress on the skyline. It is composed of perfect clean gneiss, with a vertical left wall and easy slabs to the right, a good example of a 'roche moutonee'.

Horizon Shine   25m   Difficult   (1999)

The slabs are steepest at a bulge left of the central corner which is taken by cracks straight up on excellent holds on clean rock.

NOSE BUTTRESS

This is the lowest lying of the crags here and lies above the path to the left of Blank Buttress. It has smoother brittle black rock, most but not all of which is sound. Beyond the black retaining right wall the frontal face is split into a number of narrow buttresses of overlapped rock. Routes are described right to left.

Dark Destroyer   40m   E3 5c   (2000)
To the right of the widest buttress at the lowest section of the crag is a crack running up a slight side wall beside a chimney come gully feature formed by a huge blocky rib. Climb to the crack and bridge this to a standing position on the block forming the right rib. Step into the crack and up this awkwardly to a ledge. Continue up the cracks above to heathery ground and then directly to a heather ledge. Climb the steep crack in the rib above and continue more easily to a small abseil tree.

Holly Tree Hover   50m   E2 *   (2000)
This lies on the frontal face of the widest buttress, identified by a prominent roof crack high up and a holly tree in a groove to the right. A small cleft lies to the right of the roof.
1. 30m 5c Climb the right-slanting crack just left of a shallow corner to a large flange. Climb the flange to an overlap. Climb the crack through this to below the roof and traverse horizontally right to the cleft. Step down, then climb the cleft (crux) to reach the holly tree. Climb past this on the right.
2. 20m 4c Continue up a wide crack to finish (abseil descent).

Black Beauty   20m   E1 5b **   (2000)
This excellent route climbs the right-bounding rib of the left-hand section of the crag. Slow to dry, but the climbing avoids the wettest patches. Low in the grade. Start at the base of the wall, left of a gully with weird flakes. Climb up a slight groove, then swing right to a foothold on the arete and pull into a recess. Step up onto a heather ledge. Smooth but perfect rock up the rib with good protection leads to an abseil tree on a heather terrace.

Brown Bess   25m   HVS 5a *   (2000)
Start in the middle of the left-hand section about 2m left of a shallow mossy groove. Climb a short hanging groove to gain fine cracks above leading first up, then left to the heather terrace (same tree abseil).

BEYOND BUTTRESS

This is the nose at the far left end of the crags well seen from the approach and reached by walking up to a little col beyond a vertical crag. A line of slabs lies above the col to the right of a vertical wall which ends beyond the col. This is a slow drying crag with considerable amounts of black moss which are easily removed en route.

The Pale Beyond   60m   HVS   (1999)
1. 45m 5a Climb the slab via a line of flakes and mossy cracks to near a grass patch. Step right and climb up through a heather patch to a ledge with a small dead tree; a sustained pitch.
2. 15m 4b Climb the cleaner slab right of the obvious flake-groove to heather.

LOCHEND CRAGS

(NH 003 845)   Alt 130m   West facing   Map p220

These wooded crags are obvious from the estate track below Carn Goraig, lying on the south side of Loch na Sealga, low on the spur at the end of the loch. They are somewhat vegetated, but the routes described are on mainly clean gneiss, varying from sound to superb. The crags enjoy a magnificent view to the west and may be of interest if high water prevents a crossing to Carn Goraig or Carn nan Buailtean.

Approach: Continue up the track to the end of the loch, about another 15mins by bicycle in addition to the Carn Goraig approach. The crags lie about 15mins walk up the hillside on the right.

GRUINARD CRAGS

Highland Spring   45m   HVS *   *(2000)*

Towards the right of the crags is a steep clean brown wall, with two-tiers separated by a grass ledge. This climb follows an obvious line up both tiers, taking a thin groove in the lower tier, followed by thin cracks splitting horizontal breaks in the upper tier.

1. 25m 4c Climb the lower groove on sometimes mossy rock, with very spaced protection, to a tree.

2. 20m 4c Go slightly left to a scoop, step back right on to the wall and take the line of least resistance to the topmost break, then direct up the final thin crack using a block. An excellent pitch, well protected.

Continuing up right below this wall, then coming back left above it, a clean boss of rough white gneiss is seen. It presents a steep wall to the west, standing above an attractive belvedere which receives afternoon sun. The climbs are short but nevertheless worthwhile.

Skoosh   15m   HVS 4c   *(2000)*

An obvious rightwards diagonal crack, steeper than it looks and strenuous.

Sparkle   15m   HVS 5a *   *(2000)*

Starting at the same point as the previous route, climb a strenuous vertical crack and flange, finishing up a left-trending crack.

Fizzle   12m   VS 4c   *(2000)*

At the left end of the wall is a groove leading to an unsound looking flake. Climb to the groove, then rightwards round the flake to finish.

CREAG GHIUBHSACHAIN

(NH 001 838)   Alt 270m   West facing   Map p220

This very steep gneiss crag overlooks the Allt Loch Ghiubhsachain, which flows into the upper Gruinard River. Recently discovered, there is scope for many hard routes and continued development is expected. It would appear to be quick drying. There are a few loose holds and some lichen high up; the routes have been cleaned on abseil.

Approach: Follow the Gruinard River track to a concrete bridge over the Allt Loch Ghiubhsachain, 1hr by bike. Follow the east side of the Allt, rising above a gorge section to a slight col, from where the crag is up and left, 45mins.

The left side of the crag is reddish brown and fairly smooth. The right end is pale grey and rough, with a large hole 10m up.

Seconds Best   35m   HVS 5a   *(2006)*

Start about 20m left and down from the large hole at a right to left crack leading to a short corner (cairn). Climb leftwards and make a hard move into the base of the corner. Climb this exiting leftwards to an easing of the angle and a pleasant finish.

The Fang   30m   E2 5b   *(2006)*

Start below the right side of the large hole. Climb up easily to a left-pointing fang of rock. Make a series of strenuous moves diagonally right to a ledge to the right of a large perched boulder. Move left on to this (tricky). Move off its right end and climb an overhanging crack to the top (crux).

Gruinard North

There are a number of crags spread out around the north end of Gruinard Bay. The roadside Jetty Buttress is the best known.

JETTY BUTTRESS

(NG 961 926) Alt 30m Varying aspects Maps p220, 260 Diagram p257

The rock is gneiss, generally rough but smooth on some of the steep walls. The rock dries quickly and has a wide range of grades; its convenience makes it popular. No routes are given three stars, but there are close contenders.

Approach: It is very easily seen only 50m inland from the road. Park on the verge, 30 seconds!

Descent: The easiest descent is over the top of and down beside the North Wall.

The routes are described from the top left (North Wall), down towards the road, rightwards across the Front West Wall, then up the different walls rightwards into the trees.

NORTH WALL

1 Route 1 15m Very Difficult
Start at a V-groove formed above a recess and 5m above the fallen fence situated towards the top end of the north face of the crag. Climb the groove for a short distance, go left onto the arete and then left and up by a small tree.

2 Route 2 15m Severe 4a *
Start as for Route 1, but continue up the groove to its top. Step left onto Route 1, then immediately back right across the top of the groove to the big slab on the right. Either climb the slab near its left-bounding corner (thin) or climb the wall on the left by a small groove and the slab above (airy).

3 Route 3 15m Very Difficult
Start at the same place as for Routes 1 and 2, but pull out right on to a triangular block. Step up on to a slab and finish up this.

4 Route Major 20m Hard Severe 4b *
Good but a little scary. Start approx. 8m below (towards the road) the bottom post at the start of the fallen fence where there is pale rock leading to a grey concave slab. Climb a small corner (another corner 2m right is harder), then move right and pull over a small pale wall using an embedded flake. Gain and climb the grey slab (poorly protected) passing its headwall on the left. Finish up the slabby final wall. Climbing the headwall direct is unprotected 4c.

5 Route 4 20m VS 4c
Start in the deep right-facing corner to the right of Route Major. Climb the corner to near its top (strenuous; a little wet in the back does not affect the grade), then go left onto the arete and up to the slab above. Climb the right side of the concave slab and finish by a crack in the final wall.

6 Buttress Crack 20m VS 5a
Start by climbing a detached pinnacle left of black rock in a depression. From the top of the pinnacle, climb awkwardly out right up the flaky corner and go right to the main crack in the buttress. Climb past a small tree and continue up a groove past loose sounding blocks at top.

7 Number Nine 20m E2 5b   *(1997)*
A direct line up the impressive wall right of Buttress Crack, but a little artificial. Start just right of the pinnacle and climb the smooth wall to the left end of a ledge. Continue straight up past the right end of the flaky corner of Buttress Crack and up the slabby crest to the top.

GRUINARD CRAGS

8 Route 5¹/₂ 20m   HVS 5b   *(1998)*
An easier line up the impressive wall, unfortunately neither clean nor on good rock.
Start 5m left of the black cave. From some blocks, gain a small right-slanting groove
with difficulty. From its top, step left into a small corner, then up the wall above to
reach hollow blocks on the right and a right-slanting crack in the final crest.

9 Route 6 20m   Hard Severe 4a ** **
Climbs the right side of the intimidating wall right of Buttress Crack, but the holds
are good. Start right of Buttress Crack by a small black cave, an obvious small
feature. Climb the wall just right of the cave (perhaps 4b), then step down and left
across its top on to the impressive wall. Trend left to a small groove in the centre
of the wall. Climb the groove, then a diagonal crack rightwards. Return left to
finish.
Variation: **Pikey's Wall   HVS 5a**   *(2001)*
Start more direct up the black cave and don't go right and left near the top.

10 Route 7 25m   Very Difficult
Climb black streaks 8m right of Route 6, trending left to reach and follow
rightwards a big ramp with grass ledges. Finish up a cleaner slab on the left.

11 Munroron 30m   Very Difficult ** **
Climb the centre of the obvious bottle shaped rib between Route 7 and Lilly The
Pink. Finish up the clean continuation slab on the left, as for Route 7. Nice climbing
on the rib, although it is easy to step off.

12 Lilly the Pink 30m   Hard Severe 4a *
A fine open climb. Start to the left of the north-west arete in a depression. Follow
the red quartzy rock up the centre of the depression and continue on clean slabs to
the top.

13 North-West Arete 35m   HVS 5a *
A little disappointing for such an obvious line. Climb the well defined crest
between the North and Front Walls, tenuous at first and using the corner on the
right, then directly up the slabby ground above.

FRONT WEST WALL

14 Running on Empty 35m   E2 5c   *(1998)*
An eliminate up the blank wall to the right of North-West Arete. Start just right of
the arete and climb a bouldery wall direct to beneath the widest point of the
overhang above, vital runners. Pull over this to arrive beneath a shallow black
scoop, marginal RPs only. Move up, then step left to a rounded edge and gain
easier ground common to North-West Arete.

15 Crab Crack 35m   HVS 5a *
A good start but quickly over. Start 5m right of the arete. Climb to a heather ledge
at 3m (would be better if cleaned, or start up Route 11). Step right and climb a
thin crack with a bulge at mid-height to reach slabby ground. Climb a scoop on the
right to join North-West Arete. Another crack just to the right is VS 4c but a little
overgrown.

16 Route 11 30m   VS 4b *
Start 8m right of the fence post. Climb to the right end of the heather ledge, then
go rightwards up a shallow corner come ramp taking care with a hollow block, and
continuing in the same line to easier ground. Alternatively, finish out left above the
block (4c, poorly protected).

17 Hands, Knees and Bumpsydaises 25m   E3 6a   *(1990)*
A fingery problem up the colourful bulging wall. Start 5m left of Anthrax Flake, at

JETTY BUTTRESS

4. Route Major	Hard Severe 4b *
5. Route 4	VS 4c
6. Buttress Crack	VS 5a
8. Route 5 ½	HVS 5b
9. Route 6	Hard Severe 4a **
10. Route 7	Very Difficult
11. Munroron	Very Difficult **
12. Lilly the Pink	Hard Severe 4a *
13. North-West Arete	HVS 5a *
15. Crab Crack	HVS 5a *
16. Route 11	VS 4b *
17. Hands, Knees and Bumpsydaises	E3 6a
18. Anthrax Flake	VS 4c **
20. Charlie's Corner	VS 4b **

Andy Nisbet

GRUINARD CRAGS

Ian Taylor

Anthrax Flake, VS, Jetty Buttress. Climber Hannah Burrows-Smith

a triangular spike in the ground. Gain a diagonal crack, then go up flakes passing just left of a small roof. Move left and up to a ledge with a pine. A choice of finishes.

18 Anthrax Flake   25m   VS 4c **

The classic of the crag, with some strenuous moves up the flake. Start 5m right of Route 11 at the right side of a black depression. Climb pale coloured rock up to prominent cracks and a large detached flake. Climb the left edge of the flake to its top, then finish direct.

19 Prizefighter   25m   E2 5c * *(1992/1998)*

Climbs the arete bounding Charlie's Corner on the left, then the overhanging crack immediately to the right of the Direct Finish to that route.

1. 10m 5a Climb the arete direct to a ledge.

2. 15m 5c Move up right and gain the overhanging shallow corner-crack right of the ivy choked direct finish and climb this increasingly strenuously, well protected, to a fighting finish up the overhanging crack above.

**20 Charlie's Corner   25m   VS 4b ** **

Another fine route, strenuous but good holds and protection. Start at the obvious corner to the right of Anthrax Flake by a wall and tree. Climb the corner to a ledge on the left. Continue up to the left of the main crack, then step back right into the crack above an overhang (which can be climbed direct at HVS 5a, but is overgrown with ivy).

21 Radio Gnome   25m   E3 5c * *(2000)*

Start 2m right of Charlie's Corner. Climb the vague weakness up the middle of the wall, step right onto a big flake and finish directly up the wall above.

**22 Right Charlie   20m   E2 5c ** ** *(1980s)*

The best of the harder routes; well protected. Start 8m to the right of Charlie's Corner. Pull through the initial bulge with difficulty and climb a short corner. Move left on a hollow flake and up to the big ledge above. Step right to a shallow corner directly above the start. Climb this, step left and finish directly up the obvious crack above (ignoring an escape left).

**23 Gaffers Wall   25m   E3 ** ** *(1999)*

Between Right Charlie and Dave's Dilemma is an overhanging wall providing an excellent steep route. Start 3m right of Right Charlie.

1. 10m 5b Surmount the initial overhang and step left on to a shelf. Climb up to and over a slanting flake-crack to gain the ledge just right of Right Charlie.

2. 15m 5c Climb up the shallow fault above, parallel with Right Charlie.

24 Dave's Dilemma   20m   VS 4c

Start 3m to the left of South-West Arete. Climb the crack until level with a heather ledge on the left. Cross to this ledge and then go directly up by twin cracks.

Variation: **Direct Start   E1 5b**

A short thin bulging crack in black rock and the wall above to the heather ledge.

25 South-West Arete   15m   E1 5b *

Start from large boulders at the base of the arete and climb the arete direct. Fine exposed climbing; requires small nuts, particularly RP3 or similar, for protection.

The routes on this wall are all good but a little short.

26 Bat Crack   15m   E2 5b *(2000)*

The obvious S shaped crack 3m right of South-West Arete.

27 Limited Stop   15m   VS 4b

At the centre of the wall there is a large fallen tree. From the ledge where the tree used to grow, step left to a ledge and follow a small arete, then a crack.

28 Bus Stop   15m   Severe 4a *

Start from the same ledge, pull up to the base of a big corner, hand-traverse left briefly and climb the wall to the top of the corner. Avoid the escape right and continue up cracks.

GRUINARD CRAGS

JETTY BUTTRESS

1. Route 1 — Very Difficult
2. Route 2 — Severe 4a *
3. Route 3 — Very Difficult
4. Route Major — Hard Severe 4b *
5. Route 4 — VS 4c
6. Buttress Crack — VS 5a
7. Number Nine — E2 5b
8. Route 5 ½ — HVS 5b
9. Route 6 — Hard Severe 4a **
10. Route 7 — Very Difficult
11. Munroron — Very Difficult **
12. Lilly the Pink — Hard Severe 4a *
13. North-West Arete — HVS 5a *
15. Crab Crack — HVS 5a *
16. Route 11 — VS 4b *
18. Anthrax Flake — VS 4c **
20. Charlie's Corner — VS 4b **
22. Right Charlie — E2 5c **
23. Gaffers Wall — E3 5b, 5c **
24. Dave's Dilemma — VS 4c
25. South-West Arete — E1 5b *
27. Limited Stop — VS 4b
28. Bus Stop — Severe 4a *
30. Tick Fever — Very Difficult

31. Batty — HVS 5a *
33. Starwood — HVS 5a **
35. South-West Corner — Severe 4a
36. Gogmagog — E5 6a **
37. Gruinard Corner — HVS 5a *
38. After the Storm — HVS 5b *
40. The Rowan — E1 5b *
42. Taller — Hard Severe 4c
43. Kristi Bloodstopper — E5 6b

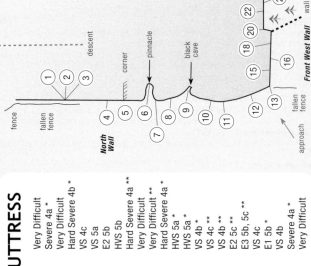

Variation: **New Millenium   Severe**   *(1999)*
Climb the corner direct.

29 Doddle   10m   Very Difficult *
Start in the same place but climb on to the face right of the corner. Continue along
a ledge for 2m and then climb an obvious crack to a large ledge and tree. Abseil
off.
Variation:
An alternative start is halfway along the face between Doddle and Tick Fever at a
dark depression. Climb this to the left of a black streak to a ledge. This is a fine
boulder problem that far exceeds the grade of the parent climb (5b).

30 Tick Fever   10m   Very Difficult
Start at the right edge of the wall by a tree and the start of the fence. Climb up and
left into an obvious crack and continue up this to a large ledge and tree. Abseil off.

SHORT WEST WALL

31 Batty   20m   HVS 5a *
Starting approximately halfway along, climb a pale wall and trend left up cracks to
a tree. Gain the next ledge and climb the wide corner-crack to the top of a huge
block, and easily thereafter. Alternatively, climb the front face of the block, trending
right to finish up the arete near Eclipse. Low in the grade.

32 Eclipse   20m   Hard Severe 4b
To the right of Batty is a prominent crack with a patch of dark rock just to its left
and a small tree at its base. Climb the crack to a tree and up the big corner behind
through jungle and loose sounding blocks.

33 Starwood   20m   HVS 5a **
The next crack right from Eclipse with a small tree growing 2m up. Fight the tree
and climb the crack with an innocuous move at the top to a ledge (possible belay).
Climb the back wall to a triangular block, trending right on to a large flake on the
arete and then up the edge of the south wall and back onto the arete to finish in
an excellent position.

SECOND SOUTH WALL

34 Kew   15m   VS 4b *
Climb the wall up to a detached block on the left-hand arete. Step right onto the
wall, up past some vegetation and left on to the large flake on the arete and finish
as for Starwood.

35 South-West Corner   15m   Severe 4a
Fight through the vegetation to reach and climb the corner where the Second South
Wall meets the Back West Wall.

BACK WEST WALL

A fine wall but sometimes mossy.

36 Gogmagog   20m   E5 6a **   *(1998)*
An impressive route up the clean left side of the wall, very bold until past the lower
roof, with good but spaced protection above. Cleaned on abseil. Climb up to the
big grassy tree filled ledge. Climb the centre of the wall above, going directly up to
a small slanting roof, which is climbed at its lower right-hand end. Move up and
right towards a big detached flake but avoid this by staying to the wall to its left to
reach a good ledge. Boldly climb the vague seam on the right on improving holds.

GRUINARD CRAGS

Allen Fyffe

The Monkey Tribe, E3, Mungasdale Crag. Climbers Andy Cunningham and Fraser Fothringham

37 Gruinard Corner   20m   HVS 5a *

Approximately halfway along the wall there is a big corner high up. Unfortunately very mossy; a good brushing would produce a two star VS 4c. Start up a small crack to the right of a hanging juniper bush and left of the start of the broken overhanging rock. Climb this right-slanting crack to a small ledge on the right. Continue up the crack above the ledge and leading into the corner which is followed to the top.

38 After the Storm   20m   HVS 5b *   *(2003)*

Start as for Gruinard Corner (the crack-line directly beneath the arete) for 5m to a shelf. Continue but before reaching the main corner, step right into the bottom of a corner on the arete above an overhang. Climb this and the arete to the top.

39 Trespass   20m   E2 5c ** * *(2001)*

The crack-line just right of the arete, with a move right after the bulge.

40 The Rowan   20m   E1 5b *   *(2001)*

Another crack-line 2m to the right.

41 Shallow End of the Gene Pool   12m   VS 4b   *(1997)*

Takes a groove come ramp-line just down and to the left of the wall's right-bounding arete and leading to a clump of trees. A good line but many loose flakes.

42 Taller   10m   Hard Severe 4c   *(1997)*

Climbs the slightly undercut arete. Start with a hard pull over the undercut into a groove in the arete, go slightly to the right to a fine crack and follow this to the ledge and trees.

THIRD SOUTH WALL

43 Kristi Bloodstopper   8m   E5 6b   *(1998)*

A broken crack-line in clean red rock to the left of an obvious big open corner. Start about 2m right of the left edge of the wall below thin cracks. Go up to a vague niche and the short groove above.

MUNGASDALE CRAG

(NG 969 928)   Alt 110m   South-West facing   Map p220

A small but very steep crag of red gneiss with incut holds, often finger holds on an overhanging wall. Those liking the style of climbing might give more stars. This area is said to derive its name from Mungo, the early Celtic saint, which may explain the theme of some of the route names.

Approach: Park in a lay-by off the A832 at NG 960 929 and walk along the road for 300m to a gate on the right. The crag can be seen in profile briefly during the walk. Head up a shallow valley to it, 15mins.

The left end of the crag is a huge block from which diminishing walls lead into the centre. The right half is an impressive overhanging wall with some flake and crack-lines belying its smooth appearance. The block dries very quickly; the rest can suffer from seepage for a day or two after rain. The crag has a pleasant outlook to Gruinard Island.

Goliath   6m   VS 4a   *(1990)*

The left end of the block (facing the sea) features a wide crack formed between it and a spear like pinnacle. Unprotected. Descend down the flake forming the back of the pinnacle into the cleft behind the block, about Moderate in ascent. This is the descent from all the routes on the block.

The arete between here and the front face is **Driving Miss Daisy** (7m 6a).

The Monkey Tribe   8m   E3 5c *   *(1999)*

The front face of the block has a prominent wide crack. The route is the central ragged crack on the wall to its left.

Soul Brothers   8m   E4 6a   *(1999)*

A thin crack-line 1m to the right (2m left of the wide crack), using holds on its right wall. Hard for the grade.

Kneel and Pray   8m   HVS 5a *   *(1991)*

The wide crack.

Bodhisattva   8m   E5 6b   *(1999)*
Use the right arete of the block to reach a break, followed by hard moves up the middle of the wall right of the wide crack to finish up a short vertical crack.

Habit Forming   8m   E1 5a   *(1999)*
Climbs the right side of the right arete of the block. More scary than hard. Holds on the right side of the arete lead to a roof. Move right past this to place runners in the crack to the right (Cloistrophobia), then return left to the arete and finish up it.

Cloistrophobia   8m   VS 4c   *(1999)*
Climb into the cleft right of the block, then the widening crack in the left wall of the block.

Achilles Heal   6m   E2 5b   *(1999)*
Cracks in the two-tiered wall some 2m right of the cleft.

Strewth   6m   VS 4c   *(1999)*
Right of Achilles Heal is a roofed alcove. Right again is another two-tiered section with a large block above the middle ledge. Climb the two walls passing over the left end of the block, with a long reach on the upper wall.

Dirty Habits   5m   VS 4c   *(1999)*
Start at a horizontal hand slot and climb the two walls near their right end (10m right of Strewth).

The following routes lie on the right-hand half, a smooth overhanging wall.

Devil Music   15m   E2 5b   *(1999)*
A flake and corner-crack above an initial roof at the left end of the overhanging wall.

Coughed up from Hell   15m   E5 6b   *(1999)*
The 'blank wall' to the right (with a small ivy plant). Wires in Genesis protect hard moves to reach the obvious hold in the middle of the wall. More long reaches gain a horizontal break. Finish slightly left and up.

Genesis   15m   E3 5c *   *(1999)*
A crack-line to the right of the 'blank wall'.

Rebirth   15m   E2 5b   *(1999)*
A hanging groove featuring a downward-pointing spike which lies to the left of a big corner with a tree and ivy.

Officer Jesus   15m   E6 6b **   *(1999)*
A fierce right-slanting diagonal crack-line starting 5m right of the corner. Sustained, a hard sequential crux with gear hard and strenuous to place.

Thelonius   12m   E4 6a **   *(1999)*
A vertical crack 10m to the right. A bold start and sustained high up, so perhaps E5. Gain the crack from the right and follow the left-hand crack above.

Walking on Water   12m   E3 5c **   *(1999)*
A shallow corner and exciting left-facing flake above.

Spioradail   10m   E5 6a *   *(2000)*
On the clean wall to the right, climb up and rightwards to a handrail, then back left into the crack.

The Road to Calvary   10m   E2 5b   *(1991)*
A crack-line above a dry stone wall which runs up to the crag.

Three Kings   10m   E5 6a ** *(2000)*
A direct line through the obvious triangular niche. Lovely climb, nippy to protect at the top.

Trumpet Brains   10m   E5 6a * *(2000)*
Start at the shot hole. Keep right at the top, finishing past a hidden horizontal jug.

Fatmouth   10m   E5 6a *(1998)*
The wall 2m left of Kind of Gentle, finishing up a short crack. Might be hard for the grade.

Kind of Gentle   8m   E3 5c * *(1999)*
A thin crack where the wall starts to diminish in height.

CARN DEARG AN DROMA

(NG 971 944)   Alt 120m   South facing   Map p220

This slabby gneiss crag lies on the westerly summit of Carn Dearg an Droma and has several routes in the easier grades; the best are described.

Approach: It is clearly seen from the lay-by near Miotag but most easily approached from the lay-by at NG 981 934. Angle up on to the crest and follow it almost to the summit. Pass this on the left and the crag is very soon visible, 20mins.

The crag is in two sections separated by a right diagonal turfy ramp with a tree at half-height. The most obvious feature on the right (higher) section is a pod with corners and a crack leading into it.

Game Boy   25m   Severe 4a *(1996)*
Start at the steep wall right of the corners and crack (Tetrus). Climb this direct, then take a crack in the wall above to join a flake-crack leading rightwards up the top slab.

Tetrus Rocket   25m   Severe 4a *(1996)*
Climb the obvious corner and deep groove line, moving right at the top of the groove to finish.

Little Faith   30m   Very Difficult * *(1996)*
Climb the pleasant rounded slabby rib which is the main feature of the left section.

Shrapnel Crack   30m   Very Difficult *(1996)*
Climb a right-slanting crack left of Little Faith.

WEIRD CRAG

(NG 974 947)   Alt 120m   South-South-West facing   Map p220

This seemingly insignificant crag lies on a knoll north of the high point of Carn Dearg an Droma; remarkable in that the 1:50000 map doesn't even mark a contour, let alone a crag. The crag is about 60m long and steadily rises from 8m at either end to a maximum height of about 18m in the middle where it is hugely undercut. It is an unusual sandstone conglomerate with sometimes huge boulders dubiously embedded in a shattered looking matrix. Contrary to first impressions, the rock is solid apart from the rotten undercut band, and runs to jugs and incuts allowing steep climbs at an amenable grade. The protection is generally very good, as are the views!

Approach: Park at NG 981 934 as above and head towards Carn Dearg an Droma. Follow a fence along the crest, then north when it leads almost to the crag, 25mins.

GRUINARD CRAGS

Near the left end of the crag is an obvious chimney set in a right-facing corner.

Blood Brothers   8m   Severe   *(2002)*
Start at the base of the chimney and climb a left-trending crack in the left wall.
Finish straight up.

Clotting Agent   10m   Hard Severe 4c   *(2002)*
About 25m right of Blood Brothers is a right-facing corner with a grassy bay near
its base. Pull over the bulge and into the grassy bay. Finish up the corner.

Wedgetarian   12m   E1 5b *   *(2002)*
About 6m right of Clotting Agent is a thin steep crack-line leading through a series
of bulges. Climb the crack direct, passing a lichenous jammed block near the top.

Burnt Offering   10m   Severe *   *(2002)*
Moving right, the base becomes a rock platform and here is a steep right-facing
corner with a bulge near the top. Climb the corner moving on to the left edge at
the bulge.

Below!   15m   E1 5a *   *(2002)*
Start about 2m right of the corner of Burnt Offering. Climb to a handrail leading
right to the edge and up this on good holds to a roof. Pull through at a short right-
facing corner and easier to finish.

Ban the Burn   18m   E1 5b *   *(2002)*
A few metres right of Below! is a wide scooped area of rock above a break in the
undercut base and a step in the ledge at the base of the crag. Pull left through the
undercut and up the scoop via good horizontal breaks to a short roof. Turn the roof
on the right, move back left above and finish direct.

At the right end of the crag is a turf fault where the undercut peters out.

Thicker Than Water   10m   Hard Severe 4b   *(2002)*
Start just left of the turfy fault below a V-groove high up. Pull over the bulge, climb
up to the V-groove and finish easily above.

Charity Crack   10m   VS 5a   *(2002)*
Start about 2m left of Thicker Than Water below a crack higher up. Pull through the
undercut and move up to the crack. Climb the crack and easier ground above.

FAERIE CRAGS

**(NG 992 912 to 991 908)   Alt 230 to 170m   West-North-West facing
Map p220**

This is a line of gneiss outcrops descending in a north to south escarpment. They
vary in height from roughly 8 to 25m and new climbs will require cleaning to give
quality climbing.

Approach: Park in a small layby at NG 993 932, from where a track leads in the
direction of a mobile phone mast. Follow this track for 500m before branching off
southwards towards the scarp, skirting round the western side of Loch an Eilich,
30mins. A more direct line from a large viewpoint layby at NG 003 928 is boggy.

CORNER CRAG

(NG 992 911)   Alt 210m   South-West facing

This is the second most significant buttress encountered approaching from the
north, with an undercut wall on the left side and a series of corners set into the

south-west edge, also boulders at their base. The climbing is excellent but the routes short considering the long approach. The following five routes are centred around the corners.

Descent: A narrow gully bounding the right side.

Sinistre Faerie   10m   HVS 5a   *(2005)*
Follows a broken corner-line where the angle of the cliff changes – just left of the first definite groove. The crux is at mid-height, moving left to gain a shelf on the arete. Slightly dirty.

Basil   10m   HVS 5a   *(2002)*
The most significant mossy left-facing corner left of the south-west edge. Climb mainly on the left wall of the corner.

Laughing Loopworm   10m   E3 5c **   *(2002)*
Climb the slim double hanging grooves just right of and overlooking the corner of Basil. Steep and awkward.

Camel Ride   10m   HVS 5a **   *(2002)*
The left-facing corner-crack set in the edge of the buttress is sustained and well protected.

Wild Goose Chase   10m   HVS 5a *   *(2002)*
Climb the crack about 2m right of the corner of Camel Ride, on the south-west side.

MYSTIC WALL

About 50m right of Corner Crag is a gully, followed by a clean reddish wall sitting high up on the hillside, identifiable by a curving slopey break running across it at mid-height. There are two thin crack-lines which run the full height of the wall. Descend to the left down the gully.

Into the Mystic   12m   E4 5c **   *(2005)*
Follows the left-hand thin crack-line, moving slightly right at one-third height to gain the slopey break. Sustained on the upper wall, but with good protection.

SLABBY WALL

About 100m further right and at the base of the scarp, is a wall with a slabby appearance, bounded on its left by a dirty corner and traversed by three parallel lines running up leftwards across it.

Faeries Fayre   18m   HVS 5a *   *(2005)*
Start at bottom right end of the wall. Climb up to join and follow the lowest of the slanting crack-lines leftwards to finish up the corner.

FAIRYMAN WALL

Further right again is a short red wall at right-angles to the main scarp, undercut at its left end, and split by a steep crack.

Don't Pay the Fairyman   15m   E1 5a *   *(2005)*
The steep central crack and its more blocky continuation above.

Barbara's Warning   15m   Severe 4b   *(2005)*
A left-facing corner bounding the wall on its right, finishing up a ramp above.

GRUINARD CRAGS

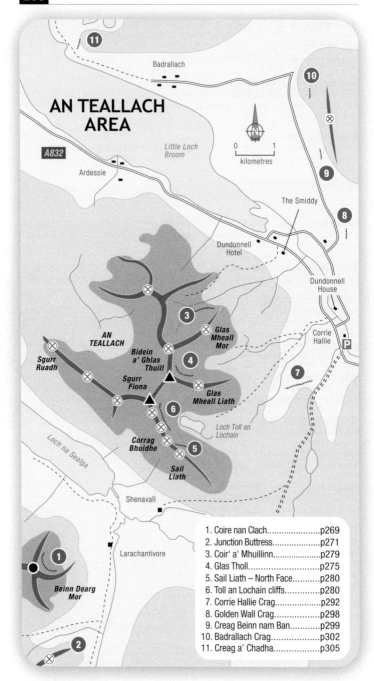

AN TEALLACH AREA

BEINN DEARG MOR

(NH 032 799)   908m

COIRE NAN CLACH

(NH 034 800)   Alt 700m   North-East facing   Maps p162, 268

This very attractive peak lies south-west of An Teallach overlooking Loch na Sealga. Coire nan Clach on its north-east side is well seen from the bothy at Shenavall and contains several large buttresses and gullies. The crags are disappointing for summer climbing, but give worthwhile winter climbs. However, they are remote and rarely visited and information is limited as a consequence.

Approach: Fairly direct from Shenavall bothy with two river crossings requiring wading. These are impossible to cross in spate and a sudden rise in water level due to thaw or rain must be guarded against.

Descent: The quickest in winter will be down one of the Grade I gullies. The south-east spur is steep and rough but slightly easier. Further deviation to the south-east eases the difficulty.

The rocks of the south peak on the left of the corrie were climbed by Sang and Morrison in 1899 and give an entertaining scramble. To the right of this mass of rock a narrow gully cuts into the cliff.

Twisting Gully   270m   IV,4 *** *(1980)*
Climb the lower reaches, which are hidden from the corrie floor. Higher up the gully splits into three parallel right-slanting branches. Take the central branch which gives the best line. Three stars is for icy conditions.

Spring Maiden   250m   V,6 ** *(1987)*
From the bottom of Twisting Gully another and easier ramp goes rightwards into the cliff. Follow this until an obvious icefall easily seen from the corrie floor, rises up on the left wall. A convenient ledge on the left allows the ice (vertical in two sections) to be climbed in two 25m pitches. Continue for a pitch up easier ground to the end of the gully. Now a short traverse to the left leads to the hidden right branch of Twisting Gully. Finish easily up this.

Fat Man's Folly   220m   III,4 *(1987)*
Below and right of the col between the south peak and the main peak is a more broken area of rock. This route starts slightly left of the lowest buttress on this face and finishes right of the col. The overhanging left wall of the third pitch means that the route is not for the stout.

Left of the massive Central Buttress (the most prominent buttress in the corrie) is the slender Flake Buttress. On its left is a gully giving the following climb.

Deranged   80m   III *(1982)*
Start to the left of Flake Buttress above a prominent spur. Climb a 6m icefall, then continue up ice for another 30m. Climb on snow and mixed ground for two pitches and finish up the left branch of the gully.

Flake Buttress   105m   Severe *(1952)*
On the first ascent this was climbed in almost snow free conditions and was considered of sustained difficulty and interest. It is questionable whether all details of the original description will be recognisable.
1. 15m Start at the left and climb a corner for 3m, then traverse delicately right to the extreme edge. Go up and round the edge to a block then back left and up to a narrow ledge.

2. 20m Go right to the edge of the buttress and around it. Traverse 6m on this flank, then 5m up a steep corner and back left on to the face of the buttress.

3. 20m Go up to a platform on the left. Make a difficult step up a wall, 2m right, then go up a slanting shelf with a crack. Go round to the right, up an exposed slab and up left to a ledge, then right to a stance below a steep wall.

4. 10m Traverse 6m on the left flank of the buttress, then up a short, steep groove for 3m. Traverse delicately left and go up to a belay in a cave below a chimney.

5. 15m Climb the chimney and exit right; go up easier rock to a ledge, then more difficult rock to another ledge.

6. 25m Continue more easily to the top of the buttress which is connected to the main mountain by a narrow ridge.

Central Gully 250m I

Between Flake Buttress and Central Buttress is a straightforward gully, although it can be made more sporting by finishing direct, particularly in lean conditions (Grade II).

The left flank of Central Buttress in winter comprises a series of snowfields separated by short vertical walls, giving a Grade II climb (1966).

Central Buttress 240m Severe   *(1953)*

The steep lower half of this buttress is bounded on the right by a gully which separates it from the right and upper parts. The original route took this gully, but that described here takes the right edge of the lower buttress, overlooking the gully.

1. 20m Start on the right. A terrace gives a footing on the buttress and a short chimney leads to the next terrace.

2. 20m Go left then back right up a deep, easy chimney.

3. 15m Slant right and up a chimney to a stance overlooking the gully.

4. 15m Climb the pillar above by chimneys on its left to a deep cleft.

5. 20m Step up a steep little wall, continue right and then left and more easily into a chimney.

6. 20m Go up the chimney with an exit on moss, and up the right side of a pillar to a conspicuous jammed block.

7. 20m Continue on the right to a steep corner.

8. etc. 130m Follow the same line to the level ridge at the top of the lower half of the buttress. The upper part of the buttress is easier.

Winter: 240m V,5 **   *(1995)*

A winter ascent of the summer line. Enjoyable climbing with amazing ambience, coming out close to the summit of Beinn Dearg Mor.

Trident Gully 260m II *

This is the obvious gully right of Central Buttress. The lower section is straightforward snow. At 90m there is a branch to the left which goes up a chimney on the right of a prominent slender buttress. The main gully continues up the right fork until at 150m it splits into three branches of about equal size. Any branch may be taken. The left branch has a pitch just above the fork and then eases off.

North Buttress 260m II

The narrow broken buttress on the right of Trident Gully has a few awkward, slabby moves low down, but most difficulties can be circumvented.

Atrial Ridge 200m III   *(2004)*

This is an indistinct ridge which is to the right of North Buttress at NH 034 804 but is better defined than it at first appears and gives an enjoyable route. The steep buttress at the foot of the ridge was climbed on the left-hand side via steep grooves and then the ridge crest was followed to the top. An escape can be made at two-thirds height into the snow gully on the right.

JUNCTION BUTTRESS

(NH 042 781)   Alt 220m   North to East facing   Maps p162, 268

This 75m crag of Lewisian gneiss, which is visible from Shenavall, stands at the junction of the Gleann na Muice and Gleann na Muice Beag. Seen from well round into the latter glen the buttress presents a slabby face on the left sloping down into Gleann na Muice, and on the right a bulging buttress facing Gleann na Muice Beag. These are separated by Pasture Gully sloping up to the left. There is no information about quality on this or The Sidings, so no stars are given.

Pasture Gully   60m   Difficult   *(1945)*
A climb for the traditionalist. The lower chockstone crowned chimney was avoided on the first ascent by using a groove on the right. After traversing back into the gully at 6m, the climb continued on "generous heather holds with occasional rock". Halfway up is a short, steep chockstone pitch. Higher up a tree had to be lassoeed. The climb finished with a pitch of vertical vegetation and a short rock chimney.

The Nose   65m   Hard Severe   *(1953)*
This climbs the buttress left of Pasture Gully. On the left side of the buttress, about 15m up, is a large terrace covered with birch trees: The Forest. The climb gains the left end of The Forest directly. Start below a steep corner, at the foot of a fierce looking layback crack.
1. 25m Climb the crack and then move right along the top of a detached flake into a steep groove. Climb this past two trees to a large holly tree. From here go left up to The Forest.
2. 40m Above is a large smooth slab. Follow a line of flakes up left to the left edge above the tip of a nose. Climb the nose past a holly and a conspicuous flake-crack to the skyline. Go round left and up easier ground. Scramble to the top.

Parker's Route   110m   Very Difficult   *(1952)*
This climb is on the crag right of Pasture Gully. Start 10m left of a corner, below a sweep of slabs.
1. and 2. 50m Climb to the left edge of the slabs.
2. 30m Move leftwards up the wall above, crossing the deep crack that slants right across the face (Rightward Slant), to a large grassy corner. Now move up the left wall by a quartzite staircase, finishing up a crack and a short wall onto a ledge.
3. 30m Move right over grass to a large block then step right and up the left edge of rough slabs to a ledge. Move right, then more slabs lead to the top.

Rightward Slant   120m   Very Difficult   *(1964)*
The obvious right-slanting line up the west (right) face of Junction Buttress.
1. 25m   Start up a steep crack, then heather and two short chimneys to a tree belay.
2. 20m   Continue up a vegetated groove on the right to a heather ledge and dubious flake.
3. 20m   Step right round a nose to another ledge. The steep chimney on the left of the ledge appears feasible, but the route goes up steeply on the right. The initial moves up the slab lead to 6m of steep climbing (crux), then easier rock to the foot of another groove.
4. 30m   Follow this groove up under a conspicuous overhang; pass this on the right and continue up to a platform.
5. 25m   Easier rock leads to the top.

Sapling Climb   85m   Very Difficult   *(1953)*
A poor route that starts 10m right of Pasture Gully.
1. 15m Climb the wall and move left to a tree belay.
2. 10m Go up the wall ahead using the heathery groove on the right, then left round a corner to another tree belay.
3. 25m Move up broken ground to a steeper wall.

4. 10m Move away from the gully and climb the left side of the wall by steep cracks, then slabs to another tree.

5. 10m Turn the wall above by the crack on its left.

6. 15m Climb the scoop above by cracks, then another little wall to heather and a tree.

THE SIDINGS

(NH 036 779)   Alt 350m   North facing

This is the next crag up Gleann na Muice Beag from Junction Buttress. The general character is slabby and uniformly steep, but there are two conspicuous features: towards the right end of the crag is a straight and narrow gully, with a well defined rib on its left, and on the left of this is a prominent curving chimney running almost the full height of the cliff.

The Funnel   110m   Severe   (1957)
Start at the foot of the curving chimney.

1. 10m Climb the chimney to an ash tree.

2. 20m Continue up the chimney past a small tree.

3. 20m Continue up the chimney, with an awkward exit.

4. 10m Climb the groove above and up to a flake belay below a steep, black chimney.

5. 15m The exit from the chimney is holdless, so traverse out left past a detached flake into the bed of a parallel chimney.

6. 15m Start on the right and climb into the chimney at 5m, then up to a large chockstone.

7. 20m Go up on the right for 6m then traverse back left across the chimney and up a short steep wall. Scrambling above.

Route 1   95m   Severe   (1952)
Start at the rib 8m left of the narrow straight gully.

1. 20m Up gentle grooves and corners.

2. 15m Continue past a stance overlooking the gully. Bear left to a triangular ledge and detached boulder. Step right to a belay overlooking the gully.

3. 10m Go up left on small holds, first a groove then a crack.

4. 25m More easily above to a heather ledge, then right to the foot of a steeper wall.

5. 25m Cross the slab on the left and round to the left of the wall. Continue easily to the top.

MULLACH COIRE MHIC FHEARCHAIR

(NH 051 735)   1019m

A mountain with a variety of rocks from sandstone on its west side, quartzite on its summit and gneiss on a sharp ridge leading east and ending at Tom an Fhiodha with some rock suspiciously like gabbro.

SGURR DUBH – NORTH FACE

NH 063 730   Alt 700m   North facing

An impressively steep cliff with much smooth clean rock but, being north facing, some vegetated sections.

Vagrants Buttress   120m   VS 4b   (1999)
The left end of the cliff holds a scree gully with a short headwall. Right of this is formed a buttress before the main face is reached; the route climbs the right edge of the buttress. Start at the right toe of the buttress and climb a steep rib to a more vegetated section. Climb direct through an overhang to a slabbier finish.

TOM AN FHIODA

(NH 075 531)   Alt 380m   North-East facing

A scrappy and often wet face overlooks the valley containing Lochan an Nid.

Nid Rib   200m   Very Difficult *(1999)*
The route is at NH 075 731 and climbs a rib near the right end of the cliff, just before it turns the corner and peters out. Here is a big wet scoop with overhangs at its top. The route climbs the rib forming its left side.

AN TEALLACH

(NH 069 843)   1062m   Map p268

This majestic mountain is one of the most sought after in the Northern Highlands. The winter traverse of its tops ranks with Liathach as the finest in the area, although it does not equal its Torridonian rivals for quality snow and ice climbs. The wonderful Torridonian sandstone architecture is disappointing for the rock climber as, like Liathach, it is too broken and vegetated to provide good summer climbs.

The main ridge runs in an east-facing crescent from gentler ground near Dundonnell in the north, over the main tops of Bidein a' Ghlas Thuill and Sgurr Fiona, then across the famous Corrag Bhuidhe pinnacles to Sail Liath in the south. Two dramatic ridges, Glas Mheall Liath and Glas Mheall Mor, run east and separate three large east facing corries, Coir' a' Mhuillinn, Glas Tholl and Toll an Lochain. The last two are major climbing venues, and Toll an Lochain in particular is a magnificent sight even when winter climbing conditions are poor.

An Teallach Ridge   II **
A long and intricate expedition with some sections of Grade II. The 'Pinnacles first' direction is easier but the 'Munros first' direction, as described, provides a good day even if discretion wins at The Pinnacles. The highest top, Bidean a' Ghlas Thuill, is easily reached, starting up a path from Dundonnell (NH 093 878). From here to Sgurr Fiona is steep but the route finding is easy (as long as one is not tricked by the more obvious east ridge towards Glas Mheall Liath). The hardest section follows, all of which is very exposed and a slip could be disastrous unless roped. There is a lot of scrambling over Lord Berkley's Seat to the Corrag Bhuidhe pinnacles. The easiest line is initially about 10m below the crest on the west (a path in summer). Fairly soon (actually about halfway along the pinnacles) there is a shallow descent gully. Go down this and traverse below the steepest rocks to bypass 'the bad step', which is the descent off the fourth pinnacle (the crest direct will require an abseil). Continuing the traverse beyond the descent gully is easier than the crest, but this will still probably require an abseil (descending from the crest but not far enough, or from beyond the descent gully, will lead on to this middle line). This whole section can be bypassed by traversing low on the west side, but it is still very exposed. Once on Cadha Gobhlach Buttress, the going is relatively straightforward.

The 'Pinnacles first' direction makes the route finding much easier and even allows the fourth pinnacle to be climbed direct but this is Grade III in full winter conditions. The easiest version is to traverse below all the pinnacles with a slight rise near their end. Lord Berkley's Seat can easily be traversed also.

COIR' A' MHUILLINN

(NH 077 862)   Map p268

The furthest north of the three corries is not as dramatic but has some climbing at its south-east end. It is only named on the 1:25,000 map.

Approach: Leave the A832 at NH 093 878 in Dundonnell and follow the main An Teallach path which runs up the north side of the corrie. Leave the path and cross to the south side to reach the climbs.

AN TEALLACH AREA

Glas Mheall Mor

Little Glass Monkey   75m   III   *(1967)*
The north-east shoulder of Glas Mheall Mor ends in a spur with two buttresses divided by a miniature corrie. The north buttress, which is easily reached from the Dundonnell path, is cleft by a Y shaped gully. This climb takes the left fork.

North Face

(NH 080 860)   Alt 600m   North-North-West facing

This is a good option with easy access when winds are high and you are getting old. If cold enough, ice forms readily producing various icefalls on the crag. The first route is to the east of a more defined section of cliff which has most of the routes.

Smear Test   150m   III   *(1999)*
Start 15m right of the lowest point, just left of an obvious corner. Climb a steep wall for 5m, move right and continue to another wall left of the corner. Continue over broken ground to a horizontal block (50m). Step left on to a small ledge and continue up a series of steps to a vertical wall (50m). Move right and take a right-slanting gully to easy broken ground.

Easily seen from the An Teallach path from Dundonnell, this cliff comes into condition during a prolonged freeze. The routes are all spring fed, giving good water ice when higher cliffs may not be in condition. The cliff is over 500m long with an easy descent at the west end. A diagonal ramp at the east end also gives a steeper descent (a short icefall joins the ramp part way up – Chairman's Choice). To the right of the ramp are a series of icy left-facing corners, then the steepest section with a hidden chimney. The centre of the crag holds the largest ice sheet of GOB. Continuing rightwards the crag gradually tapers away but contains several lower angled icefalls.
   Descriptions are from left to right starting with the short icefall on the descent ramp.

Chairman's Choice   60m   II/III   *(1999)*
This route climbs the short wide icefall on the left-hand side of the face. Climb the obvious icy slab and over a bulge to good belays on the left. Go up the ramp on the right and up the steeper wall above. Descend by ramps to the right.

Crystal Clear   100m   IV,4   *(1997)*
To the right of the previous route is a large shield of rock which contains three icy corners. This climbs the thin hanging ramp that forms the leftmost corner. Climb the ramp on ice and follow rightwards to a steep final wall. Climbed in 1999 with more ice at III,4.

Plasticity   100m   V,5   *(2004)*
About 70m right of the previous route are two parallel groove come chimney lines. Climb easy ice to gain the left-hand line, then take the chimney to a ledge below a steep ice pillar. Ascend this and easier ground above.

The Slit   100m   IV,5   *(2004)*
The right-hand line. Climb easy ice to gain a prominent V-groove and follow this to beneath a hidden icy chimney, climbed to a ledge. Finish up a steep ice column directly above and easier ground.

Resolutions   100m   IV,4   *(1997)*
Immediately to the right is an obvious icefall which forms a big open groove at the top.

GOB's Day Out   110m   IV,5   *(1997)*
Fifty metres to the right is the largest icefall, forming a wide sheet. This starts on
the left side at the foot of a diagonal fault and climbs the icefall on its left side with
two steeper sections near the top.

To the right are three other ice lines of 90m IV,4; 80m, III,4 and 80m III,4 *(1997)*.

(NH 075 845)   Alt 700m   North to East facing   Map p268   Diagram p276

The central of the three corries is more accessible but less aesthetic than Toll an
Lochain

Approach: The approach leaves the road (A832) from a small parking place
through thickets of overgrown rhododendrons near a bridge at a point opposite
Dundonnell House and about 400m on the Dundonnell side of the turn off to
Badralloch (NH 111 858). The start of the path shown on the map is no longer
used due to problems crossing the burn. Start immediately right (the other side,
north-west) of the burn and cross a broken fence. A new path (not very obvious)
soon leads to a log across a side branch of the burn. Cross this side branch and
move right to a deer fence (the continuation path is very boggy). Follow the fence
to a pine covered knoll on the left. Go round the base of this and up a little to gain
the original path on the left. Sometimes a shorter line can be taken if the
rhododendrons near the deer fence have been trimmed. Start 100m nearer
Dundonnell (another small parking spot) where the deer fence meets the road and
follow it to the knoll with pines.

Follow the path until the stream from Glas Tholl joins the main burn, just before a
big waterfall (30mins). Here the routes to the two corries diverge. For Glas Tholl,
branch off up the hillside to the east, 2hrs.

Descent: Descents can be made at a number of places. The easiest is to go to the
summit, Bidean a' Ghlas Thuill. From here, follow the ridge north, then drop down
the north flanks of Glas Mheall Mor to join a footpath leading to Dundonnell.
Alternatively, descend into Glas Tholl from the col below Glas Mheall Mor (there is
sometimes a small cornice). Hayfork Gully can also be a quick descent; climb down
to the junction and in the right conditions, glissade until well below the cliff.

A prominent feature of the south side of the corrie is the bold buttress of Major
Rib, with Minor Rib to the right and the clean line of The Alley in between. To the
left of Major Rib are a series of parallel gullies known as the Prongs, and to the
right of Minor Rib is the big Hayfork Gully leading up to an obvious notch. Right
again is North Gully which leads up to the last notch left of the summit. Below and
immediately right of the summit is a rather indistinct area of buttress and
snowfield, but further right are a number of more definite lines, the most obvious
of which is Checkmate Chimney. The climbs are described from right to left.

1 Checkmate Chimney   250m   IV,5 **   *(1969)*
A superb route unfortunately not often in condition. It is the first obvious line, a
long narrow chimney, left of the easy slopes at the back of the corrie. Climb a 10m
step, then 60m of snow to a fierce 30m icefall. This can be climbed on the left or
right according to shape. From here on the climbing is Grade III. Climb a long
enclosed chimney section with a number of short ice pitches, and finish up an easy
60m snow channel.

2 Stalemate   250m   IV,4   *(1983)*
The first line left of Checkmate Chimney runs diagonally right towards it. Gain this
line by a snowslope and follow it throughout, finishing over mixed ground directly
above.

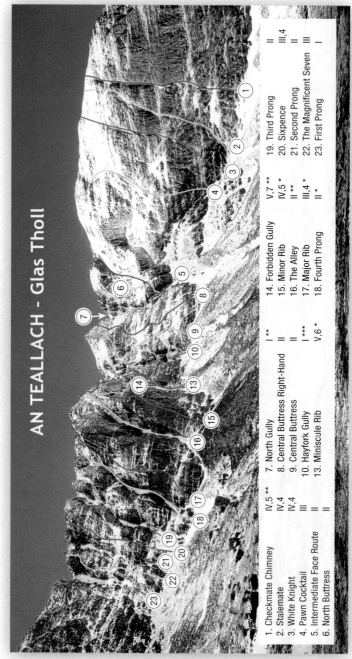

AN TEALLACH - Glas Tholl

1. Checkmate Chimney	IV,5 **	7. North Gully	I **
2. Stalemate	IV,4	8. Central Buttress Right-Hand	II
3. White Knight	IV,4	9. Central Buttress	II
4. Pawn Cocktail	III	10. Hayfork Gully	I ***
5. Intermediate Face Route	II	13. Miniscule Rib	V,6 *
6. North Buttress	II		

14. Forbidden Gully	V,7 **	19. Third Prong	II
15. Minor Rib	IV,5 *	20. Sixpence	III,4
16. The Alley	II **	21. Second Prong	II
17. Major Rib	III,4 *	22. The Magnificent Seven	III
18. Fourth Prong	II *	23. First Prong	I

Martin Moran

3 White Knight   200m   IV,4   *(1986)*
The obvious gully left of Stalemate. The difficulties are concentrated in the lower 80m.

4 Pawn Cocktail   250m   III   *(1987)*
This takes a line left of White Knight. Climb a 90m icefall to gain a right-slanting gully with easy angled ice. Where this peters out go straight up to a big tongue of rock. Go left around this to gain the ridge.

5 Intermediate Face Route   400m   II   *(1982)*
About 30m up North Gully an obvious ramp leads out right. Climb this, then follow shallow gullies and snowfields trending up right to gain an obvious line leading up right below a prominent headwall. Beyond this curve back left and climb a short gully to finish 15m right of the summit trig point.

6 North Buttress   350m   II   *(2004)*
Start up North Gully and the ramp leading out right after 30m. There is a potential direct start up a chockstone gully 10m to the right of North Gully. Leave Intermediate Face Route and head up over ice steps before going back left on snow into a narrow gully. Above this, move right into a finishing gully.

7 North Gully   300m   I *
The gully running up to the first notch left (east) of the summit of Bidein a' Ghlas Thuill is also known as Murdo's Gully, and is better seen on the approach than Hayfork Gully.

8 Central Buttress Right-Hand   300m   II   *(1997)*
Climbs the buttress between North Gully and Hayfork Gully. Central Buttress is an old name. Start at the toe of the buttress and climb easily to a steep band at half-height. Take a line leading out right to overlook North Gully, then follow a shallow gully come ramp which is formed between the crest of the buttress and North Gully to finish near the top of the latter.

9 Central Buttress   350m   II   *(1999)*
Start where the crest just right of Hayfork Gully meets the base of the buttress. Climb just right of the crest of the buttress before moving right to climb a shallow gully which leads to the steep band (perhaps a similar line to the right-hand version). Continue in the line of the gully, which passes just left of the nose of the steep band, until the upper crest on the right can be gained by the first line of weakness. Follow the upper crest to the top.

10 Hayfork Gully   300m   I **   *(1910)*
This is the deep and straightforward gully left of North Gully and right of Major and Minor Ribs. The huge vertical left wall looms over the gully which leads up to a final fork. The right branch is easier but still steep; the left branch is just Grade II. The branches finish either side of a small peak which sits in the second notch down from the summit on the east ridge of Bidein a' Ghlas Thuill. No cornice. A good descent often offering a long glissade from the fork.

11 Haystack   170m   VI,7 **   *(2000)*
A sensational route up the impressive left wall of Hayfork Gully. Start about a third of the way up Hayfork Gully at the first break in the left wall and where a gully runs up on to a platform on the rib on the left (the top of the steep wall of Miniscule Rib). Climb out left towards the gully to where a ramp leads right across the main wall (10m). Climb the ramp to below a chimney in the centre of the face (50m, 25m). Climb the steep chimney (20m). Go rightwards up a ramp then back left to the top of a crack which is the continuation of the chimney. Take a complex line through steep walls ending on the highest ledge which is above and left of the point above the continuation crack (35m). Go left round the corner past a prominent thread and climb more easily direct to the top (30m).

12 Tiny Gully   150m   IV,6   *(2000)*
The gully which cuts back left on to the rib. Gain it by a traverse and climb it past an overhanging bulge of chockstones to the platform on the rib. Traverse left to finish up the shallow gully of Minor Rib.

13 Miniscule Rib   250m   V,6 *   *(2000)*
The immediate crest left of and at times overlooking Hayfork Gully. Start up the shallow gully between Minor Rib and Hayfork. Follow this and its right branch over a bulge to reach a terrace on the right below a steep wall which overlooks Hayfork. Climb the wall by a crack right of centre, then a right-slanting flake-ramp to a niche below a wide crack (25m). Step up to the wide crack, then traverse right, up and back left to its top (actually a pinnacle). Climb a corner on the left to easy ground (20m). Move left and climb the shallow gully of Minor Rib to the top.

14 Forbidden Gully   250m   V,7 **   *(2001)*
The shallow gully between Minor Rib and Miniscule Rib. Climb a low angled ice pitch and easier snow to a fork (as for Miniscule Rib) – 60m. Take the left branch over a bulge to another fork. The left branch ends in an overhang. Climb the right branch, a chimney-corner to its top (50m). Traverse left to the left branch above its overhang. Climb a flared chimney (1PA, but it has been seen fully iced when the route would be V,5), then snow to another difficult bulge, over this and more snow until it is possible to move out left to easier ground (50m). Finish easily (this is also the optional final gully of Minor Rib).

15 Minor Rib   300m   IV,5 *   *(1956)*
The slabby rib left of Hayfork Gully. Climb the crest for 60m to a steep wall. Climb this in the centre by a crack and mantelshelf. Higher up pass a jutting fang of rock on the right. The rib now rears in a tower, climbed by a chimney on the right. Above this the ridge rises in easy steps to merge with the gully on the left (The Alley). Continue up the crest to a steep cracked wall, which may be passed by a gully on the right to reach the top.
Summer: **Very Difficult**   *(1959)*
A left-slanting crack in the tower mentioned in the winter description is the best feature of a rather vegetated climb.

16 The Alley   300m   II **   *(1978)*
The gully between Minor Rib and Major Rib gives an attractive climb, usually with some small ice pitches in the lower section, but these can disappear under heavy snow. After about 150m the gully becomes less distinct and the natural way is out right over broken rocks to the crest of Minor Rib. Continuing in the line of the gully is less interesting and can be harder.

17 Major Rib   300m   III,4 *   *(1979)*
Climb an obvious break to reach a large snowfield. Climb up and trend generally left, avoiding most obstacles, to finish up a short, stiff step near the top.

18 Fourth Prong   300m   II *   *(1959)*
A good climb immediately left of Major Rib. There is a short pitch in the lower section. Higher up climb a narrow chimney then trend right over rocks below a large buttress. Finish rightwards up easy snow.

19 Third Prong   250m   II
Again easier with more snow.

20 Sixpence   250m   III,4   *(1994)*
The widest of the inter-prong buttresses, between the Second and Third Prongs. Initially scrappy but improving to finish up a wide (3m) chimney in the centre.

21 Second Prong   250m   II
Short pitches but can bank out to grade I.

Martin Moran

Minor Rib, IV,5, Glas Tholl, An Teallach. Climber Nigel Vardy

AN TEALLACH AREA

22 The Magnificent Seven   200m   III   *(1993)*

This takes the furthest left of the narrow buttresses left of Major Rib (between First and Second Prongs). Climb the obvious line up the buttress, with an easy first pitch onto the buttress proper, and a narrow rock chimney and vertical corner on the penultimate pitch.

23 First Prong   200m   I

Straightforward on snow.

24 Cake Fork   180m   II   *(1999)*

Climb First Prong until it is possible to traverse left along a shelf (approximately 50m) to below an obvious icefall. Climb a short tapering groove to another icefall. Climb this direct, or the wall to the right (easier). Follow an open gully to the top.

Glas Mheall Liath

(NH 085 843)   Alt 530m   North facing

Rhoddies Fault   150m   III   *(1995)*

The route is situated on a north facing crag at the bottom of the eastern spur of Glas Mheall Liath and takes the obvious icy fault-line up its centre. Poor protection and belays.

TOLL AN LOCHAIN

(NH 072 832)   Map p268

The southern of the two corries, wild and extensive.

Approach: Start as for Glas Tholl (p275). From near the waterfall, continue up Coire a' Ghiubhsachain on faint paths which take a line between the two burns which lead towards the corrie, mostly following small ridges topped with bare sandstone and with occasional cairns (2 to 2hrs 30mins). The paths would be impossible to find under snow. The best path follows a rising rocky crest come escarpment which forms the left bank of the right burn. There is another path with a more obvious line of cairns which takes a more gently rising line but this peters out; it is however only marginally slower.

A longer option for Toll an Lochain, but possibly useful when starting in the dark, is to follow the Shenavall track and path, go to the lochan at NH 087 822 and traverse into the corrie (2hrs 30mins to 3hrs).

Descent (winter): The descent is longer after climbing in Toll an Lochain; the choice will depend where the route finishes. It is always possible (but steep) to descend back into the corrie from the col between Sgurr Fiona and Bidein a' Ghlas Thuill or from the southern of two Cadha Gobhlach cols between Corrag Bhuidhe and Sail Liath (the one nearest Sail Liath). Central Gully descends from the col between Corrag Bhuidhe South Buttress and Cadha Goblach Buttress, also steep snow with no pitches but much more likely to be corniced. Only the Cadha Goblach option is pleasant in summer. Otherwise, traverse the ridge in either direction and descend off Sail Liath to the Shenavall path or descend from Bidean a' Ghlas Thuill as above.

The climbs are described from left to right starting with the steep crags of Sail Liath on the extreme left of the corrie.

Sail Liath

(NH 077 825)   Alt 570m+   North facing   Diagrams p281, 285

The Sail Liath crags can be divided into three buttresses, a large dome-shaped left or frontal buttress separated from the others by a large easy snow gully. The central buttress is separated from the right by a prominent snow ramp which runs up from right to left. Near the top of the ramp three deep-cut gullies cleave the steep walls on the right, well seen on the approach to the corrie.

1 Opposition Couloir   180m   III   *(1989)*

Climbs the deep gully in the left-hand buttress, cutting up behind a pinnacle on the right side of the crag. Finish up the buttress or enter the easy gully on the right to descend.

2 Mauna Kea   400m   IV,4   *(2001)*

A scenic ramble based on a chimney on the left side of the central buttress, but never actually climbing in the chimney. A big rockfall swept the lower chimney in November 2000 and discouraged its ascent. Start up a ramp from the next bay to the right. Traverse left immediately above the rockfall scar into the chimney-line. Continue the traverse, slightly descending, until going up to a barrier wall. Climb

Andy Nisbet

AN TEALLACH
Sail Liath

1. Opposition Couloir   III
2. Mauna Kea   IV,4
3. The Forger   III
4. Counterfeit Groove   III,4
5. Kumbh Mela   V,6 **

6. Sulphur Gully   IV,6 **
7. Bottomless Gully   V,5 *
12. Elemental Gully   II

A. Forgotten Face

this with difficulty by a slight groove, then go up to the next barrier wall. Climb this and go up to a third wall, climbed by the first break left of the chimney to gain a terrace. Traverse the terrace rightwards, slightly rising to join and continue traversing as for The Forger.

3 The Forger 300m III (1988)
Climbs the most prominent ramp in the central buttress, parallel and left of the ramp which divides the central and right buttresses. Start at the right toe of the buttress. Climb a slight gully leftwards on to the left-slanting snow ramp and climb it to its end. Continue diagonally left on intricate mixed ground to a snow terrace. Follow the snow ramp left to a second terrace and climb a short chimney. Continue by mixed ground which soon leads to a traverse right to easy ground, then follow a ridge to Sail Liath.

4 Counterfeit Groove 170m III,4 (2001)
Climbs a wide but shallow groove right of The Forger. Start up and right of the big ramp of The Forger and climb the groove, or the turfy ground left of it, always trending generally left, to reach a steep capping wall. Climb this by a steep groove on the right to easy slopes on the big ramp which leads up past the three chimneys. The buttress has been climbed in this vicinity in summer by Pat Baird in the 1930s (SMCJ Vol. 20).

5 Kumbh Mela 130m V,6 ** (2001)
The left-hand and highest of the three gullies on the right-hand buttress, the central gully being Sulphur Gully. Much deeper, longer and more impressive than it looks. Start at the same place as Sulphur Gully but go left up a ramp to reach the gully. An initial chockstone was the crux, climbed on the left wall and probably Grade 7, but would become quite easy with a big build up. Thereafter it was deep and a good width for chimneying.

6 Sulphur Gully (Bowling Alley) 100m IV,6 ** (1987)
The fine central gully was climbed recently but appears to be similar to a much earlier climb. In deference to the pioneers the original name is preserved although the modern description is given. The original description mentions jammed ice axe belays and other exotica.
1. 15m Climb a very steep iced corner to the base of the gully. This is avoidable by starting up Kumbh Mela, then traversing right.
2. 40m Follow deceptively steep iced chimneys to an easier angled section.
3. 45m Steep snow leads to a steep icy section climbing underneath a prominent chockstone. Finish up easier ground. Another 100m of easy ground leads to open slopes.

7 Bottomless Gully 135m V,5 * (1988)
This is the furthest right of the three gullies. It is protected by an overhanging wall which necessitates a start 45m down the approach ramp.
1. 45m Zigzag with surprising difficulty, trending generally left, towards the base of the gully.
2. 20m Climb more easily to the gully, which is deep and narrow.
3. 30m Go up easy snow in the gully.
4. 40m A fine pitch leads out on to easy ground.

Forgotten Face

(NH 073 826) Alt 700m North facing Diagram p281, 285
The following three routes lie on the right-hand face of the right-hand buttress. The rock is good but vegetated on ledges giving pleasant climbing when the turf is bone dry (rare!). Cleaner but harder variations are possible. The winter climbs are much better on this steep open face. Although somewhat featureless, the face has two right-rising diagonal lines. The lower and right is a wide turf ramp; the left is a fault with shallow chimneys and is the start of the following two routes.

John Lyall

Monumental Chimney, V.7, Toll an Lochain, An Teallach. Climber Jonathan Preston

**8 Anvil Chorus   150m   VI,6 ** (2000)
A harder companion to Sandeman's Pinnacle, following a straight left-slanting line.
Warthogs or other turf protection are comforting. Start 30m from the left edge of
the buttress (the ramp) at a right-slanting shallow chimney, the first easily climbed
feature.
1. 50m Climb 15m up the chimney before stepping left, then up to climb a corner
(crux). Continue up the same line to a small ledge.
2. 30m Follow this turfy line to a thin slabby exit on to a ledge system.
3. 50m Continue by the same line until overlooking Bottomless Chimney, then up
awkward ground close to the crest.
4. 20m Follow the edge to easy slopes.

9 Sandeman's Pinnacle 140m VS (1999)
Start as for Anvil Chorus.
1. 40m 4a Climb the initial chimney and continue diagonally right in the same line to a big flake at the first obvious break in the steep wall above.
2. 50m 4c Move left over the flake, then up slabs to the right of a corner. Cross the corner and climb near its left edge to a big pinnacle.
3. 50m A right-trending line leads to easy ground.
Winter: **V,6 ** (1999)
As for summer except pitch 2 used a line more suited to winter. After moving left over the flake, a traverse left crossed the corner and the wall above was climbed to join the summer route. At a vertical wall about 10m below the pinnacle, a short traverse right led into the corner which was climbed on turf until a return traverse led to the pinnacle.

10 Forgotten Face 160m VS (1999)
Start in the centre of the face at a clean brown slab below the right-rising turf ramp.
1. 30m 4c Climb the slab trending left to the turf ramp, then right up the turf to above the start.
2. 25m 4b Traverse left along a clean slabby break to a large block.
3. 45m Go round the block on the left and back right above the belay by the higher of two big right-slanting ramps. Before the ramp appears to peter out, go up left on steep blocky ground.
4. 30m 4a Go up a right-slanting ramp, starting with an awkward corner to the base of a big groove (seen on the skyline from below).
5. 30m Climb the groove to scrambling.
Winter: **VI,6 *** (1999)
A line based on the summer route. The left to right turf ramp was climbed from its start. The clean slabby break has a thin line of turf but was very poorly protected (pitch 2). A more direct line was taken at the top of pitch 3 and turfy ground was climbed on the left of the final groove.

11 Monumental Chimney 115m V,7 ** (2000)
The top right end of this slabby face is bounded by a gully. Forking left from below the second ice pitch of the gully is a very steep chokestoned chimney.
1. 60m Climb the gully up a smooth corner on thin ice, then go up easy snow to the chimney.
2. 20m Go deep into the chimney and up to jammed blocks. Cut loose under these to gain the hanging chimney which is followed by a tight squeeze and awkward bulge to a ledge.
3. 35m Follow the bulging fault and gully to the top.

12 Elemental Gully 100m II (2001)
Follow the smooth corner and easy snow of Monumental Chimney, then continue up the gully on the right. The grade varies with the build up, can be Grade III.

The small pinnacle just right of Sail Liath, and to the left of the left fork of Cadha Gobhlach, has been climbed (Severe) but is dangerously loose.

Gobhlach Buttress

(NH 070 828)   Alt 650m   North-East facing   Diagram p285

Starting with the steep north-facing crags of Sail Liath on the extreme left of the corrie, to the right are easy snow slopes which lead up to the pass of Cadha Gobhlach ('the forked pass'). Right again is the rounded Gobhlach Buttress, then another col with a snow gully below (Central Gully), before the South Buttress of Corrag Bhuidhe whose rocks drop straight into the loch.

13 Gobhlach Buttress 350m IV,4 * (1999)
In the centre of the lower part of the buttress are two icefalls. The left is steep and

Andy Nisbet

AN TEALLACH
Sail Liath & Toll an Lochain - Left

7. Bottomless Gully	V,5 *	16. Central Gully	I
9. Sandeman's Pinnacle	V,6	17. Chockstone Gully	I *
10. Forgotten Face	VI,6 *	18. Original Route	II
11. Monumental Chimney	V,7 **	19. Direct Route	IV,4 **
12. Elemental Gully	II	21. Constabulary Couloir	I *
13. Gobhlach Buttress	IV,4 *	A. Forgotten Face	
14. Gobhlach Grooves	IV,4 *	B. Gobhlach Buttress	
15. Lucky Strike	II	C. Corrag Bhuidhe South Buttress	

forms two ice pillars. The right is the start of this route. Start right of the base and trend left to the icefall (or climb it from the base if formed). Climb ice, then traverse right to climb a steep iced corner. Trend left up iced grooves for two pitches to gain a right-slanting ramp which is followed easily before moving left to finish up the crest.

14 Gobhlach Grooves   350m   IV,4 *   *(1994)*
A good route in icy conditions climbing the Gobhlach Buttress via an icefall which leads over a bulge into a long obvious fault right of the crest. Start at the right corner of the buttress base up an ice ramp and mixed ground (45m). Follow the ice line left into a corner (30m). Go up steep ice bulges, then easier grooves and mixed ground trending right (45m). Continue trending slightly right to enter a gully system which leads to the top.

15 Lucky Strike   200m   II   *(1999)*
Climbs a ramp bounding the right side of Gobhlach Buttress and leading to a short gully. Gain the ramp from mid-way up the easy gully on its right (Central Gully).

16 Central Gully   300m   I
A wide gully which allows an easy route up or down from the ridge, cornice permitting. The section below the cornice is the only steep section and is usually easiest on the right (going upwards).

17 Chockstone Gully   300m   I *
A narrow gully parallel and right of Central Gully. The chockstone is near the top and the deep gully underneath it is well seen from the ridge. The gully collects a lot of snow which normally buries the chockstone.

Corrag Bhuidhe South Buttress

(NH 068 832)   Alt 650m   North-East facing   Diagram p285

An early route on this South Buttress was done by Glover and Ling. Corrag Bhuidhe South Buttress is noted in the 1936 Guide as "Difficult. It can be Very Difficult if the minimum divergence is made, which means mounting the water worn rocks directly from the loch, and negotiating a stretch of some 80 feet at three-quarter height, which is short of anchorages".

18 South Buttress, Original Route   350m   II   *(1999)*
Climbs the east face overlooking Loch Toll an Lochain, probably following the Glover and Ling original climb on this buttress. Start up a shallow gully just right of the barrier wall at the base (which drops into the lochan). Climb this and trend easily left towards a very steep wall with a ramp and obvious icefall. Make a long traverse left until it is possible to climb up mixed ground to a snowfield below the main rock barrier on the face. Traverse back right towards the crest until turfy steps lead up to a left-trending ramp come gully breaching the barrier wall. At its top, climb up left into a small basin. A short turfy groove on the left (crux) leads to easier ground. Either climb straight up to the final crest or up and left across snow to the top.

19 South Buttress Direct   350m   IV,4 **   *(1999)*
A varied line up a big buttress, even if not truly direct. Start up the gully as for the original route and trend easily left to the steep wall and icefall. Start up the icefall but soon go up a prominent diagonal line leftwards with a through route to reach a terrace. Gain the next terrace below the main rock barrier. Climb a turfy groove just left of the crest, breaking out left at half-height and returning right above. Follow the crest to the top.

20 South Buttress by the Mental Chimney   350m   V,6 *   *(1998)*
Start as for the Direct Route but continue to gain the base of a gully which is

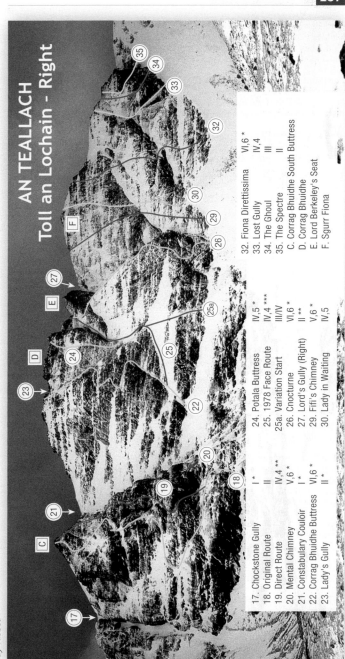

Andy Nisbet

AN TEALLACH
Toll an Lochain – Right

AN TEALLACH AREA

17. Chockstone Gully	I *		24. Potala Buttress	IV,5 *
18. Original Route	II		25. 1978 Face Route	IV,4 ***
19. Direct Route	IV,4 **		25a. Variation Start	III/IV
20. Mental Chimney	V,6 *		26. Gnocturne	VI,6 *
21. Constabulary Couloir	I *		27. Lord's Gully (Right)	II **
22. Corrag Bhuidhe Buttress	VI,6 *		29. Fifi's Chimney	V,6 *
23. Lady's Gully	II *		30. Lady in Waiting	IV,5

32. Fiona Direttissima	VI,6 *
33. Lost Gully	IV,4
34. The Ghoul	III
35. The Spectre	II
C. Corrag Bhuidhe South Buttress	
D. Corrag Bhuidhe	
E. Lord Berkeley's Seat	
F. Sgurr Fiona	

formed right of the buttress crest. A pitch with three difficult steps in the gully bed leads to two further pitches where the difficulties are passed using the rib on the right. The crest is gained soon above and followed easily to the summit. Very icy conditions might drop the grade to IV,5.

21 Constabulary Couloir　350m　I *
A long shallow couloir separates the South Buttress from the main crags of Corrag Bhuidhe, and gives the route. The couloir may have an avoidable icefall near the bottom. The rest is straightforward snow. Can be used as a descent.

Corrag Bhuidhe

(NH 066 833)　Alt 700m+　North-East facing　Diagram p287

The main face of Corrag Bhuidhe has near its base a large triangular snowfield above a short rock barrier. This may be used to locate the next four climbs. The large left-bounding buttress of the face is Corrag Bhuidhe Buttress.

22 Corrag Bhuidhe Buttress　400m　VI,6 *　　　　　　　(1999)
The line of least resistance up some very steep ground. Gain the triangular snowfield from its bottom left. Continue in the same line up a ramp which cuts up rightwards into the buttress (100m). Climb a steep step to gain an upper continuation and follow this to steeper ground. Go up a short way, then traverse sensationally left along a ledge (50m). Continue the traverse until a line back right allows an upper ledge (about 25m higher) to be reached and followed right (50m). Find a way through steep slabby ground to reach a large ledge (40m). Traverse right along the ledge to gain and follow the easier upper crest of the buttress which is left of Lady's Gully (160m).

23 Lady's Gully　350m　II *　　　　　　　　　　　　(1974)
Gain the triangular snowfield at its lower left corner and go up to the apex. Follow the left-trending gully from there to the top.
Variation: **Swiss Approach　90m　III**　　　　　　　　(2004)
A more direct approach through the rock barrier could be used for any of the routes. Start about 100m right of the left end of the barrier wall where there is an obvious line of weakness. Traverse a few metres right, then step up steeply through a rock band. Continue up and diagonally right on turf to below and left of an obvious corner (45m). Traverse right again for a few metres, then up through two rock bands to the base of the snowfield, directly below the gully.

24 Potala Buttress　240m　IV,5 *　　　　　　　　　　(1987)
This takes the V shaped rock buttress between Lady's Gully and a ramp on the right taken by 1978 Face Route. Good turf conditions are advisable. Gain the triangular snowfield at any convenient point along its base, climb up to the apex and thence to the toe of the V shaped buttress. Start 10m right of the toe.
1. 35m　Go left, up and back right by the line of least resistance to a stance overlooking the ramp of 1978 Face Route.
2. 40m　Go up slightly and traverse left to a small rock band.
3. 50m　Climb the band (sling used), then up more easily.
4. 30m　Continue without difficulty to a snowfield.
5. 50m　Go up snow trending slightly right to a weakness.
6. 35m　The line of weakness, finishing at a notch just left of the rightmost tower.

25 1978 Face Route　400m　IV,4 ***　　　　　　　　　(1978)
This atmospheric route finds a way through serious open terrain. Gain the triangular snowfield and from its apex start up Lady's Gully, then turn rightwards under a wall until below a right-sloping gully-ramp. Gain the gully-ramp (crux) and follow it for about 80m until it is easy to trend right to the crest of the buttress overlooking Lord's Gully. Either follow the crest to the top or stay in the gully and finish up it.
Variation: **Variation Start　III/IV**

Martin Moran

Lord's Gully, II, Toll an Lochain, An Teallach

A central icefall leading directly into the triangular snowfield. The grade depends on the build-up.

26 Cnocturne   450m   VI,6 *   *(1999)*

The long curving arete left of Lord's Gully and joining 1978 Face Route near its top. Climbed in poor conditions of heavy snow, much in the dark (hence the name), the route described could become a grade easier with ice on the lower pitches. A more logical but less direct start would be the short gully on the left leading to the right of the triangular snowfield; with a better build up, this would make the route IV,4. Start at the right side of the lowest rocks, and below a large right-facing corner-ramp which leads into Lord's Gully. Go up to icy ground and climb to a ledge below a steep wall (40m). Traverse left for 15m, then climb up and left on small tufts and compact rock into a scoop below a left-facing groove (serious). Gain a ledge on the left and climb up, then back right to a ledge directly above the groove (45m). Go up the steep wall above, then move left to gain the continuation groove. Climb this

Fifi's Chimney, V,6, Toll an Lochain, An Teallach. Climber Dave McGimpsey

Andy Nisbet

(technical crux), then up to the right end of the triangular snowfield (40m). Two pitches of easier turfy climbing lead up and right to the snow arete. From the top of the arete, a 40m traverse left on to 1978 Face Route was made to join and finish up this route. (A better possibility, perhaps easier than the described route in good conditions, would be to climb direct from the start of the traverse to join the ridge of 1978 Face Route higher up.)

27 Lord's Gully   400m   II ** (1923)
This is the long left-slanting gully between Corrag Bhuidhe and Sgurr Fiona. The long initial section is usually straightforward snow (and has been skied). At its top it has two branches going either side of the huge tower of Lord Berkeley's Seat. Difficulties in the right branch are often circumvented by a traverse right onto the face of Sgurr Fiona which involves some low angled ice.

Variation: **Left Branch   III *** (1973)
This branch is better defined with more interest but harder climbing.

Summer: **Severe** (1958)
Follow the line of the watercourse over many short pitches, one of which, near the top, is Severe. Go up the right branch on a steep slab. If this is wet, a traverse out right from the gully may be necessary.

28 Lord Berkeley's Seat   130m   VI,6 ** (1991)

This spectacular route up the face of the Seat is not as hard as it looks, possibly V,5 with well frozen turf and not too much snow. Start just left of the toe of the buttress.

1. 45m Climb the crest, trending slightly right until stopped by a barrier wall.
2. 35m Traverse right and climb a short slab overlooking the right branch of Lord's Gully. A series of walls leads to another barrier.
3. 25m Traverse left and climb corners just right of the crest.
4. 25m A short turfy ramp leads diagonally right to the final wall, which is finished to the right of the summit.

Sgurr Fiona

(NH 066 837)   Alt 750m   East facing   Diagram p287

The corrie face of Sgurr Fiona gives some long ice climbs in good conditions. The face is crossed by two big ramp systems which rise to the right. The higher and larger ramp starts near the base of Lord's Gully with the most obvious and regularly forming icefall above this ramp and right of centre. The distinctive features of the ice lines lie above this ramp although they have lower continuations to the base of the face.

29 Fifi's Chimney   350m   V,6 * (1999)**

The leftmost of the ice lines on the face, following a chimney which leads into a left-slanting snow ramp which finishes halfway up the crest leading from Lord Berkley's Seat up to Sgurr Fiona. Some great moves; pity the best section is short. Start just right of Lord's Gully and climb low angled ice to the upper ramp and the base of the icy chimney. A steep back and foot pitch (30m) and a pitch with three awkward bulges, the last being climbed by mixed moves on the right (30m) leads to the easier upper section.

30 Lady in Waiting   350m   IV,5 (1999)

Climbs ice which forms in a right-facing corner above the upper ramp. The lower continuation has one steep section. The corner has a considerable bulge low down which was traversed from the recess on the left (good runners) to less steep ice on its right. Continuous ice leads to a final kink right on thinner ice which gains easier upper slopes and a finish close to or just right of Sgurr Fiona.

31 Fiona Verticale   250m   III * (1994)**

Climbs the obvious icefall in the upper right sector of the face. Start where Lord's Gully becomes narrow and well defined. Strike off rightwards up the ramp and follow this to where it becomes two ramps, one set close above the other. Follow the upper ramp to its end at a large and prominent icefall covering the cliffs above. Follow the easiest line up the ice and continue up a chimney-line to finish by a narrow cleft at the north ridge of Sgurr Fiona about 70m below the summit.

32 Fiona Direttissima   400m   VI,6 * (1999)**

In good conditions a steep icefall forms over the wall below the upper ramp and icefall of Fiona Verticale. This route links this icefall with the Fiona Verticale one above to provide a long natural but escapable line to finish right of the summit of Sgurr Fiona. Start directly below the lower icefall. Climb easy iced slabs and snow for two pitches to reach the ice (the lower free-standing column was very fragile and avoided by steep snow on the right). Belay in an excellent ice cave behind the start of the ice proper. A very steep start up an icicle leads to easier climbing up and right across the icefall to finish up a steepening icy corner. Easy ground follows to a short wall 50m below Fiona Verticale. This was climbed by a wide 10m pillar (avoidable). Climb the main icefall direct to its top. To finish, a steep narrow icy chimney directly above the icefall led to mixed ground and the top (Fiona Verticale finishes further left).

AN TEALLACH AREA

33 Lost Gully   200m   IV,4 *(1999)*
Below the lower ramp which crosses Sgurr Fiona is a steep wall which bounds the cliffs on the right. This gully, well hidden from most angles, cuts through the ramp. Climb the gully, steep and poorly protected for 20m but graded for good ice, to reach the ramp. Follow the ramp rightwards on less steep ice to a short crest which leads to the slopes of Sgurr Fiona.

34 The Ghoul   180m   III *(2000)*
A left-slanting ramp, the lower of two which cut through the steep wall up right from Lost Gully, starts with an ice bulge but then becomes easier and leads on to upper slopes. Traverse left towards Lost Gully ramp, then return slightly right and climb straight up to join and finish up the crest towards Sgurr Fiona.

35 The Spectre   160m   II *(1999)*
Start further up the steep wall at a second ramp, immediately left of a big arete at its top right corner. Climb this ramp through the steep wall, then trend rightwards on mixed ground to finish up the crest above the arete.

Sgurr Ruadh

(NH 040 852)   Alt 650m   North-West facing

This is the westmost bastion of An Teallach, above the west end of Loch na Sealga. **Terminal Tower** (120m Difficult), starts at the lowest point of the rocks which face north-west (SMCJ 1954).

An Teallach – Outlying Climbs

This section includes some rock climbs on the lower slopes of An Teallach and frozen waterfalls on nearby smaller hills.

AN TEALLACH – LOWER CRAGS

Approaching Toll an Lochain up Coir' a' Ghiubhsachain a long west facing scarp of quartzite, around 60m high, offers a range of short routes. Two 'Severe' climbs have been recorded "opposite the point where the burn from Toll an Lochain turns down the corrie". (SMCJ 1946). On the southern continuation of this scarp another quartzite "nursery crag" has been climbed on, about 2km north north-east of Achneigie (NH 082 796). Three Very Difficult routes of about 60m were recorded (SMCJ 1954).

CORRIE HALLIE CRAG

(NH 104 842)   Alt 250 to 290m   North-West facing   Map p268

This quartzite scarp, which breaks off the main scarp running down Coir' a' Ghiubhsachain, has fine views to An Teallach. It catches the sun from mid-afternoon in summer and has no drainage above, so it is fairly quick to dry. The main part of the crag is just off the vertical, so the climbing is more technical than strenuous. The rock is compact with small positive edges, shallow horizontal slots and some thin vertical cracks. The face routes have few cracks but small cams, the smaller the better, and a selection of RPs provide adequate protection. A bank which runs opposite the crag provides an excellent vantage point.

Approach: The start of the crag can just be seen from the road immediately north of the craft shop as a pointed piece of clean rock. Park on the verge here. Go through a gate opposite the craft shop and follow a faint track up the west side of the burn for a short distance before striking up through the heather in the direction of the main scarp section. This leads to the bank opposite the crag, easier to identify the various walls so best for a first visit. An alternative route is much drier (unless the stream is high). Start up the Shenavall track and break off right after about 600m at a fence-line to cross the Gleann Chaorachain and reach the foot of the scarp, which can then be followed along its top or bottom. 30mins.

Descent: The only descents are at either end of the long crag, so an abseil rope is useful.

The scarp starts with small walls which provide bouldering, then a break before reaching the main wall where the ground below the crag starts to form a gully. First is a low section of wall, often damp, but increasing in height beyond the last tree on the top. The first routes are here.

Scoopy Do   10m   5b   *(2004)*
Twelve metres right of the last tree is a large but very shallow scoop in the upper half of the wall. Climb up through it.

Scraggy   10m   5a   *(2004)*
Start 4m to the right of Scooby Do. Climb directly through a horizontal break with a small clump of heather and continue up to a small left-facing corner.

Difference of Opinion   10m   VS 4c   *(2004)*
Eight metres right again. Go past a small rock scar at 3m, then directly up the wall above.

The highest section of crag starts where the gully below the crag becomes more defined and the opposite bank turns rocky with a few trees. The most obvious feature here is a white cleaned ledge before reaching the trees. About 12m left of this cleaned ledge is an area of clean lighter coloured rock.

Pale Sider   15m   VS 5a *   *(2004)*
A direct line just left of the pale rock, finishing at a small block feature on the top.

Whiter Shade of Pale   18m   HVS 5a   *(2004)*
Climb just right of the pale rock through horizontal breaks, move left into the pale rock and finish just left of heather. The first route where the crag is close to full height.

Monkeys in Bubbles   18m   VS 5a   *(2004)*
Start 5m left of Patch and climb the wall direct past the right side of a diagonal break with heather near the top to finish at the same place as Patch.

Patch   18m   Severe   *(2004)*
Climb to the white cleaned ledge, then trend slightly left through further white ledges. Technically easy but the protection is small cams.

Piff Shlapps   20m   HVS 4c   *(2004)*
This route runs through a white ledge at half-height (5m right of another white patch with moss and heather attached, also just below where a birch and a rowan grow out of the opposite wall 2m apart). Move up to where two distinct horizontal slots overlap (at one-third height) and then continue past a very small corner to the white ledge. Continue directly to the top, via a faint left-trending fracture.

Stylus   20m   E2 5b **   *(2004)*
This route starts approximately 2m right of the previous route, moving past the right end of the horizontal break emanating from the white ledge of Piff Shlapps, then following a faint right-trending crack-line.

Ullapool Fish Week   20m   VS 4c *   *(2004)*
Move up the left edge of a slightly undercut section on good holds, past a boss at half-height (small cam underneath), then trend slightly further right into and up the short right-facing corner with a flake at its base and a deep horizontal slot at its top. Finish directly.

I was Right   20m   E1 5a * *(2004)*
Opposite a large birch tree and 6m to the right, climb directly up to a narrow heathery ledge at approximately one-third height, flanked on its left by a mini corner. From the leftmost side of this ledge, move directly up towards the right end of the deep horizontal slot and continue to the top.

Tense Breakfast   20m   E1 5a *(2003)*
As for the last route up to the heathery ledge at one-third height. From its right end, move straight up to a small ledge, then up and left to the right end of the deep horizontal slot, to share the finish of I was Right.
Variation: **E1 5a** *(2004)*
From the heathery ledge, go directly up the wall above.

Half Yokin   20m   Very Difficult *(2003)*
The vegetated crack right of Tense Breakfast starts half-way up, above the obvious mid-height break and left of two full-length cracks.

Shreddies   20m   VS 4c *(2003)*
About 3m right of Half Yokin, the left-hand of the two full-height thin cracks.

Lunchtime   18m   Severe 4b *(2003)*
The right-hand crack, 3m right of Shreddies.

Slurp   18m   Severe 4a *(2004)*
Move up to join and follow the next crack which starts half-way up, above the mid-height break. Pleasant.

There is then a heathery crack at a high point in the base. The next 15m section is characterised by a series of good horizontal slots on its left edge.

Breakaway   18m   VS 4c ** *(2004)*
Start 3m from the left edge of the wall and move up through the obvious horizontal breaks.

Escoop   18m   VS 4c *(2004)*
Start 4m right of Breakaway. Go up via the right side of a shallow scoop at half-height.

Evasion   18m   VS 4c *(2004)*
A somewhat meandering line at the right end of this section. Start just left of the broken heathery section, then trend left and back right.

Next is a broken and heathery section.

Little & Large   15m   E1 5a *(2004)*
The wall about 5m right of the heathery section.

Tiffin   15m   Hard Severe 4b *(2003)*
A crack-line 4m further right, up the left boundary of more fractured rock.

Coffee Break   15m   Severe *(2003)*
Takes a route up through the right side of the fractured rock.

Inception   15m   HVS 4c * *(2004)*
Just right again, start off a small grassy mound up an obvious vertical crack to reach a short horizontal break at two-thirds height. From its right end, finish up a short crack.

Immediately right of Inception, the crag has a blockier surface for 6m, then a wall with few cracks.

King Quartz　18m　E2 5b *　　　　　　　　　　　　　　　　　*(2004)*
Start below a horizontal crack near the top (4m left of Supermatch Game). Climb a small right-diagonal ramp, then past a small red dinner-plate-sized rock scar. Continue to the second of two tiny spikes (thin sling runners). Move 3m right and back left to stand on the spike, then finish direct through the horizontal crack.

Supermatch Game　18m　E1 5b *　　　　　　　　　　　　　　*(2004)*
At the right end of this section is a low roof at 3m. Climb through the middle of this roof to a ledge above, then move up to a good nut at half-height before finishing up the middle of three faint crack-lines.

Blankety Blank　18m　E2 5a　　　　　　　　　　　　　　　　*(2004)*
The right end of the low roof forms a shallow rectangular recess. Climb rightwards through this, pass left of a mossy hole, then climb the wall trending slightly left to finish up the right-hand of the three crack-lines.

Next is a heather break with a small birch at two-thirds height. The next section is characterised by a very distinctive horizontal fault at one-third height with a vertical crack running centrally through it to about half-height. This is Bow & Arrow.

Close of Play　15m　VS 4b　　　　　　　　　　　　　　　　*(2004)*
The line to the left of Bow & Arrow.

Bow & Arrow　15m　HVS 4c *　　　　　　　　　　　　　　　*(2004)*
Climb the vertical crack running centrally through the horizontal fault. Continue directly to the top.

Busted Flush　15m　E1 5a　　　　　　　　　　　　　　　　*(2003)*
The wall between Bow & Arrow and a heathery crack, going through a ledge at two-thirds height with a small square block on its right-hand side.

Right of the heathery crack is another clean section with two obvious vertical crack-lines.

Pick the Lock　15m　E1 5a *　　　　　　　　　　　　　　　*(2002)*
The left crack, with a small ledge at one-third height.

Key Data　15m　HVS 4c *　　　　　　　　　　　　　　　　　*(2002)*
The sharper right crack.

Next is a diagonal moss and heather ledge near the base followed by a section with an arch feature at the bottom left side.

Shallow Waters　20m　E2 5b *　　　　　　　　　　　　　　　*(2004)*
Move up through the centre of the arch and climb the wall above, passing right of two small overlaps.

Alien Invasion　20m　E1 5b **　　　　　　　　　　　　　　　*(2004)*
Start 4m right of last route and take a direct central line up the seemingly blank wall, through shallow overlaps.

Sanctuary's Edge　20m　E2 5b　　　　　　　　　　　　　　　*(2004)*
Start through reddish rock just left of a moss and heather patch at 3m and 2m right of Alien Invasion. Stay just left of the easier broken ground near the top. A bit escapable.

The next section of clean rock is characterised by a double overlap feature on its right end, and a single overlap running bottom right to top left across the remainder of the wall.

Try Me   18m   VS 4b
(2004)

The crack-line just in from the left edge of the wall, passing through the left end of the single overlap.

Ron Move Wonder   18m   HVS 5a
(2004)

Climb directly up to the crack splitting the right end of the overlap and pull through to easier ground.

Move on Up   18m   E1 5b **
(2004)

A thin crack running slightly rightwards through the double overlap, then finish straight up the wall above.

Oaky Doakey   15m   Very Difficult
(2003)

This section of rock is bounded on its right by a heathery chimney with an oak tree. Climb the blocky holds to the left of the oak tree, and finish up cleaner rock above.

The next section is right of the heathery chimney with the oak tree.

Tricam   18m   E1 5b
(2004)

Start beneath the right end of a very shallow overlap which trends up to the left. Climb up to the second horizontal break at about 5m (which splits the overlap in two), then trend slightly leftwards then up through the remaining horizontal breaks towards an obvious finishing crack.

The scarp then becomes more broken for 150m until just beyond the highest point where there is another wall near where the scarp joins the main scarp running up Coir' a' Ghiubhsachain. This wall has smoother rock split by distinct vertical crack-lines.

Row yer Boat   12m   Severe 4a
(2004)

Approximately 10m left of the main wall, and left of a narrow heavily-fractured buttress, is a shorter narrow wall. Climb the cracks up this wall.

Battleship Burner   20m   HVS 5a
(2004)

On the main wall, start 3m from its left end beneath the crack-line second from left and starting at mid-height. Move directly up to the crack then continue for the top just to its right.

Ice & Sneezy   20m   VS 4c *
(2002)

The obvious crack-line immediately to the right of the previous route (and beneath a rock scar near the top of the wall). Climb the length of the crack, and then finish up the shallow corner just to the right of the rock scar.

Steelyard Blues   20m   E1 5a
(2004)

The thinner crack-line right again, trending slightly left near the top to finish up the right edge of the corner from the previous route.

The Crossing   20m   E2 5b **
(2004)

Approximately 2m right again, and just to the left of a narrow broken area, is another obvious crack which trends slightly left and runs out at about one-third height and then re-emerges at two-thirds height. Follow the crack and its upper continuation, with the crossing in the middle being bold (ground-fall potential).

Starboard Tack   18m   HVS 5a *
(2004)

Approximately 8m further right (on the other side of a narrow broken section) the wall is particularly smooth with two obvious vertical crack-lines and a ledge at half height. Start up the left crack to the ledge, then move right to finish up the right crack.

Variation: **Direct Finish   E2 5c**   *(2004)*
Continue up the left-hand crack above the ledge.

Approximately 50m downhill to the right again (looking at the scarp), there is
another substantial section which appears to lean at an easy angle into the hillside,
though it is actually steeper. The first tier provides pleasant climbing (worthy of a
star), but it is unfortunately topped by a further tier of 20 to 25m of much looser
and mossy ground which would be disconcerting without a rope.

Sleazy   35m   HVS 5a   *(2004)*
Go up the centre of a narrow section just left of the main face, following a faint
vertical line through small overlaps.

Primera   45m   VS 4c   *(2004)*
The second vertical crack-line to the right on the main face of rock. It moves up into
a more broken area next to a shallow right-facing corner after about 15m.

CARN A' BHIORAIN - COILL A' BHUN

(NH 132 837)   Alt 250m   North-West facing

A steep crag lies east of the Dundonnell river about 3km south of Dundonnell
House and is particularly obvious from the A832. The crag is composed largely of
compact schist with tree covered ledges. It has resisted one summer attempt but
provides two frozen waterfalls in the coldest of weather conditions.

Approach: A direct approach requires boulder hopping or wading. Otherwise use
a bridge at NH 127 843.

Goat Falls   100m   III *   *(1996)*
A prominent waterfall breaks through the north-eastern end of Coill a' Bhun crags
(at NH 135 840 and 500m north-east of Fain Falls). Climb an iced slab (25m). Walk
along the gully bottom for 25m. Climb another iced slab (20m) to a shelf and then
the steep shelved icefall (45m). Exit left at the top.

Fain Falls   105m   IV,4 **   *(1984)*
An impressive icefall can form a few hundred metres left of a deep obvious gully.
It gives three long steep pitches but requires wet conditions followed by cold
weather. Descent is via the deep gully.

LOCH BROOM - WEST

Bonar   200m   III   *(1994)*
An iced burn in a shallow gully west across the head of Loch Broom (NH 169 860),
and on the same grid line as Inverlael Farm. It provides short steep steps and
scrambling. Cars can be parked at NH 169 861 and a steep scramble gains the
route, 5mins. A steep line of crags, which is marked on the map, overlooks the
route to the south-east. The route is probably the same as Dutch Courage (SMCJ
1996).

Heavy Handed   90m   III   *(1996)*
Just visible from the road, this icefall at NH 162 874 is hidden by the village of
Letters. A black garage marks the starting point to walk in. Walk up to the left
shoulder and traverse in via a faint path to a bay.
1. 30m Start up thin ice to reach a tree on the right.
2. 25m Climb up more thin ice to the left of 'The Icicle'. Traverse past this (quite
tricky) to a fallen tree on the right.
3. 35m Climb 'The Icicle' direct, offering short-lived fun. Continue up another
short steep icefall to the top.

BEINN GOBHLACH - NORTH FACE

(NH 056 943)   Alt 450m   North-West facing

No Option   250m   II   *(1999)*
Approaching from the west and about halfway along is a widening gully breaching
the buttress. Climb into the narrows over a few icy steps and take the main left fork
leading easily to the top.

Baldrallach Crags

There are a number of crags approached from the road to Badrallach, offering
quartzite or Torridonian sandstone instead of the gneiss of the nearby Gruinard
crags, or as an alternative to An Teallach in cold or showery weather.

GOLDEN WALL CRAG

(NH 116 879)   Alt 230m   South-West facing   Map p268

The best of several quartzite crags which overlook Dundonnell and featuring a
golden coloured wall of smooth quartzite. The rock has positive holds typical of
quartzite and is in essence sound, although there are some loose blocks.

Approach: Leave the A832 near Dundonnell house and take the Badrallach road,
parking near the bend at NH 112 877. Cross the stream and walk up its right side
to the wall, which soon becomes prominent high on the right of the stream gorge,
20mins.

Descent: Scramble on the right.

The crag consists of a steep edge overlooking the gorge, then a right-angle turn to
form the overhanging golden wall. Further right and a little lower is another crag
of lesser angle.

Silver Shadow   25m   VS *   *(1995)*
This is on the wall facing the gorge, not far left of the edge of the golden wall. Start
a few metres left of a wide heathery crack.
1. 10m 4a Climb a slab and step right under a roof to climb a crack. Step left and
climb the crack that splits two huge flakes and belay behind them.
2. 15m 4b Step right on to the wall from the right-hand flake and climb a crack
to a small overhang. Pull through the overhang and continue in the same line to
the top.

The Golden Wall   20m   E2 5b **   *(1995)*
An exciting route up the golden wall. Start at the right edge of the wall. Climb a
line of flakes trending slightly right to the right end of a roof. Traverse under the
roof to its left end and a wedged square block. Continue rightwards up the wall
above, using a small creaking flake, to exit left at a small notch.

Old Faithful   20m   Very Difficult *   *(1995)*
This is the chimney-crack to the right of The Golden Wall. Short but good.

False Spring   35m   Severe 4a   *(1996)*
About 80m down and right of the golden wall is a rounded buttress whose right
edge is bounded by a rickety ridge and a tree. To its left is a clean slab left of a
shallow corner. Climb the slab trending leftwards to keep to the cleanest rock.

GOOSE CRAG

(NH 107 896)   Alt 240m   West facing

The closest climbing to the Badrallach road is this scruffy crag with the best looking rock on the left side.

Approach: Once the road leaves the forestry, there is a sheep fank on the left by the junction of fences. Park in the next passing place or verge on the left. The crag is directly above reached in about 10mins.

Descent: To the left.

Cow Dumped In JR's Soft-Top   40m   VS 4c   (2002)
At the left side is an undercut pillar of rock with short corners bounding either side, the left-hand corner crack has a small rowan tree at the top. Start at the lowest rocks and climb a crack to a ledge under the pillar. Move leftwards and up the corner-crack and finish easily up the slab.

CREAG BEINN NAM BAN

(NH 107 897)   Alt 280m   South-West facing   Map p268   Diagram p300

The crag is well seen from the road, a slabby wall of fine and generally sound, albeit slightly lichenous, Torridonian sandstone. Quick drying and with a fine outlook over Little Loch Broom.

Approach: Take the Badrallach road to a large lay-by just beyond the crag. Head rightwards up the hillside to a grassy gully right of the crag. Traverse a terrace left to its base, 10mins.

Descent: Either by abseil from a thread (the belay for all routes, not in situ), or make a slightly rising traverse south into the grassy gully right (looking up) of the crag.

Central to the crag is a large A shaped slab capped by a roof high up.

1 Blockbuster   40m   HVS 5a *   (1996)
An exciting swarm up jugs, but not recommended if hollow blocks make you nervous. The furthest left of several shallow corners has a steep jamming crack in its left wall. Follow this, step right on to a slab, then traverse right under an overhang. Surmount the overhang above a large block and follow the easier crack which runs up parallel with the apex of the A to the top.
Variation Finish:
Instead of traversing right, climb the rib directly above.

2 Go with the Flow   40m   E1 5b   (2002)
Right of Blockbuster is a shallow mossy groove. Climb this to the large hanging block and pass it on its right to finish as for Blockbuster.

3 Bandit Country   40m   E2 5b *   (2000)
Sustained but with adequate protection. The right wall of the shallow mossy groove leads to an arete, the route. Start up a small juggy arete leading to the main arete. Climb it fairly directly (the best line, like the protection, needs finding) to join and finish up the slab of Wendy House.

4 Wendy House   40m   VS 4b *   (1991)
A poorly protected route, but technically straightforward if the easiest line is taken (originally graded Severe). Right of the arete of Bandit Country is a two-stepped smooth corner. Start below this and climb to its base. Make an awkward move right and climb the right side of its right rib. Either step left to the top of the corner and climb up to a heather ledge (the original line) or make a thin move up from the top of the rib and then step left (a later line, cleaner but perhaps HVS 4c). Climb the slab above to a final roof (the Wendy House, original belay, is here) and turn this by a crack on the right.
Variation: **Direct Variation   E1 5a**
Climb direct from the rib to the Wendy House without going to the ledge.

AN TEALLACH AREA

CREAG BEINN NAM BAN

1. Blockbuster   HVS 5a *
2. Go with the Flow   E1 5b
3. Bandit Country   E2 5b *
4. Wendy House   VS 4b *
4a. Direct Variation   E1 5a
5. Long Distance Runner   Severe 4a *
5a. Direct Variation   VS 5a
6. Mind over Matter   HVS 5a **

Andy Nisbet

5 Long Distance Runner   40m   Severe 4a *   *(1996)*
Again poorly protected but technically straightforward and based on the shallow corner which forms the right side of an inverted V of slab. Start from a platform 5m left of the corner. Climb the steep V-slab heading towards a short crack at its apex and in the line of the corner. Climb the crack to a continuation corner. Step right, go up a slab and return left to the top of the continuation corner. Finish up a continuation crack-line.
Variation: **Direct Variation (original line)   VS 5a**
Climb the continuation corner direct (well protected).

6 Mind over Matter   45m   HVS 5a **   *(1990)*
To the right of Long Distance Runner is a steepening corner that starts above the right end of a heather band. Climb a short wall to the heather and the corner above. The corner is a sustained but well protected crux. Continue in the same line up open slabs to the top. Possibly the best route here but the other routes are close in quality.

To the right of the main crag is a gully. On the gully's right wall is a prominent pinnacle, separated from the sidewall by a chimney. To its right is another slender buttress with another bounding chimney to its right and then a broader buttress. The rock is not so good as on the main face and the routes are quite serious.

7 Hound Dog Pinnacle   15m   Severe   *(1997)*
Climb the frontal face of the pinnacle direct without using the chimney.

8 Shepherds Warning   18m   HVS 5a   *(1997)*
Climb the frontal face of the slender buttress immediately to the right of Hound Dog Pinnacle.

High above Creag Beinn nam Ban and at the top of the steep hillside is a low angled pink slab. It looks impressive in profile from the top of Fin Buttress but is rather broken with only its right end being clean and continuous. This is **Solo Slab** (50m Moderate 1998), which can be reached by continuing up the gully from Hound Dog Pinnacle until the slab is on the left.

AN TEALLACH AREA

FLUTED BUTTRESS

(NH 108 896)   Alt 380m   South-West facing
There are a number of other buttresses and walls in the vicinity. All are smaller and of poorer rock. A few lines of doubtful value have been recorded and more are possible. Right of Creag Beinn nam Ban is the gully containing Hound Dog Pinnacle. Right again is another parallel gully at the top left of which is a 15m buttress. This can be seen from the road just south of the lay-by and is characterised by left-slanting cracks and grooves. Approach up the gully, 20mins.

Put a Sock in it!   15m   Very Difficult   *(1998)*
The leftmost crack on the front face of the buttress.

Beaufort Scale   15m   Very Difficult   *(1998)*
Immediately right of the last route is a slight recess with two shallow chimneys. This is the left chimney.

Force Six Chimney   15m   Very Difficult   *(1998)*
The right chimney is rather loose.

Class Struggle   15m   HVS 5a   *(1998)*
Right of Force Six Chimney is a steep jam crack in a shallow left-facing corner. Climb the crack direct exiting right.

Prole's Crack   15m   Severe   *(1998)*
Right of this is a chimney with a rockfall scar at its base. Right again, starting from
a higher platform, is a crack in a groove, curving left towards the top (Severe).
Starting from the same platform and at the right end of the face is this route, an
undercut crack with a small square-cut overhang at half-height. Gain the crack from
the left and turn the overhanging block on its right.

FIN BUTTRESS

Left of Fluted Buttress is a small slabby buttress. Left again is a buttress with a
prominent fin of rock separating two grooves. The left-hand groove has a small tree
on its right.

Lords a Leaping   15m   VS 4c   *(1998)*
The left-hand groove. Start just left of the lowest point and climb the groove
passing the tree on its immediate left and with an awkward move right at mid-
height. An easier start is up a slab further left.

Social Climber   15m   VS 4c   *(1998)*
The right-hand groove. Start just right of the lowest point and pull up a short
bubbled wall leftwards to a slab. Move up to a groove and so to the top.

BADRALLACH CRAG

(NH 104 912)   Alt 450m   West facing   Map p268

At the north-west end of Beinn nam Ban two tiers of crags overlook the high point
of the road. The lower tier is vegetated but the upper tier contains a small slabby
crag which can be identified by a small recess at its foot. The rock is excellent rough

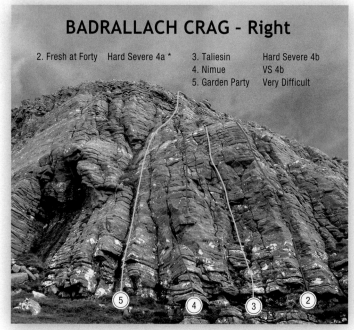

BADRALLACH CRAG - Right

2. Fresh at Forty   Hard Severe 4a *   3. Taliesin   Hard Severe 4b
                                          4. Nimue   VS 4b
                                          5. Garden Party Very Difficult

Ross Jones

BADRALLACH CRAG Left

Ross Jones

AN TEALLACH AREA

6. Lapsang Suchong	VS 4b
7. Laird's Loss	E1 5b *
8. Pillar of Society	VS 4b *
9. Poacher's Prize	VS 4b **

| 10. Hunter's Moon | HVS 4c * |
| 10a. Alternative Start | |

sandstone. The crag, which catches the afternoon and evening sun, is quick drying and offers a number of low grade routes in a fine setting.

Approach: Park at a large lay-by 300m south of the Allt na h-Airbhe hairpin bend at spot height 236 on Sheet 19. Avoid the lower tier by striking up to the north ridge on the left, then returning rightwards to the crag. 30mins.

Descent: Reverse Windy Ridge.

Routes are described from right to left.

1 Windy Ridge   70m   Easy   *(1997)*
A pleasant scramble up the blocky ridge which bounds the crag on its right. Start at the lowest rocks right of the cave.

2 Fresh at Forty   25m   Hard Severe 4a *   *(2005)*
Start 6m right of two detached blocks. Climb a small open corner for 12m. Step left and climb an arete to a halfway ledge.

3 Taliesin   25m   Hard Severe 4b   *(2005)*
Start 3m right of the detached blocks. Climb a large shallow corner direct to the halfway ledge.

4 Nimue   25m   VS 4b   *(2005)*
Climb the detached blocks and cracks on the wall left for 2m. Pull out right on to a blunt arete and to the halfway ledge. Low in the grade.

Nick Smith

Poacher's Prize, VS, Badrallach Crag. Climber Titus Murray

5 Garden Party   40m   Very Difficult   (1998)
The botanically interesting groove right of the recess.

6 Lapsang Suchong   35m   VS 4b   (1998)
Start at the right side of the recess. Climb a slab to the roof of the recess and make
a short overhanging traverse right on to an arete. Move up to easier ground, then
climb a corner which leads to the ledge.

7 Laird's Loss   35m   E1 5b *   (1998)
Climb direct to the awkward hanging groove above the centre of the recess. Climb
it (try a move on the left) to a deep crack in the slab above which leads more easily
to the ledge.

8 Pillar of Society   35m   VS 4b *   (1998)
The left wall of the recess is formed by a giant pillar. Climb the wall on mega jugs
to the top of the pillar. A crack now leads up the slab trending left. Protection is
spaced.

9 Poacher's Prize   35m   VS 4b **   (1998)
Left of the recess is a wide crack where the pillar joins the slab. Left again is a
prominent crack which runs the full height of the slab. Start steeply below the crack
and follow it to the top. Protection is spaced.

10 Hunter's Moon   30m   HVS 4c *   (1998)

At the foot of the slab and left of Poacher's Prize is a large boulder. Two cracks, one from its top and one from just below, start up the slab but run out. Start up either but end up in the left one, then continue boldly in the same line to a slight steepening which is climbed on improving holds to the ledge. Protection is spaced.

CREAG A' CHADHA

Map p268

These sandstone crags consist of hillside outcrops and some small sea-cliffs. A number of routes have been climbed with potential for more, although cleaning may be required.

Approach: From the car park at Badrallach follow the Scoraig path for 2km until the path descends close to the sea where the hillside becomes craggy. About 1hr.

CHADHA SLAB

(NH 038 928)   Alt 100m   West facing

This is the obvious cracked slab on the hillside above the path.

Descent: Down a heather rake on the right side.

Crackerjack   50m   VS 4c *   (2002)
Takes in an obvious crack up the centre of the slab. Start below an impressive roof. Climb left-trending cracks and pull through the overlap on to the slab with the crack. Climb this until the crack thins out. Belay at an obvious ledge on the right (30m). Climb up heathery ground to the top (20m).

THE SEA-CLIFFS

(NH 036 928)   Non-tidal   West facing

These small cliffs are situated down and right from the path (facing the loch) and are approached by a faint path. Unfortunately the undeveloped cliffs seem to have been inhabited by large birds with eating disorders so a power hose may be required before further development.

Soma Wall

The first feature encountered is a pink gully wall with three obvious crack-lines and the following routes. Approach down the gully to the bottom of the wall.

Desert Storm   10m   HVS 5a   (1998)
The left-hand crack.

Scoraig   10m   VS 4b   (1995)
The right-hand crack.

Eterna   10m   VS 4b   (1995)
The obvious arete on the right of the wall.

Around to the right of the wall the cliffs continue but unfortunately shorten in height. The first obvious feature is a strange eroded cave and is climbed by the following route.

The Doo Cot   7m   Very Difficult **   (1995)
Climb into the doo cot and pull out of it steeply on amazing jugs.

Kushi Doo   7m   Severe   (1995)
Climb the obvious chimney to the left of the Doo Cot.

AN TEALLACH AREA

THE FANNAICHS

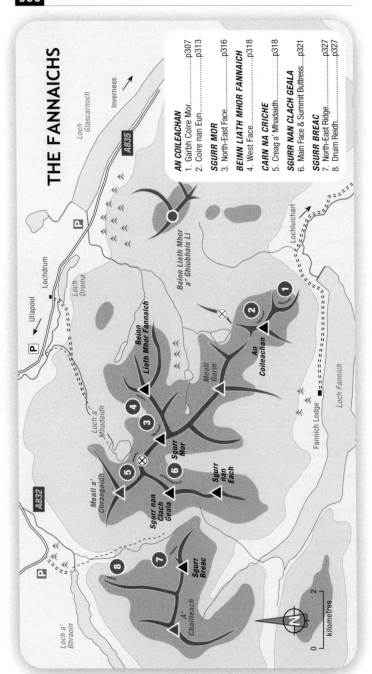

Loch Glascarnoch

Inverness

A835

Ullapool

P

Lochdrum

Loch Droma

Loch a' Mhadaidh

Loch a' Bhraoin

A832

P

Meall a' Chrasgaidh

Beinn Liath Mhor Fannaich

Beinn Liath Mhor a' Ghiubhais Li

Meall Gorm

An Coileachan

Sgurr Mor

Sgurr nan Each

Sgurr nan Clach Geala

Sgurr Breac

A' Chailleach

Fannich Lodge

Loch Fannich

Lochluichart

N

0   2
kilometres

THE FANNAICHS

The Fannaichs are the relatively remote group of mountains lying in the wedge-shaped area between the Garve to Achnasheen and the Garve to Braemore Junction roads. The line from Loch a' Bhraoin to Kinlochewe may be considered the western boundary of the group, separating it from An Teallach and Fisherfield, further west. There are several big vegetated cliffs with their inland position providing a more 'continental' climate suited to winter climbing.

AN COILEACHAN

(NH 241 680)   923m

There are two cliffs on this otherwise rounded mountain, the prominent and impressive Garbh Coire Mor and the secluded Coire nan Eun.

GARBH COIRE MOR

(NH 250 674)   Alt 600m   East facing   Diagrams p308, 310

The distinctive shape of Garbh Coire Mor is clearly seen from the Garve to Achnasheen road and easily accessible if a bike is used and the private road is clear of snow. The mixed routes are at their best when the cliff is both frozen and snowy, but this requires fairly cold conditions as it is relatively low-lying. There are also good ice climbs, which have had a few ascents due to their inclusion in Cold Climbs, but they are more rarely in condition. At these times the road is likely to be impassable.

Approach: From the south along the private estate road from Grudie (on the Garve to Achnasheen road). A locked gate at the start of this tarmaced road prevents vehicle access, but cycling is possible, after which the corrie is reached in an easy hour.

Descent: Usually down the south bounding ridge of the corrie, keeping close to the corrie rim to avoid slabby ground. The opposite side of the corrie is also possible, but usually it is uphill to reach it.

The left side of the corrie is a long and somewhat featureless slabby wall. Perhaps the best features are two shallow depressions at about one-third and two-thirds of the way along the wall but they are only seen when directly underneath.

1 Short Shrift   80m   II   *(1979)*
This is the obvious narrow gully on the extreme left of the corrie. It remains hidden throughout the approach and can hold two ice pitches.

2 Flying Carpet   150m   V,7 *   *(1995)*
Climbs the rib on the left of the left-hand depression. Access to the depression is barred by steep smooth ground, sometimes very icy. The rib on the left of this depression has a small tree. Start from the bottom left of the terrace at the base of the depression. Trend left on to the rib and up a corner to steep ground (35m). Trend back right on increasingly narrow turf ramps until next to the depression and climb a short vertical corner with a turf stripe, the flying carpet (strenuous bridging as the turf was not sufficiently solid for a direct pull) (40m). Continue just left of the depression, passing the solitary tree to big blocks (50m). Finish up a less steep turfy corner (25m).

3 Illusion Wall   150m   Very Difficult   *(1995)*
The rib on the right of the depression provides this route; the line is only obvious from its start or above, not on the approach. It provides occasional rock moves amongst the turf. Scramble on to a right-rising terrace and go up it to start well right of the rib via a ramp which slants left to the crest. Follow the crest to the top.

AN COILEACHAN - Garbh Coire Mor, left

1. Short Shrift	II	4. Quidditch	V,5	7. The Ramp Tramp	IV,4
2. Flying Carpet	V,7 *	5. Al Capone	V,6 **	8. Tormentil	IV,5 *
3. Illusion Walll	IV,5	6. The Gallous Palace	V,6 *	A. rockfall scar	

Andy Nisbet

Winter: **IV,5** *   (1995)
By the summer route except that a deviation down left from the ramp was used to
avoid a short slab on pitch 1. The short crux was a 5m wall when the crest was first
reached.

4 Quidditch 170m V,5   (2005)
A devious line up the centre of the face between the depressions. A large rockfall
scar high up and right of this route is the best locating feature. Gain and go up the
right-rising terrace to the left side of its highest section. This is about 20m left of a
point directly down from the rockfall scar. Here are two horizontal ledges leading
left, one at about 5m and one at 15m.
1. 15m Climb easily up to the right end of the second ledge.
2. 35m Follow the ledge left to its end. Move left low down, then climb up to a
higher ledge. Go left along this, then climb to a ledge below a corner capped by a
small roof.
3. 35m Climb the corner, then go right up a ramp to a chimney behind a huge
block. Climb the chimney and continue right.
4. 35m Go up steep turfy ledges to a smooth wall. Traverse left to a weakness, then
return right above the wall.
5. 50m Go right up a ramp to easier turfy ground which leads to the top.

5 Al Capone 160m V,6 **   (2001)
A fairly direct and well protected line up the right side of the face between the two
depressions, passing just right of the large rockfall scar. After a tricky wall at the
base, climb a crack and corner-line direct to the right end of a ledge above the
rockfall scar (40m). Go to the left end of the ledge and climb over two large flakes.
Return right up a ramp to below a wall which is just right of the belay (20m). Step
left into a shallow corner in the wall and make a hard move to reach turf. Continue
up to easier ground (20m). Finish up the easier ground trending slightly left (80m).

6 The Gallous Palace   150m   V,6 *   *(1999)*
Climbs the left edge of the right-hand depression, featuring a left-facing corner
which breaks through a steep band of rock. Climb up to below and just left of the
corner. Pull into the base of the corner, then climb the wall just right of it. Traverse
right to gain an easy turfy groove leading up left.

7 The Ramp Tramp   200m   IV,4   *(1985)*
This climb takes two ramps, the first going diagonally right across the right-hand
depression and the second just left of and then above a very steep section of wall
(which is left of Primrose gully). Scramble up slabs and vegetation to start under
the depression, roughly at the same point as The Gallous Palace. Gain the first ramp
and follow it rightwards to its end (50m). Above this ramp the depression is barred
by a smooth barrier wall but at the very end of the ramp there is just enough
vegetation to reach the ramp above. Follow this to broken ground, then go straight
up to the top. A left finish, going into and up the depression from part way up the
upper ramp, looks fairly straightforward.

8 Tormentil   200m   IV,5 *   *(2002)*
A narrow ramp across the steep wall parallel to and overlooking Primrose gully.
Start right of the depression and Ramp Tramp and climb steeply on turf sods to
reach the ramp. Follow it to a short corner which gives a couple of strenuous but
well protected moves to gain a continuation of the ramp, less well defined but
which leads in the same line to the top.

9 Primrose   240m   III   *(1976/1979)*
This is the gully in the back left corner of the corrie. Start up a long ice pitch to
reach the gully proper. Follow the gully until it forks at a large boulder. Either fork
may be taken, but the right fork is considered more interesting and less heavily
corniced.

10 The Primula Trap   240m   III *   *(1998)*
Climbs a ramp-line parallel and right of Primrose. Start up the long ice pitch as for
Primrose to reach a bay at the start of the ramp and about 10m below Primrose
gully. Follow the ramp, narrow at first but easier than it looks, to the top.

11 Venus Fly Trap   250m   Scottish V   *(1986)*
This is the left-hand of two icefalls running up the steep buttress right of Primrose.
After two pitches up the icefall go diagonally right on mixed ground and break
through to a broad snow ramp (right of The Primula Trap). This leads easily up right
to the top, keeping right of The Primula Trap. The icefalls rarely form so the exact
position of the route is unknown but the ice forms most readily on the left side of
the buttress, left of a band of overhangs.

12 Triffid   220m   VI,7 **   *(2003)*
Climbs the right side of the buttress, passing right of a band of overhangs which
cap the central area of the buttress. Start about 10m left of Burdock.
1. 40m Climb a groove with thin turf to the right end of an overhang. Traverse left
and pull through the left end of the overhang to another longer groove which is
followed curving right to a slight crest below steeper ground.
2. 20m Move right and climb a turfy corner. Traverse back left along a ledge for
about 10m and pull through a bulge. Traverse left again and pull leftwards through
another bulge to reach a flake below a steep corner. There may well be icicles, or
even an icefall, just right of the corner.
3. 20m Climb the steep corner (or the icefall) to turf. Continue slightly rightwards,
then up to a good ledge.
4. 50m Go rightwards, then up steep turfy ground to finish up a short bulging
chimney.
5. 50m Trend left into a broad fault and up it.
6. 40m Continue up the fault to the top.

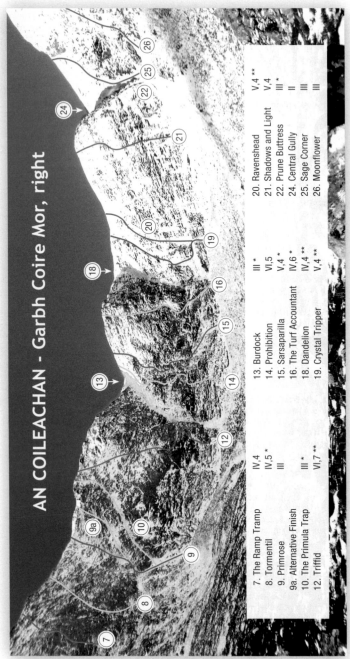

AN COILEACHAN - Garbh Coire Mor, right

7. The Ramp Tramp	IV,4
8. Tormentil	IV,5 *
9. Primrose	III
9a. Alternative Finish	
10. The Primula Trap	III *
12. Triffid	VI,7 **

13. Burdock	III *
14. Prohibition	VI,5
15. Sarsaparilla	V,4 *
16. The Turf Accountant	IV,6 *
18. Dandelion	IV,4 **
19. Crystal Tripper	V,4 **

20. Ravenshead	V,4 **
21. Shadows and Light	V,4
22. Prune Buttress	III *
24. Central Gully	II
25. Sage Corner	III
26. Moonflower	III

Erik Brunskill

13 Burdock 210m III * *(1976)*

The next gully right of Primrose. Two long ice pitches lead to easier ground. The cornice is avoidable on the right.

14 Prohibition 225m VI,5 *(2005)*

A bold route taking the faint S shaped groove system in the steep area of buttress between Burdock and Sarsaparilla. Limited rock protection; take warthogs or hooks. Start at the bottom of the slabs at a small left-facing corner directly below a prominent sapling near the bottom of the steep section of the buttress (about 30m left of the start to Sarsaparilla).

1. 45m Climb the corner and continue up the slabs (with a bold long reach for turf at 25m) towards the sapling. Belay at a horizontal flake about 10m below the sapling.

2. 55m Continue up and left through steep turfy walls and ice smears to a large recess up and left of the sapling. Step down right and traverse a black slab on tufts (directly above the sapling) and continue straight up to another smaller recess. Continue up turfy ground trending first right, then back left up the groove system to a small ledge formed by a large block at the bottom left of the next steep rocky groove.

3. 55m Move right and climb a corner to reach an overhung bay, then follow cracks on the right and turfy grooves, breaking out left at the top wall to easier ground.

4. and 5. 70m Continue easily up the right-trending shallow crest to the top or finish up Burdock.

15 Sarsaparilla 240m V,4 * *(2001)*

A line based on the groove high in the centre of the buttress between Burdock and Dandelion. Limited rock protection; take warthogs or hooks. Start roughly centrally and some 20m up and right of the lowest point of the buttress. Take a line of weakness leading diagonally left, then go straight up to steeper ground (50m). Climb a small icefall through a steep wall to a niche, then traverse right and rise right to the base of the central groove (50m). Climb the groove (ice) until the natural line leads out left (40m). Climb up and return right into the main groove (30m). Finish easily up this (70m).

16 The Turf Accountant 200m IV,6 * *(1987)*

This follows a corner-line on the right side of the steep buttress left of Dandelion, starting just to its left and aiming for a protruding block on the skyline. A fine line with a short hard crux, but the climbing is a little disappointing, being mostly easier turf.

1. 30m Climb a left-trending ramp to a terrace beneath a smooth rock band.

2. 20m Take the band direct via a sentry box (hard but well protected) to gain the bottom left-hand side of the corner-line.

3, 4. and 5. 150m Move slightly right then follow the turfy corner with increasing interest, passing just left of a square block to gain easy ground.

17 On yer Bike 200m VI,6 ** *(2001)*

A good route following an intricate line up the crest of the buttress which forms the left wall of Dandelion (i.e. right of Turf Accountant).

1. 35m Start at the bottom right edge of the buttress and climb directly up the crest to the terrace below the first rock band.

2. 30m Traverse rightwards to the end of the terrace and climb for about 5m up a right-trending ramp (overlooking Dandelion) round the rock band. Up and left is a steep cracked wall. Step up on to a pedestal and climb the wall. At its top pull out left on to a ledge on the crest of the buttress. Go up and left to a small recess above a flake-crack.

3. 50m Traverse left along the top of the flake and up a groove. Climb straight up the crest of the buttress to another smaller rock band. Climb the rock band directly up a steep flaky wall (bold). Continue up to a terrace below another large rock

band and traverse right to the edge of the buttress to a good thread below a large block (overlooking Dandelion).
4. 30m Climb up on to the block and climb the steep wall above by turfy ledges into a blocky corner-line. Climb this to its top.
5. and 6. 55m Climb up and left into an obvious open groove and follow this to the top.

**18 Dandelion   210m   IV,4 ** *(1976)*
The steep narrow gully right of Burdock. It has several ice pitches and forms more readily than the routes to its right.

To the right of Dandelion a steep icefall often forms. More rarely twin icefalls form, in which case the left one gives the next route, Crystal Tripper. If there is only one icefall it is likely to be Ravenshead. There is very little rock protection. In ideal conditions of firm snow and good ice, the routes are straightforward but this rarely happens nowadays.

**19 Crystal Tripper   240m   V,4 ** *(1979)*
Start 30m right of Dandelion at an inset corner. Climb a short ice pitch to gain a snow band. Traverse left and climb the left of twin icefalls for 30m to a belay on the left. Climb steep ice to reach rock, then make a short traverse right to gain and climb a groove which leads to a second snow band. Climb the icefall above, with a bulge at 25m, then continue up ice runnels above to a snow fan exit, which is sometimes corniced.

**20 Ravenshead   210m   V,4 ** *(1981)*
Start as for Crystal Tripper, 30m right of Dandelion. Climb up the short ice pitch to the snow band. Move right to the obvious icefall and climb this on its left side on mixed ground for 25m. Step right and gain the centre of the icefall which is followed to an obvious ice pillar. Climb this until it is possible to step left into a groove (crux) and go over a bulge to gain a belay (60m). Climb mixed ground moving right to follow an ice rake (45m). The upper bowl is gained and easier snow leads to the top.

21 Shadows and Light   240m   V,4 *(1984)*
Start about 45m left of Prune Buttress, which goes up the right edge overlooking Central Gully.
1. 15m Climb a snowslope to an obvious, steep shallow groove.
2. 45m Climb the groove over several overlaps to a large overlap.
3. 30m Pass the overlap on the right.
4. 45m Climb delicate iced slabs to a steep snow ledge.
5. 30m Traverse right to gain a shallow weakness. Follow this for a further 75m to the top.

22 Prune Buttress   210m   III * *(1979)*
This takes the edge of the buttress on the left of the large Central Gully. Various lines are possible, the best being on the extreme edge which has some impressive positions. There is a direct start just left of the edge which is harder (Grade IV).

23 Sideshow   70m   IV,5 * *(1991)*
A strenuous, well protected climb on frozen turf. Follow the easy Central Gully to a steep narrow corner in the left wall (at a point beyond where the icefalls of Sage Corner appear).
1. 15m Climb the corner over a bulge to a saddle on the right below a big spike.
2. 20m Gain the shelf above the belay, move left a few metres and attack the thin crack on the right. This leads to easier ground.
3. 35m Climb mixed ground, then traverse right below a short wall to a hanging ramp. Climb the intervening step and continue up the ramp to the top.

24 Central Gully   240m   II

The obvious wide gully in the back right of the corrie.

25 Sage Corner   165m   III   *(1979)*
About halfway up Central Gully, where it widens, break out right and climb iced slabs and snow to a prominent icefall bordered on its right by a large corner. Climb the icefall which consists of short, vertical steps and finish up snow.

26 Moonflower   240m   III   *(1984)*
Start on the right of Central Gully opposite the foot of Prune Buttress. An obvious snow ledge leads out right. Follow this to beyond the skyline then climb shallow right-trending snow grooves with short awkward steps to the top.
Variation: **Direct Start   120m   IV,3**   *(1984)*
Start about 45m left of Echo Face and climb iced slabs and grooves trending left to gain the original route.

27 Echo Face   360m   IV,3 *   *(1979)*
An atmospheric open face with minimal protection. Good snow and ice might drop the grade. Start in the centre of the large slabby face right of Central Gully. Climb icefalls then snow aiming for a groove capped by a small bulge. Surmount the bulge and climb thinly iced slabs for 90m. Above this easier ground leads via a snow funnel up and right to the top.

**28 Plumline   360m   IV,4 ** **   *(1979)*
This takes the fine corner on the right of the corrie, right of Echo Face. Climb up in three pitches to the obvious rock barrier. In some conditions this can be overcome on the left. Otherwise take an inset groove on the right, hidden from below, to reach a deep cave with an excellent pulpit stance. Step out left on steep ice and climb to another cave. Continue up the corner over occasional ice pitches to a corniced exit as for Echo Face.

COIRE NAN EUN

(NH 245 685)   Alt 700m   North facing   Map p306
A cliff well seen from Beinn Dearg but only fleetingly from the road. The first ascents were in icy conditions but should be possible as mixed routes. The icefall of Fatal Attraction is obvious from the road but the gullies are hidden.

Approach: Either a long and rough approach (7.5km, 3hr+) from the parking place on the A835 at NH 277 743, or cycle from Grudie (see Garbh Choire Mor), walk north past Garbh Choire Mor to a ridge and continue below the next corrie to another ridge, which bounds the eastern edge of the cliffs. About half way up this ridge is a large ledge, which is traversed right into the hanging corrie, 2hrs 30mins.

Descent: Either down the east side of the cliff to the approach ledge or with sufficient build-up, use Descent Gully (not a walk).

The cliffs are divided into three distinct buttresses, East, Central and West separated by two gullies, Descent Gully and Inner Sanctum.

East Buttress

Hawkwind   100m   III   *(1996)*
This route climbs an icy recess and the gully above in the centre of the east buttress, about 30m left of Descent Gully. Climb the ice recess via the right wall to gain a right-trending ramp and easier ground (40m). Continue above to a fork, take the left branch up a defined gully and finish up the right wall to the top.

Kitekat Rib   90m   II   *(2003)*
This route climbs the rib overlooking Descent Gully. Start on the right side of the buttress at the foot of Descent Gully, attain the rib and climb direct to the top.

Descent Gully   110m   I/II   *(1994)*
Towards the left end of the crag is this left-slanting snow gully. There is a short ice pitch in lean conditions.

Central Buttress

Feral Buttress   75m   III,4   *(2003)*
Start at the base of Inner Sanctum and traverse leftwards on to the front face via the obvious ledge to a large block. Climb left-trending turfy grooves to a bay below twin parallel grooves (30m). Climb the left-hand groove and continue in the same line to the top (45m).

Inner Sanctum   100m   III   *(1994)*
Twenty metres right of the easy Descent Gully is a narrower and deeper left-slanting gully which remains hidden until the corrie is entered. It has one very steep ice pitch which can be chimneyed and is much easier than it looks (assuming enough ice).

West Buttress

Slam   90m   VI,6 *   *(2003)*
This route climbs the turfy groove system on the left edge of the buttress. Protection is generally spaced and of dubious quality. Start at the bottom left toe of the buttress and climb the deceptively steep left-trending turfy groove system to a recess below the very steep upper section (50m). Continue up the continuation ramp leftwards until it levels out below a steep flaky wall. Climb thinly up this to another ledge and traverse left to a protruding block. From the top of this climb boldly up and right through the blocky overhangs to easy ground and the top (40m).

Fatal Attraction   100m   IV,4 *   *(1994)*
An icefall just right of Inner Sanctum has a similar first pitch to Slam (although on ice), but a short right traverse then leads to a continuation icefall. There were some thin sections on the only ascent in good conditions and V,4 might be more common.

Bunny Boiler   100m   III   *(2003)*
On the western side of West Buttress several icefalls form readily. This route tackles the second of two parallel falls. Climb the icefall direct and continue above trending right up a ramp to the top.

Saddle Up   120m   II/IV,4   *(2003)*
This climbs a vague right-trending icy recess starting to the right of the main icefalls at the right side of West Buttress. Climb the icy recess for 50m to a snowfield. Cross the snowfield to below two ice falls. The wide left-hand icefall is Grade II. The narrow central fall is IV,4.

FIONN BHEINN

(NH 148 621)   933m

CREAG TOLL MOR

(NH 152 621)   Alt 800m   North facing

A schist crag lies at the crest of Toll Mor quite near the east top. The schist crag is very steep and has turfy and rocky lines. Despite its meagre height the climbing is quite exciting and concentrated and in the right conditions (frozen hard and not too much snow) just about repays the walk in.

Approach: The easiest approach is from the Achnasheen road up dreary slopes and a broad ridge, 2hrs. The crag is identified from above as being the one closest to the east top.

Descent: A steep couloir to the east (Grade I) provides a handy descent to a point where a ledge curls round below the crag.

Beyond some steep rock lies the first prominent line, a steep chimney-groove above a turfy lower section.

Crystal Visions 55m IV,5 * (2002)
The hanging chimney provides the line of the crag.
1. 20m Climb the turf over a step to below the wall guarding entrance into the chimney.
2. 35m The wall provides the crux. Climb to an overlap, move back right and gain and surmount a turfy overhang to another similar overhang immediately above. Once in the chimney things ease; another short chimney can be taken on the left or avoided on the right.

Second Sight 60m IV,5 * (2005)
A good line with plenty of interest. It takes the slender groove leading out rightwards from below the crux of Crystal Visions.
1. 40m Climb the initial 10m of Crystal Visions to step right into the groove. Climb this to where it narrows, then climb the crux groove to a more open turfy section and go up this to the ramp of The Kilted Raven; belay below a steep corner.
2. 20m Climb the corner, initially tricky, to the top.

Prophetic Voices 60m IV,5 * (1999)
Roughly in the centre of the crag and 20m to the right of a chimney-groove is a stepped wall, originally identified by hanging icicles, although the crag was smothered in unconsolidated powder. Good technical climbing with easier sections.
1. 25m Climb up to the bulge containing the icicles, step up right and pull over the bulge above the icicles. Continue up a ramp (The Kilted Raven) leftwards to a saddle stance.
2. 35m A steep groove lies above, left of the corner of Crystal Visions. Climb up to a block and step right to climb a blank wall then the easier groove. Continue in the same line past a prominent block and over the cornice.

The Kilted Raven 70m II (2002)
A well defined ramp runs up right to left starting beyond Prophetic Voices. It has only one point of difficulty, a short rocky block which needs to be climbed over to reach the continuation and a finish near Crystal Visions.

Prophet of Doom 45m IV,5 * (2005)
Above the start of the ramp of The Kilted Raven is a cave 15m up. Start at the base of the ramp and climb into the cave. Exit out of its left side on unexpected holds and finish up the groove above.

Tarot 40m IV,3 * (2005)
Right of Prophet of Doom are twin right-slanting ramps. Start below the cave and climb up into the left and higher ramp. Follow this until possible to cross the wall on the left by a small ramp to finish as for the groove above the cave. Limited protection.

Sprint 45m II (2005)
Start at the same place as Tarot but follow the lower right ramp towards a rocky prow at the top of the cliff. Before reaching it, move left up a pair of interesting walls to finish back right. Despite the lowly grade, not without its moments.

The Plaid and The Bonnet 50m III (2002)
About 30m to the right of The Kilted Raven is a narrow groove leading to the rocky

THE FANNAICHS

prow, prominent from below. Some good climbing, particularly on the first pitch.
1. 30m Climb the groove over a series of short steps to below the prow.
2. 20m Continue along a dwindling ledge to a steep pull up on the left at its
termination and continue up turfy ground above.

Crescendo Groove   45m   III,4 *   (2005)
About 400m right of the last route, passing below several ridge-like outcrops, is a
longer buttress with a prominent central groove. Climb the groove with increasing
interest and difficulty, well protected where it matters, to the top.

Trig Point Direct   150m   II   (2004)
Directly below the trig point are snow slopes bottomed by a slabby tongue of rock
bordered by a shallow gully to the left. Climb up the slabby tongue by the best line
to a snow patch. Climb straight over overlaps to reach the summit slopes; continue
to the trig point. Banks out readily.

SGURR MOR

(NH 204 718)   Alt 900m   North-East facing   Map p306

The impressive north-east face of Sgurr Mor is the highest in the area, it holds snow
well and can offer a winter route into April, or even May were it to freeze. This is
a big serious face, so choose good weather and beware of windslab, cornices and
warm early morning sunshine. The better the quality of snow and ice, the easier
are the routes.

Approach: Park on the A835 (there is a good place at NH 235 759) about 3km
south-east of the Dundonnell turn off, where a small building can be seen down by
the river. This is the start of the path to Loch a' Mhadaidh, which is not obvious at
first but it is easily found at the second stream crossing after 400m, where there is
a bridge. A start at Lochdrum and across the dam is simpler but about 10mins
longer. Follow the path, then track, then path again until just short of Loch a'
Mhadaidh, then head up a vague spur and traverse to below the cliff (following the
stream to here is rougher). Allow about 2hrs 30mins.

Descent: The most pleasant descent is to head south then east to Beinn Liath
Mhor Fannaich whose Munro summit can be bagged or traversed on the left. Then
head north-east to where the track meets the stream at a bridge.

Gelid Groove   220m   III,4 *   (1991)
Climbs an ice line on the leftmost wall of the face to provide a shorter route.
Continuous ice in lean conditions (when it looks excellent) but much can bank out
under heavy snow. Start by a cave left of the icefall just left of Easter Gully. Climb
the steep initial bulge (crux), then go up pleasant ice to a belay on the left (50m).
Continue up to the top bulge and climb this to snow (40m). Move up and right to
a minor snow rib with rock islands. Between the rib and the buttress on the right
is an optional ice pitch. Above this snow leads to the top.

Easter Gully   240m   II   (1967)
This straightforward snow gully on the left (south) corner of the face often has a
big cornice. In leaner conditions it may have an ice pitch low down but perhaps the
cornice will be easier.

Transfiguration   300m   IV,5   (1998)
Climbs the left side of the Resurrection face. Start on the right side of the buttress
between Easter Gully and the dead end gully at the start of The Resurrection. Climb
a groove, then easier ground to a recess on the right which leads to easy ground
(100m). Continue up a vague rib on the right of Easter Gully to a final steepening.
This could be climbed direct to make a Grade III, perhaps even II if the left side of
the initial buttress was climbed, but a more interesting finish was to go diagonally
right on ramps into the hanging groove in the steep ground above the final
snowfield of The Resurrection. Finish up this.

Martin Moran

THE FANNAICHS

The Resurrection, III, Sgurr Mor. Climber Chris Dale

The Resurrection   300m III *   (1980)
The central route on the face provides a serious route with a great Alpine atmosphere. The last belay is the summit cairn of Sgurr Mor, the highest point in the North-West Highlands. With a big build-up, rock protection or belays tend to be buried (little exists anyway), so expect to use snow belays, possibly ice screw belays and take a warthog or two for turf, particularly at the top.

Start towards the left side of the face, at the right side of a dead-end gully right of Easter Gully. Here is a large icefall, although it may have thawed away towards the end of the season; the icefall is slightly hidden on the approach. Climb the icefall, normally 50m but it could be longer in lean conditions and steep at the bottom (Grade IV,4), to reach the base of a big snowfield. Climb 45 degree snow for two long pitches, then a short icefall gains a steeper snowfield, climbed in one long pitch to a scoop below the steep capping wall (poor rock belay here). Go diagonally right, then continue straight up to the top (55m). This pitch is not difficult but the only protection is warthogs in the turf, the rope is too short, there may be a big cornice and it's a long way to retreat. Other than that, no problem!
Variation: **Easy Start   I**
This start is particularly useful if the icefall has not formed or thawed away. Start by either of two shallow right-slanting snow runnels at the right side of the face (the easier right one is East Face) but go left across the lower snowfield to join The Resurrection. In ideal conditions, this can reduce the overall grade to II.

Variation: **Resurrection Right-Hand   300m   III** **

These are right-hand variations to The Resurrection which can give a separate route or be used as an alternative start or finish.

There are at least three icefalls in the lower wall right of the normal start, roughly Grade IV, III and II from right to left, which can be climbed to reach the big lower snowfield. Cross this to climb ice runnels in the slight buttress above the big snowfield and left of East Face to provide a more sustained line which comes directly up to finish at the same point as the normal route.

East Face   300m   III,4 *   *(1967)*

The corner come shallow gully in the face right of The Resurrection provides a fine route which requires some ice. Start up the right-hand of the two right-slanting snow runnels, then a snowslope to reach the base of the shallow gully come corner (Grade I to here). The gully has a short steep ice pitch but otherwise steep snow in ideal conditions, with an obvious finish out right.

BEINN LIATH MHOR FANNAICH

(NH 216 724)   Alt 750m   West-North-West facing   Map p306

A rather scrappy looking face which doesn't ice readily, but the routes have received few ascents so it might be worth a look. The reliable Sgurr Mor is only a little further on.

Approach: As for Sgurr Mor but leaving the path earlier.

Descent: As for Sgurr Mor.

Wot Gully   140m   II   *(1967)*

This route is on the west face of Beinn Liath Mhor Fannaich, and takes the furthest left of three gullies by an icy ramble followed by a cave pitch and steep snow.

Downward Bound   180m   II   *(1980)*

An icefall right of Wot Gully gives 60m of climbing in short steep sections. Above is a snowfield that is prone to avalanche (hence the route name). Either traverse into Wot Gully or climb the broken buttress above the snowfield.

CARN NA CRICHE

(NH 197 725)   961m

CREAG A' MHADAIDH

(NH 197 728)   Alt 550m   North-North-East facing   Map p306   Diagram 319

This is a large crag above Loch a' Mhadaidh. The crag is clearly visible from the road and ice conditions, slow to form, can be assessed. Some of the routes are on frozen turf.

Approach: As for Sgurr Mor but continue to the loch and crag.

Descent: The north-west end is less steep.

Although unimpressive from a distance, the crag is both large and steep with the lower 60m being an unbroken band of steep rock. The upper section has a central scoop bounded by ribs, and a flanking wall on the left. On the right a ramp leads up to broken ground. The upper parts of the routes are easier and variations are possible. The first two climbs are at the very left end of the lower band of the crag up a series of icefalls, about 50m left of the first of the full height routes (Blood on the Tracks). There are four lines that start about 20m left of the crag end.

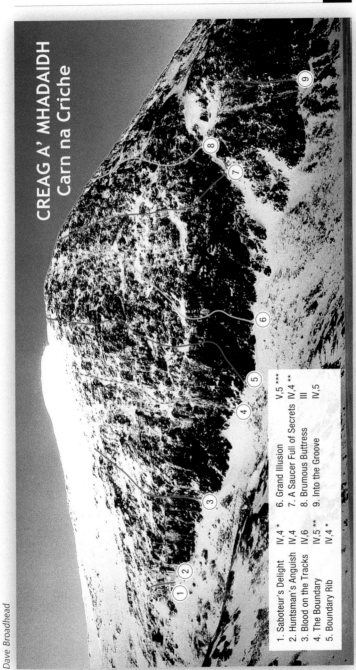

Dave Broadhead

CREAG A' MHADAIDH
Carn na Criche

1. Saboteur's Delight	IV,4 *	6. Grand Illusion	V,5 ***
2. Huntsman's Anguish	IV,4	7. A Saucer Full of Secrets	IV,4 **
3. Blood on the Tracks	IV,6	8. Brumous Buttress	III
4. The Boundary	IV,5 **	9. Into the Groove	IV,5
5. Boundary Rib	IV,4 *		

THE FANNAICHS

1 Saboteur's Delight   30m   IV,4 *   *(2002)*
The obvious left-slanting ramp is short but enjoyable.

2 Huntsman's Anguish   45m   IV,4   *(2002)*
The next unclimbed icefall is 4m right of Saboteur's Delight. This route is 4m
further right. Start just right of a slightly projecting block. Climb the lower icefalls
delicately on their left, then direct to the top. Easier if started on the left of the
block and the lower icefalls not taken direct.

A large icicle, slow to form, is another 10m right before reaching the main crag.

3 Blood on the Tracks   150m   IV,6   *(1996)*
Start towards the left end of the main crag at an obvious open chimney. Climb the
chimney, finishing direct over an overhang (crux) and exiting right on to upper
open slopes.

4 The Boundary   275m   IV,5 **   *(1983)*
About a third of the way from the left end of the lower band is an icefall which
forms regularly in cold weather. Climb the icefall for 60m with a notable bulge on
the second pitch to the top of the band. A short way above trend slightly right at
a fork and continue over an overhang and steep ground, following the obvious line
to the top.

5 Boundary Rib   310m   IV,4 *   *(1995)*
Climbs the rib bounding the left side of the central scoop. Start approximately 25m
right of the start of The Boundary at a point where the angle leading out right is
less steep.
1. 40m Climb a turf and ice groove trending right. Step left to a large ledge.
2. 50m Continue up the groove for 5m, then move right to a wide shallow gully.
3. etc. 220m Trend right to bypass a band of slabs and roofs. Continue to the top,
keeping slightly on the right side of the broad rib.

6 Grand Illusion   310m   V,5 ***   *(1991)*
This route climbs a fairly central line finishing up the central scoop. Start at a
shallow chimney a short way left of a blunt projecting rock boss.
1. 45m Climb the chimney to an overhang, then move right to a ledge on the edge
of a parallel groove. Climb the groove to the top of the rock boss, then trend left
up a turfy fault to a short narrow chimney. Climb this to a poor belay on a small
ledge.
2. 50m Climb the steep turfy groove above to an ice slot cutting through overhanging
rock. Climb this to a turf groove and the snowfield above. Trend right to a thread
belay below an obvious roof.
3. etc. 215m Climb a narrow ramp trending right, then move left and zigzag up
the central scoop to the top.

7 A Saucer Full of Secrets   240m   IV,4 **   *(1993)*
A surprisingly good route climbing to and up a groove in the right-hand upper rib.
Start at an obvious icefall halfway up the ramp that divides the main crag from the
lower right-hand wall. Climb a zigzag line up the initial icefall (45m) and continue
to a wide snow ramp. Climb this to gain and climb the long groove.

8 Brumous Buttress   190m   III   *(1991)*
This climbs the ground just right of the rib bounding the right side of the central
scoop. Climb the lower ramp and start where it begins to level off (Grade I to here).
Climb either of two breaks just right of a prominent block (45m). Traverse up and
left, then take an ice pitch in some narrows just right of a jutting buttress (50m).
Climb up to the next rock band then take the buttress on the left. One can also
traverse off right to easier ground.

9 Into The Groove 70m IV,5 *(1992)*
Lying on the lower right-hand wall (rising directly above the loch), this route climbs the groove left of centre. The groove separates steeper cleaner rock on the right from more vegetated rock to the left. Climb the groove in three pitches. Finish up a right-hand exit via a shallow blocky slot (the left-hand deeper chimney is blocked by several roofs).

SGURR NAN CLACH GEALA

(NH 184 715) 1093m

MAIN CRAG

(NH 191 717) Alt 750m East-South-East facing Map p306 Diagram p322

The fine crag on the east face of this mountain is not marked on the OS map. It is however, large and impressively steep, one of Scotland's best, and not as remote as rumour might have you believe.

The approach requires a short descent which is quite hard to find and past a possibly large cornice, so good visibility is essential for a first visit. In addition, windslab can build readily below the cornice on the sheltered east facing slopes. The cliff, and particularly the buttresses, are susceptible to sun. The best conditions are normally in the first half of the season although even then the steep buttresses can be stripped of snow by thaw or sun. The gullies reliably hold sufficient ice, although even they are thawed by the sun in March.

Approach: There are several possible approaches which can be deduced from the map. By far the best and quickest by about an hour is from the east end of Loch a' Bhraoin, reached from a track starting at NH 163 763 on the Braemore Junction to Dundonnel road. Follow the path south from the loch along a glen unnamed on the 1:50000 map, crossing the burn after 1km (about 300m after the path joins the river bank and becomes grassy). This is sometimes a boulder hop, sometimes a wade. There is a bridge a few hundred metres downstream in case of failure to cross. Continue along the path for another 1.5km before striking up east to the col between Carn na Criche and Sgurr nan Clach Geala. In reasonable conditions this takes about 2hrs 30mins.

A huge boulder forward and left of the lochan on the col, provides some shelter to gear-up (crampons are required for the descent) and a possible place to leave rucksacks. Go to the far end of the lochan and follow a shallow depression formed like an exit stream which forms a defined lowest point of the col. Descend from close to this lowest point of the col (usually easiest 10m north of the col, possible cornice/abseil) for about 50m to an easing in the slope. Follow the easing rightwards (a slightly descending traverse) to a bouldery terrace 25m below an obvious flattening in the near skyline. Cross Slanting Gully above its pitch to gain the terrace below the cliff. Descending too far below the col into the valley bottom forces the climbing of the lower tier (about 100m, Grade II) to reach the terrace below the cliff. An alternative descent close to Slanting Gully is steeper and harder to find in mist.

Descent: From the top of the climbs, descent the slopes northwards back to the lochan and boulder, then reverse the line of ascent back to Loch a' Bhraoin.

The main cliffs comprise a wedge like cluster of six narrow buttresses, numbered 1 to 6 from left to right, separated by five gullies, Alpha to Epsilon. From the top of these cliffs a graceful ridge leads south-west to the summit of the mountain, beneath which there is a more broken buttress.

1 Bungalow Buttress (No.1 Buttress) 110m IV,4 *(1998)*
Start from a small bay roughly central on the front face of the buttress. Climb a left-slanting turfy line of weakness (parallel to Alpha Gully), steeper than it looks,

SGURR NAN CLACH GEALA

1. Bungalow Buttress — IV,4
2. Alpha Crest — Very Difficult
3. Alpha Gully — II
4. Sunrise Buttress — IV,4
5. Beta Gully — III *
7. Destitution Road — V,5 **
8. Cuileag Corner — V,5 **
9. Gamma Gully — V,5 ***
10. Skyscraper Buttress — VI,7 ****
10a. Empire State Variation
11. Delta Gully — IV,4 **
13. Canary Wharf — V,5 *
14. Seller's Tower — V,6 **
15. Epsilon Gully — III
16. Slanting Gully — I
17. Fusilier — IV,5 **
18. Summiteer — II

Dave Broadhead

to finish left of the summit of the buttress. The summit, which is close to the top of Alpha Gully, is easily gained.

2 Alpha Crest   120m   Very Difficult   *(1999)*
An exposed finish, but it may not be a good route (climbed in semi-winter conditions). Follow the crest, which is very close to Alpha Gully, until it steepens. Continue just left of the crest until a grass ledge leads horizontally left to an apparent edge. Move up this, then left to finish up a turf ramp.

3 Alpha Gully   120m   II   *(1965)*
The leftmost gully. Steep snow, particularly the finish, or it may contain two small ice pitches. The gully finishes on the crest of No.2 Buttress which gives a further 120m of easy climbing (Grade I at most).

4 Sunrise Buttress (No.2 Buttress)   150m   IV,4   *(1978)*
This route follows a line in the centre of the buttress. Start at the foot of Beta Gully and climb ice bulges to gain an obvious gully system. With insufficient ice, start up Beta Gully and go left on to the buttress to a turf line leading into the gully. Turn the overhang at the top of the gully on the left and continue up the arete to the top.

5 Beta Gully   200m   III *   *(1970)*
An icefall gives access to the gully, which is straightforward up to a trifurcation. Here a short left fork goes out to No.2 Buttress, a centre fork contains a steep pitch, and a right fork avoids this pitch and rejoins the centre fork above.

6 Cuileag Buttress (No.3 Buttress)   200m   IV,5   *(1983)*
This route takes a line of low resistance but still gives good climbing in its upper half. The crux pitch is much harder than the rest. Start on the left about 20m right of Beta Gully and climb vegetation for 60m. Go left and climb a short ramp which ends on a platform close to Beta Gully. Traverse right to gain the buttress crest (40m). Climb a steep groove just left of the crest (20m, crux). Above, the angle eases and the crest is followed to the top.

7 Destitution Road   200m   V,5 **   *(1986)*
This takes the central icefall of Cuileag Buttress. Climb directly up the middle of the buttress using the general line of a shallow corner to gain the icefall. Climb this direct past a jutting nose of rock, then traverse right to gain a blocky corner cutting through the overhangs. Climb this to the easier crest of the buttress.

8 Cuileag Corner   185m   V,5 **   *(1985)*
This takes a line of discontinuous corners on the right side of Cuileag Buttress. The precise line and difficulty depends on the amount of ice.
1. 45m Climb vegetated slabs to belay under the corner system.
2. 45m Enter the corner by a thin slab and short steep wall.
3. 45m Go up the corner to a big roof. Traverse right beneath the roof and go up ice into a fault on the right edge of the buttress. Climb the fault past two steep sections.
4. 50m Continue up the fault to reach the easy ground common to all the routes on this buttress.

9 Gamma Gully   210m   V,5 ***   *(1965)*
This is probably the best of the gullies on the crag, only Grade IV in good conditions. Climb up for 30m to enter and climb a deep narrow 30m slot. Some 20m higher is the crux, a steep 10m ice pitch with smooth rock walls on either side. Another 10m ice pitch follows, then climb steep snow and occasional rock steps to gain the large scoop above Beta Gully.

THE FANNAICHS

Empire State Variation to Skyscraper Buttress, VI,7, Sgurr nan Clach Geala.
Climber Roger Everett.

Simon Richardson

10 Skyscraper Buttress 240m VI,7 **** (1978)

This magnificent sustained mixed climb is one of the finest expeditions in the Northern Highlands. Unfortunately it catches the sun and snow falls off its steep rocks, so the first half of the season is recommended for an attempt.

The best line takes the icefall at the base of the buttress, The Direct Start. This assumes both the ice to be present and the turf to be well frozen, otherwise start by the Original Route (VI,6 overall). Climb the icefall to its capping roof and move left to where the roof is quite large, or direct if the ice allows. (With no ice but the turf frozen, a possible line is to follow the turfy corner of the Right-Hand Start to its bay, then traverse left to the roof.). Pull up into a shallow undercut groove above the right end of the roof. Climb the groove (thin) to a turf ledge. The Original Route reaches this point by following Gamma Gully to the slot, then traversing easily right.

Move up again (left and up looks easier, straight up more interesting) to a traverse line beneath the steep central section of the buttress. From here, go right along the traverse line to a steep 10m high iced corner. If the corner is not iced climb a thin crack on the wall just to its left. Once past the corner it is possible to follow easier ground slightly rightwards up to the obvious series of cracks and grooves on the right side of the buttress, but this avoids the final headwall – the highlight of the climb – which is now on the left. The headwall is a slightly scooped face between two crests. The right crest with the original route is in a fairly straight line with the iced corner below and the left crest with the Empire State Variation is out to the left. Other versions may have been climbed. For the original line, take the easier ground for about a rope length, then climb a short groove on the left and traverse diagonally left to gain the right crest at a good ledge. Climb the crack above then continue directly by a series of cracks and grooves for two fine pitches. The Empire State Variation traverses left lower down to climb near the left crest. All the variations finish easily along the horizontal ridge to the plateau.

Variation: **Empire State Variation   VI,6**   *(1994)*
Climbs the left side of the headwall, very steep but the protection is excellent and the turf is very accommodating. From the belay above the crux corner, follow the easy ground up and right for 15m to a huge flake on the left. Move left around the edge above the flake to gain a small hanging snowfield, and climb a left-slanting, shallow turfy groove which cuts into the headwall looming above (50m). Climb straight up via cracks and grooves to reach a ledge and niche overlooking Gamma Gully on the left (45m). Climb a short rib on the left edge and continue up the steep groove above to ledges, then take a turfy corner leading into the centre of the final overhanging wall. Step right one metre to enter into a second groove, then trend up and left in a spectacular position to the easy horizontal ridge (45m).

Variation: **Right-Hand Start   VI,6**   *(1986)*
A sensational line; ice not required. Climb the right edge of the icefall, an iced or turfy corner, to belay in a snow bay under the biggest roof. Move out right on to the rib overlooking Delta Gully and climb an obvious groove just left of the crest. Traverse left above the roof to join the original route. Probably unrepeated.

Summer: **VS** *   *(1961/1999)*
Also a spectacular route but with vegetation and hollow blocks. Worthwhile for the adventurous, but very dry weather is recommended. The original route (Severe) followed a similar line as described in winter but taking the Gamma Gully start (which is very unpleasant). The Right-Hand Start is better. Start beside the watercourse at the base of Delta Gully. Climb the clean rib close on the left of Delta Gully, diverging and becoming more defined (4b and poorly protected), to reach a very steep section. The winter Right-Hand Start reaches here and goes left. Instead, move right into a vegetated groove and climb it until the rib can be regained on the left. The original route is joined here and the winter route soon above. Follow the Empire State Variation by going left across turf to the left-hand crest. Either follow this variation (4a) or (better) stay more directly on the left-hand crest (moves of 4b or 4c).

11 Delta Gully   240m   IV,4 *   *(1972)*
After two pleasant steep pitches, often continuous ice but susceptible to sun, the gully widens and is followed more easily with impressive rock scenery on the two enclosing buttresses.

12 Sellers' Buttress (No.5 Buttress)   140m   IV,5 *   *(1972)*
Start at the lowest rocks and climb by grooves and shallow corners always to the left of the crest. Near the top move up right to finish up the crest. About 100m of Grade I snow common to Delta and Epsilon Gullies leads to the plateau.
Summer: **Very Difficult**   *(1961)*
Start beneath a clean rock rib on the left of the buttress and follow the crest of a prominent shoulder. Continue up a shattered rib to the top.

13 Canary Wharf   140m   V,5 *   *(1998)*
Climbs the right-hand face (front face) of Sellers' Buttress, with two variations. Start below the left end of the face and slant easily up right to below a turfy line. Climb the turfy line until about 10m below the shoulder. Go diagonally right to a projecting block and swing round it to a traverse ledge which soon leads to the central corner in the upper part of the face. Climb the corner and the wall on its left to easier ground leading to the final easy crest forming the top of the buttress.

Variation:
Stand on the projecting block in order to step left into the left-hand corner. Climb this and the arete above to the top of the buttress.

**14 Sellers' Tower   160m   V,6 ** **   (1998)
The right side of the front face of Sellers' Buttress gives a fine improbable route, generally well protected. Start as for Canary Wharf but continue trending right, then curving upwards to a belay under steep ground and almost overlooking the start of Epsilon Gully (80m). Move left on to the arete of a right-facing corner and pull up to prominent turf. Traverse left along a narrow turf ledge past another corner and go up to a pedestal below the main roof system (20m). Pull through the roof (small at this point) and move left into the base of a left-facing corner, half of a pair of big corners about 5m apart and facing each other, the best indicator of the line from below. Climb this right corner, then a crack between the corners and finish up the left corner to reach easier ground. Move right and go up to a ledge below the top of the buttress (50m). Reach the final easy crest (10m).

15 Epsilon Gully   140m   III   (1974)
This starts somewhat higher up Slanting Gully, on the right of Sellers' Buttress. After a hard start the gully is straightforward.

16 Slanting Gully   300m   I   (1963)
Starts up the lower tier as a deep gully with a definite pitch which needs to be banked out to be Grade I (this is very rare). Bypassing this pitch on the right or left (via the terrace below the cliffs) restores the grade. The gully becomes shallow and slowly steepens, passing the start of Epsilon Gully.

No.6 Buttress is formed between Epsilon Gully and Slanting Gully. Its lower section is a smooth rock wall which has not been climbed.

SUMMIT BUTTRESS

(NH 184 714)   Alt 900m   North-East facing

East of the summit is a high corrie ringed by cliffs. Most of these are short but the south side of the corrie is a larger buttress which separates the corrie from the south-east face. The routes here might be in condition if the main cliff proves unfrozen (being higher) or bare (slightly better aspect).

Approach: The buttress is reached by making a descending traverse across the corrie from the top of the main cliff (Skyscraper Buttress). Alternatively, make a rising traverse south-westwards from the top of Alpha or Beta Gully, or nearly straight up from the left end of the main cliff.

Descent: Bag the Munro and walk off (not the cornice, which is near!).

**17 Fusilier   250m   IV,5 ** **   (2002)
Climbs a big groove system in the larger buttress. Much is easy but there are short steep sections which could bank up and reduce the route to Grade III. Start up the main groove to steep walls (45m). Go right up a ramp, then straight up to more steep walls (45m). Continue up a wide right-trending groove and a short steep wall (crux) to a prominent chimney (40m). The chimney is possible but it is easier to traverse right and step down on to iced slabs which are then climbed to reach an ice bulge which leads to an easier section (50m). A short steep groove leads to easier ground followed to the upper crest (45m). Finish up the crest which leads to the ridge just south of the summit (25m).

18 Summiteer   180m   II   (2004)
A route up the right face of the buttress. Start on a terrace above and right of Fusilier gully. Climb a prominent groove to a steep wall (25m). Go diagonally left, then back right to reach the top of the groove's continuation (45m). Cross a snow

ramp slightly leftwards, then move right under a wall to reach a line of weakness (40m) which leads naturally (45m) to the upper crest, and finish as for Fusilier (25m).

On the south-east face of the mountain, starting a good deal lower and to the south of the summit buttress, there is one route:

19 First Footing   400m   III   *(1982)*
The ground below the bealach between Sgurr nan Each and Sgurr na Clach Geala is bounded on its right by slabs and ledges which are often iced. Start beneath the right end of the slabs. Climb a short ice pitch to a series of easy gullies and open snowfields. Trend right for 200m, making for an obvious icefall in the headwall. Climb the icefall (40m). Continue into a narrow blind gully then traverse out left to a poor belay (30m). Move up left into then climb a hidden chimney (30m). Easy ground above.

SGURR BREAC

(NH 158 711)   Alt 999m

NORTH-EAST NOSE

(NH 162 716)   Alt 550m   North-East facing   Map p306

This hill and crag are easily reached from the glen that runs south from the east end of Loch a' Bhraoin. The lower end of its north-east ridge presents a large broken crag which is divided by a deep snow gully with a short pitch low down (Grade I/II). Left of the gully is a rather discontinuous buttress, whilst on the right is a wall split by a corner and a short deep gully near its right end.

Neverending Story   300m   II/III   *(1991)*
The buttress left of the central gully. Start under a roof just above the toe of the buttress.
1. 45m Move left and climb a snow ramp leading onto the face.
2. 45m Climb a slabby wall and snow to a cave.
3. 35m Move right into a short turfy groove. Climb this and the broken ground above to a sapling.
4. 40m Climb an obvious icy corner (well left of an icefall) and a continuation groove to a belay on the left.
5. etc. 135m Wind up between small outcrops to the top.

Turkey Time   150m   IV,4   *(1993)*
Climbs the buttress to the right of the central gully and left of Ptarmigan Corner for 90m, then an easy gully on the left to the top.

Ptarmigan Corner   110m   IV,4 *   *(1991)*
The obvious open corner on the right of the crag is climbed in three pitches.

DRUIM REIDH

(NH 155 735)   Alt 550m   North-East facing   Map p306

A small cliff on the nose of Druim Reidh overlooking the approach to Sgurr nan Clach Geala.

Heather Horror   80m   IV,5   *(2004)*
Start at the top of a small bay just left of centre. Twin grooves run the full height of the cliff. The left-hand groove has a chockstone. This route climbs the right-hand groove with a narrow chimney at half-height.

THE FANNAICHS

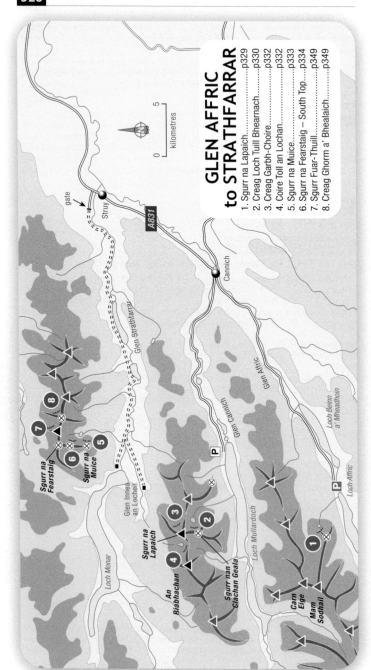

GLEN AFFRIC
to STRATHFARRAR

GLEN AFFRIC TO STRATHFARRAR

South of The Fannaichs lies an extensive mountain area, cut by five long glens stretching from the mountains to the North Sea. From south to north, these glens are Glen Affric (the longest), Glen Cannich, Strathfarrar, Glen Orrin and Strathconnon. The first three are described in this chapter.

Glen Affric

SGURR NA LAPAICH

(NH 157 243)   Alt 900m   North-East facing

A large but rather scrappy face.

Approach: From the end of the public road up Glen Affric, walk up to Loch Lapaich (NH 157 246), from where there is a good view of the face.

Descent: Climb with sacks and walk south.

Birthday Blast   80m   III   *(1999)*
A broken line up the left side of the face. Walk up to a shield of rock guarding the lower part of the left side of the corrie.
1. 30m Follow the central groove in the middle of the wall (slightly contrived – a snow gully left of the rock wall could be climbed).
2. Go up easier broken ground to the foot of the upper face (60m).
3. 50m Take a rising traverse left into a gully and follow the left branch into a wide and well protected exit chimney. The right fork is an alternative finish.

Right of Birthday Blast is an easy gully, then the main slabby face.

Punchline   120m   II/III   *(1985)*
On the left side of the main face is a slabby wall with an overhang in its centre. Climb a short chimney on the left of this to an awkward move right and follow a ramp to a corner. Climb the corner above and follow an exposed gangway to the top.

Loch Lapaich Buttress   180m   IV,5   *(2005)*
Start 15m right of the toe of the buttress.
1. 55m Go up an icy streak to reach a right-slanting ramp.
2. 30m Go right up the ramp for a few metres, then up grooves with turf tufts (just above a horizontal crack is the crux) to a left-slanting ramp with a big block.
3. 60m Go left on to an arete and follow it to another right-slanting ramp.
4. 35m Go up the ramp to a chimney-corner line. Go up this and above to finish.

Groove into 85   100m   III/IV   *(1985)*
The obvious corner-gully on the main face is the best line. The first ascent party was watched climbing it but the true grade is unknown. A recent attempt in lean frozen conditions failed on the slabby second pitch.

The narrow shallow gully right of the main face has been climbed at Grade II.

SGURR NAN CEATHREAMHNAN

(NH 055 228)   Alt 1050m   South facing

Included in this guide although it is more easily approached from Loch Cluanie (Northern Highlands South).

Cross Stone Gully   100m   II   *(1996)*
Just below and 200m east of the summit on the south face of the mountain is a steep compact cliff. It holds this deep gully which is only visible from straight on. Climb up to a steepening capped by two crossed rock slabs. Climb this strenuously on the right, then continue up easier ground to the main ridge.

Glen Cannich

The hills north of Loch Mullardoch are described under this glen, although some crags are more easily approached from Strathfarrar, the next glen to the north.

CREAG LOCH TUILL BHEARNACH

(NH 162 343)   Alt 950m   East to North-East facing   Map p328

This is the crag that lies astride the nose of the east ridge of Sgurr nan Clachan Geala (unnamed on the 1:50000 map), directly below the summit. The buttress tops out on the slope leading down from Sgurr nan Clachan Geala towards the col before Sgurr na Lapaich. Since the crag is high and remote, dry warm weather is required for summer, while good walking conditions are recommended for winter.

Approach: Park at the end of the road on the north shore of Loch Mullardoch. Take the higher of two paths (an off-road vehicle track) along the shore, then turn up the Allt Mullardoch. Cross the col south of Carn nan Gobhar and make a slightly descending traverse to the south shore of Loch Tuill Bhearnach. Go eastwards uphill, then turn north to make a traverse to the base of the crag, 3hrs 30mins.

Descent: Apart from Weary Wall and Lapland Buttress which go to the plateau, traverse off right along a wide grassy or snowy shelf in winter to descend. For Weary Wall and Lapland Buttress, it is better to climb with sacks unless the cornices are small, when descent is possible but steep on either side.

The buttress is quite prominent, almost a ridge, whose south side is more broken while the north flank offers striking grooves and ribs of considerable steepness.

1 Weary Wall   200m   III   *(2006)*
An easier line up the south side of the buttress. Start about 20m left of the toe of the buttress and gain a ledge. Traverse it right, then go up a fault trending left before going straight up to a flake. Go right up a turf ramp to a ledge below a steep wall. Pass this on the right to another ledge. Walk left, then go right up chimneys behind huge blocks to gain the easier crest and a steep finish to the plateau.

**2 Lapland Buttress   200m   IV,5 ** **   *(1989)*
This route was an attempt on the crest but was forced on to more turfy ground on the left of the ridge for a section. Start at the lowest rocks.
1. 30m Climb a V-recess then move out left.
2. 40m Climb a series of slabby cracks that lead out right back to the crest to below a steep wall.
3. 30m Climb the wall by a vertical right-facing corner, crux, which leads to a wide, left-slanting crack. Regain the crest on the right.
4. 100m Follow the much easier crest with a steep finish to the plateau.

The most obvious feature on the north flank is a slim corner-line with a roof part way up and an impressive wide crack high on its left wall.

3 Lap of the Gods   75m   HVS *   *(1997)*
This route climbs a near parallel line up the rib to the left of the obvious slim corner. Start at the foot of the rib a few metres down and left of two distinctive leaning embedded flakes.
1. 30m 5a Gain and climb a slim groove on the right side of the rib to reach a short messy diagonal fault. Move left up this to stand on a spike at the very edge. Step left to blocks on a turf ledge.
2. 15m 5b Ascend the surprisingly awkward groove above the belay then move left on to a tiny rock ledge. Pull up into an open corner and climb this to a rock ledge under a roof on the right.
3. 30m 4c Move back left into the corner, then pull up onto a turf cap. Climb a short strenuous wall, then move up into a chimney come corner. Climb this and broken ground above to the top.

CREAG LOCH
TUILL
BHEARNACH

Andy Nisbet

2. Lapland Buttress   IV,5 **
3. Lap of the Gods   HVS *
4. Lap of Honour   V,6 ***
5. Lap Dance   VI,7 **
6. Second Lap   III

4 Lap of Honour   65m   V,6 ***   *(2005)*
Excellent well protected climbing. Right of the slim corner-line is a smooth but less steep section split by a shallow narrowing chimney. This section is bounded on the right by a big left-facing corner. Start at the base of the corner and traverse a ledge left to below the chimney.
1. 30m Gain and climb the chimney until forced left into a crack-line which is followed to below a right-facing corner.
2. 35m Climb the corner with a finish on the left.

5 Lap Dance   60m   VI,7 **   *(2001)*
Sustained climbing up thinly iced corners and grooves. Start 15m up and right from the slim corner-line at the big left-facing corner, which usually holds ice low down.
1. 35m Climb the corner to a sloping ledge about halfway up the face. Gain a steep V-groove on the right, follow it into a small bay and exit via a short corner on to a huge flake.
2. 25m The steep corner immediately above leads to easier turfy ground and snow.

6 Second Lap   45m   III   *(2001)*
Near the right-hand end of the crag is a short icy square-cut chimney. Climb this and continue in the same line above.

The following route lies on a short steep buttress on the north side of the terminal end of the south-east ridge of Sgurr nan Clachan Geala (NH 168 338).

Practice Lap   120m   III,4   *(2004)*
Climb the obvious ramp past a steep rocky section to a crest and turf ledges (50m). Move up on grassy ledges to easier ground and directly to top (70m).

SGURR NA LAPAICH

(NH 161 351)   1150m

This is the beautifully shaped mountain which is the highest in the range between Glen Cannich and Strathfarrar.

Approach: It can be approached from the dam at the head of Loch Mullardoch to the south (see Creag Loch Tuill Bhearnach) but the crags on the east and north-easterly aspects are most easily reached from Strathfarrar. Drive to Loch Monar, across the dam and to the little power station at Gleann Innes an Loichel (NH 183 381) which gives access to the crags.

CREAG GARBH-CHOIRE

(NH 167 352)   Alt 750m   North facing   Map p328

The first corrie reached from Strathfarrar lies to the north of the fine east ridge of the mountain. A very prominent line follows the gully cutting the centre of the crags.

Deer Grass Gully   120m   II/III   *(1978)*
The gully gave a continuous run of water ice, with a fine 45m crux section.

COIRE NAN EACH

(NH 162 353)   Alt 1050m   East facing

These short clean cliffs lie dotted around the rim just north of the summit. They are frequently in condition but mainly bank out in heavy snow, so ideal for lean conditions. Approach up a long steepening apron of snow.

Little Corner   50m   III   *(2006)*
To the right of the left-hand buttress is a right-facing corner. Directly below is a short wide icy crack, crux, which soon leads to the easier corner and the top.

CREAG NA LAPAICH

(NH 163 348)   Alt 900m   East facing

These broken crags are not clearly marked on the map but fall steeply south-east from the main summit into a hidden corrie. The crag holds conditions and snow better than anywhere else on the mountain. Perhaps best approached from Strathfarrar via the Garbh-choire and over the Bealach na Cloiche Duibhe. Allow up to 3hrs. The crags consist of long rambling ridges that hide fine gullies. Large cornices often develop. From the summit, long steep Grade I slopes can be down climbed on the north of the corrie.

**Cool Runnings   200m   II ** **   *(2006)*
This fine narrow gully is the straightest and most central gully just left of a narrow slot. It may bank out and cornice badly. On the first ascent sun-hardened ice led for 70 to 80m to snow then up steepening turfy and icy steps. The exit was up steep snow and a small cornice.

AN RIABHACHAN

(NH 134 345)   1129m

This is the remote and flat topped mountain to the west of Sgurr na Lapaich, most easily reached from Strathfarrar. A long corrie on the north-east of the mountain has several easy climbs, not all recorded plus an icefall. The steepest section of crag however lies just west of the Sgurr na Lapaich col where a narrow buttress is split by a pronounced thin gully.

SPINDRIFT BUTTRESS

(NH 150 347)   Alt 750m   North-East facing

**Spindrift Gully   200m   II ** **   *(1969)*
The gully gradually steepens and often gives one good ice pitch in its upper half. As the name implies, the climb is often exposed to spindrift. A good scenic route.

(NH 142 352)   Alt 850m   North-East facing   Map p328

Redcoats Weep   75m   III   *(1998)*
The right-hand side of the corrie sports an obvious three tiered icefall. Climb the icefall, which is steeper on the left to a spike belay in the corner at 50m. Climb the easier icefall above, 25m.

Strathfarrar

This glen and its hills are very quiet and unspoilt and even the paths up the Munros are quite faint. The reason for this, is that the road is locked at Inchmore, about 1km west of Struy Bridge. The glen is covered by the Hillphones scheme (see p22, 01463 761360). In 2006 the arrangements for vehicle access were as follows, but it is hoped they will be relaxed in the near future.

Summer (April to October, but not on Tuesday all day or Wednesday before 1.30pm). Call in at the house beside the locked gate after 9am and a free permit will be issued. Exit must be made before 8pm, but 7pm in September and 6pm in October (daylight hours, as the worry is about poaching).

Winter (November to Easter). Phone the Mountaineering Council of Scotland office (01738 638 227) during office hours on the day before (or Friday for Sunday). They will log your name and tell you the number of a combination lock on the gate. You let yourself in and out. The number will occasionally change.

SGURR NA MUICE

(NH 227 418)   Alt 891m   Map p328

The large open corrie of Toll a' Mhuic (NH 232 420) holds some fine mixed climbing on the east faces of Sgurr na Muice and Sgurr na Fearstaig. Situated near the head of Glen Strathfarrar, this central location means that these hills hold their conditions longer than many higher westerly ones.

Approach: From a parking place at the start of the Toll a' Mhuic track. This continues into the corrie as a good path. Leave the path at its highest point before the loch, 1hr.

The cliffs of Sgurr na Muice form an arc around the east facing nose which is the area's finest looking feature. The crags form a band running below the summit with a considerable amount of steep ground below them. The usual lack of cornices on these cliffs and the grooved nature of them often means that the only significant avalanche risk is on the apron below. The crags come into condition very readily due to the grooves being lined with turf and are climbable after a good frost and minimum snow cover.

SOUTH-EAST FACE

(NH 228 415)   Alt 650m   South-East facing   Diagram p335

This is the first reached from the path. The rock is a clean compact schist, verging on gneiss with minimal protection; some pitches are also very long and a 60m rope may be an advantage. The crag is sunny and dries very quickly, although there may be drainage streaks. In winter, it is quickly stripped in thaw and does not hold snow as well as the north-east face. Unlike that face it has few grooves, mainly smooth slabs split by a central chimney come gully and with three prominent icefalls when in condition. Only the easiest and furthest left forms at all readily.

Descent: In winter, down a wide gully at the south end of the main face (see diagram). Summer descents are down ramps which lead south before cutting back to the starts. It may be preferred to scramble higher above the main slabs and descend the winter gully.

1 Pipsqueak   75m   II   *(1996)*
On the left side of the face near the exit of the descent gully that runs behind the
crags is a narrow icefall that lies at the same angle as the hillside, forming readily.
Climb the escapable icefall direct over all the bulges, steepest at the top.

The face has a large easy angled slab on the left, oval in shape and providing two
routes.

2 Pas de Bas   75m   Severe *   *(2005)*
Scrambling round the overlap of pitch 2 reduces the grade to Very Difficult.
1. 55m Start left of a rib at the lowest point of the slab. Climb up and right past
a smooth section to a corner. Continue up a pleasant slab above to below a big
overlap.
2. 20m 4a Climb the overlap on good quartz holds to easy ground.

3 Pousette   85m   Very Difficult   *(2005)*
1. 55m Start at the shallow rib right of Pas de Bas. Climb this and the clean slabs
above, always right of the last route, to under the big overlap.
2. 30m Move right past a huge block to a brown slab and climb this to the top.

4 Best Back   150m   IV,3 *   *(1979)*
This fine route is rarely in condition and can be seen as an unbroken icefall on the
left of the main slabs. An introductory pitch leads to the main icefall. The initial
30m is steep, forming the crux and after a bulge easier but continuous ice leads up
for several pitches to the top. Expect ice screw belays.

The main slabs are composed of several parallel sheets separated by vegetation.
The first sheet is the broadest and best. Walk up a ramp past a lower slab to a
puddle at the foot of the first sheet of slabs.

5 Schistomania   100m   VS **   *(2005)*
An excellent second pitch.
1. 40m 4c Start just left of the puddle at the base of the slab and friction up the
slab before moving diagonally left to the centre of a big overlap, climbed by a
groove. Continue to a bay above.
2. 45m 4a Climb the middle of the steeper but juggier slab above, over a small
overlap to below a bigger overlap,.
3. 15m Either climb the overlap or go round its right-hand end and up the slabs
above to the top.

6 Dancing On Bawbees   125m   HVS *   *(2005)*
1. 45m 4b Start right of the puddle and climb up and across rightwards via clean
sustained slabs to reach the right end of a large heather and juniper ledge. Belay
at its left end at a groove.
2. 55m 4c Climb the groove, then a steeper slab heading for some prominent
perched blocks. Move past their right side and up more slabs.
3. 25m Climb straight up to the top.

7 Middle Cut   150m   III *   *(1994)*
Mid-way between Best Back and Streaky is a narrow and well defined gully which
springs from a triangular snow patch. A pleasant route which readily comes into
condition. Reach it by following the snow ramp up right from Best Back to an icefall
which guards the entrance.
1. 30m Either climb the icefall or an easier ramp which lies a little further up the
ramp.
2. 35m The barrier immediately ahead is turned by ice on the right and the gully
followed to below a prominent ice slot.
3. 45m Climb the slot and the steepening gully above to a bottleneck exit which
sometimes forms a difficult ice bulge. Continue more easily to a short buttress.

John Mackenzie

SGURR NA MUICE
South-East Face

2. Pas de Bas   Severe *
3. Pousette   Very Difficult
5. Schistomania   VS **
6. Dancing On Bawbees HVS *

7. Middle Cut   III *
8. Streaky   IV,4 *
9. Spare Rib   III,4
10. Porker   II *

4. 40m Turn the buttress on the left and cross the snow ramp to a slabby groove which cuts across the rocks ahead (possible belay). Climb the mixed ramp to easy ground above.

8 Streaky   150m   IV,4 *   (1978)

This is a long and curved icefall near the right of the face. The icefall starts at the end of a long ramp and has several interesting pitches. Expect ice screw belays. It forms more readily than Best Back. Short ice steps lead to a flake belay on the right wall. Climb a groove (25m), then a fine icefall (40m) and its easier continuation (50m).

9 Spare Rib   200m   III,4   (2000)

To the right of the triple icefall of Streaky and to the left of the snow ramp of Porker is a buttress split by a narrow gully; this provides the line, a more or less continuous line of ice with two good final pitches. The grade assumes good icing, although the original ascent was much harder when semi-frozen and under deep powder. Approach by easy ground up the nose and head for a triangular buttress below the crags; start to the right of this.

1. 40m Climb a double icefall to easy ground

2. 40m Continue up iced slabs and steps heading for the narrow gully in the headwall.

3. 40m Climb an icefall to a rock barrier, traverse right below this and either pull over if ice exists halfway along or continue to the end and pull over there. Continue up left to below a vertical turf chimney.

4. 45m In good conditions climb the chimney or, as on the first ascent, gain a ledge just left of the chimney and climb a technical slanting crack and slab to the same point, very well protected. Climb up left to an icefall; either climb this over a bulge at the top or avoid it by a zigzag right then left.

5. 35m Climb the less steep continuation icefall direct over its final bulge to a snow ramp.

10 Porker   120m   II *   (1994)

A very exposed ramp of high angle snow without pitches leads from the easy angled central rib below the nose up and left to exit up an airy headwall left of the nose proper.

NORTH-EAST FACE

(NH 227 418)   Alt 650m   North-East facing   Diagram p338

To the right of the icefalls and the ramp of Porker is the nose of the buttress. Right of here the buttress curves around to form the steeper north-east face rising above long Grade I slopes. The left side of the North-East face is bottomed by a rock band with a girdling Snow Apron above. Above this apron the face is seamed by narrow gullies and grooves which gradually become more rocky further right. The right side of the face is bottomed by five bays. The rock is extremely sound but limited in cracks, particularly on the initial pitches.

Approach: There are four convenient approaches; for the nose an ascent up the easy angled rib is the best way, for the main face there are three shallow couloirs. The left one leads to the climbs below and left of the lower band of rock, while the middle one is best for routes further right as far as Crackling Groove whilst a shallow right-hand one is convenient for the routes right of that.

Descent: Normally climb with sacks and walk off to the south. The best descent to the base of the face (Grade I/II) is to descend to the right (looking down) of Pigsty Gully, which is north of the summit. The descent starts from a minor col a few metres north of the summit cairn and descends steep snow to near the lower half of Pigsty Gully. Curve right via a ramp that leads to the last of the five bays. This bay contains Gammon Gully tucked into the corner. The left wall of this gully blocks the traverse towards the main face and an iced slab needs to be descended (crux) to easier ground. Longer but easier is to avoid this slab by heading down soon after the ramp to lower on the hillside.

The main face (above the rock band and bays) is a series of parallel grooves either side of a lower angled central section. Identification is difficult, although there are a few prominent features. On the left of the face is a deep blocked gully come groove, Swine Fever. Well to the right of this is the twin grooved gully line of Pearls Before Swine and not far to its right is another steep rocky groove, Tusker. The face lies back in angle now as the Snow Apron stretches right to a broken edge below a prominent overlapped groove.

There now follows the series of five bays low down and right of the rock band, each with a right-facing boundary wall. The first bay is the start of Pygmalion etc. The second and biggest bay is below the steepest part of the crag with routes such as The Wolf and is floored by a usually iced slab. It ends at a more pronounced edge which drops down steeply to a deeper third bay containing a couple of grooves, also bottomed by an iced slab. The smaller fourth bay contains a slab and a wider groove and ends at another edge which leads to the fifth bay containing Gammon Gully. To reach the snow apron without climbing on the lower rock band, either approach from the left end of the tier or from the right end where there is steep snow either side of Pigsticker's initial pitch. There is much scope for getting hopelessly lost in mist!

11 Sows Ear   155m   III   (2001)
Just to the right of the ramp of Porker the nose swings to the east. Here there are three square-cut shallow gullies; this is the furthest left one. Graded for lean well frozen conditions, when it is at its best, but it banks out.
1. 45m Climb the gully to a small blockage, taken on the right wall and continue up the continuation to a big chockstone.
2. 35m Climb the crux chockstone and continue to a chimney-groove.
3. 40m Climb the chimney-groove to arrive below a slabby icefall. Climb the icefall or the dog-leg to its right which borders a buttress to arrive at a pointed block.
4. 35m Continue up left of the buttress on either snow or ice to the top.

12 Piglet   110m   II   (1994)
Piglet takes the middle of the square-cut gullies and has a lone tree-let. Climb the gully and groove for two pitches, then the more interesting buttress ahead was taken on ice rather than escaping up snow to the left.
Variation: **Direct Start   30m   III**   (2001)
To the left of the lower rock barrier is an icefall, easily formed, that goes up a groove then up a slab to below the starts of Sows Ear, Piglet and Swine Groove.

13 Cold Litter   130m   III,4 *   (2002)
The steeper and narrower gully to the right of Piglet provides excellent climbing but is escapable. It has a clutch of tiny trees in the lower groove. Climb the groove which has a steep exit near to the edge of Swine Fever. Move left to a pair of thin grooves and climb the left one to the base of a small bay. Step up right below a jutting flake to gain the base of another narrow groove which ends in a deep crack. Climb this to reach the snow ramp that runs below the top crags. Immediately above is a huge block and a recess in the wall above. Climb the crux, a thinly iced corner and step up left to climb more easily to the top.

14 Swine Fever   150m   III,4 *   (1996)
This is the first of the lines on the main north-east face, being a well pronounced gully come groove blocked by a vertical wall. It lies to the right of Piglet and can be approached either as for that route or via the lower snow ramp of Sty in the Eye. It provides some interesting but not sustained climbing, with excellent belays.
1. 15m Climb over a short bulge.
2. 25m Continue up the gully come groove to the blockage.
3. 20m   Step down and traverse across the smooth left wall, crux, short but entertaining. Continue up the groove in the arete to a flake.
4. 45m Above are two grooves. Climb the left one to an inset stance.

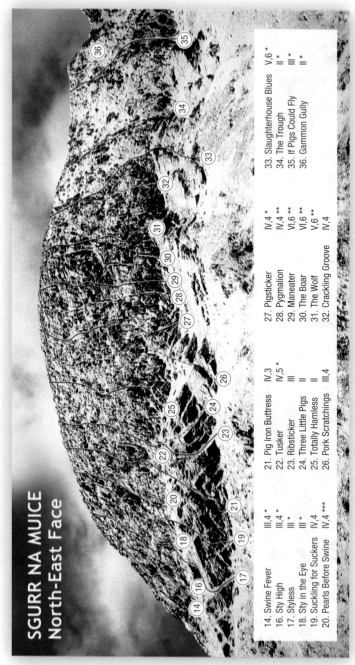

SGURR NA MUICE
North-East Face

14. Swine Fever	III,4 *
16. Sty High	III,4 *
17. Styless	III *
18. Sty in the Eye	III *
19. Suckling for Suckers	IV,4
20. Pearls Before Swine	IV,4 ***

21. Pig Iron Buttress	IV,3
22. Tusker	IV,5 *
23. Ribsticker	III
24. Three Little Pigs	II
25. Totally Hamless	II
26. Pork Scratchings	III,4

27. Pigsticker	IV,4 **
28. Pygmalion	IV,4 **
29. Maneater	VI,6 **
30. The Boar	V,6 **
31. The Wolf	V,6 **
32. Crackling Groove	IV,4

33. Slaughterhouse Blues	V,6 *
34. The Trough	II *
35. If Pigs Could Fly	III *
36. Gammon Gully	II *

John Mackenzie

5. 45m Step left and climb up to a snow ramp, cross this to the right and climb steeply up a rib which forms the left edge of a very narrow slot which runs straight up the crag.

15 Groundhog 125m III,4 ** (2005)
A fine sustained and well protected route that takes the narrow buttress just right of Swine Fever. Might be Grade IV in less favourable conditions.
1. 35m A tricky wall leads to a square chimney and groove. Climb these and step up right to the crest.
2. 40m Climb right to avoid a roof, then back left and follow a narrow turf groove to a shallow bay and a wall. Step left below the wall, then back right up a narrow groove to an easing.
3. 25m Climb the very narrow groove above to below a steeper section.
4. 25m A straight narrow groove lies above; climb this unhelpful but entertaining section with a tricky mantel out left at half-height. Move back right into the groove and grovel out at the top.

16 Sty High 190m III,4 * (1996)
A direct line up the left side of the face taking a line between Swine Fever and Sty in the Eye and providing pleasant climbing, not sustained but very enjoyable.
1. 40m Follow the left-hand couloir to the rock band and take the left-trending ramp as for Sty in the Eye.
2. 30m Climb the ice bulge on the left and gain the snow ramp above. Belay at the base of the left-hand of two grooves about 12m right of the wider entrance to Swine Fever.
3. 45m Climb up this groove, up an interesting slot and move right.
4. 45m Continue up the groove to a small overhang, turned on the left to another which is turned on the right via a spike. Continue up another steepening with chockstones.
5. 30m On the left is the final slot of Swine Fever; instead take the interesting rib to the right which has an awkward bulge and continue more easily to the top.

17 Styless 125m III * (2002)
A pleasantly sustained and well protected romp up turfy grooves, chimneys and other entertainment. To the right of Sty High is a rib that has a shallow turfy chimney-line. Climb this direct to an overhang (50m). Move right to a similar groove and up this to below a steepening (25m). Continue in the same line over various obstacles (50m). The route could be extended by one of the aforementioned starts.

18 Sty in the Eye 190m III * (1995)
A pleasant mixed climb that comes into condition rapidly and is best under hard frost and little snow. Reach the start by following the left-hand couloir to the rock band between the icefalls of Pearls Before Swine on the left and Three Little Pigs on the right.
1. 40m Climb steep snow up a ramp left of the left-hand icefall (or, harder, climb the icefall).
2. 50m Step right and climb snow or ice to the Snow Apron above and belay to the right of a dead-end snow groove which is left of Pearls Before Swine's deeper entrance gully.
3. 25m Climb up the groove, step left round the rib and traverse left to the foot of a square-cut turfy groove which lies to the right of an easier snowy one with a prominent small pinnacle.
4. 50m Climb the turfy groove up over chimneys and other narrowings; a fine pitch.
5. 25m Continue up a narrow chimney and exit up a shallow one above which is right of easier snow.

19 Suckling for Suckers 120m IV,4 (1998)
The left-bounding rib of Pearls Before Swine was climbed in poor conditions and should become a pleasant Grade III. The climb was started from the Snow Apron

but could include any of the more direct routes from below to extend the line considerably. Start just left of the gully of Pearls at the lowest rocks.

1. 45m Climb steepening ground to an overhanging wall. Surmount the left wall of this groove to follow the arete to a bay.

2. 25m Continue up the groove on thin ice to turf, then climb another thin cracked and unhelpful groove to overlook the left fork of Pearls.

3. 50m Climb the rib parallel to the left fork to a big bay above and either climb the central ice runnel or move right and up to the same place; the top is just beyond.

20 Pearls Before Swine   200m   IV,4 *** (1994)

This is a splendid route, low in the grade with varied climbing in a good position. Start by climbing the left snow couloir to below and right of a wide icefall that sometimes forms on the left side of the lower rock band.

1. 50m Climb the icefall over two steep sections to the Snow Apron.

2. 35m Continue up the apron to the hidden entrance of a deep gully on the right.

3. 35m Climb up the gully to an overhang forming a seeming impasse.

4. 50m Move right into a chimney and follow this to another overhang. Turn this on the right and follow the rib up to the final overhang which blocks the exit. Difficult moves turn this on the right. An excellent pitch.

5. 30m Continue up iced grooves more easily to the summit.

21 Pig Iron Buttress   130m   IV,3 (2000)

The buttress to the right of Pearls Before Swine, approached via the Left Start of Three Little Pigs, gives a poorly protected route. Start at the lowest rib of rock which lies closer to Tusker than Pearls.

1. 50m Climb a sustained series of grooves and awkward steps to below a steeper chimney (visible from below as a square-cut notch) which lies just left of Tusker's bigger groove.

2. 25m Climb the chimney, easier than it looks, and move up right to below a steepening groove.

3. 55m Climb the fine turfy slab and overhang on the right to easier ground; continue to the top.

22 Tusker   190m   IV,5 * (1996)

A route with well protected technical moves in a good situation.

1. 50m The centre of the lower rock band has a prominent groove with (sometimes) a run of ice. Climb the icefall to the snow terrace below a steep V-groove with a slabby side wall.

2. 35m Gain the entrance of the V-groove and climb a very thin ice runnel up its back to below an overhang. A difficult right and upwards traverse then leads to the crest of a saddle.

3. 10m Climb the scoop and crack right of a turf overhang over a bulge directly above, good hidden jug en route, to a small platform.

4. 50m Continue up an open chimney, trending slightly left near the top, to a superb cave.

5. 45m Step right from the cave and climb a blocky chimney to the summit.

23 Ribsticker   140m   III (2004)

A reasonable route starting from the terrace and climbing the shallow rib between Tusker and Three Little Pigs.

1. 50m Start below and right of Tusker at a thread and climb directly up the steepening rib over short walls.

2. 50m Continue in the same line up the rib over more short walls.

3. 40m Follow the vague crest to the top.

24 Three Little Pigs   200m   II (1995/1996)

Climb the left-hand couloir for 200m as for the previous routes to the rock band. The icefall in the rock band (used as the start of Tusker) was the original start but is slow to form and IV,4. To the right of the icefall are two left-slanting corners. The left is the better of the two starts; the right is an easier angled slabby ramp.

1. 50m Climb either of the corners.

2. 30m Continue up right past Tusker to an open chimney come gully with a block on the right skyline.

3. 50m Climb the delightful groove by jinks and turns to a small alcove on a rib on the right.

3. 70m Step left and continue in the same line to the top.

25 Totally Hamless 160m II   (1998)

The next couple of routes take lines on the easier angled central section of the face. This easier but uninspiring route climbs the next groove to the left of Pork Scratchings, unfortunately lessening in angle after 50m or so. Climb a narrow groove (which is to the right of the deeper chimney of Three Little Pigs) and step left into a turfier one. Continue on to the top.

26 Pork Scratchings 160m III,4   (1998)

Follow the right-hand couloir and turn the lower tier of crags on the right to gain the Snow Apron on the left. Pork Scratchings takes the overhang blocked groove to the left of a deeper overlapped groove.

1. 18m Climb the groove to the overhang.

2. 42m Step right and climb to a narrow slot which provides an entertaining crux; continue straight up.

3. 50m The angle now lessens but the climb takes the central groove direct which gives the most interest.

4. 50m. Continue in the same line to the summit.

Bay 1

To the right of the snow terrace cutting across the main face are five narrow bays bounded by steep right-facing walls.

27 Pigsticker 230m IV,4 *   (1996)

The next routes take steeper lines on the right side of the face. This is a fine sustained route giving good mixed climbing. Take the right-hand couloir to the lower barrier. To the right of the two left-slanting grooves used as starts to Three Little Pigs, is a shorter right-slanting one leading to the first bay.

1. 25m Climb the groove with considerable interest.

2. 25m Continue easily to a snow bay below a wide icy gully come groove.

3. 40m Climb the ice directly, then move right to the continuation.

4. 40m Climb a steep chimney and then up to an overhanging rock wall. Move left under the overhanging wall with difficulty and gain a thin turf groove on the left. Climb this to a small bay.

5. 25m Climb the deceptively sustained narrow groove above.

6. 50m Climb the wider groove to a steep section up on the left.

7. 25m Finish easily.

Bay 2

28 Pygmalion 175m IV,4 **   (1996)

An excellent climb, constantly varied and provoking all the way up. Climb the right-hand couloir for 200m to the left edge of the snow bay that forms below Pigsticker's second pitch.

1. 40m Climb the arete parallel to the first pitch of Pigsticker and belay as for that route.

2. 40m Step right over the bounding edge to the next groove. Climb up its right wall to a square-cut recess and 'kickstep' up the right wall to a rib. Climb this for a move or two, then step delicately back left to the main groove.

3. 20m Sidle left and mount a narrow turf strip to gain a prominent V-groove.

Climb this superb well protected groove.

4. 25m Above is a short but wide chimney, difficult to start. Climb this, stepping left to exit and continue up.

5. 50m Step left and climb a wide crack with a perched chockstone; continue to the top.

29 Maneater   180m   VI,6 ** (2005)

A serious and sustained route with well spaced protection but good belays. It gives fine climbing but would be easier with better ice. To the left of the big central groove (The Boar) is another pronounced groove. Climb up the iced (or snowy) slab to the icicle and thread belay that sometimes forms down the short barrier wall.

1. 45m Climb the icicle to an overhang, move left and climb the groove. Move up right steeply to welcome turf and runners, continue up the groove and follow a gangway to below a bay on the left.

2. 30m Descend a few metres and step left into a wide groove. Climb this to an overhang; step left and up into a narrow blind groove. Move across the left wall before the groove becomes vertical to a rib. Continue up a short distance to a foothold.

3. 45m Continue up a short narrow gangway overlooking the exit of the blind groove to continue up the pleasant wide groove above to below an icy slab and cul-de-sac.

4. 40m Climb the ice directly to the vertical headwall. Move left across a small groove to escape.

5. 20m Finish easily to the summit.

30 The Boar   155m   VI,6 ** (1998)

Though rarely in condition, this challenging and serious line is worth the wait. Take the right-hand approach gully to the iced slab. Climb the slab to the base of the big central groove to the left of The Wolf.

1. 50m Climb the groove which is steep, sustained and has overlaps. A thin ice runnel is essential as there is no turf apart from a central boss. Exit steeply to ice and follow to below a prominent narrow ice runnel that forms on the right wall of a shallow groove -- this is the natural continuation of the groove below.

2. 25m Climb the steep and bulging ice which can be rather thin in places, to a steep exit up right which leads to a secure recess.

3. 30m Move up left over a turfy bulge and then over snowy or iced slabs to a wide groove on the left.

4. 50m Move into the wider groove and climb this over pleasant steepenings to easy ground a short distance below the summit cairn.

31 The Wolf   165m   V,6 ** (1995)

An excellent route which is less serious than its neighbour to the left and forms more readily. Follow the right-hand couloir to a large slab below a barrier wall (the second bay). The slab is thinly iced in lean conditions. This gives 60m of Grade II or banks out under snow and leads to the base of a big V-groove in the centre of the bay (The Boar). The slab can be avoided on the right (as for Crackling Groove). To the right of the V-groove is another, which leads to an overhang.

1. 45m Climb this groove to the impasse. Traverse neatly left to a hidden groove and climb this to a slender iced groove protected by an overhang with a (usually) slender icicle. Surmount the strenuous icicle and continue up the steep V-groove above to an icefall. Step left to a snow patch. A superb sustained pitch.

2. 50m Climb the icefall to snow, then climb a groove on the left.

3. 70m Continue straight up to the summit cairn.

32 Crackling Groove   160m   IV,4 (1996)

To the right of The Wolf is a final icy groove that is bounded by an edge that borders the third and deepest bay. Climb the right-hand of the two approach couloirs and move right to more broken ground right of the iced slab, following the bounding edge of the third bay. The dead-end icy groove has a narrow subsidiary groove to its right, which gives a good first pitch. Continue in the same line to the summit cairn.

Bay 3

33 Slaughterhouse Blues 165m V,6 * *(2001)*

This good route lies in the deep bay to the right of The Wolf etc. which contains a slabby wall on the left and two groove lines to the right. This route takes the right-hand groove. Best approached from directly below via a shallow couloir to the right of the right-hand one used to gain the bays to the left.

1. 35m Climb the right-hand groove with sustained interest, good but fiddly protection, to a little cave above.

2. 40m Continue in the same line up a turfy chimney and more open ground.

3. 40m The line taken was a left-facing corner up left to a capping bulge rather than an easier direct option.

4. 50m Continue up easier ground to the top.

34 The Trough 200m II * *(2004)*

A long turfy ramp borders the right edge of the bay containing Slaughterhouse Blues and gives a pleasant excursion up a natural line. Approach for that route but start lower down and to the right of the slab which bottoms it. Easy climbing keeping to the left for two pitches arrives at a short steep wall. This is climbed centrally or on the left for most interest. The ramp now steepens and the route keeps near the rock on the left to arrive at a slabby pinnacle. Move up left to a wide groove to gradually easing ground and the top.

Bay 4

35 If Pigs Could Fly 165m III * *(2002)*

A fine route of sustained steepness in the next bay left of Gammon Gully. It holds snow readily and probably keeps its condition longer than any other route here, being very sheltered. The left recess of the bay contains the line, a fine narrow hose of ice or turf which is followed to a chimney. Turn this on the right and continue straight up to the top over turfy bulges.

Bay 5

36 Gammon Gully 100m II * *(1996)*

This narrow gully lies on the right of the face and well left of Pigsty Gully. Either climb up the right-hand couloir and traverse right or descend from the little col below the summit and descend the slopes to trend right (looking down) across a ramp to gain the bay with short steep groove lines. The icy gully lies on the left of the bay and is sometimes bottomed by a sheet of blue ice.

37 Pork Chop Grooves 100m II *(2002)*

This lies on the broken but quite steep summit buttress that lies between Gammon Gully and Pigsty Gully. It forms a good finish to Gammon Gully or can be easily reached from above by descending the snow slope (Grade I) which lies below it. Its high position means it is often in condition. Left of centre is a narrow rock rib that harbours a narrow turf groove to its right. Climb this pleasantly steep groove to its exit and then follow the continuation groove above to the top.

38 Pigsty Gully 300m II *(1978)*

To the right of the north-east face is a prominent gully with its exit up cleft walls. Minor pitches, or a continuous runnel of ice, run up to the cleft which may be corniced. Exit up the wide right-hand funnel.

Variation: **Central Exit II** *(1998)*

Climbs the central exit up very steep snow.

39 Three Little Piggies 300m II * *(2003)*

To the right of Pigsty Gully another shallow break runs up the three-tiered face, with the top tier split by a shallow gully. The climb starts opposite the northern end of the loch. The lower tier gave continuous ice at a moderate angle followed by snow to the middle tier which gave a fine 25m ice pitch to snow. Another short ice pitch above then leads to a long snow slope and the final tier split by a fine gully that gives a good mixed pitch to finish up snow.

40 Trotters Gully   240m   III   *(1978)*
This is the long shallow gully well to the right of Pigsty Gully and marks the furthest right side of the face before the easy couloir. Easy snow leads to a blockage. The left fork gives a fine steep ice pitch up a 35m chimney, the only difficulty, while the right fork gives a more direct but less interesting finish (Grade II).

SGURR NA FEARSTAIG - SOUTH TOP

(NH 226 426)   Alt 700m   East facing   Map p328   Diagram p347

The East Face above Coire Toll a' Mhuic has a shorter but steeper crag, often with cornices well above. A band of very steep snow runs from below these to the exit of the routes and care should be taken in thaw or after snowfall. The climbing is different from Sgurr na Muice in that there are few grooves but there are two deep corners and several deep gully lines. It holds snow less well than on Sgurr na Muice partially due to the cleaner rock and steeper nature. However it does have superb turf strips plus good icefalls and that coupled with a kindly rock strata gives excellent climbing when properly frozen. The climbing tends to be considerably harder when under powder snow conditions.

Approach: Follow the good track which passes right of Loch Toll a' Mhuic, then continue up broken ground. This can be heavy going in soft snow and Sgurr na Muice might be a better option in those conditions. 1hr 30mins in good conditions.

Descent: Slanting Gully by its right (furthest north) fork (Route 12, Grade I) is the quickest in good conditions. Another possibility is a shallow gully at the lowest point of the col between Sgurr na Fearstaig, South Top and Sgurr na Muice. If there is an avalanche risk, it is safest to go southwards over the top of Sgurr na Muice and walk off.

1 Red Campion   150m   II   *(1978)*
The left end of the cliff has a wide corner of snow abutting a short wall. Snow leads to the blockage, split by two grooves. The right one is easier and another short pitch leads to a fan exit.

2 Torque of the Devil   165m   IV,5 **   *(2003)*
A good natural line up the buttress right of Red Campion. The climb takes the leftmost buttress which has a conspicuous triangle of snow 50m up and is bounded on the left by the snow ramp of Red Campion. To the right of a small icefall at the toe of the buttress is a left-slanting turfy ramp.
1. 45m Follow the ramp past a bulge to traverse left along the top of the snow triangle to reach a small recess with a large block.
2. 40m Continue the traverse to the left-hand edge of the face where a prominent notch will be seen 20m up the edge. Climb up to this notch steeply to below an overhang. Twin cracks then enable difficult moves leftwards to the base of a turfy ledge, a well protected crux, and continue for 10m past a step.
3. 40m Continue left for about 10m, then climb up or near a thin ice smear and some steep mixed ground to an easing to where the summit snowfield begins.
4. 40m Continue up steepening snow to the top, sometimes corniced but usually outflanked to the left.

3 Flower of Scotland   170m   IV,5 **   *(2001)*
This is the left-hand of the two gullies which lie on the left side of the main face with a thin streak between them at half-height. The gully can be identified by a narrow slot and a chimney higher up at about half-height. A good route with lots of well protected technical mixed climbing which was climbed under ideal thin but

The Scorcerer, IV,5, Sgurr na Fearstaig. Climber John Mackenzie

John Mackenzie collection

GLEN AFFRIC TO STRATHFARRAR

well frozen conditions. Start either as for Snowdrop or to the left up mixed ground and ice.

1. 50m Climb to a corner below and left of the narrow slot.

2. 20m Move up into the slot and exit up the entertaining right wall.

3. 30m Continue to and up the next awkward chimney to an overhanging chockstone with a difficult landing. Continue up big flakes and move left around another chockstone. A great pitch.

4. 70m Continue up over a minor bump and an easy finish to the top.

4 Snowdrop   155m   III *   *(1999)*
This climb takes the main right-hand gully, much of which is hidden from below. It gave a steep and serious route in poor conditions. Climb steepening snow and ice to a point where it is possible to move right over a rib to join the rightmost gully. Climb this, moving left to a prominent saddle (60m). Continue towards the thin streak, then enter and climb the hidden gully to the right (45m). Climb a thin mixed groove to the right which ends below the girdling snow band. Climb very steep snow to a potentially large cornice.

5 Diamond Slab   90m   VS *   *(2006)*
This is the large slab that lies left of The Sorcerer's corner. Compared with Sgurr na Muice, the rock is covered in small incut holds and easier than it looks, making for a very enjoyable climb. Start well left of the right-slanting lower overhangs where a slabby wall is bounded by a grassy stepped corner on the right and a shallow corner on the left.
1. 20m 4c Climb the wall just left of the stepped corner to a below a steeper wall. Move right and climb the bold wall to a good ledge.
2. 50m 4b Move up to a shallow corner then move easily right along a shelf to a ragged crack. Follow this up the slab to a grass ledge (possible belay). Continue up and left climbing the slab left of a line of curving overlaps to a ledge. An excellent pitch.
3. 20m Continue easily to the top.

6 Sorcerer's Apprentice   160m   IV,4 *   *(1996)*
Above the ice pitch start to Slanting Gully is an icefall leading through the only break in the lower rocks to the furthest left of three big corners. This was an attempt on the corner but forced left.
1. 35m Climb moderate ice or snow to the break.
2. 25m Climb the near vertical ice funnel to reach turf, step left and curve back right past a bulge to a recess.
3. 40m Leave the line of the corner and follow a narrow left-trending ramp.
4. 30m Continue up and left in an exposed position as the ramp narrows to belay near where it ends.
5. 30m Climb a break above to the top.

7 The Sorcerer   165m   IV,5 ****   *(2001)*
The route of the crag, taking the furthest left of the three big corners direct, provides a fine route with excellent protection and belays. Graded for good conditions, with the turf well frozen and the icefall accommodating. Start as for Sorcerer's Apprentice for two pitches.
1. 35m Climb the lower icefall, sometimes covered.
2. 35m Climb the ice runnel and steep turf, stepping left then right around the bulge to continue up to a higher recess.
3. 30m Continue up turf and ice to the base of a chockstone guarding the top corner.
4. 20m Climb the interesting chockstone to continue up the corner to a chockstone just below the crux, a right-leaning right-angled corner.
5. 15m Climb the well protected corner-crack with a traditional crawl through the hole above.
6. 25m Climb a central steep wall, but it is avoidable on the left or right.

8 Rising Damp   165m   III **   *(2006)*
A varied line starting up the narrow gully below the central of three corners. Recommended for a scenic 'Cook's Tour' with an exciting finish through a tunnel.
1. 30m Climb into the gully and belay on the left 10m above an alcove.
2. 50m Enter the gully and climb it up and right below the headwall to belay on a saddle overlooking Sea Pink Gully.
3. 40m Traverse right and up into Sea Pink Gully and belay by a huge spike on the left, as for Tendril.

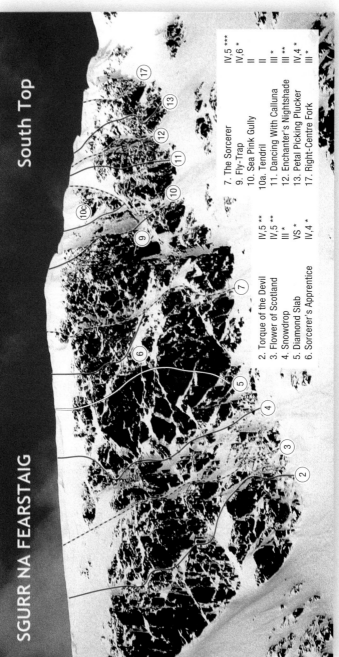

John Mackenzie

SGURR NA FEARSTAIG

South Top

2. Torque of the Devil	IV,5 **
3. Flower of Scotland	IV,5 **
4. Snowdrop	III *
5. Diamond Slab	VS *
6. Sorcerer's Apprentice	IV,4 *

7. The Sorcerer	IV,5 ***
9. Fly-Trap	IV,6 *
10. Sea Pink Gully	II
10a. Tendril	II
11. Dancing With Calluna	III *
12. Enchanter's Nightshade	III **
13. Petal Picking Plucker	IV,4 *
17. Right-Centre Fork	III *

4. 25m Climb up behind the spike and traverse left to the big corner of Fly-Trap.
5. 20m Climb through the narrow tunnel below the huge chockstone to a sudden exit. Finish directly above.

9 Fly-Trap 70m IV,6 * (2005)
The deep corner above Sea Pink Gully is the rightmost of the three corners. Carrying rucksacks is not advised!
1. 20m Climb the lower 20m of Sea Pink Gully to a rock pulpit below the corner.
2. 20m Enter the overhung chimney to a thread runner under the chockstone (not easy to arrange). Climb the overhang on ice and up the corner above trending leftwards a crevasse stance up left. A great pitch.
3. 30m The direct continuation of the corner is an off-width crack needing ice. Instead, move up and left to the crest of the buttress and mixed ground to the top.

10 Sea Pink Gully 120m II (1978)
The right corner of Fly-Trap is bottomed by a diagonal ramp leading up right. Follow Slanting Gully to a narrow gully below the corner. Climb a short ice pitch then follow the ramp rightwards to a sometimes corniced exit.
Variation: **Tendril 50m II** (2004)
About 30m up the right-slanting section of Sea Pink Gully it is possible to gain entry to the slab above. Above, move up left then back right to finish up a scoop; sometimes heavily corniced.

11 Dancing With Calluna 90m III * (2003)
The buttress that separates Sea Pink Gully from Enchanter's Nightshade has a good initial pitch.
1. 50m Start at the foot of the buttress and follow a line of weakness up left then back right to below the final step.
2. 40m The short step, then snow and a possible cornice at the top.

12 Enchanter's Nightshade 100m III ** (1978)
An exciting climb for its length, particularly under lean conditions. To the right of Sea Pink Gully is a deep steep groove. This iced groove leads for 35m to a small recess and a vertical chimney-groove. Climb this crux and exit rightwards to a steepening scoop often blocked by a huge cornice which can be turned on the left.

13 Petal Picking Plucker 80m IV,4 * (2005)
The deceptive buttress to the right of Enchanter's Nightshade, good climbing with an entertaining finish. Start 10m right of the gully below a shallow groove.
1. 45m Climb up the groove, then move right to another wider groove which is climbed on ice to give a sustained pitch.
2. 35m The easier angled ground above via a narrow groove to arrive at an arete. Follow the narrow arete to the top.

14 Slanting Gully 250m I
This is the long easy ramp that runs from bottom left to top right along the base of the previous routes, with the rightmost exit being the easiest and providing a good descent. It can disappear under heavy snow.
Variation: **Direct Start II/III**
Grade II on the left and Grade III on the right. These are optional ice pitches of around 10 and 20m that lie below the main ramp. The right-hand icefall is good when fully formed. Other icefalls can also form around here.

To the right of Petal Picking Plucker are several deep gullies providing more interesting finishes to Slanting Gully.

15 Left Fork 60m I (1978)
This is the gully immediately right of Enchanter's Nightshade.

16 Left-Centre Fork   60m   II   *(1978)*
To the right of Left Fork is a left-slanting gully which gives a pleasant but usually heavily corniced finish.

17 Right-Centre Fork   60m   III *   *(2001)*
To the right of Left-Centre Fork is a narrow groove, well iced but often with a big capping cornice, outflanked by the arete on the left.

18 Right Fork   60m   I   *(1978)*
To the right is a wide fan, often heavily corniced, which is left of Slanting Gully's easy rightmost exit.

To the right of the main crag lies a smaller crag with some steep lines. The route below is the most obvious of these.

19 Little Gem   20m   VS 4c   *(2006)*
The fine little slabby wall to the right of Right Fork is clean, sound and attractive. Start at some brown rocks, roughly in the middle and climb straight up with some boldish moves higher up.

To the right of the main crag lies a smaller crag with some steep lines. The route below is the most obvious of these.

20 A Wee Cracker   75m   III *   *(2004)*
A good steep climb with attitude. It takes the prominent narrow gully just right of a thinner cracked groove. Snow leads to a minor pitch followed by steepening snow to the obvious crux, a near vertical rocky corner. Struggle up this to finish in a good position. Often in condition.

SGURR FUAR-THUILL

(NH 237 437)   Alt 900m   North-East facing   Map p328

East of the summit, the open corrie of Fuar-Tholl Mor has mixed ground, which is good in lean conditions. Besides the route below, other much longer Grade I and possibly Grade II climbs could be made here if not banked out.

The Glass Scribe   120m   III,4 *   *(2004)*
Just left of the summit is a broken buttress with snow ramps and steps and below that another slabby buttress. Contour in or descend steep snow slopes to the foot of this. A fine icefall issuing from a spring runs down the middle of this lower buttress. Climb steeply up a groove to a large iced slab and up the middle of this to a short fat vertical pillar. Ascend this and easier ice above to snow and mixed ground to the top. A good contrasting climb with reliable ice.

CREAG GHORM A' BHEALAICH

(NH 245 435)   Alt 950m   North-East facing   Map p328

A slender ridge falls directly from the summit into upper Coire na Sguile. Either side are narrow gullies.

SE Passage   80m   I/II *   *(2004)*
The left-hand gully is scenic, quite steep and well defined having a small but interesting pitch at some narrows.

NE Passage   80m   II   *(2004)*
The right-hand gully is blocked by a rock buttress at half-height. Above are two ramps; traverse left across to the top one and make airy moves across and up to finish up the last few metres of the ridge.

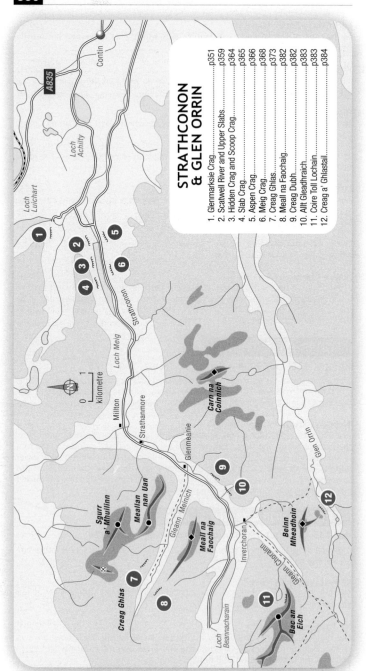

STRATHCONON & GLEN ORRIN

A835

Contin

Loch Luichart

Loch Achilty

N
0   1
kilometre

Loch Meig

Strathconon

Millton

Strathanmore

Carn na Coinnich

Glenmeanie

Glen Orrin

Sgurr a' Mhuilinn

Meallan nan Uan

Gleann Meinich

Creag Ghlas

Meall na Faochaig

Invercharron

Beinn Mheadhoin

Gleann Chorainn

Loch Beannacharain

Bac an Eich

STRATHCONON & GLEN ORRIN

These two glens are the most northerly of the five glens cutting through the mountain area south of The Fannaichs. Strathconon has a number of crags in its lower reaches (on Landranger Sheet 26) and a few lower mountain crags towards its top (on Landranger Sheet 25), including the high quality Creag Ghlas. Glen Orrin, the most southerly of the two glens, has only one crag, approached from upper Strathconon.

Strathconon

The first crag is not strictly in Strathconon but very close. Subsequent cliffs are in order as you approach up the glen.

GLENMARKSIE CRAG

(NH 383 580)   Alt 190m   South facing   Diagram p355

Once cleaned, the rock on this schist crag is impeccable. It sports pleasant middle grade wall and slab climbs and some harder routes. There is no seasonal restriction and since it gets plenty of sun, it dries quickly and is often climbable in winter. Many of the steeper climbs in the central and right-hand sections are sustained and technical. The routes are generally well protected by wires and Friends.

Approach: Turn west off the A832 beyond Contin (marked Loch Achilty) and reach a gate before the dam at Loch Luichart. The gate is unlocked from 8am to 5pm. Drive (or walk) over the dam and walk up the hillside on the right through birches before moving back left. Bracken is troublesome in the summer but improves higher up. Arrive below a scrambling groove leading to a rock glacis, 10mins.

Descent: Down the left end (facing the crag), or abseil from a concrete pillar above The Conjuror. To descend from the routes that end at the birch tree (Proteus through to Greased Lightning), abseil from the tree or scramble left to an in situ steel stake for a 20m abseil. For Top Crag, descend at either end.

Main Crag takes the form of a central slab steepening to a wall, bounded on the right by a slab and headwall. Two small crags lie above and to the right. On the left of Main Crag there is a gully with a small buttress above a rowan tree and left again a low wall that stretches up the hillside.

MAIN CRAG

The climbs are described from right to left. To the right of centre is an overhanging bay bottomed by a rock glacis with a slanting chimney on the left and a corner to the right. Right again is a slab and headwall.

1 Little Teaser   15m   E2 5c   (1990)
Just left of the small corner at the right end of the crag is a rust coloured corner above a cleaned slab. Climb the slab, then leap up overhanging corner (peg runner and RP 3) to pull on to the slab by memorable moves.

2 Hiroshima Grooves   30m   HVS 5b *   (1980)
Right of the recessed glacis is an overhanging headwall with a V-groove bottomed by a slab. Start at the bottom left of the slab beneath a big roof and follow the slab rightwards beneath the overlap to gain a shallow groove. Climb the groove which curves left to the headwall (possible belay), then climb the nicely positioned crux up through the V-groove.

3 Powder Monkey   25m   E2 6a   (1990)
The large roof on the left front face of the lower slab, below the headwall. Start just

John Mackenzie

Phobos, E2, Glenmarksie Crag. Climber Mike Haltree

left of Hiroshima Grooves and climb a short slab to the roof. Pull up and climb a thin crack to a shelf. Easy climbing either up the crack on the right or on the arete above leads to a fitting conclusion up the crux of Hiroshima Grooves.

4 Six Trees   30m   Hard Severe 4b   *(1979)*
Scramble to the rock glacis via a little groove, left of Powder Monkey. Climb the corner on the right of the bay to a slab and possible belay (4b). Traverse right across the slab to finish past trees, a good pitch.

5 Greased Lightning   35m   HVS 5a *   *(pre-1977)*
Takes the fine hanging chimney-groove on the left of the bay. Start below this in a hollow and climb the right of two flake-cracks to the glacis (4b). Take the crux wall into the chimney and past a constriction to the top (5a).
Variation: **Direct Start   HVS 5a**   *(1980)*
Climb a pinnacle left of the normal start to gain a bald slab and the glacis.

6 Strategic Arms Limitation   35m   E4 6a **   *(1989)*
The severely overhanging groove right of Greased Lightning at the back of the glacis gives a very fine route with good protection.
1. 10m 4c Start in the hollow and climb the crack left of Greased Lightning to the glacis. This pitch can be avoided by scrambling up to the glacis on the right.

2. 25m 6a Climb the strenuous and very sustained corner (which overhangs 1 in 4) to a flake at the top on the left. Mantel on to this and continue up a slab nose to the top (sometimes dirty).

7 A Bit on the Side   20m   E1 5b   *(1990)*
Climbs the area between the chimney of Greased Lightning and the curving crack of Callisto. Start at the little neck of rock at the left edge of the glacis and step on to the wall. Climb up, then step right on to the slab bordering Greased Lightning. Climb this briefly before stepping left below an overlap, then make a thin leftwards rising traverse along an undercut flake before a step left below the top overlap allows a finish as for Deimos. The top section is quite bold.

8 Callisto/Polish Peacemaker   20m   HVS 5a *   *(1982/1989)*
A fine route, sustained at VS but with one harder move on the initial traverse. Scramble up to the left edge of the glacis below the top pitch of Greased Lightning. Step left onto the wall and foot traverse left to a prominent curving crack. The crack is followed over a small overhang and where it bends back right, climb the left arete of Greased Lightning to a tree. The first pitch of Strategic Arms Limitation makes a good addition to this climb.

9 Deimos   25m   E3 5c ***   *(1990)*
The seemingly blank wall left of Callisto gives an excellent sustained climb that is well protected and low in the grade. Climb the short slanting crack left of Callisto until just right of a big triangular niche. Reach up right to a break, then traverse left along the crux quartz ripples, feet below the overhang, to a little flake and then go directly up to a hanging flake. Mantel on to the right end of a hidden ledge, traverse left along this, then climb under the overlaps rightwards to a niche. Pull over and climb straight to the tree.

10 Phobos   25m   E2 5c ***   *(1989)*
Sustained climbing, low in the grade. Start right of the central groove of Proteus at a thin crack which is climbed to an overhung ramp. Traverse left along this to a small ledge and then awkwardly into the big niche. Step out right on to the wall where hidden holds lead to another small ledge. Surmount the overlap above and climb the delicate slab which leads to the same tree as for Callisto.

11 Proteus   35m   HVS **   *(1980)*
A fine climb with much variety. Left of Phobos the wall is split by a steep groove.
1. 25m 5a Gain a ramp and step right under a roof, surmount this and climb the left rib to step right into a niche. Go up the groove and over small roofs, step up right to a shelf, then go up left to small ledge.
2. 10m 4c Climb the flake on the left and finish up a smooth slab.

12 Dynamite   35m   E2 5c *   *(1979/1990)*
Left of Proteus is a black recess topped by overhangs. Climb its slabby corner on the right over an overlap. Bridge up the overhang via thin cracks above. Climb the pleasant slab direct to the top. The original route traversed under the roof to belay on the tree (E1 5b).

13 Wild Mint   30m   Severe 4b *   *(1979)*
Left of Dynamite is a wedge with a tree on top. Undercut a big flake on the right to pull into a groove with jammed blocks which forms the right corner of the wedge, and gain the tree. Traverse right across ledges to step up at the end. Climb the slab direct to ledges as for Dynamite.

14 Glen Marxie Brothers   25m   VS 4c *   *(2006)*
A direct line through Wild Mint. Start as for Wild Mint and pull into the groove. Step right to a crack in a hanging slab and climb to the tree. Step right, then pull left into a short left-facing corner. Make thin moves up the slab above to finish up easier ledges.

15 Walk On By   45m   VS 4c *   *(1979)*
A pleasant route with a tricky start. Climb the awkward pod on the left side of the wedge to the tree. Step left to reach a niche in a corner and climb the slab on the right, then up a crack past a dead bush to the steel stake on the left. An optional second pitch, rather mossy, gains the slabby groove on the left to ledges, then moves left to a steep corner and finishes up this by a large loose slab resting on top.

Immediately left of the wedge containing Wild Mint and Walk On By is a slab with two pleasant popular routes.

16 Sickle Moon/An Feur Ghorta   25m   HVS 5a *   *(1982/1989)*
A bold lower half and an easier upper. Climb the right-slanting crack left of the wedge, then up the curving crack in the slab direct to the overhang. The original way was to move into Wild Mint before climbing the overhang, but this is inferior and much easier. Pull over this and step right, then up the left-trending ramp to the overlap. Step right and finish up the crack.

17 Selene/An Fear Feusagach   25m   HVS 5b **   *(1982/1989)*
A gentle start leads to an emphatic crux; a good route. Start 1m left of Sickle Moon and climb the wall and left-curving ramp over the small overlap. Step right above the overlap and climb direct up the shelves to a crack. The original way climbed the slab just left of the cracks. Climb the steep crux slab and finish up a crack which lies left of the top crack of Sickle Moon.

18 Sea of Tranquillity   45m   HVS ***   *(1990)*
An enjoyable climb on excellent rock. Start as for Selene.
1. 30m 5a Climb the leftward ramp to step left below a fine crack in a groove. Climb the crack, either going straight up to a ledge, inferior and easier, or step left to a flake and up the slab to the same ledge. Climb a very thin scoop leftwards to easier ledges (crux) and the short corner above. If the easier version of the crack is taken and the scoop avoided on the right award yourself a VS 4c.
2. 15m 5a Climb to and up a good crack which cuts through an overhang in the headwall above, stepping left to a small break at the top. The last move comes as a surprise.
Variation: **5c**
The unprotected and tenuous slab left of the scoop on the first pitch gives hard friction climbing.

19 The Joker   45m   E2 5c **   *(2004)*
Climb Sea of Tranquillity to the belay. Move left below a 'half-pipe' scoop left of the top pitch of Sea of Tranquillity. Surmount a small overhang and up the quartz blebbed slab to a small ledge. Climb the right wall of the scoop with interest to a horizontal fault; step left across the scoop and climb the layaways above to the top, 15m. Sustained climbing easier than it looks.

20 The Juggler   50m   HVS 5a   *(1979)*
A pleasant top pitch, otherwise very vegetated, and would benefit from a good clean. The top pitch can be reached by climbing other routes. Start at the foot of a tongue of rock, left of the corner which is left of Selene. Climb the right edge of a slab, step left beneath overlaps, then go up to a pinnacle (4a). Step right, climb a wall past heather to a block (4c). Climb a corner above, step right to heather, then go easily left to a wide crack (4c). Climb up to an inset right corner below a big roof. Step around the edge to a sloping shelf and finish up a steep slab (5a).

21 The Conjuror   40m   HVS **   *(2000)*
A fine route that climbs the slabby walls below and above the big overhangs of The Juggler. It gives two contrasting pitches with the top pitch providing the meat of the climb. Start below a short wall up left of The Juggler and down from Dog Leg.
1. 22m 5b Climb the bold wall to easier slabs which are followed to below the big roof.

Andy Nisbet

355

GLENMARKSIE
Main Crag

5. Greased Lightning	HVS 5a *
6. Strategic Arms Limitation	E4 ***
8. Callisto	HVS 5a *
9. Deimos	E3 5c ***
10. Phobos	E2 5c ***
11. Proteus	HVS **
12. Dynamite	E2 5c *

13. Wild Mint	Severe 4b *
14. Glen Marxie Brothers	VS 4c *
15. Walk On By	VS 4c *
16. Sickle Moon	HVS 5a *

17. Selene	HVS 5b **
18. Sea of Tranquillity	HVS ***
19. The Joker	E2 5c **
21. The Conjuror	HVS **

STRATHCONON & GLEN ORRIN

Helios, E2, Glenmarksie Crag. Climber John Mackenzie

John Mackenzie collection

2. 18m 5b Traverse a horizontal crack rightwards and then directly up a vertical crack to a shelf. Climb the crack up left, stepping over an overhang to finish up a rippled slabby headwall.

22 Dog Leg   40m   Very Difficult *   (1979)

A good climb with some tricky sections up the slabs on the left of the Main Crag, bordered by a gully. Takes the easiest line to the right of a steeper wall. Climb to a rust coloured corner via a short wall and curious dog shaped flake to a wide crack. Climb the wall next to the crack, then left by a horizontal break to gain a niche. A large head of rock (the Dog Head) has a V-corner on its right; climb this to finish.

23 Hot Dog   25m   E3 5c **   (2006)

A sustained and serious route with intricate technical climbing to the left of Dog Leg. Start at a central niche and move up to a short right-facing corner. Climb up to a roof, then move left (crucial Friend 0 in a horizontal slot) and up to a good hold and a prominent peg. Mantelshelf onto the good hold and move up and slightly right to a ledge. Climb the short wall above just right of a shallow corner and finish as for the top V-groove of Dog Leg.

24 Dogg'Ed   25m   VS 4c *   (1990)

A fine sustained line up the left edge of the steep wall left of Dog Leg. Start in the gully and step on to the wall and climb this via thin cracks to the traverse of Dog Mantle. Climb the wall above via wider cracks to the base of the Dog Head and finish by the right corner as for Dog Leg.

Variation: **Direct Finish   7m   E2 5b** *   *(1990)*
Climb direct the unprotected and rather spectacular arete of the Dog Head pinnacle, the final move being the crux. Harder for the short.

25 Dog Mantle   30m   Severe 4a   *(1979)*
The route starts halfway up the gully left of the Main Crag. Traverse right to a wide crack. Climb straight up the wall to a corner left of the large top overhang and finish up the corner.

**26 Helios   55m   E2 ** **   *(1993)*
This is the girdle traverse of the main crag. Despite having a contrived first pitch and the odd scrappy section, the climbing is good with an excellently sustained third pitch. Start as for Sea of Tranquillity.
1. 20m 4c Climb over the arched overlap and follow its lip to the end. Descend the corner to the birch.
2. 10m 5a Cross the slab above the overhang of Dynamite and descend Proteus to the floor of the niche.
3. 15m 5b Step down into the niche of Phobos and climb Phobos to the hidden flake hold. Step down with faith and traverse to the footledge of Deimos. Step down awkwardly to the small ledge on Callisto.
3. 10m 4c Climb up Callisto's rib to cross to the bounding edge beyond Greased Lightning at the earliest opportunity and belay on the small tree.

Left of the gully lies Small Wall, with a rowan tree at its base.

27 Small Wall Thins   12m   Severe 4a *   *(1979)*
Start right of the tree and climb up to and into a groove. Step left at the top and finish up a slab.

28 Two Step   12m   Severe 4b   *(1979)*
Climb the slab above the tree, then take the crux cracks on the right overlooking the groove of Small Wall Thins to finish up this route.

29 Staircase   10m   Very Difficult   *(1979)*
Climb pleasant rock and cracks 3m left of the tree to the top.

30 Kojak   7m   5a *   *(1979)*
A blank slab lying left of Staircase gives a neglected but splendid little problem. Gain a ledge on the left, then go either left up a thin gangway or right over a bald crest at the same grade.

Below Small Wall lies Lower Wall, a line of good bouldering rock plus several short routes, usually soloed. Near the right end is a prominent overhang.

31 Sideline   6m   4a   *(1979)*
Climb a shallow corner right of the overhang.

32 Middle Wall   5m   5a   *(1979)*
Takes a central line up the wall left of Sideline.

33 Bitter Bother   7m   4b   *(1979)*
Climb the short corner right of the overhang; finish up the top wall trending right.

34 Clutch and Thrutch   10m   5c *   *(1979)*
Start below the overhang and climb it. Once on the jutting ledge the top wall is easier. A good safe problem in an alarming position.

Walking past further small walls and just right of a tree filled corner is a curved wall, with four horizontal breaks.

35 A Touch of Class   10m   E2 5b *   *(1979)*
Climb the wall centrally using the breaks to a tenuous finish. The best of the routes on this area; the top is the crux and requires a clean.

36 Victoriana   7m   Difficult   *(1979)*
Climb the corner to the left with or without the tree.

MIDDLE CRAG & TOP CRAG

Above Main Crag lie two smaller crags, Middle Crag and Top Crag. Middle Crag is immediately up right from Main Crag. Both Middle Crag and Top Crag can be reached by scrambling up a little corner just right of Main Crag and then swinging up right over a flake; the crags are then above. This also provides the best descent. Top Crag can also be reached by walking rightwards from the top of the main crag.

Middle Crag

Currently a rather scrubby slabby crag which could be improved with a brushing. More lines await the adventurous. It is of good rock.

Trade Route   10m   Very Difficult   *(1980)*
Climb the slab left of a central groove, exiting right at top.

Central Groove   10m   Severe 4a   *(1980)*
Climb the slab right of the groove to finish up the groove.

Top Crag

Top Crag is overhanging and is split by deep cracks. It is of good rock, well protected and an excellent work-out though it takes a day to dry out after rain. It provides a complete contrast to the more delicate climbs on Main Crag.

Tiddly   4m   5b
The boulder problem on the wall just left of the left edge of the crag.

Pom   5m   VS 5b   *(1990)*
Right of the left edge of the crag are four undercut overhanging cracked corners. Pom takes the short one on the left, a good introduction to the fiercer lines to the right.

Left Unprintable   10m   E2 6b *   *(1994)*
This is the left of the two overhanging shallow corners which lie right of Pom. The crux is trying to gain and sustain the fingerlock just out of reach! The very tall will find it easier.

Right Unprintable   8m   E2 5c *   *(1991)*
The right corner is a fine test piece, which has fortunately excellent protection. It packs some punch, being sustained with an athletic start and a cruel finish.

Man o' War   15m   E4 6b **   *(1993)*
In the middle of the crag is this central roof which is split by a crack. Follow a handrail up left to the roof. The roof is the crux (Friend 4 protects) and continue up the wall to a thin exit. Puzzling climbing, currently the hardest at Glenmarksie.

Bridging the Gap   12m   E3 6a **   *(1993)*
The open groove to the right provides a fine route, less strenuous and possibly easier for the tall. A juggy start up a flake leads to technical bridging up the groove, protected by RPs or similar. Exit left under the overhang.

Gritstone Corner   12m   HVS 5a *   *(1989)*
This is the corner-crack at the right end of the crag. It provides a strenuous problem using a variety of jamming techniques.

Jumping Jack Splat   10m   E2 5c *   *(1994)*
Right of Gritstone corner is a gently overhanging wall split by a thin crack. Start in the corner below the crack and climb to a glacis. Gain the niche and jump for the jug.

Red Ant Crack   10m   VS 4b   *(1994)*
At the extreme right end of the crag lies a flake. Climb this and finish by the crack.

RIGHT CRAG

(NH 384 581)   Alt 210m   South-East facing

The crag is less obvious than the main crag but has some interesting lines requiring small items of protection. A curiosity was the in situ sheep which had lived on the same ledge for four years; this took fright and jumped but survived and restricts its diet to coarse heather.

Approach: Park as for Glenmarksie Crag but since the crag lies to the right of the main crag and at the same level as Top Crag, go directly up the hillside to it.

Optical Illusion   25m   E2 *   *(1995)*
The only route to date on the crag, possible in one pitch. Protection is very sketchy on pitch one but abundant on pitch two. Roughly at the centre and directly below a small, lonely tree, is an overhanging green wall bottomed by a clean grey slab with a guarding overhang.
1. 15m 5b Surmount the overhang at some layaways and step right. Move up left and traverse left boldly below a small overlap to below the green wall.
2. 10m 4c Climb the wall on huge holds to the tree.

SCATWELL RIVER SLABS

(NH 382 563)   Alt 40m   South facing   Map p350

These sunny slabs give unusual climbs above a delectable pool of the River Conon. Unfortunately they are prone to collecting leaves and an abseil descent for a quick brush is recommended. Despite their formidable appearance, the natural lines of weakness are climbed at quite low grades. The mica schist is exposed on the bedding plane so there are some loose flakes.

Approach: Drive 1km along the minor road from Loch Achilty towards Strathconon where there are convenient lay-bys. The slabs are hidden from view but can be reached via a vegetated 'crevasse', the outer crest of which forms the top of these impressive slabs. The slabs can be reached either by abseil off one of the handy trees or by a steep scramble down the left-hand side (looking down). Beware of sudden spates during thundery weather.

From the big central tree above, three main lines are visible. A big corner on the right, the shallow groove below the tree, a long diagonal leading to the tree from the left, and some shorter cracked corners on the left boundary. Routes are described from these, which are rather vegetated and could do with a clean.

Piccadilly Line   12m   Difficult
The first of the cracked corners. Climb the pleasant corner-crack over a steepening to the top.

Northern Line   18m   VS 4c *
The next corner to the left, follow the layback with a strenuous crux at a steepening. Finish up the corner of Circle Line. A good route.

STRATHCONON & GLEN ORRIN

Circle Line 18m Severe 4a
Start from the tree belay at the foot of Northern Line and descend a few metres. Traverse the slab leftwards to the edge (crux), then climb the pleasant crack through the overlap and up a steep little corner at the top. A much harder direct start is possible starting at the waters edge and initially following the next corner until a difficult move (5a) is made on to the slab where the parent route is joined; this variation adds another 10m on to the route.

Metropolitan and District 50m Very Difficult
The long diagonal line that starts at the water's edge and slants up left to the big tree. Climb up to a tree, then continue up the impressive slab with minimum difficulty to the tree. Unfortunately very dirty at present but if re-cleaned, then by far the best easy route on these slabs.

Scatwell Express 20m E3 5c ✶✶ *(2000)*
This provides serious slab climbing in its top section. Start from the Clapham Junction tree belay on Grand Central. Climb up and slightly right to a tree runner on the slab. Go 3m left, then directly up on thin flakes to gain the final slab directly below a large boulder on the top.

Grand Central 60m VS ✶
The central line on these slabs, taking the concave central groove that lies below the big tree. Despite few difficult moves, this is a potentially serious climb with areas of friable rock. Autumn leaves gather in the groove making spring cleaning advisable.
1. 20m Start at the water's edge and make a delightful left traverse about 6m above the pool to the haven of a group of trees (Clapham Junction).
2. 40m 4b Step down to little edges and traverse up then left to a fixed ring peg. Now climb up the groove, crux just above another fixed peg, then up the easier but very impressive groove to the big tree.

The Joust 40m E2 5c ✶✶ *(1993)*
Between The Tilting Yard and Grand Central is a cleaned area of concave slab with a prominent groove running up to a smooth headwall which provides the crux. The rock is significantly better than Grand Central. Abseil down Grand Central to the trees. Traverse left across the base of Grand Central to the start of the groove. Climb the increasingly difficult groove and flake to a small tree. Above is a blank slab with a peg runner. Gain the peg and the letterbox above, vital Friend 0 runner. The rather blank crux follows with a still interesting finish.

Flying Scotsman 30m E4 6a *(2004)*
Start as for The Joust. Follow this route to the flake (protection). Down climb a little and traverse left under a small tree, then follow intermittent cracks until above and slightly left of the small tree (peg runner). Now follow a seam up to clip the peg on The Joust. Make a hard mantel to gain small holds and finish 4m left of The Joust.

The Tilting Yard 30m E1 5b ✶✶ *(1993)*
This sustained and enjoyable route takes the big corner which bounds the west end of the slabs (right when looking down). Abseil to a ledge which is above the water. Climb the thin diagonal line into the corner and follow this tenuously past two broken blocks and then interestingly to the prominent chockstone above. Continue past a small tree to the top.

Boundary Ridge 25m VS 5a *(1993)*
This is the edge which bounds The Tilting Yard on the extreme right of the slabs (looking down). Abseil descent is possibly easier than a scramble well to the right. Climb the rib which has one awkward step.

Piles of Smiles   25m   VS 4b   (1994)
Belay as for Boundary Ridge and climb small ledges on the arete for 3m until a short traverse left leads to the base of an obvious crack 4m left of the arete. Climb this to a good ledge and move right to finish up short slabs and ledges.

Rectal Irrigation   40m   E5 6b DWS   (2000)
A very entertaining traverse from the waterfall to the tail of the large pool which sits under the crag. Abseil down The Tilting Yard to a small slab inches from water level. Step right from the slab onto an undercut traverse, smearing precariously up 3m, then right along the slab and down climb onto a small 2inch wide ledge just above the water. Make a very hard move to a hidden undercling and swing round onto a slab. Continue until under the tree belays of Grand Central to finish.

Try not to Wet your Arch   400m   VS 5b DWS   (2000)
A circular traverse of the large pool up to a natural arch, over it and back down the slab side. Abseil down slabs to rocks at the tail of the large pool. Rock hop and jump to the other side and scramble to the left of the waterfall. Traverse right just above the drink to the edge of the waterfall. Climb up and follow ledge systems and amazing rock architecture to the arch. Cross over and follow a diminishing ledge to a round bay 5m above water. Down climb and traverse onto large boulders. Go over these to a slab making a hard traverse right and down onto a scramble to the foot of Boundary Ridge. Scramble up left of this or go for the Rectal finish.

SCATWELL UPPER SLABS

(NH 381 563)   Alt 120m   South-East facing   Map p350   Diagram p362

This pleasant outcrop is composed of a rough granulitic schist, of perfect friction on the slabs, but more blocky lower down. Extraordinary friction makes it possible to climb in the rain, providing that areas of lichen are avoided.

Approach: Lies just over 1km along the minor road that connects Loch Achilty to Strathconon. A lay-by exists directly below the crag. Skirt either side of a bog to reach the slabs, 5mins.

Descent: Easiest by the open grassy gully on the left. The central chockstoned gully provides a Moderate ascent or descent to the upper crag and is useful for the routes on the right.

The crag is simple in layout, being a sweep of clean slabs bottomed by a long overhang. Shorter but steeper slabs extend rightwards from the main crag. The climbs are described first leftwards from the first route, then rightwards from it.

1 Stranger than Friction   30m   VS 5a *   (1990)
An enjoyable climb with entertaining but safe moves leading to some straightforward but unprotected slab padding. The centre of the main crag has two overhanging grooves with a more broken corner just to the right again. A drooping tree lies above the right groove. Strenuous climbing leads to the tree. Climb the initially steep slab directly behind the tree, then up and left to a heather ledge. Climb the short headwall via a niche.

2 Friction with Strangers   30m   VS 5b   (1992)
Climbs the left overhanging groove. Climb the groove to the slab above and steeply up this to easier ground.

3 Stretch   25m   HVS 5b   (1992)
Start a metre left of Friction with Strangers and climb the reachy break to much easier slabs above.

SCATWELL - Upper Slabs

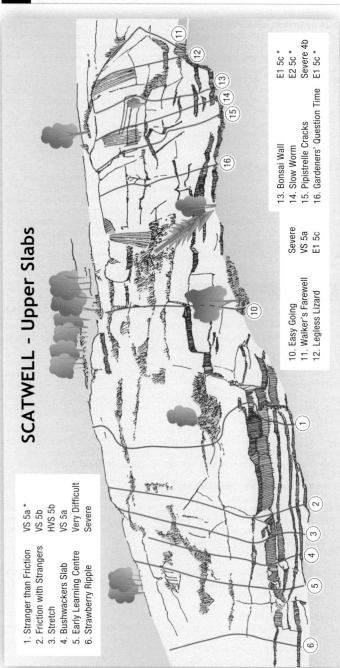

1. Stranger than Friction   VS 5a *
2. Friction with Strangers   VS 5b
3. Stretch   HVS 5b
4. Bushwackers Slab   VS 5a
5. Early Learning Centre   Very Difficult
6. Strawberry Ripple   Severe

10. Easy Going   Severe
11. Walker's Farewell   VS 5a
12. Legless Lizard   E1 5c

13. Bonsai Wall   E1 5c *
14. Slow Worm   E2 5c *
15. Pipistrelle Cracks   Severe 4b
16. Gardeners' Question Time   E1 5c *

John Mackenzie

4 Bushwackers Slab   25m   VS 5a   *(1990)*
Left of Stranger than Friction is an overhanging groove. Start a little left of this at a V-nick in the overhang and right of a similar break. Climb the overhang and little overlap above, then climb the slab between two heather bushes to finish more easily.

5 Early Learning Centre   20m   Very Difficult   *(1990)*
Just to the left of Bushwackers Slab is another break. Climb this taking the obvious line of weakness.

6 Strawberry Ripple   30m   Severe   *(1992)*
Left of Early Learning Centre is a crack trending left over little overlaps. Follow this to the top.

At the extreme left end of the slab is an overlap with a big rectangular block at the foot. The following problems start near the block.

7 Coffin Slab   8m   4c   *(1992)*
Climb over a rectangular block and surmount the overlap above on to the slab. Descend down to the left.

8 Ready and Waiting   8m   5a   *(1992)*
To the right of the block there are a couple of boulders. Step off the upper one on to slab, move up and over the overhang on finger holds on to the slab. There is no protection.

9 Alive and Kicking   10m   5b   *(1992)*
This starts to the right of Ready and Waiting

To the right of Stranger than Friction is a broken corner with a square inset section of slab with an overlap above.

10 Easy Going   30m   Severe   *(1992)*
Start right of the broken corner at a birch tree to reach a section of quite bold slab at the top which follows a cleaned line.

Above and right of the lower slab is a short steep slabby wall bordered on the right by a pale arete. This area is much more technical than the main slab but the difficulties are short, sharp and protected by RPs or equivalent.

11 Walker's Farewell   10m   VS 5a   *(1990)*
Start in a recess below the pale arete. Step over an overlap and climb the arete directly by friction, pleasant and easier than it looks.

12 Legless Lizard   15m   E1 5c   *(1992)*
Climb easily up the right-hand side of the buttress to a pine tree. Follow a thin crack between Bonsai Wall and Walkers Farewell.

13 Bonsai Wall   15m   E1 5c *   *(1990)*
Even the protection is miniature. Left of the pale arete is a small stunted pine. Start beneath this and climb slabs direct to the tree. Now climb the delectably tenuous wall above via hairline cracks.

14 Slow Worm   15m   E2 5c *   *(1992)*
A prominent water washed groove right of centre.

15 Pipistrelle Cracks   15m   Severe 4b   *(1992)*
Follow the quartz dyke just left of Slow Worm to an obvious crack left of its brown streak.

STRATHCONON & GLEN ORRIN

16 Gardeners' Question Time   20m   E1 5c * (1992)
Start at a yew tree. Climb over the overlap to a small pine left of the top wall of Pipistrelle Cracks. Climb the wall left of the crack behind the pine.

HIDDEN CRAG

(NH 372 562)   Alt 130m   South facing   Map p350

The crag is a long smooth black wall set at eighty degrees, split by several striking left-slanting crack-lines, and covered in small positive holds which give fingery yet delicate climbing. It takes drainage from the hillside and requires a day or two to dry out. A smaller outcrop adjoins the main crag to the right. There are two in situ belay spikes in the heather, one near the centre and one nearer the right-hand end of the main crag.

Approach: Take the minor road either along Strathconon and cross the Meig dam to the first large lay-by on the left opposite a Forestry Commission gate or drive along the minor road that leads to Glenmarksie and which leaves the A832 beyond Contin (signposted to Loch Achilty), to the same lay-by. Walk through the gate and follow the forest track which zigzags through the trees to exit through a gate up on the right. Hidden Crag lies down to the left, 10mins.

The routes are described from right to left.

Hoist by Ones Own Bullshit   12m   VS 5a * (1993)
A well protected crux and quick drying. Towards the right end of the main crag is a flat topped pedestal below a left-slanting crack. Start immediately right of the pedestal and climb straight up past fingery flakes. Step right to a ledge finishing up the pleasant rocks above.

Chinese Eyes   25m   HVS 5a * (1993)
A good fingery climb but slow to dry, taking the prominent left-slanting crack. Start as for Hoist... and climb to the crack, making initially difficult moves along it. The crack eases with height and then exits up the wall.

Codgers Wall   12m   Hard Severe 4b (1993)
Start to the right of Shield Bug and climb straight up the wall on surprising holds.

Shield Bug   12m   E1 5b (1993)
To the left of the left-slanting crack is a shield of flakes. Climb these and the wall above.

The Barker   12m   E1 5b ** (1993)
A sustained climb with considerable bite. To the left of the flakes of Shield Bug is a narrow crack. The crack provides most of the protection and some of the holds while the wall to the left provides most of the holds and some of the protection.

Pledge   12m   E1 5b * (1993)
Well to the left of The Barker is a smooth wall with a small overlap and ledge above at about one-third height. Climb up the smooth wall to the ledge and finish directly above. A sustained route.

Creepy-Crawly   12m   E1 5b (1993)
Near the left end of the crag is a slanting crack. Climb the wall to its right direct.

SCOOP CRAG

(NH 374 565)   Alt 200m   South facing   Map p350

A narrow slabby crag of a particularly smooth schist gives some delicate climbing. The crag is a suntrap, drying quickly and climbing is possible for much of the year.

Approach: Take the minor road either along Strathconon and cross the Meig dam to the first large lay-by on the left opposite a Forestry Commission gate or drive along the minor road that leads to Glenmarksie which leaves the A832 beyond Contin and marked Loch Achilty, to the same lay-by. Walk through the gate and follow the forest track which zigzags through the trees to exit by a gate up on the right; Scoop Crag lies up right, allow 15mins.

A sinuous curving scoop is the obvious feature with a steep headwall above, steep rock to the left and a sharp arete to the right. A shorter section of crag lies to the left of a slanting corner. A line of metal fence posts above provide good belays.

The Spike   20m   VS 4b   *(1993)*
A good line on the left of the main crag. Start below a lobe of slab right of a tree and right of the slanting corner. Climb the lobe and gain the scoop. Follow a left-slanting break on hidden holds and climb the left arete to the top.

Fleetstreet Hack   20m   HVS 5a *   *(1993)*
To the left of The Scoop is a short steep wall which gives some fine climbing. Climb the wall via an inset corner and then more easily to the headwall. Step right to its centre and climb the thin wall to a recess and the top. A high side runner in The Scoop's crack can provide the only protection until the recess.

The Scoop   25m   VS 4c **   *(1993)*
A fine delicate climb of considerable interest. The obvious scoop provides the line and is initially delicate padding to a horizontal break. Traverse left along this to the easier slab above and follow this up left to below a crack. Climb up to the crack then finish up it. A less direct variation at Severe misses out the delicate section below the break by moving left.

Brass Monkey   20m   E3 5c   *(1993)*
The bold wall to the right of Fleetstreet Hack. Climb the scoop, then up the slab to the wall. An obscure scattering of small RPs provides the only protection.

Confectionary Arete   20m   Very Difficult   *(1993)*
The attractive right arete of the crag. Start at the break a few metres up level with the top of the lower scoop. Or climb the arete from the base and risk an unprotected slither.

SLAB CRAG

(NH 358 562)   Alt 260m   South facing   Map p350
A small crag of granulitic schist that dries quickly. The climbs are quite bold and small wires may be useful.
Approach: As for Hidden Crag but continue through the woods. Once out, turn left and follow the heathery hillside for over one kilometre, 1hr.

The climbs are described from right to left.

Slab Crack   10m   VS 5a   *(1998)*
Start at an obvious crack-line 2m from the right-hand end of the slab. Climb the crack leftwards, step into a niche and finish up the crack.

Slab Corner   10m   VS 4c   *(1998)*
The main line on the crag is this corner, using its arete at intervals.

Howling Arete   10m   Severe   *(1998)*
The arete forming the left side of Slab Corner has big holds but no protection.

Polythene Pam   10m   HVS 5b   *(1998)*
Start 5m left of the arete at the foot of a small overlap and climb a prominent right-slanting crack-line.

Dandgee Crack   10m   Severe   *(1998)*
The right-slanting crack left of Polythene Pam is easier than it looks.

DAM CRAG

(NH 375 561)   Alt 70m   South facing

A curious roll of silky-smooth schist, punctuated by bore holes and occasional protruding steels it gives limited but exciting friction climbing. Due to its smoothness the slab dries almost immediately after rain. Unsatisfactory climbs have been made either side of the described routes.

Approach: Either along the Strathconon road to the dam at the east end of Loch Meig or along the road that leads from Loch Achilty and branches off on a private road near Little Scatwell. Limited parking at the dam. The crag lies below the north-east corner of the dam and is approached by traversing across scrub at the same level then descending to it, 1min.

Simple Delights   15m   Hard Severe 4b *   *(1991)*
Easier than it looks and very pleasant. Start a little right of the railings and climb straight up the slab via the bore-holes and steels, pulling over the overlap right of a bore-hole thread.

Battle of the Bulge   18m   6b *   *(1991)*
The daunting and flawless slab left of Simple Delights which sports a curved arch like overlap is seemingly protectionless and provides an excellent problem. It has yet to be led. Climb straight up to the overlap and pull through centrally. Cranking the tinies above gives an immediate manicure, be warned!

The Gulf Crisis   18m   HVS 5b *   *(1991)*
The best route here and much easier than it looks takes the slanting shallow corner left of the arched overlap. Traverse left from the railings to the foot of the groove. Climb the groove and pull onto the slab above via two drill steels. Finish more easily over the next overlap.

Thick as a Brick   18m   HVS 5b   *(1991)*
Start left of The Gulf Crisis and climb the wall immediately right of the brickwork to the top.

ASPEN CRAG

(NH 375 558)   Alt 100m   North facing   Map p350

This crag is different to the other local crags in that it is covered in incut holds, particularly in its top half. Despite its bulging nature, the climbing is easier than first appearances would suggest, giving spectacular, often strenuous moves with protection in the horizontal cracks that lie between bulges. Though it faces north, the nature of the crag and the surround of trees ensures much remains dry even in rain with finishes that are juggy enough not to be seriously affected by water.

Approach: Take the minor road down Strathconon and park in the third lay-by on the right west of the Loch Meig dam. The crag is almost obscured by trees and is less than a rope length from the lay-by, 1min.

Descent: Either by abseil or from either end.

The routes start from a shelf which lies above a scrappy lower tier.

Tantalus Groove   18m   E2 5c *   (1991)
The steep groove bounding the left of Icterus gives a bold climb with some delicate moves. Climb the groove of Icterus to just below the flat hold, then traverse left and climb a thin crack to an inset corner on the right, finishing by a tree.

Icterus   20m   E2 5c *   (1991)
Bordering the left of the crag is a beetling buttress which has a steep left-bounding corner-groove. This gives an excellent sustained climb up the lower groove which is both strenuous and technical. Start at the foot of the groove which overhangs the base. Pull up to a tiny pine, then gain the groove with difficulty. Steep moves lead to a prominent flat hold on the edge of the buttress, and the 'dragons teeth' underclings above. Step right to a flake-crack in the corner, then pull over the bulge on the left. Finish somewhat arboreally at a large birch above.

The Dark Side of Noon   20m   E3 5c *   (1992)
Takes the prominent roof left of Shadow Grasper in a direct and sustained manner. The finger slicing roof is followed by long reaches to easier ground. Climb direct to the top bulges and climb these left of a nose.

Shadow Grasper   20m   E1 5b *   (1991)
A very good and somewhat intimidating climb, technically quite easy for the grade. Climbs the bulges just right of Icterus buttress. Start below a small tree and pull over the juggy roof to it. Climb up left to a flat foothold beneath the crux bulge and gain the slab above. Climb up pleasant rock to a short corner which leads to a cramped left traverse and finish at the same tree as Icterus.

Woolly Jumper   20m   E2 5c   (1992)
Start just left of Sloshed in Action and climb through the roof at a break left of that route finishing in the same general line. The grade drops to E1 if the peg on Sloshed in Action is clipped.

Sloshed in Action   20m   E1 5b   (1992)
An exciting excursion over the overhang right of Shadow Grasper. Start at the tree belay at Meridian's start and climb up to the roof (peg runner). Surmount this on the left, then continue more easily up a groove and slab to finish up a short groove.

Gobstopper   20m   E4 5c **   (1992)
This climbs the big roof between Sloshed in Action and Licking the Lip and gives the most exciting and serious climbing here. Start at the tree as for Meridian and climb straight up to the roof and poor peg runner. Gain the lip, swing right to jugs (Friend 1 runner) and pull over. Go straight up the slab to a big tree.

Meridian   20m   VS 5a **   (1991)
An excellent introduction to the crag. Start at the base of the obvious ramp at a tree. Climb a crack behind the tree, then traverse up the ramp which gets gradually harder. Pull over the bulge in a fine position to gain a huge bucket hold on the right, then finish up the slab.

Licking the Lip   16m   HVS 5a *   (1992)
An unlikely looking climb at the lowest limit of the grade. Start to the right of Meridian's tree directly below a block beneath the roof. Climb delicately to it, step right then swing through the overhang on the largest holds on the crag, to finish up the slab above.

Underneath the Arches   15m   E1 5b *   (1991)
Start about 2m left of Mac the Knife and pull right over the roof just left of that route. Continue straight up to finish.

Mac the Knife   15m   E2 5c **   (1991)
A fine strenuous climb up a steep bulging wall 8m left of Burlesque Crack and with a small sapling high up. Start below a shallow corner and climb up to and over a bulge on the left-hand side with difficulty. Climb straight up to the sapling and overcome the top bulge.

Jumping Jack Flash   15m   E2 5c *   (1991)
Start right of Mac the Knife below the widest part of the roof. Pull straight over with long reaches and join the parent route to finish.

Creeping Stealth   15m   VS 4c *   (1991)
The lower bulge is cut by a shallow quartz groove 5m left of Burlesque Crack. Climb up to the bulge and pull over on the left. Climb straight up to a little overhanging corner at the right end of the top bulge and climb this on the left on hidden holds.

Chocks Away   14m   HVS 5a   (1991)
The thinly protected and mossy wall left of Burlesque Crack is climbed via a slight scoop, just right of Creeping Stealth. Step right and climb the bold wall direct.

Burlesque Crack   12m   Very Difficult   (1991)
Near the right end of the crag is a vertical crack, Ascend it with surprising ease.

The Aspen   14m   VS 5a   (1991)
Three metres to the right of Burlesque Crack is a thin crack leading to an overhang with a tiny aspen beneath it. Climb the crack to the overhang, move left and pull over the overhang. Climb up and right much more easily. A fine lower half makes this worthwhile.

Mid-Flight Crisis   12m   VS 5a   (1991)
A wall below the overhang lies 5m to the right of Burlesque Crack. Climb the wall and surmount the overhang centrally, continuing much more easily up the top slab and exiting as for The Aspen. Some good strenuous moves on excellent rock.

Rock and Roll Suicide   10m   HVS 5b   (1991)
Starts well right of Mid-Flight Crisis below a bulge. Climb up to and through the thin bulge and finish easily up a slab.

Uncertain Voyage   55m   E2 **   (1991)
This is the left to right girdle traverse of the crag, offering some spectacular and exciting climbing. Start left of the left edge of the Icterus buttress to belay in a tree a few metres up.
1. 10m 5b Step on to a foothold and climb the arete to flakes. Traverse right to the corner and descend awkwardly to the flat hold on Icterus. Go up right to a belay on Icterus.
2. 10m 5b Cross the slab, then descend the overhang of Shadow Grasper to the little tree below.
3. 20m 5b Traverse right and climb the ramp of Meridian to a cramped position below the top overhang. Swing down right and take a hanging belay by the sapling on Mac the Knife.
4. 15m 5b Traverse horizontally right towards Burlesque Crack but descend to handholds near the crack, then step into it and climb it to the top. It is possible but artificial to cross the break above the overhangs to the far end.

MEIG CRAG

(NH 366 557)   Alt 100m   North facing   Map p350   Diagrams p369, 371

This provides a handy roadside crag about 1km west of the Loch Meig dam on the road up Strathconon and can be easily combined with Glenmarksie for a spot of contrast.

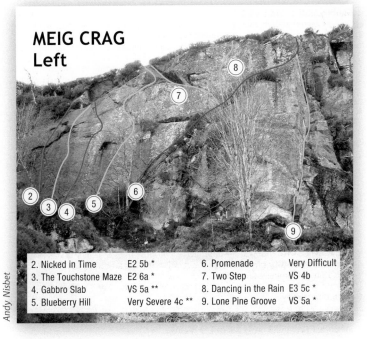

**MEIG CRAG
Left**

2. Nicked in Time	E2 5b *	6. Promenade	Very Difficult
3. The Touchstone Maze	E2 6a *	7. Two Step	VS 4b
4. Gabbro Slab	VS 5a **	8. Dancing in the Rain	E3 5c *
5. Blueberry Hill	Very Severe 4c **	9. Lone Pine Groove	VS 5a *

Andy Nisbet

Approach: After careful parking, make the short but sharp walk to the crag, beset by man-eating potholes between the boulders, 5mins.

Descent: At either end of the crag. Some routes finish on a grass ledge at three-quarters height which can be traversed onto or descended by the slab below Shy Brides Crack. Abseil descents are also common where there are trees.

The crag has a compact section at each end separated by broken ground.

LEFT SECTION

At the left end of the crag is a brown slab which is often wet, Gabbro Slab. This excellent compact slab resembles gabbro in texture and has a prominent thin crack in its left side and up the middle.

1 Sidestep   20m   VS 4c   *(1992)*
The slab is split horizontally by a break that gradually rises to meet the corner of Promenade. Follow the break to a harder section near the corner and finish up this.

2 Nicked in Time   18m   E2 5b *   *(1991)*
A fine route on excellent rock. Climb the left-hand crack to the obvious break, continue up the slab above then trend right up a groove to finish.

3 The Touchstone Maze   25m   E2 6a *   *(1994)*
Between Nicked in Time and Gabbro Slab is a smooth slab which gives the best delicate climbing on the crag. Start centrally and climb to a hole. Step right (side runners in Gabbro Slab) and pull up to a ripple. Step left and climb thinly to the break (crux), then more easily straight up to finish rightwards by a ramp to exit as for Blueberry Hill. This avoids the heather cornice and is also the best exit for Gabbro Slab.

**4 Gabbro Slab   25m   VS 5a ** ∗∗   (1992)
Well protected and on excellent rock. Climb the centre crack of the slab to a fault and step right to the cracks continuation to pull up by a small tree and heather.

**5 Blueberry Hill   25m   Very Severe 4c ** ∗∗   (1992)
The best of the easier lines on the crag, continuously interesting in a fine position. Climb the crack to the right of Gabbro Slab and follow it all the way to the top to exit up the final ramp of Promenade.

6 Promenade   20m   Very Difficult   (1991)
This is the obvious slabby rake at the right end of Gabbro Slab. A 4c variation finish takes the thin crack just left of the final edge.

7 Two Step   20m   VS 4b   (1992)
Climb Promenade to a stance below a steep headwall. Climb up a crack and traverse left into a slanting groove which is followed to the top.

8 Dancing in the Rain   20m   E3 5c ∗   (1992)
A bold and poorly protected route which takes the prominent hanging flake in the headwall. Climb Promenade to the stance and climb the crack to an undercling. The flake is then obvious but so far away!

To the right of Gabbro Slab lies a group of tall birch trees that hide a bay with a vertical corner which is normally very wet. To its left lies a two stepped corner and to its right a prominent jam crack.

9 Lone Pine Groove   25m   VS 5a ∗   (1992)
Between Gabbro Slab and the bay is a prominent corner with a solitary pine at two-thirds height. A very safe and pleasant climb with good jamming at the crux. Climb the corner past the pine to a slab and the top.

10 Correction   20m   VS 4b   (1991)
Climbs the two stepped corner left of the wet corner. Scramble up to a ledge with small trees. Climb the slabby corner past a small tree to a leaning tree. Climb up a crack to an overhang, move left to another crack, then go up to a tree and the top.

11 Erection Crack   20m   HVS 5b   (1991)
Climb a dusty wall to the crack, then the overhanging crack to an awkward landing onto a large flake. Climb a corner to trees. Finish up a short corner to a heather top.

RIGHT SECTION

A long section of broken ground now breaks the crag before reaching the right section, which has some very good crack and wall climbs. The most prominent feature is Meig Corner.

12 Sidewinder   20m   VS 4b ∗   (1992)
This lies up the buttress bounding the left of Limited Liability. Start below the corner and scramble left over blocks. Climb up and trend right towards the edge before traversing left below the final wall to finish on a grass ledge below the short top rocks. Either abseil off or traverse right to the end of the crag at this level.

The bay behind has a couple of obvious finishes, the left-bounding corner being Very Difficult and the chimney Severe.

13 The Wee Nibble   10m   HVS 5b   (1992)
Start from the ledge above the blocks of Sidewinder and climb the wall direct via a crack to the finish of Sidewinder. Only a few moves but in a good position. Low in the grade.

MEIG CRAG
Right

12. Sidewinder	VS 4b *		18. Hind Quarters	E4 6b *
13. The Wee Nibble	HVS 5b		19. Meig Corner	Hard Severe 4b *
14. Limited Liability	E2 5c **		20. The Birch	E2 5c ***
15. Casting Out	E3 5c *		21. Angst Arete	E3 6a **
16. Milk and Alcohol	E4 6a *		22. The Go-Between	VS 5a
17. Yellow Streak	E3 5b **		23. The Balance	VS
			24. Shy Brides Crack	E1 5b *

Andy Nisbet

**14 Limited Liability   20m   E2 5c ** *(1991)*
About 15m left of Meig Corner is a steep right-facing corner which has a vertical crack leading to its base. Climb the crack and corner, making use of the rib on the left, to a fine cave. The original ascent climbed the overhung corner to the left of the vertical crack and traversed delicately right to the corner, wet and 6a.

15 Casting Out   20m   E3 5c * *(1993)*
A sustained and bold pitch up a blank wall with a horizontal crack to the right of Limited Liability. Climb the vertical crack leading into Limited Liability, then traverse right (little protection) to an overhung nose at its end. Surmount the nose and gain an easier groove to finish.

16 Milk and Alcohol   20m   E4 6a * *(1994)*
This is the corner to the left of Yellow Streak. The crux is the poorly protected thin corner below the overhang. Above the overhang, finish as for Casting Out.

**17 Yellow Streak   20m   E3 5b ** *(1992)*
Between the corners of Limited Liability and Meig Corner are a central groove and a yellow streaked one to the right, both overhanging considerably. Climb the yellow streaked groove which gives serious but technically reasonable climbing (vital Rock 3 runner) to a small ledge and protection. Continue straight up the bulge above to a ledge and trees.

18 Hind Quarters   20m   E4 6b * *(1994)*
The overhanging cracked arete to the left of Meig Corner. Bold to start. Start at a spike to the right of the arete and go left into a crack and finish up this.

19 Meig Corner   30m   Hard Severe 4b *   (1979)
The fine corner with a tree at its base. Climb the corner to below a bulge (possible belay). The crux above is short.
Variation: **Severe**
Trend left to the edge at 7m, then climb to the ledge.

20 The Birch   25m   E2 5c ***   (1991)
Right of Meig Corner is a smooth and gently overhanging wall split by a striking crack. A superb and strenuous pitch, well protected.
1. 15m 5c Climb the crack to trees.
2. 10m 5a Climb the nose on the left and heather above.

21 Angst Arete   15m   E3 6a **   (1992)
This is the elegant arete to the right of The Birch, having a gash at three-quarters height. Start left of a birch tree at its foot, climbing flakes left and up to a big hold. Climb the thin well protected crack to below an overhang which is climbed on better holds to a glacis.

22 The Go-Between   10m   VS 5a   (1992)
Climb the short steep wall straight above the tree to the right of Angst Arete, with the crux at the top.

23 The Balance   30m   VS   (1979)
Climb the rust coloured corner right of Meig Corner to a tree and optional belay (4b). On the right is an arete which is followed over a huge balanced block to finish up the crux slab above (4c).

24 Shy Brides Crack   16m   E1 5b *   (1979)
To the right of The Balance and at a higher level is a cracked leaning wall. Go easily up a slab, then climb the hand crack to the top. Sustained, the difficulties increasing with height.

GEOLOGISTS SLABS

(NH 363 556)   Alt 100m   North facing

A small crag composed of the same perfect rough schist as the nearby Gabbro Slab on Meig Crag. Quartz lenses, unexpected holds and superlative friction up rippled slabs characterises the climbing here, not to mention holds composed entirely of massive brown garnets.

Approach: As for Meig Crag but 250m further west, 5mins.

Pure Gold   20m   E1 5b *   (1997)
The best route here giving varied climbing on excellent rock. Start near the left end of the crag close to an open corner and jam up the overhanging wall to a tricky landing above. Step left and climb an undercut wall and slab via twin cracks to a tree. Step left to an overlap and gain a curving thin crack which gives good climbing to the top.

Garnet Wall   20m   Hard Severe 4b   (1997)
The central slab with an overhang at three-quarters height. Start at a tree roughly in the centre and climb the slab via quartz lenses to a garnet encrusted flake. Climb this to an overhang and surmount on good holds to a tree.

BOULDERING

The best bouldering lies on the walls of the Orrin Power Station in lower Strathconon (NH 435 545). The sharp edged schist wall is about 7m at its highest and 50m in length and gives innumerable problems of which the low level traverse is but one. This varies from 4c to 5c and is hardest near the lowest end of the wall. The sandstone of the power station also gives a low level traverse, which is best done without using the horizontal foot 'ledge' at the base, when it then becomes a sustained 6a.

Other bouldering is also possible. Perhaps the best is the 6m crag 300m west of Meig Crag, which is by the road and gives several straight up routes and a traverse. The two large boulders below Gabbro Slab on Meig Crag could give a wealth of problems if cleaned of moss and loose rock.

CREAG GHLAS

(NH 246 545)   Alt 400-500m   South-West facing   Map p350

By far the biggest and most unusual crag in the area. This pair of crags, the East and West Buttresses, lie on the south-west face of Sgurr a' Mhuillin above Glen Meinich. The West Buttress has gained a good reputation, with clean rock, sustained climbing and a sunny aspect.

Approach: Park at NH 282 526 and walk or cycle along the forested glen until below either crag. Climb the 250m of steep ground fairly direct to either crag. Access to East Buttress is from directly below the crag where a new deer fence ends. West Buttress is about 500m beyond East.

EAST BUTTRESS

The East Buttress is a large somewhat triangular ramble of excellent rock with ill-defined lines and much variation but at least 250m in height.

Orient Slab

A very accessible slabby crag on a lower section of East Buttress, 5mins above the end of the fence. It lies about 60m above the track and can be seen as a pale silvery slab on the right of more broken rock. It provides some friction climbing with minimal gear. The routes are described from right to left.

Express   40m   VS 4c *   (2005)
To the right of the smoothest piece of slab is a cracked shallow corner. Climb this (good gear) to step up right beyond and follow a slab to the top.
Variation: **HVS 4c**
From near the top of the lower corner (often wet above), step right on to a steepening arete.

Inspectors Slab   45m   HVS 4c *   (2005)
Climbs the smooth slab and overlap just left. Very bold.
1. 25m 4c Friction up the lowest rocks just right of a heather clump to an easing (runner). Continue up the slab towards the overlap and just before it step left into a heathery gully to a chockstone (this is optional, depending on how brave you feel!).
2. 20m 4c Step back right, climb the overlap and continue to the top of the slab.

Murder and Mystery   20m   HVS 4c   (2005)
Left again is a brown slab. Climb it centrally, optional starts but harder to the left, and continue (a small Friend only) to a break. If the top is wet, traverse right into the heathery gully.

EAST BUTTRESS

Descent: Either on the extreme right of the crag or down the shallow gully that bounds the left edge of the crag, abseiling a short pitch from a handy tree.

STRATHCONON & GLEN ORRIN

Oh Dear   240m   Difficult to VS   *(1967)*
Climbs the left edge of the buttress. The optional crux is the first pitch, if this quite
good pitch is missed out then access can be gained from higher in the gully. Start
just right of the edge at a pair of cracks and follow the left one to a poor belay
above (4b). Follow the edge all the way to the top, rarely more than Difficult to
Very Difficult.

Oh Dearie Me   250m   VS *   *(2002)*
This gives good climbing, taking the best line up the steeper walls to the right of
Oh Dear. Climb the initial pitch of Oh Dear (4b). Move up left and up a slab and
overhang, then continue up easy ground to a steep wall. Climb the right-hand of
two cracks (crux) with fluted finishing holds (4c). Continue up several pitches on
walls separated by easy ground (4a and 4b) to arrive below a bigger wall with large
flakes at its foot. There are several lines, but possibly the best takes the rib left of
a thread around a massive flake. More easy ground leads to a vertical wall right of
an easy chimney. Climb a flake, gain a ledge on the right, step left and climb a
delicate groove (4c). Ahead is another steep but broken wall left of a more massive
one. Climb a shallow corner left of the massive wall to and up a tricky flanged crack
(4b). Scramble to a short V-chimney (4a, avoidable). The final rocks are broken but
the descent gully is most easily reached from the top rather than a precarious
scramble from below them.
Winter: **III,5 ***   *(2004)*
A technical exercise with mainly good protection. It takes the thin discontinuous
turf streaks to the right of the slab edge of Oh Dear and Oh Dearie Me and finishes
up the last two summer pitches of the latter route. Climbed with 60m ropes. The
route is probably only in condition after north-westerly blizzards.
   Turn the short bottom slab on the left and move right to the turf streak. Climb
this past a thin section to belays left of a small tree. Move right to the tree then up
increasingly tenuous slabs to a large cracked block on the left. The following crux
section can be turned on the left by more broken ground. Move right and climb a
groove, then easier ground. Take a steep short wall via a vertical ice slot followed
by easier ground to a large flake below a steep wall. Climb the corner to the right
of the flake and then the awkward crack and chockstone above – as for the summer
description of Oh Dearie Me. Now finish up the optional V-slot as for the summer
route.

Whoops   235m   HVS   *(1991)*
Takes a central line up the buttress, aiming for a rounded buttress below the
headwalls. The first and last pitches are good. As expected on this buttress, many
easier variations exist but the line chosen gives reasonably continuous climbing.
1. 40m 5a Climb the crack in the middle of the slab tongue right of the edge of
the cliff.
2. 35m Continue up right on short slabs and ledges to a ledge below a cracked
slabby wall.
3. 45m Climb the slabby walls, trending right to more walls.
4. 30m Go up the wall left of the belay to a ledge and flake below the central
rounded buttress.
5. 50m Climb the buttress above centrally on good holds, then trend right up a
wall to belay on a wide ledge at a leaning flake.
6. 35m 5a Climb a steep crack immediately above the leaning flake to a slab.
Climb this on the left to the top.
Scrambling leads to the summit.

Blue Moon   265m   III   *(1994)*
A central line up a snow strip to the right of Whoops.
1. 50m Climb the strip to poor belays on the left.
2. 50m Continue in the same line.
3. 30m Climb over a steepening to a shelf.
4. 45m Climb straight up heading for a bay to the right of the rounded buttress of
Whoops, and exit above.

5. 50m Continue to the foot of the headwall. Turn this easily on the right and climb up to a steep pair of blocky grooves.
6. 40m Climb the left-hand groove to a chockstone blocked groove above and surmount this on the left. A good top pitch.

Boulder and Bolder   330m   VS   (1978)
Climbs the right-hand edge of the buttress. Start at the base where terraces cross above smaller crags on the right (cairn beneath a short wall). Go up a wall and ribs above; take an optional crack on the left or trend right to pleasant rocks leading to a cairn. Climb the central crack up a triangular slab (4c) and go right to pale rock and up this to easier ground heading towards an arete. The climbing now follows a more natural line. To the left of this arete is a subsidiary one bounded on its left by a deep chimney. Climb this subsidiary arete and go right to a stance below a steep right wall and corner. Climb the first crack right of the corner to the arete edge, (or the crack to the right, cleaner), then climb straight up a rib left of a vegetated crack to an eyrie stance (4c). Climb the steep corner behind to reach easier ribs and the top (4b). A pleasant ramble, albeit very artificial.

Charge of the White Brigade   165m   IV,6   (1999)
This takes the right-hand face of East Buttress, following a line up the steepest part just to the right of a shallow chimney come gully. Climbed under deep soft snow which hindered rather than helped. The 'charge' was reduced to a frustrating scratching about looking for non-existent cracks in this compact schist. A good freeze would transform it into a pleasant and easier route. Approach by the easy gully that lies below this section of face and start at an easing right of a crag containing a broken chimney, approximately halfway along the face.
1. 50m Climb up to slabs and belay to the right.
2. 60m Continue up the slabs which are more difficult than they look and aim for the corner to the right of the chimney come gully. Climb a steep thin subsidiary corner which contains a couple of small trees.
3. 30m Escape up to the right via the crux wall which is short but hard. Continue straight up and exit over another corner to some flakes on the right below a wall.
4. 25m Climb the flakes and finish up above.

WEST BUTTRESS

Diagram p376
A compact mass of ribs and slabs, somewhat holdless and immaculately sound apart from exfoliating flakes, but often devoid of protection outwith cracks. There is much high angled heather between areas of spotlessly clean rock which in places resembles a high angled Etive Slabs. There are splendid jugs, however, in the most unlikely places (Evening Arete for instance) as compensation, so what looks unlikely may in fact be possible; a close up inspection and a degree of boldness helps. The upper reaches on some routes are lichenous which when wet, makes climbing exacting despite the grade. Cams of all sizes are required, particularly the smallest ones in some of the recent routes.

Descent: Either down the steep heather gully behind Spare Rib, which can be tricky in the wet, or by a shallow scree filled gully on the left of the crag. Abseils can be used for the short routes and after the main pitches of some of the longer routes.

The climbs are described from right to left.

1 Spare Rib   70m   VS   (1979)
The right edge of the cliff is bounded by a shallow gully and consists of a slab and groove with a conspicuous overhang near the top. The right-bounding edge overhangs. Start at the base.
1. 45m 4c Climb slabs on the left to heather, cross to steeper rock on the right, go past a spike to gain a bulge topped groove on the right edge. Climb this and a

STRATHCONON & GLEN ORRIN

376

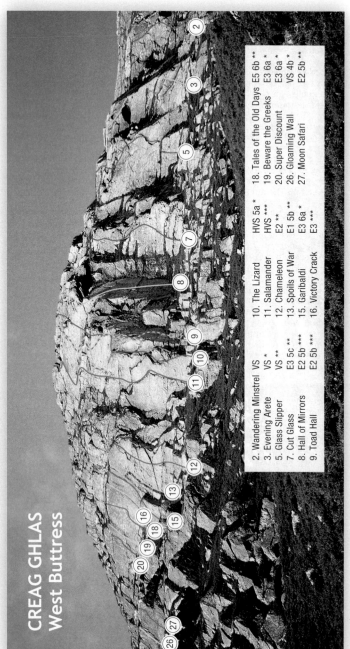

CREAG GHLAS
West Buttress

2. Wandering Minstrel	VS	10. The Lizard	HVS 5a *	18. Tales of the Old Days	E5 6b **
3. Evening Arete	VS *	11. Salamander	HVS ***	19. Beware the Greeks	E3 6a *
5. Glass Slipper	VS **	12. Chameleon	E2 **	20. Super Discount	E3 6a *
7. Cut Glass	E3 5c **	13. Spoils of War	E1 5b **	26. Gloaming Wall	VS 4b *
8. Hall of Mirrors	E2 5b ***	15. Garibaldi	E3 6a *	27. Moon Safari	E2 5b **
9. Toad Hall	E2 5b ***	16. Victory Crack	E3 ***		

John Mackenzie

delicate groove left of a heather filled one. Step right at the top to reach trees but a poor stance.

2. 25m 5a From a tree, go up a steep slab and left to a corner, traverse right under the overhang to an exposed edge and climb a groove to the top. A fine top pitch.

2 Wandering Minstrel   70m   VS   *(1992)*

This takes a pleasantly indirect line to give the easiest climbing on the face. There is little protection.

1. 35m Start as for Spare Rib, then climb broken slabs up and left to a terrace.

2. 35m 4b Above is a pale slab. Climb cracks slanting up right, then traverse up and left across the right-hand of two shallow corners. Continue traversing above the second corner to reach a square-cut sentry box on the left of the buttress. Finish up this.

3 Evening Arete   90m   VS *   *(1992)*

Left of Spare Rib is a fine looking clean-cut edge that appears, when approaching from below, to form the right-hand boundary of the cliff. Start by scrambling up broken slabs to its base.

1. 30m 4b Climb the edge awkwardly to a heathery groove, then move up this to below a prominent bollard on the arete. Climb the slab direct to the bollard.

2. 40m 4c Climb the imposing edge up a crack, then by twin cracks just right, and then boldly directly up the arete until level with the leaning overhang on the left. Follow shallow grooves that cut up left above the overhang to a belay back in the corner (Friend 4).

3. 20m Scramble up the easy gully above.

4 Thumper Groove   90m   IV,5 *   *(1993)*

This is the steep groove between Evening Arete and Glass Slipper. It produces a thin ice streak and gives very good mixed climbing of a technical but well protected nature. Start just right of Glass Slipper and climb the steep technical slab to the groove which is followed to below the steeper groove above (35m). Climb the interesting groove to exit up a narrow chimney (35m). Climb the gully above and surmount a short chimney-crack (20m).

5 Glass Slipper   65m   VS **   *(1992)*

A very fine route taking a good line. To the left of Evening Arete is a steep slab with a prominent curving overlap running up its right side. Start below an introductory slab which has a central crack.

1. 10m 4c Climb the slab by the crack to a flake below the curved overlap. Alternatively climb the right edge of the slab at 5a to the same point.

2. 20m 4c Gain the overlapped corner above by the crack and follow this tenuously to an easing and traverse left along a handrail to a narrow stance. A pitch with an interesting feel.

3. 35m 4c Climb the steepening cracks above which are well protected to a stepped ledge. Climb a spike on the right and traverse left below the top slab avoiding heather to a wide crack (optional belay). Finish easily up this. Scrambling remains.

6 Sweet Charity   115m   VS   *(1980)*

To the right of the central edge of the buttress is a long steep slab. Start at its base.

1. 40m 4c Climb to a ledge (possible belays). Move to its right edge and go up this boldly.

2. 15m 4b Climb the corner behind.

3. 30m Climb steep heather in a corner! Traverse down and right to a grim chimney.

4. 30m Break out right past a flake and up easier corners.

7 Cut Glass   90m   E3 **   *(2003)*

A good but serious route up the narrow slabby buttress to the left of Sweet Charity.

1. 45m 5b Climb the centre of the lower slab as for Sweet Charity to below the

niche where that route escapes (crucial nut runners in the niche). Step left and climb thin moves up the fine slab, past a flake to left-trending edges and go up these to follow a short heather rake to a good crack on the left.

2. 45m 5c A short wall leads to the slab. Step up on this and climb it delicately to a narrow ledge and welcome gear. Continue to the left of a steeper crack on knobbles to vital Rocks 7 and 5 runners at the end of the crack. Climb up and left delicately to a rounded horizontal edge, step up right then straight up to a tricky final move. Finish by 5m of scrambling. Escape up left to reach the descent gully.

8 Hall of Mirrors 80m E2 ***   (1993)
This route has an excellent and sustained first pitch, low in the grade, climbing the centrally placed striated sidewall left of Sweet Charity, leading to a large overhung ledge. Might be ****, but a few weeds are re-growing. The long first pitch is well protected but requires a double rack of Friends, sizes half through to 3. The pitch is often climbed alone, with an abseil descent, usually in situ but take an old sling. Start centrally below an obvious crack system.

1. 50m 5b Climb via cracks and flakes to a small overlap. Pull over and follow the main crack to a hanging belay by a small spike about 6m below the overhung ledge.

2. 30m 4a Continue to the large sloping ledge and move left on to the arete. Climb this by delightful flake-cracks to an awkward step right. Continue up and left to the right end of the heather terrace above. Either scramble down, then up to reach the descent gully or climb the following.

Variation: **Direct Finish   45m   Hard Severe**   (1993)
A scrappy finish but perhaps better than the scrambling option.

1. 15m Climb the line of flakes into a shallow corner and exit left on to a big heather terrace.

2. 30m 4b The wall of slanting cracks above has a projecting triangular block a few metres up. Climb up to and over the block and continue straight up.

9 Toad Hall   145m   E2 ***   (2000)
The right edge of the main slab offers some fine climbing, particularly on the clean first pitch. Start at a ledge beneath the central rib of the West Buttress where a broken groove (The Lizard) forms the right edge of the main slab.

1. 45m 5b Step up right on to a higher ledge, then climb to heather below the right sidewall of the rib. Step left immediately on to the sidewall and climb this, initially close to heather but soon diverging into a crack-line about a metre from the arete. Follow this, sometimes using the crack to the right, to gain the arete at a ledge. Follow the arete (crux, runners in the crack to the right) to a ledge on the left and belay as for The Lizard.

2. 20m 4c Climb the right edge of the main slab (as for The Lizard, before it moves right), then continue on the main slab trending left before returning back right to the top of the slab.

3. 20m Scramble up left to a big flake at the foot of the next slab.

4. 20m 5b Go 5m further left to gain and climb a right-slanting crack to a terrace (an initial runner high on the left is recommended).

5. 40m 4b Climb a line of flakes up the next wall. Go left to a big flake at the base of the final blocky wall. Stand on it and climb the wall above.

10 The Lizard   145m   HVS *   (1967)
Start below the groove forming the right edge of the main slab, same place as Toad Hall. Very bold for its time with the crux pitch still mossy; it deserves a good clean which would make it a two star outing.

1. 20m 4c Climb the crest of the rib to a ledge. Climb the fine curved crack which lies between two mossy corners to a ledge.

2. 30m 5a Continue up the mossy corner above to a ledge.

3. 25m 4c Step right and gain the right edge of the slab above, climbing shallow grooves to a heather exit left of a little tree to gain a terrace.

4. 25m 5a Cross the terrace and climb a slab above on the right, with an initially

delicate section up a right diagonal fault. Trend back up left, step up right, then up left following the fault. An excellent pitch.

5. 45m 4b Cross heather and climb a cracked wall, cross more heather and gain a left-slanting groove. Climb this via a crack, then climb a prominent crack to the top. An interesting pitch making the most of the final walls.

Variation Pitch 2: **The Loop Pitch   30m   E2 5b** ** *(1990)*
Shares some climbing with Toad Hall. Climb the mossy corner for a few metres, then traverse to the right arete. Climb this to a little pink ledge. Make a step left into a blind crack and layback up an improving edge to the ledge.

Variation Pitch 5: **The Big Trundle   30m   E1 5b** *(1992)*
The top pitch of The Lizard is situated above a rocky glacis. Walk left along this to reach an obvious monolithic flake at the top of the wall. Start below this and climb a rightwards-slanting crack over a bulge. Climb easier rock to the right of the flake with a strenuous finish. Quite bold.

11 Salamander   150m   HVS *** *(1994)*
An enjoyable route taking a central line and giving sustained climbing which is quick to dry. To the left of The Lizard is a sweep of smooth slabs split by a prominent dog-leg crack.

1. 40m 4c Climb the crack which is noticeably harder after the dog-leg to a narrow ledge; a superb well protected pitch.

2. 25m 4c Trend up right on hidden edges to a narrow heather ledge and creep left along this to some holds. Climb the bold slabby wall above, exiting left along a diagonal crack.

There are two methods of climbing the next pitch.

3a. 40m 5a Climb up to hollow flakes and go straight up to a curved overlap. Traverse left under this and pull over on the left to shelves. Climb up a delicate wall to a narrow rake and a hollow flake right of a hidden corner.

3b. 45m 5b Step right and climb a thin crack which is difficult for the first 6m, but eases with the lessening of angle. Take a line directly to the overlap above and turn this delicately by the right edge. Easy climbing up left leads to the hollow flake.

4. 25m 4c On the left is a hidden corner; climb up the edge and step left (often wet but possible) on to the slab and undercut into the corner. Climb this excellent corner with interest to the rock glacis below the top wall.

5. 20m 4b Left of a big block is a superb narrow chimney which narrows to a crack. Layback the edge, which is easier than it looks, to finish up a short steep crack.

Variation Pitch 4: **Legoland   20m   E3 5c** *(1998)*
A thin direct line up the slab to the right of the corner. Climb an incipient crack with occasional deviations out right. Poorly protected and tenuous.

12 Chameleon   60m   E2 ** *(1998)*
Left of the heathery corner that lies left of the Salamander slab is another steep slab with a shallow right-trending curved overlap. The route takes shallow cracks running straight through this feature. The first pitch is optional but avoids heather. Start below the overlapped slab to the right.

1. 15m 4b Climb two short slabs to move left to a short crack below the overlap.

2. 45m 5c Climb up to and through the overlap (small Friends) to the base of a thin crack. Climb this well protected crux to a wobbly flake and small ledge. Move up rightwards through an overlap and make a delicate step up right to the edge which is followed more easily to the heather ledge. An excellent sustained pitch. Either scramble off leftwards along the exposed ledge or continue to the top as for Victory Crack and Salamander.

13 Spoils of War   45m   E1 5b ** *(1995)*
This is a fine pitch up the very pronounced right-hand crack near the right edge of the long smooth slab left of Chamelion. The terrace below it can be reached by climbing a chimney come corner or more easily by the next corner left, then scrambling up a break in the wall. Start to the right of the crack to avoid heather. Traverse left by a flake hold to the main crack. Climb the crack past a wide section

to a little tree and step left to the crux section which is parallel and holdless but very well protected. Now scramble off left along a narrow ledge or continue climbing as for Victory Crack.

14 Peak Freans' Trotskyite Selection   15m   HVS 4b/6a * (1998)
This is the fine narrow slab immediately below and right of Victory Crack to which it makes an obviously direct lower pitch. The boulder problem start is climbed from the base at 6a or avoided on the left at 4b.

15 Garibaldi   40m   E3 6a * (2000)
A very fine thin crack immediately left of Spoils of War provides some thin moves. Climb Peak Freans' to the base of the thin crack (15m). Climb the crack, which is well protected by very small cams, to the ledge (25m). Rather close to Spoils of War but feeling quite independent at the crux. Scramble off left.

16 Victory Crack   70m   E3 *** (1995)
Next left is a straight crack with the crux where it should be – right at the top! The easier pitches 2 and 3 are rarely climbed. A soft touch at the grade.
1. 25m 6a Climb the crack, narrow and sustained but well protected by wires and small Friends. An abseil point is usually in place, or optional scramble left if desired.
2. 20m Step right from the belay and gain a crack that runs right of a roof forming a hidden corner. Climb the corner.
3. 25m 4b Climb up the broken slab behind the stance, reaching an unprotected quartz studded slab above which is followed to below a curving crack left of the corner pitch of Salamander. Scramble off leftwards to reach the glacis above or finish up the final two pitches of Salamander.

17 The Unknown Soldier   25m   E7 6b * (2002)
An eliminate offering extremely bold slab climbing on impeccable rock. Start 2m left of Victory Crack and just to the right of Tales of the Old Days. Climb directly up the bald slab to a quartz intrusion at 12m (RP 5). Stand on the quartz and make a long reach for a fingerhold, make a rockover on to this and stand up (crux). Reach a good hold on the left and clip the peg on Tales of the Old Days. Stand on a good hold and move diagonally left, then up to a horizontal break. Step left to a vertical crack and finish up this (as for Tales of the Old Days).

18 Tales of the Old Days   30m   E5 6b ** (1998)
A bold thin line to the left of the Victory Crack area. Start in a slabby recess below a 'crescent moon' crack above. Climb the thin slab to gain the right edge of the crack and go up this to a good pocket at half-height (first good gear). Continue up and right to an awkward mantelshelf where a long stretch or dyno gains the top break and poor cams. Follow this leftwards to a short finishing crack. Scramble off left.

19 Beware the Greeks   20m   E3 6a * (1998)
Climbs the thin crack-line 4m left of Tales of the Old Days. Climb the slab and hanging crack which can take an assortment of rather dubious gear, then climb the crack mainly by its right-hand side.

20 Super Discount   20m   E3 6a * (1998)
On the slab left of Beware the Greeks are two sets of twin cracks. This route climbs the right-hand set. Start lower down than on Beware the Greeks. Climb the left-hand crack initially to a tricky transfer to the right-hand crack, which is climbed with increasing interest to the crux moves at the top. The smallest Camalot or equivalent is required to protect the crux, otherwise add a grade.

21 Prix Choc   20m   E2 5c (2000)
Climbs the right-hand of the left set of twin cracks.

Moon Safari, E2, Creag Ghlas. Climber Robin McAllister

Below the left-hand slabs is a smaller subsidiary slabby wall seamed by cracks and with a square-cut recess near its right-hand end. Gain this by traversing heather rakes below the start of the other routes. Described left to right.

22 Centipede Crack   20m   HVS 5b   (1994)
On the left side of the slab are a heathery wide crack and a small pedestal. Start below a thin crack to its right, the leftmost of three cracks. Climb thinly up to the crack (crux) and more easily up the crack. Finish delicately.

**23 Spider in a Dark Dark Room   20m   E1 5b ** **   (1998)
The thin central crack which is sheer fun to climb, lacking only length.

24 Anonymous Chimney   20m   VS 4c   (1998)
The rather dirty and awkward right-hand crack.

25 Glazed and Confused   20m   E1 5b *   (1998)
The wide wall to the right of Anonymous Chimney is central to the crag and this

line climbs the middle section, easily at first, then over a bulge to a hairline crack and up this to a nubbin, a good ledge and the top.

26 Gloaming Wall   20m   VS 4b * *(1994)*
Left of the recess at the right end is a heathery crack. Start to the right and pull through an overlap. Climb a thin crack most pleasantly to the top.

27 Moon Safari   25m   E2 5b ** *(1998)*
An excellent and unlikely route up the largest buttress at the right end of the crag, giving technical and intricate climbing, with a serious section. The blank looking lower section is climbed left of centre, holds appearing when least expected. Move slightly rightwards to the upper section which is climbed right of centre, moving left near the top.

28 Ra-Ra Rabbit   10m   VS 5a *(1998)*
The small buttress to the right of Moon Safari which sports a ledge at two-thirds height. It has good but unprotected moves.

29 Explosive Joseph   10m   E1 5b *(1998)*
The small rightmost buttress on the crag. Climb the wall to the right of an obvious black water streak.

SGURR A' COIRE-RAINICH

(NH 247 570)   Alt 700m   North facing

Climbing on this mountain requires the dedication to walk across acres of peat-hagged heather. It may be easier to combine it with a more pleasant hillwalk over the five tops of Sgurr a' Mhuillin.

Lady's Gully   180m   II/III *(1971)*
The gully can be seen from Achanalt on the main A832 road between Garve and Achnasheen. The lower section is narrow and gives some steep ice over several pitches. Near the top the gully forks. Both forks have been climbed.

The buttress left of Lady's Gully has also been climbed. It gives indistinct climbing with optional difficulties at about Grade II.

MEALL NA FAOCHAIG - GLEANN MEINICH

NH 235 542)   Alt 400m   North-West facing   Map p350

The west end of the ridge of this hill has a broken heathery crag opposite the West Buttress of Creag Ghlas at a similar altitude. The only worthwhile conditions would be under consolidated snow, a rarity.

Approach: As for Creag Ghlas along the track in Glen Meinich but cross the burn below the crag.

Meinich Buttress   150m   III,4 *(1999)*
The line taken follows the steepest part of the crag where a shallow groove cuts up the final section just left of an apparent edge. Concave mixed ground of ice, rock and heather leads to the groove, marked by a few small trees. A broken icefall ran down the left side and gave steep awkward climbing with the crux at the top. Easy ground lies above.

CREAG DUBH

(NH 280 515)   Alt 150m   North-West facing   Map p350

This steep valley slope in upper Strathconon has four burns which in periods of frost form discontinuous icefalls of between 150 and 200m. A sustained moderate frost produces the most ice. A convenient footbridge crosses the river below the Allt Mhairi and gives access to the other falls unless the river is frozen, when it can be crossed directly.

Allt Mhairi   III/IV *
This is the burn to the left (north-east) of Creag Dubh, easily identified as being opposite the footbridge. It only forms in sustained cold weather, being lower than the other icefalls here and having a large quantity of water. It usually sports two good icefalls at the top section of the gorge; a lower 25m pitch and an impressive 40m final fall. The grade will vary according to build up

Leftfall   III *
Between the Allt Mhairi and Centrefall are two other streams. Leftfall is the one on the left which splits the highest part of the face and forms readily. Minor pitches, some steep, lead to the top section. This forms a long narrow ice hose of around 30m. From the top of Centrefall it is possible to traverse left to reach the interesting top section of this route.

Centrefall   IV,4 **
In the middle of the face are two prominent narrow streams with a steep slabby right-facing icefall above the left-hand stream. This stream contains much interest with amusing minor pitches and at least two long and steep 30m icefalls mid-way. The stream leads into a bay containing the main icefall. This forms more readily than the streams themselves and can be approached from the right if necessary. The icefall gives 60m of ice with three near vertical sections, started from the central narrow runnel. Two bulging sections above lead to the top and offer excellent climbing.

Rightfall   II/III
This lies just to the right and usually forms more readily. A series of icefalls of between 10 and 20m leads to the summit. A short traverse left then leads to the top icefall of Centrefall.

ALLT GLEADHRAICH

(NH 274 510)   Alt 150m   North-West facing   Map p350
The Strathconon Experience   III **   *(1995)*
Due to the volume of water and low altitude, this requires a sustained hard frost to fully freeze. The burn follows a steep sided deep gorge for its lower section which provided four escalating ice pitches separated by flat iced pools which provide excitement in their own way. The scenery is excellent throughout and the excursion highly recommended providing the intervening pools are frozen. Originally climbed on a day when the temperature never rose above -17, all the pitches were on superb ice that took screw runners readily.

Left Branch   40m   III/IV
If the main route is incomplete, then a narrow icefall forms low down on the left bank, variable in grade and length.

BAC AN EICH - COIRE TOLL LOCHAIN

(NH 232 486)   Alt 600m   North facing   Map p350
This scalloped corrie lies above Gleann Chorainn and presents a moderately graded slope of 150m in vertical height, the potential home of countless Grade I and II variations depending on conditions. On the upper right-hand side of the corrie is a much steeper section of about 100m; this can be identified by a thin but prominent icefall. Well right of this is a wide shallow gully with a solitary ice pitch in narrows

at the start. A nose on the extreme left of the corrie forms the south-east spur from the summit (NH 232 485), giving the following line.

Angels Delight   100m   II   (1994)
The nose has a central rocky spur, shorter than it looks. Start centrally where initially awkward slabs weave through overlaps. This promising start is not sustained and easier ground leads to a steeper turfy rib just left of a pronounced gully. Climb this rib to the top.

Cop-Out Buttress   200m   III   (2003)
Described and graded for lean and well iced conditions. Follow an iced stream and steep snow to the thin icefall. Avoid this by a hidden ramp on the right which leads to a short vertical step. Step left, then pull over to reach a narrow ledge which leads left to the snow funnel above the icefall. Follow this to the top.

Funnel Gully   200m   II   (2003)
The wide gully to the right of Cop-Out Buttress. Easy ground leads to the constriction which gives a good 20m ice pitch. Steepening snow then leads past another couple of short ice steps, the last on an outcrop that divides the gully into two exits. If the lower ice pitch is banked out then the route is no more than Grade I.

Glen Orrin

CREAG A' GHLASTAIL

(NH 265 470)   Alt 450m   South-East facing   Map p350

A vegetated crag, but with some fine ice lines in cold weather. The rock is a flaky mica-shist which is prone to sudden failure, although there is some good rock. Despite the southerly aspect the crag is quite slow to dry, three days being adequate for all except the drainage lines. Protection is generally scanty, with a paucity of decent cracks. Restrictions only allow climbing from the end of August to the end of March. Given these factors, it remains to be seen whether or not the crag develops as there are some fine looking lines.

Approach: From near the head of Strathconon leave cars before the bridge crossing the Conon and walk past the keepers house at Inverchoran. Continue over the pass between Beinn Mheadhoin and Carn na Cre on a landrover track which curves round to the foot of Creag a' Ghlastail, 1hr.

Descent: Descents off the crag is problematic. so far the best way weaves a line down steep heather shelves below and between broken crags that stretch along the hillside left of the left-boundary gully.

The crag rises above a stand of Scots pine and forms a steep 120m face of rock and mixed vegetation. It is bisected by a deep wide gully (Central Gully) that has an impressively unfriendly right wall and a high massive buttress on the left, bottomed by a long vegetated ramp rising up to the left. Below this, steep mixed vegetation surrounds a clean black slab and this mixed section ends in a steep clean buttress with a pair of drainage faults on the left of the face. This is bounded by a prominent gully with an initial waterfall pitch (Waterfall Gully). Above this, the right wall of the gully forms the most continuously steep area of clean rock, but can only be reached by climbing the waterfall pitch first. Right of the big central gully the crag becomes more vegetated and sports a stream that falls in a series of cascades down the face. The stream that cascades down the face is the Allt a' Ghlastail with the source from the lochan on Beinn Mheadhoin and has been called Orrin Falls. The left bank of Waterfall Gully involves escapades up sixty degree heather and wet rock and requires a high nerve factor. It is capped by steep rock and the only feasible escape (at half-height) is along a diminishing ledge where a small tree lies above a shallow gully. It is not possible to approach Waterfall Gully from this side.

Waterfall Gully   150m   IV,4 **   *(1994)*
On the left of the crag is this deep gully which offers unusual positions and fine
technical climbing. Vertical height not length is given. Though it can hold
continuous ice, little is visible from below. A wet autumn followed by a cold spell
is ideal. The initial chimney pitch gives about 10m of vertical ice, followed by
easier ground and then another step. More easy ground leads to a groove of about
20m which can be very hard in thaw conditions. More easy ground leads to an
amphitheatre. Climb the fine 30m icefall to below the enormous wedged
chockstone and cave. The cave is blocked except on the right where a short but
hard groove leads to the roof of the chockstone. The gully is hemmed by walls on
this side so walk along the roof of the chockstone to a cave below a fine icefall.
Either escape tamely up a ramp to the right or climb the icefall, 12m, to easier ice
and the top.

The Curates Egg   120m   VS   *(1989)*
Takes the most feasible line on the crag, the right-bounding edge of Waterfall Gully.
It is much steeper than initial appearance and there are the inevitable areas of
vertiginous heather. However there are some good moments, particularly on
pitches 3 and 4.
1. 15m Climb the flaky slab immediately right of the gully and left of the steeper
but more broken skyline rocks to a heather shelf.
2. 20m Traverse right under a tottering shelf, then stand on it from the right.
Traverse back left on better rock, then follow up and back right via a slab and
corner to reach a rectangular heather ledge.
3. 35m Climb the bounding corner of the shelf, then straight up to the central
fault-line above. Climb this steep section on flake holds to an easing and broken
ground. Scramble up and right on steep heather to a bay with small trees.
4. 20m 4c Climb the steep central break initially via the recessed jamming crack
on the right to a loose chockstone. Step left into a parallel corner and up to a steep
exit on to an easy groove.
5. 30m Step on to the rib on the right and go pleasantly up this to the heather
slopes above.

Descend by a longish traverse left across the top of Waterfall Gully and below the
top tier of crags, then heather rakes lead back down towards the gully and the
bottom.

Ghlastail G.T.X.   210m   V,5 ***   *(1990)*
An up and coming classic, with good rock belays and stances throughout; a very
fine climb whose interest increases with height. The grading assumes the top pitch
is climbed direct, otherwise Grade III. Due to its low altitude, a week's frost is
needed to bring the climb into optimum condition. Follow the burn through the
trees to the first pitch, a slabby icefall. Climb this to easy ground, then a couple of
short ice falls to the base of the mid-height slabs. Climb these in two pitches to a
bay below a narrow ice hose which forms a distinctive gully when seen from below.
Climb this to an amphitheatre below the top pitch. Take the superb ice pitch direct
just right of hanging icicles (25m, crux). This pitch can be avoided on the left by a
steep ice funnel leading to a possibly large cornice or by a tamer right traverse out
of the amphitheatre.

Three Stroke Gully   120m   II   *(1991)*
To the right of the trees and near the right-hand side of the face lies a shallow gully
which is half ice and half snow. This is the line, giving pleasant little bulges which
are not without interest. An ascent in 1996 reported Grade IV.

STRATHCONON & GLEN ORRIN

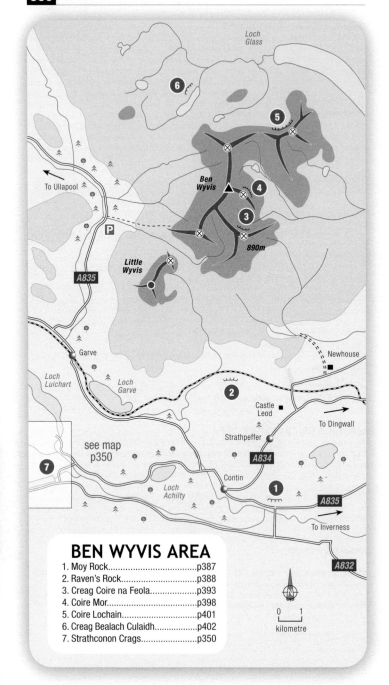

386

Loch
Glass

6

5

Ben
Wyvis

4

3

890m

Little
Wyvis

To Ullapool

P

A835

Garve

Newhouse

Loch
Luichart

Loch
Garve

2

Castle
Leod

To Dingwall

Strathpeffer

see map
p350

A834

7

Contin

Loch
Achilty

1

A835

To Inverness

A832

BEN WYVIS AREA

0   1
kilometre

BEN WYVIS AREA

First to be described are several low level crags south of Ben Wyvis, mostly around Contin. Next is Ben Wyvis itself with three main climbing corries. Finally are four smaller low level crags, widely spread but generally north of Ben Wyvis.

NORTH SUTOR CLIFFS

(NH 813 686)

The rock is a smooth and brittle undifferentiated metamorphic rock with, unfortunately, the worst properties of both granite and sandstone. Varying from brick red to yellow it is an artist's dream but, climbing wise, only some of it is solid and reliance on any single hold is risky. Protection is only as good as the rock though it can look quite convincing at times. High angled grass above the crags encouraged the pioneers to carry a short ice axe, which may prove useful.

Approach: From Nigg Ferry take a farm road east to a lay-by before the hill. Go to the beach, then a rocky scramble (at high tide) leads to grassy cliffs. The route below takes a line up the next section of more continuous crag, marked by a bright yellow arete and a right-facing chimney above a shallow cave. This cave bottoms a cleaner overhanging section of cliff that looks clean but not that enticing.

Shake, Rattle and Roll   60m   HVS 4b   *(1998)*
The cave provides two options to gain the right-facing chimney above, either straight up below it, or harder, better (and solid), climb the undercut left-slanting ramp that leads into it. Climb the chimney to a shallow cave (20m 4b). Now traverse left across the bright yellow arete and into another shallow scoop. The rock above is quite steep and very loose, crux, and leads on to the grass field which was front pointed up to an easing where a belay was taken on a broom bush and axe pick (40m, 4a).

MOY ROCK

(NH 496 550)   Alt 100m   South facing   Map p386

Moy Rock is a conglomerate cliff above the main road (A835T) just east of Contin. It is now becoming rather hidden by forestry development. The conglomerate is quite sound but the climbing is usually bold with runners often placed around the protruding 'pudding stones'. This requires long tapes and heavy karabiners. The crag also provides some low level traverses which, being sheltered, might provide some sport on a rainy retreat from the north. For reasons of conservation there is no climbing between April and July.

Approach: Cars can be left in the lay-by opposite the rock and a little further to the east. Walk back to a side road and gate and turn almost immediately left up a track, all this within 100m of the main road. Take the first fire break on the right and plug steeply up to the crag. A bird limed niche is a prominent central point and lies left of the arrival point, 5mins.

Descent: At either end.

In the centre of the face is a bird limed wall, bounded by chimney-lines and walls. On the left again a long slabby ramp forms an open corner.

Harderthanitlookscrack   40m   Severe   *(1972)*
The long ramp gives slab and corner climbing, vegetated at the top.

BIRD LIME BUTTRESS

This is the lime splashed wall between the two chimney faults. The next climb takes the deep chimney on the left.

Slanting Crack   40m   Difficult   (1972)
Follow the deep chimney left of the slab over chockstones to a bay. Straddle the chimney to a ledge. Climb the short wall above on the left to the top. A harmless introduction to conglomerate climbing.

Boggle   50m   VS *   (1978)
To the right of Slanting Crack is a slab.
1. 4b Climb the curving groove and crack to the slab and take this centrally to belays on the left below the top wall.
2. 4b Climb the steep plinth right of centre in an exposed position to reach an easy arete. Finish up Slanting Crack.

Speleological Nightmare   30m   Very Difficult   (1978)
To the right of Bird Lime Buttress is a left-slanting chimney, bordered to the right by a tree-filled gully. Start in the left chimney, climb a groove and thread a tunnel to a cave and belays. Struggle through a tight hole to reach a saddle. Finish up a wide crack and exit up Slanting Crack.

Magnificrack   50m   E3 **   (1978)
Right of the tree-filled gully is a curving flake-crack leading to a vertical wall, which gives a magnificent but serious route.
1. 5b Climb the bulging flake to its apex (long sling runner). Follow the small ragged crack up the wall to a horizontal break, crux, climb the overlap on the left and then up a slab to a small tree. Belay on a larger tree to the left.
2. Continue up the short wall above the small tree to the top.

Perigrination   40m   VS 4c   (1978)
Climb the bulging wall at the right end of the cliff to a vegetated bay. Exit on the wall right of the crack.

Perhaps rather more tempting than dicing with pebbles are three low level traverses which are all above soft grass landings. These are well sheltered behind trees, so are rarely wet, even in the rain.

Traverse 1   24m   5a
From the fire break, walk right below a vertical wall to reach a holly. Traverse back left to the gully with the crux at the end.

Traverse 2   15m   6b
From Traverse 1, walk left past the gully and start left of the slanting lower overhang. A few loose metres leads to a technical wall and hole 3m up. The crux is descending and traversing left from this.

Traverse 3   30m   5c **
The traverse of the bird limed wall is the most solid of the traverses and the best. Start by a leaning tree and continue past corners until the delicate main wall is reached. The delectable pebbles are then skipped over lightly to the end. It can also be traversed from right to left and at an easier lower level.

RAVEN'S ROCK

(NH 463 606)   Alt 120m   North facing   Map p386   Diagram p390

This extensive schist crag lies about 2km west of Achterneed along the Dingwall to Kyle railway line, 9km from Dingwall. The routes are steep with generally sound rock and were good, but the crag has not become popular, so the vegetation has regrown and routes will require cleaning on abseil for enjoyable ascents. The original stars are quoted and relate to their cleaned state. For reasons of conservation there is no climbing on this crag from April to July.

Approach: Either walk near the railway line from the former Achterneed station, or along a private road south of this, to join the track for the last 500m. Cars should be left at Achterneed, 30mins.

Descent: For most of the climbs this is via the easy but vegetated shallow gully behind the white wall, at the west end of the crag.

The cliff is in two parts. The top overhanging section of blackish rock is separated from a shorter overhanging lower wall by a grass slope. Proceeding west, roofs and cracks border a steep buttress which is in turn bordered by a corner. A black wall beyond is cut by a ramp. Further left are steep walls, then a roof topped corner. Next come a white wall and a black wall, separated by a tree-crowned ledge, which diminish in height westwards.

Most of the better climbing lies on the more accessible right side, but to get to the first climb gain the grass slope from the right to reach a minor jutting buttress beneath the great top wall. This minor buttress has a central chimney.

1 Bone Idle   15m   HVS 5b   *(1980)*
Climb the thin crack right of the chimney, step right to a ledge, crux, then go left and finish up a chimney.

2 Scorpion   50m   VS 4b   *(1971)*
A rather poor climb which takes the large slabby corner left of the prominent steep buttress which is the first major feature of the lower right section of the crag. Climb either the slab or the crack to reach a fine cave formed by blocks. Step onto a yard arm and climb a groove to mossy slabs and tree belays.

3 Tombstone Buttress   70m   E1 *   *(1978)*
This varied climb takes the fine steep buttress right of Scorpion.
1. 5b Start in the gloomy pit at the bottom right and climb the black crack and roof to a slab. Go left across the slab to a chockstone and ledge above. A short wall leads to a thin grass terrace which is traversed left to the 'tombstone' belay.
2. 5b Climb the fine steep crack to a large block. Follow the diagonal right-slanting crack; near the end, hand-traverse into a corner and spike. Climb the corner to a ledge.
3. 4b From the ledge step left to a crack splitting blocks and belay in Scorpion's cave. Finish up Scorpion.

4 Obituary   70m   E2 ***   *(1980)*
Start in the recessed right corner of Tombstone Buttress.
1. 5c Climb cracks on the left to a large roof. Traverse left to the front of the buttress and continue to a thin crack. Up this (crux), to follow holds leading to a cracked bulge on the right of the buttress. Climb the exposed crack and bulge to the second belay of Tombstone Buttress.
2. 4b Finish up Tombstone Buttress.

5 The Sting   100m   E1 *   *(1978)*
This climb takes the obvious right-slanting hanging ramp that cuts the black wall right of Tombstone Buttress.
1. 5b Climb a slab to below the ramp and take the crux bulge above on spikes to gain the ramp. Follow the easiest line on the ramp to a tree belay.
2. 4b Follow the easier slab to an overhung niche and the tree above. Climb a bulge and corner behind the tree, step right, then go up a wall of cracked blocks to a tree belay.
3. 5a Climb the steep awkward crack to a large birch tree.

6 Roots   65m   Severe   *(1978)*
1. To the right of Sting is a broken parallel groove. Climb it and traverse on to a good ledge.
2. 4a Step up right (crux) onto a prominent block, then traverse right over a good slab. Near its end climb a wall to belay below Sting's third pitch. Escape right.

BEN WYVIS AREA

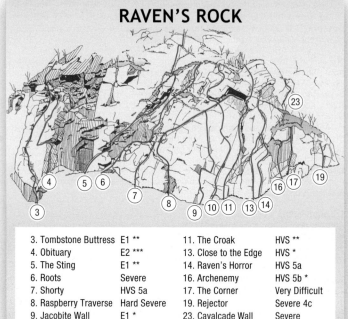

RAVEN'S ROCK

3. Tombstone Buttress	E1 **	
4. Obituary	E2 ***	
5. The Sting	E1 **	
6. Roots	Severe	
7. Shorty	HVS 5a	
8. Raspberry Traverse	Hard Severe	
9. Jacobite Wall	E1 *	
10. Kingfisher	HVS ***	
11. The Croak	HVS **	
13. Close to the Edge	HVS *	
14. Raven's Horror	HVS 5a	
16. Archenemy	HVS 5b *	
17. The Corner	Very Difficult	
19. Rejector	Severe 4c	
23. Cavalcade Wall	Severe	

John Mackenzie

7 Shorty 15m HVS 5a   *(1979)*
Right of Roots is an overhanging wall. Start below trees and gain the right-slanting
line, surmounting the crux bulge beyond a small tree and finishing rightwards.

8 Raspberry Traverse 70m Hard Severe   *(1978)*
1. 4b Right of Shorty is an inset corner. Climb this, step left and up an awkward
little wall to belay below trees.
2. 4b Traverse right around the corner and continue to a small gnarled tree. Go up
left past a niche to tree belays.
Variation: **True Finish VS 4c**
On the second pitch continue in the same line past the tree to the large corner (see
The Croak, Route 11).
Variation: **Direct Start E1 5b** *   *(1980)*
Climb the centre of the steep wall to the right to a flake, step left onto a thin ledge
and traverse into the top of the inset corner.

9 Jacobite Wall 50m E1 *   *(1979)*
Right of Raspberry Traverse is the steep wall of the Direct Start and right again a
grass mound which hides a fine cave. Jacobites are reputed to have hidden here
after the '45.
1. 5b Start left of the cave and go up to a ledge and flake. Step right to a long
ledge and traverse right to a break. Go up left to a crack and climb past a small
bent tree to belay in a crack.
2. 4b Continue up the cracked corner and finish as for Raspberry traverse.

10 Kingfisher 50m HVS ***   *(1978)*
Takes the attractive wall left of the big corner.

1. 5a Start at the raised grass mound and climb a short wall to follow the crack to a small tree. Go back up left and mantelshelf onto a slab (crux). Step up right and then climb directly up the wall to belay well left of the big roof.
2. 4c Follow a diagonal line up the overhanging headwall, starting by some blocks to reach a jutting ledge. Step up left to finish up a short wall.

11 The Croak 50m HVS ** (1978)
This climbs the steep corner right of Kingfisher.
1. 5a The lower corner is awkward and sustained but well protected. Belay on the sloping grass ledge.
2. 4b Climb the cracked slab above and swing around the corner to a tree belay.
3. 4b From the flake ledge, either climb the loose wall above on the left, or walk along the ledge to finish.

12 Fancy Tickler 30m VS (1980)
To the right of The Croak is a steep wall split by three cracks.
1. 4c Climb the short left crack to a grass ledge and tree.
2. 4c Climb the thin crack right of the arete, crux, to trend left to the tree belay on The Croak.

13 Close to the Edge 35m HVS * (1980)
1. 5a Climb the central crack in the wall, just right of Fancy Tickler to the tree belay above.
2. 4c Gain a ledge, climb up right to a niche, step right and up the crack to belay as for The Croak. Traverse off right.

14 Ravens Horror 15m HVS 5a (1978)
This climbs the third (central) crack in the wall to a jutting hold. Traverse out right to the edge and finish up this. A bold, sustained little climb.

15 Ravens Squawk 90m VS (1970)
The first and still the loosest climb on the cliff, but with some good moments. The length excludes easy ground.
1. Climb the slab and corner right of Ravens Horror to the ledge and tree belay.
2. 4a Gain the ledge and climb the wall just right of the niche of Close to the Edge to reach the flake ledge.
3. 4b Climb the crack in the roof above, crux, then the loose wall to the descent gully.
4. 4b Scramble across the gully to the back tier of cliffs. Climb either the corner or the slab to its right to step left to a tree.
5. 4b Scramble easily up the gully to a shallow groove, climb this to a ledge, traverse right to a V-crack and exit up this.

16 Archenemy 20m HVS 5b * (1978)
Right of Ravens Squawk is a slab with a crack splitting a steep wall. Climb the crack to a small tree and niche and move right, crux, to a ledge. Traverse right to a corner to finish.

17 The Corner 15m Very Difficult (1978)
Climb the lower slab and then move into and up the pleasant corner on the right to the top.

18 Midgit Corner 5m Severe 4c (1978)
The boulder problem corner left of Rejector.

19 Rejector 20m Severe 4c (1971)
An amusing short problem right of The Corner where a slabby V-groove lies right of a short steep wall. Go up the wall to enter the groove, not easy, then easily up the groove.

20 Ejector   7m   VS 5b   *(1981)*
The steep rib right of Rejector. Gain the spike, then step left to finish. A good problem, not so easy on first acquaintance.

21 Acceptor   10m   Very Difficult   *(1978)*
The pleasant groove and slab to the right of Ejector.

22 The Chimney   10m   Hard Severe 4b   *(1978)*
This climbs the good chimney-groove which lies around a corner right of the last routes. Climb it to exit left, swing back right to a ledge and up a corner to finish.

The descent gully is bordered on its true left by mossy crags. A short way up is a prominent white wall near a fallen tree.

23 Cavalcade Wall   20m   Severe   *(1978)*
Climb the white wall to a central niche and exit left to a tree.

24 Zigzag   15m   Difficult   *(1978)*
Below the white wall in the descent gully, at the gully mouth, is a curious double flake. Follow it rightwards, turn a corner then follow the flake crest back left again. Curious indeed.

There are several outcroppings of rock right of the main area. On the far right of the crag, past a white wall, is a seemingly well defined arete, Dismal Edge.

25 Black Crack   10m   Severe   *(1978)*
Right of Dismal Edge is a slanting wall with a chimney-crack to the right. Start left of this, then step into it to exit via the flakes.

26 Black Wall   10m   Severe   *(1978)*
To the right of Black Crack is a wall. Climb it and step right to flakes to exit back left.

RAVEN'S ROCK QUARRY

(NH 458 606)   Alt 120m   North facing

This lies 500m west of Raven's Rock. It is very loose but provides a fine ice climb when hard frost prevails. A good slab on the right side of the quarry used to provide pleasant climbing. Unfortunately this appears to have up and left some time ago and its current whereabouts are unknown.

Centre Fall   40m   IV,5   *(1978)*
In the centre of the quarry is a thin waterfall which freezes during a cold spell to give a fine problem, vertical low down but thin higher up.

RED ROCK

(NH 473 598)   Alt 120m   North facing

This small but imposing schist crag lies 800m east of Raven's Rock.

Approach: The approach through the forest below is tedious, so the best way is to follow the private road to near a wooden bridge and then head up and left to the crag via a fire break. There are no restrictions on access, 20mins.

The crag, which appears much larger than it is, has plenty of overhangs but since it is triangular, route possibilities are limited. The best line is the one below.

Red Wall Grooves   35m   VS 4c *   *(1978)*
The centre of the face has a prominent curving groove. Start from the ledge below where a mass of ivy festoons the left side of roofs. Climb up to the roof and Tarzan

across the ivy to a break, then climb up and step left to a ledge, belays on the right. From the left end of the ledge climb to hidden holds and reach the groove at a niche. Continue to the top in a fine position.

Variation: **Direct Start   HVS 5a**
The steep wall right of the normal start leads to the same ledge and avoids the ivy.

LITTLE RED ROCK

(NH 474 596)   Alt 150m   North facing

This is a small but technical crag a few hundred metres west of Red Rock. It has a maximum height of 12m and is about 30m long.

Approach: It is most easily reached by following the fire break from Red Rock then heading up through the trees.

Two large flakes form tight chimneys with walls in between. There are some interesting crack climbs as well as entertaining walls. Top roping is an option as not all the routes are protectable and some of the landings are decidedly bad.

Elementary Flake   10m   Severe
At the left of the crag is a flake; climb the short groove to gain the crest of the flake then take the groove on the left to finish.

The Wee Nasty   10m   E2 6a *
Climb the thin groove in the centre of the flake, with difficulty, to the crest. Finish straight up the middle of the wall. One of the better climbs but hard to protect.

Calorie Chimney   10m   Very Difficult
Climb the tight chimney at the right end of the flake to the crest. Climb the wall and slab to finish.

Medusa Crack   10m   VS 5a *
Right of Calorie Chimney is a recess with a cracked roof. Climb up to and over the roof to the top. The best climb here.

Razor Crack   10m   VS 5b
Right of Medusa Crack is a straight crack with a roof at the bottom. Climb the roof strenuously, then the crack more easily to tree belays above. The bottom roof can be taken on the right at the same grade.

Fat Ladies Chimney   10m   Severe
The tight chimney above a block right of Razor Crack.

Any Way But This   10m   E2 5c
The steep corner-groove right of the chimney, entered and followed with difficulty from the chimney. A sustained problem.

BEN WYVIS

CREAG COIRE NA FEOLA

(NH 469 668)   Alt 650m   North-East facing   Map p386   Diagram p395

A fine remote winter cliff, recently developed in Coire na Feola. Ben Wyvis seems to receive snowfall from many wind directions and often looks whiter than the mountains around. The blowing of this snow has led to a reputation for windslab avalanches and big cornices.

Approach: The corrie is remote from any direction but well worth the effort. The southern approach as described is quickest in good conditions, though the western route from Garbat and over the summit ridge is much simpler and only slightly longer in total time, since bikes are not required. For the latter, park at NH 412 673 on the south side of the Allt a' Bhealaich Mhoir. A new path follows the north side and up An Cabar. Follow the summit ridge to about NH 456 676, then head just south of east and go down a slight valley which is north of the steep part of the corrie (a cornice is possible) before descending near the stream in the base of the corrie to the cliff, 2hr30mins.

The southern approach is from Newhouse (NH 501 602), which lies off the Achterneed road. The Forestry Commission track can be cycled through the plantations, taking the first right, for 4km to a small car park. Alternatively a car can be taken, with permission, from the Forest Enterprise offices at Contin. Follow the track steeply uphill, keeping to the left. Pass the Ranger's house, bear right, taking the narrow rutted track under a tunnel on the left. When back on the main track, head right following the railway line past the cottage at Glen Sgaich. The track then winds uphill for several miles, ignoring turns off to left or right until a left turn heads towards Ben Wyvis which runs more or less parallel with the pointed hill of the Pap of Tulloch (Cioch Mor), to the small car park. This track is usually blocked in snowy weather. Cross straight across the moor to the second fire break and follow this through trees and then diagonally across more moor to join a track, exiting at a gate and a lonely SNH sign, which is diagonally to the north-east from the car park. Contour up the slopes passing east of Point 890m, rounding the shoulder into Coire na Feola. The crag is on the east wall above some small lochans. 2hrs in good conditions plus 30mins cycling.

Descent: To return to the corrie, either side of the crag is possible but cornices and avalanche conditions may force a long detour, even as far as An Socach to the north or the approach traverse to the east. Returning south to the car, the forest track can be hard to find in poor light. The Forestry Commission gate is directly below a shallow gully that splits the southern slopes left of Point 890m. Avoid the temptation to swing too far right once on the moor, but cross directly to small trees opposite and follow the moor to the narrow fire break.

After some freeze-thaw, the cliff can become very icy. It is then at its best; the stars may seem generous in mixed conditions. On the extreme left is a concave buttress topped by an easy snow arete, the line of The Snick. The main cliff has a large wedge of rock tapering to a pair of snow aretes, flanked by icefalls on the left and right. Below the main cliff is a small lochan and a minor crag with a very steep icefall. Extensive cornices run the length of the corrie and exits in some conditions may entail much traversing.

1 Four Cornice Gully 150m II (1995)
Two hundred metres left of the main crag and immediately left of a prominent narrow buttress is a deep gully. A small introductory pitch leads to straightforward snow up to the headwall, often topped by a huge and perhaps impassable cornice. The grade assumes good conditions, although on the first ascent there were four cornices and bergshrunds, extending over 25m horizontally into the plateau.

2 The Snick 200m III * (1994)
The prominent narrow buttress gives a good route to do in doubtful conditions. It has an ice bulge at half-height and is flanked by the deep Four Cornice Gully on the left and a less pronounced one to the right.
1. 35m Start below the centre of the crag and climb shelves to just below the ice bulge.
2. 25m Climb the very steep but short crux bulge to a ramp which leads to a small bay.
3. 40m Climb an iced ramp on the right, then trend back left and up to easier ground.
4. and 5. 100m The route now finishes up the broad concave rib which has only a minor cornice.

3 Hansel and Gretal 200m III (2000)
To the left of Tapered Buttress is a line of icefalls, shortest on the left. The most

BEN WYVIS
Creag Coire na Feola

3. Hansel and Gretal   III
4. Tapered Buttress Direct IV,6 *
5. Gael Force Grooves   IV,4 *
6. Discovery Buttress   IV,4 **
8. Walking On Air (finish) V,5 ***

John Mackenzie

BEN WYVIS AREA

reliable one is near the left where it is thickest and forms an ice hose bottomed by an ice corner. Start right of a narrow iced V-gully at the corner and climb ice to the hose. Climb the hose on the right to reach a snowy rake. Either descend left to the corrie floor from there or continue up either easy angled ice or snow to a steeper and possibly corniced exit.

4 Tapered Buttress Direct   280m   IV,6 *   *(2000)*
This is the narrow buttress left of the main icefalls of Gael Force Grooves. It takes a direct line up turfy ground immediately right of iced slabs. An easier route should be possible to the right bypassing the steep section on pitch two. Start at an inset corner left of the base.
1. 50m Climb this past a loose spike and a revolving chockstone to a shelf with a waist high overhang.
2. 50m The crux can be seen above on the skyline as a steep wall. Climb up to it via a narrow groove right of the iced slabs.
3. 50m The crux wall starts above a ledge and gives a vertical step with sloping holds apart from one.
4. 50m Continue easily to steepening snow.
5. 50m Continue up to a rocky arete left of a similar arete (Discovery Buttress).
6. 30m Continue up the steepening arete to a fine finish over the cornice.

5 Gael Force Grooves   225m   IV,4 *   *(1993)*
The broad icefall to the left of Discovery Buttress varies depending on build up. In full conditions a fine plume forms centrally.
1. 35m Climb the plume and traverse left.
2. 50m Go up to and climb the right side of an icefall to enter a shallow gully and ice screw belays below a fine ice pitch.
3. 50m Climb the ice pitch up left and continue up more open ground to a central rock bay.
3. 50m Climb open snow slopes.
4. 40m Climb the steepening snow to below a massive cornice, originally climbed through a deep crevasse entered via an ice tunnel. The aretes either side are an alternative option.

6 Discovery Buttress   255m   IV,4 **   *(1992)*
A good mountaineering route with turf, ice which often forms and interesting route finding. Start left of the toe of the buttress at the apex of a bay.
1. 30m Climb a right-trending groove to a snow patch.
2. 30m Move right and climb a steepening groove to a balcony stance left of an icefall.
3. 30m Climb the icefall above (or traverse right and climb iced rocks).
4. 45m Climb a narrow icefall with a steep exit on to mixed ground. Traverse left around a rock nose and gain easier ground above a short corner.
5. 60m Climb up a snowfield to a rock tower.
6. 60m Climb the left-hand runnel through the tower and gain a fine snow arete which steepens to a corniced exit.

7 Laird of the Rings   180m   V,5 **   *(2001)*
A good turfy mixed climb up the rib to the left of Walking on Air, taking the right branch of a shallow chimney to the left of the rib.
1. 20m Climb the groove 10m left of Walking on Air to an easing where the groove splits into twin chimneys. Move right to the right-hand chimney.
2. 40m Climb the chimney, exit left and surmount a steep wall using a 3m hanging icicle (a prominent feature from below) and a short ramp. Step right and continue up a steep groove and turf to a terrace.
3. 40m Turn the wall on the right and continue up turfy mixed ground.
4. 50m Move left and climb up to an icy groove which leads to the final snow slopes.
5. 30m Continue up the snow slopes to the top.

John Mackenzie collection

True Blue, IV,5, Creag Coire na Feola, Ben Wyvis. Climber John Mackenzie

8 Walking on Air 190m V,5 *** *(1993)*

A spectacular route which has been seen as continuous blue ice but at least the main icefall forms regularly. Towards the right end of the main buttress is a hanging corner which forms an icefall; this is to the left of a much shorter icy corner.

1. 40m Climb up the steepening corner to a recess on the left, then step up right to a ramp followed right.

2. 55m Climb a steepening icefall above to a water tight cave on the right.

3. 35m Climb past the cave on ice to a shelf below a steep barrier wall and traverse left to a slanting crack which lies left of centre on this wall. Climb the crack and an ice groove to the crest.

3. 35m Climb the snowfield to a groove at the right end of the summit rocks.

4. 30m Climb the pleasant groove to the plateau.

9 True Blue 210m IV,5 ** *(2001)*

To the right of Walking on Air is a concave icefall which offers some excellent ice climbing, not apparent from below. This line makes the most of the ground right of Walking on Air though it is possible to escape directly up to the right after the initial pitch.

1. 35m Climb the crux icefall, vertical at the top.

2. 40m Follow snow easily to opposite a blue icefall on the left. This can extend for a considerable distance and leads up to a narrow blue hose.

3. 50m Climb the excellent icefall to the upper hose which has a hanging icicle to its right.

4. 35m Step left past the icicle and climb the blue hose to exit on to the upper snowfield

5. 50m Go up the snow to the top.

COIRE MOR

Map p386

This is the biggest corrie on the mountain and a very remote place. Coire Mor has four diagonally raked spurs of strongly tilted moine schists leaning from left to right. These have provided some routes climbed by parties unknown in the 1950s. To the right (north) of the minor scoop of Coire an t-Socaich is No.1 spur, which is broken and grassy. Next is a long Grade I gully, which divides No.1 from No.2 spur. No.2 spur itself is split by the very narrow Fox Gully. Either side of this gully are two more interesting ridges, both of about Difficult in standard and 150m in length. Between No.3 and No.4 spurs is a fine waterfall draining Coire nan Con. No.4 spur, right of the waterfall, is a series of short rock steps and grassy ledges.

No.2 Spur

(NH 474 685)   Alt 750m   North-East facing

This pair of buttresses is blockier and turfier than the crags of Coire na Feola with the climbing being reliant on well frozen turf rather than ice. Overall the crags are steep but punctuated by delightful belvederes where one can contemplate the glories of the wind farm opposite and the mighty oil rigs in the Cromarty Firth.

Approach: Start from the Ben Wyvis car park near Garbat (NH 412 673) and follow the new path up on to Ben Wyvis; go to its summit. Head east along a ridge from the summit, then north down a slight spur before turning east at an altitude of about 900m and descending under the cliff down a gap in cliffs well marked on the map, finishing by a traverse to the routes. At least 3hrs.

The lower section of No.2 Spur, to the left of Fox Gully, is much shorter then the main upper section but has a steep frontal face. Above this steep face a long arete leads parallel to Fox Gully to the top. Being lower down it is less likely to be in condition.

1 Fox Gully Arete   200m   II   *(2004)*
This is the left bounding edge of Fox Gully clearly seen as a strip of snow or turf near the right edge of the steep face left of the gully. Scenic and a pleasant way up the cliff.
1. 50m Climb the broken walls and ledges left of the edge, steeper than they look.
2. 50m Continue up the narrow snow or turf strip and arrive at an arete.
3. 100m Continue up the level arete then over two towers, best climbed on the right, then up a steepening snow slope to finish.

2 Fox Gully   250m   I/II *   *(1950s)*
This is the steep gully that lies between the steeper but shorter left-hand buttress and the main buttress on the right. The lower section can be Grade II in certain conditions and the climb ends on snow slopes. It is steep, scenic and narrow in places and can contain an ice or turf pitch midway. It can be used as an exciting descent.

The following routes are on the main buttress to the right of Fox Gully. The main buttress has four right to left ramps, the topmost ending at the Pinnacle. To the right of these is a deep right-facing corner, roughly in the centre of the crag and also a shallow gully line leading up right. These central features start from a recessed bay. On the skyline are three prominent horns with steep corners between them. The right side of the crag is more broken.

3 High Five   245m   III,5 **   *(2006)*
This good route follows the second ramp from the bottom, starting at the lowest rocks just right of Fox Gully and briefly crossing Rampant Desire. A good route for poor snow conditions.
1. 45m Climb up shelves and short walls to trend left up a gangway.

BEN WYVIS
Coire Mor, No 2 Spur

3. High Five	III,5 **
4. Rampant Desire	III,4 *
5. The Last Resort	IV,4 **
6. Temptress	V,6 ***
7. Cock o' the North	V,5 *

John Mackenzie

2. 40m Continue more steeply leftwards up the gangway over short icy walls, then traverse right over ledges to the base of the second ramp.

3. 40m Follow the ramp up left and climb up a chimney to reach a crevasse; belays just beyond.

4. 40m Climb the steeper chimney to the crest and emerge on the face overlooking Fox Gully. Continue up the arete on the right to belay around the Pinnacle.

5. 30m The Sting in the Tail. Move down a little from the Pinnacle and enter an undercut groove (crux) and climb to a small overhang. Move left to an edge and continue up and right to a wide crack.

6. 50m Go easily up snow following the edge to an exit onto the plateau.

4 Rampant Desire   200m   III,4 *   *(2006)*

A good mountaineering route following the line of the large and lowest ramp that leads left towards Fox Gully before climbing the face overlooking the gully. Enter the ramp either from below or from the right and follow it to its apex where there is a pinnacle. Climb this in an exposed position to gain the ledge above, crux. Move up right to a recess and escape out left, second crux. Move up and right heading towards the back of the prominent Pinnacle seen from the base of the crag. Shortly before this is a mini-pinnacle on the left wall. Climb up to and squeeze past it before descending a couple of metres. Reach the next right-slanting ramp system and follow this to the turfy rib overlooking the final pitch of The Last Resort. Climb this to easy ground above. A heavy build up of snow will lessen the technical difficulty.

5 The Last Resort   200m   IV,4 **   *(2003)*

A steep and natural line up the main buttress. It is sustained at the grade and twists and turns amidst good crag scenery. To the right of the left edge, bounded by Fox Gully, is a shallow bay perhaps 30m or so right of the edge, bordered to its right by a right-slanting gully ramp. In the centre of the bay is a steep wall leading up left to a narrow ramp and chimneys below a prominent pinnacle. The climb starts up the wall and ends up on the top skyline just right of the first of three horns. The direct start is described; an easier break to the left would reduce the grade to IV.4.

1. 40m Climb a steep turfy wall that leads to the base of the left-slanting break. Follow the break up and left to chockstones in the chimney that leads to the pinnacle.

2. 45m Step down and move right along a vanishing ledge for 10m to a tricky step right. Move up and then back left along a ramp for 15m to below steep walls right of a left-slanting break. Climb the difficult stepped walls then move right.

3. 45m Above is a steep wall. Step down and move right below this to a bay and climb a splendid narrow chimney to its top. Move left past a rocking stone to gain a hidden chimney. Climb this steeply over delightful bulges and chockstones to a chockstone below the final bulge.

4. 40m Climb the tricky bulge above and then more easily an isolated outcrop.

5. 30m Steepening snow leads to the top.

6 Temptress 180m V,6 *** (2004)

The best line on the crag giving excellent varied climbing that is exposed, scenic and adequately protected and with a sensational finish. It starts up the big right-facing corner in the central bay and ends up the hanging corner by the second horn.

1. 35m Climb the corner direct to the overhanging wall. A foot traverse left to the edge is followed back right via turf. Continue up the left branch and poor belays back left on the shelf above; possibly better to belay slightly lower.

2. 50m Cross the shelf to below a left-slanting ramp. Climb the difficult wall on its right to turf and climb straight up past a serendipitous spike to and over a yellow chockstone and up into a shallow bay and ledge above.

3. 25m Move up left along a narrow shelf to a below a steep groove below the final wall. Climb the groove to a tiny shelf.

4. 20m The overhanging wall has an off-width crack and chockstone; climb the wall to its left first by turf then by torques, step right and climb the blocks and shelves in an amazing position.

5. 50m Easy snow to the top.

7 Cock o' the North 180m V,5 * (2006)

A good turfy line taking the wall and corner to the right of Temptress.

1. 40m Start right and below the big initial corner of Temptress, crossing the gully to a narrow right-facing overhanging corner which curves leftwards higher up. Climb this to the big ledge above, belaying below a turfy line.

2. 50m Climb the very steep turf line moving slightly left, then right past an overhang to ledges below a prominent chimney (taken by The Last Resort).

3. 40m Traverse right along the ledge system round the edge of the buttress above to reach a deep corner-line. Enter this more steeply to gain a stance.

4. 50m Climb the corner over a short steep wall and then to a snow fan exit.

8 Interrupted Gully 200m II * (2004)

A good interesting climb with only the start visible from below. It takes the right-slanting ramp at the right of the bay.

1. 50m Climb ice or turf up the ramp to a snow patch. Instead of continuing to its end (and a possible escape) belay below a prominent slanting flake-crack mid-way along the patch.

2. 50m Step left and climb a very awkward short wall to a ledge, crux, and then up the narrow turfy gully above which then slants right.

3. 50m The gully now jinks back left and up. Climb steeper ice or turf up the gully to a cracked block on the left.

4. 50m A steepening snow fan and probable cornice to exit.

Coire nan Con

(NH 472 691)   North to South-East facing (winter routes), South facing (summer routes).

This is the smaller hanging corrie between Nos.3 and 4 Spurs.

Approach: From the summit of Ben Wyvis, descend north-eastwards into the subsidiary hanging Coire nan Con (NH 470 690). The best rock climbing is the clean slab that lies on the north side of No.3 spur, above and left of the waterfall (facing up). It is clearly visible from below and the approach is scrambling up a wet corner.

Upper Corrie Icefalls

(NH 467 691)   Alt 800m   South-East facing

The upper corrie holds much ice early in the season, especially in the easy-angled corners on the west wall. It banks out readily under snow.

Cubs' Corner   150m   II   *(2006)*
This is the left-hand corner and holds the most ice. Easy walkable ice leads to steeper ground and the left-hand branch was taken on much ice to a snow fan exit.
Variation: **Wolf's Cascade   20m   III to IV,4 ***   *(2006)*
The right-hand and more direct line of Cubs' Corner leads past a fine cascade on the left. It varies from 75 to 90 degrees and the grade will vary according to the line taken. Continue up to join Cubs' Corner to finish.

Klettershoe Slab

The clean slab that lies on the north side of No.3 spur, above and left of the waterfall (facing up).

Klettershoe   90m   Very Difficult *   *(1970)*
Start on the clean right-hand tongue of slab and follow this direct to the arete. A shallow scoop at half-height is a landmark and the whole route is very clean. Though variation is possible, the direct line gives the best climbing.

Rubbers   90m   Severe 4b   *(1984)*
This takes the line of the central corner which arcs round rightwards at the top. There are optional starts, but the climbing improves at a red slab to the right of the corner. The bald and steeper slab right of the arched overlap gives some thin moves directly up the middle to finish just right of the overlap at the arete.

Slab Smear Left-Hand   100m   V,4   *(1986)*
A seemingly fine but unrepeated route which climbs the left-hand of the two obvious ice smears above and left of the Wyvis Waterfall, adjacent to the summer slab.

Wyvis Waterfall   50m   IV,4 *   *(1986)*
This waterfall forms the outlet of the Allt Coire nan Con at NH 473 692. It freezes readily in cold conditions. A big ice pillar on the right side of the cascade is the normal route.

COIRE LOCHAIN

(NH 487 707)   Alt 750m   North facing   Map p386

This open corrie is often in winter condition but not very steep, possibly most interesting in lean conditions. It is rather featureless with a thin stream on the left, turfy slabs in the centre and an inverted triangular buttress on the upper right-hand side. Large cornices form readily on the western half.

BEN WYVIS AREA

Approach: Request permission from the gate keeper at the gate house to drive up the long rough road past Loch Glass to Wyvis Lodge. Follow a track by the Allt Corravachie to reach the corrie by striking across the hillside. Failing permission, a massive approach over the summit of Wyvis leads to the same spot.

Cabarfeidh   150m   II   *(1982)*
The triangular buttress gives a pleasant climb with a good outlook leading to a potentially difficult cornice.

CREAG BEALACH CULAIDH

(NH 447 726)   Alt 450m   South-East facing   Map p386

This remote quartzite crag lies above its namesake loch about 4km west of Wyvis Lodge. The most distinctive features are a vertical pink holdless wall and a two-stepped corner to its left.

Badger up a Plum Tree   35m   E1 **   *(2003)*
This excellent climb takes the obvious two-stepped corner.
1. 25m 5b Climb the fine corner until it is possible to pull out left on to a slab (the lower corner-line turns into a wide messy crack above). Climb the upper corner to a grass ledge and tree.
2. 10m 4b Climb the block-filled chimney and thence to the top.

Sett Up   25m   E1 5b   *(2003)*
This route lies well to the right of the vertical pink wall on an obvious rib lying between an open vegetated groove (holding a rowan) on the left and a wide tree-filled grassy gully on the right. Start at the very toe of the rib. Climb over a huge flake, then up past a sapling to better rock. Move up to below an overhang. Traverse hard right until moves back left give access to the slabby face above. Climb the unprotected slab and vegetated ground to finish (no belay).

LOCH MORIE CRAG

(NH 543 757)   Alt 300m   South facing

There are several low crags north of the foot of Loch Morie and a much larger one. Access is from the Struie Hill road at Contullich, 3km north of the A9T junction (signposted Boath). The large crag is visible from the road but the climbing is barely worthwhile. There is another crag 2km down the valley and the following route might alternatively be on it.

Original Route   75m   Difficult   *(pre-1953)*
The western half of the crag is steep to overhanging in places but right of this it lies back and the route follows a fairly obvious line of weakness with considerable variation possible.

STRUIE HILL CRAG

(NH 657 848)   Alt 300m   South-West facing

This small conglomerate crag lies 500m east of and 100m above the summit of the A836 at Struie Hill. It has been climbed on for many years by local climbers and first ascents are not known. It gives a few pleasant climbs on its left-hand side. Others have been done but not thought worth recording.

Grey Slab Gully   25m   Difficult
Climb the narrow gully on the left of the face.

Alcove Slab   20m   VS 4c
This is the best climb here. Right of the gully is a corner and wall topped by a small

roof. Climb the corner, surmount the roof and climb a slab to exit up a steep corner.

Pink Slab   20m   Very Difficult
To the right of the last climb is a pinkish slab. Climb up to an overlap, surmount it and finish up the grey slab. A good climb.

Jungle Jim   25m   Difficult
Right again is a chimney, often wet. Climb this and the open corner to the top. A more pleasant variation is to climb the slab on the left.

Struie Icefall   25m   IV,4   (2002)
In the centre of the crag, a steepish icefall forms most winters. It is clearly visible from the road. Climb it and the heathery corner above.

BLACK BRIDGE CRAGS - STRATHVAICH

(NH 371 714)   Alt 250m   South-West facing
A group of tiered slabs well seen from the A835 Ullapool-Garve road, halfway between the Aultguish Inn and Inchbae Lodge Hotel. The Strathvaich road is followed for 400m to a car park. The climbs are on the upper tier with a maximum of route being about 15m. The rock is not that easy to protect, being a massive rippled gneiss, but is very quick drying and clean. The routes are described from right to left as one approaches.

Route One   12m   Very Difficult   (2002)
A diagonal slab with a pink scoop at the top lies to the right of a heather ledge. Start right of the pink scoop and climb juggy breaks to the top.

Route Two   15m   Severe *   (2002)
Climb up to the pink scoop either directly or from the left and climb it on good holds. Fine climbing.

The next climbs lie on the main slabby wall which is bottomed by a long overhang. The wall has two horizontal breaks and some thinner vertical cracks.

Route Three   10m   VS 4c *   (2002)
Start right of the overhang at a little corner, climb the diagonal break and up a bald slab above.

Route Four   10m   VS 4c   (2002)
The central, quartz filled crack. Surmount the overhang, climb the crack and the bold slanting break above.

Route Five   10m   VS 4b **   (2002)
Start below a thin vertical crack, reached via the overhang. Finish straight up the headwall.

Route Six   10m   VS 5a   (2002)
A squeezed in line left of Route Five but not touching the break to the left!

Route Seven   7m   Very Difficult   (2002)
Left of a broken groove and slabby cracks is a good scooped slab. Climb straight up the middle.

Kinlochewe & Loch Maree North
Glen Docherty

W	1979	Helter-Skelter	D.McCallum, D.Butterfield

Beinn a' Mhuinidh

S	1899 Easter	The West Climb	G.T.Glover, W.Inglis Clark, J.Gall Inglis
S	1910 Easter	Double Ribbon Route	C.W.Walker, W.Inglis Clark
S	1946	Bell's Variation, Route I, Route II	J.H.B.Bell, Mrs Bell
S	1949 Aug	Zigzag Gully	F.F.Cunningham, A.B.Cunningham
S	1951 Jul	Prelude	J.D.Foster, D.Leaver
S	1952 Aug 9	Tuit	J.R.Lees, D.D.Stewart
S	1958 Jul	Staircase Ridge, Stepped Chimney, Silver Slab, Pinnacle Gully, Pinnacle Face	R.Harris, P.Bamfield
S	1959 Jun 4	Miscellany, Crypton Crack	A.Ellison, J.R.Harris
S	1959 Jun 6	Climax Slab	A.Ellison, J.R.Harris
S	1967 May	Centaur	W.March, D.Campbell
S	1967 May 30	Virus	P.Nunn, C.Rowland
S	1967 Jul 1	The Alley	I.G.Rowe, A.J.Trees
S	1967 Jul 2	Safari, A Walk on the Wild Side	I.G.Rowe, A.J.Trees
S	1968 Apr	The Rebound	B.Fuller, P.Nunn
S	1969 May 26	The Tallon; The Bow	J.A.Austin, D.G.Roberts
S	1970 May 4	Coloured Corner	A.Agnew, F.Jack, G.Skelton
S	1971 May 13	Stoater, Vertigo, The Creep	J.Cunningham, W.March
S	1971 May 30	Waterfall Corner	K.Baird, P.Macdonald
S	1971 Jul 5	The Tappit Hen	B.Dunn, J.R.Houston
S	1972 Aug 5	Linea Nigra	A.C.Cain, M.Gate
S	1975 Jul 31	Spider	K.Schwartz
S	1980 Sep 30	Aquila	N.Bielby, B.Nicolson
S	1982 Jul 25	Chiaroscuro; Rainbow's End	A.C.Cain, P.Davis
W	1984 Jan 27	The Waterfall	A.Nisbet, P.Thornhill
S	1984 Sep 16	Refuse Cruise	D.Rubens, S.Pearson
S	1996 Spring	Watch Ma Sheep (Creag Ruadh)	C.French, F.Wolfenden
S	1996 Jul 17	Dream Ticket	T.Prentice, C.French
S	1996 Jul 17	Balances of Fate	C.French, T.Prentice
S	1996 Jul 17	Grades of Shey	C.French, T.Prentice

The first two pitches are similar to a line climbed by R.Everett and K.Kaiser in the late '70s, but not recorded.

S	1997 Jul 19-20	North by North-West	P.Thorburn, R.Campbell, A.D.Robertson
S	2001 May 30	The Blitz	C.Dale, P. and A.Lunn
W	2001 Dec 31	Tuit	A.Lole, G.Stein
S	2003 Jun	Scales of Justice	G.Robertson, T.Woods
S	2003 Sep	Consolation Prize	T.Fryer, I.Taylor
S	2005 Apr 26	Blanco	A.Nisbet
S	2005 May 14	Superbug, Netsky	R.I.Jones, A.Nisbet
S	2005 Jul 30	Twoo	A.Nisbet, F.Reynolds

Slioch

S	1933	Stepped Ridge	Macdougall, Cram and Blackwood
S	1952	Main Buttress	A.Parker
W	1981 Feb	Easy Gully	S.Chadwick
W	1982 Feb	Starters Gully	S.Chadwick, A.Smailes
W	1984 Mar	Surprise Gully	B.Findlay, S.Chadwick, G.Strange
S	1984 May	Pinnacle Surprise	I.Davidson, S.Chadwick

This is probably the same as Northern Pinnacles, climbed 19 Apr 1954 by D.J.Bennet and D.Mill.

S	1986 Jul 14	Skyline Highway	S.Chadwick, I.Davidson
W	1992 Dec 21	Bump Start Gully	C.Hornsby, R.Webb
W	1993 Jan 23	Skyline Highway	R.Webb, N.Wilson
S	1993 Aug 15	Stepped Ridge Direct	S.Richardson, R.Webb
W	1993 Dec	Far Away Buttress	H.Irvine, R.Webb
W	1993 Dec	Magellan's Gully	R.Webb, N.Wilson
W	1994 Jan 1	The Slioch Slim Plan	R.Webb, S.Richardson
W	1994 Apr 3	Reconciliation Gully	J.Groves, J.Fleetwood, S.Scott

W	1996 Mar 24	The Sea, The Sea	R.Webb, N.Wilson
W	2000 Apr 5	Stepped Ridge	N.Wilson, R.Webb
W	2000 Apr 15	Main Buttress	N.Wilson, R.Webb
W	2001 Apr 28	1949 Route	V.Chelton, N.Johnson, D.McGimpsey, S.Mearns
W	2004 Feb 1	Avalanche Goose	I.Small, N.Wilson
W	2004 Feb 1	Pinnacled Gully	C.Cartwright, R.Webb
W	2005 Jan 23	Big Pinnacle Route 1	R.Webb
W	2005 Feb	Xenephon, Big Pinnacle Route 2	S.Richardson, R.Webb
W	2005 Feb	Big Pinnacle Route 3	H.Irvine, R.Webb
W	2006 Mar 18	On a Flat Day you can see America, Top Tower Gully, Right-Hand Finish	R.Webb, S.M.Richardson

Furnace Crags

S	1984 May 20	The Mad Fencer	A.C.Cain, J.Davies
S	1984 Jun 17	Skeleton Lum	A.C.Cain, B.Ledingham, B.Kennedy
S	1984 Jun 24	Caisteal Mor	A.C.Cain, B.Ledingham, B.Kennedy
S	1984 Jul 22	Soft Shoulder	A.C.Cain, B.Ledingham, B.Kennedy, J.Cheesemond
S	1985 May 4	Norse Requiem	I.Davidson, S.Chadwick
S	1985 May 12	Riabhach Slab	A.C.Cain, J.Davies
S	1985 Sep 29	Indian Summer	J.Davies, A.C.Cain
S	1985 Sep 29	Phew	A.C.Cain, J.Davies
S	2001 Jun 27	Brown Slabs routes	J.R.Mackenzie
S	2001 Jun 27	Creag Mhor Cracks	J.R.Mackenzie
S	2001 Jul	Left Wall, The Mad Fencer Direct, Creag Mhor Wall, Crevasse Wall, Sidewinder	J.R.Mackenzie and party

Ardlair Crags

S	1990s	Flying Buttress	R.Brown, G.Cullen
S	1999 Mar 26	The Wreckie	J.R.Mackenzie, D.S.B.Wright
S	1999 May 14	Slattadale Pillar	J.R.Mackenzie, D.S.B.Wright
S	2001 Jun	The Corner, Left Wall	P.Tattersall, F.Fotheringham
S	2001	Where Eagles Nest, Serious Adventure	J.R.Mackenzie and party

Kinlochewe & Loch Maree South
Meall an Ghiubhais, Ruadh Stac Beag

S	1980s	Traveller	S.Chadwick, I.Davidson
S	1983 Sep	The Long Stroll	K.Anderson, S.Chadwick
W	1986 Jan 26	Outrider	S.Chadwick, C.Morrison, A.Taylor
W	1996 Feb 5	Bhanamhoir Fall	S.Chadwick, M.E.Moran
		Resignation Variation by N.Johnson, V.Chelton, B.Timms on 10 Feb 2001	
W	1999 Feb 6	Ruadh Ridge Beag	A.Nisbet
S	1999 May 1	Persecution Rib, Money Lenders Slab, Path Buttress	J.R.Mackenzie
S	1999 May 1	Great Expectations	J.R.Mackenzie
		Variation 1 by D.Morrison, R.Simpson, 26 Mar 2000	
		Variation 2 by A.Nisbet, 9 Oct 2000	
S	2000 Mar 26	Chasm Pinnacle	D.Morrison, R.Simpson
S	2000 Oct 9	Pawn Broker	A.Nisbet
S	2000 Oct 20	Lonesome Pine	A.Nisbet
W	2001 Feb 10	On the Skyline	N.Johnson, V.Chelton, B.Timms.

Coble Crags

S	1998 Aug 4	Alter Ego	J. and M.Buchanan
S	1997 Aug 19	Mutant Gene, Prodigal Sun, Blunt Edge	J.Buchanan, S.Maclean
S	1999 Jun 23	On the Pavement	D.McGimpsey, S.Leggatt, J.Preston
S	1999 Jun 23	Solid Gold	G.Ettle, S.Gillies
S	1999 Jun 23	Anxiety, Wasted	J.Preston, D.McGimpsey
S	1999 Jun 23	Little Jack Horner, The Flakiest, Ripsnorting	J.Preston, S.Leggatt, D.McGimpsey

Stone Valley Crags

S	1984	Open Secret, Dome Corner	S.Chadwick and partner
S	1989 Jan 3	Central Corner (Creag nan Cadhag)	T.Doe, A.Brooks
S	1989 Jun 18	The Trail of the Lonesome Pine Martin	T.Doe, A.Brooks
S	1995 May 14	Stone Diary, Inside Information, Rum Doodle Arete	R.Brown, J.R.Mackenzie
S	1995 May 14	Open Secret (as described)	R.Brown, J.R.Mackenzie

Starting up the musical corner of Bald Eagle; finishing by Open Secret, named Singing Stone Slab, by A.Brooks, T.Doe, D.Jones on 18 Jun 1989. The musical block has been trundled by someone unaware of its history.

Direct Start to Open Secret by J.R.Mackenzie and partner, Apr 2001

S	1995 May 20	The Thin Red Line, Totters Slab	A.Nisbet, G.Nisbet
S	1995 Jun 11	Hidden Agenda, Touch and Go, Bald Eagle, Flaming June	R.Brown, J.R.Mackenzie
S	1995 Jun 24	Melting Pot	J.R.Mackenzie, R.Brown, G.Cullen
S	1996 Mar 10	Cheesegrater Slab, Divided Loyalty, Updraught	J.R.Mackenzie, R.Brown
S	1996 Mar 24	No Beef	R.McHardy, R.Brown
S	1996 May 3	Gas Bubble Wall, Lucky Strike, Short Sharp Shock, Pink Wall	R.Brown, J.R.Mackenzie
S	1996 May 9	Bold as Brass, The Thug	R.Brown, J.R.Mackenzie
S	1996 Jun 9	Questionable Crack, The Lum (as described)	R.Brown, J.R.Mackenzie

The Lum pitch 1, then Questionable Crack pitch 2 (named Peregrine Crack) by A.Brooks, T.Doe, D.Jones on 18 Jun 1989

S	1996 Jun 18	Controlled Steering, Mellow Ambler	R.Brown, J.R.Mackenzie, D.Wilby
S	1996 Jul 24	Juniper Slab, Roman Wall, Demon Razor, Lumside Phew	R.Brown, J.R.Mackenzie
S	1996 Aug 11	Chleirical Error	R.Brown, J.R.Mackenzie
S	1996 Aug	The Beer Bottle Dilemma	I.Taylor
S	1997 Mar	Wander at Will	R.Brown, C.White
S	1997 Mar 11	Percussion Crack, Syncopation Wall, Stratospheric Pachyderms	R.Brown, J.R.Mackenzie
S	1997 May 30	Strike Two, Playtime Wall, Blood Feud	J.R.Mackenzie, D.S.B.Wright
S	1997 Jun 10	Curse you Red Barn!, Hun in the Sun, Lilly of the West, Veinous Fly Trap, Blood Red Roses	G.Ettle, D.S.B.Wright
S	1997 Jun 10	Flying Circus, A Load of Old Bosche, Rock around the Block, Blyth Spirit, Tormentil Grooves, Mountain Everlasting	R.Brown, J.R.Mackenzie
S	1997 Jun 14	The Flashing Blade, The Domino Effect, Golden Eagle	G.Ettle, I.Taylor
S	1997 Jun 16	The Wallace, The Bruce	G.Ettle, D.S.B.Wright
S	1997 Jun 24	Cat Burglar	I.Taylor, G.Ettle, R.Brown
S	1997 Jun	The Time Warp	G.Ettle, D.S.B.Wright
S	1997 Aug 25	Atlantic Wall routes	L.Cannon, J.R.Mackenzie, D.S.B.Wright
S	1998 Jun 2	Burnt Offering, Flaming Crack	G.Ettle, D.S.B.Wright
S	1998 Jun 3	Scraggy Slab	G.Ettle, D.S.B.Wright, K.Grindrod
S	1998 Jun 14	Helga`s First Time	D.S.B.Wright, A.K.R.Parker
S	1998 Jun 18	Uphellya, Little Valhalla, Schiltrom	G.Ettle, D.S.B.Wright
S	1998 Jun 18	Norse Face Route	G.Ettle (unsec)
S	1999 Sep 21	Fisherboys, Then What?, Go Lightly	P.Tattersall
S	2000 May 7	School's Out	R.Anderson
S	2000 May 7	Primary Care	R. and C. Anderson
S	2000 Jun 3	No Robins	G.Ettle, J.Lyall

S	2001 Mar 19	White Lining, Avoid the Paint	P.Tattersall, J.Buchanan
S	2001 Apr 7	Doodles	B.Fyffe, A.Cunningham
S	2001 Apr 7	Heavyweights	A.Cunningham, B.Fyffe
S	2001 Apr 27	No Mutton	S.A.Blagbrough, G.McEwan
S	2001 Apr	Long Walk, Short Climb	J.R.Mackenzie and partner
S	2001 May 6	Gotta Feeling, Busy Day, Crowded Out, Better Things to Do, Dear Trees, So What	Dundonnell MRT
S	2001 Aug 18	The Valley Walls routes	R. and C.Anderson
S	2001 Nov 12	Tall Tail	P.Tattersall
S	2005 Apr 26	Sun Due	J.Preston, J.Lyall
S	2006 Jun 2	Benny Blanco from the Bronx, Gailes, Giggling Cairn	P.Macpherson

Baosbheinn

W	1987 Mar	Baosbheinn NW Face routes	S.Chadwick
W	1999 Jan	Direct Route (Baosbheinn NE Face)	R.G.Webb, N.Wilson
W	2001 Feb 8	North-West Ridge	D.McGimpsey
W	2001 Feb 8	Beachcomber	V.Chelton, N.Johnson, D.McGimpsey
W	2001 Mar 3	Scalagwag, Right Icefall	D.McGimpsey, A.Nisbet
W	2002 Mar 12	Merlinswanda	E.Brunskill V.Chelton D.McGimpsey

Gairloch Crags
Raven's Crag

S	1981 Aug	Charlestone	S.Chadwick, H.Emerson
S	1982 Jul	Hydro Hek	G.Powell, S.Chadwick
S	1982 Aug	Badachro	G.Powell, S.Chadwick
S	1982 Sep	Ken's Joy	S.Chadwick, K.Anderson
S	1982	Leac McCac, Flakes, Special K, Ricicles	D.Neville, S.Chadwick
S	1983 Jun	Lonmore	A.Smailes, S.Chadwick
S	1984 Sep	Lucy, Gem	S.Chadwick, I.Davidson
		The direct line as described by D.Lang in 1991 and named Mountain Ash.	
S	1984 Sep	Rainbow Pink	S.Chadwick, I.Davidson
S	1985 Apr	Stage Fright	I.Davidson, S.Chadwick
S	1986 Apr 3	Entasis	M.McKay, R.A.Napier
		Variation by D.Conway, R.A.Napier, 6 Apr 1986	
S	1986 Apr 3	Far Post	M.McKay, R.A.Napier
S	1986 Apr 6	Groove Climb	E.Simpson, G.Callander
S	1991	Jutting Blocks, Two Guns	D.Lang
W	1995 Jan 1	Bright Star	I.Davidson
W	1995 Jan 2	Constabulary Slab	I.Davidson, J.Fraser
S	1995 May 21	Shield Direct, The Morning After	S.Richardson, R.Webb
S	1997 Jun 15	Crack Climb	A.Nisbet, G.Nisbet
S	1997 Jun 15	Bunny Slabs	G.Nisbet

Fruity Crag

S	1991 Sep 15	Apples, Pears	T.Doe
S	1991 Sep 15	Lemon	T.Doe, A.Brooks
S	1991 Sep 15	Fruit Chimney	R.James, K.Lacey
S	1991 Sep 15	Swapped	A.Brooks, R.James
S	1996 Jun 15	Orange, Mango, Lime	N.Hodgson, B.Williamson
S	1998 Mar 21	Passion Fruit	G.Robertson
S	1998 Mar 21	Starfruit	A.Crofton
S	1998 Mar 21	Paw-paw	T.Rankin, D.Laing
S	2000 Oct 9	Blaeberry	A.Nisbet
S	2001 Feb 13	Jam, Bananas	P.Tattersall
S	2001 Feb 17	Mulled, Cloudberries, Raspberries	P.Tattersall, J.Buchanan
S	2001 Apr 12	Shrot, Plump	T.Doe, P.Tattersall
S	2001 Aug 19	Fruit-case	R. and C.Anderson
S	2002 Jul 30	Banana Cake Conspiracy	R.Beaumont

Sneaky Crag

S	2001 Mar 17	Dave the Miller, Mighty Mo, Dog Pete	T.Doe
S	2001 Apr 12	Mad John	T.Doe, P.Tattersall
S	2001 Apr 12	Screwy Louis, Bad Bob	P.Tattersall

Druid Rock & Echo Valley

S	1990s	"Chinese" routes by I.Davidson, with A.Wilson or J.Fraser, 1995 to 1999	
S	2001 Feb 19	Shaman, Totem, Taboo, Voodubh, Acorn Slab	P.Tattersall, J.Buchanan
S	2001 Mar 24	Prophet and Loss	P.Tattersall, J.Buchanan
S	2001 Mar 24	Sultan of Swing, Crooked Willie	T.Doe, J.Buchanan
S	2001 Jun 12	Freeks and Mayonnaise, Poirot Woz Here	J.Buchanan, L.Vanhelsuwe
S	2001 Jul 19	Burnt Offering, Alchemy, Healing Touch, Sundance	J. and D.Preston

Vegie Crag

S	1998 Mar 21	Neep	A.Crofton, D.Laing
S	1998 Mar 21	Swede	A.Crofton, D.Laing, T.Rankin
S	1998 Mar 21	Sweet Potato	T.Rankin, D.Laing, A.Crofton
S	1998 Mar 21	Turnip	T.Rankin

Routes on Lochan Fuar Crag and Loch Braigh Horrisdale Crag by T.Doe, A.Brooks, 17 Oct 1999.
Heather Gem (Diamond Crag) by I.Davidson, 1993.
Solitaire and routes on Back Country Crag and Cadfael Crag by A.Nisbet, 7 Aug 2005.
Routes on Badachro Crag by I.Davidson, A.Wilson, 2000.

An Groban

Some routes were climbed by a Glenmore Lodge party in 1971 but were not recorded.

S	1973 May	Slipway, Blackgang, Hatman, Straker	D.McArthur, C.Higgins
S	1994 Jun 25	Alleyway	D.F.Lang
S	1998 Apr 29	Growbag Grooves	A.Nisbet, G.Nisbet

Flowerdale Bastion

Routes by J.R.Mackenzie, D.S.B.Wright, 16 Jun 2000

Sidhean Mor

Middle Rib by I.Thow in Jun 2000. The HVS by A.Jones, date unknown.

Aztec Tower

S	1996 Aug	Torn Heart, Cortes	J.Buchanan, M.Buchanan
S	1997 Apr	Human Sacrifice	A.Gorman, J.Buchanan
S	1997 Apr	Warrior God	J.Buchanan, A.Gorman
S	1997 Jun 27	Conquistador	J.Lines, S.Chadwick, A.Nisbet
S	1997 Nov	Horse Feather	P.Tattersall, A.Katzenmeier
S	1998 Aug 24	Sun God, Infanta	R.Weld, J.R.Mackenzie
S	2001 Jun 6	Quickstep, Two Step	N.McAdie

Routes on Sunset Crag were climbed by S.Allan, K.Grindrod on 14 and 17 Apr 2005
Routes on Grass Crag by P.Tattersall and others, Jan and Feb 2006.

Creag Bhadan an Aisc

S	2000 Apr 30	Handbagged, Blondes Don't Reverse, 5.10 Stilettos, Lip Gloss	C.Maclellan, R.J.F.Brown, D.S.B.Wright
S	2001 May 11	Curtain Wall, The Crack	R.A.Biggar, C.Maclellan
S	2002 Mar 19	Windhover	P.Tattersall, J.Buchanan
S	2002 Jun 10	Hobbyhorse	P.Tattersall
S	2003 Feb 18	Tired of Creation	P.Tattersall T.Doe
S	2005 Mar 29	Dark Roots	S.Allan, K.Grindrod
S	2005 Jun 11	Ante Naval Base	R.Wallace

Rubha Reidh

S	1990s	A' Staca Dubh	S.Chadwick
S	2005 Mar 26	The Levitant	R.I.Jones, C.Las Heras
S	2005 Apr 24	South Stack	R.I.Jones
S	2005 Apr 24	The Storyteller, The Calm Sea	R.I.Jones, C.Las Heras
S	2005 Apr 24	The Book, Hidden Story	C.Las Heras, R.I.Jones
S	2005 May 21	Landward Face (North Stack), The Watchman, Beaten by the Tide, Stac 'n Arbhair	R.I.Jones, J.H.Stocks
S	2005 May 22	The Sleeping Sentinel	R.I.Jones, J.H.Stocks
S	2005 May 22	A' Staca Ghibnich	R.I.Jones
S	2005 May 22	The Ogre Within	R.I.Jones (unsec)
S	2005 May 20	Silent Wisdom, South Face	R.I.Jones, M.Dent

Poolewe & Tollaidh Crags
Loch Tollaidh Crags

S	1940s	Raven's Edge, Assault Slab	Highland Field Craft Training Centre
S	1981	In the Pink	S.Chadwick, G.Powell
S	1982	Ewephoria	S.Chadwick, G.Powell
S	1991 Apr	Sage Bush Rider	P.Tattersall, A.Katzenmeier
S	1991 Jul	Someone Else's Dream	P.Tattersall, A.Katzenmeier
S	1992 Jun	Kermit	J.Buchanan, J.Henderson
S	1992 Jun	Sprocket	J.Buchanan, J.Robinson
	Direct as described, by R. and C.Anderson, 13 Aug 1995		
S	1992 Jul	Fozzy Bear, Dr Beaker	D.Neville, J.Buchanan
S	1992 Jul 4	Gonzo, Scooter, Miss Piggy, Animal, Doozer	J.Buchanan, M.Buchanan
S	1992 Jul	Waldorf	J.Buchanan, J.Henderson
S	1992	Flushed Out	J.Buchanan, D.Neville
S	1992	Red Faced	K.Clark, I.Davidson
S	1992 Nov	Eight Below	J.Buchanan, M.Buchanan
S	1992	Rushed-up	S.Chadwick, G.Iseli
S	1993 May	Cookie Monster	T.Doe, J.Buchanan
S	1994 Apr	Buena Vista	A.Winton, S.Chadwick
S	1994 Aug	Water Lily	A.Winton, A.Gorman
S	1994 Oct	Malpasso	A.Winton, J.Buchanan
S	1994	The Ramp, After Eight, Eighted, Mint	A.Winton
S	1994	Zig-Zag	S.Chadwick, A.Winton
S	1995 Jun	Fraggle Roll	T.Doe, J.Buchanan
	Direct Finish (Roll Up) by L.Hughes, A.Cunningham on 27 Apr 2001		
S	1995 Aug 12	Heave-ho	R. and C.Anderson
S	1995 Aug 13	Lean-to, Peek Practice, Reddy Ribbed	R. and C.Anderson
S	1995 Sep 17	Crack Bush Chimney Route, Scarlatina, Rouged-up	R. and C.Anderson
S	1996 Feb	Path	P.Tattersall, A.Katzenmeier
S	1996 May 11	Old El Pastis	R.Anderson, D.Cuthbertson
S	1996 May 12	El Passe	D.Cuthbertson, R.Anderson
S	1996 May 18	Avoidance	R.and C.Anderson
S	1996 May 19	Balding Oldie	R.and C.Anderson
S	1996 May 20	First Amendment, Third Degree, Fourth Dimension, One Up, Two Down, Three Across	R. and C.Anderson
S	1996 May 20	Second Charge	R. and C.Anderson
	Direct variation by J.Preston, D.McGimpsey, 23 Apr 2000		
S	1996 May 25	The Drying Game, Inclement Proposal, Dangerous Lesions	R. and C.Anderson
S	1996 May 26	The Imposter	R.Anderson
S	1996 May 26	Aging Bull	R. and C.Anderson
S	1996 Jun 8	Ewereka, Pump Action, White Fright	R. and C.Anderson
S	1996 Jun 15	Strip-teaser, Temptress	R. and C.Anderson
S	1996 Jun 16	Lorelei	R. and C.Anderson

S	1996 Jul 21	Slowed-down	R. and C.Anderson
S	1996 Jul 22	Squeezed-in, Boldered-out	R. and C.Anderson
S	1996 Jul 24	Descent Gully Rib, Hollow Heart, Simple Mind	R. and C.Anderson
S	1996 Jul 26	Tortured Soul	R. and C.Anderson
S	1996 Aug 8	Super Sleuth	R. and C.Anderson
S	1996 Aug 8	Semi-Automatic	R.Anderson, D.Cuthbertson, C.Anderson
S	1996 Aug 16	Feathering the Nest	R. and C.Anderson
S	1996 Aug 17	Rock Bottom, Zeazy Top	R. and C.Anderson
S	1996 Sep	Conquistador	D.Cuthbertson
S	1997 Apr	Smokescreen	P.Tattersall
S	1997 Jun 28	The Snake	A.Nisbet, J.Lines
S	1997 Aug 26	Blow-out	B.Birkett, T.Rogers
S	1998 Apr	Crossroads, Alien Spacemen	P.Tattersall
S	1998 Apr	Joyful Departure	P.Tattersall, A.Katzenmeier
S	1998 May	Distraction	P.Tattersall, A.Katzenmeier
S	1999 Apr 25	The Snapper, Pieces of Eight	A.Fyffe, A.Cunningham
S	1999 Apr	Frog Dance	P.Tattersall, A.Katzenmeier
S	1999 Jun 23	Mud Wrestler	A.Cunningham, A.Fyffe, B.Fyffe
S	1999 Jun	Eights and Reel	T. Doe
S	1999 Jun	MacDonald	P.Tattersall, A.Katzenmeier
S	1999 May 30	The Bulge	J. and D.Preston
S	1999 May	May Election	G.Ettle, J.Lyall
S	1999	Chitin	A.Cunningham, D.Gemmell
S	2000 Apr 16	Fifth Wave	P.Tattersall
S	2000 Apr 23	Underneath the Arches, Pullover	J.Preston, D.McGimpsey
S	2000 Apr 29	They Think it's all Overhang	J. and D.Preston
S	2000 May 3	Yabbandit	G.Ettle, D.S.B. Wright
S	2000 May 3	Wild Iris	P.Thorburn, A.Gorman
S	2000 May 12	Tasty Little Number, Mother Earth	P.Tattersall, J.Buchanan
S	2000 Jun	Bluenote	P.Tattersall
S	2000 Jun 24	Strongbow, Dreamcoat	G.Ettle, D.S.B.Wright
S	2000 Jun 29	Rosie, Viagara Falls, Brewer's Droop	P. Tattersall, J. Buchanan
S	2000 Jul 23	Welcome Home	P.Tattersall
S	2000 Jul 28	Social Club	P.Tattersall, L.N.Hughes
S	2000 Aug 23	Lifeline	P.Tattersall, C.Meek
S	2000 Aug 23	Breac, Bradan	C.Meek, P.Tattersall
S	2000 Aug 23	Rockspawn, Horny Handed	P.Tattersall, J.Buchanan
S	2000 Aug 25	Lewd Behaviour	J.Buchanan, A.Gorman
S	2000 Aug 25	Stiff Egg White	P.Tattersall, A.Katzenmeier, C.Meek
S	2000 Aug 25	Prickly Pair	A.Gorman, J.Buchanan
S	2000 Sep 23	New Horizons, Incisor	T.Doe, A.Tooth
S	2000	Blast Off	P.Tattersall
S	2001 Mar 21	Ewe Tree Slab, Foot in Mouth	P.Tattersall
S	2001 Apr 7	Barking Shark, Arctic Dreams	P.Tattersall, T.Doe
S	2001 Apr 7	Low	T.Doe, P.Tattersall
S	2001 Apr 8	Shotgun Wedding	P.Tattersall
S	2001 Apr 11	Unrepeatable	P.Tattersall, T.Doe
S	2001 Apr 12	Gutbuster	P.Tattersall, T.Doe
S	2001 Apr 16	Gaugely, Babyface, The Upsetter, Large Libido	P.Tattersall
S	2001 Apr 16	Molly Moo's Posse	M.Tozer, D.S.B.Wright, K.Grindrod
S	2001 Apr 20	Deliver Me	L.Johnson, F.Bennet
S	2001 Apr 25	Wedgie	A.Cunningham, S.Blagbrough, G.McEwan
S	2001 Apr 29	Balls of Fire, Yabugga	P.Tattersall, T.Doe
S	2001 Apr	Unnamed	A.Cunningham, L.Hughes
S	2001 May 1	For Schny Dung, Fill An Der	P.Tattersall, C.Meek
S	2001 May 4	Recessed Groove	A.Cunningham, L.Hughes
S	2001 May 7	Chopsticks	P.Tattersall, T.Doe
S	2001 May 8	Deathmarch	P.Tattersall, T.Doe
S	2001 May 9	Mary, Mary	C.Maclellan, D.S.B.Wright
S	2001 Jun 23	Bound and Gagged, Rubberist	R.and C.Anderson

S	2001 Jun 24	Silky Smooth	R. and C.Anderson
S	2001	Bitches from Hell	M.Garthwaite, C.Smith
S	2002 Mar 23	The Wild Bunch	T.Doe, J.Buchanan
S	2002 Apr 4	Primrose Slab	K. and G.Latter
S	2002 Apr 6	Off The Bone, Monte Cristo	R. and C.Anderson
S	2002 Apr 7	Left Out	R.Anderson, M.Garthwaite
S	2002 Apr 7	Nippy Heed, Itty Bitty Gritty, Peweky	M.Garthwaite R.Anderson
S	2002 Apr 8	Right On	R.Anderson, M.Garthwaite
S	2002 Apr 8	Ming Mong	M.Garthwaite, R.Anderson
S	2002 Apr 10	The Walline, The Nextline, The Crackline	R. and C.Anderson
S	2002 Apr 13	BaBa	P.Tattersall
S	2002 May 19	Reeperbahn	P.Tattersall
S	2002 Jul 16	Steer Clear	P.Tattersall
S	2002 Jul 20	Tall in the Saddle (top-rope practised)	P.Tattersall
S	2002 Aug 20	Frozen in Time	T.Doe, A.Gorman
S	2003 May 4	Back to Business	F.Fotheringham, A.Tattersall
S	2004 Jun 6	Hypocrites and Bastards	D.Porter, B.Sparham
S	2005 Apr 22	U2	A.Fyffe, A.Cunningham
S	2005 Sep 3	Animal Instinct	R.I.Jones, R.Benton
S	2006 May 20	The Rub, Bog Bean	J. and D.Preston
S	2006 May 20	Out of the Mire, Bog Trot, Bog Trot Direct	J.Preston

Leth Chreag

Early ascents possibly by Highland Field Craft Training Centre during World War Two (certainly used for abseiling).

S	1980 Jun	Sky Walk	G.Powell, S.Chadwick

Direct Line by A.Nisbet, S.Chadwick, J.Lines, 27 Jun 1997

S	1985 May	Spider Corner	T.Doe, J.Buchanan
S	1992 Jul	Oregon Bend	B.McMillan, S.Chadwick
S	1992 Jul	Sooper-gloo and a route either side	J.Buchanan, M.Buchanan
S	1992 Jul	Spiral Staircase	J.Buchanan, M.Buchanan

Variation start by S.Chadwick, J.Iseli in August 1992

S	1992 Aug	Kiwi Cruise Control	J.Iseli, S.Chadwick
S	1995 Jun	The Roof	C.Hills, S.Chadwick
S	2005 May 13	The Long Wait	T.Doe, J.Buchanan

The name refers to 20 years after Spider Corner, but probably climbed before.

Creag Fhada

S	1989 May	The Great White Whale	A.Fraser, J.Dickson
S	1992 Jun	Sunday Lies, Gneiss Groove	D.Neville, S.Chadwick
S	1992 Jul 11	Toe Route	I.Davidson, A.Martin, S.Chadwick
S	1992 Jul 11	Break Out	S.Chadwick, A.Martin
S	1992 Jul 11	Route 66	I.Davidson, S.Chadwick, A.Martin
S	1992 Aug	Break In	I.Davidson, S.Chadwick
S	1992 Aug	Midsummer Wallpaper	A.Martin, S.Chadwick

Creag a' Mhic Talla

S	1999 Aug 6	Bowel Crusher, Felso Belsik	P.Tattersall, A.Katzenmeier

The narrow red slab climbed by I.Davidson, A.Martin in 1992

Creag nan Luch

The original route, now retro-bolted as Old Snapper, was Hit the Dog (E4 5c), by P.Tattersall, J.Buchanan, Aug 26 2002. Sport routes in 2004 and 2005, mainly P.Tattersall, with C.Meek, R.Wilby, D.Chisolm, P.Thorburn, T.Doe, J.Buchanan, A.Charmings and M.Jamieson to varying degrees.

Creag Mhor Thollaidh

S	1966 May 10	Knickerbocker Glory	B.Robertson, T.W.Patey, M.Galbraith
S	1966 May 11	Anti Gravity	B.Robertson, M.Galbraith

S	1966 May 15	The Hand Rail	T.W.Patey, M.Galbraith
S	1967 May 21	The Ugly Duckling	J.Renny, J.Porteous
S	1967 Jun	Hoax	W.Sproul, A.Ewing, J.Brumfitt
S	1967 Jun	Rumple Fyke	I.G.Rowe, A.J.Trees

3PA; FFA: J.Lamb, P.Whillance 17 June 1975

S	1967 Sep 7	The Trip	C.Jackson, B.Andrews

(1PA); FFA unknown

S	1967 Sep 8	Teddy Bears Picnic	C.Jackson, B.Andrews

Pitches 2,3 by C.Jackson, R.Conway 30 Jun, 1985
Pitch 1 variation: R.Anderson, C.Greaves 21 May 1988

S	1968 Jun 1	Cocaine	M.Curdy, R.McHardy, P.Nunn, A.Wright
S	1968 Jun	Siren	R.McHardy, P.Nunn, C.Rowland
S	1968 Jun	The Left Arete	M.Curdy, A.Wright
S	1968 Aug 1	Catastasis	B.Andrews, C.Jackson
S	1969	King Prawn, Shazam, Soft Option	Mr and Mrs F.W.Harper

An Alien Heat finish to Shazam by R.Conway, C.Jackson, 29 Jun 1985

S	1970 May 9	Stoney Broke	J.Cunningham, W.March
S	1970 Jul 18	Pokey Hat	D.C.Forrest, D.M.Jenkins
S	1971 Aug 2	Minute	M.Horsburgh, K.Schwartz
S	1971 Aug 17	Toady	C.Jackson, T.Proctor
S	1971 Aug 18	Gudgeon	C.Jackson, T.Proctor

FFA: R.Anderson, C.Greaves 22 May 1988

S	1974 Jun 11	The Bug	P.Botterill, J.Lamb
S	1975 Jun 17	Friday The Thirteenth	J.Lamb, P.Whillance
S	1975 Jul 31	Second	R.Morrow, K.Schwartz
S	1983 May	Decadent Days	R.Anderson, M.Hamilton
S	1983	Hamilton's Groove and Arete	M.Hamilton, D.Dinwoodie
S	1983	Murrays Arete	M.Hamilton
S	1985 Jun 28	Trick of the Light	R.Conway, C.Jackson
S	1985 Jun 28	Sailing to Byzantium	R.Conway, C.Jackson

Climbed with the direct start by A.Cunningham, I.Rea, A.Fyffe, 1993

S	1985 Jun 29	Edge Clipper	R.Conway, C.Jackson
S	1987 Apr 18	Big Toe	R.Anderson, S.Pearson, A.Conkie
S	1987 May 9	Cloud Cuckoo Land	G.Nicoll, R.Anderson
S	1987 May 10	Second Coast	G.Nicoll, R.Anderson
S	1987 May 10	Loctite, Uhu, The Heretic	R.Anderson, G.Nicoll

Heresy variation to The Heretic climbed later by K.Howett.
The Heretic originally climbed by C.Jackson, R.Conway, 30 Jun 1985; line uncertain but less direct.

S	1987	Spirit Air, Destitution Man, Blasad Den Iar	K.Howett
S	1987	Jarldom Reach	K.Howett, A.Nelson
S	1987 Aug 27	Rain-In-The-Face, Each Uisge	D.Dinwoodie, A.Ross

Direct Start: Across the Lines R.Anderson, C.Greaves 8 Jul 1988

S	1988 May 22	Home Start	R.Anderson, C.Greaves
S	1988 Jul 3	Gulf Coast Highway	R.Anderson, C.Greaves
S	1988 Jul 4	Love is the Drug	A.Tibbs, A.Milne
S	1991 May 12	North-West Orient	R. and C.Anderson
S	1992 May 30	Arial	K.Howett, G.Ridge, J.Horrocks
S	1992 Jun 6	Pagan Love Song	K.Howett, G.Ridge
S	1992 Jun 7	The Shimmer	K.Howett, J.Horrocks
S	1993 May 26	Hostile Witness	A.Fyffe, A.Cunningham
S	1997	Diagonal Fault (Loch Maree Crag)	M.Morton, D.Borthwick
S	1998 Jun 4	Sarah'n'Dipity and the Forgotten Pill	S.Hill, D.S.Shepherd
S	1999 Sep 18	Fatg	P.Benson, A.Reid

Croft Crag

S	2003 Feb 15	The Gay Waiver	P.Tattersall, C.Meek

Cliff Hill, Theatre of Dreams

S	2001 Apr 26	Memory Gland	J.Buchanan
S	2001 Jul 29	Zap the PRAM	J.Buchanan, T.Doe
S	2001 Aug 3	Silicon Implant, Alien Skin	J.Buchanan, A.Gorman

S	2002 Mar 30	Erebus	P.Tattersall, T.Doe
S	2003 Feb 12	Bats the Size of Woodcocks, Glassbeads	P.Tattersall, A.Cunningham
S	2003 Feb 12	The Learning Curve	A.Cunningham, P.Tattersall
S	2003 Feb 15	Wishful Thinking	C.Meek, P.Tattersall
S	2003 Feb 15	The Outwit	P.Tattersall
S	2003 Feb 16	Itchy Trigger Fingers	P.Tattersall, C.Meek
S	2003 Feb 18	Ship of Fools	P.Tattersall, T.Doe
S	2003 Feb 18	Disillusion Crack	T.Doe, P.Tattersall
S	2003 Feb 18	Out of Control, The Pillar	P.Tattersall, T.Doe, J.Buchanan
S	2003 Jul 21	Cleavage, Full Frontal	P.Tattersall, T.Doe
S	2003 Jul 28	34D	T.Doe, P.Tattersall
S	2003 Jul 29	Left It	P.Tattersall, T.Doe
S	2003 Jul 29	Pair Shaped	P.Tattersall

Loch Chriostina Crags

S	1997 Aug 29	Rainbow Alliance	D.S.B.Wright, K.Grindrod
S	1997 Sep 2	The Scorcher	G.Ettle, D.S.B.Wright
S	1998 Sep 17	Candle Buttress	J.R.Mackenzie, D.S.B.Wright
S	1999 Aug 11	Boor Constrictor, Left Crack	J.R.Mackenzie, D.S.B.Wright
S	1999 Aug 11	The Mission	D.S.B.Wright, J.R.Mackenzie
S	2000 May 11	Blinding Crack	G.Ettle, D.S.B.Wright
S	2001 Apr 30	One for Angus	C.Maclellan, R.J.F.Brown, D.S.B.Wright
S	2001 May 9	Isle of Ewe Pillar	C.Maclellan, D.S.B.Wright

Rubha Mor

S	1980s	Beer Belly, Heron Crack, The Pit	J.Henderson, J.Buchanan
S	1980s	Intimate Ending	J.Henderson, J.and M.Buchanan
S	1980s	Birthday Treat, Jagged Edge, Lunar Dance, Bum Thrust, Head Case, Gutbuster, The Gash, Endless	J. and M.Buchanan
S	1980s	Walk on the Wild Side, Malignant Tumour, Bum Thrust Direct	J.Robinson, D.Neville
S	1980s	Wild Thing, Drilling the Nerve, Laughing Gas, Painkiller	D.Neville, J.Henderson
S	1980s	Munich Man	J.Henderson, N.Brack
S	1980s	Twinkle Toes, Nuptial Flight	J.Buchanan, J.Henderson
S	1980s	Birthday Hangover, The Dog, The Seal, Cavity Corner	J.Henderson, D.Neville
S	1980s	SNP, Labour, Lib/Dem, Tory	D.Neville, J.Robinson

Members of the local MRTs were quietly active climbing around Dundonnell, Gruinard, Greenstone and Gairloch in the 1980's. A Slaggan climbing guide, with diagrams, was produced by Jim Henderson in the late 1980s.

S	1990 Jul	Cheech, Chong	A.Cunningham, J.Pickering
S	1994 Aug	Shagger's Route	K.Geddes, D.Horsburgh
S	1994 Aug	Coach's Climb	D.Horsburgh, K.Geddes
S	1994 Aug	Anuna, Look Left	A.Cunningham, J.Pickering, M.Blyth
S	1994 Aug	Hourglass Cracks	M.Blyth, J.Pickering, A.Cunningham
S	1994 Aug	The Gentleman Adventurer	A.Cunningham, M.Blyth, K.Geddes
S	1996 Jul	Sore Finger, Sore Thumb	J.Henderson, J.Buchanan

The first recorded routes on Boom Crag. The name Boom Crag comes from the fact that during WWII there was a defence boom strung across Loch Ewe narrows from Mellon Charles, to protect the anchored fleet in Loch Ewe from U-boat submarine attack.

S	1997 Jun	Black Rib, Pampers Groove	A.Cater, A.Cunningham
S	1997 Jun	Calum's Corner, First Born,	
S		Frontpack	A.Cunningham, A.Cater
S	1997 Aug	Mexican Wave, Two Shakes, Third Class	A.Cunningham, F.Curtler
S	1997 Aug	A Good First, Poor Second	F.Curtler, A.Cunningham
S	1998 Apr	Climb and Enjoy Fatboy	P.Tattersall, A.Katzenmeier
S	1998 Sep	Heather's a Blether	D.McGimpsey, J.Lines, R.McAllister
S	1998 Sep	Chrome Melons	D.McGimpsey

S	1998 Sep	Melons in a Muddle	J.Lines, D.McGimpsey, R.McAllister
S	1998 Sep	Old Salt, Balancing Act, Ambling Gambler	D.McGimpsey, N.Harrison
S	1998 Sep	Surf's Out, Flotsam, Jetsam, Drunken Sailor, Squid, Shark's Fin	J.and M.Buchanan
S	1998 Sep	Aquanox, Neptune's Ladder, MC's Chicken, Barnacle, Mother Carey	P.Tattersall, A.Katzenmeier
S	1998 Dec	O La La, Wild Sex, Wild Eyes, Boundless, Writers Block	P.Tattersall, A.Katzenmeier
S	1999 Apr 2	Wrack and Tangle, Precision Decision, Opinan Corner, Westward Ho!	J.R.Mackenzie
S	1999 Jun	Head Games	A.Cunningham, J.Pickering
S	1999 Jun	Cacofinix, Asterix, Dogmatix, Vitalstatistix, Cleverdix	C.Meek, D.Neville, J.Robinson
S	1999 Jun	Getafix	J.Robinson, D.Neville, C.Meek
S	1999 Jun	Obelix	D.Neville, J.Robinson, C.Meek
S	1999 Aug 16	Gung Ho!, Nut Juggler, Carapace Crack	J.R.Mackenzie, I.McWhirter
S	1999 Sep 26	What Ho!, Sea Monster	J.R.Mackenzie, R.Brown
S	1999 Sep 26	Left Crack	J.R.Mackenzie
S	1999 Sep 26	Jugs Galore	R.Brown, J.R.Mackenzie
S	1999 Oct	Tat's Route	P.Tattersall
S	1999 Nov 12	Mermaid's Slab, Torpedo, Consolation Corner	R.Goolden, D.S.B.Wright, J.R.Mackenzie
S	1999 Nov 12	Depth Charge	J.R.Mackenzie, R.Goolden, D.S.B.Wright
S	1999 Nov 12	Blasted Wall	D.S.B.Wright, R.Goolden, J.R.Mackenzie
S	1990s	Huckleberry Fin	N.Ritchie, B.Lawrie

The pair also climbed on a headland close by, but memory fades with old age!

S	2000 Sep 25	Sandpaper, Fair Lady Slab, Black Hearted Bitch, Femme Fatale	J.R.Mackenzie, D.S.B.Wright
S	2000 Sep 25	Wandering Wifie	D.S.B.Wright, J.R.Mackenzie
S	2003 Jan 7	Black Ice, Winter Break, Cranreuch Cauld	A.Cunningham
S	2003 Jan 7	Skid, Icicle Works, Mr Freeze, Numb Nuts, To Infinity....	L.Hughes
S	2003 Jan 7	Baltic, Traction Control	L.Hughes, A.Cunningham
S	2003 Jan 7	Am I a Woman?	P.Tattersall
S	2003 Jan 9	Salary Man, Skint	A.Cunningham, P.Tattersall
S	2003 Jan 9	Same Old Song, Hard Up	P.Tattersall, A.Cunningham
S	2003 Jan 20	Fat Man's Fingers	A.Cunningham, L.Hughes
S	2003 Jan 20	A Long Way Off, On The Fringes	L.Hughes
S	2003 Feb 13	Zurg, Nice Melons!, Buzz Lightyear	A.Cunningham, L.Hughes
S	2003 Feb 13	The Stamp of Australia, Green Goblin	L.Hughes, A.Cunningham
S	2003 Mar 15	Slinky, Slotted Pig	A.Cunningham, A.Fyffe
S	2003 Mar 15	The Snout, Time and Tide, A New Day Yesterday	A.Fyffe, A.Cunningham
S	2003 Apr 7	A Blip In A Sea Of Mediocrity	A.Fyffe, A.Cunningham
S	2003 Apr 7	Sitting Duck, Decoy Cafe	A.Cunningham, A.Fyffe
S	2003 Apr 12	Why Not?, Friendly Fire, Collateral Damage, Held to Account	A.Cunningham, M.Blyth
S	2003 Apr 12	Minister of Information	M.Blyth, A.Cunningham
S	2003 Apr 14	Six Different Ways, What Not, An Ill Wind, Funfest, Glabrous Crack	A.Cunningham
S	2003 Apr	Pauper's Corner, Lightning Cracks	P.Tattersall, T.Doe
S	2003 May	Spit and Polish, Terms and Conditions	A.Cunningham, A.Fyffe
S	2003 May	Lady Luck, Scurvy, Scabious	A.Fyffe, A.Cunningham

S	2003 May	Meloncholy, Melodrama	N.McAdie
S	2003 Jun	Mileage, Witz	P.Tattersall
S	2003 Jun	Call Out, Nato Crack, Battle Stations	T.Doe, J.Buchanan
S	2003 Sep	Lost Friends	A.Cunningham
S	2004 Apr 4	Damp Start, The Contract	A.Cunningham, L.Hughes
S	2004 Sep	Surf Direct, Rungs Missing, Fishnet	P.Tattersall

Carnmore & Fisherfield
Beinn Airigh Charr

S	1909 May	Eastern Buttress	G.T.Glover, W.N.Ling
S	1910 March	Original Route	G.T.Glover, H.Walker, R.Corry, W.N.Ling

This name seems to ignore the 1909 climb, but for consistency with earlier guides it has been retained.

S	1947	Glasgow Ridge (Meall Mheinnidh)	W.D.Blackwood, D.Parlane, B.Wright
S	1951 Jul 4	Lower Buttress Direct	C.G.M.Slesser and party
S	1951 Jul 18	Square Buttress	J.C.Stewart, S.McPherson, W.D.Brooker, J.W.Morgan
W	1964 Mar	Staircase Gully	P.N.L.Tranter, N.Travers
S	1971 Oct	The Beanstalk	D.Bathgate, P.F.Macdonald

Also climbed by P.Buckley, M.Goad in Jun 1971, when it was known as Brooker's Blade, although Brooker hadn't climbed it.

S	1974 Apr	The Roc	M.Boysen, P.Braithwaite, P.Nunn
S	1977 Jul	Lower Buttress	W.D.Brooker, A.G.Cousins
W	1988 Feb 5	Comic Relief	D.Broadhead, I.Dalley
W	1999 Dec 29	Original Route	J.Lyall, R.Webb
W	2003 Dec 29	2003 Route	M.Shaw, I.Humberstone

Beinn Lair

S	1951 Jun 3	Angel Buttress Ordinary	Miss A.Hood, J.S.Orr
S	1951 Jun 6	Ordinary variation	Miss A.Hood, J.S.Orr
S	1951 Aug 17	Wrangham's variation	E.A.Wrangham, F.Adams
S	1951 Jun 3	Pilgrim's Progress	J.S.Orr, Miss A.Hood
S	1951 Jun 3	Molar Buttress, Route I	D.C.Hutchinson, B.S.Smith
S	1951 Jun 3	Rose Route	J.Smith, N.A.Todd
S	1951 Jun 4	Cavity Chimney	D.C.Hutchinson, B.S.Smith
S	1951 Jun 4	Wisdom Wall	D.C.Hutchinson, B.S.Smith
S	1951 Jun 4	Wisdom Buttress	J.Smith, Miss A.Hood, J.S.Orr
S	1951 Jun 6	Bat's Gash	B.S.Smith, D.C.Hutchinson
S	1951 Jun 7	The Tooth	D.C.Hutchinson, B.S.Smith, Miss A.Hood, J.S.Orr
S	1951 Jul 5	West Chimney Route	C.G.M.Slesser, G.Dutton, J.Wight
S	1951 Jul 9	Marathon Ridge	W.D.Brooker, S.McPherson, J.W.Morgan, J.C.Stewart
S	1951 Aug 16	Left-Hand Route	F.Adams, E.A.Wrangham
S	1951 Aug 20	Right-Hand Route, Y Buttress	E.A.Wrangham, F.Adams
S	1951 Aug	Stag Buttress, Sesame Buttress, Central Route	J.D.Foster, D.Leaver
S	1951 Aug	Falstaff, Rainbow Wall	D.Leaver, J.D.Foster
S	1952 Mar	Excalibur	E.A.Wrangham, A.B.Clegg
S	1953 Dec 3	Right Wing, Butterfly Buttress	E.A.Wrangham, D.St.J.R.Wagstaff
S	1953 Dec 5	Olympus	E.A.Wrangham, D.St.J.R.Wagstaff
S	1957 Apr 8	North Summit Buttress	Miss M.M.Langmuir, M.J.O'Hara
S	1967 Jul 6	Left Wing, Butterfly Buttress	I.G.Rowe
W	1969 Feb 26	Easachan	Q.T.Crichton, G.N.Hunter
W	1969 Feb 27	Geodha Ban	Q.T.Crichton, G.N.Hunter
W	1978 Feb 18	Cabbage White	R.McHardy, A.Nisbet
W	1978 Feb 19	North Summit Buttress	J.Anderson, R.McHardy, A.Nisbet, J.Unwin
W	1978 Apr	Butterfly Gully	D.Dinwoodie, R.Renshaw
S	1980 Aug	Tower Ridge	I.Thow
W	1988 Feb 7	Left Wing, Butterfly Buttress	D.J.Broadhead, I.Dalley

W	1997 Feb 2	Bat's Gash	F.Bennet, J.Fisher
W	1997 Feb 3	Dragon's Lair	F.Bennet, J.Fisher
W	1998 Apr 11	Y Gully, Left Fork	P.F.Macdonald, C.G.M.Slesser
W	1998 Apr 11	Angel Buttress, Ordinary Route by Wrangham's variation	R.F.Allen, R.Richardson
W	2005 Feb 20	Right Wing, Butterfly Buttress	J.Higham, I.Young

Creag na Gaorach

S	1957 Apr 8	Jealousy	M.J.O'Hara, Miss M.M.Langmuir
S	1957 Apr 9	Zebra Slabs	M.J.O'Hara, Miss M.M.Langmuir
S	1967 May 22	Rainbow's End	P.J.Sugden, J.R.Sutcliffe
S	1967 May 22	Unnamed Rib	D.Chapman, P.A.Haigh
S	1978 May 30	Denizen	R.A.Croft, J.R.Sutcliffe
S	1994 Jul 24	Ugly Duckling, The Little Mermaid, Red Shoes	S.Kennedy, D.Ritchie

Creag Poll Fraochain

S	1957 Aug 10	Temerity	D.Ashton, P.C.Machen
S	1958 Apr	Right End Rib	E.A.Wrangham, P.E.Evans
S	1972 Jun	Central Groove	P.Buckley, P.Gray
S	1988 May 26	Little Big-Horn	D.Dinwoodie, A.Nisbet

Aid was used to clean part of the top groove before free-climbing it.

S	1994 May 29	Into the Valley	P.Thorburn, R.Campbell, C.Forrest
S	1994 May	Left Crack	C.Forrest, S.Turner
S	1994 May	Right Crack	R.Campbell, P.Thorburn

Hanging Crag

S	1988 May 26	Causeway Corner	W.McCrae, N.Wilson
S	1988 May 26	Changing Face	N.Wilson, W.McCrae

Ghost Slabs & Creag Dubh-dearg

S	1958 Apr	Left-Hand Route	E.A.Wrangham, P.Nelson
S	1958 Apr	Right-Hand Route	G.T.Fraser, P.E.Evans, M.Fraser
S	1967 Aug 2	Doodle	R.Carrington, M.Shaw
S	1967 Aug 2	Leviathan	J.R.Jackson, I.Fulton
S	1988 May 23	Moby Dick, Black Rain, Tannasg Dubh	D.Dinwoodie, A.Nisbet
S	2001 Jul	Sprit of Letterewe	J.R.Mackenzie and partner

Carnmor

S	1952 Mar 31	Diagonal Route	E.A.Wrangham, A.B.Clegg

Initiated Cambridge University's long association with the crag. Carnmor Corner was the lure.

S	1954	Poachers' Route	C.J.S.Bonington and party
S	1956 Mar	Thrutch	M.J.O'Hara, Miss M.M.Langmuir
S	1956 Mar 29	Original Route	G.J.Fraser, M.J.O'Hara
S	1956 Mar 31	Happy Wanderer	M.J.O'Hara, Miss M.M.Langmuir
S	1956 Jun 17	Botanist's Boulevard	J.H.Longland, M.J.Clay, H.B.Carslake, .Rhodes
S	1956 Jun 17	Red Scar Entry	M.J.O'Hara, R.E.Kendell
S	1957 Mar 29	Needle	S.G.M.Clark, M.J.O'Hara
S	1957 Apr 2	Tinkerbell	M.J.O'Hara, Miss M.M.Langmuir
S	1957 Apr 7	Fionn Buttress	M.J.O'Hara, W.D.Blackwood

A very fine discovery

S	1957 Apr 20	Fionn Castle Variation	G.J.Fraser, J.D.C.Peacock, M.J.O'Hara
S	1957 Apr 22	Dragon	G.J.Fraser, M.J.O'Hara

O'Hara took a cat's cradle belay on a leaf peg under the roof. A great ascent of an intimidating route, which O'Hara still thinks is E1.

S	1957 Jun	Grey Ridge	M.J.O'Hara, N.C.Peacock, R.G.Hargreaves
S	1957 Jun 24	Avoidance	G.Burns, D.Leaver
S	1957 Aug 8	Initiation	D.Ashton, P.C.Machen, C.B.Harris
S	1960 Apr	Gob	D.Haston, R.Smith
S	1962 Apr	Yogi	D.Haston, A.Wightman
S	1966 May	Balaton, Boo-Boo, The Kady	W.Gorman, C.Higgins

S	1966 Jun 19	Black Mischief	B.E.H.Maden, R.D.Sykes
S	1966 Jul 22	Abomination	J.McLean, A.Currey, J.Cunningham
S	1967 May	Green Corner	A.G.Cram, R.Schipper, W.Young

The main pitch had been climbed before in 1963 by P.Buckley and J.Budd.

S	1967 May 28	St George	A.G.Cram, R.Schipper
S	1967 Jun	Kaleidoscope, Strawberry Fields	G.Macnair, R.Jones
S	1967 Jun	Connie-Onnie	R.Jones, G.Macnair
S	1967 Jun	Penny Lane	R.J.Isherwood, E.Birch
S	1967 Jun	The Cracks	E.Birch, R.J.Isherwood
S	1967 Jun	Trampoline	R.Jones, G.MacNair

Direct Finish (Proprietor): G.Latter, L.Arnott, 22 Jul 1997

S	1967 Jun	The Sword	R.J.Isherwood, E.Birch

Climbed late in the day after Penny Lane and The Cracks. About three aid points were used. A fine achievement on a very difficult route.
FFA: G.Duckworth, R.Kerr, May 1980.

S	1968 Jun 19	Carnmor Corner	R.Carrington, J.R.Jackson

A long standing problem. One aid point was used on the ramp below the roof.
Probable FFA: R.Perriment, A.Hodges 1975
Direct Start: G.Latter, L.Arnott 22 Jul 1997

S	1974 Apr 15	Purple Wall	P.Buckley, B.E.H.Maden, M.J.O'Hara
S	1974 Apr	Odyssey	P.Buckley, B.E.H.Maden, M.J.O'Hara
S	1974 Apr 16	Ring of Bright Water	A.Faller, M.Harris
S	1975 May 25	Achilles	P.Buckley, C.Warnham

Most pitches had been climbed on previous occasions by Buckley with O'Hara, Maden and Smith.

S	1975 May	Ulysses	P.Buckley, C.Warnham
S	1976 Spring	Claymore	S.B.Thomas, R.B.Evans
S	1980 May	Wilderness	M.Lawrence, D.Mullin

Climbed on sight. A very bold ascent.

S	1981 Apr 1	Running Bear	D.Dinwoodie, J.Wyness

First pitch originally climbed with a detour into Boo-Boo.
Direct ascent: D.Dinwoodie, A.Nisbet 20 May 1988.

S	1981 Apr 2	Naughty Alien	D.Dinwoodie, J.Wyness
S	1982 May 20	Black Magic	C.Dale, A.Dytch

A similar line was climbed by P.Buckley and B.E.H.Maden in 1974.

S	1982 May 21	Dandelion Days	C.Dale, A.Dytch

Climbed earlier by M.Hamilton and P.Whillance, but unrecorded.

S	1984 Aug 1	Break In	A.Tibbs, A.Winton
S	1984 Aug 2	999	A.Tibbs, A.Winton
S	1985 Jun 15	Crackers	D.Hawthorn, C.Maclean
S	1985 Jun 16	The Orange Bow	D.Dinwoodie, D.Hawthorn

Left-hand start: D.Dinwoodie, A.Nisbet 22 May 1988

S	1985 Jun 16	Curare	D.Dinwoodie, D.Hawthorn

Probably the first pre-cleaned routes at Carnmor.

S	1986 Aug 8	Beastmaster	D.Dinwoodie, G.Livingston
S	1986 Aug 9	Lion Rampant	G.Livingston, D.Dinwoodie
S	1986 Aug 9	Death-Wolf	G.Livingston, D.Dinwoodie

Climbed over two days, a nut being left in place overnight at the lip.

S	1986 Aug 10	Ride of the Valkyrie	D.Dinwoodie, G.Livingstone
S	1987 Apr 28	Jivaro Crack	D.Dinwoodie, D.Hawthorn
S	1987 Jun 21	It Was Twenty Years Ago Today	D.Rubens, S.Pearson
S	1988 May 21	Red Crack	D.Dinwoodie, A.Nisbet
S	1988 May 22	Quagga	A.Nisbet, D.Dinwoodie
S	2000 Jun 4	Fian Grooves	T.Rankin, G.Robertson
S	2000 Jun 5	Firecracker	T.Rankin, G.Robertson

Torr na h-Iolaire

S	1933 Jun 22	Baird's Route	P.D.Baird, J.W.Crofton, E.J.A.Leslie
S	1951 Jul 3	Skyline Route, West Face Ledge Route, Tantivy Tower	C.G.M.Slesser, G.Dutton, J.Wight
S	1956 Mar 27	Ipswich Rib	G.J.Fraser, P.R.Steele
S	1956 Mar 29	Shark's Tooth	P.R.Steele, Miss M.M.Langmuir
S	1957 Apr 19	Red Admiral	G.J.Fraser, J.D.C.Peacock, M.J.O'Hara
S	1957 Apr 19	Hieroglyphics	M.J.O'Hara, J.D.C.Peacock, G.J.Fraser
S	1957 Apr 22	Wester, Goat's Groove	J.D.C.Peacock, A.Finlay
S	1957 Jun 23	Sigma	M.J.O'Hara, D.Fagan, B.E.H.Maden

The route described was climbed by D.J.Broadhead and G.Cohen while writing the guide.

S	1957 Jun 23	Sunday Climb	G.Burns, D.Leaver
S	1957 Jun 23	Rainbow Corner	B.E.H.Maden, M.J.O'Hara, D.Fagan
S	1957 Jun 25	Sarcophagus	D.Fagan, M.J.O'Hara
S	1957 Jun 25	Intimidation	M.J.O'Hara, D.Fagan
S	1957 Jun 25	Mica Rib	B.E.H.Maden
S	1957 Jun 25	Rose Rib	D.Fagan, M.J.O'Hara
S	1957 Jun 29	Frogmarch	G.G.Hargreaves, N.C.Peacock
S	1957 Jun 29	Juniper Groove	D.Fagan, M.J.O'Hara
S	1957 Jun 30	The Long Reach	D.Fagan, N.C.Peacock
S	1959 Apr	Suspension	G.McCallum, C.Pollock
S	1966 Mar	The Trees	G.Macnair, B.E.H.Maden
S	1966 Jun 20	Sickle, Sapros	B.E.H.Maden, R.D.Sykes
S	1967 Aug 1	Skeleton Corner	J.R.Jackson, M.Shaw
S	1967 Aug 3	Skull, Wishbone Rib	J.R.Jackson, R.Carrington
S	1970 Jun 18	Eryr	C.L.Jones, C.F.Walmsley
S	1978 May 22	The Eyrie	G.Cohen, G.Macnair, R.J Archbold
S	1978 May 22	Holly Tree Wall	R.J.Archbold, G.Cohen, G.Macnair
S	1978 May 22	Cadaverous Crack	G.Macnair, G.Cohen
	On the first ascent aid was used while gardening the top of the crack.		
S	1988 May 20	Cleopatra	D.Dinwoodie, A.Nisbet
S	1988 May 20	Toad Hall	A.Nisbet, D.Dinwoodie
S	1988 May 20	Carnivorous Crack	D.Dinwoodie, A.Nisbet
S	1988 May 20	Hyena Corner	A.Nisbet, D.Dinwoodie
S	2001 Aug 8	Tiger Lily	A.Nisbet

Maiden Buttress & Carnan Ban

S	1955 Apr 10	Dishonour	M.J.O'Hara, Miss M.M.Langmuir
S	1955 Aug 18	Tweedledee	M.J.O'Hara, R.E.Kendell
S	1955 Aug 19	Modesty, Tweedledum	R.E.Kendell, M.J.O'Hara
S	1955 Aug 19	Strewth	M.J.O'Hara, R.E.Kendell
S	1955 Aug 20	Cakewalk	R.E.Kendell, M.J.O'Hara
S	1955 Aug 20	Ecstasy	M.J.O'Hara, R.E.Kendell
S	1956 Mar 28	Barndance	M.J.O'Hara, Miss M.M.Langmuir
S	1956 Mar 28	Doddle	G.J.Fraser, P.R.Steele
S	1956 Mar 31	Practice Precipice Climbs	G.J.Fraser, P.R.Steele
S	1967 Jul 17	Strider, Balrog	D.T.McLennan, D.C.Forrest
S	1994 May 24	Eastern Wall	M.Litterick, B.R.Shackleton
S	2001 Aug 8	Blind Date, Sleeping Beauty	A.Nisbet

A' Mhaighdean

S	1933 Jun 23	Baird, Crofton and Leslie's Route	P.D.Baird, J.W.Crofton, E.J.A.Leslie
S	1950	Pillar Buttress	Dr. and Mrs. J.H.B.Bell
S	1951 Jul 2	West Face Climb	C.G.M.Slesser, G.Dutton, J.Wight
	The lower part of this face is very indefinite and the account has not proved adequate for identification.		
S	1951 Aug	Leeds Variation (direct start)	J.D.Foster, D.Leaver
S	1951	Triple Cracks Route	A.J.Bennett and party
	Possibly the same line as "The Slot", climbed (in descent) by M.J.O'Hara and R.G.Hargreaves, Jun 30 1957.		
S	1954 Apr 17	Red Slab	D.J.Bennet, D.Mill
S	1957 Mar 31	Conglomerate Arete	M.J.O'Hara, M.M.Langmuir
S	1957 Apr 21	Doe Crack	M.J.O'Hara, G.J.Fraser
S	1957 Apr 21	Windslab	M.J.O'Hara, G.J.Fraser
S	1957 Apr 21	Whitbread's Aiguille	M.J.O'Hara, G.J.Fraser
S	1957 Jun 30	Vole Buttress	M.J.O'Hara, R.G.Hargreaves
S	1957 Jun 30	Eagle Grooves	M.J.O'Hara, R.G.Hargreaves
S	1959 Apr 1	Fahrenheit	F.Green, G.McCallum
S	1959 Apr 3	Soh What?	K.Torrance, A.Currie
S	1965 Mar 31	Kraken	W.D.Fraser, D.Martin
S	1966 Aug 15	Gladiator	J.R.Sutcliffe, D.Chapman
S	1966 Aug 15	Goats' Ridge, Hodge's Pinnacle	D.Chapman, J.R.Sutcliffe
S	1967 May 24	Trident Gully Buttress	J.R.Sutcliffe, P.J.Sugden
S	1967 Jun	Compensation	R.J.Isherwood, E.Birch
W	1978 Apr 29	Ermine Gully	R.F.Allen, M.G.Geddes
S	1988 May 24	The Cave Mouth, Mossy Bower	D.Dinwoodie, A.Nisbet

S	1988 May 24	The Cave	D.Dinwoodie
S	1988 May 24	Gearradh	A.Nisbet, D.Dinwoodie
S	1988 May 24	Purity	D.Dinwoodie, A.Nisbet

Probably climbed before

| W | 2000 Jan | A Ridge Too Far | M.Hind, R.Webb |

Na Bearta Buttress & Creag Toll a' Mhadaidh

| S | 1955 Aug 22 | Ricepaper | R.E.Kendell, M.J.O'Hara |

One PA used on crux crack owing to vegetation
FFA: A.Hardwick, A.Nisbet, Jul 1989

| S | 1956 30 Mar | Wallflower | M.J.O'Hara, Miss M.M.Langmuir |

One PA used, probably unrepeated

| S | 1956 Mar 30 | Good Friday Climb | G.J.Fraser, P.R.Steele |

Some pitches near top avoided on lead and top-roped by second.

S	1957 Jul 3	Sanctuary Slabs	M.J.O'Hara
S	1999 Jul 12	Good Friday Direct	A.Nisbet
S	2000 May 7	My Fair Lady, Crucifer	A.Nisbet
S	2000 Jul 22	Rough Bounds	R.and C.Anderson
S	2000 Aug 13	Twice Bitten	R.and C.Anderson

Gruinard Bay Crags
Car Park Area

S	1994 May 1	Small but Perfectly Formed, Not Bad	J.R.Mackenzie
S	1994 May 8	Two Minute Slab	J.R.Mackenzie
S	1994 May 8	Five Minute Crack, Flaky Wall, Gneiss Groove, Gneiss, Gneisser, Gneissest	G.Cullen, J.R.Mackenzie

Molly's Ridge, Mutt's Crack and routes on Flake Buttress by J. and P.Richards, J. and K.Bolger, C. and S.Steer on 23 Jun 1996. 1999 routes by J.R.Mackenzie on 5 Aug 1999.

Beach & Birch Crag

S	1998	Armburger	F.Fotheringham, I.Brodie
S	1998 Apr 19	Beach Groove Garden, Capillary Wall	A.Cunningham, L.Hughes
S	1998 Apr 19	Dechno	L.Hughes, A.Cunningham,
S	1999 Apr 30	Aorta, Adalat, Voltarol	A.Cunningham, D.Neville
S	2001 Apr 12	Sheepless in Seattle	A.Cunningham, B.Gordon
S	2002 Mar 17	Hatrick for Patrick	P.Tattersall, T.Doe, J.Buchanan, A.Tattersall
S	2002	Saga of Sewage	P.Tattersall
S	2005 Mar 28	Cowrie	P.Tattersall, T.Doe
S	2005 Apr 24	Childs Play	A.Cunningham, A.Fyffe, L.Hughes, J.Cunningham
S	2005 Apr 24	Family Fun	A.Cunningham, A.Fyffe, L.Hughes, J.Cunningham, C.Meek
S	2005 Apr 24	Panick Beach Teacher	C.Meek P.Tattersall
S	2005 Apr 24	50 Gallon Drum	P.Tattersall, C.Meek

Road Crag

S	1999 Mar 25	Celtic Ray	P.Holmes, A.Cunningham
S	1999 Mar 25	Raglan Road	A.Cunningham, P.Holmes
S	2000 Jun 4	Ataka, Trojan	R. and C.Anderson
S	2000 Sep	Tom Jones	A.Cunningham, L.Hughes
S	2000 Sep	Mongo	L.Hughes, A.Cunningham
S	2003 Mar 23	Pockets of Resistance	A.Fyffe, A.Cunningham
S	2003 Mar 23	On the Road to Baghdad	A.Cunningham, A.Fyffe
S	2003 Apr 10	Roadkill	A.Cunningham, A.Fyffe

Post Crag

S	2000 Jun 26	Billet Dubh, Hate Mail	J.R.Mackenzie, D.S.B.Wright
S	2000 Aug 31	Scoobie Dubh	L.N.Hughes, D.S.B.Wright
S	2002 Apr 5	Post-it	G. and K.Latter
S	2002 May 23	Instantly Forgettable	A.Cunningham, J.Dale

Bog Meadow Wall

S	2000 Jul 30	Summer Breeze, Last Tango	R.Anderson
S	2002 May 23	Bloody Flake	A.Cunningham, J.Dale

Gruinard Crag

S	1994 May 14	Halcyon Days, Utopia, Simple Perfections	R.Brown, J.R.Mackenzie
S	1994 May 23	Paradise Regained, The Big C	R.Brown, J.R.Mackenzie
S	1994 May 28	Baywatch, Red John of the Battles, Overlord	R.Brown, J.R.Mackenzie, A.Nisbet
S	1997 May 24	Stand and Deliver	R.Anderson
S	1997 May 25	Quick on the Draw	R.Anderson
S	1997 May 25	Pistolero	R. and C.Anderson
S	1997 Jul 27	How the West was Won	R. and C.Anderson

Direct version redpointed by P Thorburn, J.Lowther on 16 Aug 1998

S	1997 Aug	Ueejit	N.Morrison, J.Reed
S	1998 Jun 16	Coupe du Monde, Quail	G.Ettle, D.S.B.Wright
S	1999 May 16	Who Shot JR	D.Allan, R.Plenderleith

Reference to the disappearance of Jon Robinson from the Gruinard scene.

S	1999 May 31	Breakpoint	R.Anderson, D.McCallum, S.Anley
S	2000 Apr 30	Off-shore	P.Thorburn, G.Ettle
S	2000 Apr 30	Gunslinger	G.Ettle, J.Preston, D.McGimpsey, P.Thorburn

Inverianvie Crag

S	1990	Gneiss and Easy	J.Robinson and party

Variation 1: D.S.B.Wright, J.Grindrod, D.Willis, 28 Mar 2000
Variation 2: The Pleasure Beach G.Ettle, D.S.B.Wright, 21 May 1998

S	1990	Double Matured	J.Robinson and party
S	1990	Cask Conditioned	J.Robinson and party
S	1995 Aug 3	Barrel of Fun, Root Beer	C. and R.Anderson
S	1998 May 10	The Dundee Dram	A. and G.Nisbet
S	1998 May 21	The Parting Glass	G.Ettle, D.S.B.Wright
S	1998 Aug 25	Shadow	A.Cunningham, I.B.B.Hunter
S	1998 Aug 31	Decommissioned Arms	A.Cunningham

Easy start by A.and G.Nisbet on 10 May 1998

S	2000 Mar 28	Slippery Nipple	C.Grindrod, J.Grindrod, J.R.Mackenzie
S	2000 Mar 28	Tuppenny Tipple	D.S.B.Wright, D.Willis
S	2000 Apr 30	Perihelion	J.Preston
S	2000 May 11	Gill, Synoptical, Double Vision	G.Ettle, D.S.B.Wright
S	2000 Jul 4	Something Completely Different	A.Cunningham, A.Fyffe
S	2000 Jul 4	Temporary Beauty	A.Fyffe, A.Cunningham
S	2001 Aug 10	Coffin Dodgers Eliminate	R.J.F.Brown, D.S.B.Wright
S	2001 Oct 19	Cerebral Harmer	P.Tattersall, T.Doe
S	2001 Oct 19	Something Karma, Welly or Wonty	J.Buchanan, A.Gorman
S	2001 Oct 19	Serial Farmer, Farmer Giles	J.Buchanan, T.Doe
S	2001 Oct 19	Winter Park	T.Doe, J.Buchanan
S	2001 Oct 19	The Wee Jumper	P.Tattersall
S	2002 May 12	The Saloon of Life	P.Tattersall, T.Doe
S	2002 Jun 16	Predator	P.Tattersall, A.Tattersall, T.Doe
S	2002 Jun 16	Bloomsday	P.Tattersall, T.Doe
S	2003 Mar 30	Lock-in	C.Cartwright, N.Wilson, S.Campbell

Fox's Buttress

S	2000 Apr 16	Glacier Mint	A.Cunningham, A.Fyffe
S	2000 Apr 16	Vulpine Groove	A.Fyffe, A.Cunningham
S	2000 Jul 4	Gone to Ground	A.Cunningham, A.Fyffe
S	2001 Jun 16	Foxtrot	J.Lyall, J.Preston
S	2001 Jun 16	Barking	J.Preston, J.Lyall
S	2001 Jul 14	Diamond Slab, Earth Matters	J. Preston

Dog Crag

Lassie, Tess, K9, Inverianvie Corner, Slab Crack, Wanderlust were climbed by J.S.Robinson

and D.Neville before 1988.
Second pitch of K9 by R.Anderson, C.Anderson on 1 Aug 1995
Second pitch of Inverianvie Corner by A.Cunningham, J.Pickering in Jun 1990, named
Spotty Dog

S	1990 Aug	Pluto, Down Shep, Cailleach	A.Cunningham, J.Pickering
S	1996 Jun 20	Prospectors Rib	G.Nisbet
S	1999 Apr	Crab Slack	A.Nisbet
S	2000 Jul 4	Dogged Persistence	A.Cunningham, A.Fyffe
S	2000 Aug 21	Pig Monkey Bird	P.Tattersall, A.Katzenmeier

Two unnamed boulder problems at left end by P.Tattersall, Aug 2000

Riverside Slabs
Routes by A Cunningham, A.Fyffe on 9 Oct 2002

Lochan Dubh Crag

S	1989	The Crack	Dundonnell Mountain Rescue Team
S	1989	Edged Out	Dundonnell Mountain Rescue Team
S	1989	Beat the Beak	D.Neville, J.Robinson

Later climbed and called Abrasion Cracks

S	1989	Nick the Niche	J.Robinson, D.Neville

Later climbed and called Grand Recess

S	1990	Edgebiter	J.Robinson, D.Neville 1990
S	1994 Apr 14	The Silk Road	J.R.Mackenzie, R.Brown
S	1994 May 8	Abrasion Cracks	J.R.Mackenzie, R.Brown
S	1994 May 14	Scrabble	R.Brown, J.R.Mackenzie
S	1995 Apr 28	Call of the Wild	M.Moran, M.Welch

Variation start by G.Latter, P.Thorburn on 12 May 1996

S	1995 May 26	The Missing Link	A.Andrew, M.Moran

Pitch 2 by J.Robinson, D.Neville in 1990, named Raid the Ramp

S	1995 Aug 3	Major Domo	R. and C.Anderson
S	1995 Aug 6	Smashy, Gneissy	C. and R.Anderson
S	1995 Aug 6	Dead Calm	R. and C.Anderson
S	1996 May	Sunk Without Trace	P.Thorburn, N.Craig
S	1996 May	Flawed by Design	P.Thorburn, R.Campbell
S	1996 Jun 20	The Recess	J.Lyall, A.Nisbet, A.T.Robertson
S	1996 Jun 20	The Slab	G.Nisbet
S	1996 Jun 20	Raid the Recess	A.Nisbet, G.Nisbet

The route includes part of an original line out of the niche, by J.Robinson, 1989.

S	2000 May 6	Ducks with Attitude	R. and C. Anderson
S	2001 Oct 12	Sunset Song	A.Cunningham, A.Fyffe

Creag Carn an Lochan Duibh
S	1994 May 14	Pink Streak	J.R.Mackenzie, R.Brown

Chimney Crag

S	1995 Sep 16	Glam Rock, Grunge	R.Anderson, C.Anderson
S	2001 Jul 14	Not in Vein	J.Preston
S	2004 Feb 14	New Forest Gateaux,	
		The King's Hat	T.Doe, P.Tattersall.
S	2004 Feb 14	The Intrusion	P.Tattersall, T.Doe

Gruinard River Crags
Goat Crag

S	1946 Aug	Unrecorded route on the left end	J.H.B.Bell and Mrs Bell
S	1963 Aug 11	Missile	J.Hinde, D.Bottomer, R.Sadler
S	1966	Breach Route	T.W.Patey
S	1971	Liquidator	A.J.Anderson, M.B.Hall (some aid)

Route as described by R.McAllister, A.Nisbet in Jun 1998 (1 rest)
FFA: P.Tattersall Summer 2000

S	1974	Barefoot in the Park	P.Boardman, A.J.Anderson

Pitch 2 by R.McAllister, A.Nisbet in Jun 1998

S	1974	Meridian	M.B.Hall, B.A.James
S	2000 Apr	Tatapult	P.Tattersall, L.Hughes
S	2000 Oct	Commonsense	P.Tattersall, L.N.Hughes

S	2000 Oct	Homosuperior	P.Tattersall, L.N.Hughes
S	2000 Oct	Freakshow	P.Tattersall
S	2000 Oct	Twilo Thunder	L.Hughes, C.Meek
S	2000 Nov 11	B Movie	P.Tattersall

Sport climbs on Am Fasgadh by P.Tattersall in 2002 and 2003 except for the middle 7c by L.N.Hughes in 2005.

Carn Goraig

S	1987 Mar 11	Wailing Wall	F.Fotheringham, A.Taylor
S	1995 Jul	Ramadan	A.Cunningham, F.Fotheringham
S	1998 Sep 6	Return to Mecca	F.Fotheringham, A.Taylor
S	1998 Sep 29	Alba	J.R.Mackenzie, D.S.B.Wright
S	1998 Oct 2	Olden Glory	D.S.B.Wright, R.Brown
S	1998 Oct 7	The Fatwah, Dispossessed, Call of the Muwazzin	A.Cunningham, F.Fotheringham
S	1998 Oct 7	The Highland Cragsman	J.R.Mackenzie, D.S.B.Wright
S	1998 Oct 13	Whoopers	G.Latter, A.Siddons
S	1999 Jul 9	The Wicked	G.Ettle, P.Thorburn, D.S.B.Wright
S	2000 May 6	Bootless Crow, Old Goats	A Cunningham and R Baines
S	2000 May 13	Slideline	R. and C.Anderson
S	2000 May 31	Crusader	J.R.Mackenzie, D.S.B.Wright

Saracens Variation by G. and K.Latter, 6 Apr 2000

| S | 2000 Jun 18 | Climbing with Heather | J.R.Mackenzie, D.S.B.Wright |

Carn nam Buailtean

S	1999 Jun 11	Sylph	J.R.Mackenzie, R.Biggar
S	1999 Jun 17	Nymph, Point Blank	R.Biggar, J.R.Mackenzie
S	1999 Jun 17	Rock of Ages	J.R.Mackenzie, R.Biggar
S	1999 Jun 25	Satyr, Stealth Fighter, Glistering Slab	J.R.Mackenzie, D.S.B.Wright
S	1999 Jun 25	Foxbat	D.S.B.Wright, J.R.Mackenzie
S	1999 Jul 30	Step Dance	J.R.Mackenzie, D.S.B.Wright
S	1999 Jul 30	Heart of Gold	D.S.B.Wright, J.R.Mackenzie
S	1999 Oct 18	Golden October, Horizon Shine, The Pale Beyond	J.R.Mackenzie, D.S.B.Wright
S	2000 May 9	Shogun, Terrano, Freelander, Terra Nova	G.Ettle, D.S.B.Wright
S	2000 May 9	Eternal Cleft, Holly Tree Hover	R.Biggar, J.R.Mackenzie
S	2000 May 9	Blanked Out	J.R.Mackenzie, R.Biggar
S	2000 May 9	Brown Bess	G.Ettle
S	2000 May 13	Black Beauty	G.Ettle, L.Noble
S	2000 Jun 3	Gossamer	R. and C.Anderson
S	2000 Jun 3	Dark Destroyer	R.Anderson

Lochend Crags

Routes by G.Ettle, D.S.B.Wright on 4 Jun 2000

Creag Ghiubhsachain

| S | 2006 Apr 16 | Seconds Best | B.Hard, R.J.F.Brown |
| S | 2006 Jun 11 | The Fang | R.J.F.Brown, B.Hard |

Gruinard North
Jetty Buttress

S	1946 Aug	Two routes by J.H.B.Bell and Mrs Bell, including Red Slab Route (Very Difficult!), now named Lilly the Pink (Hard Severe). Also another Very Difficult to its left.
S	1960s and 70s	Many routes by military personnel, particularly A.Anderson.
S	Late 80s	Right Charlie	F.Fotheringham, J.Robinson
S	1990	Hands, Knees and Bumpsydaises	A.Ravenhill
S	1992 Nov	Prizefighter pitch 2	G.Ettle, J.Findlay
S	1997 May	Number Nine	P.Tattersall, A.Katzenmeier, K.Noble, A.Charmings
S	1997 Aug	Shallow End of the Gene Pool, Taller	T.Archer
S	1998 Apr 26	Running on Empty, Prizefighter	

		pitch 1, Route 5fi	J.R.Mackenzie, R.Brown
S	1998 May	Gogmagog, Kristi Bloodstopper	P.Tattersall, A.Katzenmeier
S	1999 Jan 1	New Millenium?	C.McNee, D.Kirk
S	1999 May 16	Gaffers Wall	J.R.Mackenzie, R.Biggar
S	2000 Jun 26	Radio Gnome	P.Tattersall, A.Katzenmeier
S	2000	Bat Crack (free)	P.Tattersall
S	2001 May 5	Trespass	C.Meek
S	2001 May 20	The Rowan	C.Meek, C.Dryer
S	2001 May	Pikey's Wall	G.Ettle, J.Lyall
S	2003 Apr 12	After the Storm	R.I.Jones, S.J.McNaught

Mungasdale Crag

S	1990	Goliath	D.Neville
S	1991	The Road to Calvary	F.Fotheringham, D.Neville
S	1991	Kneel and Pray	S. and J.Heap O'Neill
S	1998 Oct 5	Fatmouth, Kind of Gentle	P.Tattersall, A.Katzenmeier
S	1999 Apr 17	The Monkey Tribe	P.Tattersall, A.Katzenmeier
S	1999 Apr 24	Habit Forming, Cloistrophobia	C.Meek, D.Neville
S	1999 Apr 30	Thelonius	P.Tattersall, A.Katzenmeier
S	1999 Apr 30	Walking on Water	C.Meek, A.Katzenmeier, P.Tattersall
S	1999 May	Bodhisattva, Coughed up from Hell	P.Tattersall
S	1999 May	Devil Music	P.Tattersall, A.Katzenmeier
S	1999 May	Genesis	C.Meek, A.Katzenmeier, P.Tattersall
S	1999 May	Rebirth	P.Tattersall, A.Katzenmeier
S	1999 May	Officer Jesus	P.Tattersall
S	1999 Jul	Soul Brothers	P.Tattersall, A.Katzenmeier
S	1999 Jul	Strewth	P.Tattersall, A.Katzenmeier, J.Robinson
S	1999 Oct	Achilles Heal, Dirty Habits	A.Cunningham, F.Fotheringham, A.Fyffe
S	2000 Mar	Spioradail, Three Kings, Trumpet Brains	P.Tattersall, C.Meek

Carn Dearg an Droma

Routes by J.Richards and S.Steer on 29 Aug 1996
Routes on Weird Crag by M.Blyth, A.Cunningham, 11 May 2002
"A few short climbs" had previously been climbed by J.H.B. and Mrs. Bell in Aug 1946

Sheiling Crags

S	2002 May 12	Basil, Laughing Loopworm, Camel Ride, Wild Goose Chase	M.Blyth, A.Cunningham
S	2005 Jun 18	Sinistre Faerie	B.Sparham, D.Porter
S	2005 Apr 24	Faeries Fayre, Don't Pay the Fairyman, Barbara's Warning	D.Porter, B.Sparham
S	2005 Jun 18	Into the Mystic	S.Clarke, D.Porter

An Teallach Area
Beinn Dearg Mor

	1899	South Peak	Sang and Morrison
S	1952 Easter	Flake Buttress	A.Parker, J.Derris, I.Richards
S	1953 Apr 5	Central Buttress	A.Parker and party
W	1963 Dec	Trident Gully, Central Branch	P.N.L.Tranter, N.Travers
W	1966 Nov	Left Flank of Central Buttress	A.McKeith, I.G.Rowe
W	1980 Jan 19	Twisting Gully	M.G.Geddes, C.Higgins, A.Walne
W	1982 Jan 1	Deranged	J.Bennet, L.Bowie
W	1987 Mar 23	Fat Man's Folly	A.Todd, W.Curr
W	1987 Apr 2	Spring Maiden	G.Taylor, A.Todd
W	1995 Feb	Central Buttress	C.Cartwright, I.Stevens
W	2004 Nov 27	Atrial Ridge	J.Higham, C.Gilmore

Junction Buttress & The Sidings

S	1945	Pasture Gully	E.C.Pyatt, E.C.King
S	1952 Easter	Parker's Route	A.Parker, J.Derris, I.Richards

S	1952 Mar 30	Route 1	E.A.Wrangham, A.B.Clegg
S	1953 Apr 3	The Nose, Sapling Climb	H.G.Nicol, D.St.J.R.Wagstaff, E.A.Wrangham
S	1956	Rowell's Route	H.Rowell
S	1957 Dec 6	The Funnel	E.A.Wrangham, D.St.J.R.Wagstaff
S	1964 Apr 10	Rightward Slant	G.A.Watt, G.W.Jack

Mullach Coire Mhic Fhearchair

S	1999 May 14	Nid Rib (Tom an Fhioda)	A.Nisbet
S	1999 May 14	Vagrants Buttress (Sgurr Dubh)	A.Nisbet

An Teallach, Coir' a' Mhuillinn

The north face of Glas Mheall Mor had been climbed on before, notably by Kinloss MRT but also others, but routes have not been recorded.

W	1967	Little Glass Monkey (see SMCJ 1967)	
W	1997 Jan 2	Crystal Clear	I.Small, I.Collier
W	1997 Jan 1	Resolutions, Three ice lines	I.Small
W	1997 Jan 2	GOB's Day Out	D.McQuaker, A.McQuaker, D.Martin, I.Collier, I.Small
W	1999 Dec 19	Smear Test	S.Price, J.Coats
W	1999 Dec 19	Chairman's Choice	P.Greening, A.Barnyard, D.Whalley
W	2004 Feb 28	Plasticity, The Slit	I.Small, A.Hume

Glas Tholl

W	1910 Mar 26	Hayfork Gully	G.Sang, W.A.Morrison
S	1945 Jun 10	Major Rib	E.C.Pyatt, K.C.King
W	1956 Apr 15	Minor Rib	R.Barclay, W.D.Brooker
S	1959 Sep 21	Minor Rib	F.Henderson, G.Sim, R.Sim

An 'inviting crack' avoided on this ascent was climbed by T.W.Patey, N.Drasdo, C.M.Dixon at Severe in May 1962

W	1959 Feb 15	Fourth Prong	T.M.Lawson, R.J.Tanton, J.Clarkson
W	1969 Mar 3	Checkmate Chimney	T.W.Patey, C.J.S.Bonington
W	1978 Dec 18	The Alley	R.Baker, A.McCord
W	1979 Feb	Major Rib	I.L.Dalley, J.Grant
W	1982 Dec	Intermediate Face Route	D.Butterfield, J.Elliot, P.Savill
W	1983 Feb	Stalemate	K.Schwartz, J.Mount
W	1986 Feb 23	White Knight	M.Fowler, C.Watts
W	1987 Jan 18	Pawn Cocktail	C.Forrest, W.Moir
W	1993 Mar 25	The Magnificent Seven	N.Kekus, A.Andrew, D.Taylor, C.Brook, T.Wagg, I.Forth, P.Buck
W	1994 Mar 9	Sixpence	M.Johnstone, A.Nisbet, D.Thompson
W	1997 Jan	Central Buttress Right Hand	A.Cunningham, F.Fotheringham, D.Williamson
W	1999 Dec 18	Cake Fork	P.Greening, T.Moore
W	1999 Dec 24	Central Buttress	A.Nisbet
W	2000 Jan 3	Miniscule Rib	D.McGimpsey, A.Nisbet
W	2000 Jan 6	Haystack	D.McGimpsey, A.Nisbet
W	2000 Apr 5	Tiny Gully	B.Davison, D.McGimpsey, A.Nisbet
W	2001 Mar 24	Forbidden Gully	D.McGimpsey, A.Nisbet
W	2004 Mar	North Gully	P.Raistrick

Toll an Lochain

W	1923 Easter	Lord's Gully, Right branch	J.H.B.Bell, E.E.Roberts
S	1958 Aug 9	Lord's Gully, Right branch	D.Robertson, F.Old
W	1973 Feb 17	Lord's Gully, Left branch	A.Borthwick, F.Fotheringham
W	1974 Dec 30	Lady's Gully	F.Fotheringham, J.R.R.Fowler

Swiss Approach by J.Preston, M.Hirsbrunner, C.Koenig, 26 Jan 2004

W	1978 Feb 19	1978 Face Route	M.Freeman, N.Keir

Variation Start: D.Gardner, E.Lynch, Feb 1994

W	1987 Jan 31	Potala Buttress	D.Rubens, D.Broadhead

Sling for aid. Unrepeated?

W	1987 Apr 12	Bowling Alley	M.Fowler, C.Watts
W	1988 Mar 13	Bottomless Gully	M.Fowler, D.Wilkinson
W	1988 Mar	The Forger	J.Lyall, S.Spalding

W	1989 Feb	Opposition Couloir	J.Lyall
W	1991 Jan 28	Lord Berkley's Seat	S.Jenkins, A.Nisbet
W	1994 Jan 29	Gobhlach Grooves	N.Kekus, M.Welch
W	1994 Apr 13	Fiona Verticale	M.E.Moran, D.Litherland
W	1995 Jan 28	Rhoddies Fault	E.W.Brunskill, H.Ellen
W	1998 Dec 28	Corrag Bhuidhe, South Buttress	
		by the Mental Chimney	D.McGimpsey, A.Mullin, A.Nisbet
W	1999 Jan 10	Cnocturne	N.Johnson, D.McGimpsey
W	1999 Jan 19	Lost Gully, The Spectre	D.McGimpsey, A.Nisbet
W	1999 Jan 24	Corrag Bhuidhe Buttress	D.McGimpsey, A.Nisbet
W	1999 Feb 23	Fifi's Chimney, Lady in Waiting	D.McGimpsey, A.Nisbet
W	1999 Feb 24	Corrag Bhuidhe South Buttress,	
		Original Route	V.Chelton, R.McAllister,
			D.McGimpsey, S.Mearns
W	1999 Feb 24	Lucky Strike	V.Chelton, R.McAllister,
			D.McGimpsey, S.Mearns
W	1999 Feb 26	Corrag Bhuidhe, South Buttress	
		Direct	D.McGimpsey, A.Nisbet
W	1999 Mar 7	Fiona Diretissima	B.Davison, D.McGimpsey
S	1999 Aug 8	Forgotten Face, Sandeman's	
		Pinnacle	D.McGimpsey, A.Nisbet
W	1999 Dec 5	Forgotten Face	D.McGimpsey, A.Nisbet
W	1999 Dec 12	Sandeman's Pinnacle	D.McGimpsey, A.Nisbet
W	1999 Dec 20	Gobhlach Buttress	D.McGimpsey, A.Nisbet
W	2000 Dec 15	Monumental Chimney	J. Lyall, J. Preston
W	2000 Dec 19	Anvil Chorus	J.Lyall, J.Preston
W	2000 Apr 5	The Ghoul	B.Davison, D.McGimpsey, A.Nisbet
W	2001 Jan 7	Counterfeit Groove, Kumbh	
		Mela	D.McGimpsey, A.Nisbet
W	2001 Jan 18	Elemental Gully	J.Lyall
W	2001 Mar 1	Mauna Kea	A.Nisbet

An Teallach - Outlying Climbs
Corrie Hallie Crag

S	2002 Sep 20	Pick the Lock, Key Data	C.Meek, M.Holmes
S	2002 Oct 20	Ice and Sneezy	P.Tattersall, C.Meek
S	2003 May	Tense Breakfast	C.Meek, R.Wilby
	Variation by S.Ritchie, D.Porter, 9 May 2004		
S	2003 May	Half Yokin	R.Wilby, M.Holmes
S	2003 May	Shreddies	C.Meek, M.Holmes
S	2003 May	Lunchtime, Coffee Break	M.Holmes, R.Wilby
S	2003 May	Tiffin	R.Wilby, C.Meek
S	2003 May	Busted Flush	C.Meek
S	2003 May	Oaky Doakey	M.Holmes, H.Meek
S	2004 May 8	Inception	D.Porter, S.Clark
S	2004 May 8	Close of Play, Sanctuary's Edge	S.Ritchie, D.Porter
S	2004 May 8	Bow and Arrow	D.Porter, S.Ritchie
S	2004 May 8	Shallow Waters, Move on Up,	
		Tricam	S.Clark, D.Porter
S	2004 May 9	Piff Shlapps, Little and Large	S.Ritchie, D.Porter
S	2004 May 9	I was Right, Obvious, Ron Move	
		Wonder	D.Porter, S.Ritchie
S	2004 May 14	Scoopy Do	D.Porter
S	2004 May 14	Difference of Opinion	D.Porter, S.Clark
S	2004 May 14	Stylus	S.Clark, B.Sparham, D.Porter
S	2004 May 14	Ullapool Fish Week	B.Sparham, D.Porter
S	2004 May 14	Slurp	D.Porter, B.Sparham
S	2004 May 15	Breakaway, Try Me, The Crossing	D.Porter, J.George
S	2004 May 15	Starboard Tack	D.Porter, J.George
	Direct Finish by S.Clarke, D.Porter, 5 Sep 2004		
S	2004 May 15	Alien Invasion, Battleship Burner,	
		Steelyard Blues	J.George, D.Porter
S	2004 May 15	Row yer Boat	D.Porter
S	2004 May 22	Escoop, Supermatch Game,	
		Blankety Blank	D.Porter, B.Sparham

S	2004 May 22	Evasion	B.Sparham, D.Porter
S	2004 Aug 28	Scraggy	D.Porter
S	2004 Aug 28	Pale Sider, Monkeys in Bubbles	D.Porter, A.Nisbet
S	2004 Aug 28	Patch, Whiter Shade of Pale, King Quartz	A.Nisbet, D.Porter
S	2004 Sep 5	Sleazy, Primera	D.Porter, S. Clarke

Outlying Winter Routes

W	1984 Jan 21	Fain Falls	B.Findlay, S.Kennedy, R.Ross, G.S.Strange
W	1994 Feb 26	Bonar	M.Buddle, B.Sparham
W	1996 Jan 8	Heavy Handed	D.Whalley, K.Holland ,I.McPherson
W	1996 Feb 4	Goat Falls	M.Caroll, N.Kenworthy
W	1999 Mar 1	No Option (Beinn Gobhlach)	A.Cunningham, F.Curtler

Badrallach Crags
Golden Wall Crag
Routes by R.Brown, J.R.Mackenzie on 5 May 1995 except False Spring by G.Cullen, J.R.Mackenzie on 3 Mar 1996

Creag Beinn nam Ban Area

S	1990	Mind over Matter	D.Neville, J.Robinson
S	1991	Wendy House	J.Robinson, D.Neville
S	1996 Apr 6	Blockbuster	G.Cullen, J.R.Mackenzie
S	1996 Apr 6	Long Distance Runner	J.R.Mackenzie, G.Cullen
S	1996 Aug 13	Hound-Dog Pinnacle	J.R.Mackenzie, R.Brown
S	1996 Aug 13	Shepherds Warning	J.R.Mackenzie, R.Brown
S	1998 May 3	Put a Sock in it!	N.J.Smith
S	1998 May 4	Beaufort Scale	T.A.Murray, C.A.Watt
S	1998 May 4	Force Six Chimney, Class Struggle, Prole's Crack, Social Climber, Lords a Leaping	N.J.Smith, J.R.Mackenzie
S	1998 Jun 5	Solo Slab	N.J.Smith
S	2000 Jul 2	Bandit Country	D.McGimpsey, A.Nisbet
S	2002 Jun 7	Go with the Flow	G.E.Little, R.Wilby
S	2002 Sept 13	Cow Dumped In JR's Soft-Top (Goose Crag)	A.Cunningham, K.Geddes

Badrallach Crag

S	1997 Jul 5	Windy Ridge	N.J.Smith
S	1998 May 1	Garden Party, Lapsang Suchong, Laird's Loss	T.A.Murray, N.J.Smith, C.J.Watt
S	1998 May 2	Pillar of Society, Poacher's Prize, Hunter's Moon	T.A.Murray, N.J.Smith, C.J.Watt
S	2005 Aug 6	Fresh at Forty, Taliesin, Nimue	R.I.Jones, R.H.McArthur

Creag a' Chadha

S	1995 Jun	Scoraig, The Doo Cot	E.Brunskill, S.Mearns
S	1995 Jun	Kushi Doo	S.Mearns, E.Brunskill
S	1995 Jun	Eterna	K.Anderson, H.Ellen
S	1998 Sept	Desert Storm	R.McAllister, S.Mearns
S	2002 Aug 17	Crackerjack	E.Brunskill, D.McGimpsey

The Fannaichs
An Coileachan, Garbh Choire Mor, Coire nan Eun

W		Central Gully	N.S.Tennant and party
W	1976	Dandelion	C.Rowland and party
W	1976 Dec	Burdock	C.Rowland, S.Rowland, D.Scott
W	1976	Primrose (left fork)	C.Rowland, M.Anthoine
W	1979	Primrose (right fork)	D.Butterfield, C.Frazer, D.McCallum, J.R.Mackenzie
W	1979 Jan 13	Echo Face	J.R.Mackenzie, D.McCallum
W	1979 Jan 27	Short Shrift	J.R.Mackenzie, R.Brown

W	1979 Feb 10	Plumline	J.R.Mackenzie, R.Brown
W	1979 Feb 11	Prune Buttress	R.Butler, D.Howard, D.McCallum, C.Roylance
W	1979 Feb 17	Crystal Tripper	J.R.Mackenzie, D.McCallum
W	1979 May 5	Sage Corner	J.R.Mackenzie, D.Butterfield
W	1981 Feb 28	Ravenshead	D.McCallum, A.Russell
W	1984	Moonflower Direct	D.Butterfield, A.Hayward
W	1984	Shadows and Light	D.Butterfield, A.Hayward
W	1985 Jan 19	The Ramp Tramp	C.Maclean, A.Nisbet
W	1986 Feb 28	Venus Fly-Trap	D.Dinwoodie, D.Hawthorn
W	1987 Dec 9	The Turf Accountant	S.Jenkins, M.E.Moran
W	1991 Nov 17	Sideshow	G.Cullen, J.R.Mackenzie
W	1994 Mar 26	Inner Sanctum, Fatal Attraction, Descent Gully	A.Nisbet
S	1995 Aug 18	Illusion Wall	A.Nisbet, G.Nisbet
W	1995 Nov 18	Illusion Wall	A.Nisbet, S.Richardson
W	1995 Dec 9	Flying Carpet	J.Allott, A.Nisbet
W	1996 Jan 28	Hawkwind	B.S.Findlay, G.S.Strange
W	1998 Feb 4	The Primula Trap	B.Davison, A.Nisbet
W	1999 Dec 14	The Gallous Palace	D.McGimpsey, A.Nisbet
W	2001 Jan 12	Al Capone	D.McGimpsey, A.Nisbet
W	2001 Jan 19	Sarsaparilla	D.McGimpsey, A.Nisbet
W	2001 Feb 3	On yer Bike	E.Brunskill, D.Morris
W	2002 Nov 18	Tormentil	A.Nisbet
W	2003 Jan 4	Triffid	D.McGimpsey, A.Nisbet
W	2003 Jan 10	Feral Buttress, Slam	E.Brunskill, D.Morris
W	2003 Feb 1	Kitekat Rib	D.Morris, H.Stagg
W	2003 Feb 15	Bunny Boiler, Saddle Up	D.Morris, H.Stagg
W	2005 Mar 6	Prohibition	E.Brunskill, G.Hughes
W	2005 Nov 19	Quidditch	J.Lyall, A.Nisbet, J.Preston

Fionn Bheinn, Creag Toll Mor

W	1999 Dec 12	Prophetic Voices	J.R.Mackenzie, R.Biggar
W	2002 Dec 10	The Kilted Raven	J.R.Mackenzie
W	2002 Dec 14	Crystal Visions	D.Allan, J.R.Mackenzie
W	2002 Dec 14	The Plaid and The Bonnet	J.R.Mackenzie, D.Allan
W	2004 Dec 11	Trig Point Direct	J.R.Mackenzie
W	2005 Jan 14	Tarot, Crescendo Groove, Sprint	J.R.Mackenzie, A.Nisbet
W	2005 Jan 25	Prophet of Doom, Second Sight	J.R.Mackenzie, A.Nisbet

Beinn Liath Mhor Fannaich, Sgurr Mor, Carn na Criche

W	1967 Apr 9	Wot Gully	R.Graham, R.Warrack
W	1967 Apr 10	Easter Gully	B.Brand, O.Bruskeland
W	1967 Apr 11	East Face	R.Graham, R.Warrack
W	1980 Jan 19	Downward Bound	J.R.Mackenzie, D.Gilbert
W	1980 Mar 14	The Resurrection	J.R.Mackenzie, D.Butterfield

The Resurrection Right-Hand: the upper part by M.Moran and party in 1997

W	1983 Feb 19	The Boundary	D.Rubens, D.J.Broadhead
W	1990 Jan 12	Brumous Buttress	G.Cullen, J.R.Mackenzie
W	1991 Jan 27	Gelid Groove	J.R.Mackenzie, G.Cullen
W	1991 Feb 14	Grand Illusion	G.E.Little, J.M.G.Findlay
W	1991 Dec 21	Into the Groove	J.M.G.Finlay, G.E.Little
W	1993 Jan 31	A Saucer Full of Secrets	J.M.G.Finlay, G.E.Little
W	1995 Jan 2	Boundary Rib	J.M.G.Finlay, A.Huntington
W	1996 Dec 28	Blood on the Tracks	F.Bennet, J.Fisher
W	1998 Feb 5	Transfiguration	B.Davison, A.Nisbet
W	2002 Mar 1	Saboteur's Delight	W.Deadman, R.I.Jones
W	2002 Mar 1	Huntsman's Anguish	R.I.Jones, W.Deadman

Sgurr nan Clach Geala

| S | 1961 Apr 3 | Skyscraper Buttress | T.W.Patey, J.M.Taylor, J.White, G.K.Annand |

Right-Hand Start: A.Nisbet, 10 Aug 1999

| S | 1961 Apr 16 | Sellers' Buttress | T.W.Patey, R.Harper |

First ascent probably made in 1960 by R.H.Sellers and J.Smith. No details are available. Buttress named after Sellers who was killed later that year.

W	1963 Dec 7	Slanting Gully	P.N.L.Tranter
W	1965 Mar 6	Alpha Gully	P.Baker, D.S.B.Wright
W	1965 Mar 6	Gamma Gully	P.N.L.Tranter, I.G.Rowe
W	1970 Feb 28	Beta Gully (centre fork)	P.F.Macdonald, J.Porteous
W	1970 Feb 28	Beta Gully (right fork)	I.G.Rowe, W.Sproul
W	1972 Feb 19	Sellers' Buttress	G.S.Strange, D.Stuart
W	1972 Mar	Delta Gully	D.Dinwoodie, M.Freeman
W	1974 Mar 16	Epsilon Gully	M.Freeman, N.Keir
W	1978 Feb 18	Skyscraper Buttress	R.J.Archbold, M.Freeman, J.C.Higham, R.A.Smith

Direct Start: D.Dinwoodie, C.Jamieson, K.Murphy, 9 Feb 1986
Right-Hand Start: D.Dinwoodie, D.Hawthorn, 26 Feb 1986
Empire State Variation: R.Everett, S.M.Richardson, 13 Feb 1994

W	1978 Feb 18	Sunrise Buttress	P.R.Baines, D.M.Nichols
W	1982 Jan 2	First Footing	N.Halls, A.Kimber, R.Townsend
W	1983 Feb 13	Cuileig Buttress	R.Arnott, A.Nisbet
W	1985 Jan 18	Cuileig Corner	C.Maclean, A.Nisbet
W	1986 Feb 19	Destitution Road	D.Dinwoodie, K.Murphy
W	1998 Nov 18	Canary Wharf	D.McGimpsey, A.Nisbet; A.Clarke, R.McAllister (by the variation)
W	1998 Dec 6	Bungalow Buttress	A.Nisbet
W	1998 Dec 22	Sellers' Tower	R.McAllister, D.McGimpsey, A.Nisbet
S	1999 Apr 19	Alpha Crest	A.Nisbet
W	2002 Jan 31	Fusilier	D.McGimpsey, A.Nisbet
W	2004 Jan 26	Summiteer	D.McGimpsey, A.Nisbet

Sgurr Breac

W	1991 Feb 16	Neverending Story	J.M.G.Findlay, J.G.Findlay, G.E.Little
W	1991 Feb 16	Ptarmigan Corner	J.M.G.Findlay, G.E.Little
W	1993 Dec	Turkey Time	G.Ettle, J.M.G.Finlay
W	2004 Jan 28	Heather Horror	I.Taylor, T.Fryer

Glen Affric to Strathfarrar
Glen Affric / Sgurr na Lapaich, An Riabhachan

W	1969 Apr 12	Spindrift Gully	D.Smith, J.G.Stewart
W	1978 Feb 25	Deer-Grass Gully	J.R.Mackenzie, D.Langudge
W	1985 Jan 1	Punchline	G.Szuca, P.Hyde
W	1985 Jan 1	Groove into 85	Unknown Party
W	1989 Dec 22	Lapland Buttress	J.Lyall, A.Nisbet
W	1996 Mar 7	Cross Stone Gully	M.Welch, I.Douglas, J.King, C.Trotter
S	1997 Jun 12	Lap of the Gods	G.E.Little, J.Finlay
W	1998 Feb 1	Redcoats Weep	R Bale, K.McKintosh; N.Kenworthy, C.Wright (next day)

Also possibly ascended by T.McDonald and party in the 1980s.

W	1999 Feb 19	Birthday Blast	C.Jones, A.MacDonald
W	2001 Feb 18	Lap Dance	B.Davison, D.McGimpsey
W	2001 Feb 21	Second Lap	D.Allen, D.McGimpsey, J.Preston
W	2004 Feb 17	Practice Lap	A Hume, I.Small
W	2005 Jan 25	Loch Lapaich Buttress	D.Moy, S.Maclean
W	2005 Dec 6	Lap of Honour	S.Allan, A.Nisbet
W	2006 Jan 14	Weary Wall	J.Lyall, A.Nisbet
W	2006 Feb 1	Little Corner, Cool Runnings	J.R.Mackenzie

Sgurr na Muice, Sgurr na Fearstaig, Sgurr Fuar-Thuill, Creag Ghorm a' Bhealaich

W	1978 Jan 22	Sea Pink Gully	T.Anderson, J.R.Mackenzie
W	1978 Feb 15	Red Campion, Enchanter's Nightshade	J.R.Mackenzie
W	1978 Feb 18	Streaky	J.Smith, J.R.Mackenzie
W	1978 Feb 19	Trotters Gully	J.R.Mackenzie, T.Anderson
W	1978 Feb 19	Slanting Gully, by Left Fork	T.Anderson, J.R.Mackenzie

By Left-Centre Fork, also Right Fork by J.R.Mackenzie, C.Norman, 19 Mar 1978

By Right-Centre Fork by J.R.Mackenzie, 17 Jan 2001

W	1978 Mar 19	Pigsty Gully	J.R.Mackenzie, C.Norman

Central Exit by J.R.Mackenzie, D.Broadhead, 31 Jan 1998

W	1979 Feb 18	Best Back	J.R.Mackenzie, D.McCallum
W	1994 Feb 13	Pearls Before Swine	G.Cullen, J.R.Mackenzie
W	1994 Feb 13	Piglet	J.R.Mackenzie, G.Cullen

Direct Start: J.R. Mackenzie, R.Weld, 20 Feb 2001

W	1994 Mar 12	Middle Cut	J.R.Mackenzie, P.Moffat
W	1995 Feb 10	The Wolf	J.R.Mackenzie, R.Brown, G.Cullen
W	1995 Feb 10	Three Little Pigs	G.Cullen, J.R.Mackenzie

Route as described was climbed by J.R.Mackenzie, G.Cullen, 28 Jan 1996

W	1995 Mar 11	Sty in the Eye	G.Cullen, I.M.F.Smith
W	1996 Jan 28	Tusker	J.R.Mackenzie, G.Cullen
W	1996 Feb 3	Pigsticker	D.J.Broadhead, J.R.Mackenzie
W	1996 Feb 11	Crackling Groove	R.Weld, J.R.Mackenzie
W	1996 Feb 11	Pipsqueak	J.R.Mackenzie, R.Weld
W	1996 Feb 13	Sorcerer's Apprentice	J.R.Mackenzie, R.Weld
W	1996 Mar 15	Pygmalion	D.J.Broadhead, J.R.Mackenzie
W	1996 Nov 24	Swine Fever	J.R.Mackenzie, G.Cullen
W	1996 Dec 29	Sty High	G.Cullen, J.R.Mackenzie
W	1996 Dec 29	Gammon Gully	G.Cullen, J.R.Mackenzie
W	1998 Jan 10	The Boar	J.R.Mackenzie, D.J.Broadhead
W	1998 Jan 24	Pork Scratchings	P.Whitfield, J.R.Mackenzie
W	1998 Jan 31	Totally Hamless	J.R.Mackenzie, D.Broadhead
W	1998 Mar 10	Suckling for Suckers	J.R.Mackenzie, P.Whitfield
W	1999 Mar 9	Snowdrop	C.Grindrod, J.R.Mackenzie
W	2000 Jan 15	Pig Iron Buttress	J.R.Mackenzie, R.Biggar
W	2000 Feb 13	Spare Rib, Porker (in descent)	G.Cullen, J.R.Mackenzie
W	2001 Jan 9	Slaughterhouse Blues	R.Biggar, J.R.Mackenzie
W	2001 Jan 14	Flower of Scotland	J.R.Mackenzie, R.Richard
W	2001 Jan 17	The Sorcerer	J.R.Mackenzie, R.Biggar

An attempt in Feb 1996 by Mackenzie and R Weld reached a point 5m from the end of the difficulties.

W	2002 Feb 16	Styless	D.Broadhead, J.R.Mackenzie
W	2001 Feb 20	Sows Ear	R.Weld, J.R.Mackenzie
W	2002 Mar 2	Pork Chop Grooves, Cold Litter	J.R.Mackenzie
W	2002 Mar 21	If Pigs Could Fly	J.R.Mackenzie
W	2003 Feb 9	Torque of the Devil	D.Broadhead, J.R.Mackenzie
W	2003 Feb 22	Three Little Piggies	D.Broadhead, J.R.Mackenzie
W	2003 Feb 22	Dancing With Calluna	J.R.Mackenzie, D.Broadhead
W	2004 Jan 11	The Trough	J.R.Mackenzie, D.Broadhead
W	2004 Mar 6	Tendril	D.Allan, J.R.Mackenzie
W	2004 Mar 24	Ribsticker	J.R.Mackenzie, A.Nisbet
W	2004 Feb 21	A Wee Cracker, The Glass Scribe, SE Passage, NE Passage	J.R.Mackenzie
W	2005 Feb 23	Maneater	J.R.Mackenzie, K.V.Crocket
W	2005 Mar 6	Fly-Trap	J.R.Mackenzie, D.Broadhead
W	2005 Mar 6	Petal Picking Plucker	D.Broadhead, J.R.Mackenzie
S	2005 Jul 6	Pas de Bas, Pousette, Schistomania, Dancing On Bawbees	J.R.Mackenzie, A.Nisbet
W	2005 Dec 29	Groundhog	D.Broadhead, J.R.Mackenzie
W	2006 Feb 18	Rising Damp	D.Broadhead, J.R.Mackenzie
S	2006 Jul 15	Little Gem, Diamond Slab	J.R.Mackenzie, A.Nisbet

Strathconon & Glen Orrin
Glenmarksie Crag

S	1970s	Greased Lightning	I.Ruscoe and Inverness MC

Direct Start: J.R.Mackenzie, M.Birch, Apr 1980

S	1979 Jun 4	Dog Leg	M.Birch, D.Gilbert, J.R.Mackenzie
S	1979 Jun 18	Wild Mint	D.Butterfield, J.R.Mackenzie, D.McCallum
S	1979 Jun 30	Six Trees, Walk on By	J.R.Mackenzie, D.McCallum.
S	1979 Jul 2	Dynamite	J.R.Mackenzie, D.McCallum

Direct (as described): R.Brown, J.R.Mackenzie, 22 Apr 1990

S	1979 Jul 3	The Juggler	M.Birch, J.R.Mackenzie
S	1979 Sep 23	Small Wall Thins	J.R.Mackenzie, D.Gilbert
S	1979 Sep 23	Two Step, Staircase	D.Gilbert, J.R.Mackenzie
S	1979 Sep 23	Kojak, Clutch and Thrutch, A Touch of Class	J.R.Mackenzie
S	1979 Sep 23	Sideline, Middle Wall, Bitter Bother, Victoriana	J.R. Mackenzie
S	1979 Oct 27	Dog Mantle	M.Birch, J.R.Mackenzie
S	1980 Apr 26	Hiroshima Grooves, Central Groove	J.R.Mackenzie, D.Butterfield
S	1980 Apr 26	Proteus	J.R.Mackenzie
S	1980 Apr 26	Trade Route, Central Groove	D.Butterfield, J.R.Mackenzie
S	1982	Callisto	B.McDermott, D.Butterfield

Variant: Polish Peacemaker R.Brown, C.White, 10 Jun 1989

S	1982	An Feur Ghorta	B.McDermott, D.Butterfield

Variant: Sickle Moon J.R.Mackenzie, G.Cullen 25 Nov 1989

S	1982	An Fear Feusagach	B.McDermott, D.Butterfield

Variant: Selene G.Cullen, J.R.Mackenzie 25 Nov 1989

S	1989 Jun 19	Phobos	J.R.Mackenzie, R.Brown
S	1989 Aug 26	Strategic Arms Limitation	J.R.Mackenzie, R.Brown
S	1989 Sep 30	Gritstone Corner	J.R.Mackenzie, P.Figg
S	1990 Mar 12	Sea of Tranquillity	J.R.Mackenzie, G.Cullen
S	1990 Jun 3	Little Teaser	J.R.Mackenzie, R.Brown
S	1990 Jun 10	Dogg'Edd	G.Cullen, P.Whitefield

Direct version: G.Cullen, J.R.Mackenzie, R.Brown 17 Jul 1990

S	1990 Aug 24	Deimos	J.R.Mackenzie, R.Brown
S	1990 Sep 16	A Bit on the Side	J.R.Mackenzie, R.Brown
S	1990 Sep 16	Powder Monkey	J.R.Mackenzie, R.Brown
S	1990 Oct 10	Pom	J.R.Mackenzie, G.Cullen
S	1991 Apr 14	Right Unprintable	J.R.Mackenzie, R.Brown
S	1993 Jun 8	Bridging the Gap	J.R.Mackenzie, R.Brown
S	1993 Jun 28	Man o'War	J.R.Mackenzie, R.Brown
S	1993 Sept 16	Helios	J.R.Mackenzie, R.Brown
S	1994 May 3	Left Unprintable	J.R.Mackenzie, J.Finlay
S	1994 May 25	Red Ant Crack	R.Biggar
S	1994 Sep 3	Jumping Jack Splat	J.R.Mackenzie, R.Brown
S	1995 Apr 2	Optical Illusion	R.Brown, J.R.Mackenzie
S	2000 Mar 30	The Conjuror (top pitch)	R.Biggar, J.R.Mackenzie

Lower Pitch: R.Biggar and partner, 2000

S	2004 Jun 2	The Joker	J.R.Mackenzie, E.Naismith
S	2006 Jun 11	Glen Marxie Brothers	J.R.Mackenzie, A.Nisbet
S	2006 Sep 16	Hot Dog	J.R.Mackenzie, J.Preston, A.Nisbet

Scatwell River Slabs

S	1980s	Early lines were climbed by M.Birch, D.Butterfield and B.McDermott
S	1993 Nov 3	The Joust	J.Finlay, J.R.Mackenzie
S	1993 Sep 17	The Tilting Yard	J.R.Mackenzie, J.Finlay
S	1993 Oct 30	Boundary Ridge	M.Hind, J.Lowe
S	1994 Apr 15	Piles of Smiles	J.Finlay, D.Henderson
S	2000 Jul	Scatwell Express	R.Mackenzie, D.Ostler
S	2000 Jul	Rectal Irrigation, Try not to Wet your Arch	R.Mackenzie
S	2000 Aug	Flying Scotsman	R.Mackenzie, P.Freaudanthal

Scatwell Upper Slabs

S	1990 Mar 18	Stranger than Friction	R.Brown, J.R.Mackenzie
S	1990 Summer	Early Learning Centre	G.Cullen, J.R.MacKenzie
S	1990 Sep 23	Bushwackers Slab, Bonsai Wall	J.R.Mackenzie, A.Walker
S	1990 Sep 23	Walkers Farewell	A.Walker, J.R.Mackenzie
S	1992 Aug 1	Legless Lizard, Slow Worm	M.Hind, S.Lockhard
S	1992 Aug 2	Strawberry Ripple, Coffin Slab, Ready and Waiting, Alive and Kicking, Easy Going	M.Hind
S	1992 Aug 4	Pipistrelle Cracks	M.Hind, S.Lockhard
S	1992 Aug 10	Gardeners' Question Time	J.R.MacKenzie, C.Fox

S	1992 Aug 14	Friction with Strangers	J.R.MacKenzie, R.Brown
S	1992 Aug 14	Stretch	R.Brown, J.R.MacKenzie

Hidden Crag

S	1993 Feb 7	Hoist by Ones Own Bullshit	R.Brown, J.R.Mackenzie, G.Cullen
S	1993 Feb 9	Pledge, Creepy-Crawly, Shield Bug	M.Hind
S	1993 Mar 7	Chinese Eyes	R. Brown, J.R.Mackenzie
S	1993 Mar 7	The Barker	R.Brown, J.R.Mackenzie, R.Scott
S	1993 Jun 20	Codgers Wall	R.Brown, R.Abbott

Scoop Crag

S	1993 Feb 23	The Spike	R.Brown, J.R.Mackenzie
S	1993 Mar 7	Fleetstreet Hack, The Scoop	R.Brown, J.R.Mackenzie, R.Scott
S	1993 Mar 14	Brass Monkey	M.Hind
S	1993 Mar 12	Confectionary Arete	J.R.Mackenzie, R.Brown

Slab Crag

Routes soloed by A.Mullin in Jun 1998.

Dam Crag

S	1991 May 15	Simple Delights	G.Cullen, J.R.Mackenzie
S	1991 May 17	The Gulf Crisis, Battle of the Bulge (top-rope)	M.Hind, J.R.Mackenzie
S	1992 Summer	Thick as a Brick	M.Hind

Aspen Crag

S	1991 Jun 23	Meridian, The Aspen	J.R.Mackenzie, G.Cullen
S	1991 Jun 23	Burlesque Crack	G.Cullen, J.R.Mackenzie
S	1991 Jun 28	Icturus	R.Brown, J.R.Mackenzie
S	1991 Jul 3	Tantalus Groove	M.Hind, J.R.Mackenzie
S	1991 Jul 3	Shadow Grasper	J.R.Mackenzie, M.Hind
S	1991 Jul 17	Mac The Knife	M.Hind, J.R.Mackenzie
S	1991 Jul 17	Creeping Stealth, Mid-Flight Crisis	J.R.Mackenzie, M.Hind
S	1991 Jul 21	Uncertain Voyage	J.R.Mackenzie, R.Brown
S	1991 Aug	Chocks Away	M.Hind
S	1991 Sep 8	Underneath the Arches, Jumping Jack Flash, Rock and Roll Suicide	M.Hind
S	1992 Apr 29	Sloshed in Action	J.R.Mackenzie, M.Hind
S	1992 Apr 29	Licking the Lip	R.Brown, J.R.Mackenzie
S	1992 May 16	Gobstopper	R.Brown, J.R.Mackenzie
S	1992 Aug 22	The Dark Side of the Moon, Woolly Jumper	M.Hind, R.Brown

Meig Crag

S	1979 Jun 30	Meig Corner, The Balance	J.R.Mackenzie, D.McCallum
S	1979 Jun 30	Shy Brides Crack	D.McCallum, J.R.Mackenzie
S	1991 May 23	The Birch	J.R.Mackenzie, M.Hind
S	1991 May 23	Limited Liability	M.Hind, J.R.Mackenzie
S	1991 Aug 21	Erection Crack	J.R.Mackenzie, G.Cullen, M.Hind
S	1991 Sep 1	Correction	R.Brown, T.W.Brown
S	1991 Sep 11	Nicked In Time	M.Hind
S	1991 Summer	The Rake	M.Hind
S	1992 Jan 19	Angst Arete	J.R.Mackenzie, R.Brown, G.Cullen
S	1992 Jan 28	Lone Pine Groove	G.Cullen, J.R.Mackenzie
S	1992 May 13	Sidewinder	M.Hind
S	1992 May 26	The Go-Between	M.Hind, R.Scott
S	1992 Jun 10	Yellow Streak	M.Hind, R.Brown
S	1992 Jun 11	Gabbro Slab	J.R.Mackenzie, G.Cullen
S	1992 Jun 14	The Wee Nibble	M.Hind, J.R.Mackenzie
S	1992 Jul 2	Promenade, Two Step	M.Hind
S	1992 Jul 3	Dancing in the Rain	M.Hind, J.R.Mackenzie

S	1992 Jul	Sidestep	M.Hind
S	1992 Jul 31	Blueberry Hill	M.Hind, S.Lockhart
S	1993 Oct 30	Casting Out	M.Hind
S	1994 Jun	Milk and Alcohol	N.Main, S.Raw
S	1994 Jun	Hind Quarters	N.Main, K.Grant
S	1994 Aug 22	The Touchstone Maze	J.R.Mackenzie, R.Brown

Geologists Slabs
Routes by R.Brown, J.R.Mackenzie on 20 Apr 1997.

Sgurr a' Mhuilinn, Creag Ghlas

S	1967 Aug	Oh Dear	J.Renny, M.Strong
S	1967 Aug	The Lizard	D.Bathgate, R.N.Campbell

The Loop Pitch: M.Selwood, J.R.Mackenzie, 28 Jul 1990
The Big Trundle: M.Hind, R.Brown, Jul 1992

S	1978 May 28	Boulder and Bolder	M.Birch, J.R.Mackenzie
S	1979 Oct 2	Spare Rib	R.McHardy, J.R.Mackenzie
S	1980 May 15	Sweet Charity	J.R.Mackenzie, D.Butterfield
S	1991 Aug 25	Whoops	G.Cullen, J.R.Mackenzie
S	1992 May 20	Evening Arete	R.Brown, J.R.Mackenzie
S	1992 Jun 7	Wandering Minstrel	M.Hind
S	1992 Jun 7	Glass Slipper	R.Brown, J.R.Mackenzie, M.Hind
W	1993 Jan 8	Thumper Groove	M.Hind, J.R.Mackenzie
S	1993 Oct 30	Hall of Mirrors	R.Brown, G.Cullen, J.R.Mackenzie

Direct Finish: G.Cullen, J.R.Mackenzie, R.Brown, 30 Oct 1993

W	1994 Jan 1	Blue Moon	G.Cullen, J.R.Mackenzie
S	1994 Aug 12	Salamander	J.R.Mackenzie, R.Brown, C.Powell

Route as described by same party on 24 Sep 1994
Legoland: D.McGimpsey, R.McAllister, Aug 1998

S	1994 Sep 24	Gloaming Wall	R.Brown, J.R.Mackenzie
S	1994 Sep 24	Centipede Crack	J.R.Mackenzie, R.Brown
S	1995 Aug 20	Victory Crack	J.R.Mackenzie, R.Brown
S	1995 Nov 4	Spoils of War	R.Brown, J.R.Mackenzie
S	1998 Aug 24	Peak Freans' Trotskyite Selection	R.McAllister
S	1998 Aug 31	Chameleon	J.R.Mackenzie, R.Brown
S	1998 Sep 19	Super Discount	D.McGimpsey, R McAllister, A.Fraser
S	1998 Sep 20	Spider in a Dark Dark Room	A.Fraser, R.McAllister, D.McGimpsey
S	1998 Sep 20	Anonymous Chimney	D.McGimpsey, A.Fraser, R.McAllister
S	1998 Sep 20	Glazed and Confused	A.Fraser, R.McAllister, D.McGimpsey
S	1998 Sep 20	Moon Safari	R.McAllister, D.McGimpsey, A.Fraser
S	1998 Sep 20	Ra-Ra Rabbit	R.McAllister, D.McGimpsey
S	1998 Sep 20	Explosive Joseph	R.McAllister
S	1998 Sep	Tales of the Old Days	R.McAllister, D.McGimpsey, M.Harrison
S	1998 Sep	Beware the Greeks	J.Lines, R.McAllister, D.McGimpsey
W	1999 Feb 28	Charge of the White Brigade	J.R.Mackenzie, R.Biggar
S	2000 Aug 29	Garibaldi	D.McGimpsey, A.Nisbet
S	2000 Sep 3	Toad Hall	D.McGimpsey, A. and G.Nisbet
S	2000 Sep 3	Prix Choc	D.McGimpsey, A.Nisbet
S	2002 Jul 17	Oh Dearie Me	J.R.Mackenzie, A.Mackenzie, C.Tarbat

Most of the individual pitches have been climbed before by J.R.Mackenzie and partners in the 1980s.

S	2002 Jul 18	The Unknown Soldier	J.Lines, R.A.Biggar

Perhaps the first new E7 climbed on sight in Scotland

S	2003 Jun 25	Cut Glass	R.Brown, J.R.Mackenzie
W	2004 Feb 9	Oh Dearie Me	A.Dennis, J.R.Mackenzie
S	2005 Jun 19	Express	S.Jensen, J.R.Mackenzie
S	2005 Jun 19	Inspectors Slab, Murder and Mystery	J.R.Mackenzie, S.Jensen

Sgurr a' Coire-rainich

W	1971 Jan 5	Lady's Gully	Mrs. N.Tennent, J.R.Mackenzie

Meall na Faochaig, Gleann Meinich

W	1999 Dec 20	Meinich Buttress	J.R.Mackenzie

Bac an Eich, Coire Toll Lochain

W	1994 Dec 27	Angels Delight	J.R.Mackenzie
W	2003 Feb 19	Cop-Out Buttress, Funnel Gully	J.R.Mackenzie

Creag Dubh (Upper Strathconon)

Most of the climbs were ascended by members of the Inverness MC in the 1970s.

Allt Gleadhraich (Upper Strathconon)

W	1995 Dec 29	The Strathconon Experience	J.R.Mackenzie, G.Cullen

Creag a' Ghlastail

S	1989 Sep 24	The Curate's Egg	J.R.Mackenzie, R.Brown
W	1990 Feb 16	Ghlastail GTX	G.Cullen, J.R.Mackenzie
W	1991 Feb 17	Three Stroke Gully	G.Cullen, J.R.Mackenzie, M.Hind
W	1994 Feb 24	Waterfall Gully	J.R.Mackenzie, P.Moffat

Ben Wyvis Area
Raven's Rock & Raven's Rock Quarry

S	1970 Jun 22	Ravens Squawk	J.R.Mackenzie, A.Finlay-Sherris
S	1970	Pad Slab	J.R.Mackenzie, R.Richard
S	1971 Sep 18	Scorpion	J.R.Mackenzie, A.Ross
S	1971	Rejector	J.R.Mackenzie
S	1978 Jan 14	The Chimney	J.R.Mackenzie, T.Anderson
W	1978	Centre Fall	R.Brown, J.R.Mackenzie
S	1978 Apr 23	Tombstone Buttress	J.R.Mackenzie, M.Birch
S	1978 May	Cavalcade Wall	J.Smith, T.Anderson, R.Brown, C.Fraser, J.R.Mackenzie
S	1978 Jul 2	Zigzag	J.R.Mackenzie
S	1978 Jul 7	The Croak	J.R.Mackenzie, M.Birch
S	1978 Jul 16	The Sting	J.R.Mackenzie, M.Birch
S	1978 Aug 12	Ravens Horror	J.R.Mackenzie
S	1978 Sep 8	Raspberry Traverse	R.Brown, J.R.Mackenzie
S	1978 Sep 16	Archenemy	J.R.Mackenzie, M.Birch
S	1978 Sep 16	The Corner	M.Birch, J.R.Mackenzie
S	1978 Sep 23	Kingfisher	J.R.Mackenzie, F.Adams
S	1978 Sep 23	Black Crack	F.Adams, J.R.Mackenzie
S	1978 Sep 23	Black Wall	J.R.Mackenzie
S	1978 Sep 23	Midgit Corner	F.Adams, J.R.Mackenzie
S	1978 Nov 17	Roots	R.Brown, J.R.Mackenzie
S	1978	Acceptor	J.R.Mackenzie
S	1979 Jul 27	Jacobite Wall	J.R.Mackenzie, P.Goodwin
S	1979 Jul 29	Shorty	P.Goodwin, J.R.Mackenzie
S	1980 May 13	Close to the Edge	J.R.Mackenzie, M.Birch
S	1980 Aug 9	Bone Idle	J.R.Mackenzie, R.Brown
S	1980 Summer	Fancy Tickler	C.Roylance, J.R.Mackenzie
S	1980 Summer	Obituary	D.McCallum, D.Butterfield
S	1981 Jun 27	Ejector	J.R.Mackenzie

Red Rock

S	1978 Apr 21	Red Wall Grooves	J.R.Mackenzie, M.Birch

Moy Rock

S	1972 Apr 29	Harderthanitlookscrack, Slanting Crack	J.R.Mackenzie
S	1978 May 2	Boggle	J.R.Mackenzie, M.Birch
S	1978 May 6	Speleological Nightmare, Peregrination	M.Birch, J.R.Mackenzie
S	1978 May 31	Magnificrack	J.R.Mackenzie, R.McHardy, M.Birch

Ben Wyvis

W	1950s	Fox Gully	Unknown
S	1970 Jun 20	Klettershoe	J.R.Mackenzie
W	1982 Dec 31	Caberfeidh	J.R.Mackenzie, G.Gorner
S	1984 Jul 7	Rubbers	J.R.Mackenzie
W	1986 Feb 19	Wyvis Waterfall	A.Winton, D.Bond
	Probably first climbed in the 1960s		
W	1986 Feb 20	Slab Smear Left-Hand	A.Winton, D.Bond
W	1992 Dec 29	Discovery Buttress	D.Broadhead, J.R.Mackenzie
W	1993 Jan 31	Gael Force Grooves	J.R.Mackenzie, M.Hind
W	1993 Feb 28	Walking on Air	G.Cullen, J.R.Mackenzie
W	1994 Feb 3	The Snick	J.R.Mackenzie, P.Moffat
W	1995 Apr 28	Four Cornice Gully	J.R.Mackenzie, J.Finlay, J.Finlay
W	2000 Apr 5	Hansel and Gretal	J.R.Mackenzie, R.Biggar
W	2000 Apr 5	Tapered Buttress Direct	R.Biggar, J.R.Mackenzie
W	2001 Jan 7	Laird of the Rings	C.Cartwright, S.M.Richardson
W	2001 Feb 18	True Blue	J.R.Mackenzie, R.Weld
W	2003 Mar 13	The Last Resort	J.R.Mackenzie, D.Allan
W	2004 Feb 18	Fox Gully Arete, Interrupted Gully	J.R.Mackenzie, D.Allan
W	2004 Mar 8	Temptress	J.R.Mackenzie, A.Dennis
W	2006 Jan 4	Cubs' Corner, Wolf's Cascade, Rampant Desire	J.R.Mackenzie
W	2006 Jan 8	Cock o' the North	J.R.Mackenzie, R.Webb, N.Wilson
W	2006 Mar 18	High Five	J.R.Mackenzie, N.Wilson

North Sutor Cliffs

S	1998 Aug 19	Shake, Rattle and Roll	J.R.Mackenzie, R.Weld

Ben Wyvis Outlying Crags North

S	pre-1953	Original Route (Loch Morie Crag)	D.H.Maling, W.T.Cowe
W	2002 Jan 3	Struie Icefall	D.Allan
	Other routes at Struie Hill Crag unknown.		
S	2002 Jul 13	Routes 1,3,4,5,7 (Black Bridge Crags)	J.R.Mackenzie, A.Mackenzie
S	2002 Sep 29	Routes 2,6	J.R.Mackenzie, C.Tarbat, E.Stuart-Richardson
S	2003 Jun 7	Badger up a Plum Tree	G.E.Little, J.Lowther
S	2003 Jun 7	Sett Up	J.Lowther, G.E.Little

SCOTTISH MOUNTAINEERING CLUB
SCOTTISH MOUNTAINEERING TRUST

Prices were correct at time of publication, but are subject to change

CLIMBERS' GUIDES

Glen Coe	£20.00
Ben Nevis	£20.00
Northern Highlands North	£20.00
Northern Highlands Vol. 1	£13.00
Lowland Outcrops	£20.00
Arran, Arrochar and Southern Highlands	£15.00
The Cairngorms Vol. 1	£11.00
The Cairngorms Vol. 2	£12.00
Highland Outcrops	£17.50
North-East Outcrops	£19.00
Scottish Winter Climbs	£19.00
Scottish Rock Climbs	£21.00
Skye	£11.00
Scottish Sports Climbs	In preparation

HILLWALKERS' GUIDES

The Munros	£20.00
The Munros CD-ROM	£40.00
Munros GPS data disk – from SMC website	£10.48
The Corbetts & Other Scottish Hills	£20.00
The Corbetts & Other Scottish Hills CD-ROM	£30.00
North-West Highlands	£22.00
The Cairngorms	£18.00
Central Highlands	£18.00
Islands of Scotland Including Skye	£20.00
Southern Highlands	£17.00

SCRAMBLERS' GUIDES

Highland Scrambles North	£18.00
Skye Scrambles	£15.50

OTHER PUBLICATIONS

Hostile Habitats – Scotland's Mountain Environment	£15.00
Munro's Tables	£16.00
A Chance in a Million? Avalanches in Scotland	£15.00
The Munroist's Companion	£16.00
Ben Nevis – Britain's Highest Mountain	£15.00
Ski Mountaineering in Scotland	£13.00

Visit our website for more details and to purchase on line:
www.smc.org.uk

Distributed by:
Cordee Ltd, 3a De Montfort Street, Leicester LE1 7HD
(t) 0116 254 3579 (f) 0116 247 1176
www.cordee.co.uk

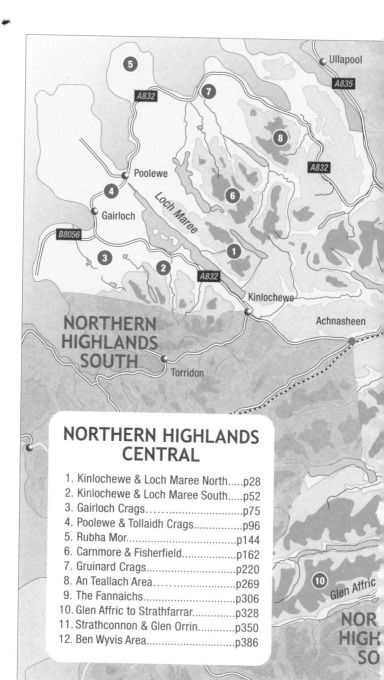

Ullapool

A835

⑤

A832

⑦

⑧

A832

Poolewe

④

Loch Maree

⑥

Gairloch

B8056

③

②

①

A832

Kinlochewe

Achnasheen

NORTHERN
HIGHLANDS
SOUTH

Torridon

NORTHERN HIGHLANDS
CENTRAL

⑩ Glen Affric

NOR
HIGH
SO